CRIMINAL PROCEDURE

THEORY AND PRACTICE

Jefferson Ingram

University of Dayton

PEARSON

Prentice
Hall

Upper Saddle River, New Jersey 07458

Library of Congress Cataloging-in-Publication Data

Ingram, Jefferson.
  Criminal procedure : theory and practice / Jefferson Ingram.—1st ed.
    p. cm.
  Includes index.
  ISBN 0-13-098760-3
  1. Criminal procedure—United States. 2. Criminal procedure—United States—Cases.
  3. Civil rights—United States. 4. Civil rights—United States—Cases. I. Title.
  KF9619.I544 2005
  345.73'05—dc22

                                                        2004003622

Executive Editor: Frank Mortimer, Jr.
Assistant Editor: Korrine Dorsey
Managing Editor: Mary Carnis
Production Liaison: Brian Hyland
Manufacturing Buyer: Cathleen Petersen
Director of Manufacturing and Production: Bruce Johnson
Design Director: Cheryl Asherman
Senior Design Coordinator: Miguel Ortiz
Cover Design: Carey Davies
Cover Photo: Richard T. Nowitz/CORBIS
Composition/Full-Service Project Management: nSight/Laserwords
Printer/Binder: Courier Westford
Cover Printer: Coral Graphics

10 9 8 7 6 5 4 3 2 1
ISBN 0-13-098760-3

For my parents:
Dr. Ernagene F. Ingram and
Dr. Lewis K. Ingram.

Contents

5   SPECIAL PROBLEM SEARCHES: ADMINISTRATIVE, INVENTORY, SCHOOL, AIRPORT, AND WORK SEARCHES   129

**6   PRINCIPLES OF THE EXCLUSIONARY RULE: REMEDIES
          AND EXCEPTIONS TO CONSTITUTIONAL VIOLATIONS   173**

9   **IDENTIFICATION PROCEDURES: CONSTITUTIONAL
            CONSIDERATIONS**   **279**

10   **THE DECISION TO PROSECUTE: INDICTMENT AND INFORMATION   305**

11   PLEA BARGAINING AND GUILTY PLEAS: CONSTITUTIONAL STANDARDS   333

12   PRETRIAL CRIMINAL PROCEDURE: PRELIMINARY HEARING, BAIL, RIGHT TO COUNSEL, SPEEDY TRIAL, DOUBLE JEOPARDY, AND COLLATERAL ESTOPPEL   365

13   THE TRIAL: CONSTITUTIONAL RIGHTS AND TRIAL PRACTICE: JURY TRIAL, RIGHT TO COUNSEL, DUE PROCESS, AND EQUAL PROTECTION   407

Preface

The field of criminal procedure provides part of the matrix of fairness and justice that promotes equality of treatment for persons accused of crime; therefore, it occupies an important position in the field of criminal justice. Since its genesis comes from both the Constitution of the United States and the constitutions of the several states, its substance and application will vary in some fashion from jurisdiction to jurisdiction. The decisions made by the Supreme Court of the United States, when speaking on federal constitutional issues, are binding on state criminal justice practice. Although constitutional decisions are mandatory on the states, such decisions dictate the minimal legal protections required under our federal system. Every state may go beyond the basic federal guarantees by offering an accused greater state constitutional rights; it also may grant enhanced criminal procedure protections based on state constitutional and statutory law.

The constitutional and statutory rules that make up the body of law known as criminal procedure regulate how state and federal governments must treat persons accused or suspected of committing crimes. Rules dictating the way law enforcement officials interact with individuals who are mere suspects for particular crimes restrain the activities and approaches that can be followed prior to the initiation of formal criminal prosecutions. When investigations have moved beyond their initial stages to the point where criminal suspects have been identified, the rules of criminal procedure provide a road map that all law enforcement officials must follow. Where officials fail to observe recognized criminal procedural rules, such deviation may jeopardize any eventual successful criminal prosecution by opening the conviction to appellate attack.

Similarly, when law-enforcement officials have turned their work product over to the prosecutor's office, the personnel presenting the government's case must carefully follow additional rules regulating fair conduct in order to accord due process to the accused. Defense attorneys have a role within the rules of criminal procedure to ensure that the government has played fairly during the investigation, pretrial, and trial phases; they also are obligated to provide a vigorous defense consistent with the Constitution and state rules and regulations.

During criminal trials, judges must carefully weigh the arguments of the contending parties, whether they are arguing over criminal procedural issues relative to the admission of evidence or over more traditional admission of evidence under evidence codes. Whether a judge presides over pretrial issues, the trial itself, or posttrial motions, or serves on an appellate panel reviewing trial-level judicial decisions, every judge possesses a duty of due process to both the prosecution and the defense. Roughly translated, due process implies fundamental fairness and fair dealing during all important portions of the criminal justice process.

The study of criminal procedure traditionally follows a case method of instruction, where students read previously decided criminal cases that instruct by using concrete examples covering criminal procedure issues. By learning both earlier case precedents and the latest pronouncements on a particular topic, the student can develop a historical context for the important concepts and theories in criminal procedure, as well as knowledge about the direction where the jurisprudence may be developing. The most significant developments, changes, and corrections in criminal procedure have generally come from landmark case decisions of the Supreme Court of the United States. Implementation of the rules contained within Supreme Court case decisions has largely been delegated to state legal systems, where state courts have developed slightly divergent interpretations and applications of these legal principles. The Federal Rules of Criminal Procedure and state rules of criminal procedure owe much of their content to the codification of legal principles announced by the Supreme Court of the United States and to common-law practice. Whereas the Federal Rules of Criminal Procedure are fairly detailed, state process varies from very detailed rules to an outline system of procedural rules.

While the traditional study of criminal procedure follows the case method, learning criminal procedure through reading narrative material provides an alternative with which many students feel an appropriate level of comfort. Arguably, both the case and text methods of instruction and learning possess benefits and some challenges. A textual pedagogy allows the rapid introduction of more complete concepts that students may quickly grasp, but it does not grant the depth of knowledge required to make analogies easily between similar cases. The case method usually presents discrete legal concepts that the student must mentally organize and categorize as the course progresses, but until the discrete components materialize to compose the complete legal picture, some students may experience frustration during the learning process. This book has taken both the text and the case approach in an effort to introduce and place in context larger related blocks of material, reinforcing that understanding with relevant cases that are followed by related questions and other instructional material. Organizing such material presents challenges concerning whether to follow a conceptual or a chronological approach, since legal concepts and procedures develop in a random or piecemeal order. In years when the Supreme Court takes groups of cases containing related legal issues and decides them in novel ways, new concepts are quickly recognized and placed within the legal matrix. More often, the Court accepts cases that have little relation to each other, but taken individually, each case may modify criminal procedure in subtle ways and answer questions the Court formerly left unresolved. Although the chapters generally follow a chronological order, where a different order made pedagogical sense, I followed that deviation. For example, although *Miranda* warnings are often given very early in the criminal justice process, this book presents the *Miranda* material immediately prior to the section on the right against self-incrimination, since conceptually the two topics are interrelated.

Each of the fourteen chapters of this book begins with an outline of the topics covered in that chapter, as well as key terms that are important to an understanding of the chapter. Each chapter begins with a preview that includes a broad overview of the legal principles that will be covered and offers detailed textual explanations that demonstrate the interrelationship of various legal concepts. Where an understanding of the developmental history of a particular concept or legal theory seems important, an effort has been made to trace the development from its genesis to the present time. For example, the exclusionary rule used to enforce the requirements of the Fourth Amendment is more fully comprehended if one has an understanding of its historical background. Likewise, historical knowledge and case law development facilitate an understanding of the *Miranda* warnings, since the warnings have experienced some evolution and clarification from the initial court decision to the present application in a variety of contexts. Footnotes and citations allow the reader avenues for additional study, as well as provide clarification for some of the more arcane areas of criminal procedure. The cases that follow the textual presentation have been selected for their prominence and for their influence in the particular subfield of criminal procedure. In many instances, older cases have been presented because they represent the landmark decisions in that particular area or are indicative of major departures or initiatives taken by the Supreme Court of the United States. The book presents many updated and current cases where judicial activity has refined or changed the direction of a particular point of law. In some areas of criminal procedure, such as the right to counsel under the Sixth Amendment, the concepts seem to be relatively settled and there has been little major judicial activity in recent years. Where settled legal principles exist, the text and the comments following the cases attempt to illustrate present application of those principles and to suggest or challenge the student to consider possible changes that should or could be made.

This book begins with an introductory section that theoretically could have been its first chapter, but I felt that many students at this level have covered most of this material in an introductory course in criminal justice or the legal process. The introduction provides an element of the history of criminal procedure from its basis in the federal Constitution and case law cited by the United States Supreme Court. Clear effort has been made to indicate that we have a federal system of criminal justice in which the states have historically possessed the primary responsibility for investigating and prosecuting criminal activity. This introduction reinforces the concept that the states and the federal government operate parallel criminal justice systems that have overlapping jurisdiction in many instances. Crucial to an understanding of the evolution of criminal justice is the concept of the selective incorporation of the Bill of Rights into the Fourteenth Amendment and its effect on local criminal procedure. Included within this introduction is a review of the chronology of the typical criminal process from arrest to final adjudication.

Chapter 1 presents the initial materials dealing with the Fourth Amendment as it relates to searches, seizures, and the requirement of a warrant. This chapter covers matters relating to the specificity requirement of a warrant and the occasions when a warrant is an absolute necessity. The chapter also discusses some of the requirements for obtaining a warrant when the use of informants proves necessary to the development of probable cause. Concepts of probable cause, knock and announce, and exceptions to the warrant requirement receive significant textual and case treatment.

Chapter 2 covers the concept of stop and frisk and the development of its attendant case law. From the initial *Terry v. Ohio* case to the most recent situations in which it has been applied, the text explores the twists and turns and interesting nuances faced by a police officer when making the decision to stop a person for an initial investigation. The chapter presents the thought process and the factoring of the information that an officer must make to determine whether to conduct a subsequent frisk based on the correct level of suspicion that criminal activity may be afoot. Included within this chapter is the development of the stop and frisk concept to include "frisks" of motor vehicles, the plain feel doctrine, and the expansion of *Terry* to persons not under suspicion.

Chapter 3 explains the concept of arrest and illustrates its legal standards. While the plain meaning of the Fourth Amendment would indicate that a warrant is required for an arrest, case law and practice indicate otherwise. This chapter investigates the development of probable cause in an individual case, the sources of probable cause, the need for a warrant in some cases, the concept of stale probable cause, and arrests within the suspect's home. Exceptions to the warrant requirement such as hot pursuit and exigent circumstances are discussed and analyzed within this chapter.

Chapter 4 covers searches of homes and motor vehicles, as well as searches incident to arrest. Assuming the existence of probable cause, this chapter probes deeply into the reasonableness of searches and how they are conducted. It investigates the scope and extent of motor vehicle searches permitted with probable cause and illustrates the more limited scope of search where probable cause does not exist. This chapter discusses the concept of consent searches and the factors under the totality of the circumstances used to determine whether the consent was voluntarily and freely given or whether coercion may have prevented the giving of voluntary consent. Searches of containers, inventory searches, consent searches, and searches of vehicles under forfeiture may not require warrants and in some cases may not include the requirement of probable cause for search. This chapter offers additional insights into the plain view doctrine allowing a search without probable cause and its corollary doctrine, the plain feel doctrine.

Chapter 5 considers a variety of searches that are different from and outside the usual scope of typical searches designed to produce evidence of criminal wrongdoing. Modern governments sometimes must conduct surveys or searches in order to enforce zoning requirements and municipal programs; schools and governmental employers have reasonable needs to secure safe school environments or work situations, which may include searching some students and employees in some contexts. This chapter notes that although the Fourth Amendment requires probable cause to search, and warrants in many cases, there are administrative situations in which the concept of probable cause has been somewhat redefined downward to a lower standard, making search warrants easy to obtain. The Fourth Amendment regulates workplace searches, both in public-sector jobs and in private workplaces where the employer is required by the government to conduct a search. This chapter illustrates some of the legal justifications for airport passenger searches, international border searches, and various types of emergency searches.

Chapter 6 discusses the exclusionary rule promulgated by the United States Supreme Court in an effort to enforce the constitutional guarantees of the Fourth Amendment. It presents the theoretical basis for the exclusionary rule, along with its history from the early federal rule applicable only in federal courts to the present-day standard that excludes evidence illegally seized from use in either state or federal courts. This chapter covers situations in which the exclusionary rule has an expansive effect: where it not only excludes illegally seized evidence but also removes from court consideration evidence that has been derived by using illegally seized evidence to secure other evidence. This chapter notes the existence of a variety of exceptions to the exclusionary rule and explains their legal and theoretical justifications. Alternative remedies to violations of the Fourth Amendment receive attention, as do limitations introduced by the concept of standing.

Chapter 7 presents the warnings that are required to be offered to every person in custody before law enforcement officials conduct an interrogation. The *Miranda* warnings must be offered to anyone facing custodial interrogation; if they are not, any evidence derived will generally be excluded from court for proof of guilt. This chapter devotes significant effort to determining when a person is in custody and to analyzing what the Supreme Court meant by the term *interrogation*. This chapter notes the existence of public safety exceptions to the *Miranda* warnings that have been construed somewhat differently in some jurisdictions. The most recent case to be decided by the Supreme Court of the United States indicated that the *Miranda* warnings possessed constitutional dimension and were required to be offered by the Constitution of the United States.

Chapter 8 covers the concept of the confession and the constitutional privilege against compelled testimonial self-incrimination. The authors of the Fifth Amendment intended the amendment to limit the federal government and did not envision that it would be applied to state government practice. The Supreme Court of the United States deemed the self-incrimination portion of the Fifth Amendment so important to liberty and the fair administration of justice that the Court decided that by implication it should be incorporated into the Due Process Clause of the Fourteenth Amendment. This chapter surveys the distinction between testimonial and nontestimonial evidence, as well as the forums in which the privilege against self-incrimination may be asserted. Even where the privilege against self-incrimination has been appropriately raised, immunity from prosecution or its lesser cousin, use immunity, may operate in such a manner that the person must offer evidence that otherwise would have been incriminating. Where an accused chooses not to stand on constitutional rights but instead desires to confess to a crime, to be admissible, such confession must have been given freely and voluntarily. This chapter investigates the requirements for voluntariness of a confession and the procedural requirements for a court to follow in admitting the confession into evidence. Confessions taken in violation of *Miranda* may be admissible in court for impeachment purposes, since they were not taken involuntarily when evaluated by the Fifth Amendment privilege.

Chapter 9 considers the use of identification procedures with a view to ensuring that in a court identification, due process has been followed and the identification offered meets a minimum standard of accuracy. Intimately involved in the identification process is the requirement that an attorney have represented the accused if the accused was indicted or where the government had filed an information prior to the in-person identification process. This chapter surveys the use of photographic arrays and in-person lineups and the requirement of fundamental fairness that must exist prior to allowing a jury to hear identification evidence. This chapter surveys the requirements necessary to admit eyewitness testimony against a defendant under the *Neil* five-factors test and demonstrates the process for determining whether an identification procedure may be discussed in court when a subject was not represented by counsel at an identification procedure.

Chapter 10 covers the methods and constitutional rules governing the initiation of serious and less serious criminal charges in both state and federal prosecutions. While this chapter discusses the grand jury and how it operates, it notes that the grand jury is not a federal constitutional requirement for state criminal justice, since this part of the Fifth Amendment has never been applied to modify state criminal justice practice. Grand jury secrecy, its purposes, and its limitations are covered in this chapter, along with the fact that a grand jury may hear and consider improperly seized evidence. Witnesses may be compelled to testify before a grand jury, but the prosecution may have to offer some level of immunity prior to requiring testimony. This chapter notes that occasionally grand juries have been affected by racial discrimination, either in the initial selection or subsequently, and covers the constitutional remedy where proven or admitted racial discrimination has infected the charging portion of the criminal justice process.

Chapter 11 covers plea bargaining, the remedy for breached plea bargains, and the procedure for entering a guilty plea to a criminal charge. As this chapter discusses, where a defendant decides to enter a plea of guilty to an indictment, information, or other formal charge, he or she relinquishes various rights and privileges under the Constitution. This chapter notes that, as a general rule, a judge who accepts a guilty plea must address the defendant and be certain that the defendant understands the constitutional rights that are being relinquished. Where a government or a defendant breaches a plea bargain, both sides possess remedies that may have drastic effects on the other. This chapter notes that, in most jurisdictions, a defendant may plead guilty to the charges while at the same time continuing to profess innocence without destroying the validity of the guilty plea.

Chapter 12 introduces numerous pretrial procedures that may have a significant impact on a criminal defendant and that generally must be pled and/or initiated prior to the time of trial. Generally a defendant must raise speedy trial issues, collateral estoppel, and double jeopardy allegations prior to trial, since, if these allegations are sustained, no trial will be necessary. Bail concerns and the desire for a preliminary hearing, where permitted, should be addressed in the period prior to trial. Pretrial procedures deemed to be mandatory involve issues that tend to become moot once a case proceeds to trial. This chapter introduces the concept of when jeopardy first attaches, when it ends, and what requirements need to be proven to demonstrate that a trial truly involves a second trial over the same offense. Using the *Blockburger* test for separate offenses, separate trials covering the same physical act, if prosecuted by two separate sovereignties, will not trigger a successful double jeopardy argument.

Chapter 13 encompasses various constitutional rights that have primary effect at a criminal trial. This chapter teaches that the right to a jury trial is not absolute in all situations and that a jury may not mean exactly the same thing in every jurisdiction. Juries are not routinely offered for petty offenses in all jurisdictions, but some offenses deemed rather petty may carry a right to a jury trial. This chapter introduces the concept that a jury may vary from the traditional size of twelve and may lawfully involve merely six members. Some juries may not have to come to a unanimous decision to produce a valid verdict. A central concept of justice, that a jury should be selected from a fair cross section of the community, enhances the chance of a fair trial. Although the right to counsel exists in various stages and in various specific contexts in the criminal justice system, it is primarily a right that exists during a criminal trial. Due process requires that the right to counsel be recognized in many pretrial proceedings, but the necessity of an attorney in those proceedings helps assure that a trial attorney can offer effective legal assistance. Although constitutional rights are important and desirable, this chapter accentuates the concept that constitutional and statutory rights can be waived by competent defendants.

Chapter 14 introduces the criminal procedural remedies that a convicted defendant may pursue following a conviction. Since no system of justice can be perfect and free from substantial errors in every case, methods of error correction permit convicted defendants to request an appellate court to review the proceedings that resulted in a criminal adjudication. This chapter introduces the concept that every person who has been convicted of a crime possesses at least one absolute right to have an appeals court review the conviction. The convicted defendant may pursue the first level of appeal as a matter of statutory legal right, although nowhere in the Constitution of the United States is such a right specifically mentioned. This chapter explains that to have an effective appeal, legal representation is a virtual necessity; for that reason, case law from the Supreme Court of the United States has determined that in all serious cases, the right to the assistance of an attorney for an appeal involving incarceration is constitutionally mandated and an attorney is available free of charge to the indigent. During the trial, the attorney must make a clear effort to preserve the trial record for appellate purposes. While direct appeal beyond the first appeal rests within a higher court's discretion, other avenues of relief involving habeas corpus may follow an unsuccessful appellate effort.

While every book has its limitations, every effort has been expended here to include text and appropriate case illustrations that clearly demonstrate the present requirements of criminal procedure from the initiation of a criminal prosecution to a conviction and on to the appellate stage. Although every nuance and small deviation of fact pattern from those presented in these cases may dictate a different outcome, the cases have been selected to cover the most general situations and to present the rules for dealing with them. The major cases of all areas of criminal procedure covered within this book have been presented in an edited case format designed to isolate one primary issue. I selected representative subsidiary cases that modify the major cases with the intention of offering continuity with the primary cases. The subsidiary cases offer more recent jurisprudence that takes the teaching of the primary case in a subtle new direction or reaffirms the basic decision with renewed clarity. When the text portion of each chapter has been digested along with the cases and other materials presented, the reader will have developed a basic understanding and appreciation of the principles presented within the section. The comments, notes, and questions that follow each case have been designed to demonstrate the effect of subtle changes in fact patterns and to provide additional information in a more specific sense. The questions presented after each case have been designed to challenge the inquiring student with some additional food for thought and to foster the ability to make analogies among discrete concepts and apply them in a novel fashion to future criminal procedural problems.

Because the text and cases presented here represent a point along the evolving path of criminal procedure, additional resources and updates are available on the Internet at various addresses. Additional material and updates coordinated with this book can be found at http://www.criminalprocedurebyingram.com. As court decisions dictate that additional case or text material needs to be added to this book, new material will be found updated and organized with hyperlinks in a table of contents that mirrors the actual table of contents of this book. One click will take the student to the latest material essential to understanding criminal procedure.

Just as criminal procedure changes and evolves, rendering some material obsolete, so is the Internet at the mercy of changes that affect validity of addresses and content. For all these Internet addresses, be sure to ignore any punctuation following the address. Some of the general addresses that are useful for students of criminal procedure include http://www.findlaw.com, http://www.findlaw.com/casecode, http://www.law.cornell.edu, http://www.lawsource.com, and http://www.lexisone.com. Many of these addresses contain links to more useful and specific information. For access to the Constitution of the United States and the amendments regulating some aspects of criminal procedure, go to http://www. findlaw.com/casecode/constitution and click on the various entries of interest.

To access the Supreme Court of the United States, go to http://www. supremecourtus.gov; for Supreme Court Decisions since 1893, searchable by full text, volume, year, or citation, go to http://www.findlaw.com/casecode/supreme. html. For decisions since 1990, go to http://supct.law.cornell.edu/supct/. For decisions issued between 1937 and 1975, go to http://www.fedworld.gov/supcourt/ index.htm. To consult cases of the federal courts of appeal, try http://www.aele. org/Lawlinks.html.

For the student desiring recent full-text United States Supreme Court cases in a searchable database of at least 23,326 of the cases since 1870, as well as some earlier classic cases, go to http://www.usscplus.com, where a CD-ROM is available for a reasonable fee. All the cases of the current term of the Supreme Court are available free in both PDF and ASCII formats.

Sources for state laws and constitutions and relevant links are available at http://www.law.cornell.edu/states, where the information for a particular state can be obtained by a mouse click. In addition, state criminal procedure codes for most states are available by going to http://www.law.cornell.edu/topics/state_statutes2. html#criminal_procedure and selecting the appropriate state criminal procedure code.

If the glossary at the back of this book fails to cover an essential entry, please consult one of the following on-line law dictionaries: http://dictionary.law.com, http://www.lectlaw.com/def.htm, or http://www.lawinfo.com/lawdictionary. Each one has some significant differences in approach, but all of them will prove quite useful. Instructors adopting this book might want to consider adding one or more of the dictionaries to a Web syllabus to further assist the student.

The author is indebted to Maureen Doyle-Warren of Prentice Hall who saw early merit to this project and introduced me to Acquisitions Editor Kim Davies. Discussions with Kim Davies led to the book's approval, and her encouragement in starting the project proved essential.

I wish to thank Susan Beauchamp of Prentice Hall for assistance in organization and for managing blind reviews of portions of the manuscript. Suggestions made by the reviewers have been incorporated within the text and followed in other ways. I would also like to thank the reviewers themselves: Barbara Belbot of the University of Houston–Downtown, Wojciech Cebulak of Minot State University, Alex del Carmen of the University of Texas at Arlington, George Dery of California State University–Fullerton, Shaun Gabbidon of Penn State University–Capital College, Lonn Laza-Kaduce of the University of Florida, and Donna Nicholson of Manchester Community College. Following the reviews, Susan Beauchamp offered strong suggestions for reorganization and helped keep the project on a reasonable schedule.

Korrine Dorsey of Prentice Hall provided direction to the author in developing the instructor's manual and test bank. She encouraged the development of the PowerPoint slides that will assist and accompany the marketing of this book. Many thanks go out to the numerous other Prentice Hall associates who have placed the finishing touches on the book and had a part in bringing it to its present state.

Special thanks goes to the extremely competent people at nSight, Inc. Associate Project Manager Robert Saley deserves special recognition. He kept the final production of this book on schedule without any sacrifice in quality. He kept the author on task, and did so with a sense of humor that promoted editing, rewrites, and other changes in a tolerable manner. The detailed efforts of copy editor Susan Ecklund transformed this book from a raw literary effort to a readable text possessing excellent continuity. Her suggestions enabled the author to say what he meant and to state it with clarity in ways that readers will be able to understand. Finally, the strong attention to detail by proofreader Catherine Cooker deserves full praise in correcting many errors. Without her efforts, mistakes created by the author would be numerous and probably pervasive. Any remaining errors are the full responsibility of the author, who has endeavored to minimize their presence and their effect on the overall book.

Jefferson Ingram
March 2004

Introduction

Introduction to the Criminal Process: History and Overview of Criminal Procedure

All civilized societies recognize certain norms of human behavior and have developed methods for dealing with those individuals whose conduct seriously deviates from the expected level of behavior. For societies that wish to deal with criminal deviancy and related behavior in a fair manner, some sort of standardized process must evolve that treats each individual in a substantially similar way, no matter what the criminal charge may involve.

Within the United States, rules of conduct that government agents must follow have evolved from practices inherited from the British common law, modified by colonial legislative enactments, and altered by early state governmental practices. Some additional rules of procedure and practice emanate from the United States Constitution, from constitutions of the several states, and from case law decided in both federal and state court systems. In the latter half of the twentieth century, the Supreme Court of the United States rendered a series of opinions that recognized new rules of criminal procedure and in some cases applied old federal requirements of criminal procedure to the states. Most of these opinions were decided during the period when Earl Warren served as chief justice. Later cases expanded and reinterpreted some of the Warren Court decisions in ways that sometimes restricted the effect but in some cases expanded the scope of Warren Court decisions, enhancing many rights accorded to persons accused of crime. Continued litigation in both state and federal courts has added significant gloss to many criminal procedure legal theories. As a result, the student of criminal procedure is required to read and digest the most significant of these legal cases.

The legal cases presented in this book have had their facts rewritten with a view toward presenting the necessary information to allow the reader to understand the substance of what gave rise to the case. Although there may be many legal issues in a particular criminal appellate case, the legal question in each case has been narrowly phrased to direct the reader to the main issue. The case presentation provides an answer to the legal question and follows it with an edited version of the Court's opinion. This practice allows the reader to focus on the essence without running the risk of becoming involved in collateral matters, which are present in every legal case.

One method commonly used by students who study both text and cases is to take the case as presented and reduce it to what is called a brief (see Figure 1). A student

Carroll v. United States
Supreme Court of the United States
267 U.S. 132 (1925)

FACTS:

A federal prosecutor obtained an indictment against Carroll and another man for illegally transporting intoxicating liquor in violation of federal law. The defendants filed an unsuccessful motion to suppress the evidence of illegal alcohol that had been taken by agents following a search of their automobile. After their conviction by a jury, the defendants appealed.

The basis for their appeal involved an allegation that the police had no right to stop and search their automobile, since probable cause did not exist to believe that they were doing anything illegal. Agents gained their interest in Carroll following an attempted purchase of illegal spirits from Carroll and his associate. Although the sale was never completed, agents believed that Carroll and the identified vehicle were involved in illegal alcohol sales. At another time, the agents observed the same vehicle traveling along the road used by smugglers but lost track of the vehicle. Two months after the prior sighting, the agents were successful in stopping the vehicle. Because the car was traveling the route used by alcohol smugglers, and since it was the Oldsmobile car involved in the earlier attempted sale, and since Carroll had a reputation as a bootlegger, the agents contended that they possessed probable cause to search the vehicle. The agents searched the Oldsmobile without a warrant.

Carroll contended that there was no probable cause to stop and search the vehicle and that the evidence should have been suppressed under the federal rule that excludes illegally seized evidence. The Supreme Court granted certiorari.

PROCEDURAL ISSUE:

If federal agents or police possess probable cause to search a moving vehicle, may they seize the vehicle and conduct a warrantless search of the vehicle?

HELD: Yes.

RATIONALE:

1. As a general rule, probable cause is necessary to search a motor vehicle.

2. The agents possessed probable cause to believe that the vehicle might be carrying illegal liquor because they had dealt with Carroll and the car earlier; they had attempted to purchase illegal alcohol for Carroll in a failed buy; they had observed it traveling the route favored by smugglers of alcohol; and they knew Carroll had a reputation as a bootlegger and seller of illegal alcohol.

3. Probable cause can be defined as existing when the facts and circumstances within the officers' knowledge and of which they had reasonably trustworthy information were sufficiently strong and reliable to warrant officers of reasonable caution in the belief that intoxicating liquor was being transported in the automobile that they stopped and searched.

4. Under the circumstances, obtaining a warrant for a fleeting target moving through the state of Michigan would have been impractical, since after obtaining the warrant the vehicle would be long gone and lost to law enforcement.

5. Therefore, under the circumstances obtaining in this case where probable cause exists to search a moving vehicle that may easily be lost to law enforcement agents if not immediately stopped and searched, the warrantless stop and search of the motor vehicle was reasonable under the Fourth Amendment and the evidence of illegal liquor should not have been suppressed.

Conviction affirmed by the Supreme Court of the United States.

Figure 1. Sample brief from the first case in chapter 1 (Case 1.1)

brief usually has four components, the facts, the issue, how the court decided the issue, and the rationale. While the facts of the cases in this book have been reduced and rewritten from the originals, the student may wish to reduce them further on paper to their barest essentials under the heading FACTS. The legal issue has been presented in a fairly narrow form, but the student may wish to reduce this to a more succinct question under the heading PROCEDURAL ISSUE. The issue should always be phrased in the form of a question that can be answered yes or no; this answer, which follows the heading HELD, indicates the Court's holding, which is, in effect, the answer posed by the procedural question. The RATIONALE section of the brief presents the legal reasoning employed by the Court to reach its decision. In a written case brief, the RATIONALE section usually is the longest section; its goal is to reduce the Court's decision in a manner that makes logical sense to the reader and still captures the essence of the lesson offered by the decision.

As the case brief in Figure 1 demonstrates, the brief should be written in a manner that allows it to fit completely on the front side of a page. This enables a reader to refer to the page during class discussion, to use the brief for the purpose of asking questions during class, and to easily review the brief when studying for an examination.

CRIMINAL PROCEDURE: WHAT TO CONSIDER AT THE BEGINNING

Since criminal procedure in the United States is regulated ultimately by the United States Constitution, an understanding of this document as it relates to criminal procedure suggests a logical beginning. It should be noted at the outset that criminal procedure as regulated by the United States Constitution dictates only the minimum standard of governmental conduct and of the rights possessed by the accused. Governmental practice, whether state or federal, must meet only the minimum constitutional standards, but governmental units are free to give an accused greater rights and enhanced protections. Some states restrict their law enforcement agencies with rules and limitations that are not necessarily required by the United States Constitution but might be required under a state constitution, state case law, or state legislative law. While the federal Constitution sets the minimum standards, not all the standards required by the Constitution for the federal government are binding on state governments, and in some cases, the requirements on state governments may operate in a different manner.

THE CONSTITUTION OF THE UNITED STATES

With the ratification of the Constitution of the United States, the nation embarked upon a new chapter in an ongoing legal and governmental experiment. The Articles of Confederation had proven to be less than ideal, and it was hoped that the Constitution would provide cures for the deficiencies that had become obvious in running a national government under the articles. To enhance the chances that the proper number of states would ratify the United States Constitution and have it replace the

Articles of Confederation,[1] a Bill of Rights was proposed as the first series of amendments to limit the powers of the government. If federal government powers were limited and some guarantees given to the states concerning their powers, acceptance by a sufficient number of states of the new national government seemed more likely. These initial amendments to the Constitution that we know as the Bill of Rights are simply the ones that received approval among others that were offered.

The limited national government, organized under the Articles of Confederation and existing before the ratification of the Constitution of the United States, possessed inherent power and jurisdiction to investigate, apprehend, try, and convict those accused of crimes and to punish transgressions of federal criminal law. The state governments possessed inherent power to punish violations of state law. States did not obtain power to govern from the federal government because state authority and power predated the existence of both the Articles of Confederation and the Constitution[2] and were not altered when the states ratified the Constitution. Inherent to a sovereign government is the power to defend itself not only against external enemies but also against internal enemies, who might be called criminals. Thus the federal government under the Articles of Confederation and under the Constitution of the United States possessed the power to define criminal deviancy and to provide for its punishment. The federal power to prosecute criminal activity coexisted with the power possessed by state governments to define and regulate deviant conduct.[3]

SEPARATION OF POWERS DOCTRINE

The Constitution of the United States separates the powers of the government into three coequal branches, the legislative, the executive, and the judicial. Under this separation of powers theory, the legislature makes law, the executive branch enforces law, and the judicial branch interprets law. In Article 1 of the United States Constitution, the powers of the legislature are conferred and described in general terms, with some requirements specifically mentioned. Article 2 provides for the basic organization of the executive branch and gives it rough parameters of power and responsibility. In Article 3, the Framers of the Constitution established a Supreme Court and permitted Congress to create other inferior courts as the Congress might later authorize. Basic jurisdiction and some limitations on the judicial power of the federal courts were enshrined within the Constitution by the Framers. For example, in court cases involving ambassadors and other public consuls, and in cases where a state is a party, the Supreme Court of the United States was given original jurisdiction. The federal court system was given jurisdiction

---

[1]Constitution of the United States, Article 7. The document provided that a new government would be established among the states when nine states had ratified.

[2]*Heath v. Alabama,* 474 U.S. 82, 89 (1985). Justice O'Connor, writing for the Court, stated, "The States are no less sovereign with respect to each other than they are with respect to the Federal Government. Their powers to undertake criminal prosecutions derive from separate and independent sources of power and authority originally belonging to them before admission to the Union and preserved to them by the Tenth Amendment."

[3]Ibid. "[T]he Court has uniformly held that the States are separate sovereigns with respect to the Federal Government because each State's power to prosecute is derived from its own 'inherent sovereignty,' not from the Federal Government."

over controversies in which the United States government might be a party, in cases where one state sues another state, in cases where a citizen of one state sues a citizen of a different state, and to all cases in law or equity arising under the Constitution. Some cases may be considered nonjusticiable when the issues involve political questions where there is a textually demonstrable constitutional commitment to another branch of the government. Over the years, the Supreme Court of the United States and inferior federal courts have taken steps to ensure that they do not encroach on matters that the Constitution has left to another coordinate branch of government.

SOURCES OF LAW

The federal and state governments get their law from a variety of sources, including their respective state and federal constitutions, state and federal legislative enactments, state and federal court decisions, and decisions made by administrative bodies. The initial and paramount source of law for federal courts comes from the United States Constitution. In an effort to supplant one of the deficiencies of the Articles of Confederation, the Constitution within its text declares that the document is the supreme law of the land.[4] When Congress exercises the powers granted to it under the Constitution, it may use the full extent of the power granted but must not exceed that power. Pursuant to this power, Congress may create federal crimes by describing them and attaching punishments to them. Congress has the power to prescribe rules of evidence and promulgate rules of criminal procedure, both of which it has done.

THE COMMON LAW AND MODERN LAW

The original state governments inherited the British common-law tradition,[5] with their general law initially derived from the common law in force on the date of American independence. Colonial legislative law as modified by the states following the Declaration of Independence formed the basic law of the states under the Articles of Confederation and, later, under the present Constitution. As Justice Field explained the sources of our law in the *Slaughterhouse Cases:*

> The common law of England is the basis of the jurisprudence of the United States. It was brought to this country by the colonists, together with the English statutes, and was established here so far as it was applicable to their condition. That law and the benefit of such of the English statutes as existed at the time of their colonization, and which they had by experience found to be applicable to their circumstances, were claimed by the Congress of the United Colonies in 1774….83 U.S. 36, 104 (1872).

---

[4]Constitution of the United States, Article 6. "This Constitution, and the laws of the United States which shall be made in pursuance thereof; and all treaties made, or which shall be made, under the authority of the United States, *shall be the supreme law of the land;* and the judges in every State shall be bound thereby, anything in the Constitution or laws of any State to the contrary notwithstanding" (emphasis added).
[5]The states of the United States follow the British common-law tradition, with the exception of the state of Louisiana, which follows the civil law system, largely based on the French Code of Napoleon.

Each state has a constitution that gives a basic framework of law in which the document allocates powers among the three coequal branches of government. State legislatures are permitted to fully use the powers possessed by them subject to the limitation that they may not usurp the powers not granted to them by their constitutions. A further limitation on state legislatures prohibits the assumption of authority that is inconsistent with powers granted to the national government under the United States Constitution, federal law, or federal treaty.

States create new law pursuant to their respective constitutions by passing bills through their legislatures with the concurrence of their governors. If the law defines and describes prohibited conduct and attaches a punishment, it will be considered an addition to the state's criminal code.

CONCURRENT JURISDICTION

Under our federal form of government, the states and the federal government have concurrent jurisdiction over many crimes. This means that criminal activity by one individual might violate both state and federal criminal law, and both jurisdictions could prosecute this individual for distinct federal and state crimes. For example, possession of various recreational pharmaceuticals offends both federal and state law, and an individual could be prosecuted first in a state court and later in a federal court. Armed bank robbery is an offense against the United States as well as an offense against any state in which the bank might be located. Successive state prosecution and federal prosecution for the possession of recreational pharmaceuticals and for bank robbery would be appropriate and would not offend any federal constitutional provision.[6] In a slightly different context, criminal activity might transgress the laws of two separate states, each of which may prosecute the individual for the violation of that state's law.[7]

Some criminal offenses are recognized only in a particular state and may not be considered as offenses by the federal government or by other state governments. For example, speaking on a cellular telephone while driving an automobile has been prohibited by New York law, but this practice is perfectly legal under the laws of many other states and is not illegal under federal criminal law. In a different context, possession of medicinal marijuana has been approved under a state statutory scheme in California, whereas the possession of the same medicinal marijuana has been prohibited by federal law.

---

[6]See *Bartkus v. Illinois,* 359 U.S. 121 (1959). Bartkus was acquitted of federal bank robbery charges and subsequently charged and convicted of state bank robbery charges involving the same physical conduct. The Court found no constitutional difficulty, since the one act (bank robbery) had been a crime against two separate sovereigns.

[7]See *Heath v. Alabama,* 474 U.S. 82 (1985). The dual sovereignty doctrine provides that, when a defendant in a single act violates the "peace and dignity" of two separate sovereigns by breaking the laws of each, he or she has committed two separate and distinct crimes. The crucial determination is whether the two governments that seek successively to prosecute a defendant for the same course of conduct can be termed separate sovereigns. This determination turns on whether the prosecuting entities' powers to undertake criminal prosecutions derive from separate and independent sources. The Court has traditionally held that state power to prosecute for crime is derived from its own inherent sovereignty and not from the federal government.

Thus, concurrent jurisdiction allows the federal government, a state government, or both to prosecute an individual act that transgresses the law of both jurisdictions. This practice is simply the recognition of a federal system involving states that have individual sovereignty in all criminal prosecutions involving a breach of state law.

PARALLEL COURT SYSTEMS

Courts within the United States are generally organized into a three-tiered system, with trial courts on the bottom, intermediate appellate courts in the middle, and a final supreme court at the apex. The trial courts, which generally have original jurisdiction for most cases, are the most numerous and are found throughout each state and throughout the jurisdiction of the United States. The trial court is the place where attorneys present evidence, witnesses are heard, criminal defendants appear with counsel, and juries hear evidence, deliberate, and render verdicts. Appeals from these trial courts are directed to the intermediate appellate courts, which have little discretion concerning which cases they will hear. Appellate courts hear oral arguments based on submitted legal briefs by counsel for criminal defendants. Typically, appellate courts have odd numbers of judges on the bench so as to produce a decision. Appealing a case from an appellate court to a supreme court is not automatic, and a supreme court generally uses discretion in deciding whether to hear a case.

In federal criminal prosecutions, the government initiates a case in a federal district court, which may sit with or without a jury depending on a defendant's wishes. If the federal government wins a conviction, the defendant has a statutory right to an appeal to a federal circuit court of appeal. This court must entertain the appeal and has no discretion to reject the case. If the defendant remains dissatisfied with the outcome, the defendant may ask that the Supreme Court of United States hear the case. This court generally has discretion to grant certiorari, which means that at least four justices have voted to hear the case. Justices often vote to hear a case where there is a conflict in legal principle between two circuit courts of appeal or where there is a case of special importance that the justices believe needs to be heard. When the Supreme Court decides a case involving an interpretation of the United States Constitution, there is no further appeal in any court. However, if the case involved an interpretation of a federal law, Congress possesses the power to change the interpretation given it by the Supreme Court by rewriting the law in a different manner with explicit instructions on interpretation.

In most instances, the state courts operate as a parallel legal system to the federal courts. State trial courts possess original jurisdiction over offenses against that particular state. Many state trial courts are divided into courts that primarily hear felony cases and other courts that hear misdemeanor cases. State trial courts go by a variety of names, with some called courts of common pleas, superior courts, circuit courts, and district courts, to name a few. Courts hearing misdemeanors often are municipal courts, county courts, and city courts. State criminal courts having felony jurisdiction often sit with juries as the finder of fact, unless the defendant has waived a trial by jury. As is the case with federal trial courts, a defendant who is dissatisfied with the outcome has a legal right to one appeal as a matter of law. The highest court in each state has discretion as to whether to hear most cases; it may accept or reject any case for any reason but is most likely to accept a case that involves an important legal issue needing clarification or where lower appellate courts in that state have decided a similar issue with conflicting results. Where a criminal defendant has been successful in having the highest court in the state consider his or her case and if the defendant remains dissatisfied with the outcome, an appeal to the United States Supreme Court is possible if the error involves a federal question. The defendant must allege that the criminal justice system of that state in some fashion has violated a federal right belonging to the defendant, and four justices of the Supreme Court of the United States must agree to hear the case.

CRIMINAL PROCEDURE PRIOR TO SELECTIVE INCORPORATION OF THE BILL OF RIGHTS

Until the late 1930s, the federal courts, including the Supreme Court, generally did not get involved in state criminal procedure. Some avenues were available to the federal courts following the Civil War, and some of these legal theories were put forth in the *Slaughterhouse Cases,* 83 U.S. 36 (1872). There the litigants argued that various provisions of the Fourteenth Amendment to the Constitution gave new rights to individuals in the states. Litigants contended that the constitutional amendments following the Civil War were intended to alter the relationship between the states and the national government. According to the Court:

> [W]e do not see in those amendments any purpose to destroy the main features of the general system. Under the pressure of all the excited feeling growing out of the war, our statesmen have still believed that the existence of the State with powers for domestic and local government, including the regulation of civil rights—the rights of person and of property—was essential to the perfect working of our complex form of government, though they have thought proper to impose additional limitations on the States, and to confer additional power on that of the Nation. *Slaughterhouse Cases,* 83 U.S. 36, 82 (1872).

Arguments concerning equal protection, privileges and immunities, and due process of law were lodged to no avail with the Supreme Court, which gave a rather narrow reading to the post–Civil War amendments. For many years after the 1870s, the Court ignored legal theory that could have allowed it to be more involved in state criminal procedure.

Where the Court did hear state criminal procedure cases, they typically involved egregious conduct on the part of various state functionaries in the criminal justice system. Demonstrative of this practice is the case of *Moore v. Dempsey,* 261 U.S. 86 (1923), where a mob improperly influenced the conviction and sentencing to death of five black men convicted of murder. According to the Court, a trial for murder in a state court in which the accused were hurried to conviction under mob domination without regard for their rights is without due process of law and absolutely void. Here and elsewhere, the Supreme Court proved willing to reverse cases where the conduct created miscarriages of justice, but the Court was not amenable to wholesale alteration of the constitutional system by applying the Bill of Rights to limit state criminal justice.

While the Court was not willing to incorporate specific guarantees of the Bill of Rights into the Due Process Clause of the Fourteenth Amendment, it was willing to say that some types of outrageous conduct by those clothed with state authority could violate that clause. In *Rochin v. California,* 342 U.S. 165 (1952), police officers, without a warrant, entered the home where Rochin lived and forced open the bedroom where Rochin and his wife were present. When police observed two capsules on a bedside table and asked him what they were, Rochin grabbed them and swallowed them. Police removed Rochin to a hospital, had his stomach pumped, and recovered the capsules of morphine. Later the morphine was introduced against him at his trial for possession of a controlled substance. Rochin successfully pursued his appeal to the United States Supreme Court, which ruled in his favor. As Justice Frankfurter said:

> …[W]e are compelled to conclude that the proceedings by which this conviction was obtained do more than offend some fastidious squeamishness or private sentimentalism about combating crime too energetically. This is conduct that shocks the conscience. Illegally breaking into the privacy of the petitioner, the struggle to open his mouth and remove what was there, the forcible extraction of his stomach's contents—this course of proceeding by agents of government to obtain evidence is bound to offend even hardened sensibilities. They are methods too close to the rack and the screw to permit of constitutional differentiation. 342 U.S. 165, 172.

Even though the Supreme Court ruled in Rochin's favor, it did not determine that the Fourth Amendment guarantee against unreasonable searches and seizures should be incorporated into the Due Process Clause of the Fourteenth Amendment and be applied so as to limit state law enforcement activity. This step was left for another day.

SELECTIVE INCORPORATION OF THE BILL OF RIGHTS

With changes in court personnel and the passage of time, the Supreme Court embarked on the path of selective incorporation of the Bill of Rights into the Fourteenth Amendment's Due Process Clause. Demonstrative of this process is the landmark case of *Mapp v. Ohio,* 367 U.S. 643 (1961), where the Court overruled an earlier case and instituted a rule of exclusion of illegally seized evidence. Mapp's home had been searched without a warrant, and evidence was seized and used against her in a criminal trial. She had been unsuccessful in her quest to have the Ohio courts overturn her conviction based on her allegation of an illegal search and seizure at her home. The Supreme Court granted certiorari, heard the case, and reversed her conviction. The *Mapp* Court held that the Fourth Amendment applied to the states and that evidence illegally seized should be excluded from trial to prove guilt.

In deciding to adopt the exclusionary rule for state prosecutions, the Court reexamined the constitutional underpinnings of an earlier case and determined that a new rule of criminal procedure should be applied to state prosecutions. In looking at the practice of many states in excluding illegally seized evidence from trial, the Court decided that all evidence obtained by searches and seizures in violation of the requirements of the Fourth Amendment should be excluded from state criminal trials, just as evidence illegally seized had been excluded from federal criminal trials since 1914.[8] The *Mapp* case incorporated the Fourth Amendment and its jurisprudence into the Due Process Clause of the Fourteenth Amendment and made the Fourth Amendment limitations on searches and seizures applicable to the states just as if the words of the Fourth Amendment had been written originally within the Fourteenth Amendment.

The process whereby the Supreme Court took a particular case in which an argument had been made that one of the guarantees of the Bill of Rights should be incorporated into the Due Process Clause and made enforceable against the states continued during the 1960s and 1970s. Supreme Court jurisprudence on a case-by-case basis has selectively incorporated most of the guarantees of the Bill of Rights into the Due Process Clause of the Fourteenth Amendment and made them applicable to state law enforcement and judicial processes.

STEPS IN THE CRIMINAL PROCESS

Introduction to the Criminal Process

As is indicated by its title, which refers to criminal procedure, this book is concerned with a system that processes people through the justice system and with the legal and constitutional rules that regulate how our criminal justice system operates. The remaining sections of this introduction outline in a rough chronological order the way a person enters the criminal justice system and is processed through it. Most American state jurisdictions and the federal jurisdictions follow a similar process from the initial investigation to the final disposition of a criminal case. Many of the rules and regulations that guide the various officials in delivering criminal justice services have developed through a series of cases, some on the federal level and some on the state level. State legislatures and the United States Congress have had a role in shaping the criminal justice system by passing laws that modify the criminal process to reflect changed perceptions of justice.

The Initial Encounter with the Justice System

The first time a person has contact with a member of the criminal justice system, a law enforcement official probably has been motivated by an official complaint; a personal observation of a crime by a police officer; an observation that, though not necessarily criminal, deserves some further investigation; or an arrest pursuant to a grand jury indictment or prosecutor's information. In other situations,

---

[8]See *Weeks v. United States*, 232 U.S. 383 (1914).

the individual may have contact with a police officer when a search warrant is executed or an arrest warrant is served. In other situations, a law enforcement officer processes some discretion concerning whether to pursue additional investigation, to make an immediate arrest, to defer the arrest to a later time, or to offer a warning or corrective suggestion to the individual. In other situations the law enforcement officer has little or no discretion concerning an arrest, such as where the officer possesses an arrest or search warrant and must reasonably follow the command of the warrant.

Following the discretionary path, under the stop and frisk rationale, if the officer has observed unusual conduct that, in light of the officer's experience and training, would lead a reasonable person to conclude that criminal activity may be afoot, the officer may approach the individual and make a reasonable inquiry. If the individual who has exhibited unusual behavior offers an objectively reasonable explanation for his or her conduct, that should end this brief encounter, and the officer should allow the citizen to go free and continue the activity. The encounter with the officer and the detention of the individual must be fairly brief, given the circumstances, or the officer may face the position of having, in effect, made an arrest without probable cause.

The Concept of Arrest

An arrest is a type of governmental seizure regulated by the Fourth Amendment,[9] which requires that probable cause exist prior to the time the law enforcement agent takes a person into physical custody. Probable cause is said to exist when the law enforcement official believes that the facts and circumstances known to that officer are based on trustworthy information and are sufficient to warrant a person of reasonable caution in believing that the suspect had committed or was committing an offense that dictated a full-custody arrest.

Miranda and Related Problems

Subsequent to arrest, the officer may ask questions concerning the person's name, residence, and general identity. However, if there is a desire to ask substantive questions of the arrestee concerning the suspected crime, the officer must carefully offer legal warnings required by the case of *Miranda v. Arizona*. The necessity of conveying these legal warnings arises when the officer has custody of the individual and wishes to interrogate that person. If the officer has custody but has no plans to ask questions, the *Miranda* warnings need not be given. If an arrest has not occurred and the officer wishes to ask questions of a person not in custody, no warnings are necessary.

The *Miranda* warnings are designed to convey to the arrestee his or her right to remain silent under the Fifth Amendment and the right to consult with counsel, protected under the Sixth Amendment. Prior to interrogation, the person in custody must be clearly informed of the right to remain silent, and that anything he or she says may be used against him or her in a court of law. The individual must be

---

[9]Through the process of selective incorporation of various of the first eight amendments into the Due Process Clause of the Fourteenth Amendment, the guarantees of the Fourth Amendment are applicable against state action. See chapter 4 for additional information on the doctrine of selective incorporation.

clearly informed of the right to consult with a lawyer and to have the lawyer present during interrogation, and that a lawyer will be appointed if the accused is indigent. At the conclusion of the warnings, if the individual indicates, prior to or during questioning, the wish to remain silent, the interrogation must cease; if the accused states that he or she wants an attorney, the questioning must cease until an attorney is present.

A person is in police custody when he or she is not free to leave or to otherwise go about his or her business. Two separate inquiries are often used to resolve the question of custody. First, what were the circumstances surrounding the interrogation? Second, given those circumstances, would a reasonable person have felt at liberty to terminate the interrogation and leave? Where the answers to the questions indicate both custody and interrogation, *Miranda* warnings become mandatory criminal practice.

A similarly difficult determination centers around the issue of interrogation and whether the activities of police constitute true questioning. Interrogation has been interpreted in a broader context than mere questioning and extends to intentional actions by police that are designed to elicit a verbal response indicative of crime. According to the courts, interrogation may include conversations between police officers that can be overheard by an arrestee. If the substance of this conversation is designed to elicit an incriminating response from the arrestee, the conversation of the police within earshot of the arrestee maybe deemed the "functional equivalent" of interrogation and run afoul of the *Miranda* prohibition.

Collection of Evidence

Following an arrest, the investigatory stage of the process continues, including gathering evidence at the arrest location, searching the person of the arrestee, and evidentiary searches at derivative locations. The scope of a search incident to a lawful arrest extends to any objects on the person or within the arrestee's clothing and to the area under the arrestee's immediate dominion and control; it may include a full search and inventory of any personal possessions of the arrestee. An arrest within or near an automobile allows a fairly broad search of the area within the immediate dominion and control of the arrestee. The postarrest process of searching normally concludes with an inventory search of the arrestee's personal property when the arrestee undergoes the booking procedure at the local jail.

Initial Judicial Appearance and Preliminary Hearing

Where a person has been arrested pursuant to warrant, an initial court determination of probable cause is not necessary, since a neutral and detached judicial official has previously made that determination prior to issuing an arrest warrant. However, if the arrest has been based on a police officer's determination of probable cause, a judicial official must hold a hearing to make a determination of the existence of probable cause[10] within forty-eight hours of arrest.[11]

---

[10]See *Gerstein v. Pugh,* 420 U.S. 103 (1975).
[11]See *County of Riverside v. McLaughlin,* 500 U.S. 44 (1991).

If the hearing involves a determination of issues beyond simply deciding probable cause, it may be called a preliminary hearing in many jurisdictions. Since local practice varies so widely, a preliminary hearing not only may determine probable cause but also may deal with and dispose of a larger number of issues. If legal counsel has not been appointed previously, the judge will appoint counsel for the detainee. The prosecution may be required to put on a prima facie case by calling witnesses who can be cross-examined by the defendant. A failure to present a prima facie case usually results in a dismissal of the prosecution's case. At some preliminary hearings the issue of bail may be considered and the defendant may be required to enter a plea and to offer notice of the intent to use some affirmative defenses.

The Grand Jury and Filing an Information

Unless a defendant waives the right to a grand jury indictment, in federal prosecutions, the prosecutor must initiate a serious criminal case through a grand jury indictment. However, the Fifth Amendment requirement of a grand jury indictment does not apply to the individual states of the United States; states are free to use their version of a grand jury system or to initiate criminal prosecutions by the use of an information.

Where a prosecutor convenes a grand jury, the practice is fairly similar, regardless of the jurisdiction. A grand jury is composed of citizens who hear evidence against an accused and come to a determination concerning whether probable cause exists to believe that a person has committed a crime or crimes. The grand jury members may ask questions of the witnesses who appear before the grand jury, and grand juries have the power to subpoena papers and documents from virtually any person, company, or legal entity. As is frequently the case, the target of the grand jury's investigation may be unaware that the grand jury is considering an indictment against the individual.

Where the prosecutor files an information against a defendant, it generally consists of a recitation in plain English, accusing a particular person of committing a particular crime or crimes. It will include the dates, times, and operative facts concerning the alleged crime in order to give a defendant fair notice of what he or she must defend against.

Plea Bargaining and Plea Negotiation

The concept that a prosecutor and defense counsel would both take a close look at a pending criminal case and come to some agreement concerning its disposition without trial received judicial approval by the Supreme Court in 1971.[12] This process involves consultation between the defense counsel and the client, on one side, and the prosecutor's office, on the other. The defense may have to plead

---

[12]See *Santobello v. New York,* 404 U.S. 257 (1971).

to the charges as brought if there are no defense witnesses and the defendant believes that the government will prevail at trial. On the other side of the equation, the prosecutor who understands that there are weaknesses in the case and that a conviction at the level charged is unlikely will be more inclined to allow a defendant to plead guilty to some lesser included offense or to offer reduced sentencing recommendations to assure the certainty of a conviction.

Pretrial Motions

While efforts directed toward the defense of the client begin the moment the attorney is appointed by the court or is hired by the defendant, significant defense strategy begins to emerge following the preliminary hearing. The evidence presented by the prosecutor during a preliminary hearing also gives the defense attorney considerable insight into the theory that the prosecution will likely pursue at trial. Upon request, the defense counsel is usually allowed to see a considerable amount of the evidence that prosecution possesses but does not have a similar duty to disclose defense evidence and strategy.

Some constitutional issues must be raised prior to trial or they are deemed to have been waived. For example, where a defendant believes that he or she has been the victim of an illegal search and seizure in violation of the Fourth Amendment, this issue should be raised and resolved prior to trial. If the defendant's attorney is successful in having such an issue resolved in the defendant's favor prior to trial, it may result in a dismissal of the case. If the defendant wins on some issues and loses others, it may make his or her pretrial position stronger to the point that a plea bargain may be attainable.

Similarly, any Fifth Amendment issue involving the defendant's privilege not to incriminate him- or herself should be resolved prior to trial because it will result in evidence being excluded from the prosecution's use. Closely allied to Fifth Amendment concerns are issues involving warning of the right to counsel and the right to silence under the case of *Miranda v. Arizona*. Whether the exclusion results in a different disposition of the case in the pretrial stage, most exclusion of evidence should work to the defendant's benefit.

Trial by Jury

According to the Sixth Amendment, "In all criminal prosecutions, the accused shall enjoy the right to a speedy and public trial, by an impartial jury of the State and district wherein the crime shall have been committed." This particular legal right has been found to be binding not only on the federal government but on all state governments as well,[13] but that right may not always entitle a state court defendant to a jury of twelve members or to a jury in which a unanimous decision is required. However, where the potential sentence is more than six months, a federal criminal defendant receives a twelve-person jury, which must reach a verdict by a unanimous vote.

---

[13]See *Duncan v. Louisiana,* 391 U.S. 145, 156 (1968).

Trial to a Judge

Although there is a constitutional right under the Sixth Amendment to a trial by jury, whether in a federal or state court, many defendants decide to waive their rights to a jury and have the case decided by a judge or, in some cases, a three-judge panel. Where a defendant selects this approach, such a decision is usually the result of careful deliberation by the defendant and his or her legal counsel. Where the judge hears the case, he or she rules on admission or exclusion of evidence, listens to opening and final arguments from both sides, and acts as a jury of one. The judge makes the decision on guilt or innocence by evaluating the facts as a jury would have otherwise done.

The Trial

Following pretrial maneuvers, motions, and judicial rulings, the defendant and the prosecution begin the trial by selecting the jury and proceeding to opening arguments. While the attorneys for both sides may have had a chance to influence the jurors slightly during the jury selection process, the first real chance they have to offer the jury their respective theories of the case is during the opening statement. The prosecution and defense initiate opening arguments by explaining what each side expects to prove and the methods by which the evidence will be presented.

During the case in chief, the prosecution will introduce evidence from witness observation, physical evidence, or demonstrative evidence. Evidence presented must meet the test of relevancy or, stated another way, must be of sufficient importance to be worth allowing the jury to consider. Even where evidence may prove to be quite important, it may still be excluded if, upon proper objection, the judge rules that its prejudicial effect outweighs its probative value.

When both the prosecution and the defense have presented their cases in chief and the jury has heard the closing arguments by the prosecutor and by defense counsel, the judge instructs the jury concerning the legal theory governing the case. The judge's instructions consist of an explanation of the law applicable to the case at bar. When the jury reaches a verdict beyond a reasonable doubt and by the appropriate number of jurors necessary to produce a decision, it returns to court to render its verdict.

Criminal Appeal Process

Although no federal constitutional right to an appeal exists, all states in the United States and the federal government grant the right to appeal a criminal conviction either by statute or by state constitution. A person convicted in federal court has a right of appeal to a federal circuit court of appeal. Where an indigent wishes to make the first appeal as of right, the government must supply appointed legal counsel for appellate purposes at no cost to the indigent litigant. The successful appellant, whether indigent or otherwise, faces the possibility of a second trial and must be prepared to go through the criminal justice system one more time.

Subsequent to successful appeal by a defendant, the prosecution must reevaluate the strength of its case and the challenges presented by a retrial. The prosecution may select a retrial, the defense may attempt to negotiate a plea, or the prosecutor decline to pursue the case further. In some instances, an appellate court may remand the case to the trial court with instructions to dismiss the case. Not infrequently, the defendant prevails at the first appellate level only to have the prosecution pursue the case one level higher to a state supreme court or the top federal court. The prosecution's pursual of an appeal to a higher court poses no double jeopardy problem because the original conviction may be reinstated in situations where the government ultimately prevails.

CHAPTER 1

The Fourth Amendment Standards: Probable Cause to Search, Searches, Warrants, and Exceptions to the Legal Requirements

Chapter Outline

Key Terms

Affidavit for a warrant
Knock and announce
Open fields doctrine
Particularity of description
Probable cause

Scope of search
Stale probable cause
Totality of the circumstances test
Two-pronged test
Warrant

1. INTRODUCTION AND HISTORY: GENERALLY

Amendment Four

The right of the people to be secure in their persons, houses, papers, and effects, against unreasonable searches and seizures, shall not be violated, and no Warrants shall issue, but upon probable cause, supported by Oath or affirmation, and particularly describing the place to be searched, and the persons or things to be seized.

The Fourth Amendment, which became effective in 1791, had been ratified as part of the first ten amendments, which were designed to limit the power of the federal government. The first ten amendments were part of a package of amendments that had been offered as an inducement to get the proper number of states to approve what is known now as the Constitution of the United States. When the proposed constitution had been presented to the states and to the people for ratification, there was a fear, in many significant circles, that the central government would become too powerful. As a result, some limitations upon the power of the proposed national government in the form of a Bill of Rights would help enhance the arguments in favor of ratification and allay the fears that blanket searches similar to those conducted by the British colonial government might return under a new national government.

From its inception, the authors of the Fourth Amendment intended to place restrictions on federal government agents when conducting searches and seizures against the people of the United States. In pre–Revolutionary War days, Crown officers of the British government had been allowed to search colonial homes looking for papers and other effects with what amounted to blanket search warrants. These blank search warrants, called writs of assistance, and the purpose and location of the search were filled out by government agents following the conclusion of a search. The colonists protested against such conduct by Crown officials and argued that because the colonists possessed the rights of Englishmen and that such a search would have been illegal in England itself, the rights of the colonists were being violated by the British Crown. This deep distrust of a national government carried over to the proposed stronger national government under the United States Constitution. With this history in mind, some limitations on the power of the central government were thought to be necessary to prevent future difficulties along the lines of those experienced by the colonists in the pre–Revolutionary War days.

The Fourth Amendment, from its inception, applied only to federal government officials and had no effect on state law enforcement practice. By its terms, the amendment was to limit law enforcement officials in the exercise of their duties by not allowing them to search in areas where a person might have a right expectation of privacy.[1] Thus, an individual might protect his person, house, and personal items from scrutiny or disclosure to an agent of the federal government. The fact that one

---

[1] The word *privacy* is not mentioned in the text of the Fourth Amendment. However, through judicial interpretation and a common practice it is believed that the Fourth Amendment protects an individual's expectation of privacy in a variety of contexts. The expectation of privacy and its link with the Fourth Amendment have been mentioned by the Supreme Court of the United States as recently as *Kyllo v. United States,* 533 U.S. 27 (2001), and as early as 1911 in *Flint v. Stone Tracy Co.,* 220 U.S. 107.

could expect what we now call privacy from government scrutiny was not a limitless right but could be overcome if the government used proper evidence and followed proper procedure. According to the Fourth Amendment, only *unreasonable* searches and seizures were prohibited, which gives rise to the concept that *reasonable* searches and seizures were perfectly permissible. Naturally, the difficulty arises in determining when a search is reasonable and when it crosses the line and becomes unreasonable. History has left this determination to law enforcement officials in many situations, but in general the requirement is that a judge or magistrate must authorize a search or seizure for its legality to be assured.

Where a judicial official is asked to issue a warrant for a search, seizure, or arrest, the legal standard that must be met is called *probable cause,* which is mentioned in the text of the Fourth Amendment. Although probable cause is not defined within the amendment, judicial construction through case law has given content to the concept. In *Brinegar v. United States,* probable cause to search was stated to exist "where the known facts and circumstances are sufficient to warrant a man of reasonable prudence in the belief that contraband or evidence of a crime will be found."[2] In a similar fashion, probable cause to seize a human was deemed to exist where "the facts available to the officers at the moment of the arrest would 'warrant a man of reasonable caution in the belief' that an offense has been committed."[3] The probable cause threshold where an officer has sufficient proof to search or seize has been stated as "whether the facts available to an officer at the moment of the arrest would warrant a person of reasonable caution to conclude that an offense has been committed or that seizable property may be found in a particular place or on a particular person." Probable cause must be greater than mere suspicion and more than a hunch, but it need not rise to the level of proof beyond a reasonable doubt.

For an arrest or search warrant to issue, probable cause under the Fourth Amendment must be supported by the sworn oath of an officer, who must carefully describe the location of the place to be searched and particularly describe the object or objects to be seized. If it is a person, the officer must carefully describe the individual sufficiently so that the target person may be identified without being confused with other people. This concept of particularity appears to have been designed to remove any arguments that might indicate that the warrant process possesses any similarity to the blank warrants used prior to the Revolutionary War. Where the judicial official agrees with the officer that probable cause exists, the judge or magistrate has the power to issue a warrant for a search or an arrest.

The text of the Fourth Amendment provides the basic framework for searches, seizures, and arrests, but the actual mechanics and practice of searches and seizures have seen extensive adjustments and alteration through case law decided since 1791. The addition of the Fourteenth Amendment, subsequent to the War between the States, containing a due process clause, gave rise to an argument that due process should include the guarantees of the Fourth Amendment protecting individuals against unreasonable searches and seizures. While these arguments were not initially

---

[2] *Brinegar v. United States,* 338 U.S. 160 at 175–176 (1949).
[3] *Beck v. Ohio,* 379 U.S. 89 (1964).

persuasive,[4] eventually the Supreme Court of the United States determined that the guarantees of the Fourth Amendment were, in reality, part of due process and should be considered enforceable against the states[5] and should limit state law enforcement practices.

2. THE FOURTH AMENDMENT: PROBABLE CAUSE TO SEARCH

"The right of the people to be secure in their persons, houses, papers, and effects, against unreasonable searches and seizures, shall not be violated, and no warrants shall issue, but upon probable cause."[6] The language of the Fourth Amendment describes rights possessed by people, but it does not define all its terms, and it is not self-enforcing. While basically describing some sort of a right of privacy, it does so without mentioning the word *privacy.* As a general rule, we are guaranteed the right to keep objects and personal effects from governmental inquiry and scrutiny unless there exist powerful reasons for the government to intrude on our personal lives. When governmental agents believe that these powerful reasons are present, procedures have evolved to test the validity of the reasons and to allow searches and seizures in many cases where the governmental need outweighs our right to expect, for lack of a better term, our right of privacy. According to *Carroll v. United States,* 267 U.S. 132, 162 (1925), in a case involving transportation of untaxed alcoholic beverages, probable cause to search existed when police officers possessed "facts and circumstances within their knowledge and of which they had reasonably trustworthy information [that those facts] were sufficient, in themselves, to warrant a man of reasonable caution in the belief that intoxicating liquor was being transported in the automobile which they stopped and searched" (see Case 1.1).

With some exceptions,[7] probable cause must exist before any search may lawfully occur, whether the search is pursuant to a warrant or otherwise. To paraphrase *Carroll v. United States,* 267 U.S. 132, 162 (1925), probable cause has been said to exist when the facts and circumstances within the officers' knowledge are sufficient to warrant a person of reasonable prudence in the belief that contraband or evidence of a crime will be found in a particular place or on a particular person. This standard of belief rises above a mere hunch but falls far short of proof beyond a reasonable doubt. Probable cause is based on an objective standard and not on the subjective belief of the particular police officer. While a police officer may believe that probable cause to search exists, further steps are required to be analyzed prior to making a search. Some searches may be conducted with probable cause but without a warrant; the general rule, however, is that warrantless searches inside a home are presumed to be unreasonable, in violation of the Fourth Amendment.[8]

---

[4]See *Wolf v. Colorado,* 328 U.S. 25 (1949).
[5]See *Mapp v. Ohio,* 367 U.S. 643 (1961).
[6]Amendment Four, United States Constitution.
[7]Exceptions to the requirement of probable cause include brief stop and frisks under *Terry v. Ohio,* 392 U.S. 1 (1968); sweeps of real estate under *Maryland v. Buie,* 494 U.S. 325 (1990); and brief sobriety stops of motorists under *Michigan v. Sitz,* 496 U.S. 444 (1990).
[8]*Coolidge v. New Hampshire,* 403 U.S. 443 (1971).

Since the Fourth Amendment protects against unreasonable searches and seizures, reasonable searches are permitted. As a general rule, where a judicial official has issued a search warrant, the search conducted pursuant to it is presumed to be reasonable. Case law permits warrantless searches of motor vehicles given probable cause to search on the theory that such searches are reasonable under the circumstances. Similarly, an open field, where there is little expectation of privacy, may be searched without a warrant, given probable cause. As exceptions to the general rule, searches incident to arrest, inventory searches, and emergency searches may be conducted without warrants.

3. SPECIFICITY OF SEARCH; PARTICULARITY OF DESCRIPTION

Under the Fourth Amendment, to obtain a search warrant, there must be sufficient specificity describing the location of the object to be seized. The specificity of description requirement can be satisfied where "the description is such that the officer with a search warrant can with reasonable effort ascertain and identify the place intended."[9] A warrant for which the supporting documentation indicates probable cause to search the garage and the area of the home used for business purposes is specific enough to allow a search of the entire building.[10] In a case[11] where police officers obtained and executed a search warrant for a search of a described person as well as premises known as "2603 Park Avenue third floor apartment" for drugs was held to be sufficiently specific, even though, unknown to officers, there was more than one apartment on the third floor (see Case 1.3). Where a building or real estate is the subject of the search, proper description such as the mailing address and its location at the corner of specific streets will generally be specific enough to withstand a court challenge to the validity of the search. A description of an object needs to be as specific as possible; it need not be perfect, just sufficiently detailed given the nature of the object of the search. Obviously, a serial number would not be expected for a search for a quantity of drugs, and gambling records do not allow precise description, but a search for a stolen firearm might well include a serial number, caliber, type of weapon, and manufacturer.

4. REQUIREMENT OF A WARRANT

To conduct a legal search, absent some well-defined exception, a search warrant from a neutral and detached judicial official is required under the dictates of the Fourth Amendment. In addition, as a practical matter, where a search is conducted pursuant to a warrant, the warrant assures the individual whose property is being searched or being seized of the lawful authority of the law enforcement officer, the need to search, and the limits of the officer's power to search. The procedure to obtain a

---

[9] *Steele v. United States,* 267 U.S. 498, 503 (1925).
[10] Ibid. According to the *Steele* Court and stated with approval, "A warrant was applied for to search any building or rooms connected or used in connection with the garage, or the basement or subcellar beneath the same. It is quite evident that the elevator of the garage connected it with every floor and room in the building, and was intended to be used with it."
[11] *Maryland v. Garrison,* 480 U.S. 79 (1987).

warrant to search must begin with a police officer making a determination, based on facts and circumstances known to the officer, that probable cause exists. The officer, sometimes with assistance from a prosecutor's office, prepares an affidavit for a search warrant in which the operative facts and details are recited. The officer (affiant) must swear that the facts are true as far as he or she knows. Since the Fourth Amendment requires specificity concerning the object and location of the search, detailed information proves essential in the process of obtaining a search warrant. If an informant has been used to establish or help establish probable cause, the facts elicited from that person will be recounted along with reasons the judge should believe the informant's conclusions. The role of the judge is not to "rubber-stamp" the conclusions of police but to exercise independent judgment in rendering a decision concerning the existence of probable cause. If the judge concurs with police that probable cause exists to believe that seizable property will be found at a particularly described place or on a particular person, he or she will sign a warrant to search. The search warrant issued by a neutral and detached judicial official upon a finding of probable cause is a court order to law enforcement officials to search and seize specifically described and located property.

5. SOURCES OF PROBABLE CAUSE: THE INFORMANT

Where the foundation of probable cause rests on information from an informant, earlier case law from the Supreme Court of the United States suggested that the police and judges use a two-pronged test[12] to determine whether that information demonstrated probable cause. The police officers in *Aguilar v. Texas*[13] obtained a warrant based on a defective affidavit in which they swore that they had "received reliable information from a credible person and do believe that heroin, marijuana, barbiturates" were located within a residence. The *Aguilar* Court noted that the officers failed to state facts or circumstances from which the magistrate could have independently concluded that probable cause existed, *and* they neglected to offer any evidence that could have given credibility to the informant's conclusion that drugs were located in a particular place. To establish probable cause using an informant, the two-pronged test had to be met or police risked obtaining a defective warrant.

Under the *Aguilar* test, an informant's veracity and reliability had to be determined prior to a finding that the informant's information supplied probable cause. The police had to prove that the informant was a believable person. An informant might be believed to be truthful if he or she had given reliable information in the past or had implicated him- or herself in a crime by conveying the information to the police. If the informant were the local priest, mayor, or another police officer, his or her believability would not likely be questioned. The second prong required that police present facts to the judge or magistrate which demonstrated that the informant possessed a basis from which one could reasonably conclude that probable cause existed.

---

[12]The two-pronged test was developed in *Aguilar v. Texas,* 378 U.S. 108 (1964), and refined somewhat in *Spinelli v. United States,* 393 U.S. 410 (1969), before being dropped by the Court in *Illinois v. Gates,* 462 U.S. 213 (1983).
[13]378 U.S. 108 (1964).

In summary, to demonstrate probable cause based on an informant's information, the police must establish the basis of knowledge of the informant. First, police must understand the particular means by which the informant came by the information; second, there must exist supporting facts that prove either the veracity of the informant or the specific reliability of the information in the particular case. Unacceptable facts were bald and unilluminating conclusions offered by an informant that were not supported by the facts he or she provided.[14] For judicial approval, the police officer must include some of the underlying circumstances that would allow the judicial official to independently assess the validity of the informant's conclusions.

6. THE DEMISE OF THE TWO-PRONGED TEST

In attempting to follow the dictates of *Aguilar*, state courts generated significant litigation centering on application of aspects of the two-pronged test. Subsequent to deciding *Aguilar*, the Court reaffirmed the two-pronged test in *Spinelli v. United States,* 393 U.S. 410 (1969). In *Spinelli,* officers investigating interstate gambling relied partly on information supplied by an informant and partly on personal investigation. In preparing the affidavit for a search warrant for Spinelli's apartment, the officers neglected to state facts that could have permitted the magistrate to independently conclude that the informant was reliable. The Court held that the officers neglected to state facts that would lead one to believe that probable cause existed, and they failed to state facts that supported the reliability of the informant. On the face of the affidavit, the officers should have noted why they concluded that the informant should have been believed. In overturning the search pursuant to the warrant, the Court reaffirmed the continued validity of the *Aguilar* decision.

Convinced that the *Aguilar* test was not being applied properly in a number of cases, and deciding to revisit the issue of informant production of probable cause, the Court overruled the *Aguilar* two-pronged test in *Illinois v. Gates,* 462 U.S. 213 (1983), and adopted a totality of the circumstances test (see Case 1.2). Under the totality of the circumstances approach, a judge must look at the information offered by the informant and consider all relevant information, including facts supporting the believability and truthfulness of the informant, in reaching a decision. The *Gates* Court noted that under the totality of the circumstances analysis, "a deficiency in one may be compensated for, in determining the overall reliability of a tip, by a strong showing as to the other, or by some other indicia of reliability."[15] What the Court was attempting to avoid was a mechanical application of the two-pronged test. Under the totality of the circumstances test, if an informant had no past record of reliability or honesty but gave a detailed account of facts that indicated probable cause, the wealth of detail should overcome the lack of a proven record of honesty.

---

[14]For a more detailed explanation of the history of the two-pronged test, see *Aguilar v. Texas,* 378 U.S. 108 (1964), and *Spinelli v. United States,* 393 U.S. 410 (1969). The two-pronged test was officially overruled in *Illinois v. Gates,* 462 U.S. 213 (1983), but courts still look to both factors in determining the value of an informant's information.

[15]*Gates* at 233.

Following *Gates,* a judicial officer may look at all the evidence pointing toward probable cause and come to a determination, without having to satisfy unrealistic pigeonhole standards. An informant's evidence may meet the probable cause standard by virtue of his or her past record as an informant, the extensive detail of the information conveyed, the surrounding circumstances, or any combination of these.

Although *Gates* abandoned strict adherence to the two-pronged test in determining probable cause under the Fourth Amendment, some state jurisdictions continued to apply the old *Aguilar* rule requiring a reason to believe the informant and dictating close scrutiny to deciding whether the substance of what the informant offered equaled probable cause. If state courts rely on their individual interpretation of state law and continue to apply *Aguilar,* there is no problem. Although *Gates* demolished the *Aguilar* test, many state courts continued to apply it, as if it remained good law. In an effort to bury the *Aguilar* two-pronged test, the Supreme Court reaffirmed the *Gates* decision and the demise of the two-pronged test in *Massachusetts v. Upton,* 466 U.S. 727 (1984).

In *Upton,* the state court had continued to interpret the Fourth Amendment as requiring the two-pronged test of *Aguilar* when making determinations on whether an informant's information equaled probable cause. According to the *Upton* Court:

> Prior to *Gates,* the Fourth Amendment was understood by many courts to require strict satisfaction of a "two-pronged test" whenever an [informant helps supply probable cause]…in the particular case. The Massachusetts court apparently viewed *Gates* as merely adding a new wrinkle to this two-pronged test: where an informant's veracity and/or basis of knowledge are not sufficiently clear, substantial corroboration of the tip may save an otherwise invalid warrant.
>
> > We do not view the *Gates* opinion as decreeing a standardless "totality of the circumstances" test. The informant's veracity and basis of his knowledge are still important but, where the tip is adequately corroborated, they are not elements indispensible [*sic*] to finding of probable cause. It seems that, in a given case, the corroboration may be so strong as to satisfy probable cause in the absence of any other showing of the informant's "veracity" and any direct statement of the "basis of [his] knowledge." 390 Mass. At 568, 458 N.E.2d at 721.
>
> We think that the Supreme Judicial Court of Massachusetts misunderstood our decision in *Gates.* We did not merely refine or qualify the "two-pronged test." We rejected it as hypertechnical and divorced from "the factual and practical considerations of everyday life on which reasonable and prudent men, not legal technicians, act." Quoting *Brinegar v. United States,* 338 U.S. at 175 (1949).[16]

Consistent with principles of federalism, state courts relying on their individual state constitutional provisions are free to continue to use the two-pronged test to determine probable cause, but they can no longer use the test as a determinative for probable cause under the Fourth Amendment.

---

[16]466 U.S. 727 at 731, 732.

7. SOURCES OF PROBABLE CAUSE: POLICE OFFICERS AND OTHERS

In a large number of cases, the evidence presented to the judicial official in an affidavit for a search warrant comes from the personal observation of police officers and reports of other officers. Since courts assume that a sworn affidavit of personal knowledge offered by a police officer contains true information, the problems associated with the use of anonymous or questionable informants do not arise. Where the text of the affidavit for a search warrant includes information provided by fellow officers, the credibility of those officers does not come into question unless factually incredible evidence has been included. Generally, the judge need only consider the information contained within the affidavit to make an informed judgment concerning whether the facts support the existence of probable cause. If the judge determines from the affidavit that probable cause exists, he or she will sign the warrant authorizing the search of particularly described premises or person.

8. THE AFFIDAVIT FOR A WARRANT

As a general rule, a search warrant will not be issued until the judge or magistrate has considered the facts contained within the affidavit presented by the police. In addition to a description of why probable cause exists, the affidavit must particularly describe the place,[17] person, or property to be searched or the object to be seized. In most jurisdictions, the affiant must state the offense to which the seized property is believed to relate. The judicial official may agree with the officer's probable cause conclusions and issue the warrant. Alternatively, the judge or magistrate may require additional evidence before being convinced that probable cause exists. If the evidence must be added to the affidavit, generally it must be provided in writing as an amended affidavit or as an addendum to the original.

9. THE SEARCH WARRANT: A COURT ORDER

A warrant is a court order directed to the law enforcement official that recites the material facts alleged in the affidavit and carefully describes the place to be searched and particularly describes the objects to be seized. The warrant commands the officer to search the place or person or described property and bring any items seized to the court. The warrant requires the person or persons in control of the particular premises to allow the search to be conducted. Since a warrant is a lawful court order, no one possesses any right to resist the execution of a search warrant, but

---

[17]Specificity concerning the place to be searched is a requirement under the Fourth Amendment according to the Court in *Maryland v. Garrison,* 480 U.S. 79, 84 (1987), where Justice Stevens, writing for the Court, stated:

The Warrant Clause of the Fourth Amendment categorically prohibits the issuance of any warrant except one "particularly describing the place to be searched and the persons or things to be seized." The manifest purpose of this particularity requirement was to prevent general searches. By limiting the authorization to search to the specific areas and things for which there is probable cause to search, the requirement ensures that the search will be carefully tailored to its justifications, and will not take on the character of the wide-ranging exploratory searches the Framers intended to prohibit.

there is no duty to affirmatively assist in the search. The officer or officers executing the warrant give the person in control of the premises a copy of the warrant and, later, a list or inventory of items seized. If no one is present, the inventory is affixed to the premises that have been searched.

10. THE SEARCH WARRANT: THE TIME OF EXECUTION

Police officers must follow several rules and requirements during the execution of the warrant. The warrant must be executed within a reasonable time or within the time limits dictated by state law[18] if it specifies a time limit. A warrant executed later than what is considered as reasonable or as specified is invalid and does not produce good evidence. The general preference for executions of warrants is that they be served during daytime hours, but most jurisdictions allow requests for night executions, and, significantly, most states do not invalidate a night search whether or not it had been requested pursuant to state law.

11. FOURTH AMENDMENT REQUIREMENT: KNOCK AND ANNOUNCE

Many jurisdictions require a knock and announce before beginning a search, but this requirement may be ignored if following it would subject the officers to greater danger (see Case 1.4).[19] In fact, some state laws allow the affiant to request in the affidavit approval for a nonconsensual entry where the officer has reason to believe that a knock and announce procedure will pose a greater danger to the officers executing the warrant. Nonconsensual or dynamic entries to execute search warrants have been approved[20] by the United States Supreme Court as being consistent with the Fourth Amendment. In addition to the general knock and announce requirement, police may detain persons who are present or who come to the premises during the execution of the search warrant.[21] Police officers may detain persons connected to the place of search, but they may not search the persons[22] of the seized individuals unless some other legal theory permits a search or searches. In some situations, when police have probable cause and are awaiting the arrival of a search warrant, they may prohibit unaccompanied reentry to premises by the occupant. Such brief seizure of the property until a judge issues a warrant has been deemed reasonable under the Fourth Amendment.[23]

---

[18]Demonstrative of the time limit is the Ohio Revised Code, Section 2933.24, which requires the search to be completed within three days of the issuance of the warrant. Other states have similar statutes.

[19]See *Wilson v. Arkansas,* 514 U.S. 927 (1995), where the Court held that the Fourth Amendment included the knock and announce requirement because of common-law practice. However, the Court also held that a search and seizure in a dwelling might be reasonable without a prior announcement due to the circumstances of a reasonable belief of enhanced peril if done openly. This issue will be litigated on a case-by-case basis.

[20]Ibid.

[21]See *Michigan v. Summers,* 452 U.S. 692 (1981).

[22]See *Ybarra v. Illinois,* 444 U.S. 85 (1979).

[23]See *Illinois v. McArthur,* 531 U.S. 326 (2001).

12. SCOPE OF SEARCH

The extent of a search, or its scope, as it is often called, is dictated by the size and type of object that is the goal of the search, as well as the location where the search is to occur. Obviously, powdered recreational pharmaceuticals might be hidden in any location; thus, a warrant ordering the search and seizure of drugs would allow police officers to search virtually anywhere in a motor vehicle or residence. On the other hand, because a larger object such as a computer or a rifle could not be stored in an automobile console or a bathroom medicine chest in a residence, a search for such an object in those areas would exceed the lawful scope of the search. As Justice Stevens explained the concept of the scope of a lawful search in the context of a container search:

> The scope of a warrantless search of an automobile thus is not defined by the nature of the container in which the contraband is secreted. Rather, it is defined by the object of the search and the places in which there is probable cause to believe that it may be found. Just as probable cause to believe that a stolen lawnmower may be found in a garage will not support a warrant to search an upstairs bedroom, probable cause to believe that undocumented aliens are being transported in a van will not justify a warrantless search of a suitcase. *United States v. Ross,* 456 U.S. 798, 824 (1982).

Generally, once the object of the search has been described, the scope of the search is limited to areas and places where that object might reasonably be located. To search in areas where the object might not reasonably be located could constitute an unreasonable search under the Fourth Amendment and might result in the object being excluded from use in evidence at trial.

13. STALE PROBABLE CAUSE

While warrants are valid for a reasonable time or for a set period of time, the problem of stale probable cause may undercut the validity of a warrant-based search conducted after probable cause has ceased to exist. The objects of many searches possess ready mobility, so that what may be true today will not necessarily be true later. A seller of recreational pharmaceuticals must turn over the inventory rather than hoard or store the product. Where the police have presented probable cause to believe that a particular home contains illegal drugs, the situation may change within a short time so that probable cause quickly becomes stale.[24] Probable cause to believe that a stolen forty-ton punch press has been installed in an industrial building would remain for quite some time, since the press is not readily movable without obvious expenditure of observable effort. Similarly, business records required for everyday transactions at an ongoing commercial enterprise are not likely to be moved between the time probable cause matures and the time the warrant is executed. In these and similar situations, stale probable cause should not pose a problem for law enforcement or the prosecution.

---

[24]Continuing enterprises may keep probable cause from becoming stale. See, e.g., *United States v. Greany,* 929 F.2d 523, 525 (9th Cir. 1991), where two-year-old information relating to an ongoing marijuana operation was not deemed stale, and *Rivera v. United States,* 928 F.2d 592, 602 (2d Cir. 1991), where that court noted that in drug-trafficking cases involving repeated conduct, information may be months old and not stale.

Whether probable cause continues to exist must be determined by an examination of the facts of each case.[25] Staleness cannot be determined by any mechanical formula such as the passage of time alone. Whether a tip equaling probable cause may be said to be stale depends on the nature of the tip and the time it is used to procure a warrant. A tip about repetitive and continued criminal behavior may last for an extended period, especially when some of the conduct may be readily observable. The lapse of time is least important when the suspected criminal activity is continuing in nature and when the property or contraband is not likely to be destroyed, consumed, or dissipated.

14. WARRANTS NOT ALWAYS REQUIRED FOR SEARCHES

Warrants are not required for abandoned property or for property over which no one has a legitimate expectation of privacy. When one throws away a soft drink can containing a sample of fingerprints, vacates a motel room and leaves behind incriminating evidence[26] in a trash can, or takes the license plates from a vehicle and leaves with no intent to have anything to do with the car in the future, such conduct indicates that the property has been abandoned. Property over which no one presently possesses any expectation of privacy or has any rights under the Fourth Amendment is subject to search and seizure at any time without probable cause and/or a warrant.

Even property over which a person possesses a general right of privacy may be searched without a warrant in some circumstances. In *United States v. Dunn,* 480 U.S. 294 (1987), the Supreme Court reaffirmed the doctrine that an occupier of fenced farm land does not have an expectation of privacy in fenced, but otherwise open, fields unless steps are taken to keep people out of the area or to keep others from observing the fields directly (see Case 1.5).

Demonstrative of the principle that no one has privacy rights in abandoned property is the case of *California v. Greenwood,* 486 U.S. 35 (1988), where the Court approved a warrantless police search of residential trash canisters that had been placed near the public street for a private trash hauler to pick up. A high volume of vehicle and pedestrian traffic around the residence had caused Greenwood's neighbors to complain to police that he might be dealing in recreational pharmaceuticals. Without a warrant, the police arranged for the private trash collector to pick up Greenwood's waste in an empty truck and to deliver the contents to the police. Inspection of the truck's contents indicated the presence and probable use of illegal drugs at the residence.

The police used the trash evidence as part of the basis for developing probable cause to search Greenwood's residence. A judge issued a search warrant, and the subsequent search revealed illegal drugs. The *Greenwood* Court approved the warrantless search of the trash on the theory that the act of placing the trash for pickup indicated that the occupants had abandoned the property and possessed no Fourth Amendment expectation of privacy[27] in connection with the contents of the trash container.

---

[25]*United States v. Webster,* 734 F.2d 1048, 1056 (5th Cir. 1984).

[26]See *Abel v. United States,* 362 U.S. 217 (1960), where the Court held that Abel had abandoned papers by placing them in a trash can in his motel room, which he later vacated, never to return.

[27]A case could be made that Greenwood had an expectation of privacy under California law and case law. In *People v. Krivda,* 5 Cal.3d 357, 486 P.2d 1262 (1971), the California Supreme Court previously held that warrantless trash searches violate the Fourth Amendment

15. SUSPICIONLESS SEARCHES OF PRIVATE AND GOVERNMENT EMPLOYEES

In other contexts, the Fourth Amendment has been judicially construed to regulate governmental conduct that requires probable cause or reasonable basis to suspect criminal activity but does not dictate the use of a warrant. In some limited situations, courts have approved warrantless and suspicionless searches as reasonable under the Fourth Amendment. Warrantless drug testing of commercial transportation workers involved in interstate commerce, especially railroad and airline employees, may be required. According to *Skinner v. Railway Labor Executives' Association,* 489 U.S. 602 (1989), probable cause to believe that an employee is drug impaired is not required as a prerequisite to conducting a search of body fluids. The *Skinner* Court developed a balancing test to weigh the need for the testing against the infringement of the Fourth Amendment rights of the employees. Due to the compelling and paramount interest of the federal government in safety and in having unimpaired individuals operating the nation's transportation system, the privacy interests of employees must give way to government dictates.

Some governmental employees possess a reduced level of protection under the Fourth Amendment by virtue of their employment situation. The federal government initiated a mandatory policy requiring that United States Customs Service employees submit to a drug test if they were seeking transfer or promotion to positions having a direct involvement in drug interdiction or requiring the incumbent to carry firearms or to handle classified material. The federal government did not require probable cause or a warrant to conduct the tests. In *National Treasury Employees Union v. Von Raab,* 489 U.S. 656 (1989), the Court held that the program passed constitutional muster because the searches were reasonable under the Fourth Amendment due to the needs of the government and the fact that the tests could not be used in criminal prosecutions. According to the Court, a warrant would provide little or no additional protection of personal privacy, since the government program defines narrowly and specifically the circumstances justifying testing and the permissible limits of such intrusions. Since the affected employees become aware that they must be tested and understand the testing procedures that the government will follow, the Court approved the approach taken by the federal government as being reasonable under the Fourth Amendment.

16. WARRANTLESS AND SUSPICIONLESS SEARCHES AT SCHOOLS

Other searches without probable cause and in the absence of any compelling interest by any level of government have been approved. In *Vernonia School District 47J v. Acton,* 515 U.S. 646 (1995), the Court upheld a mandatory random drug test program for student athletes merely because the individuals were involved in sports.

---

and the California constitution. Following *Krivda,* the California constitution was altered to bar the suppression of illegally seized evidence, but *Krivda* continued to allow suppression under the United States Constitution. Thus, one could have reasonably possessed an expectation of privacy in California trash.

The Court believed that the drug searches were constitutional as it discovered a decreased student expectation of privacy, since athletes routinely dress and undress in front of each other, the collection of urine was done in a reasonable manner, and the conditions of urine collection were nearly identical to those typically encountered in public rest rooms. In *Vernonia*, students could avoid the drug testing program by not playing any sport or related activity.

Taking the drug testing further down the path it started in *Vernonia,* in *Board of Education v. Earls,* 536 U.S. 822 (2002), the Court approved of requiring consensual drug testing for middle and high school students who wanted to participate in any extracurricular school activity. The board policy required students to consent to urinalysis prior to the start of the school activity and to agree to random tests throughout the season and upon any reasonable suspicion of drug use. Earls contended that nonathletes possessed a greater expectation of privacy than did athletes, since academic activities such as the Latin club or chess club did not involve communal disrobing. The Court noted that the minimal intrusion on schoolchildren, when weighed against the perceived epidemic of drug use among secondary students, suggested that drug testing under the circumstances was reasonable. As in *Vernonia,* the student could avoid urinalysis drug screening by deciding not to engage in any extracurricular activity.

17. WARRANTLESS SEARCHES OF POLITICAL CANDIDATES REJECTED

Despite Court approval for searches in the drug arena where probable cause was lacking and no warrant was required, the Court backed off of suspicionless testing in the political arena. The State of Georgia enacted a law that required candidates for specific state offices to certify that they have taken a urinalysis drug test within thirty days prior to qualifying for nomination or election and that the test result was negative. In *Chandler v. Miller,* 520 U.S. 305 (1997), the Supreme Court deemed the warrantless and suspicionless search of the body fluids of candidates as unreasonable under the Fourth Amendment as applied to the states through the Fourteenth Amendment. The Court distinguished *Skinner* and *Von Raab* on the grounds that the individuals seeking elective office in Georgia did not have sensitive positions, did not have access to classified material, and did not carry firearms. Thus, there was not any substantial risk to public safety where a suspicionless search could be arguably reasonable.

In other contexts, beyond those mentioned here, warrants may not be essential to conducting searches and seizures. Emergency searches, *Terry* stop and frisk searches, motor vehicle searches, searches incident to arrest, inventory searches, and consent searches are examples of searches that may be conducted without a warrant in the proper circumstances. Such exceptions are discussed in other chapters of this book.

MAJOR CASES

CASE 1.1

Probable Cause Defined

Carroll v. United States
Supreme Court of the United States
267 U.S. 132 (1925)

FACTS

A federal prosecutor in Michigan indicted George Carroll and John Kiro and won convictions against both men for transporting intoxicating liquor, in violation of the National Prohibition Act. The defendants appealed their convictions in the federal court system, and the Supreme Court of the United States granted certiorari. Carroll and Kiro alleged that the search and seizure of their motor vehicle were in violation of their constitutional rights under the Fourth Amendment and that use of the seized intoxicating liquor as evidence constituted reversible error. A motion to suppress the evidence was made by the defendants that all the liquor seized be returned to the defendant. This motion was denied, and the evidence was used against Carroll and Kiro.

Carroll and a friend of his had made an earlier attempt to sell intoxicating liquors to law enforcement agents, but because the identity of law enforcement agents may have become known to Carroll, the sale was never completed. During this encounter, the law enforcement agents observed the physical characteristics of Mr. Carroll, the make and model of his motor vehicle, and the identity of one of his associates. Carroll had a reputation as a bootlegger who sold and trafficked in distilled spirits in violation of federal law. A month or so later, the same agents observed the Oldsmobile roadster containing Carroll and John Kiro headed eastward from Grand Rapids, Michigan, toward Detroit, a well-known liquor smuggling route. Officers followed but lost sight of the vehicle. Two months later, officers spotted the same vehicle traveling westward toward Grand Rapids and were successful in stopping it. With the reputation as bootleggers that Carroll and Kiro possessed, the fact that they were using the same Oldsmobile which was used in the aborted earlier sale, the fact that they were driving the same vehicle seen several months earlier traveling along the smuggling route, and the fact that they were once again traveling along a liquor trafficking highway route, gave the officers

probable cause to stop the automobile. The same facts generated probable cause to believe that the motor vehicle contained contraband. A warrantless search of the motor vehicle revealed 68 bottles of intoxicating liquor carried in violation of federal law. The officers were not anticipating that Carroll and Kiro would be driving down the highway at that time, but when they observed them in the same car, they believed they were carrying liquor, and as a result the officers made the stop, search, seizure, and arrest of Carroll and Kiro.

PROCEDURAL ISSUE

Where a person has a reputation for illegal activity of a specific type and has attempted to commit a crime involving a federal officer, and where the same government agent observes the person apparently plying his trade openly, does such conduct meet the standard of probable cause under the Fourth Amendment?

HELD: YES.

RATIONALE

Chief Justice Taft delivered the lead opinion.

★ ★ ★

It would be intolerable and unreasonable if a prohibition agent were authorized to stop every automobile on the chance of finding liquor, and thus subject all persons lawfully using the highways to the inconvenience and indignity of such a search. Travelers may be so stopped in crossing an international boundary because of national self-protection reasonably requiring one entering the country to identify himself as entitled to come in, and his belongings as effects which may be lawfully brought in. But those lawfully within the country, entitled to use the public highways, have a right to free passage without interruption or search unless there is known to a competent official authorized to search, probable cause for believing that their vehicles are carrying contraband or illegal merchandise.

★ ★ ★

It follows from this that, if an officer seizes an automobile or the liquor in it without a warrant and the facts as subsequently developed do not justify a judgment of condemnation and forfeiture, the officer may escape costs or a suit for damages by a showing that he had reasonable or probable cause for the seizure. *Stacey v. Emery,* 97 U.S. 642. The measure of legality of such a seizure is, therefore, that the seizing officer shall have reasonable or probable cause for believing that the automobile which he stops and seizes has contraband liquor therein which is being illegally transported.

We here find the line of distinction between legal and illegal seizures of liquor in transport in vehicles. It is certainly a reasonable distinction. It gives the owner of an automobile or other vehicle seized under Section 26 of the [National Prohibition Act], in absence of probable cause, a right to have restored to him the automobile, it protects him under the *Weeks* and *Amos* cases from use of the liquor as evidence against him, and it subjects the officer making the seizures to damages. On the other hand, in a case showing probable cause, the Government and its officials are given the opportunity which they should have, to make the investigation necessary to trace reasonably suspected contraband goods and to seize them.

Such a rule fulfills the guaranty of the Fourth Amendment. In cases where the securing of a warrant is reasonably practicable, it must be used, and when properly supported by affidavit and issued after judicial approval, protects the seizing officer against a suit for damages. In cases where seizure is impossible except without warrant, the seizing officer acts unlawfully and at his peril unless he can show the court probable cause. *United States v. Kaplan,* 286 Fed. 963, 972.

★ ★ ★

Finally, was there probable cause? In *The Apollon,* 9 Wheat. 362, the question was whether the seizure of a French vessel at a particular place was upon probable cause that she was there for the purpose of smuggling. In this discussion, Mr. Justice Story, who delivered the judgment of the Court, said (page 374):

> It has been very justly observed at the bar that the Court is bound to take notice of public facts and geographical positions, and that this remote part of the country has been infested, at different periods, by smugglers, is a matter of general notoriety, and may be gathered from the public documents of the government.

We know in this way that Grand Rapids is about 152 miles from Detroit, and that Detroit and its neighborhood along the Detroit River, which is the International Boundary, is one of the most active centers for introducing illegally into this country spirituous liquors for distribution into the interior. It is obvious from the evidence that the prohibition agents were engaged in a regular patrol along the important highways from Detroit to Grand Rapids to stop and seize liquor carried in automobiles. They knew or had convincing evidence to make them believe that the Carroll boys, as they called them, were so-called "bootleggers" in Grand Rapids, i.e., that they were engaged in plying the unlawful trade of selling such liquor in that city. The officers had soon after noted their going from Grand Rapids half way to Detroit, and attempted to follow them to that city to see where they went, but they escaped observation. Two months later, these officers suddenly met the same men on their way westward, presumably from Detroit. The partners in the original combination to sell liquor in Grand Rapids were together in the same automobile they had been in the night when they tried to furnish the whisky to the officers which was thus identified as part of the firm equipment. They were coming from the direction of the great source of supply for their stock to Grand Rapids, where they plied their trade. That the officers, when they saw the defendants, believed that they were carrying liquor we can have no doubt, and we think it is equally clear that they had reasonable cause for thinking so. Emphasis is put by defendants' counsel on the statement made by one of the officers that they were not looking for defendants at the particular time when they appeared. We do not perceive that it has any weight. As soon as they did appear, the officers were entitled to use their reasoning faculties upon all the facts of which they had previous knowledge in respect to the defendants.

The necessity for probable cause in justifying seizures on land or sea, in making arrests without warrant for past felonies, and in malicious prosecution and false imprisonment cases has led to frequent definition of the phrase. In *Stacey v. Emery,* 97 U.S. 642, 645, a suit for damages for seizure by a collector, this Court defined probable cause as follows:

> If the facts and circumstances before the officer are such as to warrant a man of prudence and caution

in believing that the offense has been committed, it is sufficient.

★ ★ ★

[I]t is clear the officers here had justification for the search and seizure. This is to say that the facts and circumstances within their knowledge and of which they had reasonably trustworthy information were sufficient, in themselves, to warrant a man of reasonable caution in the belief that intoxicating liquor was being transported in the automobile which they stopped and searched.

★ ★ ★

The judgment is
Affirmed.

COMMENTS, NOTES, AND QUESTIONS

1. What factor "tipped" the scale for the Court to find probable cause in the *Carroll* case? Was it the fact that Carroll had a reputation as a bootlegger? Should reputation alone be sufficient for a finding of probable cause to search the automobile? What additional facts helped to develop probable cause for a search? What conduct of Carroll and Kiro was significant for the Court? Does probable cause mature because of all the various facts that came together the moment the police discovered Carroll's Oldsmobile being driven on the bootlegger highway?

2. *Carroll* has become an often cited case for probable cause. The *Carroll* Court, quoting *Stacey v. Emery*, 97 U.S. 642, at 645 (1878), defined probable cause as follows: "If the facts and circumstances before the officer are such as to warrant a man of prudence and caution in believing that the offense has been committed, it is sufficient."

3. Would probable cause to search in *Carroll* have been more difficult to determine if a portion of the information necessary to mature probable cause came from an informant? Would it make a difference if the informant was a priest or a drug addict? Why or why not?

4. The officers possessed probable cause to believe that the car contained contraband liquor. How far can they search, given probable cause? The general rule is that where law enforcement officers have probable cause to

search an entire vehicle, they may conduct a warrantless search of the vehicle and its contents, including all containers and packages, that may reasonably conceal the object of the search. Also see Case 4.5, *United States v. Ross,* 456 U.S. 798 (1982).

CASE 1.2

Probable Cause for a Search: Using Informants—The Development of the Standard

Illinois v. Gates
Supreme Court of the United States
462 U.S. 213 (1983)

FACTS

On May 3, 1978, the Police Department of Bloomingdale, Illinois, received an unsolicited and anonymous letter which contained statements alleging that Mr. and Mrs. Gates were engaged in the selling of drugs and that they possessed a quantity of drugs worth over $100,000 in the basement of their dwelling. The letter contained the information that the wife of Lance Gates would normally drive the family automobile to Florida to be loaded with drugs and Lance would normally fly down to drive it back to Illinois. The letter noted that a trip was soon to take place and gave the precise date of the trip. The writer included information that the pair bragged about drug selling, never having to work, and making their money from drug pushers. Police received the following letter:

> This letter is to inform you that you have a couple in your town who strictly make their living on selling drugs. They are Sue and Lance Gates, they live on Greenway, off Bloomingdale Rd. in the condominiums. Most of their buys are done in Florida. Sue his wife drives their car to Florida, where she leaves it to be loaded up with drugs, then Lance flys [*sic*] down and drives it back. Sue flys [*sic*] back after she drops the car off in Florida. May 3 she is driving down there again and Lance will be flying down in a few days to drive it back. At the time Lance drives the car back he has the trunk loaded with over $100,000.00 in drugs. Presently they have over $100,000.00 worth of drugs in their basement.

They brag about the fact they never have to work, and make their entire living on pushers.

I guarantee if you watch them carefully you will make a big catch. They are friends with some big drug dealers, who visit their house often.

Lance & Susan Gates

Greenway

in Condominiums

Subsequent to some preliminary inquiries, police contacted an informant and discovered that Lance Gates had an airplane reservation to Florida near the date mentioned in the anonymous letter. Bloomingdale police contacted the Drug Enforcement Administration, which observed Lance Gates. The DEA surveillance disclosed that Lance Gates took a flight to Florida, stayed overnight in a motel room registered in his wife's name, and left the following morning with a woman in a car bearing an Illinois license plate issued to Lance Gates. The automobile started north on an interstate highway used by travelers to the Bloomingdale area. Numerous facts mentioned in the letter received corroboration by state and federal agents.

On the basis of the anonymous letter, the information from the informant of the Bloomingdale police, and corroborative information from the Drug Enforcement Administration, the Bloomingdale police obtained a search warrant for both the home of Lance and Susan Gates and their automobile. The resulting search produced marijuana and other contraband in the home and the automobile.

The grand jury indicted Lance and Susan Gates for violation of state drug laws. Prior to trial the Gateses successfully filed a motion to suppress evidence seized during this search. The trial court ordered suppression of all the items seized due to a lack of probable cause, and the Illinois Appellate Court affirmed. The Illinois Supreme Court affirmed the decision of the lower state appellate court holding that the anonymous letter and affidavit were inadequate to sustain a determination of probable cause for issuance of the search warrants under *Aguilar v. Texas*, 378 U.S. 108, and *Spinelli v. United States*, 393 U.S. 410 (1969). The Supreme Court of the United States granted certiorari.

PROCEDURAL ISSUE

Where the basis for probable cause necessarily includes information from an informant, shall the two-pronged test developed to determine probable cause to search under *Aguilar* and *Spinelli* be abandoned in favor of a "totality of the circumstances" test to determine probable cause?

HELD: YES.

RATIONALE

Justice Rehnquist delivered the opinion of the Court.

We granted certiorari to consider the application of the Fourth Amendment to a magistrate's issuance of a search warrant on the basis of a partially corroborated anonymous informant's tip.

★ ★ ★

We…conclude that the Illinois Supreme Court read the requirements of our Fourth Amendment decisions too restrictively.

★ ★ ★

The [anonymous] letter was referred by the Chief of Police of the Bloomingdale Police Department to Detective Mader, who decided to pursue the tip. Mader learned from the office of the Illinois Secretary of State, that an Illinois driver's license had been issued to one Lance Gates, residing at a stated address in Bloomingdale. He contacted a confidential informant, whose examination of certain financial records revealed a more recent address for the Gateses, and he also learned from a police officer assigned to O'Hare Airport that "L. Gates" had made a reservation on Eastern Airlines flight 245 to West Palm Beach, Fla., scheduled to depart from Chicago on May 5 at 4:15 p.m.

Mader then made arrangements with an agent of the Drug Enforcement Administration for surveillance of the May 5 Eastern Airlines flight. The agent later reported to Mader that Gates had boarded the flight, and that federal agents in Florida had observed him arrive in West Palm Beach and take a taxi to the nearby Holiday Inn. They also reported that Gates went to a room registered to one Susan Gates and that, at 7:00 a.m. the next morning, Gates and an unidentified woman left the motel in a Mercury bearing Illinois license plates and drove northbound on an interstate frequently used by travelers to the

Chicago area. In addition, the DEA agent informed Mader that the license plate number on the Mercury was registered to a Hornet station wagon owned by Gates. The agent also advised Mader that the driving time between West Palm Beach and Bloomingdale was approximately 22 to 24 hours.

Mader signed an affidavit setting forth the foregoing facts, and submitted it to a judge of the Circuit Court of DuPage County, together with a copy of the anonymous letter. The judge of the court thereupon issued a search warrant for the Gates' residence and their automobile. The judge, in deciding to issue a warrant, could have determined that the *modus operandi* of the Gateses had been substantially corroborated. As the anonymous letter predicted Lance Gates had flown from Chicago to West Palm Beach late in the afternoon of May 5th, had checked into a hotel room registered in the name of his wife, and, at 7:00 a.m. the following morning, had headed north, accompanied by an unidentified woman, out of West Palm Beach on an interstate highway used by travelers from South Florida to Chicago in an automobile bearing a license plate issued to him.

At 5:15 a.m. on March 7th, only 36 hours after he had flown out of Chicago, Lance Gates, and his wife, returned to their home in Bloomingdale, driving the car in which they had left West Palm Beach some 22 hours earlier. The Bloomingdale police were awaiting them, searched the trunk of the Mercury, and uncovered approximately 350 pounds of marijuana. A search of the Gates' home revealed marijuana, weapons, and other contraband. The Illinois Circuit Court ordered suppression of all these items, on the ground that the affidavit submitted to the Circuit Judge failed to support the necessary determination of probable cause to believe that the Gates' automobile and home contained the contraband in question. This decision was affirmed in turn by the Illinois Appellate Court and by a divided vote of the Supreme Court of Illinois.

The Illinois Supreme Court concluded—and we are inclined to agree—that, standing alone, the anonymous letter sent to the Bloomingdale Police Department would not provide the basis for a magistrate's determination that there was probable cause to believe contraband would be found in the Gates' car and home. The letter provides virtually nothing from which one might conclude that its author is either honest or his information reliable; likewise, the letter gives absolutely no indication of the basis for the writer's predictions regarding the Gates' criminal activities. Something more was required,

then, before a magistrate could conclude that there was probable cause to believe that contraband would be found in the Gates' home and car. See *Aguilar v. Texas,* 378 U.S. 108, 109, n.1 (1964); *Nathanson v. United States,* 190 U.S. 41 (1933).

The Illinois Supreme Court also properly recognized that Detective Mader's affidavit might be capable of supplementing the anonymous letter with information sufficient to permit a determination of probable cause. [Citation omitted.] In holding that the affidavit in fact did not contain sufficient additional information to sustain a determination of probable cause, the Illinois court applied a "two-pronged test," derived from our decision in *Spinelli v. United States,* 393 U.S. 410 (1969). The Illinois Supreme Court, like some others, apparently understood *Spinelli* as requiring that the anonymous letter satisfy each of two independent requirements before it could be relied on....According to this view, the letter, as supplemented by Mader's affidavit, first had to adequately reveal the "basis of knowledge" of the letter writer—the particular means by which he came by the information given in his report. Second, it had to provide facts sufficiently establishing either the "veracity" of the affiant's informant, or, alternatively, the "reliability" of the informant's report in this particular case.

We agree with the Illinois Supreme Court that an informant's "veracity," "reliability" and "basis of knowledge" are all highly relevant in determining the value of his report. We do not agree, however, that these elements should be understood as entirely separate and independent requirements to be rigidly exacted in every case, which the opinion of the Supreme Court of Illinois would imply. Rather, as detailed below, they should be understood simply as closely intertwined issues that may usefully illuminate the common-sense, practical question whether there is "probable cause" to believe that contraband or evidence is located in a particular place.

★ ★ ★

As these comments illustrate, probable cause is a fluid concept—turning on the assessment of probabilities in particular actual contexts—not readily, or even usefully, reduced to a neat set of legal rules. Informants' tips doubtless come in many shapes and sizes from many different types of persons. As we said in *Adams v. Williams,* 407 U.S. 143, 147 (1972):

Informants' tips, like all other clues and evidence coming to a policeman on the scene, may vary greatly in their value and reliability.

Rigid legal rules are ill-suited to an area of such diversity. "One simple rule will not cover every situation." Ibid.

Moreover, the "two-pronged test" directs analysis into two largely independent channels—the informant's "veracity" or "reliability" and his "basis of knowledge." There are persuasive arguments against according these two elements such independent status. Instead, they are better understood as relevant considerations in the totality of circumstances analysis that traditionally has guided probable cause determinations: a deficiency in one may be compensated for, in determining the overall reliability of a tip, by a strong showing as to the other, or by some other indicia of reliability. [Citations omitted.]

★ ★ ★

We also have recognized that affidavits "are normally drafted by nonlawyers in the midst and haste of a criminal investigation. Technical requirements of elaborate specificity once exacted under common law pleading have no proper place in this area." Likewise, search and arrest warrants long have been issued by persons who are neither lawyers nor judges, and who certainly do remain abreast of each judicial refinement of the nature of "probable cause." See *Shadwick v. City of Tampa,* 407 U.S. 345, 348–350 (1972). The rigorous inquiry into the *Spinelli* decision cannot be reconciled with the fact that many warrants are—quite properly, 407 U.S. at 348-350—issued on the basis of nontechnical, common-sense judgments of laymen applying a standard less demanding than those used in more formal legal proceedings. Likewise, given the informal, often hurried, context in which it must be applied, the "built-in subtleties," *Stanley v. State,* 313 A.2d 847, 860 (Md. App. 1974), of the "two-pronged test" are particularly unlikely to assist magistrates in determining probable cause.

★ ★ ★

Finally, the direction taken by decisions following *Spinelli* poorly serves "the most basic function of any government": "to provide for the security of the individual and of his property." *Miranda v. Arizona,* 384 U.S. 436, 539 (1966) (White, J., dissenting). The strictures that inevitably accompany the "two-pronged test" cannot avoid seriously impeding the task of law enforcement....If, as the Illinois Supreme Court apparently thought, that test

must be rigorously applied in every case, anonymous tips would be of greatly diminished value in police work. Ordinary citizens, like ordinary witnesses,...generally do not provide extensive recitations of the basis of their everyday observations. Likewise, as the Illinois Supreme Court observed in this case, the veracity of persons supplying anonymous tips is by hypothesis largely unknown, and unknowable. As a result, anonymous tips seldom could survive a rigorous application of either of the *Spinelli* prongs. Yet, such tips, particularly when supplemented by independent police investigation, frequently contribute to the solution of otherwise "perfect crimes." While a conscientious assessment of the basis for crediting such tips is required by the Fourth Amendment, a standard that leaves virtually no place for anonymous citizen informants is not.

For all these reasons, we conclude that it is wiser to abandon the "two-pronged test" established by our decisions in *Aguilar* and *Spinelli.* In its place we reaffirm the totality of the circumstances analysis that traditionally has informed probable cause determinations. The task of the issuing magistrate is simply to make a practical, common-sense decision whether, given all the circumstances set forth in the affidavit before him, including the "veracity" and "basis of knowledge" of persons supplying hearsay information, there is a fair probability that contraband or evidence of a crime will be found in a particular place. And the duty of a reviewing court is simply to ensure that the magistrate had a "substantial basis for... conclud[ing]" that probable cause existed. We are convinced that this flexible, easily applied standard will better achieve the accommodation of public and private interests that the Fourth Amendment requires than does the approach that has developed from *Aguilar* and *Spinelli.*

Reversed.

COMMENTS, NOTES, AND QUESTIONS

1. Could the "totality of the circumstances" test used to evaluate informant evidence be used as a standardless measure of probable cause to search? The Supreme Court answered in the negative in *Massachusetts v. Upton,* 466 U.S. 727 (1984), where the Court reaffirmed its decision in *Gates* in which it abandoned the two-pronged test of *Aguilar v. Texas,* 378 U.S. 108 (1964).

2. Could the judge or magistrate, when evaluating an affidavit for a search warrant, merely cite the various factors which caused that judicial official to conclude that probable cause was present? Could an appellate court do the same, especially where seizable evidence was discovered?

Would a reviewing court be more likely to uphold a borderline search based on an informant's information when contraband has been seized pursuant to the warrant?

3. Do you think that this "totality of the circumstances" test will be easy to apply? The Court seemed to think so, since it stated that "this flexible, easily applied standard will better achieve the accommodation of public and private interests." The Court seemed to indicate that the "totality of the circumstances" test would include the veracity (truthfulness) and basis for knowledge that was the foundation for the two-pronged test. Is the Court merely giving some "wiggle room" for trial and appellate courts for cases with fact patterns that could be decided either way?

4. If a police officer does not possess probable cause to conduct a search and does not possess an alternative theory that would allow the search, the subsequent search does not produce admissible evidence because of a violation of the Fourth Amendment. In *Knowles v. Iowa*, 525 U.S. 113 (1998) (Case 4.3), a police officer stopped Mr. Knowles for speeding and issued a traffic citation for that offense. Iowa law allowed the officer the option of making an arrest or issuing a citation under such circumstances. Additionally, Iowa law permitted the officer to conduct a full search of the vehicle where the officer could have arrested the driver but did not arrest. The officer conducted a full search of the car, and under the driver's seat he found a bag of marijuana and a pipe used for smoking the contraband. The officer arrested Knowles and charged him with violation of state laws dealing with controlled substances. The Supreme Court reversed the drug conviction because the officer failed to possess probable cause for a search of the motor vehicle driven by Knowles. It rejected Iowa's argument that since the officer could have arrested for the traffic offense based on probable cause, the officer possessed the power to make a search incident to arrest even in the absence of an arrest.

CASE 1.3

Specificity of Description of Place and Scope of Search

Maryland v. Garrison
Supreme Court of the United States
480 U.S. 79 (1987)

FACTS

Police obtained a warrant to search specified premises known as 2036 Park Avenue, the third floor apartment, to look for and seize marijuana, marijuana paraphernalia, other drugs, papers, and photographs dealing with the illegal distribution of marijuana. It was noted that the numbers 2036 were presently affixed to the side of the property within the city of Baltimore, Maryland. At the time the police conducted the search of the Park Avenue address they had reason to believe that there was only one apartment at the property described by the affidavit for a warrant. Before the officers executing the warrant became aware that they were in a separate apartment occupied by respondent, they had discovered the contraband that provided the basis for respondent's conviction. The trial court found, and the appeals courts agreed, that after the police made a reasonable investigation prior to the search, which included the verification of information which came from a reliable informant, an examination of the exterior of the building, and an inquiry of the utility company, the police reasonably concluded that the third floor apartment contained only the apartment of McWebb. When police executed the search, they thought that they were searching the residence of McWebb and did not know initially that they were in the apartment of anyone else.

The trial court denied respondent Garrison's motion to suppress the evidence, and the Maryland Court of Special Appeals affirmed. The Maryland Court of Appeals reversed and remanded for a new trial, but the Supreme Court granted certiorari.

PROCEDURAL ISSUE

Where police officers have developed appropriate probable cause, have specifically described the location of the search, and have described with particularity the object of the search, does the fact that the warrant authorized a search which turned out to be ambiguous in scope invalidate the warrant?

HELD: NO

RATIONALE

Justice Stevens delivered the opinion of the Court.

★ ★ ★

I

The Warrant Clause of the Fourth Amendment categorically prohibits the issuance of any warrant except one "particularly describing the place to be searched and the persons or things to be seized." The manifest purpose of this particularity requirement was to prevent general searches. By limiting the authorization to search to the specific areas and things for which there is probable cause to search, the requirement ensures that the search will be carefully tailored to its justifications, and will not take on the character of the wide-ranging exploratory searches the Framers intended to prohibit. Thus, the scope of a lawful search is

> defined by the object of the search and the places in which there is probable cause to believe that it may be found. Just as probable cause to believe that a stolen lawnmower may be found in a garage will not support a warrant to search an upstairs bedroom, probable cause to believe that undocumented aliens are being transported in a van will not justify a warrantless search of a suitcase. *United States v. Ross*, 456 U.S. 798, 824 (1982).

In this case, there is no claim that the "persons or things to be seized" were inadequately described or that there was no probable cause to believe that those things might be found in "the place to be searched" as it was described in the warrant. With the benefit of hindsight, however, we now know that the description of that place was broader than appropriate because it was based on the mistaken belief that there was only one apartment on the third floor of the building at 2036 Park Avenue. The question is whether that factual mistake invalidated a warrant that undoubtedly would have been valid if it reflected a completely accurate understanding of the building's floor plan.

Plainly, if the officers had known, or even if they should have known, that there were two separate dwelling units on the third floor of 2036 Park Avenue, they would have been obligated to exclude respondent's apartment from the scope of the requested warrant. But we must judge the constitutionality of their conduct in light of the information available to them at the time they acted. Those items of evidence that emerge after the warrant is issued have no bearing on whether or not a warrant was validly issued. Just as the discovery of contraband cannot validate a warrant invalid when issued, so is it equally clear that the discovery of facts demonstrating that a valid warrant was unnecessarily broad does not retroactively invalidate the warrant. The validity of the warrant must be assessed on the basis of the information that the officers disclosed, or had a duty to discover and to disclose, to the issuing Magistrate. On the basis of that

information, we agree with the conclusion of all three Maryland courts that the warrant, insofar as it authorized a search that turned out to be ambiguous in scope, was valid when it [was] issued.

II

The question whether the execution of the warrant violated respondent's constitutional right to be secure in his home is somewhat less clear. We have no difficulty concluding that the officers' entry into the third-floor common area was legal; they carried a warrant for those premises, and they were accompanied by McWebb, who provided the key that they used to open the door giving access to the third-floor common area. If the officers had known, or should have known, that the third floor contained two apartments before they entered the living quarters on the third floor, and thus had been aware of the error in the warrant, they would have been obligated to limit their search to McWebb's apartment. Moreover, as the officers recognized, they were required to discontinue the search of respondent's apartment as soon as they discovered that there were two separate units on the third floor and therefore were put on notice of the risk that they might be in a unit erroneously included within the terms of the warrant. The officers' conduct and the limits of the search were based on the information available as the search proceeded. While the purposes justifying a police search strictly limit the permissible extent of the search, the Court has also recognized the need to allow some latitude for honest mistakes that are made by officers in the dangerous and difficult process of making arrests and executing search warrants.

In *Hill v. California*, 401 U.S. 797 (1971), we considered the validity of the arrest of a man named Miller based on the mistaken belief that he was Hill. The police had probable cause to arrest Hill, and they in good faith believed that Miller was Hill when they found him in Hill's apartment. As we explained:

> The upshot was that the officers in good faith believed Miller was Hill, and arrested him. They were quite wrong, as it turned out, and subjective good-faith belief would not in itself justify either the arrest or the subsequent search. But sufficient probability, not certainty, is the touchstone of reasonableness under the Fourth Amendment, and, on the record before us, the officers' mistake was understandable and the arrest a reasonable response to the situation facing them at the time. *Id.* at 803–804.

While *Hill* involved an arrest without a warrant, its underlying rationale that an officer's reasonable misidentification of a person does not invalidate a valid arrest is equally applicable to an officer's reasonable failure to appreciate that a valid warrant describes too broadly the premises to be searched. Under the reasoning in *Hill,* the validity of the search of respondent's apartment pursuant to a warrant authorizing the search of the entire third floor depends on whether the officers' failure to realize the overbreadth of the warrant was objectively understandable and reasonable. Here it unquestionably was. The objective facts available to the officers at the time suggested no distinction between McWebb's apartment and the third-floor premises

For that reason, the officers properly responded to the command contained in a valid warrant even if the warrant is interpreted as authorizing a search limited to McWebb's apartment, rather than the entire third floor. Prior to the officers' discovery of the factual mistake, they perceived McWebb's apartment and the third-floor premises as one and the same; therefore their execution of the warrant reasonably included the entire third floor. Under either interpretation of the warrant, the officers' conduct was consistent with a reasonable effort to ascertain and identify the place intended to be searched within the meaning of the Fourth Amendment.

The judgment of the Court of Appeals is reversed, and the case is remanded for further proceedings not inconsistent with this opinion.

It is so ordered.

COMMENTS, NOTES, AND QUESTIONS

1. Consistent with the rationale of the majority opinion in *Maryland v. Garrison,* could one argue that the Fourth Amendment rights of Mr. Garrison were either violated or did not exist because of the police mistake? Should Fourth Amendment rights be dependent on whether police make mistakes? On the mistakes of court data entry workers? In *Arizona v. Evans,* 514 U.S. 1 (1995), Mr. Evans was arrested by Phoenix police during a routine traffic stop when a patrol car's computer indicated that there was an outstanding misdemeanor warrant for his arrest. A search incident to arrest revealed marijuana for which he was to be tried. Ultimately, the Supreme Court in *Evans* held that the drug evidence should have been admitted against Evans because the erroneous information resulted from clerical errors of court

employees and not by police. Thus, a mistake can result in the loss of Fourth Amendment expectations of privacy and the evidence being admitted against the one with the right of privacy.

2. Would Fourth Amendment rights be more appropriately protected if errors or wrongdoing, whether innocent or intentional, by any governmental official resulted in an invalid search? Would every functionary in the justice system act more carefully so that errors would not result in bad searches and seizures? Is it possible that errors that result in erroneous probable cause determinations are so rare as to be acceptable in our justice system? Why or why not? Would it matter if your rights were the ones being lost through carelessness of public servants?

3. In dissent in *Garrison,* on the merits, Justice Blackmun contended that the search of Garrison's apartment was invalid under the Fourth Amendment. Blackmun observed that the

> words of the warrant were plain and distinctive: the warrant directed the officers to seize marijuana and drug paraphernalia on the person of McWebb and in McWebb's apartment, i.e., "on the premises known as 2036 Park Avenue third floor apartment."

Blackmun failed to see how a warrant for one person's apartment could support the search of a different person's apartment. A separate warrant would have been needed for Garrison's place of residence on the third floor.

Was Justice Blackmun correct, in your view? Should the good faith of the officers conducting the search make a difference? Does it help that when the officers discovered their mistake, they ended the search at once?

4. Should a citizen have a remedy when law enforcement agents violate the Fourth Amendment? Where federal agents broke the requirements of the Fourth Amendment by conducting an unreasonable search in an unreasonable manner, should money damages be awarded to compensate for a Fourth Amendment wrong? In *Bivens v. Six Unknown Named Agents,* 403 U.S. 388 (1971), the Court permitted a civil suit for damages to go forward against agents of the predecessor of the Drug Enforcement Administration where they had wrongly entered a residence of an innocent family and acted in less than a professional manner. There was no evidence to suppress, since the family was not involved in criminal activity, and suppression of the evidence (which did not exist) would have afforded no remedy.

CASE 1.4

Knock and Announce Requirement

Wilson v. Arkansas
Supreme Court of the United States
514 U.S. 927 (1995)

FACTS

During the latter part of 1992, Ms. Wilson made a series of sales of recreational pharmaceuticals to undercover agents working with the Arkansas State Police. One of these informants arranged to purchase some marijuana and, at the consummation of the sale, Wilson threatened to kill the informant if she were working for the police.

Law enforcement agents applied for and obtained warrants for search of Wilson's home as well as an arrest warrant for Wilson and an associate. When the police arrived to execute the search and arrest warrants, Wilson's front door was unlocked and wide open, but entry was blocked by a screen door. The police opened the screen door and entered the residence while identifying themselves as police officers. In plain view the officers discovered a virtual pharmacy of drugs. Police seized marijuana, methamphetamine, Valium, narcotics paraphernalia, a gun, and ammunition. They also found Ms. Wilson in her bathroom, flushing marijuana down the toilet.

Prior to trial, Ms. Wilson's attorney filed a motion to suppress the evidence seized during the search. The motion alleged that the search was invalid because the officers had failed to "knock and announce" before entering her home. Her motion was denied, the evidence was introduced against her at trial, and the Supreme Court of Arkansas affirmed her conviction upon appeal. The Supreme Court of the United States granted certiorari.

PROCEDURAL ISSUE

Under the Fourth Amendment, and where it is reasonable to do so, must police officers executing a search or arrest warrant first knock and announce their presence and purpose prior to entering a home?

HELD: YES.

RATIONALE

Justice Thomas delivered the opinion of the court.

★ ★ ★

II

The Fourth Amendment to the Constitution protects "[t]he right of the people to be secure in their persons, houses, papers, and effects, against unreasonable searches and seizures." In evaluating the scope of this right, we have looked to the traditional protections against unreasonable searches and seizures afforded by the common law at the time of the framing. See *California v. Hodari D.*, 499 U.S. 621, 624 (1991); *United States v. Watson*, 423 U.S. 411, 418–20 (1976); *Carroll v. United States*, 267 U.S. 132, 149 (1925). "Although the underlying command of the Fourth Amendment is always that searches and seizures be reasonable," *New Jersey v. T.L.O.*, 469 U.S. 325, 337 (1985), our effort to give content to this term may be guided by the meaning ascribed to it by the Framers of the Amendment. An examination of the common law of search and seizure leaves no doubt that the reasonableness of a search of a dwelling may depend in part on whether law enforcement officers announced their presence and authority prior to entering.

Although the common law generally protected a man's house as "his castle of defence and asylum," 3 W. Blackstone, Commentaries 288 (hereinafter Blackstone), common law courts long have held that,

> when the King is party, the sheriff (if the doors be not open) may break the party's house, either to arrest him, or to do other execution of the K[ing]'s process, if otherwise he cannot enter. *Semayne's Case,* 5 Co.Rep. 91a, 91b, 77 Eng.Rep. 194, 195 (K.B. 1603).

To this rule, however, common law courts appended an important qualification:

> But before he breaks it, he ought to signify the cause of his coming, and to make request to open doors…, for the law without a default in the owner abhors the destruction or breaking of any house (which is for the habitation and safety of man) by which great damage and inconvenience might ensue to the party, when no default is in him; for perhaps he did not know of the process, of which, if he had notice, it is to be presumed that he would obey it…. *Ibid.* 77 Eng.Rep. at 195–196.

See also Case of Richard Curtis, Fost. 135, 137, 168 Eng.Rep. 67, 68 (Crown 1757) ("[N]o precise form of words is required in a case of this kind. It is sufficient that the party hath notice, that the officer cometh not as a mere trespasser, but claiming to act under a proper authority…"); *Lee v. Gansell,* Lofft 374, 381–382, 98 Eng.Rep. 700, 705 (K.B. 1774) ("[A]s to the outer door, the law is now clearly taken" that it is privileged; but the door may be broken "when the due notification and demand has been made and refused").

Several prominent founding-era commentators agreed on this basic principle. According to Sir Matthew Hale, the "constant practice" at common law was that

> the officer may break open the door, if he be sure the offender is there, if, after acquainting them of the business and demanding the prisoner, he refuses to open the door.

See 1 M. Hale, Pleas of the Crown 582. William Hawkins propounded a similar principle: "the law doth never allow" an officer to break open the door of a dwelling "but in cases of necessity," that is, unless he "first signify to those in the house the cause of his coming, and request them to give him admittance." 2 W. Hawkins, Pleas of the Crown, ch. 14, § 1, p. 138 (6th ed. 1787). Sir William Blackstone stated simply that the sheriff may "justify breaking open doors if the possession be not quietly delivered." 3 Blackstone 412.

The common law "knock and announce" principle was woven quickly into the fabric of early American law. Most of the States that ratified the Fourth Amendment had enacted constitutional provisions or statutes generally incorporating English common law, see, e.g., N.J.Const. of 1776, § 22, in 5 Federal and State Constitutions 2598 (F. Thorpe ed. 1909) ("[T]he common law of England…shall still remain in force, until [it] shall be altered by a future law of the Legislature") … [Other examples omitted.]

Our own cases have acknowledged that the common law principle of announcement is "embedded in Anglo-American law," *Miller v. United States,* 357 U.S. 301, 313 (1958), but we have never squarely held that this principle is an element of the reasonableness inquiry under the Fourth Amendment. We now so hold. Given the long-standing common law endorsement of the practice of announcement, we have little doubt that the Framers of the Fourth Amendment thought that the method of an officer's entry into a dwelling was among the factors to be considered in assessing the reasonableness of a search or seizure. Contrary to the decision below, we hold that in some circumstances an officer's unannounced entry into a home might be unreasonable under the Fourth Amendment.

This is not to say, of course, that every entry must be preceded by an announcement. The Fourth Amendment's flexible requirement of reasonableness should not be read to mandate a rigid rule of announcement that ignores countervailing law enforcement interests. As even petitioner concedes, the common law principle of announcement was never stated as an inflexible rule requiring announcement under all circumstances.

★ ★ ★

Thus, because the common law rule was justified in part by the belief that announcement generally would avoid "the destruction or breaking of any house…by which great damage and inconvenience might ensue," *Semayne's Case, supra,* at 91b, 77 Eng.Rep. at 196, courts acknowledged that the presumption in favor of announcement would yield under circumstances presenting a threat of physical violence. See, e.g., *Read v. Case,* 4 Conn. 166, 170 (1822) (plaintiff who "had resolved…to resist even to the shedding of blood…was not within the reason and spirit of the rule requiring notice"); *Mahomed v. The Queen,* 4 Moore 239, 247, 13 Eng.Rep. 293, 296 (P. C. 1843) ("While he was firing pistols at them, were they to knock at the door, and to ask him to be pleased to open it for them? The law, in its wisdom, only requires this ceremony to be observed when it possibly may be attended with some advantage, and may render the breaking open of the outer door unnecessary").

★ ★ ★

We need not attempt a comprehensive catalog of the relevant countervailing factors here. For now, we leave to the lower courts the task of determining the circumstances under which an unannounced entry is reasonable under the Fourth Amendment. We simply hold that, although a search or seizure of a dwelling might be constitutionally defective if police officers enter without prior announcement, law enforcement interests may also establish the reasonableness of an unannounced entry.

★ ★ ★

The judgment of the Arkansas Supreme Court is reversed, and the case is remanded for further proceedings not inconsistent with this opinion.

It is so ordered.

COMMENTS, NOTES, AND QUESTIONS

1. Does a knock and announce rule add to the dangers faced by law enforcement officers when executing search warrants? One could argue that when the occupants of a dwelling or warehouse become aware that the police are outside, they would be more likely to resist entry by the law enforcement officers. If this is routinely the case, should we dispense with the knock and announce requirement under the reasonableness of the Fourth Amendment? Why or why not? What argument could you construct advocating the knock and announce requirement?

2. Is the Court too far removed from the real-life law enforcement experience? Are most drug offenders dangerous in many situations? Or has the Court managed to keep the concept of reasonableness alive in Fourth Amendment jurisprudence and apply it properly?

3. An exception to the knock and announce rule may be observable on a case-by-case basis, but the Court was not willing to allow *all* drug searches to constitute an exception to the historical evidence of the knock and announce requirement. According to the Court in *Richards v. Wisconsin,* 520 U.S. 385, 391, 392 (1997):

> We recognized in *Wilson* that the "knock and announce" requirement could give way "under circumstances presenting a threat of physical violence," or "where police officers have reason to believe that evidence would likely be destroyed if advance notice were given." 514 U.S. at 936.

The Court considered that felony drug investigations may frequently involve situations involving the destruction of evidence or a threat of harm, but that each case must be determined on its own facts and that there was to be no blanket exemption by virtue of the type of case involved or the way criminals of a certain type frequently act.

CASE 1.5

Searches Not Requiring Probable Cause

United States v. Dunn
Supreme Court of the United States
480 U.S. 294 (1987)

FACTS

The Drug Enforcement Administration (DEA) discovered that respondent Dunn and a another defendant appeared to be in the process of manufacturing amphetamine and phenylacetone in a barn on Dunn's property. In addition, it appeared that Dunn was in possession of amphetamine tablets with intent to distribute. With the goal of ascertaining the truth and to develop probable cause for a search warrant, DEA agents entered respondent's 198-acre ranch. The agents crossed a perimeter fence and an interior fence where they were able to detect an odor of phenylacetic acid emanating from the barn. The officers proceeded to the larger barn, which required that they cross Dunn's barbed wire fence and his wooden fence.

When in front of one of the barn's entrances, the officers peered inside the barn and observed what seemed to be a phenylacetone laboratory. The officers returned twice more, but never entered the barn prior to executing a search warrant issued on the basis of their observations. An additional source of probable cause, on which the judge who issued the search warrant relied, arose from two locating beepers originally legally installed in cans of the precursor chemicals which ended up at the ranch.

Although the District Court refused to suppress the evidence seized pursuant to the search warrant, the Court of Appeals concluded that the warrant had been based on the agents' illegal entry on the respondent's property. Following a variety of appellate maneuvers, the Supreme Court granted certiorari to consider the issue of whether respondent had an expectation of privacy in fields outside the curtilage of his ranch home. (At common law the curtilage included the area around a dwelling house which might actually be fenced or could reasonably be fenced but was not actually fenced.)

PROCEDURAL ISSUE

Where a barn and other outbuildings are located in a field beyond the curtilage of a home, does the occupier of the land have an expectation of privacy in those fields absent an effort to prevent observation of the fields?

HELD: NO.

RATIONALE

Justice White delivered the opinion of the Court.

★ ★ ★

II

The curtilage concept originated at common law to extend to the area immediately surrounding a dwelling house the same protection under the law of burglary as was afforded the house itself. The concept plays a part, however, in interpreting the reach of the Fourth Amendment. *Hester v. United States,* 265 U.S. 57, 59 (1924), held that the Fourth Amendment's protection accorded "persons, houses, papers and effects" did not extend to the open fields, the Court observing that the distinction between a person's house and open fields "is as old as the common law. 4 Bl. Comm. 223, 225, 226."

★ ★ ★

Drawing upon the Court's own cases and the cumulative experience of the lower courts that have grappled with the task of defining the extent of a home's curtilage, we believe that curtilage questions should be resolved with particular reference to four factors: the proximity of the area claimed to be curtilage to the home, whether the area is included within an enclosure surrounding the home, the nature of the uses to which the area is put, and the steps taken by the resident to protect the area from observation by people passing by. [Citations omitted.]

★ ★ ★

First. The record discloses that the barn was located 50 yards from the fence surrounding the house, and 60 yards from the house itself. Standing in isolation, this substantial distance supports no inference that the barn should be treated as an adjunct of the house.

Second. It is also significant that respondent's barn did not lie within the area surrounding the house that was enclosed by a fence. We noted in *Oliver, supra,* that

> "for most homes, the boundaries of the curtilage will be clearly marked; and the conception defining the curtilage—as the area around the home to which the activity of home life extends—is a familiar one easily understood from our daily experience." 466 U.S., at 182, n. 12.

Viewing the physical layout of respondent's ranch in its entirety, see 782 F.2d, at 1228, it is plain that the fence surrounding the residence serves to demark a specific area of land immediately adjacent to the house that is readily identifiable as part and parcel of the house. Conversely, the barn—the front portion itself enclosed by a fence—and the area immediately surrounding it, stands out as a distinct portion of respondent's ranch, quite separate from the residence.

Third. It is especially significant that the law enforcement officials possessed objective data indicating that the barn was not being used for intimate activities of the home. The aerial photographs showed that the truck Carpenter had been driving that contained the container of phenylacetic acid was backed up to the barn, "apparently," in the words of the Court of Appeals, "for the unloading of its contents." 674 F.2d, at 1096. When on respondent's property, the officers' suspicion was further directed toward the barn because of "a very strong odor" of phenylacetic acid. App. 165. As the DEA agent approached the barn, he "could hear a motor running, like a pump motor of some sort.…" *Id.,* at 17. Furthermore, the officers detected an "extremely strong" odor of phenylacetic acid coming from a small crack in the wall of the barn. *Ibid.* Finally, as the officers were standing in front of the barn, immediately prior to looking into its interior through the netting material, "the smell was very, very strong…[and the officers] could hear the motor running very loudly." *Id.,* at 18. When considered together, the above facts indicated to the officers that the use to which the barn was being put could not fairly be characterized as so associated with the activities and privacies of domestic life that the officers should have deemed the barn as part of respondent's home.

Fourth. Respondent did little to protect the barn area from observation by those standing in the open fields. Nothing in the record suggests that the various interior fences on respondent's property had any function other than that of the typical ranch fence; the fences were designed and constructed to corral livestock, not to prevent persons from observing what lay inside the enclosed areas.

III

★ ★ ★

Oliver reaffirmed the precept, established in *Hester,* that an open field is neither a "house" nor an "effect," and, therefore,

> "the government's intrusion upon the open fields is not one of the 'unreasonable searches' proscribed by the text of the Fourth Amendment." 466 U.S., at 177.

The Court expressly rejected the argument that the erection of fences on an open field—at least of the variety involved in those cases and in the present case—creates a constitutionally protected privacy interest. *Id.,* at 182–193.

"[T]he term 'open fields' may include any unoccupied or undeveloped area outside of the curtilage. An open field need be neither 'open' nor a 'field' as those terms are used in common speech." *Id.* at 180, n. 11

★ ★ ★

Under *Oliver* and *Hester,* there is no constitutional difference between police observations conducted while in a public place and while standing in the open fields.

The officers lawfully viewed the interior of respondent's barn, and their observations were properly considered by the magistrate in issuing a search warrant for respondent's premises. Accordingly, the judgement of the court of Appeals is reversed.

COMMENTS, NOTES, AND QUESTIONS

1. Do most people really expect some privacy in a large parcel of land? Does society view a large estate as having a better level of privacy than a small house in a plat? Why or why not? Could Dunn have posted guards on his land to keep out interlopers, including police investigators? Why or why not? Does the Court say that Dunn had no expectation that someone would not walk across his fenced land?

2. The "open fields" doctrine followed in *Dunn* originated in *Hester v. United States,* 265 U.S. 57 (1924), which held that government agents who trespass over open fields do not violate the restrictions of the Fourth Amendment and need no search warrant to search or enter open areas. Open fields include fenced areas unless extreme measures have been taken by the occupier of the land. The Supreme Court reaffirmed *Hester* in *Oliver v. United States,* 466 U.S. 170 (1984), by declaring that open fields are not within the coverage of the Fourth Amendment because fields are not persons, houses, papers, or effects.

3. May police, in the absence of a search warrant, overfly a backyard where there was some evidence of marijuana cultivation? Many people would consider what occurs inside a walled backyard to be private activity, such as might occur in a hot tub or swimming pool. If the backyard of a home is considered legally an open field, some police activity may appear to constitute a search and, yet, not be ruled a search. The open fields doctrine may include areas where the occupant has made little effort to shield illegal activities for airborne surveillance. In *California v. Ciraolo,* 476 U.S. 207 (1986), police inspected the backyard of the house while flying in a fixed-wing aircraft above one thousand feet elevation. With the naked eye the officers saw what they concluded was marijuana growing in the yard.

The Supreme Court held that the inspection was not a search subject to the Fourth Amendment. The Court stated that, although the yard was within the curtilage of the house and was shielded by a fence from observation from the street, the occupant's subjective expectation of privacy was not reasonable. Essentially, the *Ciraolo* Court did not believe that a naked-eye police inspection of the backyard of a house from a fixed-wing aircraft at one thousand feet constituted a search. Anyone could look at Ciraolo's backyard if no fence had existed, and anyone was free to fly over the backyard, including police. The evidence obtained from the air search and a subsequent ground-level search was properly admitted at trial. Is this appropriate, or does a person really have some expectation against observation from the area above one's property? Should society recognize an expectation of privacy from the air?

4. The home and its curtilage (the area around it that might reasonably be fenced) are not necessarily protected under the Fourth Amendment from inspection that involves no physical invasion. In *Florida v. Riley,* 488 U.S. 445 (1989), Riley had been suspected of cultivating marijuana in his greenhouse behind his trailer home. Police flew a helicopter at four hundred feet elevation to observe growing marijuana through holes in the greenhouse roof. This information was the basis for an affidavit for a warrant and resulted in a search warrant being issued. Riley had no expectation of privacy from the air so long as the aircraft was being operated legally and within the dictates of federal authorities who regulate air navigation. Riley was bound by the same theory as was Ciraolo, and the evidence should have been admitted against him.

5. According to Justice O'Connor, concurring in *Florida v. Riley,* "[I]t is unreasonable for persons on the ground to expect that their curtilage [the area around a home] will not be observed from the air." *Riley* at 488 U.S. 453. The principle that there is no expectation of privacy under the Fourth Amendment in open fields (*Dunn*) or in backyards open to the air (*Riley*) allows police to make warrantless reasonable searches. In such a case, the concept of probable cause and the necessity of obtaining a search warrant do not apply. However, the usual rules covering the search of a building within the confines of an open field require a warrant or some exception to that requirement. To search Dunn's barn would have required a warrant, as a general rule.

The Concept of Stop and Frisk

Chapter Outline

Key Terms

Drug courier profile
Frisk
Limitations on scope
Plain feel doctrine
Reasonable basis to suspect
Reasonable suspicion

Scope of frisk
Stop
Stop and identify
Time limitations on detention
Unexplained flight
Weapons frisk of automobile

1. INTRODUCTION TO STOP AND FRISK

Every society has individuals whose conduct attracts attention of the law enforcement community but may or may not involve criminality. Historically, an encounter with a justice official and brief questioning involves the Fourth Amendment if the subject is not free to walk away. The case law appears to recognize three types of police-citizen contact. The first situation involves the officer merely exchanging pleasantries with a person, with neither one being under any obligation to converse with the other, and each free to go on his or her way. Since no seizure has occurred, the Fourth Amendment has no application to the encounter. In a second situation, where the facts suggest that the officer has an obligation to make some investigation of conduct that could be criminal, a stop and (where the facts indicate some reasonable fear that the individual may be armed) a frisk may be appropriate. In this situation, the jurisprudence of the Fourth Amendment regulates the conduct of an officer who has momentarily made a seizure of a person. The third situation involves an arrest in which the individual comes under the total physical control of the officer following the development of probable cause to arrest.

2. STOP AND FRISK

As a legal concept, the stop and frisk doctrine constitutes the least intrusive search that an officer may be permitted to make of a person for whom the officer has some suspicion of criminality. The stop allows a cursory investigation sufficient to determine whether additional steps are appropriate. The frisk, where allowed, permits a police officer to determine whether a person poses a danger to the officer or to other citizens by discerning whether the individual is armed with some sort of weapon. The concept involves several steps, each one dependent on the outcome of the prior step, until the person may be initially searched in a limited fashion by a pat-down of the outer garments. As a general rule, the officer must possess a reasonable suspicion that a person may be armed. This suspicion must be an objectively reasonable one judged by the surrounding facts and circumstances. This reasonable suspicion may be negated by an objectively credible explanation offered by the person for his or her "unusual conduct." A stop and frisk involves situations that do not certainly appear criminal but that deserve some further scrutiny by law enforcement to determine whether or not criminality exists.

The Fourth Amendment[28] prohibition against unreasonable searches and seizures, as incorporated into the Fourteenth Amendment's Due Process Clause, has been determined to regulate the brief police-citizen encounters in stop and frisk situations, *Terry v. Ohio,* 392 U.S. 1 (1968) (see Case 2.1). When a police officer restrains an individual from walking away, a Fourth Amendment seizure has occurred, and, to be lawful, the manner of seizure, its duration, and any subsequent search must be "reasonable." The police officer does not need traditional probable cause for arrest in order to briefly detain a suspicious person, merely a reasonable suspicion that criminal activity might be afoot. The Supreme Court of the United States held that this limited seizure of the person does not require a warrant and that, similarly, where reasonable, a limited search does not necessitate a warrant.

The officer who observes unusual conduct which suggests that criminal activity may be happening or has just occurred may detain the person involved and inquire into what he or she has observed. If the explanation does not resolve the concern, and if the officer has reason to fear that the person may be armed, it is permissible to make a pat-down of the individual's outer clothing. According to *Terry* and its progeny, the officer is permitted to look for weapons by searching the outer garments of the detainee. If no "weapon-like lump" is discovered and no

---

[28]Amendment Four (1791). The right of the people to be secure in their persons, houses, papers, and effects, against unreasonable searches and seizures, shall not be violated, and no warrants shall issue, but upon probable cause, supported by Oath or affirmation, and particularly describing the place to be searched, and the persons or things to be seized.

other evidence of criminality comes to the knowledge of the officer, the individual must be allowed to continue to his or her destination.

Prior to *Terry v. Ohio,* police routinely conducted brief investigative encounters with citizens where police observed facts indicating suspicious circumstances. The location of the subject in a high-crime area late at night,[29] the experience of the police officer,[30] attempts at flight upon sight of the officer,[31] and acting strangely[32] are all factors that may be used by an officer to conclude that a brief investigation is warranted. Some of these unusual situations prove to be readily explainable by the persons involved, but other police-citizen encounters dictate additional scrutiny. A brief conversation and sometimes a limited search of the person may dispel any legitimate curiosity, while other *Terry* searches produce evidence sufficient for probable cause for arrest. Out of the Court's decision in *Terry* emerged definite and generally clear guidelines for the conduct of stop and frisk searches. Following *Terry,* courts have adapted the stop and frisk rationale to situations involving automobiles and airport detentions.

3. THE *TERRY* LEGAL STANDARD

The *Terry* Court held that wherever and whenever an officer observes unusual conduct that, in light of the officer's experience, leads him or her to reasonably conclude, based upon articulated facts, that criminal activity might be afoot, the officer is permitted to lawfully stop the person and make an inquiry. A reasonable level of force may be used to effectuate the stop if the individual proves resistant. If not in uniform, the law enforcement officer must convey to the subject that the person conducting the stop is a police officer. The subject may be questioned briefly concerning the unusual conduct; if the explanation proves unreasonable, and where the officer reasonably believes the person is armed and dangerous, he or she may conduct a limited search of the outer clothing. This search is intended to protect the officer and those in the immediate vicinity from danger or harm.

Chief Justice Warren, writing for the majority, stated the Court's essential holding in *Terry:*

> We merely hold today that, where a police officer observes unusual conduct which leads him reasonably to conclude in light of his experience that criminal activity may be afoot and that the persons with whom he is dealing may be armed and presently dangerous, where, in the course of investigating this behavior, he identifies himself as a policeman and makes reasonable inquiries, and where nothing in the initial stages of the encounter serves to dispel his reasonable fear for his own or others' safety, he is entitled for the protection of himself and others in the area to conduct a carefully limited search of the outer clothing of such persons in an attempt to discover weapons which might be used to assault him. 392 U.S. 1, 30.

---

[29]See *Adams v. Williams,* 407 U.S. 143 (1972).
[30]See *Terry v. Ohio,* 392 U.S. 1 (1968).
[31]See *Illinois v. Wardlow,* 528 U.S. 119 (2000).
[32]Ibid.

The *Terry* Court determined that a stop and frisk can be legitimately conducted on less evidence than would be required for probable cause for arrest or for a traditional search of a house or motor vehicle. Consistent with the reasonableness requirement of the Fourth Amendment, the search is restricted to tactics designed to discover weapons. Even though a stop and frisk requires only "reasonable suspicion" as justification, in situations where the pat-down reveals a lump or bulge that could reasonably be construed as a weapon, the officer may reach inside the clothing. While some weapons are easily discerned, other lumps within clothing do not lend themselves to quick determination. In *United States v. Campbell,* 178 F.3d 345 (1999), the Court approved a search within a pocket where a police officer removed a bulge from a bank robbery suspect. Contained within the bulge were $1,400 in cash, a gold cardboard jewelry box containing some gold chain, and some change. The Court felt that the money could have been hiding a weapon. However, if an officer concludes that the object felt through the clothing could not reasonably be construed as a weapon, further searching cannot proceed. In *Minnesota v. Dickerson,* 508 U.S. 366 (1993), the Court held that a police officer cannot manipulate an object (crack cocaine) from outside a suspect's pants pocket to discern the identity of the pocket's contents. The officer never entertained the thought that the lump was a weapon and did not immediately recognize it as rock cocaine. As a general rule, where the protective search goes beyond what is necessary to determine whether the suspect is armed, the search cannot be valid under *Terry,* and its fruits should be suppressed.[33]

In a companion case to *Terry, Sibron v. New York,*[34] where the facts were held not to be sufficient to allow a frisk, the Court held that evidence obtained from the frisk had been obtained in violation of the Fourth Amendment as applied to the states. In *Sibron,* which had facts possessing some similarity to those in *Terry,* a uniformed police officer observed Sibron from four o'clock in the afternoon until midnight. Sibron conversed with known narcotics addicts, but the officer did not observe any transfer or sale of drugs or see anything approaching illegality.

Late in the evening, Sibron entered a restaurant. The officer observed Sibron speak with three more known addicts inside the restaurant. Once again, nothing was overheard, and nothing was seen to pass between Sibron and the addicts. Sibron sat down and ordered pie and coffee, and, as he was eating, the officer approached him and told him to come outside. Once outside, the officer said to Sibron, "You know what I am after." According to the officer, Sibron "mumbled something and reached into his pocket." At the same time the officer put his hand into the same pocket, and together they removed several glassine envelopes containing heroin. At no time did the officer state that he was fearful of Mr. Sibron or believed that Sibron might be armed and dangerous.

When Sibron's case reached the Supreme Court of the United States, his contention that the officer's search of his person was unreasonable under the circumstances

---

[33]See *Florida v. J.L.,* 529 U.S. 266 (2000). In this case, an anonymous informant conveyed news to police that a specifically described young male, wearing a plaid shirt, was standing at a particular bus stop and illegally carrying a concealed firearm. The Court held that an uncorroborated tip from an unknown informant could not justify a frisk.

[34]392 U.S. 40 (1968).

prevailed. The distinction between the *Terry* case and Sibron's situation turns on the issue of whether the officer could have developed a reason to suspect Sibron of criminal activity and to have concluded that Sibron might be armed and dangerous. No evidence pointed to any reasonable suspicion of criminal activity by Sibron, and there existed no reason to believe that he was armed. Therefore, the search by the officer was illegal under the Fourth Amendment, and the evidence of heroin possession should have been suppressed from his trial.

4. FACTS INDICATING UNUSUAL CONDUCT

The facts that generate a police officer's reasonable basis to suspect criminal activity may be derived from the officer's personal observation, from informant information, from a dispatcher message, or from a combination of two or more sources. In *Terry v. Ohio,* the police detective observed two men apparently "casing" a store by repeatedly walking past the store window and conferring with each other. This conduct demanded some inquiry by the detective and allowed him to briefly stop the two men for questioning. Personal observation of furtive and evasive behavior by a passenger following a routine traffic stop can create a reasonable basis to suspect criminal behavior. According to the Florida court of appeals in *Brown v. State,* 2004 Fla. App. LEXIS 254 (2004), police officers could justify a frisk of a passenger where his evasive movements while in the vehicle suggested that he might be trying to hide something and that he might be armed. A police officer may also obtain information from an informant, as happened in *Adams v. Williams,* 407 U.S. 143 (1972), where the officer received the information from a reliable informant[35] that a man was armed, selling drugs, and sitting in an automobile late at night (see Case 2.2). Information giving rise to "reasonable basis to suspect" may come from more than one source. In *Alabama v. White,* 496 U.S. 325 (1990), the Court approved the stop of a moving automobile on the stop and frisk rationale where the police obtained some information from an anonymous informant and verified some of the information by personal observation (see Case 2.3). Thus, the stop and frisk standard of proof may be met by virtue of information supplied by an informant alone or may be combined with personal observations of the officer to reach the proper level of proof.

Representative of a fact situation that aroused suspicion from personal observations by the officer but failed to meet the *Terry* standard of reasonable basis to suspect criminal activity occurred in a Missouri case. One morning, a police officer noticed a truck drive up and park in a shopping center at 12:30 A.M. on a side of the center where no entrances to the stores were located. The shopping center had not experienced any recent elevated criminal activity. The light from streetlights was sufficient to enable the officer to keep the truck under surveillance at all times, and the officer observed that the driver did nothing unusual. When the driver started the vehicle and drove away, the officer stopped the truck and found that the driver was under the influence of alcohol.

---

[35]There must be objective reasons to believe an informant. An anonymous tip from a telephone caller telling police that a young male standing at a particularly described bus stop illegally possessed a firearm was insufficient to permit a stop and frisk for the weapon. In *Florida v. J.L.,* 529 U.S. 266 (2000), the Court held that because police had no means to test the unknown informant's knowledge and credibility, the tip lacked sufficient indicia of reliability to provide reasonable suspicion necessary to make a *Terry*-type stop.

According to trial testimony, the officer stated that he just wanted to get a name in case some crime had been committed. In reversing the conviction for driving while under the influence of alcohol, the appellate court agreed with the defendant's pretrial and trial contentions made during a motion to suppress the evidence of intoxication. The court held that the officer lacked any articulable and reasonable suspicion that could be construed as consistent with *Terry* that the truck or driver may have offended the law, and he should not have stopped the defendant.[36]

Merely being in a high-crime area with a bulge in one's pants does not rise to the level of reasonable basis to suspect criminal activity. In a Maryland case, while cruising in an unmarked car, officers noticed a man standing on the street who looked at them; the officers concluded that a bulge in the man's pants could be a gun. One officer approached the man and initiated a pat-down but started at the waist and did not initially direct his focus at the bulge. When the officer discovered a smaller, until then unknown, bulge that contained drugs, he placed the subject in custody and completed a full search incident to arrest. In evaluating the reasonable basis to suspect standard under the totality of the circumstances, the appellate court held that the officers failed to possess sufficient evidence to meet the *Terry* standard authorizing an initial stop.[37]

5. FLIGHT UPON SEEING AN OFFICER AS UNUSUAL CONDUCT

Mere flight upon seeing a police officer, without more, may not give rise to the observation of unusual conduct that might be indicative of crime. However, flight upon sight plus other factors may give an officer the sufficient level of reasonable suspicion necessary for a *Terry* stop. In *Michigan v. Chesternut,* 486 U.S. 567 (1988), while observing the approach of a police car on routine patrol, Chesternut began to run in the opposite direction. The police followed him "to see where he was going"; after catching up with him and driving alongside him for a short distance, they observed him discarding a number of packets. Believing that the packets contained drugs, the police alighted from the cruiser, examined them, and concluded that they contained narcotics. The police arrested Chesternut. According to the Court, any determination concerning whether police conduct amounts to a seizure implicating the Fourth Amendment must take into account "'all of the circumstances surrounding the incident'" in each individual case. Thus, flight plus questionable conduct permitted the police to make a stop under the *Terry* standard.

Flight alone would not be sufficiently suspicious, but almost any added factor seems to meet the *Terry* standard. In *Illinois v. Wardlow,* 528 U.S. 119 (2000), the subject initiated flight upon seeing a caravan of police cars converging on a Chicago street in an area known for heavy drug trafficking (see Case 2.5). He was holding an opaque bag and, upon spotting the police, began to run away. Officers caught the subject and discovered a revolver during a pat-down of his person and bag. Ultimately, the Supreme Court upheld the stop of the suspect under *Terry,* since the

[36] *Missouri v. Schmutz,* 100 S.W.3d 876, 880, 881 (2003).
[37] *Ransome v. Maryland,* 373 Md. 99, 108, 109; 816 A.2d 901, 905, 906 (2003).

otherwise innocent flight upon seeing the police was accompanied by another factor: being in a high drug crime area. The *Wardlow* Court noted that "the determination of reasonable suspicion must be based on common sense judgments and inferences about human behavior."[38] In essence, flight alone probably would not be sufficient to conduct a stop of a person, but where it is accompanied by almost any other action of a suspicious nature, an officer may make a lawful *Terry* stop of the person without running afoul of the Fourth Amendment.

State courts have generally followed the *Wardlow* rationale in permitting stops and frisks where unexplained flight occurs. A citizen complaint that a specifically described individual possessed a handgun at a particular street intersection, coupled with that individual's flight upon seeing an officer approach, can be sufficient to warrant a stop and frisk. In a Pennsylvania case, the court ruled that a complaint about a handgun, coupled with the initial encounter between the suspect and the officer, could not justify a stop. However, that same information added to the subject's flight upon the officer's approach justified the stop and the subsequent frisk that revealed the concealed weapon.[39]

6. FRISK MAY NOT ALWAYS ALLOW ADDITIONAL SEARCH

Judicial clarifications on stop and frisks where courts disagree with law enforcement officials are rather limited when compared with decisions approving police pat-downs. In *Sibron v. New York,* 392 U.S. 40 (1968), a companion case to *Terry* and noted earlier in this chapter, the Court held that reasonable basis to suspect was not reached where an officer watched a known drug addict talk to several other known addicts over a period of several hours; did not see anything given to him; and did not overhear any conversation that would indicate criminality. Similarly, a pat-down of a bar patron for weapons during the execution of a search warrant for the premises was improper, since no individualized suspicion existed that a particular patron or anyone was armed.[40] Some searches conducted following a lawful *Terry* stop may exceed permissible bounds. A Florida court of appeal held that an officer had no authority to look inside a box of cigarettes taken from a frisked participant at a fight scene. Since the officer had no reason to suspect that a knife or gun was hidden inside the cigarette box, the court held that looking inside the cigarette box exceeded the scope of searches permissible under the Fourth Amendment.[41]

Because a stop may not justify a frisk, and a frisk may not justify a more intrusive search, a police officer must possess the proper quantum of evidence prior to proceeding to the next step under the *Terry* rationale. Demonstrative of this principle, the officer in *Alexander v. Florida,* 616 So. 2d 540 (1993), stopped the defendant because a reliable informant had told the officer that a specific car had some cocaine

---

[38]528 U.S. at 124.

[39]*In the Interest of D.M.* 566 Pa. 445; 781 A.2d 1161 (2001).

[40]See *Ybarra v. Illinois,* 444 U.S. 85 (1979). The Court determined that a *Terry*-type frisk of all patrons of a bar for which a search warrant had been issued was unreasonable, since no individualized suspicion existed for any particular patron. Police conducted a pat-down of the customers and returned to make a more extensive search on Ybarra by reaching inside his clothing when there was no reason to suspect him of any wrongdoing.

[41]*Harford v. State,* 816 So. 2d 789 (Fla. 2002).

inside it. Following a stop of the vehicle, the officer conducted a pat-down of the driver and discovered a hard, cylindrical object two or three inches long and a half inch in diameter in the area of his pant's crotch. When the officer finally obtained the object, it proved to contain cocaine. The court of appeals reversed conviction based on the evidence obtained from the stop and frisk search and seizure on the theory that removal of the object was unreasonable, since the officer had no information that the object might be a weapon. According to the court:

> Assuming that the informant's tip, that he had seen a large amount of cocaine in the car driven by Alexander, provided reasonable suspicion that a crime was being committed, thereby justifying a stop of the vehicle, neither the facts nor the law supports the remainder of the trial court's finding, that the pat-down search was justified because the informant's tip gave the officer "probable cause to believe that defendant may have been armed and dangerous" because he was engaged in a drug transaction involving a large quantity of narcotics and a large sum of money. 616 So.2d 540, 541, 542.

Thus, the officer's conduct failed to meet the requirements for a search under the stop and frisk rationale.

In a slightly different context, a Florida court overturned a conviction based on a failed stop and frisk. The police initiated the encounter when a bicyclist, in an area known for narcotics dealing, leaned toward the interior of an automobile and reached inside. No exchange was observed, but the officer recognized the bicyclist as a purchaser of drugs on prior occasions. Police attempted to stop the bicyclist, who initiated flight from the officers. Ultimately, the officers caught him after a short foot chase. Opening his hand, they found a baggie containing a trace of cocaine. The Florida Court of Appeals reversed the conviction of the defendant on the basis that the initial detention was not valid. According to the court:

> A stop is not warranted solely upon an officer's observation of a black male in a high-crime district leaning into the window of a white man's car stopped in the middle of the street who walks away upon seeing an officer approach. *Winters v. State,* 578 So.2d 5 (Fla. 2d DCA 1991). Nor is a stop warranted where the defendant engages in such activity while in the presence of known drug dealers. [Citations omitted.] Thus, the fact that the appellant had merely been present at other drug transactions does not raise the basis for the officers' suspicion to the level required for detention under the stop and frisk law. *Shackelford v. Florida,* 579 So. 2d 306, 307 (1991).

While not all courts would follow the logic as applied to the facts in the foregoing cases, the rationale points out that police officers need to be aware that the facts necessary to justify the initial stop must be more than a mere hunch, that not all stops will mature into pat-down searches, and that even fewer will allow a deeper search once the officer is reasonably satisfied that the individual is not armed.

7. *TERRY* STOPS UNDER A DRUG COURIER PROFILE

If a person fits the "drug courier profile," under the *Terry* rationale, a brief stop of the person and a brief investigation have been held to be appropriate. In *Florida v.*

Royer, 460 U.S. 491 (1983), the defendant, an airline passenger, attracted the attention of drug enforcement agents because of his appearance, mannerisms, luggage, and actions, and by the purchase of a one-way airline ticket—all hallmarks of the drug courier profile (see Case 2.4). The agents properly detained him to ask questions but exceeded the length of time that was considered reasonable under the circumstances. Similarly, in *United States v. Sokolow,* 490 U.S. 1 (1989), the defendant met the drug courier profile by paying cash for a plane ticket from Hawaii to Florida, traveling under a name that did not match his phone number, stayed in a drug source city for less than forty-eight hours, appeared nervous during the trip, and had no checked luggage. When met at the Honolulu airport by police, the defendant and his girlfriend were briefly detained so that a drug-sniffing dog could check their carry-on luggage. Two warrants were later issued to search both bags to which the dog alerted. Ultimately, this stop and frisk sniff of the bags by the dog was held to be appropriate, and the conviction was reinstated by the Supreme Court of the United States.

Under the drug courier profile theory of stop and frisk, a person may be detained briefly, without probable cause to arrest, but the curtailment of his or her liberty by the police must be supported at least by a reasonable and articulable suspicion that the person seized may be engaged in criminal activity. The principle allows a brief encounter due to the drug courier profile but does not permit a lengthy detention of the person or luggage unless probable cause for arrest or search of the luggage quickly matures. In *United States v. Place,* 462 U.S. 696 (1983), police officers believed that Place met the drug courier profile and sought additional information from him. Following Place's brief initial encounter with the law enforcement officers at New York's La Guardia Airport, officers requested permission to search his luggage. When Place refused to grant consent, the officers removed his luggage to a secure area to await a search until police procured a warrant. The agents then took the luggage to Kennedy Airport, where it was subjected to a "sniff test" by a trained narcotics dog, which reacted positively to one of the suitcases. At this point, ninety minutes had elapsed since the seizure of the luggage. At some time later, the warrant arrived, and agents executed it, revealing cocaine.

The trial court admitted the drug evidence against Place, but the court of appeals reversed on the ground that the time limits of a *Terry* investigative stop had been exceeded. The Supreme Court affirmed the reversal of the conviction. The Court held that where an officer reasonably believes that a person carries luggage that contains narcotics, a brief seizure of the luggage may be justified under the dictates of *Terry.* Where police seize personal articles, the time limitations applicable to detentions of people apply to investigative detentions of a person's property. Thus, in Place's situation, the seizure of his luggage became unreasonable at some point during the seizure of an hour-and-a-half's duration. The Court noted that the agents had sufficient time to have a dog ready to sniff the luggage when it arrived in New York, since they knew when and where the plane would land.

Ultimately, the Supreme Court of the United States upheld the reversal of Place's conviction due to the illegal search of the luggage. Police did not have probable cause to arrest Place or to search his luggage until the dog alerted. By that time, the length of detention of the luggage under the *Terry* standard had become unreasonable under the Fourth Amendment. The lesson of *Place* allows police to follow a drug courier profile while making brief stops to gain additional information, but the detention must be both brief and reasonable unless probable cause to arrest or to search the person or luggage develops. If the initial encounter does not resolve the officer's suspicions, but no additional evidence surfaces, the subject must be allowed to continue his or her journey.

8. SUBJECT MUST BE AWARE OF OFFICER'S STATUS

The *Terry* standard requires that the person being stopped be knowledgeable that the person with whom he or she is dealing is a law enforcement officer. In most situations, the identity will be readily apparent by virtue of the officer's uniform. However, as in the original *Terry* case, the detective was in plain clothes and needed to identify himself as a police officer. Once the individual has knowledge that the person is a police officer, submission to authority should be a reasonable approach rather than flight, which could be understandable if the person were not an officer. The person stopped has no duty to submit to alleged authority if he or she possesses no knowledge of the status of the officer.

9. OFFICER MUST HAVE REASON TO BELIEVE THAT THE PERSON MAY BE ARMED AND DANGEROUS

The circumstances faced by the officer must give rise to the idea that the person with whom he is dealing may be armed and dangerous, according to the *Terry* standard. A situation where a robbery may be under way (*Terry*) would give rise to the conclusion that the perpetrator might be armed, whereas a person who has passed an airport security checkpoint prior to boarding could not reasonably be believed to be armed. See *Florida v. Royer,* 460 U.S. 491 (1983). In *Michigan v. Long,* 463 U.S. 1032 (1983), the Court held that the *Terry* rationale does not restrict a pat-down search of the person of a detained suspect even when the detainee is under the control of the officer and could not gain access to a weapon. The *Long* Court concluded it was reasonable under *Terry* to allow officers to conduct an area search of the passenger compartment of a vehicle to uncover weapons, as long as the officers possess an articulable and objectively reasonable belief that the suspect was potentially dangerous. In a slightly different situation, *New York v. Reyes,* 651 N.Y.S.2d 431 (1996), pursuant to a specific citizen complaint, an officer conducted a pat-down of a person who had a gun. The officer approached and noticed a bulge in the person's front coat pocket, tapped the bulge, felt something hard, and, believing that it was a gun, properly pulled out a package of drugs. Similarly, a police officer may order the driver of a lawfully stopped car to exit the car and submit to a pat-down if there exists a reasonable suspicion that the driver may be armed and dangerous. See *Pennsylvania v. Mimms,* 434 U.S. 106 (1977). Consistent with *Mimms,* an officer may order passengers from a stopped vehicle and perform a pat-down upon reasonable suspicion that they may be armed and dangerous. See *Maryland v. Wilson,* 519 U.S. 408 (1997).

As a general rule, the officer's fear that the person may be armed and dangerous must be a reasonable one under the circumstances. In *New York v. Hill,* 1999 N.Y. App. Div. LEXIS 7469 (1999), the court held that police acted lawfully when they stopped two individuals, where the police encountered the men late at night at a location where several vehicles had recently been burglarized. The officer engaged one of the two subjects in a conversation and observed a bulge in the front pocket of his jacket. The officer conducted a pat-down of the front of the jacket. He discovered several cassette tapes in the front pocket and continued the pat-down until he felt something hard near the small of the defendant's back, which turned out to be a gun. Prior to the pat-down, the defendant provided straightforward answers to the police officer's questions about where he was going, where he had been, and the identity of his companion. The court held that the information possessed by the police officer may have provided, at most, an unfounded suspicion that criminal activity was afoot, thereby activating the common-law right to inquire. The court ruled that the pat-down violated the Fourth Amendment. The police officer's authority to pat down or frisk a defendant is dependent on the right to stop and detain, which authority is activated only by a reasonable suspicion of criminality, which the *Hill* court found lacking.

The reality of the reasonable belief that an individual may be armed and dangerous has a rather low threshold; thus, only rarely is evidence suppressed due to an unreasonable fear that the person may be armed and dangerous. In *Michigan v. Summers,* 452 U.S. 692 (1981), the Court approved the detention of a man who was leaving a home that was the subject of a warrant-based search. The Court based its rationale on whether it was reasonable to detain someone who had a connection with the home and who might have been involved in the suspected criminality within the home. According to the Court, three police interests were furthered by the detention: preventing flight in the event incriminating evidence was found, minimizing risk of harm to the officers, and facilitating an orderly search through cooperation of the occupants. Note that in *Summers,* there was barely any thought that the individual might have been armed, yet the detention gained Court approval. However, Summers had a greater and more significant connection to the house being searched than a bar patron who merely happened to be on the premises when a search of the bar occurred.

Demonstrative of how minimal the fear may be that a subject may be armed is the case of one of the New York World Trade Center bombing conspirators. In *United States v. El-Gabrowny,* S.D.N.Y., 825 F. Supp. 38 (1993), the court denied a motion to suppress evidence obtained by officers in a pat-down search of one of the defendants.[42] Officers were executing a search warrant of the defendant's apartment when he approached them with his hands in his pockets. One officer removed the defendant's hands from the pockets and proceeded with a pat-down search. The officer discovered and removed a yellow envelope that was folded and fastened with rubber bands. It proved to contain forged and altered passports and birth certificates.

---

[42]The Second Circuit Court of Appeals upheld the eventual conviction of El-Gabrowny, including, by implication, the search of El-Gabrowny's clothing prior to arrest in *United States v. El-Gabrowny,* 189 F.3d 88, 1999 U.S. App. LEXIS 18926 (CA2 1999).

The court held that the search was reasonable to ensure the officers' safety despite the absence of any fear that the packet was a weapon.

As appears from the case law, courts take different approaches concerning when a situation appears to indicate that criminality might be afoot and the subjects involved may be armed and dangerous. Predicting the outcome of a particular set of circumstances under the stop and frisk doctrine can prove to be a risky proposition due to the varying interpretations courts have given to substantially similar situations.

10. INVESTIGATION MUST NOT DISPEL THE FEAR THAT THE SUBJECT MAY BE ARMED AND DANGEROUS

Although the original *Terry* case held that, prior to conducting a pat-down, the officer must have a reasonable belief that the subject was armed and dangerous, many court cases construing this requirement have not been as demanding as the original case. In fact, the person on whom police would like to conduct a pat-down need not be personally believed to be armed; it is only necessary that an individual in a similar position might be armed. As mentioned earlier, in *Michigan v. Summers,* 452 U.S. 692 (1981), the Court approved a seizure of a man for whom no reason existed to believe that he was armed; he merely had connections to a home that was being searched pursuant to a warrant.

Suspicion of drug trafficking allows police to stop automobiles and trucks for brief investigations where there exists reason to suspect criminal activity but where there is no individualized suspicion that the person may be armed and dangerous. See *United States v. Sharpe,* 470 U.S. 675 (1985). In *Sharpe,* a Drug Enforcement Administration (DEA) officer followed an overloaded pickup truck with a camper shell that appeared to be traveling in tandem with a car. The truck was so overloaded that it did not sway or move up or down when encountering bumps in the road. The agent followed the vehicles for twenty miles and made the determination to make a *Terry* investigatory stop in concert with local police. The DEA agent walked to the rear of the truck, where he smelled marijuana, and opened the rear of the camper, which revealed bales of the drug. The Supreme Court believed that the *Terry* standard for a stop had been met. As the Court stated in footnote 3 of *Sharpe:*

> Agent Cooke had observed the vehicles traveling in tandem for 20 miles in an area near the coast known to be frequented by drug traffickers. Cooke testified that pickup trucks with camper shells were often used to transport large quantities of marihuana. Savage's pickup truck appeared to be heavily loaded, and the windows of the camper were covered with a quilted bed-sheet material, rather than curtains. Finally, both vehicles took evasive actions and started speeding as soon as Officer Thrasher began following them in his marked car. Perhaps none of these facts, standing alone, would give rise to a reasonable suspicion; but taken together as appraised by an experienced law enforcement officer, they provided clear justification to stop the vehicles and pursue a limited investigation.

While the Supreme Court appeared to have little difficulty in making a decision in *Sharpe* and approving the stop and frisk of the truck, the officer in the field must put the discrete facts together to determine whether the *Terry* standard has been met and whether additional information may be required prior to making a stop.

11. THE PLAIN FEEL DOCTRINE

In making a frisk, an officer may feel objects that, while not likely to be weapons, may be indicative of criminal activity. In *Minnesota v. Dickerson,* 508 U.S. 366 (1993), the Court expanded the scope of a *Terry* stop and frisk by permitting the officer to reach inside the clothing of a detainee if the officer reasonably believed, by the feel of the object, it constituted seizable material. In *Dickerson,* the subject had been detained on suspicion of drug possession. The pat-down conducted by an officer revealed a small lump, and the officer made the determination that it was crack cocaine wrapped in cellophane because the officer manipulated the object between his thumb and index finger. According to the Court in *Dickerson,* the officer went beyond the allowable search permitted by *Terry,* and the evidence should have been suppressed. Had the officer merely felt an object whose criminal identity was readily apparent, the pat-down would have been permissible; manipulating the object was a greater search than allowed by *Terry.* However, *Dickerson* recognized a new area of seizable property under *Terry* that did not exist previously. This expansion of *Terry* has been variously referred to as the "plain touch" or the "plain feel" doctrine.

Many state courts have followed *Dickerson* in allowing officers to extend the scope of a search when an object's identity has been discovered during a pat-down. In a Texas drug investigation, an officer frisked the suspect for weapons but felt a large amount of cash in the pants pocket. The officer justified the frisk of the outer clothing on the theory that drug dealers are often armed with guns and other weapons, but the suspect argued that the scope of the frisk proved too extensive. The court upheld the frisk since the officer had testified that he immediately recognized that the bulge was currency from the way it felt, creating the justification for going in the pocket to retrieve it. In upholding the search, the Texas court quoted *Minnesota v. Dickerson,* stating, "if a police officer lawfully pats down a suspect's outer clothing and feels an object whose contour or mass makes its identity immediately apparent, there has been no invasion of the suspect's privacy beyond that already authorized by the officer's search for weapons."[43] The court distinguished the facts in its case from those of the *Dickerson* case: in *Dickerson,* the officer manipulated the contents of the pocket, and in the Texas case, the officer did not manipulate the currency. He instantly knew the identity of the bulge by its feel.[44]

12. EXPANSION OF THE STOP AND FRISK BEYOND ITS GENESIS

The Supreme Court of the United States and other courts began to approve stops in situations where there was no belief that the individual person was armed or

---

[43]508 U.S. 366 at 375.
[44]*Carmouche v. State,* 10 S.W.3d 323 (Tex. Crim. App. 2000).

dangerous. Courts have approved short seizures of luggage where police have reasonable basis to suspect that criminal activity might be ongoing. Where police seize luggage on less than probable cause, the limitation concerning the length of the detention of the personal articles has been construed to follow the same standards as the stop of a person. See *Florida v. Royer,* 460 U.S. 491 (1983). In such a situation the initial stop and subsequent seizure must actually be of a temporary nature and exist no longer than reasonably necessary to effectuate the purpose. Where the seizure extends longer than reasonably required, the seizure may be declared as unreasonable and the evidence suppressed.[45]

The Court extended the stop and frisk rationale to cover the situation where police have lawfully detained an automobile and possessed an articulate fear that the occupant might obtain a weapon while searching for his driver's license. See *Michigan v. Long,* 463 U.S. 1032 (1983). Two police officers noticed a vehicle driving erratically and at an excessive rate of speed in a rural area late at night. After the officers saw the car go off the road and into a ditch, they stopped to investigate. Long, the driver, met the officers at the rear of the car and seemed to be under the influence of some intoxicant. When Long began walking toward the open door of the car to obtain the vehicle registration, the officers followed him and saw a hunting knife on the floorboard of the driver's side of the car. The officers then stopped the respondent and subjected him to a pat-down search, which revealed no weapons, but one of the officers noticed what appeared to be a baggie of marijuana protruding from under the armrest of the seat. The officers also conducted a limited weapons search of the interior of the auto. The *Long* Court approved this "*Terry* pat-down" of the passenger compartment of the vehicle because there existed a reasonable suspicion that the driver might gain immediate control of a weapon.

However, not every encounter between a police officer and an individual gives the officer the right to detain and frisk. In *Kolender v. Lawson,* 461 U.S. 352 (1983), police stopped and arrested a person who had no identification. The individual was walking alone and did not appear about to commit a crime. Pursuant to a California statute, any person who loiters or wanders about the streets must identify him- or herself to police upon request and account for his or her presence, even in the absence of any reasonable basis to suspect criminal activity. A failure to make a "credible and reliable" identification when asked to "stop and identify" could result in an arrest for violating the statute. The Supreme Court of the United States determined that the law was unconstitutionally vague on its face within the meaning of the Due Process Clause of the Fourteenth Amendment. Thus, a person is not subject to stop, arrest, or search for merely walking or loitering without appropriate identification; some reasonable basis to suspect individual criminal activity must be demonstrably present in order to justify a stop and frisk. Similarly, an officer may not stop a motor vehicle for which there was no reasonable basis to suspect that the driver was committing any type of criminal activity. In *Delaware v. Prouse,* 440 U.S. 468 (1979), the court disapproved a stop of Prouse's automobile for no reason. The officer had randomly decided to stop the car to check the vehicle's registration and had no individualized suspicion of criminal activity. This practice ran afoul of the

---

[45]*United States v. Place,* 462 U.S. 696, 709, 710 (1983).

Fourth Amendment and the *Terry* line of cases requiring individualized suspicion of criminal activity.[46]

13. EXPANSION OF *TERRY* TO INDIVIDUALS NOT UNDER SUSPICION

More recently, the Court arguably retreated from requiring individualized suspicion in situations similar to stop and frisks. In *Maryland v. Wilson*, 519 U.S. 408 (1997), a police officer who had validly stopped the vehicle in which Wilson was a passenger ordered Wilson to exit the automobile. As Wilson complied, some crack cocaine fell to the ground in full view of the officer. Prior to his trial, Wilson argued that the officer's act of ordering him out of the car constituted an unreasonable seizure, since he was not suspected of any wrongdoing at that time. Ultimately, the Supreme Court held that the reasonableness of a seizure depends on a balance between the needs of the public interest and the individual's right to personal security free from arbitrary interference by law enforcement officials. The Court noted that traffic stops are dangerous to police officers because drivers or passengers may assault officers. The added safety to police compared with the relatively small inconvenience of exiting a motor vehicle means that requiring a passenger to exit is reasonable during a routine traffic stop.[47] Although the Court does not require individualized suspicion to force an occupant to leave the vehicle, what is not clear is whether the passenger may leave the scene or if instead he or she has actually been seized and may be frisked if suspicions are legitimately aroused.

In cases where police have no individualized suspicion, they are free to enter into discussions with individuals of their choosing. This suspicionless inquiry has been determined not to constitute a seizure under the Fourth Amendment or a *Terry* stop under the stop and frisk standard. In one instance, police entered an interstate bus to talk with passengers on the bus during a stop. In *United States v. Drayton*, 536 U.S. 194 (2002), two police officers stationed themselves one at each end of the aisle of a bus, while the third officer began talking to passengers concerning transportation of drugs and guns. First appearances would indicate that the persons on the bus were not free to leave and effectively had been seized since police officers blocked both means of egress. However, passengers were in fact free to enter or leave the bus, but the officers did not inform them of this freedom. When an officer spoke to passenger Drayton and requested permission to pat him down, Drayton consented. The officer discovered bulky items on his inner thighs where drug smugglers normally carry contraband. Drayton and his traveling companion were arrested, tried, and convicted of drug offenses, but a federal court of appeals reversed the convictions. The Supreme Court reversed the court of appeals and ruled that the men had never been seized and were free to go at any time until the point of arrest.

---

[46]Not all seizures require "individual suspicion" despite the *Terry* requirement. In *Michigan v. Sitz*, 496 U.S. 444 (1990), the Court upheld the use of "sobriety checkpoints" where the stop was extremely brief, officers stopped every vehicle, and the intrusion was outweighed by the state's interest in reducing drunken driving. Such stops did not involve any individualized suspicion of any particular driver but served as a screen to find impaired motor vehicle operators.

[47]See *Wyoming v. Houghton*, 526 U.S. 295 (1999), where the Court noted that a passenger is often engaged in a common enterprise with the same goals as the driver of a vehicle and shares a reduced expectation of privacy while traveling in a motor vehicle. To require the passenger to exit the vehicle is reasonable under the circumstances.

According to the Court, police officers do not do not violate the Fourth Amendment's prohibition of unreasonable seizures merely by approaching individuals on the street or in other public places and putting questions to them if they are willing to listen. The fact that Drayton, who the Court noted was free to leave, consented to a search of his person ended his argument that he had been improperly seized under the Fourth Amendment.

MAJOR CASES

CASE 2.1

Initial Court Approval for Stop and Frisk

Terry v. Ohio
Supreme Court of the United States
392 U.S. 1 (1968)

FACTS

While on routine, non-uniformed patrol, detective Martin McFadden of the Cleveland Police Department observed two men acting in a strange fashion. One of the men under McFadden's view repeatedly walked partway down one block, peered in a store window, walked a bit further, returned to look in the window a second time, and then retraced his steps to confer with the unknown subject. The second man repeated the conduct of the first and then returned for a conference. This conduct repeated several times until a third man joined them. When the third man left the company of the first two men, they repeated their unusual conduct. Detective McFadden observed all of this activity to the point that it aroused his suspicions.

Officer McFadden, based on his 35 years as a police detective, believed that the men were "casing a job, a stick-up" and that the conduct warranted further investigation. When the third man rejoined the first two, McFadden approached the three men, made his identity known to the men, and asked them for their names. When the three mumbled inaudible replies, McFadden grabbed Terry and spun him around so that McFadden could view Chilton and the other man while he conducted a limited search of Terry's outer garments.

The pat-down search revealed to McFadden the fact that Terry possessed a pistol in an inside pocket of an overcoat. Prior to removing Terry's overcoat, McFadden patted only the outer garments and did not reach inside until he felt the "weapon-like" lump. He ordered all three

men inside the nearest store where a further pat-down of the three produced one more weapon.

After he had been charged with carrying a concealed weapon and prior to a trial on the merits, Terry filed a motion to suppress the evidence uncovered by McFadden. He alleged that Officer McFadden had no probable cause for arrest and, therefore, the search of his person exceeded the bounds permitted by the Fourth Amendment as applied to the states. The trial court agreed with Terry that probable cause for arrest did not exist but held the opinion that Detective McFadden had the right to pat down the men for his own protection. The trial court held that, under the circumstances, such conduct was reasonable under the Fourth Amendment and refused to suppress the weapon evidence from trial.

Subsequent to the trial court's denial of Terry's pre-trial motion to suppress the revolver, Terry elected a bench trial and he was convicted. The Court of Appeals affirmed and the Supreme Court of Ohio dismissed their appeal on the ground that it involved no "substantial constitutional question." The Supreme Court of the United States granted Terry's petition for certiorari.

PROCEDURAL ISSUE

Where a police officer has observed unusual conduct which led him to reasonably conclude that criminal activity might be afoot or has occurred and that the person with whom he was dealing may be armed and dangerous, where, during the course of the encounter, he identified himself as an officer, and where his fear for his safety remains, may the officer conduct a limited pat-down of the subject's outer clothing in order to discover weapons?

HELD: YES

RATIONALE

Mr. Chief Justice Warren delivered the opinion of the Court.

★ ★ ★

The Fourth Amendment provides that "the right of the people to be secure in their persons, houses, papers, and effects, against unreasonable searches and seizures, shall not be violated...."This inestimable right of personal security belongs as much to the citizen on the streets of our great cities as to the homeowner closeted in his study to dispose of his secret affairs.

★ ★ ★

Unquestionably petitioner was entitled to the protection of the Fourth Amendment as he walked down the streets in Cleveland. The question is whether in all the circumstances of this on-the-street encounter, his right to personal security was violated by an unreasonable search and seizure.

We would be less than candid if we did not acknowledge that this question thrusts to the fore difficult and troublesome issues regarding a sensitive area of police activity—issues which have never before been squarely presented to this Court....

On the one hand, it is frequently argued that in dealing with the rapidly unfolding and often dangerous situations on city streets the police are in need of an escalating set of flexible responses, graduated in relation to the amount of information they possess. For this purpose it is urged that distinctions should be made between a "stop" and an "arrest" (or a "seizure" of a person), and between a "frisk" and a "search." Thus, it is argued, the police should be allowed to "stop" a person and detain him briefly for questioning upon suspicion that he may be connected with criminal activity. Upon suspicion that the person may be armed, the police should have the power to "frisk" him for weapons. If the "stop" and the "frisk" give rise to probable cause to believe that the suspect has committed a crime, then the police should be empowered to make a formal "arrest," and a full incident "search" of the person. This scene is justified in part upon the notion that a "stop" and a "frisk" amount to a mere "minor inconvenience and petty indignity," which can properly be imposed upon the citizen in the interest of effective law enforcement on the basis of a police officer's suspicion.

On the other side the argument is made that the authority of the police must be strictly circumscribed by the law of arrest and search as it has developed to date in the traditional jurisprudence of the Fourth Amendment. It is contended with some force that there is not—and cannot be—a variety of police activity which does not depend solely upon the voluntary co-operation of the citizen and yet which stops short of an arrest based upon probable cause to make such an arrest. The heart of the Fourth Amendment, the argument runs, is a severe requirement of specific justification for any intrusion upon protected personal security, coupled with a highly developed system of judicial controls to enforce upon the agents of the State the commands of the Constitution. Acquiescence by the court in the compulsion inherent in the field interrogation practices at issue here, it is urged, would constitute an abdication of judicial control over, and indeed an encouragement of, substantial interference with liberty and personal security by police officers whose judgment is necessarily colored by their primary involvement in "the often competitive enterprise of ferreting out crime." *Johnson v. United States,* 333 U.S. 10, 14, 68 S.Ct. 367, 369 (1948). This, it is argued, can only serve to exacerbate police-community tensions in the crowded centers of our Nation's cities.

★ ★ ★

[W]e approach the issues in this case mindful of the limitations of the judicial function in controlling the myriad daily situations in which policemen and citizens confront each other on the street. The State has characterized the issue here as:

> the right of a police officer...to make an on-the-street stop, interrogate and pat down for weapons (known in street vernacular as "stop and frisk").

But this is only partly accurate. For the issue is not the abstract propriety of the police conduct, but the admissibility against petitioner of the evidence uncovered by the search and seizure. Ever since its inception, the rule excluding evidence seized in violation of the Fourth Amendment[48] has been recognized as a principal mode of discouraging lawless police conduct. Thus, its major thrust is a deterrent one,...and experience has taught that it is the only effective deterrent to police misconduct in the criminal context, and that, without it, the constitutional

---

[48]See *Weeks v. United States,* 232 U.S. 383 (1914), and *Mapp v. Ohio,* 367 U.S. 643 (1961), for discussion on the rule of exclusion for federal courts and state courts, respectively, adopted by the Supreme Court of the United States in cases involving illegal searches and seizures.

guarantee against unreasonable searches and seizures would be a mere "form of words." *Mapp v. Ohio,* 367 U.S. 643, 655 (1961). The rule also serves another vital function—"the imperative of judicial integrity." Courts which sit under our Constitution cannot and will not be made party to lawless invasions of the constitutional rights of citizens by permitting unhindered governmental use of the fruits of such invasions.

★ ★ ★

II

Our first task is to establish at what point in this encounter the Fourth Amendment becomes relevant. That is, we must decide whether and when Officer McFadden "seized" Terry and whether and when he conducted a "search." There is some suggestion in the use of such terms as "stop" and "frisk" that such police conduct is outside the purview of the Fourth Amendment because neither action rises to the level of a "search" or "seizure" within the meaning of the Constitution. We emphatically reject this notion. It is quite plain that the Fourth Amendment governs "seizures" of the person which do not eventuate in a trip to the station house and prosecution for crime—"arrests" in traditional terminology. It must be recognized that whenever a police officer accosts an individual and restrains his freedom to walk away, he has "seized" that person. And it is nothing less than sheer torture of the English language to suggest that a careful exploration of the outer surfaces of a person's clothing all over his or her body in an attempt to find weapons is not a "search." Moreover, it is simply fantastic to urge that such procedure performed in public by a policeman while the citizen stands helpless, perhaps facing a wall with his hands raised, is a "petty indignity." It is a serious intrusion upon the sanctity of the person, which may inflict great indignity and arouse strong resentment, and it is not to be undertaken lightly.

★ ★ ★

In this case there can be no question, then, that Officer McFadden "seized" petitioner and subjected him to a "search" of his clothing. We must decide whether at that point it was reasonable for Officer McFadden to have interfered with petitioner's personal security as he did. And in determining whether the seizure and search were "unreasonable" our inquiry is a dual one—whether the officer's action was justified at its inception, and whether it was reasonably related in scope to the circumstances which justified the interference in the first place.

★ ★ ★

III

★ ★ ★

In order to assess the reasonableness of Officer McFadden's conduct as a general proposition, it is necessary "first to focus upon the governmental interest which allegedly justifies official intrusion upon the constitutionally protected interests of the private citizen," for there is no ready test for determining reasonableness other than by balancing the need to search [or seize] against the invasion which the search [or seizure] entails. And, in justifying the particular intrusion, the police officer must be able to point to specific and articulable facts which, taken together with rational inferences from those facts, reasonably warrant that intrusion. The scheme of the Fourth Amendment becomes meaningful only when it is assured that, at some point, the conduct of those charged with enforcing the laws can be subjected to the more detached, neutral scrutiny of a judge who must evaluate the reasonableness of a particular search or seizure in light of the particular circumstances. And, in making that assessment, it is imperative that the facts be judged against an objective standard: would the facts available to the officer at the moment of the seizure or the search "warrant a man of reasonable caution in the belief" that the action taken was appropriate? Anything less would invite intrusions upon constitutionally guaranteed rights based on nothing more substantial than inarticulate hunches, a result this Court has consistently refused to sanction. And simple

> "good faith on the part of the arresting officer is not enough."…If subjective good faith alone were the test, the protections of the Fourth Amendment would evaporate, and the people would be "secure in their persons, houses, papers, and effects," only in the discretion of the police. *Beck v. Ohio,* 379 U.S. at 97 (1964).

Applying these principles to this case, we consider first the nature and extent of the governmental interests involved. One general interest is, of course, that of effective crime prevention and detection; it is this interest which underlies the recognition that a police officer may, in appropriate circumstances and in an appropriate manner, approach a person for purposes of investigating possibly criminal behavior even though there is no probable cause to make an arrest. It was this legitimate investigative function Officer McFadden was discharging when he decided to approach petitioner and his companions. He had observed Terry, Chilton, and Katz go through a series of acts, each of them perhaps innocent in itself, but which, taken together, warranted further investigation....It would have been poor police work indeed for an officer of 30 years' experience in the detection of thievery from stores in this same neighborhood to have failed to investigate this behavior further.

The crux of this case, however, is not the propriety of Officer McFadden's taking steps to investigate petitioner's suspicious behavior, but, rather, whether there was justification for McFadden's invasion of Terry's personal security by searching him for weapons in the course of that investigation. We are now concerned with more than the governmental interest in investigating crime; in addition, there is the more immediate interest of the police officer in taking steps to assure himself that the person with whom he is dealing is not armed with a weapon that could unexpectedly and fatally be used against him....

IV

We must now examine the conduct of Officer McFadden in this case to determine whether his search and seizure of petitioner were reasonable, both at their inception and as conducted. He had observed Terry, together with Chilton and another man, acting in a manner he took to be preface to a "stick-up." We think on the facts and circumstances Officer McFadden detailed before the trial judge a reasonably prudent man would have been warranted in believing petitioner was armed and thus presented a threat to the officer's safety while he was investigating his suspicious behavior. The actions of Terry and Chilton were consistent with McFadden's hypothesis that these men were contemplating a day-light robbery—which, it is reasonable to assume, would be likely to involve the use of weapons—and nothing in their conduct from the time he first noticed them until the time he confronted them and identified himself as a police officer gave him sufficient reasons to negate that hypothesis. Although the trio had departed the original scene, there was nothing to indicate abandonment of an intent to commit a robbery at some point. Thus, when Officer McFadden approached the three men gathered before the display window at Zucker's store he had observed enough to make it quite reasonable to fear that they were armed; and nothing in their response to his hailing them,

identifying himself as a police officer, and asking their names served to dispel that reasonable belief.

★ ★ ★

The sole justification of the search in the present situation is the protection of the police officer and others nearby, and it must therefore be confined in scope to an intrusion reasonably designed to discover guns, knives, clubs, or other hidden instruments for the assault of the police officer.

The scope of the search in this case presents no serious problem in light of these standards. Officer McFadden patted down the outer clothing of petitioner and his two companions. He did not place his hands in their pockets or under the outer surface of their garments until he had felt weapons, and then he merely reached for and removed the guns. He never did invade...[the third gentleman's] person beyond the outer surfaces of his clothes, since he discovered nothing in his pat down which might have been a weapon. Officer McFadden confined his search strictly to what was minimally necessary to learn whether the men were armed and to disarm them once he discovered the weapons. He did not conduct a general exploratory search for whatever evidence of criminal activity he might find.

V

We conclude that the revolver seized from Terry was properly admitted in evidence against him. At the time he seized petitioner and searched him for weapons, Officer McFadden had reasonable grounds to believe the petitioner was armed and dangerous, and it was necessary for the protection of himself and others to take swift measures to discover the true facts and neutralize the threat of harm if it materialized. The policeman carefully restricted his search to what was appropriate to the discovery of the particular items which he sought. Each case of this sort will, of course, have to be decided on its own facts. We merely hold today that where a police officer observes unusual conduct which leads him reasonably to conclude in light of his experience that criminal activity may be afoot and that the persons with whom he is dealing may be armed and presently dangerous; where in the course of investigating this behavior he identifies himself as a policeman and makes reasonable inquiries; and where nothing in the initial stages of the encounter serves to dispel his reasonable fear for his own or others' safety, he is entitled for the protection of himself and others in the area to conduct a carefully limited search of the outer clothing of such persons in an attempt to discover weapons which might be used to assault him. Such a search is a reasonable search under the Fourth Amendment, and any weapons seized may be properly introduced in evidence against the person from whom they were taken.

Affirmed.

COMMENTS, NOTES, AND QUESTIONS

1. Suppose that Mr. Terry offered an objectively reasonable explanation for his conduct and that of his friends. Consistent with the *Terry* Court, would Detective McFadden have been permitted to conduct a frisk (search) of their outer clothing? Why or why not? There is a subtle distinction between the legal authority to stop and the reasonableness of a frisk. Every stop does not allow an automatic frisk, a fact often missed by police officers and citizens alike. The *Terry* case represents a situation in which the lawfulness of the stop coupled with subsequent events allowed the frisk of Terry and his associates. The *Terry* Court approved not only the stop but also the subsequent frisk of Terry and his two accomplices. Only where the explanation does not suffice to dispel the fear that a person with whom the officer is dealing may be armed and dangerous may the officer conduct the pat-down search.

2. Consider the situation where a person with several convictions for narcotics use has been observed in the company of a known drug dealer. The two were together for several hours, but the police officer observing them was unable to see everything the two men did. Later, the known narcotics user and his friend walked through a high-crime area late at night; both of them hugged and then chatted with a friend who had just exited a suspected crack house. Both the user and the dealer carried over-the-shoulder backpacks and had used cell phones that had been stored in the backpacks. Has the officer seen enough to make a stop under the *Terry* theory? If so, explain what factors led you to this conclusion. If there has not been enough information to allow a stop and perhaps a frisk, what additional factors would you need to justify a *Terry* stop? What additional information would a police officer need to conduct a lawful frisk of the known user?

3. Reconsider the basic facts of the scenario in question 2. Would sudden flight upon seeing the officers have added anything to your consideration of whether the officers possessed reasonable basis to suspect criminal activity? Are there ever legitimate reasons to avoid contact with a law enforcement officer? What would they be?

Should sudden flight upon making eye contact with a police officer, without more, be sufficient for additional investigation? See *Illinois v. Wardlow,* 528 U.S. 119 (2000), Case 2.5, where unexplained flight upon seeing a police officer, with additional circumstances, permitted an investigatory stop and frisk.

4. In the early years following the *Terry* decision, officers were often required to clearly demonstrate "reasonable basis to suspect criminal activity" to justify stops that culminated in pat-down searches. Consider the situation where two police officers observed two men, late at night, walking away from each another in an alley in an area with a high incidence of drug traffic. The area has been noted for drug trafficking and sexual offenses in a nearby park. Neither officer had any specific reason to suspect either man of specific wrongdoing or to suspect that either man might be armed. The officers stopped and asked one man to identify himself and explain what he was doing. The man refused to identify himself, and the officers arrested him for violating a state statute that required individuals to give a name and address when requested by a peace officer. Under *Terry,* did the officers have sufficient reason to force the man to stop? What crime could the officers have reasonably believed that the man might have committed? Would this conduct, including refusing to identify himself, be sufficient for a pat-down? Why or why not? The main facts of this scenario are similar to those of *Brown v. Texas,* 443 U.S. 47 (1979), where the Supreme Court held that the application of the Texas statute to detain Brown and to require him to identify himself violated the Fourth Amendment because the officers lacked any reasonable suspicion to believe that appellant was engaged in or had engaged in criminal conduct. According to the Court, detaining Brown under the circumstances constituted an illegal seizure of his person and transgressed the requirement of reasonableness under the Fourth Amendment and *Terry.*

CASE 2.2

Extension of Stop and Frisk Rationale to Automobiles

Adams v. Williams
Supreme Court of the United States
407 U.S. 143 (1972)

FACTS

Sgt. John Connolly was alone early in the morning on car patrol duty in a high-crime area of Bridgeport,

Connecticut. An informant, known to Connolly, spoke with the officer and stated that a specifically described individual parked in a nearby automobile was carrying narcotics and possessed a gun at his waist.

Following a call for backup, Connolly approached the subject in the car, tapped on his window, and asked respondent Williams to open the door. Instead of obeying the command, Williams rolled down the window. Connolly reached inside the auto and inside Williams' pants and removed a pistol located where the informant had stated. A search incident to arrest disclosed a quantity of heroin on Williams' person and found a machete and a second revolver hidden in the automobile.

Williams claimed that his Fourth Amendment rights as set forth in *Terry v. Ohio,* 392 U.S. 1 (1967), had been violated on the theory that absent a more reliable informant or additional corroboration of the tip, Sgt. Connolly's search was unreasonable because Connolly did not have reasonable basis to suspect criminal activity. The trial court rejected Williams' allegations that, absent a more reliable informant or some additional corroboration of the tip, the policeman's actions were unreasonable under the standards announced in *Terry v. Ohio.* The court convicted Williams of illegal possession of a handgun and of possession of heroin.

Williams unsuccessfully pursued his state remedies and was denied certiorari by the Supreme Court of the United States. Williams requested a writ of habeas corpus from a federal district court but the writ was denied. However, the Court of Appeals for the Second Circuit granted the requested relief. The Supreme Court of the United States granted certiorari.

PROCEDURAL ISSUE

When a police officer receives a tip from a known reliable informant that a specifically described man is sitting in an automobile possessing a handgun as well as narcotics, may the officer, consistent with *Terry v. Ohio,* make an immediate but limited search for the weapon?

HELD: YES

RATIONALE

Mr. Justice Rehnquist delivered the opinion of the Court.

★ ★ ★

Respondent Williams contends that the initial seizure of his pistol, upon which rested the later search and seizure of other weapons and narcotics, was not justified by the informant's tip to Sgt. Connolly. He claims that absent a more reliable informant, or some corroboration of the tip, the policeman's actions were unreasonable under the standards set forth in *Terry v. Ohio.*

In *Terry* this Court recognized that

"a police officer may in appropriate circumstances and in an appropriate manner approach a person for purposes of investigating possible criminal behavior even though there is no probable cause to make an arrest."

The Fourth Amendment does not require a policeman who lacks the precise level of information necessary for probable cause to arrest to simply shrug his shoulders and allow a crime to occur or criminal to escape. On the contrary, *Terry* recognizes that it may be the essence of good police work to adopt an intermediate response. A brief stop of a suspicious individual, in order to determine his identity or to maintain the status quo momentarily while obtaining more information, may be most reasonable in light of the facts known to the officer at the time.

★ ★ ★

Applying these principles [of *Terry v. Ohio*] to the present case we believe that Sgt. Connolly acted justifiably in responding to his informant's tip. The informant was known to him personally and had provided him with information in the past. This is a stronger case than obtains in the case of an anonymous telephone tip. The informant here came forward personally to give information that was immediately verifiable at the scene. Indeed, under Connecticut law, the informant might have been subject to immediate arrest for making a false complaint had Sgt. Connolly's investigation proven the tip incorrect (for false reporting of a crime). Thus, while the Court's decisions indicate that this informant's unverified tip may have been insufficient for a narcotics arrest or search warrant,[49] the information carried enough indicia of reliability to justify the officer's forcible stop of Williams.

---

[49]The Court notes that the informant's tip may not have been sufficient for an arrest or search because those activities require a higher level of proof than is minimally necessary to conduct a stop and frisk. Probable cause requires that the informant have given some

In reaching this conclusion, we reject respondent's argument that reasonable cause for a stop and frisk can only be based on the officer's personal observation, rather than on information supplied by another person. Informants' tips, like all other clues and evidence coming to a policeman on the scene, may vary greatly in their value and reliability. One simple rule will not cover every situation. Some tips, completely lacking in indicia of reliability, would either warrant no police response or require further investigation before a forcible stop of a suspect would be authorized. But in some situations—for example, when the victim of a street crime seeks immediate police aid and gives a description of his assailant, or when a credible informant warns of a specific impending crime—the subtleties of the hearsay rule should not thwart an appropriate police response.

While properly investigating the activity of a person who was reported to be carrying narcotics and a concealed weapon and who was sitting alone in a car in a high crime area at 2:15 in the morning, Sgt. Connolly had ample reason to fear for his safety.…Under these circumstances the policeman's action in reaching to the spot where the gun was thought to be hidden constituted a limited intrusion designed to insure his safety, and we conclude that it was reasonable. The loaded gun seized as a result of this intrusion was therefore admissible at Williams' trial.

★ ★ ★

The fruits of the search were therefore properly admitted at Williams' trial, and the Court of Appeals erred in reaching a contrary conclusion.

Reversed.

COMMENTS, NOTES, AND QUESTIONS

1. Was there sufficient reason to believe the informant in *Adams*? What factors would you argue made the *Adams* informant a believable person? How important to meeting the "reasonable basis to suspect" standard was the fact that Officer Connolly verified some facts alleged by the informant? Would the frisk have been reasonable if there had been only a female parked in a large diesel pickup truck? What arguments could you make directed toward meeting the stop and frisk standard?

2. *Adams* involved an informant, a complicating factor not present in the original *Terry* case. How should an officer evaluate the information offered by an informant? Should the officer have some reason to believe an informant? Since the stop and frisk standard is a lower level of proof than probable cause, should the informant meet the same standards required of informants when evaluating their evidence to determine probable cause? In *Adams,* the officer had some prior experience with the informant, but one may wonder whether it was sufficient to believe him. On the witness stand, the officer noted that the informant had given him information on homosexual activity, but no arrests followed based on that information. Would this be sufficient to believe that an informant was telling the truth? Why or why not? Would a longer "track record" with the informant make you more likely to believe the informant when he conveyed information about Williams?

3. Would a police officer have any problem if the information came from a fellow officer rather than an informant? Should an officer's word be good? The general rule is that the credibility of a police officer is not normally questioned concerning his or her believability, but an informant requires some additional scrutiny.

4. It is possible to contend that the Court extended the stop and frisk rationale to a new set of facts that were not contemplated by the original *Terry* court. A stop and frisk can now be conducted of persons when occupying automobiles so long as there is reasonable basis to suspect criminal activity. The information sufficient for a stop may come to the officer by an informant or from personal observation. The *Adams* majority did not concern itself with the fact that the officer did not make a reasonable inquiry or frisk prior to seizing the weapon. The Court seems to be saying, though not directly, that when a firearm is involved, the officer may not have to make an inquiry, or to frisk first, if the location of the gun has been communicated to the officer.

---

reason to be believed and that the detail of the facts given by the informant give rise to an independent determination by the officer that probable cause exists. If the officer knows the informant has given reliable information in the past or has implicated himself in a crime by talking to the officer, such facts would make the officer more likely to conclude that probable cause existed. Since the stop and frisk is based on a lower level of proof, a shady informant who had no "track record" with the officer or who had not always told the truth in the past might still be able to offer evidence sufficient to allow a lawful stop and frisk.

5. Consider this situation: police are dispatched to a bus stop following an anonymous telephone call which stated that a particularly described young man was carrying a concealed firearm in a state where concealed firearms are permitted for adults. There was no verification of the informant's truthfulness and no way to identify the informant. May the police approach and conduct a stop and a subsequent frisk on this level of knowledge? Why or why not? If not, what are police lacking to conduct a stop? Or would you allow a stop but not a frisk unless other factors become apparent? This situation could be evaluated by reference to *Florida v. J.L.,* 529 U.S. 288 (2000).

CASE 2.3

Moving Motor Vehicles May Be Stopped under the **Terry** *Rationale*

Alabama v. White
Supreme Court of the United States
496 U.S. 325 (1990)

FACTS

Officers in the Montgomery [Alabama] Police Department received an anonymous telephone tip that respondent Vanessa White would be leaving a named apartment building at a particular time in a uniquely described vehicle which had a broken right taillight lens. Further the caller said that Ms. White would be going to Dobey's Motel and that she would be in possession of an ounce of cocaine. Two officers immediately proceeded to the apartment building, saw a vehicle matching the caller's description, observed White as she left the building and entered the vehicle, and followed her along the most direct route to the motel. Although the police did not observe Ms. White take anything from the apartment to her vehicle, they decided to stop her vehicle just short of the motel. Corporal Davis asked respondent to step to the rear of her car, where he informed her that she had been stopped because she was suspected of carrying cocaine in the vehicle. He asked if they could look for cocaine, and Ms. White indicated her consent. The officers found a locked brown attaché case in the car and, upon request, respondent provided the combination to the lock. The officers found marijuana in the attaché case and

placed respondent under arrest. In a search incident to arrest, cocaine was found in her purse.

The prosecution charged Ms. White with possession of marijuana and cocaine. The trial court rejected her motion to suppress evidence and she pled guilty, reserving the right to appeal the legality of the stop and search of her automobile and the search incident to arrest.

The Court of Criminal Appeals of Alabama reversed her conviction on possession charges, holding that the trial court should have suppressed the marijuana and cocaine because the officers did not have the reasonable suspicion necessary under *Terry v. Ohio,* 392 U.S. 1 (1968), to justify the investigatory stop of the vehicle. The Supreme Court of Alabama denied the government's petition for certiorari. The Supreme Court of the United States granted certiorari to the State of Alabama.

PROCEDURAL ISSUE

May an anonymous telephone tip alleging criminal activity, when substantially corroborated by observations by police officers, produce "reasonable basis to suspect criminal activity" sufficient to make an investigatory stop of a person in a moving motor vehicle?

HELD: YES

RATIONALE

Justice White delivered the opinion of the Court.

[The Supreme Court in] *Adams v. Williams,* 407 U.S. 143 (1972), sustained a *Terry* stop and frisk undertaken on the basis of a tip given in person by a known informant, who had provided information in the past. We concluded that, while the unverified tip may have been insufficient to support an arrest or search warrant, the information carried sufficient "indicia of reliability" to justify a forcible stop. We did not address the issue of anonymous tips in *Adams,* except to say that "[t]his is a stronger case than obtains in the case of an anonymous telephone tip," *id.,* at 146.

[Similarly, the Court in] *Illinois v. Gates,* 462 U.S. 213 (1983), dealt with an anonymous tip in the probable cause context. The Court there abandoned the "two-pronged test"[50] of *Aguilar v. Texas,* 378 U.S. 108 (1964),

---

[50]In *Aguilar v. Texas,* 378 U.S. 108 (1964), the Court appeared to adopt a "two-pronged test" to determine whether an informant could offer evidence that would give probable cause to search (or arrest, since the standard of proof is the same). It required that the

and *Spinelli v. United States,* 393 U.S. 410 (1969), in favor of a "totality of circumstances" approach to determining whether an informant's tip establishes probable cause. *Gates* made clear, however, that those factors that had been considered critical under *Aguilar* and *Spinelli*—an informant's "veracity," "reliability," and "basis of knowledge"—remain "highly relevant in determining the value of his report." 462 U.S., at 230. These factors are also relevant in the reasonable suspicion context, although allowance must be made in applying them for the lesser showing required to meet that standard.

The opinion in *Gates* recognized that an anonymous tip alone seldom demonstrates the informant's basis of knowledge or veracity inasmuch as ordinary citizens generally do not provide extensive recitations of the basis of their everyday observations and given that the veracity of persons supplying anonymous tips is "by hypothesis largely unknown, and unknowable."

★ ★ ★

As there was in *Gates,* however, in this case there is more than the tip itself. The tip was not as detailed, and the corroboration was not as complete, as in *Gates,* but the required degree of suspicion was likewise not as high.

★ ★ ★

Reasonable suspicion [required under *Terry*] is a less demanding standard than probable cause not only in the sense that reasonable suspicion can be established with information that is different in quantity or content than that required to establish probable cause, but also in the sense that reasonable suspicion can arise from information that is less reliable than that required to show probable cause.... Thus, if a tip has a relatively low degree of reliability, more information will be required to establish the requisite quantum of suspicion than would be required if the tip were more reliable.... Contrary to the court below, we conclude that when the officers stopped respondent, the anonymous tip had been sufficiently corroborated to furnish reasonable suspicion that respondent was engaged in criminal activity and that the investigative stop therefore did not violate the Fourth Amendment.

It is true that not every detail mentioned by the tipster was verified, such as the name of the woman leaving the building or the precise apartment from which she left; but the officers did corroborate that a woman left the 235 building and got into the particular vehicle that was described by the caller. With respect to the time of departure predicted by the informant, Corporal Davis testified that the caller gave a particular time when the woman would be leaving, but he did not state what the time was. He did testify that, after the call, he and his partner proceeded to the Lynwood Terrace Apartments to put the 235 building under surveillance. Given the fact that the officers proceeded to the indicated address immediately after the call and that respondent emerged not too long thereafter, it appears from the record before us that respondent's departure from the building was within the time frame predicted by the caller. [The Court felt that the prediction of her destination was sufficiently corroborated by her act of driving toward the described motel.]

★ ★ ★

The Court's opinion in *Gates* gave credit to the proposition that because an informant is shown to be right about some things, he is probably right about other facts that he has alleged, including the claim that the object of the tip is engaged in criminal activity. [*Illinois v. Gates*] 462 U.S., at 244. Thus, it is not unreasonable to conclude in this case that the independent corroboration by the police of significant aspects of the informer's predictions imparted some degree of reliability to the other allegations made by the caller.

We think it is also important that, as in *Gates,* "the anonymous [tip] contained a range of details relating not just to easily obtained facts and conditions existing at the time of the tip, but to future actions of third parties ordinarily not easily predicted." *Gates,* 462 U.S., at 245. The fact that the officers found a car precisely matching the caller's description in front of the 235 building is an example of the former. Anyone could have "predicted" that fact because it was a condition presumably existing at the time of the call. What was important was the caller's ability to predict respondent's *future behavior,* because it

---

informant be proven to be reliable and honest in what information was being relayed to law enforcement. Additionally, the facts offered by the informant had to be evaluated to determine whether probable cause existed. Under *Aguilar,* mere conclusions of fact given by the informant were insufficient. The Court overruled *Aguilar* and abolished the "two-pronged test" in *Illinois v. Gates,* 462 U.S. 213 (1983), by substituting the "totality of the circumstances" test to determine the existence of probable cause. However, the honesty and facts presented by an informant still must be evaluated to determine probable cause.

demonstrated inside information—a special familiarity with respondent's affairs.

★ ★ ★

When significant aspects of the caller's predictions were verified, there was reason to believe not only that the caller was honest but also that he was well informed, at least well enough to justify the stop.

Although it is a close case, we conclude that under the totality of circumstances the anonymous tip, as corroborated, exhibited sufficient indicia of reliability to justify the investigatory stop of respondent's car. We therefore reverse the judgment of the Court of Criminal Appeals of Alabama and remand for further proceedings not inconsistent with this opinion.

So ordered.

Justice Stevens, with whom Justice Brennan and Justice Marshall join, dissenting.

Millions of people leave their apartments at about the same time every day carrying an attache case and heading for a destination known to their neighbors. Usually, however, the neighbors do not know what the briefcase contains. An anonymous neighbor's prediction about somebody's time of departure and probable destination is anything but a reliable basis for assuming that the commuter is in possession of an illegal substance—particularly when the person is not even carrying the attache case described by the tipster.

★ ★ ★

Anybody with enough knowledge about a given person to make her the target of a prank, or to harbor a grudge against her, will certainly be able to formulate a tip about her like the one predicting Vanessa White's excursion. In addition, under the Court's holding, every citizen is subject to being seized and questioned by any officer who is prepared to testify that the warrantless stop was based on an anonymous tip predicting whatever conduct the officer just observed.

COMMENTS, NOTES, AND QUESTIONS

1. In the principal case, Justice Stevens noted that any person could have a neighbor stopped by police by giving details of the neighbor's work schedule and related habits as long as the informant made an allegation of a crime. Could anyone have a neighbor or enemy stopped by police by anonymously making criminal allegations? Were the future activities of Ms. White, which were predicted to police, merely the details that any observant neighbor could have given? Is Justice Stevens' concern, that the standard has been lowered too far, a reasonable one? Why or why not? Would it be important that police verify some of the allegations prior to making a stop? Why or why not?

2. May officers stop an automobile with less information concerning criminality than they possessed in the case *Alabama v. White,* 496 U.S. 325 (1990)? Must police possess some level of suspicion that a crime has occurred or is about to occur? In *Delaware v. Prouse,* 440 U.S. 648 (1979), an officer made a traffic stop where the officer testified that he "had observed neither traffic or equipment violations nor any suspicious activity, and that he made the stop only in order to check the driver's license and registration."[51] Clearly, the officer had no reason to stop Prouse that could have even approached the facts and level of suspicion which the officers possessed in *Alabama V. White.* In cases where police do not possess individualized suspicion of criminal activity, a stop of an automobile cannot be made on a guess or mere hunch; the reasonable basis to suspect criminal activity threshold of *Terry* must be met. As the Court stated in *Prouse:*

> [E]xcept in those situations in which there is at least articulable and reasonable suspicion that a motorist is unlicensed or that an automobile is not registered, or that either the vehicle or an occupant is otherwise subject to seizure for violation of law, stopping an automobile and detaining the driver in order to check his driver's license and the registration of the automobile are unreasonable under the Fourth Amendment.

Thus, the Court approved the finding that the police stop of Prouse violated the requirements of the Fourth Amendment as applied to the states.

3. What about a situation where local law enforcement agents set up roadblocks to detect alcohol-impaired or chemically impaired drivers? Would there be any individualized suspicion that every driver who is stopped is impaired? Could such a practice be reasonable, since most

---

[51] *Delaware v. Prouse,* 440 U.S. 648, 650 (1979).

states have a significant problem with impaired drivers? What if the police just waved most people through the roadblock and stopped only people who had old cars or were not dressed extremely well? Or stopped only young drivers? Despite the *Terry* decision allowing brief seizures only upon reasonable basis to suspect, the Court has approved some very brief seizures that could not rise to the level of proof needed for a stop and frisk. In *Michigan v. Sitz,* 496 U.S. 444 (1990), the Court allowed the practice where the Michigan State Police initiated roadblocks for motorists in order to check for impaired drivers. The police stopped every driver but detained each one only briefly without any reason to suspect that any particular driver was driving under the influence. In permitting the seizure without suspicion, the Court balanced the state's interest in preventing drunken driving against the degree of intrusion upon individual motorists who are briefly stopped and found that the seizures weighed in favor of the state program.

CASE 2.4

Evolution of the Terry Rationale to the Drug Courier Profile

Florida v. Royer
Supreme Court of the United States
460 U.S. 491 (1983)

FACTS

After purchasing a one-way airline ticket to New York City at Miami International Airport under an assumed name and checking his two suitcases bearing identification tags with the same assumed name, Mark Royer went to the concourse leading to the airline boarding area. Unknown to Royer, two detectives used a "drug courier profile"[52] to isolate Royer from other passengers planning to fly from Miami International Airport to New York's La Guardia Airport. The detectives approached Mr. Royer and asked to see his airline ticket

and some identification. The ticket bore the name of one "Holt" which was different from the name on Mr. Royer's driver's license. After listening to Royer offer a brief explanation which did not dispel the detectives' suspicions of narcotics trafficking, they suggested that Royer accompany them to a small room. At this point the detectives told Mr. Royer that they suspected that he was transporting contraband drugs and asked him to accompany them to a small room adjacent to the airport concourse.

Royer's airline ticket, boarding pass, and driver's license remained in the possession of the detectives during the forty-foot walk to the room. Royer appeared to voluntarily walk with the officers to the room, but did not orally consent. With Royer still in the room, one of the detectives, without the consent of Royer, used his luggage claim checks to obtain Mr. Royer's luggage from the airline.

When asked if he would give consent to a search of the luggage, Royer did not verbally agree, but he offered a key and unlocked one suitcase that he did not open. One detective, in the absence of any oral consent, opened that suitcase, revealing a quantity of marijuana. When asked if the detectives could open the second suitcase, Royer explained that he did not know the combination but that it was all right with him if they opened it. One of the detectives forcibly opened the second item of luggage, disclosing more marijuana. Approximately fifteen minutes had elapsed from the time the detectives initially stopped Mark Royer until his arrest upon the discovery of the contraband.

Prior to his trial for possession of marijuana, Royer filed a motion to suppress the marijuana alleging that since the officers detained him too long under the stop and frisk theory, the conduct violated the Fourth Amendment. He pled no contest to the drug possession charge while reserving his right to appeal the denial of his Fourth Amendment claim.

The Florida District Court of Appeal held that Royer had been involuntarily confined within the small room without probable cause and that the involuntary detention had exceeded the limited time of restraint

---

[52]The concept of a "drug courier profile" involves a determination of what stereotypes and characteristics are generally possessed by the person who transports drugs. The factors will vary depending on whether the location is an airport, a motor home, or a city known to be a drug origination source. Typically an airport courier may pay for a ticket in cash with large bills and purchase only a one-way fare. This individual will normally be fairly young (twenty-five to thirty-five) but carry expensive luggage, if luggage is used at all. Some legs of a courier's trip may involve no luggage, checked or otherwise. Staying for a short time in a drug origination city, traveling under an assumed name, and nervous demeanor are all additional factors police use to make the local drug courier profile. Criticism has been directed at using such stereotypes, since they also fit many law-abiding citizens.

permitted by *Terry v. Ohio*. The United States Supreme Court granted certiorari.

PROCEDURAL ISSUE

Where government officials detain a subject for fifteen minutes, remove him to an interrogation room, and retrieve his luggage from an airline on the basis that he fits a "drug courier profile," does such conduct exceed the time limits of a permissible scope of a stop under the stop and frisk doctrine?

HELD: YES

RATIONALE

Justice White announced the judgment of the Court and delivered an opinion, in which Justice Marshall, Justice Powell, and Justice Stevens joined.

★ ★ ★

II

Some preliminary observations are in order. First, it is unquestioned that, without a warrant to search Royer's luggage and in the absence of probable cause and exigent circumstances, the validity of the search depended on Royer's purported consent. Neither is it disputed that, where the validity of a search rests on consent, the State has the burden of proving that the necessary consent was obtained and that it was freely and voluntarily given, a burden that is not satisfied by showing a mere submission to a claim of lawful authority.

Second, law enforcement officers do not violate the Fourth Amendment by merely approaching an individual on the street or in another public place, by asking him if he is willing to answer some questions, by putting questions to him if the person is willing to listen, or by offering in evidence in a criminal prosecution his voluntary answers to such questions. *Terry v. Ohio,* 392 U.S. at 31, 32–33. Nor would the fact that the officer identifies himself as a police officer, without more, convert the encounter into a seizure requiring some level of objective justification. The person approached, however, need not answer any question put to him; indeed, he may decline to listen to the questions at all, and may go on his way. *Terry v. Ohio,* 392 U.S. at 32–33. He may not be detained even momentarily without reasonable, objective grounds

for doing so; and his refusal to listen or answer does not, without more, furnish those grounds. *United States v. Mendenhall,* supra, at 556 (opinion of Stewart, J.). If there is no detention—no seizure within the meaning of the Fourth Amendment—then no constitutional rights have been infringed.

Third, it is also clear that not all seizures of the person must be justified by probable cause to arrest for a crime. Prior to *Terry v. Ohio, supra,* any restraint on the person amounting to a seizure for the purposes of the Fourth Amendment was invalid unless justified by probable cause. *Dunaway v. New York, supra,* at 207–209. Terry created a limited exception to this general rule: certain seizures are justifiable under the Fourth Amendment if there is articulable suspicion that a person has committed or is about to commit a crime.

★ ★ ★

Fourth, *Terry* and its progeny nevertheless created only limited exceptions to the general rule that seizures of the person require probable cause to arrest. Detentions may be "investigative," yet violative of the Fourth Amendment absent probable cause. In the name of investigating a person who is no more than suspected of criminal activity, the police may not carry out a full search of the person or of his automobile or other effects. Nor may the police seek to verify their suspicions by means that approach the conditions of arrest.

III

The State proffers three reasons for holding that when Royer consented to the search of his luggage, he was not being illegally detained. First, it is submitted that the entire encounter was consensual and hence Royer was not being held against his will at all. We find this submission untenable. Asking for and examining Royer's ticket and his driver's license were no doubt permissible in themselves, but when the officers identified themselves as narcotics agents, told Royer that he was suspected of transporting narcotics, and asked him to accompany them to the police room, while retaining his ticket and driver's license and without indicating in any way that he was free to depart, Royer was effectively seized for the purposes of the Fourth Amendment. These circumstances surely amount to a show of official authority such that "a reasonable person would have believed he was not free to leave." *United States v. Mendenhall,* 446 U.S., at 554 (opinion of Stewart, J.) [footnote omitted].

Second, the State submits that if Royer was seized, there existed reasonable, articulated suspicion to justify a temporary detention and that the limits of a *Terry*-type stop were never exceeded. We agree with the State that when the officers discovered that Royer was traveling under an assumed name, this fact, and the facts already known to the officers—paying cash for a one-way ticket, the mode of checking the two bags, and Royer's appearance and conduct in general—were adequate grounds for suspecting Royer of carrying drugs and for temporarily detaining him and his luggage while they attempted to verify or dispel their suspicions in a manner that did not exceed the limits of an investigative detention.... We have concluded, however, that at the time Royer produced the key to his suitcase, the detention to which he was then subjected was a more serious intrusion on his personal liberty than is allowable on mere suspicion of criminal activity.

★ ★ ★

What had begun as a consensual inquiry in a public place had escalated into an investigatory procedure in a police interrogation room, where the police, unsatisfied with previous explanations, sought to confirm their suspicions. The officers had Royer's ticket, they had his identification, and they had seized his luggage. Royer was never informed that he was free to board his plane if he so chose, and he reasonably believed that he was being detained. At least as of that moment, any consensual aspects of the encounter had evaporated, and we cannot fault the Florida Court of Appeal for concluding that *Terry v. Ohio* and the cases following it did not justify the restraint to which Royer was then subjected. As a practical matter, Royer was under arrest. Consistent with this conclusion, the State conceded in the Florida courts that Royer would not have been free to leave the interrogation room had he asked to do so.

★ ★ ★

We also think that the officers' conduct was more intrusive than necessary to effectuate an investigative detention otherwise authorized by the *Terry* line of cases. First, by returning his ticket and driver's license, and informing him that he was free to go if he so desired, the officers may have obviated any claim that the encounter was anything

but a consensual matter from the start to finish. Second, there are undoubtedly reasons of safety and security that would justify moving a suspect from one location to another during an investigatory detention, such as from an airport concourse to a more private area. There is no indication in this case that such reasons prompted the officers to transfer the site of the encounter from the concourse to the interrogation room. It appears, rather, that the primary interest of the officers was not in having an extended conversation with Royer but in the contents of his luggage, a matter which the officers did not pursue orally with Royer until after the encounter was relocated to the police room.

★ ★ ★

IV

The State's third and final argument is that Royer was not being illegally held when he gave his consent because there was probable cause to arrest him at that time.... We agree with the Florida Court of Appeal, however, that probable cause to arrest Royer did not exist at the time he consented to the search of his luggage. The facts are that a nervous young man with two American Tourister bags paid cash for an airline ticket to a "target city." These facts led to inquiry which in turn revealed that the ticket had been bought under an assumed name. The proffered explanation did not satisfy the officers. We cannot agree with the State, if this is its position, that every nervous young man paying cash for a ticket to New York City under an assumed name and carrying two heavy American Tourister bags may be arrested and held to answer for a serious felony charge.

V

Because we affirm the Florida Court of Appeal's conclusion that Royer was being illegally detained when he consented to the search of his luggage, we agree that the consent was tainted by the illegality[53] and was ineffective to justify the search. The judgment of the Florida Court of Appeal is accordingly

Affirmed.

COMMENTS, NOTES, AND QUESTIONS

1. A police officer faces a difficult task in determining what conduct falls into the category of reasonable

---

[53]See *Wong Sun v. United States,* 371 U.S. 471 (1963), for a discussion of the "fruit of the poisonous tree" doctrine and the exclusion of derivative evidence.

basis to suspect criminal activity. Obviously, outrageous and egregious conduct will trigger the legal right to stop, but conduct that does not clearly rise to that level will cause difficulty. Consistent with the lesson of *Royer,* how could the police have conducted the encounter to produce admissible evidence? If you were to advise airport officers, how long would you tell them that they could keep control of a person in Mr. Royer's shoes? How should this be evaluated? Should you tell him that he was free to leave? Would this help? How?

2. As the principal case demonstrates, not only is a "reasonable basis to suspect criminal behavior" of crucial concern for *Terry* stops, but thorny legal problems beyond the appropriate length of a detention involving the location, the atmosphere, and the coerciveness of the encounter all create challenges for law enforcement officials. What factors should determine whether a given location of the encounter with law enforcement officials affects the reasonableness of the detention? What facts should a police officer consider? How important is the fact that police officers possess a detainee's luggage? Do you think that the Court offered a great deal of guidance concerning how to conduct operations that involve stopping airport travelers? How has the concept of airport searches changed since September 11, 2001? Significant litigated cases have yet to reach the upper levels of the state or federal appellate system, and new legislation is in the process of being implemented that may alter the way a stop and frisk operates in the context of sensitive areas.

3. Consent to remain with the police might be a way to ensure that the subject had no objection to remaining in close proximity to police officers. Alternatively, if the police had told Royer that he was free to leave and restored his luggage to the airline luggage system, there would not have been an illegal detention. Consent to search the luggage might have been a proper approach if requested quickly. In *Royer,* the state attempted to justify the search based on the theory that Royer consented to a search when he unlocked one suitcase while inside the airport security room. Since consent, inter alia, must be voluntarily given, under the "totality of the circumstances," would it seem that Royer granted voluntary consent? Using the "totality of the circumstances," a test

for consent[54] announced in *Schneckloth v. Bustamonte,* 412 U.S. 218 (1973) (see case 4.8), did Royer consent to a search of either piece of luggage? Did Royer feel free to either give or withhold consent? Do you agree with the Court and Justice White? Why or why not? In consent search cases, the burden of proving the existence of a free and voluntarily given consent rests with the government. See *Bumper v. North Carolina,* 391 U.S. 543, 548 (1968).

4. Consider a situation in which the individual was suspected of carrying narcotics from an airport in one state to an airport destination in a different state. When the suspect refused to grant consent to search his luggage, officers took it from him and transported the luggage to a third airport, where a drug-sniffing dog alerted to the baggage, giving probable cause to search. The subject was "free to go," but the government had all his luggage. If all the baggage seizure happened within ninety minutes, would this be an unreasonable detention of the luggage in violation of the *Terry* standard? What factors would you consider? Would a traveler feel free to continue his travels? These facts were present in *United States v. Place,* 462 U.S. 696 (1983), mentioned in the textual material for this chapter.

5. In *United States v. Acosta-Colon,* 157 F.3d 9 (1998), the defendants were about to board an airplane from Puerto Rico to New York when customs agents stopped them. A canine unit had alerted to their bags. Acosta was placed in handcuffs, involuntarily transported (in restraints) to an official holding area some distance from the place of the original stop, confined to a small interrogation room for more than fifteen minutes, and kept there under observation for additional time. Acosta was never informed how long he would be detained or told that he was not under arrest, but agents testified that he would not have been free to leave. Acosta also missed his flight to New York.

The court of appeal felt that the case was covered by *Florida v. Royer* and determined that the level of custody and its length exceeded the permissible time allowed under *Terry* and *Royer.* Are there any real differences between this case and *Royer?* Did the fact that the dog alerted to some of the luggage make any difference? Should it?

---

[54]The "totality of the circumstances" test for consent announced in *Schneckloth v. Bustamonte* focuses on several factors, some of which may be present in a given case. Some factors that have been taken into consideration include the youth of the accused, the lack of education, the presence of low intelligence, the ignorance of constitutional rights, the length of detention, the repeated and prolonged nature of interrogation, the use of physical coercion, knowledge of the right to refuse consent, and whether the subject was under arrest.

CASE 2.5

Unexplained Flight upon Sight of Police Officer Can Create Reasonable Basis to Suspect

Illinois v. Wardlow
Supreme Court of the United States
528 U.S.119 (2000)

FACTS

Defendant Wardlow had been convicted of unlawful use of a weapon by a felon at a bench trial in Cook County, Illinois. He appealed his two-year sentence on the basis that the trial court should have excluded the evidence against him and not have entered a verdict of guilt.

The police officers who arrested Wardlow were among eight officers in four cars traveling in Chicago with the purpose of investigating narcotics sales. One officer stated that he was working in uniform but did not recall whether the police car he drove, the last in the "caravan," was marked or unmarked. The officers had spotted Wardlow standing on the street in front of a building and did not appear to be violating any law. As the officers' car got closer to Wardlow, he appeared to look in their direction and then "ran southbound through a gangway and then through an alley. Officer Nolan stated that defendant, who was carrying a white opaque bag under his arm, was cornered after they had alighted from their cruiser in an effort to intercept his path of flight. The police also observed Wardlow carrying a white opaque bag under his arm, but its contents were not visible.

Following the stop of Wardlow, an officer conducted a frisk of his person and "fluffed" the opaque bag by squeezing it. From the feel of the bag, the officer believed that a weapon was secreted inside the bag, so the officer opened the bag and revealed a .38 caliber handgun which was loaded. The officers immediately arrested Wardlow on an illegal weapons charge.

Wardlow contended, unsuccessfully in the trial court, that the stop and frisk was unlawful under the Fourth Amendment and that the evidence should not have been introduced against him at his bench trial. He contended that the trial court erred in denying his motion to suppress because his presence in a high-crime area and flight from police were insufficient to justify his investigatory stop and the subsequent frisk.

The intermediate appellate court in Illinois reversed the conviction, holding, among other things, that unprovoked flight is insufficient to justify a stop and frisk under the circumstances. The Supreme court of Illinois affirmed the appellate court result and held that Wardlow gave no outward indication of involvement in illicit activity prior to the approach of the police vehicle. The court noted that Wardlow was simply standing in front of a building when the officers drove by. Since the court majority held that the police were not able to point to specific facts corroborating the inference of guilt gleaned from Wardlow's flight, the police stop, frisk, and subsequent arrest of Wardlow were in conflict with the Fourth Amendment. The appellate reversal of the trial court's conviction was upheld by the Illinois Supreme court.

The Supreme Court of the United States granted certiorari to consider the contentions of the State of Illinois that the stop and frisk of Wardlow were constitutional under the Fourth Amendment.

PROCEDURAL ISSUE

Consistent with the Fourth Amendment, is an individual's flight upon the approach of a police vehicle patrolling a high-crime narcotics area sufficient to justify an investigative stop of the person?

HELD: YES

RATIONALE

Chief Justice Rehnquist delivered the opinion of the Court.

★ ★ ★

This case, involving a brief encounter between a citizen and a police officer on a public street, is governed by the analysis we first applied in *Terry*. In *Terry*, we held that an officer may, consistent with the Fourth Amendment, conduct a brief, investigatory stop when the officer has a reasonable, articulable suspicion that criminal activity is afoot. While "reasonable suspicion" is a less demanding standard than probable cause and requires a showing considerably less than preponderance of the evidence, the Fourth Amendment requires at least a minimal level of objective justification for making the stop. *United States v. Sokolow,* 490 U.S. 1, 7 (1989). The officer must be able to articulate more than an "inchoate and unparticularized suspicion or 'hunch'" of criminal activity.

Nolan and Harvey were among eight officers in a four car caravan that was converging on an area known for heavy narcotics trafficking, and the officers anticipated encountering a large number of people in the area, including drug customers and individuals serving as lookouts. App. 8. It was in this context that Officer Nolan decided to investigate Wardlow after observing him flee. An individual's presence in an area of expected criminal activity, standing alone, is not enough to support a reasonable, particularized suspicion that the person is committing a crime. *Brown v. Texas,* 443 U.S. 47 (1979). But officers are not required to ignore the relevant characteristics of a location in determining whether the circumstances are sufficiently suspicious to warrant further investigation. Accordingly, we have previously noted the fact that the stop occurred in a "high crime area" among the relevant contextual considerations in a *Terry* analysis. *Adams v. Williams,* 407 U.S. 143, 144 and 147–148 (1972).

In this case, moreover, it was not merely respondent's presence in an area of heavy narcotics trafficking that aroused the officers' suspicion, but his unprovoked flight upon noticing the police. Our cases have also recognized that nervous, evasive behavior is a pertinent factor in determining reasonable suspicion. Headlong flight—wherever it occurs—is the consummate act of evasion: it is not necessarily indicative of wrongdoing, but it is certainly suggestive of such....

Such a holding is entirely consistent with our decision in *Florida v. Royer,* 460 U.S. 491 (1983), where we held that when an officer, without reasonable suspicion or probable cause, approaches an individual, the individual has a right to ignore the police and go about his business. And any "refusal to cooperate, without more, does not furnish the minimal level of objective justification needed for a detention or seizure." *Florida v. Bostick,* 501 U.S. 429, 437 (1991). But unprovoked flight is simply not a mere refusal to cooperate. Flight, by its very nature, is not "going about one's business"; in fact, it is just the opposite. Allowing officers confronted with such flight to stop the fugitive and investigate further is quite consistent with the individual's right to go about his business or to stay put and remain silent in the face of police questioning.

Respondent and amici also argue that there are innocent reasons for flight from police, and that therefore flight is not necessarily indicative of ongoing criminal activity. This fact is undoubtedly true, but does not establish a violation of the Fourth Amendment....

In allowing such detentions, *Terry* accepts the risk that officers may stop innocent people. Indeed, the Fourth Amendment accepts that risk in connection with more drastic police action; persons arrested and detained on probable cause to believe they have committed a crime may turn out to be innocent. The *Terry* stop is a far more minimal intrusion, simply allowing the officer to briefly investigate further. If the officer does not learn facts rising to the level of probable cause, the individual must be allowed to go on his way. But in this case, the officers found respondent in possession of a handgun, and arrested him for violation of an Illinois firearms statute. No question of the propriety of the arrest itself is before us.

The judgment of the Supreme Court of Illinois is reversed, and the cause is remanded for further proceedings not inconsistent with this opinion.

It is so ordered.

COMMENTS, NOTES, AND QUESTIONS

1. Suppose that an officer on a college campus observed an individual finishing stretching exercises under a streetlight and, upon noticing the officer, started running in the opposite direction down a jogging trail. Should this type of activity allow a police officer to make a stop of the jogger? Would a person's flight upon seeing a police officer allow the officer to stop if it appeared that the person had initiated his or her jogging routine in a high-crime area? Would it matter if it were in the evening? What other factors could you add that might allow a stop? How contextual is the right to stop upon flight? Consider *California v. Hodari D.,* 499 U.S. 621 (1991), a case in which a juvenile ran at the sight of a police officer and was captured just after tossing away a rock of crack cocaine. The issue of flight of the defendant did not play a role in the case from the defendant's perspective, but the officer clearly initiated pursuit because of the defendant's flight. The *Hodari D.* Court held that the juvenile had not been seized at the time the officer initiated the chase, but that such seizure occurred when the officer had dominion and control over the juvenile. The defendant did not argue that the police officer should not have given chase when observing unusual conduct by a person who took flight at the sight of the officer under suspicious circumstances.

2. What other factors accompanied by flight allow a police officer to make a *Terry*-type stop? What about a situation in which a person starts to move away from police and begins to empty his or her pockets while observing police in close proximity? Would it make a difference what type of objects were being discarded? What if the objects being thrown away appeared to be packets of drugs? Or just paper? In *Michigan v. Chesternut,* 486 U.S. 567 (1988), while observing the approach of a police car on routine patrol, Chesternut began to run. The police

followed alongside him for a short distance "to see where he was going," and, after catching up with him, observed him discarding a number of packets. Believing that the discarded packets contained drugs, the police alighted from the cruiser, examined them, and concluded that they contained narcotics. Police chased and arrested Chesternut. According to the Court, any determination concerning whether police conduct amounts to a seizure implicating the Fourth Amendment must take into account "'all of the circumstances surrounding the incident'" in each individual case. *INS v. Delgado,* 466 U.S. 210, 215 (1984), quoting *United States v. Mendenhall,* 446 U.S. 544, 554 (1980) (opinion of Stewart, J.). The Court adhered to its traditional contextual approach and determined that, in *Chesternut,* the police conduct in question did not amount to a seizure until Chesternut was under police control. Unexplained flight accompanied by other suspicious activity allowed police to stop him, but in this case, probable cause for arrest had also matured by that time.

Arrest and Seizure of the Person

Chapter Outline

Key Terms

Arrest

Arrest in the home

Arrest in third-party home

Exceptions to warrant

Exigent circumstances

Expectation of privacy

Hot pursuit

Neutral and detached judicial official

Probable cause to arrest

Seizure

Stale probable cause

Standing

Warrant to arrest

1. PROBABLE CAUSE ARRESTS: THE LEGAL STANDARD

While many stop and frisk situations do not escalate to the next level, evidence discovered during a valid stop and frisk may mature probable cause for an arrest. Where the officer's reasonable suspicion has been satisfied, the encounter must end and the detainee allowed to continue with the prior course of conduct. However, if evidence unearthed during a *Terry* stop and frisk rises to the level of probable cause for an arrest, the officer may effectuate the arrest or make some other disposition of the subject. Probable cause for arrest[55] is said to exist where the officers at the moment of arrest have facts and circumstances available to them as would "warrant a man of reasonable caution in the belief" that an offense has been committed or is being committed. *Carroll v. United States,* 267 U.S. 132, 162 (1925).

---

[55]Probable cause for arrest has been phrased similarly to *Carroll*. In *Beck v. Ohio,* probable cause for an arrest was said to exist if "at the moment the arrest was made…the facts and circumstances within [the arresting officers'] knowledge and of which they had reasonably trustworthy information were sufficient to warrant a prudent man in believing that the [suspect] had committed or was committing an offense." 379 U.S. 89 (1964).

2. THE CONCEPT OF PROBABLE CAUSE FOR ARREST

An arrest is a seizure under the Fourth Amendment where an individual person, against his or her will, comes under the total physical control of a governmental agent. There must be either a submission to the will of the law enforcement official or a physical application of force sufficient to put the person in the custody of the officer. Merely chasing a suspect does not constitute a seizure or an arrest until the individual is physically caught or when he or she submits to the lawful authority of the officer. See *Michigan v. Chesternut,* 486 U.S. 567 (1988) and *California v. Hodari D.,* 499 U.S. 621 (1991). To be lawful, probable cause must exist, and the manner of the seizure must be reasonable under the circumstances. The Fourth Amendment provides that "no Warrants shall issue, but upon probable cause" which means that where a court is to issue an arrest warrant, it must make a finding that a strong fact pattern indicates that powerful reasons exist to think a person has committed a particular crime for which taking the person into custody would be reasonable.

3. PLAIN MEANING OF THE FOURTH AMENDMENT

When one reads the Fourth Amendment, a reasonable interpretation with logical inferences would appear to require that a warrant would have to have been issued in compliance with the dictates of the amendment prior to each and every arrest. Since colonial times, arrests have been made under the common law without the use of warrants, and a warrant is not presently a necessity for felony arrests. In *United States v. Watson,* 423 U.S. 411 (1976), the Court approved of the constitutionality of warrantless arrests, holding that the Fourth Amendment reflected the ancient common-law rule that a law enforcement official had the power to arrest without a warrant for a misdemeanor or a felony committed in his presence, as well as for a felony not committed in his presence if there was reasonable ground (probable cause) for making the arrest. According to *Watson,* a warrant is not generally required even where the officer has adequate time to procure one. By the lesson of history,[56] legislation passed by the Framers of the Fourth Amendment, and settled usage,[57] police officers may make warrantless arrests given the presence of probable cause.

4. PROBABLE CAUSE DEFINED

Although the Fourth Amendment spoke of probable cause, it did not define it or give it any parameters. Probable cause need not rise to the level of proof beyond a reasonable doubt but must be sufficient that the level of proof is beyond a mere hunch or guess. To establish probable cause, as the Supreme Court noted, "requires

---

[56]"The rule of the common law, that a peace officer or a private citizen may arrest a felon without a warrant, has been generally held by the courts of the states to be in force in cases of felonies punishable by the civil tribunals." See *Kurtz v. Moffitt,* 115 U.S. 487, 504 (1885).

[57]Many federal law enforcement officers have been expressly authorized by statute to make felony arrests on probable cause but without a warrant. This is true of United States marshals, 18 U.S.C. § 3053, and of agents of the Federal Bureau of Investigation, 18 U.S.C. § 3052; the Drug Enforcement Administration, 84 Stat. 1273, 21 U.S.C. § 878; the Secret Service, 18 U.S.C. § 3056(a); and the Customs Service, 26 U.S.C. § 7607.

only a probability or substantial chance of criminal activity, not an actual showing of such activity."[58] Settled usage of the time (1791) provided content and definition, while later court cases have construed and refined the meaning. Probable cause has been defined as where the facts and circumstances within the officer's knowledge are sufficient in themselves to warrant a prudent person of reasonable caution in believing that a particular person is committing or has committed a particular offense.[59] See Case 3.1, *Beck v. Ohio,* 379 U.S. 89 (1964).

In *Beck,* the arresting officer had a picture of the arrestee, knew what he looked like, knew some of his prior convictions, and had "heard reports" that Beck was running numbers. The Court held that these facts did not rise to probable cause and that the arrest of Beck had been unlawful. The level of belief required to meet probable cause is much more than a mere hunch, as in *Beck,* but falls far below proof sufficient for guilt beyond a reasonable doubt.

In determining whether an officer possesses sufficient evidence to make a warrantless arrest, the Supreme Court of Michigan suggested an inquiry concerning

> whether an officer had probable cause to make an arrest is whether there are any facts which would lead a reasonable person to believe that the suspected person has committed a felony. Secondly, a police officer's belief that a defendant has committed a felony must be based on facts which are present at the moment of the arrest.[60]

The court noted that when courts review probable cause determinations by police, they must analyze whether the facts sufficient to establish probable cause existed at the moment of the arrest that would justify a fair-minded person of reasonable caution and of normal intelligence in believing that the person with whom the officer was dealing had committed a felony. All the facts and circumstances known to the officer at the moment of arrest can and should be considered.

In the case the Michigan court had under review against a claim by the defendant that the arresting officers lacked probable cause, the officers knew the defendant had been stalking and threatening the deceased, understood that the smell of gasoline had been detected near the home, and observed that the defendant did not seem upset at news that his girlfriend had died in a fiery blaze. According to the court, the collective information known to the police offered probable cause to arrest for stalking,[61] at a minimum, and probable cause to arrest for murder also may well have existed.

5. SOURCES OF PROBABLE CAUSE TO ARREST

The information that matures probable cause to arrest may have a variety of sources. The officer may have personally observed the facts creating probable cause,

---

[58] *Illinois v. Gates,* 462 U.S. 213 (1983).
[59] In *Carroll v. United States,* 276 U.S. 132 (1925), which offered a definition of probable cause in the context of a bootleg liquor search, the Court stated: "This is to say that the facts and circumstances within their [the police] knowledge and of which they had reasonably trustworthy information were sufficient, in themselves, to warrant a man of reasonable caution in the belief that intoxicating liquor was being transported in the automobile which they stopped and searched." The legal standard for a search is the same level of proof as for an arrest.
[60] *Michigan v. Davis,* 660 N.W.2d 67, 69 (2003).
[61] *Davis* at 70.

have received information from a fellow officer,[62] have received some or all information from an informant, or a combination of all of these. If an informant supplied the basis for probable cause, courts (and police) generally want to know what facts the informant observed and why the court (and police) should believe the particular informant. In *Draper v. United States,* 358 U.S. 307 (1959), an informant of known reliability gave excellent information concerning drug trafficking, and a law enforcement official later corroborated the facts (see Case 3.2). The information matured probable cause to arrest because of its detail and its reliable source and because a reasonable person would have arrived at the conclusion that Draper was probably carrying drugs. Probable cause may be established based on the collective knowledge of the officers involved rather than only the knowledge personally obtained by the arresting officer.[63]

Where an informant is involved, developing probable cause for an arrest involves virtually identical legal considerations as are involved in developing probable cause for a search. There needs to be sufficient reason to believe that the information given by the informant equals probable cause, and the informant must be believable as a person. This basic two-pronged test for evaluating an informant's information arose in *Aguilar v. Texas*[64] and was reviewed and altered in *Illinois v. Gates*[65] when the Court replaced the two-pronged *Aguilar* test with a totality of the circumstances test. *Gates* lowered the level of reliability demanded of an informant by allowing a weak showing of honesty to be cured by minute details that would be known only by one close to the situation. When determining probable cause to arrest based on an informant's information, it remains important to evaluate the informant's trustworthiness and to carefully consider what information has been communicated. Under the totality of the circumstances test, the officer needs to make a practical, commonsense determination whether, considering all the information available, probable cause to arrest exists while giving due consideration to the informant's information.

As a general rule, probable cause may be based on hearsay statements or declarations contained within a criminal complaint or attached to an affidavit for a warrant as long as there is a substantial reason for believing that the source of the hearsay evidence is believable and that a factual basis exists for the information. Arrest probable cause may exist following the evaluation of wiretap information obtained pursuant to a federal or state warrant. Research in public records, when combined with other information, may also indicate probable cause to arrest.

Although the majority of arrests occur without the utilization of a warrant, the existence of probable cause for an arrest remains an absolute prerequisite for a valid seizure of a person. Where the police arrest an individual without a warrant, the Fourth Amendment requires a judicial determination of probable cause within a reasonable time. According to the Court in *Riverside v. McLaughlin,* 500 U.S. 44 (1991),

---

[62]*United States v. Perkins,* 994 F.2d 1184 (6th Cir. 1993).
[63]See *Collins v. Nagle,* 892 F.2d 489, 495 (6th Cir. 1989).
[64]378 U.S. 108 (1964).
[65]462 U.S. 213 (1983).

the judicial determination of probable cause must generally be made within forty-eight hours following a warrantless arrest.

6. STALE PROBABLE CAUSE

Where probable cause to arrest exists at a particular point in time, it will not subsequently cease to exist, as a general rule. If police have obtained information that indicates an individual is subject to arrest for a particular crime, the passage of time and continued police effort are most likely to generate more evidence of guilt rather than produce exculpatory evidence. In some cases, however, the original grounds supporting probable cause for arrest could be disproved by subsequent investigation that at the same time turns up wholly new evidence supporting probable cause to arrest a different person. In that type of situation, probable cause could become stale because it was based upon information now discredited. The outer time limitation for arrest, once probable cause to arrest has been established, is the passage of the statute of limitations, if any, for the particular crime. Once the statute of limitations has expired, probable cause, in the legal sense, no longer exists, and the person may not be arrested.

Probable cause may become stale because the underlying crime may have been resolved or the reason for arrest no longer exists. For example, in *Arizona v. Evans,* 514 U.S. 1 (1995), a justice of the peace issued an arrest warrant for the defendant, which was duly logged into the police computer. Several days after the warrant had been issued, the defendant appeared before the justice of the peace and resolved matters. The judicial official had the warrant quashed (extinguished) because probable cause had ceased to exist. A police officer later arrested Evans because, although the warrant had been quashed, the record of the arrest warrant erroneously remained in the police department computer, giving what appeared to be probable cause to arrest to any officer who read the computer data. In essence, the probable cause had become stale by the passage of more recent events.[66] Even though probable cause in *Evans* became stale, in most cases, stale probable cause will not become a legal issue.

7. ARREST PURSUANT TO A WARRANT

An arrest warrant[67] is a court order directed toward law enforcement officers to take into custody a particularly described individual. In order for a judicial official to

---

[66]The case, *Arizona v. Evans,* dealt primarily with the application of the exclusionary rule of the Fourth Amendment, but it serves as an example of stale probable cause.

[67]An arrest warrant is an order of court issued by a neutral and detached judicial official who has determined that probable cause for arrest exists. The warrant directs law enforcement officers to take into custody a particularly described individual for having committed a specifically described crime where the evidence would permit a person of reasonable caution to believe that the described person has committed the crime or crimes.

issue an arrest warrant, the judge[68] or magistrate must be personally convinced that probable cause to arrest exists for a specifically described individual. Arrest warrants are often issued when the subject is known and has been indicted but his or her exact location is not known. There is a procedural advantage to arresting a person pursuant to a warrant: if the arrestee later wishes to contest the validity of probable cause, the burden of proof is on the defendant and not on the prosecution. Where a warrantless arrest has occurred without the benefit of a judicial decision, the prosecution must prove arrest probable cause by a preponderance of the evidence.

An arrest warrant typically contains the name of the defendant and/or a clear description from which he or she can be positively identified with reasonable certainty. The warrant should describe the offense for which the defendant has been charged and may have a copy of the complaint or indictment attached to it. The arrest warrant commands the person executing it to seize the person named and bring that individual before the court that issued the warrant without needless delay. Where a law enforcement officer makes the arrest and does not have a copy of the arrest warrant, the officer should inform the arrestee of as much of the information contained within the warrant as is known, but a failure to inform does not invalidate the arrest or otherwise affect the warrant to arrest.

When an officer has an arrest warrant or believes probable cause to arrest exists, the legal authority to make the arrest carries with it the power to make the arrest effective. The level of force necessary to effectuate an arrest differs significantly from case to case. At times significant force may be required; even deadly force may be necessary where the defense of the officer or others dictates its use. In *Tennessee v. Garner,* 471 U.S. 1 (1985), the Court held that a police officer, who had probable cause to arrest, used an unreasonable level of force when he observed an apparently unarmed suspected felon in the act of escaping and shot and mortally wounded the suspect to prevent the escape. On the other hand, the Court would have approved the use of deadly force to prevent the escape of a suspected felon if the officer had good cause to believe that the fleeing felon would pose a serious threat of death or serious injury to police or other persons.

8. REQUIREMENTS FOR ARREST WITHOUT A WARRANT

A warrantless arrest is permissible if there exists sufficient probable cause. See Case 3.1, *Beck v. Ohio,* 379 U.S. 89 (1964). Under the common law and the general practice in effect at the time of the adoption of the Constitution of the United States, a peace

---

[68]The general rule is that an arrest warrant or search warrant must be issued by a judge or magistrate. See *Coolidge v. New Hampshire,* 403 U.S. 443 (1971). Justice Stewart wrote the lead opinion for the *Coolidge* Court, which invalidated a search warrant because it had not been issued by a neutral and detached judicial official. In the context of a search warrant, in Justice Brennan's dissent in *Horton v. California,* 496 U.S. 128 at 148 (1990), he noted that generally, "The Fourth Amendment demands that an individual's possessory interest in property be protected from unreasonable governmental seizures, not just by requiring a showing of probable cause but also by requiring a neutral and detached magistrate to authorize the seizure in advance." Arrest warrants are not required so long as probable cause exists, but where an arrest warrant is to be issued, a member of the judicial branch must make the probable cause determination.

officer or a private citizen could arrest a felon without a warrant. This practice has generally been upheld by both state and federal courts.[69]

Demonstrative of this principle is *United States v. Watson,* 423 U.S. 411 (1976), where the defendant had been arrested for a felony without a warrant. The arresting officer possessed probable cause due to earlier investigative efforts. Although the officer had time to procure an arrest warrant, he chose not to obtain one prior to effectuating the arrest. The *Watson* Court approved of the warrantless arrest so long as probable cause existed, largely by citing historical precedent. Although the Fourth Amendment could be interpreted as requiring a warrant for arrests, the *Watson* Court considered the practice at the time of the adoption of the Fourth Amendment and attempted to discern the intent of the Framers. The Court noted that the Second Congress passed legislation giving United States marshals the same power as local peace officers to arrest without warrant. It also noted that the warrantless arrest practice has continued to the present for state, local, and federal officers. As a strong general rule, warrantless arrests may be made outside the home of the arrestee based solely upon probable cause.

A recent court case reinforces the principle that probable cause to arrest is all that a police officer constitutionally needs to make an arrest outside the home of the arrestee. In *Atwater v. City of Lago Vista,*[70] the defendant was driving her pickup truck with her children unrestrained, contrary to Texas law, when a police officer stopped her (see Case 3.3). After calling for backup, he arrested her in front of her children and took her to jail because of her apparent violation of the transportation code. Subsequent to her legal troubles, Atwater filed a civil suit against the jurisdiction alleging that the warrantless arrest for the seat belt violation violated her Fourth Amendment rights to be free from unreasonable seizure. The *Atwater* Court held that the Fourth Amendment does not forbid a warrantless arrest for a minor criminal offense punishable only by a fine. Central to the Court's rationale was the belief that, although some support existed for the concept that a police officer historically could not arrest for a misdemeanor not committed in the presence of the officer, a survey of English and American history and the weight of authority permitted an arrest without warrant. Early state practice permitted warrantless misdemeanor arrests, and Congress in 1792 gave federal marshals the same power to make warrantless arrests, which included misdemeanors. With this historical record, whether or not warrantless misdemeanor arrests are practically appropriate or intelligent in all cases, the practice passed constitutional muster. Thus, given probable cause to arrest for any criminal offense, a warrant is not a constitutional requirement to arrest outside of a home.

One primary limitation on arrest procedure is that the manner of apprehension must be reasonable under the Fourth Amendment. Clearly, an officer may not effectuate the arrest by killing the subject,[71] absent self-defense or where the subject

---

[69]See *United States v. Watson,* 423 U.S. 411 (1976) and *Atwater v. City of Lago Vista,* 532 U.S. 318 (2001).
[70]532 U.S. 318 (2001).
[71]In *Tennessee v. Garner,* 471 U.S. 1 (1985), the Court held that using deadly force against an apparently unarmed, nondangerous fleeing suspect for whom probable cause existed cannot be justified as reasonable under the Fourth Amendment, unless necessary to prevent an escape from arrest where the officer has probable cause to believe that the suspect poses a significant threat of death or serious

presents a significant threat to others. The force used must be necessary to accomplish the arrest, but it must not be outrageously excessive when measured by the level of force, if any, offered in resistance.

Following an arrest without a warrant, the arresting officer or another officer should bring the arrested person, without undue delay, before a court of competent jurisdiction for a judicial consideration of probable cause. In *Gerstein v. Pugh*, 420 U.S. 103 (1975), in addressing the Fourth Amendment's prohibition against unreasonable seizures, the Court determined that a police detention of an arrestee requires a prompt judicial determination of probable cause following an arrest made without a warrant. In arrest situations, where police alone have determined probable cause, a judge or magistrate must reconsider whether probable cause exists, and the judge must do so within a reasonable time following the arrest. See *Riverside v. McLaughlin,* 500 U.S. 44 (1991). According to the *Riverside* Court, a reasonable time to be incarcerated on less than a judicial showing of probable cause or a grand jury indictment was forty-eight hours.[72] As a practical matter, charges that support the arrest should be filed by the officer or one acting on behalf of the officer within a reasonable time, but a judicial official should rule on probable cause within the two-day period.

9. REQUIREMENTS FOR ARRESTS WITHIN THE HOME

The Fourth Amendment has been judicially construed to prohibit a warrantless arrest within one's home unless exigent circumstances, destruction of evidence, hot pursuit, or some other exception applies. In construing the Fourth Amendment, the Court emphasized in *Coolidge v. New Hampshire,* 403 U.S. 443 (1971), that there was

> a distinction between searches and seizures that take place on a man's property—his home or office—and those carried out elsewhere. It is accepted, at least as a matter of principle, that a search or seizure carried out on a suspect's premises without a warrant is per se unreasonable, unless the police can show that it falls within one of a carefully defined set of exceptions based on the presence of "exigent circumstances."

In a case in the Second Circuit Court of Appeal, the court reaffirmed its view that a home arrest requires a warrant when it stated:

> To be arrested in the home involves not only the invasion attendant to all arrests, but also an invasion of the sanctity of the home. This is simply too substantial an invasion

---

physical injury to the officer or others. According to the *Garner* Court, "The use of deadly force to prevent the escape of all felony suspects, whatever the circumstances, is constitutionally unreasonable."

[72]When the forty-eight-hour period of custody without a judicial determination of probable cause is violated, the remedy is not clear. In *United States v. Alvarez-Sanchez,* 511 U.S. 350 (1994), the arrestee argued on appeal that his rights were violated, since he had not been given a hearing within forty-eight hours of arrest and had made incriminating statements while being held illegally under *McLaughlin*. The Court held that he had waived the argument by not raising it in the lower courts. Thus, the remedy for a violation of the forty-eight-hour period is not clear at this point, but it would appear that a successful litigant would have to show prejudice.

to allow without a warrant, at least in the absence of exigent circumstances, even when it is accomplished under statutory authority and when probable cause is clearly present. *United States v. Reed,* 572 F.2d 412, 423 (CA2 1978).

As noted in *Coolidge* and *Reed,* the expectation of privacy in the home has been so protected from intrusion that even police with probable cause to arrest may not transgress the home boundaries without a warrant or some emergency circumstance.[73] The Court of Appeals for the Fourth Circuit found a violation of the Fourth Amendment when a police officer with probable cause entered the home of the suspect without a warrant to make an arrest. The officer knocked at the door with the result that the suspect answered the door. The officer went inside to complete the arrest after telling the subject that he was under arrest. Absent hot pursuit or exigent circumstances, the arrest was unreasonable due to the lack of a warrant.[74]

In *Payton v. New York,*[75] police officers had developed probable cause to arrest Payton for murder, but they entered his home illegally without a warrant. The Court held that the officers needed an arrest warrant to enter the home, and that by entering without a warrant, they had violated Payton's Fourth Amendment rights[76] in warrantlessly seizing evidence. The need for a warrant to make an arrest was reaffirmed in *Kirk v. Louisiana,*[77] where police warrantlessly entered, arrested Kirk, and searched his residence with probable cause to believe that drugs were being sold on the premises. In a per curiam decision, the *Kirk* Court held that a warrantless entry to search and/or arrest requires a warrant or some exception to the warrant requirement; it sent the case back for further proceedings consistent with *Payton v. New York.*[78] (The principle that one may not be lawfully arrested in one's own home without a warrant may not always apply to the arrest of casual visitors and does not apply to trespassers who may be found in the home.) Similarly, in *Welsh v. Wisconsin,* 466 U.S. 740 (1984), officers had probable cause to arrest Welsh for driving while intoxicated. Police gained entry to Welsh's home and arrested him in his bed, even though there had been no immediate or continuous pursuit (no hot pursuit) of Welsh from the scene of the crime. The Court held that, under the circumstances of the case, the arrest of Welsh in his own bed was illegal under the Fourth Amendment.

10. REQUIREMENTS FOR ARRESTS WITHIN A THIRD PARTY'S HOME

Where police have an arrest warrant for one person but want to look in the home of a second person in an effort to find the first person, a warrant to enter the home is required. This merely restates the general rule that absent exigent circumstances or

---

[73]See *Payton v. New York,* 445 U.S. 573 (1980).
[74]*Sparing v. Village of Olympia Fields,* 266 F.3d 684, 691 (2001).
[75]Ibid.
[76]An illegal arrest does not prevent the government from convicting the individual whose rights have been violated. See *Frisbie v. Collins,* 342 U.S. 519 (1952). The effect of the illegal arrest inside the home is that evidence which has been observed or seized within the home as a result of the illegal arrest will be suppressed from prosecutorial use at trial for proof of guilt.
[77]536 U.S. 635 (2002).
[78]See *Payton v. New York,* 445 U.S. 573 (1980).

consent, a home may not be searched without a warrant. In *Steagald v. United States,* 451 U.S. 204 (1981), Drug Enforcement Administration (DEA) agents entered Steagald's home to search for another man without first obtaining a search warrant for Steagald's residence. Although DEA agents possessed a warrant for the individual they wished to arrest, they arrested Steagald after warrantlessly entering his home and after it appeared that he possessed illegal recreational pharmaceuticals and other contraband. The *Steagald* Court held that the entry and search of Steagald's home and the arrest of Steagald were illegal and contrary to the requirements of the Fourth Amendment in the absence of exigent circumstances or consent. To have lawfully searched Steagald's home for the target of the arrest, law enforcement officials would have had to have procured a search warrant for the home.

Possession of an arrest warrant indicates that a judicial official has determined that circumstances reasonably permit the seizing of the person wherever the individual may be located, including within the suspect's home. The arrest warrant carries with it the power to make it effective by using a reasonable level of force, if necessary. Without an arrest warrant, the burden is on the government to demonstrate exigent circumstances that overcome the presumption of unreasonableness and illegality that attach to all warrantless home arrests.

MAJOR CASES

CASE 3.1

Threshold Level of Proof: Probable Cause to Arrest

Beck v. Ohio
Supreme Court of the United States
379 U.S. 89 (1964)

FACTS

Police officers signaled William Beck to pull over and park his automobile because they suspected that he was involved in gambling. Although the officers had neither arrest nor search warrant, the officers immediately arrested Beck and conducted a search of his person and of his automobile which revealed nothing indicative of criminal activity. At a nearby police station, a second search of his person revealed an envelope containing a number of clearing house slips "beneath the sock of his leg."

According to testimony, the officers initially decided to stop Beck if they saw him make a "numbers" stop in a bar or tavern. The officers' actual decision to stop Beck was partially based on knowledge that he had a prior record involving gambling, knowledge of his identity from a picture, and the fact that they had "heard reports"

that someone reliable had stated that Beck possessed clearing house slips. The officers conducted this individual stop, search, and arrest in the absence of any probable cause or warrant either for a search or an arrest. Even the arresting officer who testified at the trial said no more than that someone (he did not say who) had told him something (he did not say what) about the petitioner being involved in gambling.

The prosecutor charged Beck with possession of clearing house slips in Cleveland Municipal Court. His counsel filed a motion to suppress based on the allegation that the evidence seized from the search of his person incident to his arrest had been seized in violation of his Fourth Amendment rights. The argument that probable cause to arrest was absent was rejected by the court and motion to suppress evidence was overruled. A guilty verdict followed. An Ohio Court of Appeals affirmed the municipal court conviction and the Supreme Court of Ohio upheld the decision. The United States Supreme Court granted Beck's petition for certiorari.

PROCEDURAL ISSUE

Where police possessed a photograph of a person, where they heard from unnamed and unsubstantiated sources that the person possessed illegal gambling materials, where they knew the person had a reputation for illegal gambling, and where police initiated an arrest based upon such data, has sufficient information been obtained to constitute probable cause to arrest?

HELD: NO

RATIONALE

Mr. Justice Stewart delivered the opinion of the Court.

★ ★ ★

The trial court made no findings of fact in this case. The trial judge simply made a conclusory statement: "A lawful arrest has been made, and this was a search incidental to that lawful arrest." The Court of Appeals merely found "no error prejudicial to the appellant." In the Supreme Court of Ohio, Judge Zimmerman's opinion contained a narrative recital which is accurately excerpted in the dissenting opinions filed today. But, putting aside the question of whether this opinion can fairly be called the opinion of the court, such a recital in an appellate opinion is hardly the equivalent of findings made by the trier of the facts. In any event, after giving full scope to the flexibility demanded by "a recognition that conditions and circumstances vary just as do investigative and enforcement techniques," we hold that the arrest of the petitioner cannot on the record before us be squared with the demands of the Fourth and Fourteenth Amendments.

The [factual] record [in this case] is meager, consisting only of the testimony of one of the arresting officers, given at the hearing on the motion to suppress. As to the officer's own knowledge of the petitioner before the arrest, the record shows no more than that the officer "had a police picture of him and knew what he looked like," and that the officer knew that the petitioner had "a record in connection with clearing house and scheme of chance." Beyond that, the officer testified only that he had "information," that he had "heard reports," that "someone specifically did relate that information," and that he "knew who that person was." There is nowhere in the record any indication of what "information" or "reports" the officer had received, or beyond what has been set out above, from what source the "information" and "reports" had come. The officer testified that when he left the station house, "I had in mind looking for [Defendant Beck] in the area of East 115th Street and Beulah, stopping him if I did see him make a stop in that area." But the officer testified to nothing that would indicate that any informer had said that the petitioner could be found at that time and place. And the record does not show that the officers

saw the petitioner "stop" before they arrested him, or that they saw, heard, smelled, or otherwise perceived anything else to give them ground for belief that the petitioner had acted or was then acting unlawfully.

No decision of this Court has upheld the constitutional validity of a warrantless arrest with support so scant as this record presents. . . . [T]he record in this case does not contain a single objective fact to support a belief by the officers that the petitioner was engaged in criminal activity at the time they arrested him.

An arrest without a warrant bypasses the safeguards provided by an objective predetermination of probable cause, and substitutes instead the far less reliable procedure of an after-the-event justification for the arrest or search, too likely to be subtly influenced by the familiar shortcomings of hindsight judgment. "Whether or not the requirements of reliability and particularity of the information on which an officer may act are more stringent where an arrest warrant is absent, they surely cannot be less stringent than where an arrest warrant is obtained." [Citation omitted.]

★ ★ ★

Where the constitutional validity of an arrest is challenged, it is the function of a court to determine whether the facts available to the officers at the moment of the arrest would "warrant a man of reasonable caution in the belief" that an offense has been committed. *Carroll v. United States,* 267 U.S. 132, 162. If the court is not informed of the facts upon which the arresting officers acted, it cannot properly discharge that function. All the trial court was told in this case was that the officers knew what the petitioner looked like and knew that he had a previous record of arrest or convictions for violations of the clearing house law.

★ ★ ★

It is possible that an informer did in fact relate information to the police officer in this case which constituted probable cause for the petitioner's arrest. But when the constitutional validity of that arrest was challenged, it was incumbent upon the prosecution to show with considerably more specificity than was shown in this case what the informer actually said, and why the officer thought the information was credible. We may assume that the officers acted in good faith in arresting the petitioner. . . . If subjective good faith alone were the test, the protections of the Fourth Amendment would evaporate, and the people would be "secure in their persons, houses, papers, and effects," only in the discretion of the police.

Reversed.

COMMENTS, NOTES, AND QUESTIONS

1. Assume that, prior to the arrest, the officers in *Beck* had presented to a judicial official their evidence for why they believed Beck was subject to arrest. Would that official have issued a warrant for the arrest of defendant? Why or why not? Do you believe that probable cause existed? The legal standard for issuance of an arrest warrant has been stated as "whether the facts available to an officer at the moment of the arrest would warrant a person of reasonable caution to conclude that an offense has been committed." What should be done if the officers had additional information but did not include it in the application for an arrest warrant? Could it be told to the trial court to save the arrest by a later demonstration of probable cause? Hypothetically, what other facts could the officers have added to convince a judicial official that minimal probable cause for an arrest existed?

2. Did any problem arise from the fact that the officers in *Beck* did not obtain an arrest warrant? Must law enforcement officials obtain an arrest warrant where there is sufficient time and no emergency exists? By its terms, the Fourth Amendment could be construed to require an arrest warrant absent an emergency. "[N]o warrants shall issue, but upon probable cause…particularly describing the place to be searched, and the persons or things to be seized" is what the Fourth Amendment requires. The Court in *United States v. Watson,* 423 U.S. 411 (1976), upheld the warrantless nonemergency arrest of a United States Post Office employee who was suspected of being involved in credit card theft. Essentially, the Court said that given probable cause to arrest, either course of action—using a warrant or deciding not to obtain a warrant—is reasonable under the Fourth Amendment.

3. Consider a situation in which the police are close to possessing probable cause to arrest but are a bit short of meeting the legal standard. If the police arrest anyway and find incriminating evidence that clearly completes the probable cause requirement, should they be able to use what evidence they have discovered in retroactively establishing probable cause? In legal theory, facts establishing probable cause may not be discovered *after* arrest; the facts and circumstances giving rise to probable cause must be apparent to a reasonable officer *prior* to the arrest. If

someone appears guilty of a crime, why not use the facts disclosed subsequent to the arrest to establish probable cause for the arrest?

4. What happens to police officers who have a genuinely mistaken belief that probable cause to arrest exists, but a judge or magistrate later disagrees? Are police officers liable civilly for mistakes in judgment? In *Hunter v. Bryant,* 502 U.S. 224 (1991), local police and Secret Service agents believed that probable cause existed to believe that Bryant had made credible threats against the president of the United States. Police arrested Bryant on, arguably, less than probable cause. When the charges were dropped, Bryant sued the Secret Service officers. The Supreme Court ultimately held that

> [T]he Secret Service agents are entitled to qualified immunity. Even if we assumed, arguendo, that they (and the magistrate) erred in concluding that probable cause existed to arrest Bryant, the agents nevertheless would be entitled to qualified immunity because their decision was reasonable, even if mistaken.
>
> The qualified immunity standard "gives ample room for mistaken judgments" by protecting "all but the plainly incompetent or those who knowingly violate the law." See *Malley v. Briggs,* 475 U.S. at 343, 341 (1986).

Where police officers make an arrest on less than probable cause and such error is reasonable under the circumstances, the general rule is that qualified immunity from civil or criminal prosecution exists so long as the error was a reasonable one. In *Bryant,* the error of caution was an overriding desire to protect the president from harm, and a bit of error was reasonable given the laudable goal. For a case in which law enforcement conduct became outrageous and probable cause never existed, consider *Bivens v. Six Unknown Named Agents,* 403 U.S. 388 (1971). The *Bivens* Court created a court-generated cause of action that permitted the allegedly wronged party to sue the agents involved for civil damages.

5. May police make a valid arrest when the information they have been provided purports to give probable cause for an arrest but the information is stale? See *Arizona v. Evans,* 514 U.S. 1 (1995). Phoenix police arrested Evans following a routine traffic stop when a patrol car's computer indicated that there was an outstanding misdemeanor warrant for his arrest. A lawful search of his car following his arrest on the outstanding warrant revealed a recreational amount of marijuana. When the police notified the court that Evans had been arrested, the court discovered that the arrest warrant previously had

been quashed, and so advised the police. Evans argued that, because his arrest was based on a warrant that had been quashed seventeen days prior to his arrest, the marijuana seized incident to the arrest should be suppressed as the fruit of an unlawful arrest. Although the *Evans* Court failed to expressly reach the issue of whether the arrest was invalid due to stale information, it did determine that the search following the arrest was valid and the marijuana was properly introduced against Evans. Would you argue that the information received by the police gave them probable cause to arrest under the authority of an outstanding warrant? Would police have been derelict in their duty had they not arrested Evans when their information indicated an outstanding arrest warrant? Why or why not?

CASE 3.2

Reliability of Informants When Establishing Probable Cause to Arrest

Draper v. United States
Supreme Court of the United States
358 U.S. 307 (1959)

FACTS

A federal narcotics agent with 29 years' experience, Marsh, arrested Draper for possession of heroin as he alighted from a train. The warrantless arrest had been prompted by information given to the agent by an informant, Hereford, who "worked" for the Bureau of Narcotics. Hereford, the "special employee," related to agent Marsh that Draper had gone to Chicago by train to purchase three ounces of heroin and that he would return by train on one of two different mornings. The "special employee" offered a complete physical description of Draper including minute details of clothing he would be wearing, facts which only a person intimately involved with Draper could know.

On one of the mornings suggested by the informant Hereford, a person matching Draper's description emerged from the Chicago train and rapidly strolled away. Agent Marsh and a police officer arrested Draper based on Hereford's description of Draper coupled with his visual and personal validation of these significant details. Subsequent to the arrest, Marsh conducted a search of Draper's person which disclosed two envelopes of heroin and a hypodermic needle.

Contending that police lacked probable cause to arrest him as he exited the train, Draper filed a motion to suppress the evidence of heroin based on an alleged illegal arrest under the Fourth Amendment. The trial court held that probable cause for an arrest existed and that the heroin was properly admitted as a search incident to a lawful arrest. At Draper's trial, the prosecutor introduced the drug evidence against Draper, who was convicted of violating federal law by knowingly concealing and transporting narcotic drugs in interstate commerce. The Court of Appeals affirmed the conviction and the Supreme Court of the United States granted certiorari.

PROCEDURAL ISSUE

Where an informant, known to the police, has given reliable information in past cases, and where the informant offered a detailed description of a suspected criminal and his criminal activities which were later validated by an agent personally present, does informant's information coupled with the verifications of the officer equal probable cause for an arrest?

HELD: YES

RATIONALE

Mr. Justice Whittaker delivered the opinion of the Court.

★ ★ ★

Petitioner…contends that the information given by Hereford to Marsh was "hearsay" and, because hearsay is not legally competent evidence in a criminal trial, could not legally have been considered, but should have been put out of mind, by Marsh in assessing whether he had "probable cause" and "reasonable grounds" to arrest petitioner without a warrant, and that, even if hearsay could lawfully have been considered, Marsh's information should be held insufficient to show "probable cause" and "reasonable grounds" to believe that petitioner had violated or was violating the narcotic laws and to justify his arrest without a warrant.

★ ★ ★

[The Court reaffirmed that hearsay evidence may be a factor in determining probable cause for an arrest.]

★ ★ ★

[The Court could not] agree with petitioner's second contention that Marsh's information was insufficient to show probable cause and reasonable grounds to believe that petitioner had violated or was violating the narcotic laws and to justify his arrest without a warrant. The information given to narcotic agent Marsh by "special employee" Hereford may have been hearsay to Marsh, but coming from one employed for that purpose and whose information had always been found accurate and reliable, it is clear that Marsh would have been derelict in his duties had he not pursued it. And when, in pursuing that information, he saw a man, having the exact physical attributes and wearing the precise clothing and carrying the tan zipper bag that Hereford had described, alight from one of the very trains from the very place stated by Hereford and start to walk at a "fast" pace toward the station exit, Marsh had personally verified every facet of the information given him by Hereford except whether petitioner had accomplished his mission and had the three ounces of heroin on his person or in his bag. And surely, with every other bit of Hereford's information being thus personally verified, Marsh had "reasonable grounds"[79] to believe that the remaining unverified bit of Hereford's information—that Draper would have the heroin with him—was likewise true.

> In dealing with probable cause,…as the very name implies, we deal with probabilities. These are not technical; they are the factual and practical considerations of everyday life on which reasonable and prudent men, not legal technicians, act.

Brinegar v. United States, supra, at 175. Probable cause exists where

> the facts and circumstances within their [the arresting officers'] knowledge and of which they had reasonably trustworthy information [are] sufficient in themselves to warrant a man of reasonable caution in

the belief that an offense has been or is being committed. *Carroll v. United States,* 267 U.S. 132, 162, 45 S.Ct. 280, 288. [(1925).]

We believe that, under the facts and circumstances here, Marsh had probable cause and reasonable grounds to believe that petitioner was committing a violation of the laws of the United States relating to narcotic drugs at the time he arrested him. The arrest was therefore lawful, and the subsequent search and seizure, having been made incident to that lawful arrest, were likewise valid. It follows that petitioner's motion to suppress was properly denied and that the seized heroin was competent evidence lawfully received at the trial.

Affirmed.

COMMENTS, NOTES, AND QUESTIONS

1. Why was the informant in *Draper* to be believed? At what point was the informant's information believable? Did either officer have probable cause until Mr. Draper alighted from the train dressed as predicted? Why or why not? What factors pointing toward the development of probable cause to arrest could you remove and still have probable cause to arrest Draper?

2. In making a determination of the existence of probable cause when based, either totally or partially, on an informant's information, the evaluation must be considered with *Illinois v. Gates,* 462 U.S. 213 (1983) (see case 1.2). *Gates* involved the maturing of probable cause for a search based on an anonymous letter in which the informant was unknown and uncorroborated. Additional information was corroborated by police, but not every detail. Prior to *Gates,* the reliability of an informant was evaluated on two levels: was there a reason to believe this particular informant, and, if the informant was to be believed, did the facts offered by the informant equal probable

---

[79]The term *reasonable grounds* and the term *probable cause* are often treated as synonymous, a practice continued by Justice Whittaker writing for the *Draper* Court, above. In most instances, one could consider that the terms are rough synonyms. However, some of the members of the Supreme Court of the United States have proven less than clear when writing opinions using the two terms and have intended different concepts in some cases. Justice Harlan, in a concurring opinion in *Sibron v. New York,* 392 U.S. 40 (1968), referred to "reasonable grounds" as being the standard necessary for a stop and frisk. Similarly to Justice Harlan, in *Maryland v. Wilson,* 519 U.S. 408 (1997), Justice Kennedy used "reasonable grounds" as if it were equal to the legal standard necessary for a stop and frisk. Consider *New Jersey v. T.L.O.,* 469 U.S. 325 (1985), where Justice Blackmun seemed to believe that "reasonable grounds" inferred a lower and different standard than probable cause. Justice White, in dissent, in *Welsh v. Wisconsin,* 466 U.S. 740 (1984), quoted state law, which referred to an arrest being permissible on "reasonable grounds" when, more often, the term *probable cause* is used in the arrest context. It appears that sometimes the justices are neither consistent nor clear in using the terms, with the result that confusion can easily be interjected into court opinions, blurring the distinctions between the quantum of proofs necessary for an arrest and a stop and frisk.

cause for an arrest or a search? See *Aguilar v. Texas,* 378 U.S. 108 (1964). *Gates* lowered the level of reliability demanded of an informant by allowing a weak showing of honesty to be cured by the informant's offering minute details that would be known only to one close to the situation. Alternatively, probable cause based on an informant's information may be constructed by an impeccably honest informant whose rendition of the facts may not sound exactly correct. The essence of *Gates* was to make the future procurement of probable cause for arrest and for search warrants significantly easier and less contestable where an informant's information has been necessary to the development of probable cause.

3. When police have probable cause to arrest, what level of force is reasonable under the Fourth Amendment? Should police be allowed to use deadly force to protect society from felons who want to resist arrest? Would it be reasonable to use deadly force to apprehend an unarmed fleeing felony suspect? Sometimes? What if the officer did not know if the fleeing suspect was armed? Could you be sure that the fleeing felon would not kill or seriously injure another person if the escape proved successful? In *Tennessee v. Garner,* 471 U.S. 1 (1984), a police officer's use of deadly force was ruled excessive and unreasonable where the officer shot and killed a fleeing, unarmed, youthful burglary suspect. According to the *Garner* Court, determining whether a particular seizure is reasonable requires that the method of seizure and the rights of the individual be balanced against governmental interests in effective law enforcement. Nonwithstanding probable cause to arrest, the Court felt that deadly force could not be used to prevent the escape of all felony suspects.

4. May an officer enter a home to make a warrantless arrest? Should it make a difference if screams were coming from within the home? What is the reasonable approach under the Fourth Amendment? Absent exigent (emergency) circumstances or hot pursuit, the Court in *Payton v. New York,* 455 U.S. 573 (1980), determined that in-home arrests generally require arrest warrants. According to the *Payton* Court, warrantless, nonconsensual arrests are prohibited even where the probable cause is for a felony. The Court reaffirmed the necessity of an arrest warrant in *Welsh v. Wisconsin,* 466 U.S. 740 (1984), where the *Welsh* Court ruled as illegal the warrantless arrest inside the defendant's home for a nonjailable traffic offense. Significantly, *Welsh* did not involve hot pursuit or exigent circumstances.

5. Suppose that an estranged wife told police that she knew that her husband had illegal drugs within their trailer home when she asked police to stand nearby while she picked up some of her belongings. Should this give police probable cause to arrest the husband? Would probable cause to arrest exist prior to searching the trailer home and finding marijuana? If the same level of informant involvement gave rise to probable cause to search, would it not also give probable cause to arrest? Could the officers arrest if the man was outside his trailer home and the subject had been prevented from reentering while a search warrant was being procured? See *Illinois v. McArthur,* 531 U.S. 326 (2001), where the Court held that probable cause did exist to search the trailer home and that police could prevent the occupant from reentering his home while a warrant was being obtained.

CASE 3.3

Arrest Constitutionally Permitted for Any Offense

Atwater v. City of Lago Vista
Supreme Court of the United States
532 U.S. 318 (2001)

FACTS

While on patrol, a Lago Vista police officer, Bart Turek, observed the driver of a pickup truck who was not wearing a safety belt as required by Texas law. Accordingly, he stopped the driver, Gail Atwater, and arrested her for the crime of not wearing a seatbelt and for not requiring her children to wear appropriate child restraints. The officer berated and handcuffed Atwater and placed her in a cruiser. A friend heard of her plight and came to take charge of the children. Following her ride in handcuffs to the local lockup, police had her remove her shoes, jewelry, and eyeglasses prior to taking her mug shot and placing her in a cell. Atwater eventually pled guilty to a misdemeanor seatbelt offense and paid a fifty-dollar fine, the maximum penalty permitted under Texas law.

Subsequently, Atwater sued the City of Lago Vista, essentially alleging that her rights[80] under the Fourth Amendment as applied to the states had been violated.

---

[80]Atwater and her husband filed a civil rights suit in a Texas state court under 42 U.S.C. § 1983 against Turek, the City of Lago Vista, and the chief of police. The city removed the case to the United States District Court for the Western District of Texas.

The trial court dismissed the suit, but a three-judge panel of the Fifth Circuit Court of Appeal reversed, concluding that an arrest for a first-offender violation of a seatbelt ordinance was an unreasonable seizure under the Fourth Amendment. The en banc Fifth Circuit Court of Appeal reversed the three-judge panel on the theory that the officer had probable cause to arrest and that there was no evidence that the arrest had been done in an extraordinary manner which might have been unusually harmful to Atwater. The United States Supreme Court granted certiorari.

PROCEDURAL ISSUE

Does the Fourth Amendment, by incorporating common law restrictions on misdemeanor arrests or by some other legal theory, limit a police officer's authority to arrest for misdemeanors, with probable cause in the absence of a warrant, when the offense does not amount to a breach of the peace?

HELD: NO

RATIONALE

Justice Souter delivered the opinion of the court.

★ ★ ★

II

The Fourth Amendment safeguards "[t]he right of the people to be secure in their persons, houses, papers, and effects, against unreasonable searches and seizures." In reading the Amendment, we are guided by "the traditional protections against unreasonable searches and seizures afforded by the common law at the time of the framing," *Wilson v. Arkansas,* 514 U.S. 927, 931 (1995), since

> [a]n examination of the common law understanding of an officer's authority to arrest sheds light on the obviously relevant, if not entirely dispositive, consideration of what the Framers of the Amendment might have thought to be reasonable. *Payton v. New York,* 445 U.S. 573, 591 (1980) (footnote omitted).

Thus, the first step here is to assess Atwater's claim that peace officers' authority to make warrantless arrests for misdemeanors was restricted at common law (whether "common law" is understood strictly as law judicially derived or, instead, as the whole body of law extant at the time of the framing). Atwater's specific contention is that "founding era common law rules" forbade peace officers

to make warrantless misdemeanor arrests except in cases of "breach of the peace," a category she claims was then understood narrowly as covering only those nonfelony offenses "involving or tending toward violence." Brief for Petitioners 13. Although her historical argument is by no means insubstantial, it ultimately fails.

A

We begin with the state of pre-founding English common law and find that, even after making some allowance for variations in the common law usage of the term "breach of the peace," the "founding era common law rules" were not nearly as clear as Atwater claims; on the contrary, the common law commentators (as well as the sparsely reported cases) reached divergent conclusions with respect to officers' warrantless misdemeanor arrest power. Moreover, in the years leading up to American independence, Parliament repeatedly extended express warrantless arrest authority to cover misdemeanor-level offenses not amounting to or involving any violent breach of the peace.

1

★ ★ ★

On one side of the divide there are certainly eminent authorities supporting Atwater's position. In addition to Lord Halsbury, quoted in Carroll, James Fitzjames Stephen and Glanville Williams both seemed to indicate that the common law confined warrantless misdemeanor arrests to actual breaches of the peace. See 1 J. Stephen, A History of the Criminal Law of England 193 (1883) ("The common law did not authorise the arrest of persons guilty or suspected of misdemeanours except in cases of an actual breach of the peace either by an affray or by violence to an individual"); G. Williams, Arrest for Breach of the Peace, 1954 Crim.L.Rev. 578, 578 ("Apart from arrest for felony…, the only power of arrest at common law is in respect of breach of the peace"). See also Queen v. Tooley, 2 Ld.Raym. 1296, 1301, 92 Eng.Rep. 349, 352 (Q.B. 1710) ("[A] constable cannot arrest, but when he sees an actual breach of the peace; and if the affray be over, he cannot arrest").

Sir William Blackstone and Sir Edward East might also be counted on Atwater's side, although they spoke only to the sufficiency of breach of the peace as a condition to warrantless misdemeanor arrest, not to its necessity. Blackstone recognized that, at common law, "[t]he constable…hath great original and inherent authority with regard to arrests," but with respect to nonfelony offenses, said only that "[h]e may, without warrant, arrest anyone for breach of the peace, and carry him before a justice of the peace." 4 Blackstone 289. Not long after the framing of the Fourth Amendment, East characterized peace officers' common law arrest power in much the same way:

> A constable or other known conservator of the peace may lawfully interpose upon his own view to prevent a breach of the peace, or to quiet an affray.... 1 E. East, Pleas of the Crown § 71, p. 303 (1803).

The great commentators were not unanimous, however, and there is also considerable evidence of a broader conception of common law misdemeanor arrest authority unlimited by any breach of the peace condition. Sir Matthew Hale, Chief Justice of King's Bench from 1671 to 1676, wrote in his History of the Pleas of the Crown that, by his "original and inherent power," a constable could arrest without a warrant "for breach of the peace and some misdemeanors, less than felony." 2 M. Hale, The History of the Pleas of the Crown 88 (1736).

★ ★ ★

As will be seen later, the view of warrantless arrest authority as extending to at least "some misdemeanors" beyond breaches of the peace was undoubtedly informed by statutory provisions authorizing such arrests, but it reflected common law in the strict, judge-made sense as well, for such was the holding of at least one case reported before Hale had even become a judge but which, like Hale's own commentary, continued to be cited well after the ratification of the Fourth Amendment.

★ ★ ★

We thus find disagreement, not unanimity, among both the common law jurists and the text writers who sought to pull the cases together and summarize accepted practice. Having reviewed the relevant English decisions as well as English and colonial American legal treatises, legal dictionaries, and procedure manuals, we simply are not convinced that Atwater's is the correct, or even necessarily the better, reading of the common law history.

2

A second, and equally serious, problem for Atwater's historical argument is posed by the "divers Statutes," M. Dalton,

Country Justice ch. 170, § 4, p. 582 (1727), enacted by Parliament well before this Republic's founding that authorized warrantless misdemeanor arrests without reference to violence or turmoil. Quite apart from Hale and Blackstone, the legal background of any conception of reasonableness the Fourth Amendment's Framers might have entertained would have included English statutes, some centuries old, authorizing peace officers (and even private persons) to make warrantless arrests for all sorts of relatively minor offenses unaccompanied by violence. The so-called "nightwalker" statutes are perhaps the most notable examples. From the enactment of the Statute of Winchester in 1285 through its various readoptions and until its repeal in 1827, night watchmen were authorized and charged "as...in Times past" to "watch the Town continually all Night, from the Sun-setting unto the Sun-rising" and were directed that "if any Stranger do pass by them, he shall be arrested until Morning...." 13 Edw. I, ch. 4, §§ 5–6, 1 Statutes at Large 232–233; see also 5 Edw. III, ch. 14, 1 Statutes at Large 448 (1331) (confirming and extending the powers of watchmen). Hawkins emphasized that the Statute of Winchester "was made" not in derogation, but rather "in affirmance of the common law," for "every private person may by the common law arrest any suspicious night-walker, and detain him till he give good account of himself...." 2 Hawkins, ch.13, § 6, p. 130. And according to Blackstone, these watchmen had virtually limitless warrantless nighttime arrest power:

> Watchmen, either those appointed by the statute of Winchester...or such as are merely assistants to the constable, may *virtute officii* arrest all offenders, and particularly nightwalkers, and commit them to custody till the morning. 4 Blackstone 289; see also 2 Hale, History of the Pleas of the Crown at 97 (describing broad arrest powers of watchmen even over and above those conferred by the Statute of Winchester).

★ ★ ★

Nor were the nightwalker statutes the only legislative sources of warrantless arrest authority absent real or threatened violence, as the parties and their amici here seem to have assumed. On the contrary, following the Edwardian legislation and throughout the period leading up to the framing, Parliament repeatedly extended warrantless arrest power to cover misdemeanor-level offenses not involving any breach of the peace. One 16th-century statute, for instance, authorized peace officers to arrest persons playing "unlawful game[s]" like bowling, tennis, dice, and cards, and for good measure extended the authority beyond players to include persons "haunting" the "houses, places, and alleys where such games shall be suspected to be holden, exercised, used or occupied." 33 Hen. VIII, ch. 9, §§ 11–16, 5 Statutes at Large 84–85 (1541).

★ ★ ★

The significance of these early English statutes lies not in proving that any common law rule barring warrantless misdemeanor arrests that might have existed would have been subject to statutory override; the sovereign Parliament could of course have wiped away any judge-made rule. The point is that the statutes riddle Atwater's supposed common law rule with enough exceptions to unsettle any contention that the law of the mother country would have left the Fourth Amendment's Framers of a view that it would necessarily have been unreasonable to arrest without warrant for a misdemeanor unaccompanied by real or threatened violence.

B

An examination of specifically American evidence is to the same effect. Neither the history of the framing era nor subsequent legal development indicates that the Fourth Amendment was originally understood, or has traditionally been read, to embrace Atwater's position.

1

To begin with, Atwater has cited no particular evidence that those who framed and ratified the Fourth Amendment sought to limit peace officers' warrantless misdemeanor arrest authority to instances of actual breach of the peace, and our own review of the recent and respected compilations of framing era documentary history has likewise failed to reveal any such design. See The Complete Bill of Rights 223–263 (N. Cogan ed. 1997) (collecting original sources); 5 The Founders' Constitution 219–244 (P. Kurland & R. Lerner eds. 1987) (same).

★ ★ ★

The evidence of actual practice also counsels against Atwater's position. During the period leading up to and surrounding the framing of the Bill of Rights, colonial and state legislatures, like Parliament before them, supra at 333–335, regularly authorized local peace officers to make warrantless misdemeanor arrests without conditioning

statutory authority on breach of the peace. See, e.g., First Laws of the State of Connecticut 214–215 (Cushing ed. 1982) (1784 compilation; exact date of Act unknown) (authorizing warrantless arrests of "all Persons unnecessarily travelling on the Sabbath or Lord's Day"); id. at 23 ("such as are guilty of Drunkenness, profane Swearing, Sabbath-breaking, also vagrant Persons [and] unseasonable Night-walkers"); Digest of the Laws of the State of Georgia 1755–1800, p. 411 (H. Marbury & W. Crawford eds. 1802) (1762 Act) (breakers of the Sabbath laws); id. at 252 (1764 Act) (persons "gaming…in any licensed public house, or other house selling liquors"); Colonial Laws of Massachusetts 139 (1889) (1646 Act) ("such as are overtaken with drink, swearing, Sabbath breaking, Lying, vagrant persons, [and] night-walkers"); [other examples omitted].

★ ★ ★

…[A] number of state constitutional search and seizure provisions served as models for the Fourth Amendment, see, e.g., N.H. Const. of 1784, pt. I, Art. XIX; Pa. Const. of 1776 (Declaration of Rights), Art. X, and the fact that many of the original States with such constitutional limitations continued to grant their own peace officers broad warrantless misdemeanor arrest authority undermines Atwater's contention that the founding generation meant to bar federal law enforcement officers from exercising the same authority. Given the early state practice, it is likewise troublesome for Atwater's view that, just one year after the ratification of the Fourth Amendment, Congress vested federal marshals with

> the same powers in executing the laws of the United States as sheriffs and their deputies in the several states have by law in executing the laws of their respective states. Act of May 2, 1792, ch. 28, § 9, 1 Stat. 265.

Thus, as we have said before in only slightly different circumstances, the Second Congress apparently "saw no inconsistency between the Fourth Amendment and legislation giving United States marshals the same power as local peace officers" to make warrantless arrests. *United States v. Watson,* 423 U.S. 411, 420 (1976).

★ ★ ★

Nor does Atwater's argument from tradition pick up any steam from the historical record as it has unfolded since the framing, there being no indication that her claimed rule has ever become "woven…into the fabric" of American law. *Wilson [v. Arkansas], supra,* at 933; see also *Payton v. New York,* 445 U.S. at 590 (emphasizing "a clear consensus among the States adhering to [a] well settled common law rule"). The story, on the contrary, is of two centuries of uninterrupted (and largely unchallenged) state and federal practice permitting warrantless arrests for misdemeanors not amounting to or involving breach of the peace.

First, there is no support for Atwater's position in this Court's cases (apart from the isolated sentence in *Carroll [v. United States,* 267 U.S. 132 (1925)], already explained). Although the Court has not had much to say about warrantless misdemeanor arrest authority, what little we have said tends to cut against Atwater's argument.

★ ★ ★

Second, and again in contrast with Wilson, it is not the case here that "[e]arly American courts…embraced" an accepted common law rule with anything approaching unanimity. *Wilson v. Arkansas,* 514 U.S. at 933. To be sure, Atwater has cited several 19th-century decisions that, at least at first glance, might seem to support her contention that "warrantless misdemeanor arrest was unlawful when not [for] a breach of the peace." Brief for Petitioners 17 (citing *Pow v. Beckner,* 3 Ind. 475, 478 (1852), *Commonwealth v. Carey,* 66 Mass. 246, 250 (1853), and *Robison v. Miner,* 68 Mich. 549, 556–559, 37 N.W. 21, 25 (1888)).

★ ★ ★

The reports may well contain early American cases more favorable to Atwater's position than the ones she has herself invoked. But more to the point, we think, are the numerous early- and mid-19th-century decisions expressly sustaining (often against constitutional challenge) state and local laws authorizing peace officers to make warrantless arrests for misdemeanors not involving any breach of the peace. *See, e.g., Mayo v. Wilson,* 1 N.H. 53 (1817) (upholding statute authorizing warrantless arrests of those unnecessarily traveling on Sunday against challenge based on state due process and search and seizure provisions); *Holcomb v. Cornish,* 8 Conn. 375 (1831) (upholding statute permitting warrantless arrests for "drunkenness, profane swearing, cursing or sabbath-breaking" against argument that "[t]he power of a justice of the peace to arrest and detain a citizen without complaint or warrant against him, is surely not given by the common law"); *Jones v. Root,* 72 Mass. 435 (1856) (rebuffing constitutional challenge to

statute authorizing officers "without a warrant [to] arrest any person or persons whom they may find in the act of illegally selling, transporting, or distributing intoxicating liquors"); [other examples omitted].

★ ★ ★

Accordingly, we confirm [that]…[i]f an officer has probable cause to believe that an individual has committed even a very minor criminal offense in his presence, he may, without violating the Fourth Amendment, arrest the offender.

IV

Atwater's arrest satisfied constitutional requirements. There is no dispute that Officer Turek had probable cause to believe that Atwater had committed a crime in his presence. She admits that neither she nor her children were wearing seat belts, as required by Tex. Tran. Code Ann. § 545.413 (1999). Turek was accordingly authorized (not required, but authorized) to make a custodial arrest without balancing costs and benefits or determining whether or not Atwater's arrest was in some sense necessary.

Nor was the arrest made in an "extraordinary manner, unusually harmful to [her] privacy or…physical interests." *Whren v. United States,* 517 U.S. at 818.…The arrest and booking were inconvenient and embarrassing to Atwater, but not so extraordinary as to violate the Fourth Amendment.

The Court of Appeals' en banc judgment is affirmed.

It is so ordered.

Justice O'Connor, with whom Justice Stevens, Justice Ginsburg, and Justice Breyer join, dissenting.

★ ★ ★

A custodial arrest exacts an obvious toll on an individual's liberty and privacy even when the period of custody is relatively brief. The arrestee is subject to a full search of her person and confiscation of her possessions. *United States v. Robinson, supra.* If the arrestee is the occupant of a car, the entire passenger compartment of the car, including packages therein, is subject to search as well. *See New York v. Belton,* 453 U.S. 454 (1981). The arrestee may be detained for up to 48 hours without having a magistrate determine whether there in fact was probable cause for the arrest. *See Riverside v. McLaughlin,* 500 U.S. 44 (1991). Because people arrested for all types of violent and nonviolent offenses may be housed together awaiting such review, this detention period is potentially dangerous. Rosazza & Cook, Jail Intake: Managing a Critical Function—Part One: Resources, 13 American Jails 35 (Mar./Apr. 1999). And once the period of custody is over, the fact of the arrest is a permanent part of the public record. *Cf. Paul v. Davis,* 424 U.S. 693 (1976).

We have said that

> the penalty that may attach to any particular offense seems to provide the clearest and most consistent indication of the State's interest in arresting individuals suspected of committing that offense. *Welsh v. Wisconsin,* 466 U.S. 740, 754, n. 14 (1984).

If the State has decided that a fine, and not imprisonment, is the appropriate punishment for an offense, the State's interest in taking a person suspected of committing that offense into custody is surely limited, at best. This is not to say that the State will never have such an interest. A full custodial arrest may on occasion vindicate legitimate state interests, even if the crime is punishable only by fine. Arrest is the surest way to abate criminal conduct. It may also allow the police to verify the offender's identity, and, if the offender poses a flight risk, to ensure her appearance at trial. But when such considerations are not present, a citation or summons may serve the State's remaining law enforcement interests every bit as effectively as an arrest. *Cf.* Lodging for *Amici Curiae* State of Texas *et al.* (Texas Department of Public Safety, Student Handout, Traffic Law Enforcement 1 (1999)) ("Citations…Definition—a means of getting violators to court without physical arrest. A citation should be used when it will serve this purpose except when by issuing a citation and releasing the violator, the safety of the public and/or the violator might be imperiled as in the case of D.W.I.").

Because a full custodial arrest is such a severe intrusion on an individual's liberty, its reasonableness hinges on "the degree to which it is needed for the promotion of legitimate governmental interests." *Wyoming v. Houghton,* 526 U.S. at 300. In light of the availability of citations to promote a State's interests when a fine-only offense has been committed, I cannot concur in a rule which deems a full custodial arrest to be reasonable in every circumstance. Giving police officers constitutional carte blanche to effect an arrest whenever there is probable cause to believe a fine-only misdemeanor has been committed is irreconcilable with the Fourth Amendment's command that seizures be reasonable.

COMMENTS, NOTES, AND QUESTIONS

1. Joe and Habib were driving from New Orleans through the state of Texas and headed to Galveston for spring break. After finishing eating a bag of fast food, Joe, the driver, attempted to close the bag, but a napkin accidentally blew out the car window. As luck would have it, a police officer noticed the apparent littering by the driver of the out-of-state motor vehicle. Assume that littering is an offense punishable by fine only on the first offense.[81] May the police officer arrest Joe and take him to jail? From what you have read to this point, is there probable cause to arrest Joe? Why or why not? Is this as clear-cut a case as the principle case involving Mrs. Atwater? Why or why not?

2. As the *Atwater* case demonstrated, probable cause to believe that a crime has been committed is all that is minimally required to allow an arrest if the state or local law permits arrests for minor offenses. If you were the police chief in Lago Vista or a similar city, would you want all your officers to follow the lead of Officer Turek? Why or why not? What are the practical ramifications if all your officers enforced the city misdemeanor ordinances in this manner? Does the *Atwater* decision allow police officers to arrest those they would like to harass or those individuals for whom a closer look would be desired? Could discriminatory law enforcement result from this decision? Could an officer tell a speeder that, in exchange for allowing the officer to look in the car's trunk, he or she will not be arrested for speeding and will receive only a ticket?

3. One could contend that to take a person into custody constituted a greater penalty than was authorized by the law Atwater was accused of breaking. Justice O'Connor dissented from the majority because she felt that the practice of arresting a person for whom a fine was the sole punishment was "unreasonable" under the Fourth Amendment. Was Justice O'Connor substituting her personal view for that of the Framers of the Fourth Amendment? Is the question really whether it is reasonable to arrest for minor offenses not involving incarceration? Or is the

---

[81]Justice O'Connor noted, "In several States, for example, littering is a criminal offense punishable only by fine. See, e.g., Cal.Penal Code Ann. § 374.7 (West 1999); Ga.Code Ann. § 16-7-43 (1996); Iowa Code §§ 321.369, 805.8(2)(af) (Supp. 2001)." *Atwater v. City of Lago Vista,* 532 U.S. 318 at 371 (2001).

question more along the lines of what was the original intent of the writers and adopters of the Fourth Amendment: what would they have wanted under the circumstances?

Which view should prevail: the original intent or a newer interpretation of the Fourth Amendment that recognizes modern realities?

Fourth Amendment Searches and Seizures: Houses, Persons, Motor Vehicles, and Effects

Chapter Outline

Key Terms

Consent search
Infrared scan
Inventory search: motor vehicle
Inventory search: possessions
Plain feel search
Plain view seizure
Scope of search: home

Scope of search: motor vehicle
Search for arrestee
Search incident to arrest
Thermal imaging
Vehicle forfeiture search
Warrant exception for vehicles
Warrant requirement for house

1. SEARCHES OF HOUSES

In 1604, an English court made the now-famous observation that "the house of every one is to him as his castle and fortress, as well for his defence against injury and violence, as for his repose." *Semayne's Case,* 5 Co.Rep. 91a, 91b, 195, 77 Eng.Rep. 194, 195 (K.B.).[82]

In his *Commentaries on the Laws of England,* William Blackstone noted that

> the law of England has so particular and tender a regard to the immunity of a man's house that it stiles it his castle, and will never suffer it to be violated with impunity, agreeing herein with the sentiments of [ancient] Rome....For this reason no doors can in general be broken open to execute any civil process, though, in criminal causes, the public safety supersedes the private. 4 *Commentaries on the Laws of England* 223 (1765–1769).[83]

Since the Framers of the Fourth Amendment understood much of the legal philosophy of the English and shared many abusive experiences recent to them, one of the reasons for adopting the Fourth Amendment involved the security of one's home. Consistent with the British view, it would be reasonable to expect that the place where one resides should have a great level of protection from governmental intrusion. A strong general rule has developed through case law that a private home shall not be entered by a governmental agent unless he or she possesses a search or arrest warrant that allows the intrusion.[84] Subject to a few limited exceptions, the question whether a warrantless search of a home is reasonable and, therefore, constitutional must be answered with a strong "no." When the police officer displays a properly drawn search warrant, the occupier is on notice that proper procedure has been followed and that the officer has carefully delineated authority to search in a particular place while looking for particularly described objects. A warrant is a court order directed to an officer or officers to perform a search for particular objects and to seize them if they are discovered. The home occupier has no right to resist the lawful probing of a police officer or officers when they operate pursuant to a search warrant.

Where the Fourth Amendment has been interpreted to allow for a departure from the warrant requirement, there has usually been an exigency making an intrusion into a dwelling imperative to the health or safety of the police and/or community. For example, in *Warden v. Hayden,* 387 U.S. 294 (1967), police were permitted to follow a suspect into a private dwelling without a warrant under the theory of "hot pursuit"; in *Michigan v. Tyler,* 436 U.S. 499 (1978), the Court approved a building search by law enforcement officials because the structure was burning and there was a dire need for official action; and in *Maryland v. Buie,* 494 U.S. 325 (1990), police were permitted to warrantlessly sweep the house to make sure there were no other suspects present who might harm them.

---

[82]*Wilson v. Layne,* 526 U.S. 603, 609 (1999), Chief Justice Rehnquist quoting *Semayne's Case* as cited internally above.
[83]Ibid. at 610.
[84]See *Payton v. New York,* 445 U.S. 573 (1980), where the Court held that a warrant was a requirement to validly arrest within the subject's home unless special circumstances were present. According to Justice Stevens, "Unreasonable searches or seizures conducted without any warrant at all are condemned by the plain language of the first clause of the Amendment." 445 U.S. 573, 584.

2. WARRANT TO SEARCH AND ARREST INSIDE THE HOME

Demonstrative of the concept that police officers and other law enforcement personnel may not enter a private residence without an arrest or search warrant is the case of *Payton v. New York,* 445 U.S. 573 (1980) (see Case 4.1). Police officers developed probable cause that Payton had committed murder of a gas station attendant. Several officers went to Payton's apartment for the purpose of arresting him, but they failed to obtain either a search warrant or an arrest warrant, despite the fact that there was probable cause for his arrest. When neither Payton nor anyone else responded to the officers' repeated knocks on the door, the officers summoned assistance and brought down the door with a crowbar. When it became obvious that no one was home, police seized a .30-caliber shell casing that was later linked to the murder and was admitted against Payton at his homicide trial.

In rejecting Payton's motion to suppress the shell casing taken from his apartment, the trial judge cited two theories justifying the warrantless intrusion. The trial court held that exigent circumstances (an emergency) excused the officers' failure to announce their presence prior to entry and that New York law permitted the warrantless probable cause entry into the apartment. Exigent circumstances were not argued as justification for the warrantless entry into Payton's residence. New York appellate courts upheld the admission of evidence, but the Supreme Court of the United States reversed Payton's conviction.

The *Payton* Court noted, "Unreasonable searches or seizures conducted without any warrant at all are condemned by the plain language of the first clause of the Amendment."[85] According to the Court, the language of the Fourth Amendment applies equally to seizures of persons as to seizures of property and that a basic principle of the Fourth Amendment dictates that searches and seizures inside a home without a warrant are presumptively unreasonable. The purpose of the decision was not to protect the person of the suspect but to protect his home from entry in the absence of judicial finding of probable cause. Since there was an absence of proof of exigent circumstances for the arrest of Payton and because warrantless arrests inside the home are presumptively illegal, the Court reversed Payton's conviction.

Payton stands for the age-old principle that a man's home is his castle and should not have its walls breached by the government in the absence of some clear emergency unless the government agent possesses a warrant to arrest or to search the private premises.

The Supreme Court recently reaffirmed the rationale of *Payton* in *Kirk v. Louisiana,* 536 U.S. 635 (2002), where police arrested the defendant without a warrant after entering his place of residence. After law enforcement officials observed drug purchases made out of Kirk's apartment and arrested a customer, they knocked on the door of the apartment and arrested defendant, Kirk. A search incident to arrest revealed cocaine and money. Citing *Payton v. New York*[86] and its well-settled theory that, absent exigent or emergency circumstances, police may not enter a private

[85] *Payton v. New York,* 445 U.S. 573, 585 (1980).
[86] 445 U.S. 573 (1980).

dwelling without an arrest or search warrant, the Supreme Court reversed Kirk's conviction of possession of cocaine with intent to distribute.

Even though a man's home may be his castle, neither the home nor all the surrounding objects are beyond the capacity of being searched under proper circumstances. Where police officers possess a warrant to search a particular home, the warrant may extend to include vehicles parked within the structure and those parked nearby if the objects of the search warrant could be hidden within the vehicle or vehicles. Since the goals of a search might be frustrated if vehicles were not searched and because vehicles can be used as storage areas, a vehicle on searched premises should be treated and searched just like other personal effects found on the searched premises that could contain the contraband or evidence. In a Michigan case, the officers searched a vehicle located on the premises and partially on the driveway as part of their search of the home. When the searching officers found drugs within the vehicle, the defendant moved to suppress the drugs from trial, alleging an unreasonable search and seizure under the Fourth Amendment. In approving a vehicle search, at least where the police had a search warrant for the home and found the vehicle on the searched premises, a Michigan court of appeals noted, "Although Michigan has not ruled on the precise issue raised by defendant, nearly all jurisdictions that have decided the question have held a search warrant for 'premises' authorizes the search of all automobiles found on the premises."[87] Part of the rationale for allowing a search anywhere on the premises where the object physically could have been hidden has, as its basis, some language from the Supreme Court in *United States v. Ross* (see Case 4.5).[88] In permitting the search of a motor vehicle for which probable cause existed, the *Ross* Court noted:

> A lawful search of fixed premises generally extends to the entire area in which the object of the search may be found and is not limited by the possibility that separate acts of entry or opening may be required to complete the search. Thus, a warrant that authorizes an officer to search a home for illegal weapons also provides authority to open closets, chests, drawers, and containers in which the weapon might be found....A warrant to search a vehicle would support a search of every part of the vehicle that might contain the object of the search.[89]

By analogy, if the object could be hidden within the car on the premises, the car should be treated just like a medicine chest or a closet.

While police and other law enforcement agents may not enter private premises in the absence of a warrant to arrest or to search, mere presence on private apartment property will not give an individual an expectation of privacy while inside the property. In *Minnesota v. Carter,* 525 U.S. 83 (1998), an officer observed Mr. Carter and some associates dividing cocaine into separate containers. The officer was looking through a street-level window, which contained a gap in the curtains. Upon observing sufficient information for probable cause to search the apartment, the officer procured a warrant and searched the apartment. The Supreme Court held that Carter had no expectation of privacy within the apartment because he did not live

---

[87]*Michigan v. Jones,* 249 Mich. 131, 137; 640 N.W.2d 898, 900, 901 (2002).
[88]456 U.S. 798 (1982).
[89]Ibid. at 821.

there; he had not stayed there overnight; and he was only using the apartment for the purposes of a commercial drug trade. Had the officers immediately entered the apartment without a warrant, at first blush, it would seem like Carter could make an argument similar to that made by Payton and with it successfully have the cocaine evidence suppressed. The difference here was that Carter had an insufficient connection to the apartment to claim a right of privacy under the Fourth Amendment, whereas Payton lived in his apartment and possessed a traditional expectation of privacy, which the Court recognized.

If Carter could have been lawfully arrested inside an apartment without a warrant because of insufficient expectation of privacy, some additional connection to real estate should arguably create an expectation of privacy close to that observed in *Payton v. New York*. The case of *Minnesota v. Olson,* 495 U.S. 91 (1990), provides a suitable benchmark for the minimum connection to property sufficient to produce an expectation of privacy under the Fourth Amendment. In *Olson,* police developed probable cause for Olson's arrest and discovered that he was believed to be in a particular home where he had been staying. Without permission or a warrant, but with probable cause for arrest, police entered the home and arrested Olson. During a subsequent interrogation, Olson made an inculpatory statement, which he argued should have been suppressed from his trial.

Prior to trial, the trial court refused to suppress Olson's statement on the ground that he possessed no expectation of privacy at another person's home. The Minnesota Supreme Court reversed[90] the conviction because it believed that Olson had an expectation of privacy even though he was never left alone in the home or given a key. The Supreme Court of the United States affirmed the Minnesota court because it believed that Olson had a sufficient connection to the property to have an expectation of privacy and, secondarily, there existed no emergency exception to allow the warrantless arrest within the home.

3. MODERN TECHNOLOGY AND WARRANTLESS HOME SEARCHES

While physical intrusions into the home have historically been the focus of Fourth Amendment litigation, new methods to search humans, buildings, homes, and cars have recently been developed. In *Kyllo v. United States,* 533 U.S. 27 (2001), federal agents had become suspicious that marijuana was being cultivated with the use of high-intensity lamps in the residence of Mr. Kyllo (see Case 4.2). In order to determine whether the high-intensity lamps were actually being used, federal agents determined to conduct an infrared scan, creating a thermal image of the outside of the home that could measure heat emanating from the interior. The scan of Kyllo's home took only a brief time to complete and was performed from across the street from the front of the house. The infrared scan showed that the roof over the garage and a side wall of the home were relatively hot compared with the rest of the home and substantially warmer than neighboring homes subjected to thermal imaging. The information from the scan along with other evidence produced probable cause

---

[90]436 N.W.2d 92 (1989).

for a search warrant. Evidence obtained from the search warrant was used against Kyllo at his trial for growing marijuana. The court of appeals affirmed the conviction, but the Supreme Court of the United States reversed.

At first blush, it would seem that there was no search of Kyllo's home because the agents did not enter the home in any form or fashion. In a case involving a similar principle, a luggage sniff by a drug-locating dog had been determined not to be a search of the interior of the luggage, since the dog reacted only to odors outside the luggage.[91] On those grounds, the government could certainly argue that there was no search of the interior of the home and that the only evidence collected from the infrared scan was heat that had escaped from within the home, which the agents collected and measured on the outside with thermal imaging equipment. Kyllo contended that the process constituted a search because details of his private life within the home became observable to the government due to the use of advanced technology to obtain evidence previously unknowable without a physical intrusion.

Justice Scalia, writing for the *Kyllo* Court, in reversing the lower federal courts, noted:

> Where, as here, the Government uses a device that is not in general public use, to explore details of the home that would previously have been unknowable without physical intrusion, the surveillance is a "search" and is presumptively unreasonable without a warrant.
>
> Since we hold the Thermovision imaging to have been an unlawful search, it will remain for the District Court to determine whether, without the evidence it provided, the search warrant issued in this case was supported by probable cause—and if not, whether there is any other basis for supporting admission of the evidence that the search pursuant to the warrant produced.[92]

Even with newer technology that would allow the government access to information emanating from the home, the Supreme Court of the United States has seen fit to return to the philosophy and jurisprudence of the early Fourth Amendment. The Court, by giving protection to those individuals within homes and buildings who possess an expectation of privacy that society is prepared to recognize, gives effect to the original intent of the Framers of the Fourth Amendment. At that time, no one would have envisioned that a law enforcement official would be able to discern the interior of the house without looking in a window or walking through the entrance.

4. SEARCH INCIDENT TO ARREST

It is well settled that a search incident to a lawful arrest is a traditional exception to the warrant requirement of the Fourth Amendment. The arrest consists of the law enforcement officer taking physical control over the person and determining where, when, and how a person moves from or stays in a particular location. When an arrest is made, courts have universally considered it to be a permissible practice

---

[91]See *United States v. Place,* 462 U.S. 696 at 707 (1983).
[92]*Kyllo v. United States,* 533 U.S. 27, 40 (2001).

for the arresting officer to search the person of the arrestee. In addition, a search may be made of the area within the immediate dominion and control of the arrestee. The search incident to arrest has been determined as reasonable under the Fourth Amendment because the privacy interest protected by that constitutional guarantee is subordinated to legitimate and paramount governmental concerns. Courts have also considered it entirely reasonable for the arresting officer to seize any evidence of criminality on the arrestee's person to prevent its concealment and/or destruction.[93] There are two historical rationales[94] for allowing the search incident to arrest exception to the search warrant requirement: the need to disarm the suspect in order to take him into custody and the necessity of preserving evidence for later use at trial.

A search incident to a lawful arrest would, by its definition, appear to require a valid arrest as a foundation for conducting a search following an arrest. In *Knowles v. Iowa,* 525 U.S. 113 (1998), a police officer conducted a search of a motor vehicle's interior with probable cause to arrest the driver but without making the actual arrest (see Case 4.3). The Supreme Court held that the search was invalid under the Fourth Amendment since there was no other rationale to justify the vehicle search other than a search incident to an arrest, and there had never been a valid arrest on which to base the subsequent vehicle search. The clear lesson from *Knowles* is that an actual arrest is a necessary step prior to conducting a search incident to an arrest.

5. SEARCH INCIDENT TO ARREST: NO WARRANT REQUIREMENT

A search incident to a lawful arrest has been recognized as an exception to the warrant requirement since 1914, and by actual practice prior to that time.[95] See *Weeks v. United States,* 232 U.S. 383. Whereas the *Weeks* Court approved of warrantless searches of the arrestee's person and effects, the Court expanded the scope of the search incident to arrest in *Marron v. United States,* 275 U.S. 192 (1927). There the Court enlarged the permitted scope of a search incident to an arrest to include personal effects not described in a search warrant but seized on the premises. The *Marron* Court asserted that police have authority to search incident to arrest that includes all parts of the premises used for the unlawful purpose. The Court subsequently approved of an expanded warrantless search incident to arrest in *United*

---

[93]*Chimel v. California,* 395 U.S. 752 at 762–763 (1969).

[94]In *United States v. Robinson,* 414 U.S. 218 at 234 (1973), the Court approved the full search of a driver of an automobile for whom probable cause to arrest existed. Immediately following the arrest, the officer conducted a search of the inner pockets and personal effects of the arrestee and discovered heroin. The *Robinson* Court quoted then Associate Judge Cardozo of the New York Court of Appeals as he explained the justification of a search incident to arrest. Cardozo stated, "The peace officer empowered to arrest must be empowered to disarm. If he may disarm, he may search, lest a weapon be concealed. The search being lawful, he retains what he finds if connected with the crime." *People v. Chiagles,* 237 N.Y. 193, 197;142 N.E. 583, 584 (1923).

[95]In *Payton v. New York,* 445 U.S. 573 at 610 (1980), the Court quoted with approval an early Massachusetts case, *Rohan v. Swain,* 59 Mass. 281 at 282 (1851), which upheld the practice of warrantless arrests:

"It has been sometimes contended that an arrest…without a warrant, was a violation of the great fundamental principles of our national and state constitutions, forbidding unreasonable searches and arrests except by warrant founded upon a complaint made under oath.…They do not conflict with the authority of constables or other peace officers…to arrest without warrant those who have committed felonies. The public safety, and the due apprehension of criminals, charged with heinous offences, imperiously require that such arrests should be made without warrant by officers of the law."

States v. Rabinowitz, 339 U.S. 56 (1950), where the police were permitted to search the entire premises that the suspect occupied at the time of the arrest. The police obtained a warrant for Rabinowitz's arrest, but they did not procure a search warrant. When they arrested him in his place of business, they searched not only his person but also the desk, safe, and file cabinets; they also seized 573 forged postage stamps as incident to arrest. The Court approved the search of the business premises without a warrant as incident to the warrant-based arrest. The rule derived from *Rabinowitz,* later overruled, allowed the complete warrantless search of business premises based on an arrest and could easily be applied to private homes.

6. GENERAL SCOPE OF THE SEARCH INCIDENT TO ARREST

While *Rabinowitz* authorized an extensive search following arrest, the virtually unlimited search permitted there has subsequently seen restriction. In more recent cases, the Court significantly reduced the scope of the search incident to arrest. In *Chimel v. California,* 395 U.S. 752 (1969), the Court reconsidered the extensive searches approved in *Rabinowitz* and *Marron* and effectively overruled the *Rabinowitz* and *Marron* approval of extensive searches incident to arrest.

The *Chimel* police went to the defendant's home to arrest him pursuant to a warrant, but they had to wait for defendant to arrive home from work. Mrs. Chimel allowed the officers to enter the home and wait for her husband. When Chimel arrived, police arrested him and conducted a warrantless search of his home. Accompanied by Chimel's wife, the officers looked through the entire three-bedroom house, including the attic, the garage, and a small workshop. The officers directed her to open drawers and to physically move contents of the drawers from side to side so that they might view any items that would have come from the burglary of which Mr. Chimel had been accused. The search revealed primarily coins but also several medals, tokens, and a few other objects. The entire search took less than an hour. The *Chimel* Court rejected the extensive scope of the search and held that the search conducted by the officers was unreasonable under the Fourth Amendment. To meet the requirements of the Fourth Amendment, the Court redefined the extent of a search incident to an arrest by limiting it to the area under the defendant's immediate dominion and control. The portions of the home that remained beyond Chimel's immediate control should not have been searched as incident to the arrest.

Chimel continued to recognize the principle that an arrest that occurs within a home allows search of portions of the home that would not be permissible if the individual had been arrested on the public street. Under *Chimel,* an object, indicative of criminality, that comes into view during a search incident to arrest where the search has been appropriately limited in scope may be seized without a warrant. In the absence of any additional suspicion following an in-home arrest, police officers are permitted a limited search beyond the person of the arrestee. This ancillary search includes looking into closets, cabinets, and other spaces immediately adjoining the place the arrestee occupies following the arrest. This additional search is justified, since a weapon could be stored nearby, a confederate might exit a closet and attempt to frustrate arrest, or some other hidden danger could present harm to the officers or others within the home. This area around the arrestee has often been known as the "lunge area," the area from which an arrestee might abruptly grab a weapon or destroy evidence. The search should be limited to the area into which an arrestee might reach. As a practical matter, the lunge area encompasses the area within the arrestee's immediate dominion and control, but it generally would not include a basement,[96] an attic, or a separate room of the home inaccessible by the arrestee. According to the general rule, where police are lawfully searching incident to arrest, an object that comes into view which is indicative of criminality may be seized without a warrant.

A search incident to a valid arrest has often been called a full search of the person; it is not limited to a frisk of the suspect's outer clothing and removal of such weapons as the arresting officer may reasonably believe that the suspect has in his possession. The absence of probable fruits or further evidence of the particular crime for which the arrest is made does not narrow the permissible scope of the search. The officer not only may frisk the individual but also is entitled to conduct a complete search of the person, a complete search of clothing, and a complete search of the effects with the arrestee. Naturally, the search must be reasonable in the manner in which the officer conducts the quest. Clearly, an individual cannot be forced to completely disrobe on a public street corner to facilitate a clothing search without violating the Fourth Amendment's requirement that searches be reasonable. Similarly, a body cavity or other extensive personal search must have additional justification beyond the usual probable cause to arrest.

7. SEARCHES OF MOTOR VEHICLES

The mobile nature of motor vehicles dictates that search and seizure issues under the Fourth Amendment take a different route than for homes and buildings. Naturally, most motor vehicles are mobile and could pass through a court's jurisdiction before a warrant could be obtained. Since all motor vehicles have windows, arguably a lower expectation of privacy may be expected by persons who are inside vehicles and who have placed personal items within the interior of the vehicle. Motor vehicles, as well as their operators, have been subject to extensive regulation by the states almost from their introduction as self-powered means of conveyance. Court interpretation of the right to be secure against unreasonable searches in one's papers and effects when they are contained within a motor vehicle indicates that a person has a reduced expectation of privacy[97] in a motor vehicle.

---

[96]Some searches may be permissible following an arrest within the home that are not necessarily incident to arrest as the term is now understood. In *Maryland v. Buie,* 494 U.S. 325 (1990), the Court approved of a properly limited protective sweep of the rooms in conjunction with an in-home arrest when the searching officer possessed a reasonable belief based on specific and articulable facts that the area to be swept could harbor an individual posing a danger to those on the arrest scene. The justification for such an extensive sweep is decidedly not automatic; the sweep may be conducted only when justified by a reasonable suspicion on behalf of the officers.

[97]The Fourth Amendment by its words does not speak of a right of privacy being guaranteed to individuals, but the amendment has been interpreted over the years as giving some level of privacy that varies with the fact situation and location. For some discussion of privacy and the Fourth Amendment in two different contexts, consult Justice Scalia's opinion in *Wyoming v. Houghton,* 526 U.S. 295 (1999), and Justice White's lead opinion in *California v. Greenwood,* 486 U.S. 35 (1988).

Despite a diminished level of Fourth Amendment protection where motor vehicles are concerned, the general rule requires that, prior to a search, the governmental agent possess probable cause. Although the level of privacy is reduced in a motor vehicle, the level of probable cause remains identical to that for any other search where evidence of criminality is being sought. Probable cause may mature due to a police officer's observations, reports from other officers, information from informants, or a combination of all these factors. For example, in *Carroll v. United States,* 267 U.S. 132 (1925), police officers had convincing evidence that the Carrolls were transporting illegal liquor in violation of federal law because the men had offered illegal liquor to be sold to the officers at an earlier time. When the officers identified the Carrolls traveling along the same route frequented by illegal bootleggers, in the same car, they possessed probable cause to stop and search the vehicle.[98] Under the Court's interpretation of *Carroll,* the presence of probable cause permitted the officers to search the vehicle without a warrant.

8. VEHICLE SEARCHES GENERALLY DO NOT REQUIRE WARRANTS

Although the Fourth Amendment speaks of no warrants being issued except upon probable cause, the literal reading of the amendment might indicate that a warrant would be required for a search of a motor vehicle. The reality is that the Supreme Court has determined that a warrant is not a usual requirement of a vehicle search. The operative difficulty with motor vehicles revolves around their inherent mobility and the fact that a court has a limited jurisdiction in which its search warrant may be executed. A court in California cannot issue a warrant that would be valid in Nevada—whether to search a building or an automobile. If a police officer possessed probable cause and wished to search a motor vehicle, the vehicle could leave the jurisdiction if a warrant were a necessity. Alternatively, an officer could seize the vehicle and immobilize it until a warrant had been procured, but a warrantless seizure would still run afoul of the literal meaning of the Fourth Amendment. Since the Fourth Amendment requires a reasonable approach to searches and seizures, one could contend that an immediate search with probable cause would be more reasonable and less of an inconvenience to the driver and occupants than immobilizing the vehicle while other officers procure a search warrant. According to the Court in *Chambers v. Maroney,* 399 U.S. 42 (1970), where the police possessed probable cause to stop a car matching the description of a robbery getaway vehicle, the Court approved an immediate warrantless search of that car (see Case 4.4). According to the *Chambers* Court:

[A]n immediate search is constitutionally permissible. Arguably, because of the preference for a magistrate's judgment, only the immobilization of the car should

---

[98]In enforcing the Fourth Amendment's prohibition against unreasonable searches and seizures, the Court has insisted upon probable cause as a minimum requirement for a reasonable search permitted by the Constitution. As a general rule, it has also required the judgment of a magistrate on the probable cause issue and the issuance of a warrant before a search is made. Only where an emergency exists and in a few other exceptional situations, the judgment of the police as to probable cause may serve as a sufficient authority for a warrantless search. *Carroll* held that a search warrant was unnecessary where there is probable cause to search an automobile stopped on the highway where the car is movable and the car's contents may never be found again if a warrant must be obtained. Hence, an immediate search is constitutionally permissible.

be permitted until a search warrant is obtained; arguably, only the "lesser" intrusion is permissible until the magistrate authorizes the "greater." But which is the "greater" and which the "lesser" intrusion is itself a debatable question, and the answer may depend on a variety of circumstances. For constitutional purposes, we see no difference between, on the one hand, seizing and holding a car before presenting the probable cause issue to a magistrate and, on the other hand, carrying out an immediate search without a warrant. Given probable cause to search, either course is reasonable under the Fourth Amendment. *Chambers v. Maroney,* 399 U.S. 42, 52 (1970).

Following *Chambers,* which built on the doctrine of *Carroll,* where police have probable cause to search a motor vehicle, the search may be conducted immediately[99] so long as good probable cause exists at the time of the search. In support of the concept, the Supreme Court, in *Maryland v. Dyson,* 527 U.S. 465 (1999), in a per curiam opinion reaffirmed that a search warrant generally is not a requirement for a vehicle search. It noted that a vehicle search is not unreasonable if based on facts that would have justified the issuance of a warrant, even though a warrant was never obtained. In most cases, if the officers desire, a warrant may be first procured and the search conducted pursuant to the warrant. Essentially, where a motor vehicle is involved, the officer has a choice whether to conduct a search with or without a warrant, since either course has been determined to be reasonable given the presence of probable cause.

Although most searches of motor vehicles do not require warrants,[100] in *Coolidge v. New Hampshire,* 403 U.S. 443 (1971), the Court identified a situation wherein a search warrant was required for a motor vehicle. While the facts in *Coolidge* were somewhat unique and the case may stand only for a situation exactly on point with *Coolidge,* the case has not been overruled and remains good law. In *Coolidge,* the police suspected the defendant of murder, the defendant had no control over the car, and there were no exigent or emergency circumstances that justified an immediate warrantless search. The *Coolidge* Court invalidated the searches of the automobile because a valid warrant had not been obtained prior to the police search of the car. The Court distinguished this case from *Carroll v. United States* (the *Carroll* doctrine) by noting that the defendant had ample time to destroy any evidence in his car, he had no access at the time of search, and the car was not capable of going anywhere, unlike the Carroll automobile, which was actually being driven at the time it was seized. One concept that arises from *Coolidge* is that automobiles that cannot be moved under their own power may require a search warrant or some recognized exception to the warrant requirement in order to be lawfully searched. Most assuredly, to protect the admissibility of evidence in motor vehicles that are not readily mobile, the possibility of procuring a warrant

---

[99]There is no requirement that police procure a search warrant for a motor vehicle even where there is ample time to do so. In a per curiam opinion in *Pennsylvania v. Labron,* 518 U.S. 938 (1996), the Court clearly rejected the Pennsylvania Supreme Court's attempt to require that police obtain vehicle search warrants where time permits.

[100]In a per curiam opinion the Court stated in *Maryland v. Dyson,* 527 U.S. 465, 467 (1999), "We made this clear in *United States v. Ross,* 456 U.S. 798 (1982), when we said that in cases where there was probable cause to search a vehicle 'a search is not unreasonable if based on facts that would justify the issuance of a warrant, even though a warrant has not been actually obtained.'"

prior to conducting a search supported by probable cause should be considered by law enforcement officers.

9. LIMITED VEHICLE SEARCHES ON LESS THAN PROBABLE CAUSE

In addition to complete motor vehicle searches based on probable cause, a governmental agent may make limited warrantless searches of moving vehicles in the absence of any probable cause where the government is searching for evidence of alcohol or drug impairment by car and truck drivers. In *Michigan v. Sitz,* 496 U.S. 444 (1990), the Court gave approval to the practice in which police stopped all vehicles passing through a checkpoint as a way to screen for alcohol-impaired drivers. Following this plan, the police made a limited seizure in the absence of probable cause and in the absence of any individualized suspicion of intoxication or impairment. The *Sitz* Court approved the brief seizures by balancing the state's interest in reducing impaired driving against the minimal intrusion upon members of the motoring public who were briefly stopped. The Court determined that the short stop to discern sobriety was reasonable under the Fourth Amendment.

10. VEHICLE INVENTORY SEARCHES

Some vehicle searches may follow valid arrests of the driver or passenger using the theory of search incident to arrest,[101] while other warrantless searches may be justified under an inventory search theory.[102] In a search incident to arrest in a motor vehicle, the officers are permitted to search the interior of the vehicle where the arrestee might reasonably make a grab or lunge to obtain a weapon or destroy evidence. The inventory search[103] stands on a different theoretical basis and is designed to "protect an owner's property while it is in the custody of the police, to insure against [false] claims of lost, stolen, or vandalized property, and to guard the police from danger";[104] it also is intended to protect property custodians from any dangerous substance or ordinance that might be transported to a property room from an impounded vehicle. The Supreme Court approved inventory searches in *Colorado v. Bertine,* 479 U.S. 367 (1987), where the search parameters were directed by a written policy. Where an automobile has been lawfully impounded, courts will generally uphold inventory searches as reasonable, even in the absence of search probable cause.

---

[101]For examples of searches incident to arrest of drivers of motor vehicles, see *United States v. Robinson,* 414 U.S. 218 (1973), and *Gustafson v. Florida,* 414 U.S. 260 (1973).

[102]In many situations, probable cause for a search, the justification for an inventory search, and consent may all coexist, giving a prosecutor several legal theories on which to argue in favor of admission of the evidence. Where one theory allows admission, the evidence will generally be admitted.

[103]An inventory search may be conducted after an automobile has been lawfully impounded, as occurred in *Florida v. White,* 526 U.S. 559 (1999), where the officers, conducting a routine inventory search, discovered illegal drugs within the automobile.

[104]*Benson v. State,* 342 Ark. 684, 30 S.W.3d 731 (2000).

An inventory search of a motor vehicle requires that the police agency have and follow an inventory search policy. In the absence of a policy regulating this process, individual officers would have unlimited discretion so that a particular inventory search could evolve into a ruse for conducting a general search. The policy regulating inventory searches must be designed to produce an inventory rather than permitting the inventory officer so much latitude that no standards exist. The absence of a policy on inventory searches or a defective policy can create difficulties for the prosecution. In *Florida v. Wells,* 495 U.S. 1 (1990), an arrested driver gave police permission to open the trunk of his impounded car. An inventory search of the car revealed marijuana within a suitcase. The *Wells* Court approved the state court decision holding that the evidence should have been suppressed on the grounds that the Florida Highway Patrol possessed no governing standards covering the opening of closed containers found within motor vehicles. A search of this nature was not deemed to be reasonable under the Fourth Amendment.

Clear examples of the appropriate use of an inventory search theory occur following many traffic accidents where the vehicles need to be removed from the roadway for safety reasons. When police officers conduct an inventory search with a view to securing valuables, the basic reasonableness of such a search becomes obvious. In an Arkansas case, a woman drove her car from the highway in a one-car accident that involved a rollover of the vehicle. Her injuries dictated hospitalization and that she be removed from the scene of the accident. The police engaged a wrecker service to remove the vehicle from the accident location but conducted an inventory search prior to the car being towed. According to the police officer on the scene, it was the written policy of the police to impound a vehicle involved in an accident if it would otherwise have been left unattended on or near the roadway. The inventory search disclosed some recreational quantities of marijuana and methamphetamine. According to the court of appeals, the trial court properly refused to suppress the evidence, citing the reasonableness of the inventory policy even where the officer may have possessed a secondary investigatory motive.[105]

11. SCOPE OF MOTOR VEHICLE SEARCH

Given the existence of probable cause to search a vehicle, the police need to determine the extent of the lawful search permitted. Clearly, probable cause to search a car will not, without significantly more evidence, justify a search of the driver's home, especially without a warrant. The general rule concerning scope of a search dictates that the area of the automobile to be searched depends upon the nature of the object that is the goal of the search. For example, if the police possessed probable cause to search a car for a stolen desktop computer system, a look in the trunk of the vehicle would be appropriate, but sifting through the ashtray near the driver's seat would not be likely to reveal a computer and would be an unreasonable search. Following similar logic, if there were probable cause to search for some recreational pharmaceuticals, a search in virtually any part or location of the vehicle would be

---

[105] *Bratton v. Arkansas,* 77 Ark. App. 174; 72 S.W.3d 522 (2002).

reasonable, since drugs may be secreted in any small or large area of the car. Given probable cause to search a motor vehicle, police may search in any location in the vehicle where the object of the search might reasonably be located.

12. SCOPE OF SEARCH OF CONTAINERS WITHIN MOTOR VEHICLES

Where containers are not associated with motor vehicles, individuals possess a Fourth Amendment right to expect that governmental agents will not look through luggage, backpacks, grocery bags, and similar articles without probable cause and without a warrant unless special circumstances exist.[106] Different rules have developed when the same containers are stowed or hidden in motor vehicles. When police encounter luggage and similar containers within motor vehicles, the jurisprudence has followed a complicated path as courts struggled to produce coherent, consistent, and unified rationales consistent with the Fourth Amendment.

In *Carroll v. United States,* 267 U.S. 132 (1925), the Court approved a general search of the vehicle on probable cause that it held untaxed liquor in some sort of container or containers. Consistent with *Carroll* was *United States v. Ross,* 456 U.S. 798 (1982), where the Court gave approval to a probable cause warrantless search of the interior of a car, its trunk, a closed brown paper bag, and a zippered leather pouch. In *Ross,* the police had probable cause to believe that Ross had been selling drugs from the car and that additional drugs were contained within the car with the exact location unknown. The *Ross* Court allowed a search anywhere within the automobile where drugs might reasonably be hidden, which naturally included a search of any containers.

When the police do not have probable cause to search an entire vehicle, but only a container, a different rule has been applied, but it is not current law.[107] In *Arkansas v. Sanders,* 442 U.S. 753 (1979), the police, acting on an informant's information that Sanders, upon arriving at an airport, would be carrying a green suitcase containing marijuana, placed him under surveillance. When Sanders placed a green suitcase in the trunk of a taxi, police stopped the vehicle, opened the unlocked suitcase, and discovered marijuana. The police conducted the vehicle search without a warrant,[108] based on the justification of the *Carroll* vehicle doctrine permitting warrantless searches of vehicles on probable cause. Since there was probable cause for not only the vehicle stop and search but probable cause to search the luggage, the

---

[106]Emergency situations, airport searches, consent searches, school searches, border searches, postarrest searches, and some stop and frisk situations may allow an officer to search personal belongings as exceptions to the general rule that probable cause and warrants are necessary.

[107]The current law is expressed by *United States v. Ross,* 456 U.S. 798 (1982). The *Ross* Court concluded that officers who have legitimately stopped an automobile and who possess probable cause that seizable matter is concealed somewhere within the vehicle may conduct a warrantless search of the vehicle that is as thorough as a judge or magistrate could have authorized by warrant, even though no warrant has been obtained.

[108]The *Sanders* police would have been on notice that a search of a piece of luggage generally required a warrant in addition to probable cause. In *United States v. Chadwick,* 433 U.S. 1 (1977), with probable cause but without a warrant, police seized and opened a piece of luggage that had traveled from San Diego to Boston on a train. The *Chadwick* defendants had just placed the luggage in the trunk of a car. In substance, the *Chadwick* Court held that the warrant clause of the Fourth Amendment required a warrant to search luggage absent exigent circumstances or some other exception and that merely touching a car with the luggage did not trigger the *Carroll* doctrine.

connection of the luggage to the vehicle seemed sufficient to allow a warrantless search of the luggage under the *Carroll* doctrine. The Supreme Court disagreed on the legality of the search, holding that in the absence of exigent circumstances, police are required to obtain a warrant before searching luggage taken from an automobile properly stopped and searched for recreational pharmaceuticals. In *Sanders,* the probable cause extended only to the luggage, and merely touching a motor vehicle with luggage did not turn the search into a *Carroll* search, for which no warrant would have been required. The Court made a distinction between a probable cause search of an automobile that coincidentally turned up a container and a similar search of a container that coincidentally ended up in an automobile. Thus, at the time of *Sanders,* the evidence had to be suppressed, since police needed a warrant to search luggage taken from a motor vehicle.

That theory changed when the Court decided *United States v. Ross,* 456 U.S. 798 (1982), where the Court held that given probable cause to search a container within a motor vehicle, no warrant was required to conduct the search. To the extent that *Ross* was inconsistent with *Sanders* and other similar cases, the Court seems to have overruled that line of cases and substituted the rule of *Ross.* The Court reasoned that where a home search has been authorized, a search for a small object would include looking inside containers and closets. Therefore, where a vehicle search for an easily hidden object is appropriate, looking inside containers, as in a house search, should be reasonable.

The problem with the court cases centered on the concept that a search of luggage or other container would be illegal if conducted without a warrant where probable cause extended only to a search of the luggage, but the same piece of luggage could be lawfully searched without a warrant if encountered inside a vehicle during a search as in *Ross.* The Supreme Court attempted to clarify the case law so that Fourth Amendment protections would not turn on the happenstance of the location of the luggage at the time probable cause matures. As the *Ross* Court stated:

> When a legitimate search is under way, and when its purpose and its limits have been precisely defined, nice distinctions between closets, drawers, and containers, in the case of a home, or between glove compartments, upholstered seats, trunks, and wrapped packages, in the case of a vehicle, must give way to the interest in the prompt and efficient completion of the task at hand. *Ross* at 821.

The newer theory applied where there was probable cause to search the automobile, but it did not clearly address a situation where there was probable cause only to search a particularly described container within the vehicle, as was the case in *Arkansas v. Sanders.*

In *California v. Acevedo,* 500 U.S. 565 (1991), police made a controlled delivery of drugs to an apartment (see Case 4.6). Acevedo arrived, entered, and exited the apartment quickly while carrying a brown paper bag of the size delivered to the apartment. With probable cause to search the bag but not the car, police waited until Acevedo placed the bag within his automobile and drove away. Police stopped him and conducted a warrantless search of the brown paper bag. The police followed the search practice, which transgressed the outdated theory of *Sanders,* by searching a container because it had come in contact with a motor vehicle. In order to provide one rule for searches of containers discovered in automobiles, the *Acevedo* Court held that the police may search an automobile and the containers within it where they have probable cause to believe contraband or evidence is contained somewhere within the motor vehicle. Under this view, the search of the luggage in *United States v. Chadwick* would have been lawful in the absence of a warrant, and the search of the luggage in *Arkansas v. Sanders* would have produced lawfully seized evidence.

13. OTHER THEORIES OF VEHICLE SEARCHES AND SEIZURES

The Fourth Amendment allows officials to conduct warrantless searches of motor vehicles based on probable cause to search, pursuant to an inventory search, incident to lawful arrest, based on consent, and, to a limited extent, at sobriety checkpoints. Limited searches are permitted under the stop and frisk rationale where police officers possess reasonable basis to suspect that criminal activity might be afoot. Automobile inventory searches require that the law enforcement agency have and routinely follow a written inventory policy. Exigent circumstances might allow a vehicle search where life was clearly at risk.

Searches of motor vehicles following a lawful arrest[109] of the driver or passenger follow the general rules for searches incident to arrest.[110] The primary goal of such a search is to remove any weapons over which an arrestee might gain control. Where the arrest occurs while a driver is seated, the area inside the passenger compartment may be searched, since the arrestee might be able to grab a gun or other weapon or destroy evidence. Naturally, the driver's person may be searched following an arrest within a motor vehicle.

Limited motor vehicle searches have been approved on less than probable cause where the state was attempting to detect drug- or alcohol-impaired drivers. In *Michigan v. Sitz,* 496 U.S. 444 (1990), the Supreme Court approved a police plan in which automobile drivers were stopped briefly while officers attempted to observe traits that indicated impairment. The *Sitz* Court held that, although such stops were Fourth Amendment seizures, they constituted reasonable seizures when balanced between the state's grave and legitimate interest in curbing drunken driving and the minimal intrusion on and inconvenience for the motorist. According to the Court, the use of sobriety checkpoints is reasonable where all the motorists are briefly screened for drug or alcohol use and only those who appear impaired are subject to additional inquiry.

If an effort to detect drinking drivers passed muster under the Fourth Amendment on less than probable cause or reasonable basis to suspect criminal activity, it would seem as if the interdiction of a drug-carrying or drug-using motorist might

---

[109]The basis for a search of a motor vehicle following an arrest of the driver requires an actual arrest of the driver. In *Knowles v. Iowa,* 525 U.S. 113 (1998), where a police officer possessed probable cause to arrest but issued only a citation and then searched the automobile because the officer *could* have arrested Mr. Knowles, the Court held the search to be unreasonable under the Fourth Amendment.

[110]For a case detailing the scope of a search incident to an arrest involving a motor vehicle, consult *United States v. Robinson,* 414 U.S. 218 (1973).

win court approval. In *Indianapolis v. Edmond,* 531 U.S. 32 (2000), the Court ruled against the practice of setting up roadblocks on public highways so that police could inspect the interiors of automobiles and observe drivers while a drug-sniffing dog walked around the vehicle (see Case 4.7). The locations where automobiles would be stopped were marked by highway signs. Police practice involved stopping a group of cars and allowing all others to proceed while the officers processed the stopped vehicles. There was no particular reason to stop any car. The officers conducted each stop in the same manner until and unless particularized suspicion developed. The officers possessed no discretion to stop any vehicle out of sequence.

In failing to approve the practice in *Edmond,* the Court distinguished *Michigan v. Sitz* on the ground that the program in *Sitz* was

> clearly aimed at reducing the immediate hazard posed by the presence of drunk drivers on the highways, and there was an obvious connection between the imperative of highway safety and the law enforcement practice at issue. The gravity of the drunk driving problem and the magnitude of the State's interest in getting drunk drivers off the road weighed heavily in our determination that the program was constitutional. *Michigan v. Sitz,* 496 U.S. 444, 451 (1990).

The stop in *Sitz* was quite brief, the carnage on highways from impaired drivers was well documented, and the Court felt the stop at the checkpoint was reasonable under the Fourth Amendment. The gravity of the drunk driving problem and the extent of the state's interest in getting drunk drivers off of the road weighed heavily in the Court's determination that the *Sitz* program was constitutional. In contrast in *Edmond,* the primary purpose was the interdiction of narcotics and other illegal drugs and the arrest of drug offenders. Such a goal was more of a general crime-fighting activity, which, if the drug stops were upheld, could be considered for other types of crime using roadside stops. Since the primary purpose involved a general interest in crime control, the Court declined to suspend the general requirement of individualized suspicion normally required to seize a person.

While receiving mixed reviews in the drug and alcohol context, the roadblock screen has constitutional vitality in some other limited contexts, especially where an emergency dictates that reasonable police practice requires some minimal scrutiny of vehicles leaving an area. In a Massachusetts case, after three o'clock in the morning, police received numerous 911 calls concerning a series of multiple gunshots from a cul-de-sac and found fifty or more people milling about. Since some of the individuals were attempting to leave the area in vehicles, the police decided to take a look at each vehicle passing out of the cul-de-sac. During the brief questioning of each occupant, an officer noticed a firearm in one of the vehicles and eventually arrested the occupants, charging one with illegal possession of a firearm. When the subject filed a motion to suppress the evidence, the court noted that, although normally articulable suspicion is required to make a vehicle stop, on some occasions the intrusion is limited and serves a crucial public need that cannot be easily met in any other manner. The court held the initial stop and intrusion were reasonable given the fact that the police knew a crime had been committed but possessed no individually particularized suspicion. The reasonableness required a balancing of the public interest against the right of a person to be free from arbitrary seizure by law enforcement personnel. In upholding the brief stop, the court of appeals noted that "the facts indicate this was a deliberate emergency police effort to apprehend one or more fleeing suspects as to whom the police had no physical description, no information as to their number, and indeed no indication as to whether they were fleeing on foot or by vehicle."[111]

14. SEARCHES FOLLOWING VEHICLE FORFEITURES

In some cases, a state government may possess a complete right of ownership of a car[112] and not merely a right under the Fourth Amendment to search it. Where a motor vehicle's status allows it to be seized as forfeitable contraband, no warrant is required prior to taking control of the vehicle and searching the interior. In *Florida v. White,* 526 U.S. 559 (1999), police officers observed White using his car to deliver cocaine on three separate occasions, thus developing probable cause to believe that the automobile was subject to forfeiture under Florida law. Several months later, police had probable cause to arrest White on charges unrelated to his cocaine dealing. During the arrest process, police noticed the car, which they believed was subject to forfeiture, and immediately, without a warrant, seized the vehicle.[113] The Supreme Court of the United States reversed the Florida Supreme Court's holding that a warrant was required under the Fourth Amendment to seize the car. According to the *White* Court, since there was probable cause to believe that the car was contraband, having been used in a drug delivery, and since it was mobile and in a public place, the vehicle could be reasonably seized without a warrant under the Fourth Amendment as interpreted by the *Carroll* doctrine.

15. SEARCHES BASED ON CONSENT

Where law enforcement officials wish to search a particular area for which no probable cause exists or where probable cause may exist, but the officer possesses no required search warrant, there exists a possibility of searching by the use of the theory of consent. Like many personal constitutional rights, the Fourth Amendment guarantees are waivable if the parties involved follow appropriate steps.

The first requirement in acquiring consent dictates that the *proper person* give consent. This person must have sole dominion and control over the property or must share dominion and control with another person or persons. Apartment dwellers may not own the real estate, but since the dweller has dominion and control over the property at the moment, that individual is a proper person from whom

---

[111]*Commonwealth v. Grant,* 57 Mass. App. Ct. 334, 339; 783 N.E.2d 455, 459, 460 (2003).

[112]Justice Thomas explained, "The Florida Contraband Forfeiture Act [Florida Contraband Forfeiture Act, Fla. Stat. § 932.701 *et seq.* (1997)] provides that certain forms of contraband, including motor vehicles used in violation of the Act's provisions, may be seized and potentially forfeited." *Florida v. White,* 526 U.S. 559, 561 (1999).

[113]Mr. White also developed other troubles subsequent to his arrest when the police subjected his forfeited vehicle to an inventory search that revealed two rocks of crack cocaine. The inventory search could have been justified as a routine inventory search for which neither probable cause nor a warrant would be required. An alternative manner of justifying the search finds no expectation of privacy in the automobile by Mr. White, since, at the time of the search, it belonged to the government of Florida under the forfeiture law. See Florida Contraband Forfeiture Act, Fla. Stat. § 932.701 *et seq.* (1997).

consent may be granted. Personal property generally falls into the same set of rules. The person possessing dominion and control over the subject property may give consent to search a car, backpack, shoulder bag, purse, or other container. In a Minnesota case, a driver of an automobile gave consent to a police officer to search the vehicle, which had been stopped for having a broken headlight. The officer searched the locked trunk area and opened a passenger's suitcase, revealing controlled substances. According to the appellate court, the results of the search should have been suppressed from admission into evidence, since the prosecution failed to demonstrate that the third-party driver of the vehicle had dominion and control over the property or shared common authority over the suitcases. The appellate court took the position that a driver's consent to search a motor vehicle should not be construed automatically to extend to property owned and controlled by passengers where the passengers were present and available to grant or withhold consent to the search of their property.[114] Even though Fourth Amendment rights are generally considered personal and cannot be asserted vicariously, some jurisdictions allow vicarious waiver and would allow a driver to consent to a search of the passenger's belonging under the foregoing circumstances[115] due to a reduced expectation of privacy in motor vehicles.

There may be occasions on which the proper person purports to have dominion and control over the property, especially real estate, but the individual is being untruthful or the police are relying on reasonable appearances. In *Illinois v. Rodriguez,* 497 U.S. 177 (1990), a former girlfriend of Rodriguez used her key to allow police to enter an apartment to arrest Rodriguez, who had drugs in plain view. The woman represented that the apartment was "ours" and that she had clothes and furniture there. The general rule is that a warrantless entry is valid when based on the consent of a third party if the police reasonably believe that the third party possesses common dominion and control over the premises.[116] The *Rodriguez* Court held, essentially, that if police had a good faith reasonable belief that the individual with the key possessed dominion and control, that fact could support a consent search if all the other components were present.

The second requirement under the Fourth Amendment for a valid consent to search is that the consent be given freely and voluntarily. Voluntariness is a question of fact to be determined from all the circumstances surrounding the situation, but knowledge of the right to refuse consent is not an absolute requirement.[117] The factors to be considered include the level of education and general intelligence of the consenting party, the coerciveness of the circumstances, whether the individual was under arrest, whether the person knew about the right to refuse to grant consent, whether the police indicated a search would be conducted anyway, and whether

---

[114]*Minnesota v. Frank,* 650 N.W.2d 213 (2002), and see *Brown v. Florida,* 7879 So.2d 1021, 1021, 1023 (Fla. Dist. Ct. App. 2001), where a driver's consent to search a vehicle did not extend to personal items like purses and backpacks.

[115]See *United States v. Navarro,* 169 F.3d 228, 230 (5th Cir. 1999), and *Wisconsin v. Matejka,* 241 Wis.2d 52; 621 N.W.2d 891 (2001); cert. denied 532 U.S. 1058 (2001). Note: In *Wyoming v. Houghton,* 526 U.S. 295 (1999), the Court approved of the search of a woman passenger's purse, but the distinction involved the presence of probable cause to search rather than consent to search.

[116]*Illinois v. Rodriguez,* 497 U.S. 177, 182–189 (1990).

[117]The Court in *Schneckloth v. Bustamonte,* 412 U.S. 218, 226, 227 (1973), held that knowledge of the right to refuse to grant consent was not essential to offering valid consent; it was but one of several factors in the totality of the circumstances test.

police falsely stated that they possessed a warrant. Although these factors are not exclusive, they demonstrate the usual considerations that courts use in determining whether consent was voluntarily given.

Where a question arises concerning the validity of a consent search, the prosecution must demonstrate that the proper person gave consent and that it was given freely and voluntarily under the totality of the circumstances. Demonstrative of these principles is *Schneckloth v. Bustamonte,* 412 U.S. 218 (1973), where police lawfully stopped a vehicle during the early morning hours (see Case 4.8). The driver had no license and most of the six men had no identification. Officers requested permission from the owner's brother, Alcala, to search the car. A police backup unit arrived with more officers, creating a slightly coercive atmosphere. As the proper person to give consent, Alcala agreed to allow a search of the vehicle. Criminal charges eventually resulted against passenger Bustamonte, who contended that the evidence seized had been discovered during an illegal search involving a lack of consent.

The driver apparently did not possess dominion and control over the vehicle since Alcala, the owner's brother, made decisions involving the car's operation. The real issue involved whether Alcala gave a free and voluntary consent under the totality of the circumstances. Alcala's educational level was not known, but he appeared to be of normal intelligence. There was no indication that anyone was initially threatened with arrest or that the numbers of officers present indicated a coercive atmosphere. Under the circumstances, the Supreme Court upheld the conviction and ruled that the consent had been freely and voluntarily offered by the proper person.[118]

Assuming the proper party voluntarily and freely grants consent, the person may offer a complete or a limited right to search in respect to the length of the search or its scope. Once given, consent may be withdrawn at any time. If police exceed the scope of the consent, items seized in violation of the limitations may be excluded from use as evidence. The scope of consent may be informed by the object of the search. In *Florida v. Jimeno,* 500 U.S. 248 (1991), a police officer informed a motorist that the officer had reason to believe that the automobile contained narcotics. The officer explained that the driver did not have to consent to a search of the car. After the driver stated that he had nothing to hide, he granted the officer permission to search the automobile. When a folded brown bag in the car proved to contain cocaine, the driver contended that his consent did not extend to the closed paper bag. While Jimeno had success in the Florida state courts, the Supreme Court held that the consent covered the paper bag. Justice Rehnquist, writing for the Court, held that consent to search for drugs would allow the officer to open and look into any containers within the car that could reasonably conceal drugs.

---

[118]When a court decides whether to suppress evidence, an important question to deal with is which person possesses standing to contest an alleged illegal search and seizure. Normally, only a person with an expectation of privacy as recognized by Fourth Amendment case law will be permitted to argue the merits of a motion to suppress. Applying modern standing rules of *Rakas v. Illinois,* 439 U.S. 128 (1978), to *Schneckloth v. Bustamonte,* the passenger, Bustamonte, who was eventually prosecuted, might not have any expectation of privacy since he did not own or lease the vehicle. Under such circumstances, the passenger would not have any legal right to contest the validity of the search and seizure.

Where the consenting party gave a free and voluntary consent to search property under that party's control and where police do not exceed the bounds of the consent given, any evidence seized may be used in court unless excluded for evidentiary reasons unrelated to the Fourth Amendment. Consent to search for an object or material extends to any place where the property may be hidden or stored within reasonable bounds.

16. REQUIREMENTS FOR THE PLAIN VIEW DOCTRINE

The "plain view" doctrine constitutes an exception to the warrant requirement for a search, but, standing alone, the doctrine does not allow an officer to immediately enter private premises to effectuate a seizure. As a general rule, law enforcement officials may make warrantless seizures of evidence in plain view when the officer observes the object of the seizure from a lawful vantage point, the incriminating nature of the object or its clear connection to crime is immediately apparent, and the officer can acquire dominion over and control of the object without a violation of the Fourth Amendment.

An object subject to police seizure may present itself during a search for some different object, a stop and frisk, a routine traffic stop, hot pursuit, or at any other time where a law enforcement officer lawfully observes evidence indicative of criminality. Under this legal theory police may be permitted to seize an object without a warrant where the officer is lawfully in a position to view it, if the object's incriminating character is clearly and immediately apparent, and if the police have a lawful right of access to the item. The legal theory behind the plain view doctrine is that

> if contraband is left in open view and is observed by a police officer from a lawful vantage point, there has been no invasion of a legitimate expectation of privacy, and thus no "search" within the meaning of the Fourth Amendment—or at least no search independent of the initial intrusion that gave the officers their vantage point. *Minnesota v. Dickerson,* 508 U.S. 366, 375 (1993).

The usual legal standards for a valid plain view seizure as described in *Coolidge v. New Hampshire,* 403 U.S. 443 (1971), required that the police officer observe the seizable evidence from a position the officer had a lawful right to occupy; that the officer's discovery was unexpected or inadvertent; and that the incriminating nature of the evidence be clearly apparent to the officer. This final requirement merely restates the necessity of probable cause to seize the evidence. Under *Coolidge,* if the officer expected to find a particular item of evidence at a particular place, the "discovery" of the evidence could not be sustained under the plain view doctrine due to the absence of inadvertent discovery.

In a classic case in which the plain view had application, in the early morning hours a police officer observed a vehicle traveling at about ninety miles per hour in a forty-five-miles-per-hour zone with a flat tire and sparks coming from the rim of the tire wheel. The officer made a probable cause stop of the vehicle, and the driver subsequently opened the driver's door and fell out of the car onto the road. When one officer smelled a strong odor of marijuana coming from the vehicle, he looked inside the passenger compartment and observed plastic baggies containing what the officer recognized as marijuana. The appellate courts upheld the seizure under the plain view theory, since the officers had a lawful vantage point outside the vehicle; the nature of the object clearly offended the law; and in a vehicle context, they were lawfully allowed to enter the premises and make a seizure.[119]

17. INADVERTENT DISCOVERY: NO LONGER REQUIRED

Subsequent to the *Coolidge* plain view doctrine case, police officers were permitted to seize evidence if they were lawfully on the premises and discovered evidence that had not been anticipated but was clearly indicative of criminal activity. The reality, of course, was that officers legitimately on the premises would pretend to inadvertently discover evidence they may have expected to discover on the premises but for which they lacked probable cause. The fact that probable cause did not exist for the expected objects meant that the affidavit could not have mentioned such evidence and the warrant would not have included a description of the evidence.

Almost twenty years later, the Supreme Court reexamined the legal elements of the plain view doctrine in *Horton v. California,* 496 U.S. 128 (1990) (see Case 4.9). In *Horton,* police determined that there was probable cause to search Horton's residence for the proceeds of a robbery and weapons used in the robbery. Police obtained a search warrant that covered the proceeds of the robbery but did not mention a handgun that police believed would likely be present. The search revealed a handgun but no evidence of the robbery proceeds. The Supreme Court held that even if the discovery of the handgun was expected and not inadvertent, the evidence was properly seizable under the plain view doctrine. According to the Court, inadvertent discovery no longer was a requirement for use of the plain view doctrine.

18. OFFICER NEEDS TO BE LAWFULLY PRESENT

Following *Horton,* the requirements for the use of the plain view doctrine dictate that the officer was lawfully on the premises or at a lawful vantage point; that probable cause for seizure be clearly apparent; and that the officer have a lawful method of gaining access to the seizable property.

The evidence must be clearly visible and not in a location where the officer must manipulate or minutely examine the evidence to determine whether the property is seizeable. If the officer needs to move the property to find a serial number to determine whether the property was stolen[120] or needs to open a container to observe the incriminating item, such conduct constitutes a separate search and cannot meet the dictates of the plain view doctrine. Demonstrative of the proposition that the property and its seizable qualitites must be clearly visible to the officer is *Arizona v. Hicks,* 480 U.S. 321 (1987), where police were lawfully on the premises

[119]*Pennsylvania v Ballard,* 2002 PA Super 283; 806 A.2d 889, 892 (2002).
[120]See *Arizona v. Hicks,* 480 U.S. 321 (1987).

following reports of a shooting. One of the officers noticed some expensive stereo components that looked out of place in such a squalid apartment and concluded that they might have been stolen. The officer moved the components so that he could see their serial numbers and recorded them for future use. The equipment later proved to be stolen property, but the *Hicks* Court concluded that the warrant that had been issued on the basis of the serial numbers had been improperly obtained by virtue of the officer's warrantless search for the serial numbers. In effect, the plain view doctrine requires that the relevancy of the evidence be readily apparent prior to seizure, and even a warrantless search for serial numbers could not be justified under the plain view doctrine.

Whereas the evidence must be in plain view, the officer remains free to lawfully take a position that permits the best vantage point. For example, in *California v. Ciraolo,* 476 U.S. 207 (1986), following reports from neighbors that Ciraolo was cultivating marijuana in his backyard, police boarded an aircraft to search the yard from a lawful altitude. Officers observed marijuana growing inside the defendant's yard behind a privacy fence. While officers expected to find marijuana growing in the backyard plot, and while the discovery was not inadvertent, the Court upheld the search even though *Ciraolo* was decided four years prior to *Horton.* So long as the place or position that the officer takes is a lawful one, the observations made can properly be the basis for the use of the plain view doctrine.

19. THE PLAIN FEEL DOCTRINE

Under the stop and frisk doctrine, police officers often discover items that are not reasonably considered weaponlike lumps but that, to a trained and experienced officer, may seem to be contraband. Consider the situation in which an officer notices what seems to be contraband through the sense of touch during an otherwise lawful pat-down. Such a search may allow the officer to enter the inner clothing if he or she has felt an object whose contour or mass makes its identity immediately apparent. Under these circumstances, there has been no illegal invasion of the suspect's privacy beyond that already authorized by the search for weapons under a stop and frisk.

In *Minnesota v. Dickerson,* 508 U.S. 366 (1993), a police officer was conducting a lawful stop and frisk. As he patted down a suspect who had been lawfully seized, the officer felt what he thought was a rock of crack cocaine, a determination made only after manipulating it between his thumb and index finger. The Supreme Court agreed that a plain feel doctrine would allow a seizure under the circumstances where a police officer lawfully patted down a suspect's outer clothing and felt an object whose contour or mass makes its identity as contraband immediately apparent. The *Dickerson* Court recognized there would have been no invasion of the suspect's privacy beyond that already authorized by the officer's search for weapons. If the object reasonably seems to be contraband, the seizure by the officer would be justified by the same practical considerations that inhere in the plain view context. Justice White, writing the lead opinion in *Dickerson,* held that the officer's manipulation of the object in the subject's pants constituted a search beyond the stop and frisk and could not be considered as lawfully seized following the plain feel doctrine. A seizure would be permitted only where the lawful touch allowed the officer to instantly develop a reasonable belief that the object offended the law.

MAJOR CASES

CASE 4.1

Arrest within the Home Generally Requires Arrest or Search Warrant

Payton v. New York
Supreme Court of the United States
445 U.S. 573 (1980)

FACTS

New York detectives gathered evidence sufficient to establish probable cause to believe that Theodore Payton had murdered the manager of a gas station several days earlier. Without a warrant for search or arrest, six officers went to the apartment rented by Mr. Payton and although the sound of music could be heard playing from inside the apartment, no one answered the door. Eventually the door of the apartment was broken open and the officers entered but found no one home. In plain view, the officers observed a .30-caliber shell casing, which they seized and which the trial court later admitted into evidence at Payton's murder trial. The trial judge believed that the warrantless and forcible entry was authorized by New York law and that the shell had been lawfully seized. The trial resulted in a verdict of guilty. The Appellate Division and the New York Court of Appeals affirmed the admission of evidence and the verdict. Neither court relied on exigent circumstances for its decision.

Payton appealed to the Supreme Court of the United States and offered the argument that under the Fourth Amendment, a warrant to enter a home should be required in order to arrest or seize a person, unless there are exigent circumstances present. The Supreme Court of the United States granted certiorari.

PROCEDURAL ISSUE

Must law enforcement agents possess either a search or an arrest warrant in order to make a lawful arrest of a resident inside a home or search of a home absent exigent circumstances?

HELD: YES

RATIONALE

Mr. Justice Stevens delivered the opinion of the Court.

★ ★ ★

It is familiar history that indiscriminate searches and seizures conducted under the authority of "general warrants" were the immediate evils that motivated the framing and adoption of the Fourth Amendment. Indeed, as originally proposed in the House of Representatives, the draft contained only one clause, which directly imposed limitations on the issuance of warrants, but imposed no express restrictions on warrantless searches or seizures. As it was ultimately adopted, however, the Amendment contained two separate clauses, the first protecting the basic right to be free from unreasonable searches and seizures and the second requiring that warrants be particular and supported by probable cause. The Amendment provides:

> The right of the people to be secure in their persons, houses, papers, and effects, against unreasonable searches and seizures, shall not be violated, and no Warrants shall issue, but upon probable cause, supported by Oath or affirmation, and particularly describing the place to be searched, and the persons or things to be seized.

It is thus perfectly clear that the evil the Amendment was designed to prevent was broader than the abuse of a general warrant. Unreasonable searches or seizures conducted without any warrant at all are condemned by the plain language of the first clause of the Amendment.

★ ★ ★

The simple language of the Amendment applies equally to seizures of persons and to seizures of property. Our analysis in this case may therefore properly commence with rules that have been well established in Fourth Amendment litigation involving tangible items. As the Court reiterated just a few years ago, the "physical entry of the home is the chief evil against which the wording of the Fourth Amendment is directed." *United States v. United States District Court,* 407 U.S. 297, 313. And we have long adhered to the view that the warrant procedure minimizes the danger of needless intrusions of that sort.

It is a "basic principle of Fourth Amendment law" that searches and seizures inside a home without a warrant are presumptively unreasonable.

★ ★ ★

The Fourth Amendment protects the individual's privacy in a variety of settings. In none is the zone of privacy more clearly defined than when bounded by the unambiguous physical dimensions of an individual's home—a zone that finds its roots in clear and specific constitutional terms: "The right of the people to be secure in their…houses…shall not be violated." That language unequivocally establishes the proposition that,

> [a]t the very core [of the Fourth Amendment] stands the right of a man to retreat into his own home and there be free from unreasonable governmental intrusion. *Silverman v. United States,* 365 U.S. 505, 511.

In terms that apply equally to seizures of property and to seizures of persons, the Fourth Amendment has drawn a firm line at the entrance to the house. Absent exigent circumstances, that threshold may not reasonably be crossed without a warrant.

★ ★ ★

[W]e note the State's suggestion that only a search warrant based on probable cause to believe the suspect is at home at a given time can adequately protect the privacy interests at stake, and since such a warrant requirement is manifestly impractical, there need be no warrant of any kind. We find this ingenious argument unpersuasive. It is true that an arrest warrant requirement may afford less protection than a search warrant requirement, but it will suffice to interpose the magistrate's determination of probable cause between the zealous officer and the citizen. If there is sufficient evidence of a citizen's participation in a felony to persuade a judicial officer that his arrest is justified, it is constitutionally reasonable to require him to open his doors to the officers of the law. Thus, for Fourth Amendment purposes, an arrest warrant founded on probable cause implicitly carries with it the limited authority to enter a dwelling in which the suspect lives when there is reason to believe the suspect is within.

Because no arrest warrant was obtained in either of these cases, the judgments must be reversed and the cases remanded to the New York Court of Appeals for further proceedings not inconsistent with this opinion.

It is so ordered.

COMMENTS, NOTES, AND QUESTIONS

1. Could you make an argument that arresting a suspected murderer constitutes an emergency so that to attempt to arrest the individual at his home should not require a warrant so long as there is probable cause for the arrest? Does it seem like Payton was the kind of person who might commit new serious crimes if he were not apprehended quickly? Would some suspected murderers be so dangerous that capturing that kind of individual would clearly be supportable as an emergency? What about a person who has killed several members of his or her immediate family, and it appears that there may be others on the suspected killer's list? Could this constitute an emergency that should relieve the police of obtaining an arrest warrant if they arrest the individual inside his or her home? Why or why not?

2. If police had conducted a "hot pursuit" of Payton from the crime scene to his apartment, they could have entered immediately without the need of a warrant. This situation constitutes an example of an emergency situation where the need for an arrest warrant to arrest within the home in not a requirement. See *Warden v. Hayden,* 387 U.S. 294 (1967), where the Court approved of the practice of allowing police to enter a home without a warrant to find an accused robber on the run. What if Payton had been home and the police asked him to step outside? Could Payton have been properly arrested at that moment without an arrest warrant? When police possess probable cause to arrest, may police step just inside a suspected drug dealer's doorway and make a warrantless arrest within the home? See *Kirk v. Louisiana,* 536 U.S. 635 (2002). Could this be considered an example of hot pursuit?

3. A clear case in which there would be no doubt concerning a lawful warrantless arrest within the arrestee's home would be where police have entered following a shootout with a person inside the home or where a person had a hostage within the home while holding police at bay with a weapon or by threatening the well-being of the hostage. An arrest that follows one of these situations would be lawful in the absence of a warrant to enter the home. The theory allowing an immediate entry would involve hot pursuit in the shooting situation and exigent circumstances (emergency) in the hostage scenario.

CASE 4.2

Fourth Amendment Expectation of Privacy in Particular Places

Kyllo v. United States
Supreme Court of the United States
533 U.S. 27 (2001)

FACTS

An agent of the Department of the Interior of the United States developed suspicions that one Danny Kyllo might have been growing and might continue to grow marijuana in one apartment of a triplex in Florence, Oregon. Indoor cultivation of marijuana typically requires high intensity lamps that substitute for sunlight and which create a warmer atmosphere than is usually kept in private homes. In an effort to measure the amount of excess heat that might be escaping from Kyllo's place of residence, the agent from the Department of the Interior, associated with another law enforcement agent, procured an Agema Thermovision 210 thermal imaging scanner to scan Kyllo's home. The image produced by the scanner portrayed shades of grey that represented relative temperatures of the residence. White portions of the image indicated warm surfaces while black portions indicated cold surfaces. The agents performed the scan from across the street from Kyllo's home and from an automobile and did not invade the home in any way. The machine read escaping heat and did not intrude into the home. The scan revealed that Kyllo's garage roof and the side wall were relatively hot compared to the rest of his home and substantially warmer than the signature offered by neighboring residential units.

The scan was done without a warrant and not under circumstances indicating an emergency, but produced sufficient evidence to permit a federal judicial official to issue a warrant for a traditional search of Kyllo's home. The search pursuant to the warrant disclosed more than 100 marijuana plants growing inside the home.

Kyllo tendered a conditional guilty plea, reserving his right to appeal the search and seizure issue. The Ninth Circuit Court of Appeal remanded the case for a determination concerning the intrusiveness of the imaging machinery. The District Court found that the Agema 210 was not a device that intruded into the inside of a home; it did not show people or activity within the home; and it did not reveal intimate human conduct. The Ninth Circuit subsequently found that there had been no violation of the Fourth Amendment in the original scan of the home and that the warrant had been properly issued. The Court upheld the conviction.

The Supreme Court granted certiorari to Kyllo's petition for review of the decision of the Ninth Circuit Court of Appeal.

PROCEDURAL ISSUE

Where police make a warrantless scan of the exterior of a home using non-intrusive imaging devices that read only heat emanated from a residential structure, does such practice constitute a search of a home for which a warrant is traditionally required under the Fourth Amendment?

HELD: YES

RATIONALE

Justice Scalia delivered the opinion of the Court.

⋆ ⋆ ⋆

II

The Fourth Amendment provides that "[t]he right of the people to be secure in their persons, houses, papers, and effects, against unreasonable searches and seizures, shall not be violated." "At the very core" of the Fourth Amendment "stands the right of a man to retreat into his own home and there be free from unreasonable governmental intrusion." *Silverman v. United States,* 365 U.S. 505, 511 (1961). With few exceptions, the question whether a warrantless search of a home is reasonable and hence constitutional must be answered no. See *Illinois v. Rodriguez,* 497 U.S. 177, 181 (1990); *Payton v. New York,* 445 U.S. 573, 586 (1980).

On the other hand, the antecedent question of whether or not a Fourth Amendment "search" has occurred is not so simple under our precedent. The permissibility of ordinary visual surveillance of a home used to be clear because, well into the 20th century, our Fourth Amendment jurisprudence was tied to common law trespass. See, e.g., *Goldman v. United States,* 316 U.S. 129, 134–136 (1942); *Olmstead v. United States,* 277 U.S. 438, 464–466 (1928). Cf. *Silverman v. United States,* supra, at 510–512 (technical trespass not necessary for Fourth Amendment violation; it suffices if there is "actual intrusion into a constitutionally protected area"). Visual surveillance was unquestionably lawful because "'the eye cannot by the laws of England be guilty of a trespass.'" *Boyd v. United States*, 116 U.S. 616, 628 (1886) (quoting *Entick v. Carrington*, 19 How.St.Tr. 1029, 95 Eng.Rep. 807 (K.B. 1765)). We have since decoupled violation of a person's Fourth Amendment rights from trespassory violation of his property, see *Rakas v. Illinois*, 439 U.S. 128, 143 (1978), but the lawfulness of warrantless visual surveillance of a home has still been preserved. As we observed in *California v. Ciraolo*, 476 U.S. 207, 213 (1986),

> [t]he Fourth Amendment protection of the home has never been extended to require law enforcement officers to shield their eyes when passing by a home on public thoroughfares.

One might think that the new validating rationale would be that examining the portion of a house that is in plain public view, while it is a "search" despite the absence of trespass, is not an "unreasonable" one under the Fourth Amendment. See *Minnesota v. Carter*, 525 U.S. 83, 104 (1998) (Breyer, J., concurring in judgment). But in fact we have held that visual observation is no "search" at all—perhaps in order to preserve somewhat more intact our doctrine that warrantless searches are presumptively unconstitutional. In assessing when a search is not a search, we have applied somewhat in reverse the principle first enunciated in *Katz v. United States*, 389 U.S. 347 (1967). Katz involved eavesdropping by means of an electronic listening device placed on the outside of a telephone booth—a location not within the catalog ("persons, houses, papers, and effects") that the Fourth Amendment protects against unreasonable searches. We held that the Fourth Amendment nonetheless protected Katz from the warrantless eavesdropping because he "justifiably relied" upon the privacy of the telephone booth. *Id.* at 353. As Justice Harlan's oft-quoted concurrence described it, a Fourth Amendment search occurs when the government violates a subjective expectation of privacy that society recognizes as reasonable. See *id.* at 361. We have subsequently applied this principle to hold that a Fourth Amendment search does not occur—even when the explicitly protected location of a house is concerned—unless "the individual manifested a subjective expectation of privacy in the object of the challenged search," and "society [is] willing to recognize that expectation as reasonable." *Ciraolo, supra*, at 211. We have applied this test in holding that it is not a search for the police to use a pen register at the phone company to determine what numbers were dialed in a private home, *Smith v. Maryland*, 442 U.S. 735, 743–744 (1979), and we have applied the test on two different occasions in holding that

aerial surveillance of private homes and surrounding areas does not constitute a search, *Ciraolo, supra; Florida v. Riley*, 488 U.S. 445 (1989).

The present case involves officers on a public street engaged in more than naked-eye surveillance of a home.... While we upheld enhanced aerial photography of an industrial complex in *Dow Chemical*, we noted that we found "it important that this is *not* an area immediately adjacent to a private home, where privacy expectations are most heightened," 476 U.S. at 237, n. 4 (emphasis in original).

[The government argued that the conviction should be upheld, since the imaging only detected heat that radiated from the residence and was not an intrusive search of the interior of the home. The Court rejected the mechanical analysis, since more sophisticated equipment in the near future may be capable of "looking" inside the home without any physical intrusion. The Court rejected the government contention that the imaging of the home met constitutional standards, since it did not detect private activities occurring in private areas of the home. Additionally, were the Court to enter the labyrinth of determining which activities within the home deserve "private" protection, the door would have been opened to endless litigation.]

We have said that the Fourth Amendment draws "a firm line at the entrance to the house," *Payton*, 445 U.S. at 590. That line, we think, must be not only firm, but also bright—which requires clear specification of those methods of surveillance that require a warrant. While it is certainly possible to conclude from the videotape of the thermal imaging that occurred in this case that no "significant" compromise of the homeowner's privacy has occurred, we must take the long view, from the original meaning of the Fourth Amendment forward.

> The Fourth Amendment is to be construed in the light of what was deemed an unreasonable search and seizure when it was adopted, and in a manner which will conserve public interests as well as the interests and rights of individual citizens. *Carroll v. United States*, 267 U.S. 132, 149 (1925).

Where, as here, the Government uses a device that is not in general public use, to explore details of the home that would previously have been unknowable without physical intrusion, the surveillance is a "search" and is presumptively unreasonable without a warrant.

Since we hold the Thermovision imaging to have been an unlawful search, it will remain for the District Court to determine whether, without the evidence it provided, the search warrant issued in this case was supported by probable cause—and if not, whether there is any other basis for supporting admission of the evidence that the search pursuant to the warrant produced.

★ ★ ★

The judgment of the Court of Appeals is reversed; the case is remanded for further proceedings consistent with this opinion.

It is so ordered.

COMMENTS, NOTES, AND QUESTIONS

1. Under the decision, the *Kyllo* Court held that thermal imaging of a home requires a warrant if the goal is to produce admissible evidence. Do you believe that measuring heat leaving a home must be equated with looking into the interior of a home? Did the Court make a mistake in determining that imaging requires a warrant? Or does the practice of scanning a home for heat emanation constitute the collection of the same information that the officers could otherwise obtain only by a physical entry? If so, then the Court may be right, since the imaging machine produces evidence that could have been obtained only from within the home. Could the Court have noted that any information the officers could have collected by the unassisted senses would be admissible but that sensations or perceptions obtained by enhanced means transgress the expectation of privacy? Would this approach make sense under the Fourth Amendment?

2. Under normal circumstances, merely looking at a house or apartment would not constitute a search by law enforcement agents. Were officers to observe evidence of criminality or suspicions of criminality, there would be no reason not to act on the information. Observing the heat from a home, arguably, should not be any different, since the officers are merely looking at a home with a device that enables them to "see" the heat leaving the home and not to see inside the home. Since no intrusion occurred, why should this activity be labeled a search? Consult the *Katz* case mentioned in *Kyllo*, where the officers did not make a physical trespass to a protected area but were deemed to have violated the privacy of Katz. Concepts of trespass for property law may indicate a starting point for some Fourth Amendment evaluations but may not always resolve the issue of whether an expectation of privacy is reasonable under the circumstances.

3. Kyllo could have enhanced his expectation of privacy under Fourth Amendment interpretations by insulating his home to prevent the heat from escaping, thus preventing the creation of an image on the Thermovision device. Would his claim under the Fourth Amendment have been even stronger if he had taken steps to contain the heat or insulate his house against heat loss? If the heat went through his roof, according to the instant case, would there be any expectation of privacy? How would you argue in Kyllo's case if the police had used the thermal imager from the air? Would the principles of *Kyllo* lawfully allow a thermal scan from an aircraft? Why or why not?

CASE 4.3

Search Incident to Arrest Requires an Arrest

Knowles v. Iowa
Supreme Court of the United States
525 U.S. 113 (1998)

FACTS

A Newton, Iowa, police officer stopped Knowles for speeding and issued the standard speeding ticket. Although Iowa law gave the officer the option of issuing a speeding ticket or arresting a speeder, the officer did not arrest Knowles. Subsequent to the stop, the officer conducted a full search of Knowles' automobile and found a bag of marijuana and a pipe used for smoking marijuana. The officer arrested Knowles and charged him with violation of state laws dealing with controlled substances.

Prior to trial, Knowles filed a motion to suppress the evidence of drug use on the theory that the search was not justified as incident to arrest under *United States v. Robinson,* 414 U.S. 218 (1973) since he had not been arrested. The officer conceded that he had neither Knowles' consent nor probable cause to conduct the search but contended that, since Iowa law allowed a search anytime he could have made an arrest, the search was lawful. Iowa provides that Iowa peace officers having probable cause to believe that a person has violated any traffic or motor vehicle equipment law may arrest that person and immediately take that person before a magistrate. Iowa law also authorizes the far more usual practice of issuing a traffic citation in lieu of making an arrest. The Iowa Supreme Court had approved the use of full searches where the officer declined to make an arrest but had issued a citation. The trial court denied the motion to suppress the drug evidence.

The Supreme Court of Iowa affirmed the trial court, holding that so long as the officer had probable cause to make an arrest, there need not in fact have been a custodial arrest to justify the search. The Supreme Court of the United States granted certiorari.

PROCEDURAL ISSUE

Consistent with the Fourth Amendment, may probable cause to arrest an automobile driver justify a full search of an automobile incident to probable cause to arrest where the police never arrest the driver?

HELD: NO

RATIONALE

Chief Justice Rehnquist delivered the opinion of the court.

★ ★ ★

In [*United States v. Robinson,* 414 U.S. 218 (1973)], we noted the two historical rationales for the "search incident to arrest" exception: (1) the need to disarm the suspect in order to take him into custody, and (2) the need to preserve evidence for later use at trial. 414 U.S. at 234. *See also United States v. Edwards,* 415 U.S. 800, 802–803 (1974); *Chimel v. California,* 395 U.S. 752, 762–763 (1969); [other citations omitted]. But neither of these underlying rationales for the search incident to arrest exception is sufficient to justify the search in the present case.

We have recognized that the first rationale—officer safety—is "'both legitimate and weighty,'" *Maryland v. Wilson,* 519 U.S. 408, 412 (1997) (quoting *Pennsylvania v. Mimms,* 434 U.S. 106, 110 (1977) (*per curiam*)). The threat to officer safety from issuing a traffic citation, however, is a good deal less than in the case of a custodial arrest. In *Robinson,* we stated that a custodial arrest involves "danger to an officer" because of "the extended exposure which follows the taking of a suspect into custody and transporting him to the police station." 414 U.S. at 234–235. We recognized that

> "[t]he danger to the police officer flows from the fact of the arrest, and its attendant proximity, stress, and uncertainty, and not from the grounds for arrest." Id. at 234, n. 5.

A routine traffic stop, on the other hand, is a relatively brief encounter, and "is more analogous to a so-called 'Terry stop'…than to a formal arrest." *Berkemer v. McCarty,* 468 U.S. 420, 437 (1984). See also *Cupp v. Murphy,* 412 U.S. 291, 296 (1973) ("Where there is no formal arrest…, a person might well be less hostile to the police and less

likely to take conspicuous, immediate steps to destroy incriminating evidence").

This is not to say that the concern for officer safety is absent in the case of a routine traffic stop. It plainly is not. But while the concern for officer safety in this context may justify the "minimal" additional intrusion of ordering a driver and passengers out of the car, it does not, by itself, justify the often considerably greater intrusion attending a full field-type search. Even without the search authority Iowa urges, officers have other, independent bases to search for weapons and protect themselves from danger. For example, they may order out of a vehicle both the driver, *Mimms, supra,* at 111, and any passengers, *Wilson, supra,* at 414; perform a "pat-down" of a driver and any passengers upon reasonable suspicion that they may be armed and dangerous, *Terry v. Ohio,* 392 U.S. 1 (1968); conduct a "*Terry* pat-down" of the passenger compartment of a vehicle upon reasonable suspicion that an occupant is dangerous and may gain immediate control of a weapon, *Michigan v. Long,* 463 U.S. 1032, 1049 (1983); and even conduct a full search of the passenger compartment, including any containers therein, pursuant to a custodial arrest, *New York v. Belton,* 453 U.S. 454, 460 (1981).

Nor has Iowa shown the second justification for the authority to search incident to arrest—the need to discover and preserve evidence. Once Knowles was stopped for speeding and issued a citation, all the evidence necessary to prosecute that offense had been obtained. No further evidence of excessive speed was going to be found either on the person of the offender or in the passenger compartment of the car.

Iowa nevertheless argues that a "search incident to citation" is justified because a suspect who is subject to a routine traffic stop may attempt to hide or destroy evidence related to his identity (e.g., a driver's license or vehicle registration), or destroy evidence of another as-yet undetected crime. As for the destruction of evidence relating to identity, if a police officer is not satisfied with the identification furnished by the driver, this may be a basis for arresting him rather than merely issuing a citation. As for destroying evidence of other crimes, the possibility that an officer would stumble onto evidence wholly unrelated to the speeding offense seems remote.

In *Robinson,* we held that the authority to conduct a full field search as incident to an arrest was a "bright-line rule," which was based on the concern for officer safety and destruction or loss of evidence, but which did not depend in every case upon the existence of either concern. Here, we are asked to extend that "bright-line rule" to a situation where the concern for officer safety is not present to the same extent, and the concern for destruction or loss of evidence is not present at all. We decline to do so. The judgment of the Supreme Court of Iowa is reversed, and the cause remanded for further proceedings not inconsistent with this opinion.

It is so ordered.

COMMENTS, NOTES, AND QUESTIONS

1. What are some of the reasons to search an arrestee after an arrest? What are the odds that a person may be armed? Or dangerous? Or carrying contraband? Would some arrestees be more likely to be armed than others? Would it be reasonable to search only those arrestees for whom there is a special reason to believe they might be armed? According to *United States v. Robinson,* 414 U.S. 218, 234 (1973), there are two reasons to search the person of the arrestee: the need to disarm the suspect in order to take him into custody and the need to preserve evidence for later use at trial. Could you think of other perfectly reasonable arguments in support of searching the person of the arrestee? What would they be?

2. On the merits of the *Knowles* case, would you advocate arresting every single driver for whom probable cause to arrest existed? Would that solve the problem in *Knowles* of the validity of a search incident to arrest? Why or why not? Could this be extended to loitering, jaywalking, and similar minor offenses for which local law might permit an arrest? From a police operational perspective and as a practical matter, what problems might this "arrest everyone" policy create?

CASE 4.4

Automobile Search Requires Probable Cause but Not a Warrant

Chambers v. Maroney
Supreme Court of the United States
399 U.S. 42 (1970)

FACTS

Two males robbed the attendant operating a gasoline station in North Braddock, Pennsylvania. The robber in charge instructed the station employee to place the coins in his right-hand glove, which was then stolen by the robber. Kovacich, the station employee, described one of the robbers as wearing a green sweater while his companion sported a trench coat. Additional information was supplied by two teenagers who had reported observing two men fitting the description of the robbers driving away in a blue station wagon.

Police officers spotted and stopped a blue station wagon matching the witnesses' description. The four males traveling in the automobile were stopped for further inquiry. Two of the male occupants' descriptions matched those given by Kovacich. Police noticed that Chambers was seated inside the automobile while wearing a green sweater. The police arrested the occupants and had the station wagon removed to the police station.

A complete search of the automobile at the police station disclosed two .38-caliber revolvers, a right hand glove complete with small change, and cards bearing the name of an attendant who had been the victim of a robbery a week earlier. While the station house search of petitioner Chambers' automobile was conducted without a warrant, the police conducted a subsequent search of his home pursuant to a warrant issued for that purpose. Ammunition for the gun found in the auto was discovered during the search of his home.

At the trial, the prosecutor introduced the evidence from both the automobile and from his home against Frank Chambers. Through counsel, he objected to the admission of the evidence from his automobile since the search had been conducted without a warrant and Chambers alleged that there existed no proper excuse for failure to obtain one.

Chambers' efforts at judicial relief proved less than successful so he filed a petition for habeas corpus in the appropriate federal court. When the court denied the initial petition, Chambers appealed to the Court of Appeals for the Third Circuit. The Court of Appeals affirmed and the Supreme Court of the United States granted certiorari to consider his claims.

PROCEDURAL ISSUE

Following a probable cause arrest where the arrestees have been removed from an automobile for which probable cause to search exists, must police officers obtain a search warrant prior to conducting a valid search of the automobile?

HELD: NO

RATIONALE

Mr. Justice White delivered the opinion of the Court.

★ ★ ★

We pass quickly the claim that the search of the automobile was the fruit of an unlawful arrest. Both the courts below thought the arresting officer had probable cause to make the arrest. We agree. Having talked to the teen-age observers and to the victim Kovacich, the police had ample cause to stop a light blue compact station wagon carrying four men and to arrest the occupants, one of whom was wearing a green sweater and one of whom had a trench coat with him in the car.

Even so, the search that produced the incriminating evidence was made at the police station some time after the arrest and cannot be justified as a search incident to an arrest: "Once an accused is under arrest and in custody, then a search made at another place without a warrant, is simply not incident to the arrest." *Preston v. United States,* 376 U.S. 364, is to the same effect; the reasons that have been thought sufficient to justify warrantless searches carried out in connection with an arrest no longer obtain when the accused is safely in custody at the station house.

There are, however, alternative grounds arguably justifying the search of the car in this case. In *Preston, supra,* the arrest was for vagrancy; it was apparent that the officers had no cause to believe that the evidence of crime was concealed in the auto….Here the situation is different for the police had probable cause to believe that the robbers, carrying guns and the fruits of the crime, had fled the scene in a light blue compact station wagon which would be carrying four men, one wearing a green sweater and another wearing a trench coat. As the state courts correctly held, there was probable cause to arrest the occupants of the station wagon that the officers stopped; just as obviously was there probable cause to search the car for guns and stolen money.

In terms of the circumstances justifying a warrantless search, the Court has long distinguished between an automobile and a home or office. In *Carroll v. United States,* 267 U.S. 132 (1925), the issue was the admissibility in evidence of contraband liquor seized in a warrantless search of a car on a highway. After surveying the law from the time of the adoption of the Fourth Amendment onward, the Court held that an automobile and other conveyances may be searched without a warrant in circumstances which would not justify the search without a warrant of a house or an office, provided that there is probable cause to believe that the car contains the articles that the officers are entitled to seize.

★ ★ ★

On the facts before us, the blue station wagon could have been searched on the spot when it was stopped since there was probable cause to search and it was a fleeting target for a search. The probable cause factor still maintained at the station house and so did the mobility of the car unless the Fourth Amendment permits a warrantless seizure of the car and the denial of its use to anyone until a warrant is secured.

[The Court approved the warrantless arrests of the defendants on the theory that police possessed probable cause for the arrests. Since probable cause to stop the vehicle to arrest the occupants existed, and the subsequent warrantless arrests and motor vehicle search proved legal, the Court upheld the convictions. The Court affirmed the legality of the search of the automobile at the police station because a warrant is not generally needed for a search of an automobile.]

COMMENTS, NOTES, AND QUESTIONS

1. What was the rationale of the *Chambers* Court for not requiring a warrant for the typical motor vehicle search? Does the easy mobility of the vehicle play a role in allowing a warrantless search? Since the Fourth Amendment did not mention motor vehicles, has the Court created an exception to the general requirement of a warrant under the Fourth Amendment? One clear factor in allowing warrantless vehicle searches concerns the difficulty of obtaining a warrant in one jurisdiction only to find that the vehicle had moved out of the jurisdiction to where the warrant would not be lawful. Would seizing and immobilizing the vehicle on the street be reasonable while police wait for a warrant? The Fourth Amendment also regulates seizures, which must be reasonable under the circumstances. Would such a seizure be reasonable under the teaching of *Chambers*? Consider *Carroll v. United States,* 267 U.S. 132 (1925), where the Court approved an immediate, warrantless, probable cause search of a vehicle believed to be transporting illegal alcoholic beverages. Hence, the vehicle exception to the Fourth Amendment requirement of a warrant has often been called the "*Carroll* doctrine," at least when applied to a vehicle that is actually moving.

2. Could you conceive of a situation in which a motor vehicle search should require a warrant? What about a motor home that has no engine or wheels and has been placed on cement blocks and used for seasonal hunting? Should a search of the vehicle require a warrant? It has more in common with a home than with a motor vehicle. Should that make a difference? What about searching a

motor home parked in a beach parking area where the police had information that the occupier was trading marijuana for sexual contact with teenagers? Should the motor home be subject to a search without a warrant? Does this situation seem to be similar to that for any motor vehicle? What if police have observed the driver attempting to drive away, but it becomes obvious that the motor home will not start? Should that make a case for a warrant to search? Some motor homes and similarly situated vehicles might not require any more than probable cause in order to conduct a valid search. For a case that had similar facts, see *California v. Carney,* 471 U.S. 386 (1985).

3. Should a warrant be required to search a car when the owner of the car is already in police custody? In *Coolidge v. New Hampshire,* 403 U.S. 443 (1971), police searched a vehicle for evidence in a homicide case. The vehicle had been parked in front of the suspect's home when the police became interested in its contents. When the warrant that purported to authorize the search proved invalid, the prosecution sought to justify the search on the basis of the *Carroll* doctrine, which allowed the warrantless search of an automobile given probable cause. The Court refused to extend *Carroll* to an automobile that had not been stopped while being driven on the highway, where the police had full control of the automobile, and where the suspect already had full opportunity to tamper with any evidence that might have been present. The *Coolidge* Court distinguished *Carroll* by stating that in *Coolidge* there was "no alerted criminal bent on flight, no fleeting opportunity on an open highway after a hazardous chase, no contraband or stolen goods or weapons, no confederates waiting to move the evidence and no other reasons to bring *Coolidge* within the vehicle exception to the warrant requirement."

CASE 4.5

Probable Cause to Search Motor Vehicle May Permit Container Search

United States v. Ross
Supreme Court of the United States
456 U.S. 798 (1982)

FACTS

Officer Marcum, a District of Columbia policeman, received information from an informant of proven past

reliability that a specifically described person known as "Bandit" was selling narcotics from a trunk of a particularly described automobile parked in front of 439 Ridge Street. Marcum and other officers initiated an investigation concerning the license plate number, the registered owner of the vehicle, and the personal description.

Upon first inspection by Marcum, no one seemed to be involved with the automobile, but five minutes later the officer observed the defendant driving the auto down the street. Since the subject matched the earlier description, the officers stopped the car. A complete probable cause search of the vehicle's interior revealed a cartridge on the front seat and a brown paper bag containing glassine packets of heroin. A subsequent warrantless search of the car's trunk at the police station disclosed a zippered leather pouch that contained a quantity of cash.

Police charged Ross with possession of heroin with intent to distribute and he was convicted. His argument, that the heroin was illegally seized and should not have been introduced into evidence, failed. The Court of Appeals reversed the conviction on the theory that, although the officers had proper legal authority to stop and search the automobile, the search exceeded permissible scope of a lawful search because police looked inside the brown paper bag. The Court of Appeals concluded that Ross had an expectation of privacy within the containers and that neither container should have been opened without a warrant or other proper legal theory.

PROCEDURAL ISSUE

In the absence of a search warrant, may police officers who have probable cause to search a motor vehicle for a particular object search any place within the vehicle where the object of the search could have been hidden?

HELD: YES

RATIONALE

Justice Stevens delivered the opinion of the Court.

★ ★ ★

III

The rationale justifying a warrantless search of an automobile that is believed to be transporting contraband arguably applies with equal force to any movable container that is believed to be carrying an illicit substance. That argument, however, was squarely rejected in *United States v. Chadwick*, 433 U.S. 1 (1977).

Chadwick involved the warrantless search of a 200-pound footlocker secured with two padlocks. Federal railroad officials in San Diego became suspicious when they noticed that a brown footlocker loaded into a train bound for Boston was unusually heavy and leaking talcum powder, a substance often used to mask the odor of marijuana. Narcotics agents met the train in Boston and a trained police dog signaled the presence of a controlled substance inside the footlocker. The agents did not seize the footlocker, however, at this time; they waited until respondent Chadwick arrived and his footlocker was placed in the trunk of Chadwick's automobile. Before the engine was started, the officers arrested Chadwick and his two companions. The agents then removed the footlocker to a secured place, opened it without a warrant, and discovered a large quantity of marijuana.

★ ★ ★

The Court in *Chadwick* specifically rejected the argument that the warrantless search was "reasonable" because a footlocker has some of the mobile characteristics that support warrantless searches of automobiles. The Court recognized that "a person's expectations of privacy in personal luggage are substantially greater than in an automobile," and noted that the practical problems associated with the temporary detention of a piece of luggage during the period of time necessary to obtain a warrant are significantly less than those associated with the detention of an automobile. In ruling that the warrantless search of the footlocker was unjustified, the Court reaffirmed the general principle that closed packages and containers may not be searched without a warrant. In sum, the Court in *Chadwick* declined to extend the rationale of the "automobile exception" to permit a warrantless search of any movable container found in a public place.

The facts in *Arkansas v. Sanders*, 442 U.S. 753 (1979), were similar to those in *Chadwick*. In *Sanders*, a Little Rock police officer received information from a reliable informant that Sanders would arrive at the local airport on a specified flight that afternoon carrying a green suitcase containing marijuana. The officer went to the airport. Sanders arrived on schedule and retrieved a green suitcase from the airline baggage service. Sanders gave the suitcase to a waiting companion who placed it in the trunk of a taxi. Sanders and his companion drove off in the cab; police officers followed and stopped the taxi several blocks

from the airport. The officers opened the trunk, seized the suitcase, and searched it on the scene without a warrant. As predicted, the suitcase contained marijuana.

The Arkansas Supreme Court ruled that the warrantless search of the suitcase was impermissible under the Fourth Amendment, and this Court affirmed....

★ ★ ★

It is clear, however, that in neither *Chadwick* nor *Sanders* did the police have probable cause to search the vehicle or anything within it except the footlocker in the former case and the green suitcase in the latter.

Robbins v. California, 453 U.S. 420, however, was a case in which suspicion was not directed at a specific container. In that case the Court for the first time was forced to consider whether police officers who are entitled to conduct a warrantless search of an automobile stopped on a public roadway may open a container found within the vehicle. In the early morning of January 5, 1975, police officers stopped Robbins' station wagon because he was driving erratically. Robbins got out of the car, but later returned to obtain the vehicle's registration papers. When he opened the car door, the officers smelled marijuana smoke. One of the officers searched Robbins and discovered a vial of liquid; in a search of the interior of the car the officer found marijuana. The police officers then opened the tailgate of the station wagon and raised the cover of a recessed luggage compartment. In the compartment they found two packages wrapped in green opaque plastic. The police unwrapped the packages and discovered a large amount of marijuana in each.

Robbins was charged with various drug offenses and moved to suppress the contents of the plastic packages. The California Court of Appeal held that the "[s]earch of the automobile was proper when the officers learned that appellant was smoking marijuana when they stopped him" and that the warrantless search of the packages was justified because

> "the contents of the packages could have been inferred from their outward appearance, so that appellant could not have held a reasonable expectation of privacy with respect to the contents." 103 Cal.App.3d 34, 40, 162 Cal.Rptr. 780, 783 (1980).

This Court reversed. Writing for a plurality, Justice Stewart rejected the argument that the outward appearance of the packages precluded Robbins from having a reasonable expectation of privacy in their contents.... The plurality concluded that the warrantless search was impermissible because *Chadwick* and *Sanders* had established that

> "a closed piece of luggage found in a lawfully searched car is constitutionally protected to the same extent as are closed pieces of luggage found anywhere else." 453 U.S., at 425, 101 S.Ct., at 2845.

★ ★ ★

Unlike *Chadwick* and *Sanders,* in this case police officers had probable cause to search respondent's entire vehicle. Unlike *Robbins,* in this case the parties have squarely addressed the question whether, in the course of a legitimate warrantless search of an automobile, police are entitled to open containers found within the vehicle. We now address that question. Its answer is determined by the scope of the search that is authorized by the exception to the warrant requirement set forth in *Carroll.*

IV

★ ★ ★

A lawful search of fixed premises generally extends to the entire area in which the object of the search may be found and is not limited by the possibility that separate acts of entry or opening may be required to complete the search. Thus, a warrant that authorizes an officer to search a home for illegal weapons also provides authority to open closets, chests, drawers, and containers in which the weapon might be found. A warrant to open a footlocker to search for marijuana would also authorize the opening of packages found inside. A warrant to search a vehicle would support a search of every part of the vehicle that might contain the object of the search. When a legitimate search is under way, and when its purpose and its limits have been precisely defined, nice distinctions between closets, drawers, and containers, in the case of a home, or between glove compartments, upholstered seats, trunks, and wrapped packages, in the case of a vehicle, must give way to the interest in the prompt and efficient completion of the task at hand.

★ ★ ★

The scope of a warrantless search of an automobile thus is not defined by the nature of the container in which the contraband is secreted. Rather, it is defined by the object of the search and the places in which there is probable cause to believe that it may be found. Just as probable cause to believe that a stolen lawnmower may be found in a garage will not support a warrant to search an upstairs bedroom, probable cause to believe that undocumented aliens are being transported in a van will not justify a warrantless search of a suitcase. Probable cause to believe that a container placed in the trunk of a taxi contains contraband or evidence does not justify a search of the entire cab.

V

Our decision today is inconsistent with the disposition in *Robbins v. California* and with the portion of the opinion in *Arkansas v. Sanders* on which the plurality in *Robbins* relied. Nevertheless, the doctrine of *stare decisis* does not preclude this action. Although we have rejected some of the reasoning in *Sanders,* we adhere to our holding in that case; although we reject the precise holding in *Robbins,* there was no Court opinion supporting a single rationale for its judgment and the reasoning we adopt today was not presented by the parties in that case. Moreover, it is clear that no legitimate reliance interest can be frustrated by our decision today. Of greatest importance, we are convinced that the rule we apply in this case is faithful to the interpretation of the Fourth Amendment that the Court has followed with substantial consistency throughout our history.

★ ★ ★

The exception recognized in *Carroll* is unquestionably one that is "specifically established and well-delineated." We hold that the scope of the warrantless search authorized by that exception is no broader and no narrower than a magistrate could legitimately authorize by warrant. If probable cause justifies the search of a lawfully stopped vehicle, it justifies the search of every part of the vehicle and its contents that may conceal the object of the search.

The judgment of the Court of Appeals is reversed. The case is remanded for further proceedings consistent with this opinion.

COMMENTS, NOTES, AND QUESTIONS

1. If police have probable cause to believe that a twenty-year-old driver has alcohol inside her automobile, may the police search her purse and the automobile's

glove box? What arguments would you use to allow a search of the containers without a warrant? Does an adult female have some expectation of privacy in her purse? How does the *Ross* case help you argue in favor of a search of the purse? *Ross* permitted a search in any location within the vehicle where the object might be hidden, including separate containers. Given probable cause to search a motor vehicle, what is the extent of the permissible search? Can any closed container be legally opened by police? Does the scope of the search depend on the object of the search and the size of the area being searched?

2. From your reading of *Robbins* contained within *Ross,* did the Court successfully distinguish its holding in *Ross* from the holding in *Robbins v. California,* 453 U.S. 420? Has *Ross* overruled *Robbins*? Is that the operative effect?

3. The Court in *Chambers v. Maroney,* 399 U.S. 42 (1970), held that motor vehicles stopped on the road could be searched with or without a warrant so long as probable cause existed. This holding follows an earlier case[121] and excused the use of a warrant in *Ross.* On the same logic, could a home be searched without a warrant? Is there a Fourth Amendment distinction? Why should homes and motor vehicles be treated differently? Are the law enforcement interests similar when considering both searches?

4. How long should probable cause to search a vehicle exist? Should it remain several hours later when the vehicle has been in police custody the entire time? If probable cause originally existed, what could change to the point where probable cause no longer exists with respect to the vehicle? Where a warrantless search of an automobile happens incident to the arrest of the passenger in control of the vehicle, the legal authority to search an automobile stopped on the road remains for a period of time once police have full control over the vehicle according to the Supreme Court of the United States. Where police officers were justified in conducting an inventory search prior to towing a car within their custody, the discovery of two bags of marijuana in the unlocked glove compartment gave rise to probable cause to believe that the car might contain further contraband. A warrantless search of the air vents under the dashboard was held to have been proper. *Michigan v. Thomas,* 458 U.S. 259 (1982).

CASE 4.6

Warrantless Probable Cause Vehicle Container Searches

California v. Acevedo
Supreme Court of the United States
500 U.S. 565 (1991)

FACTS

A federal drug enforcement agent in Hawaii contacted Santa Ana, California, police that the government had seized drugs from the Federal Express system which were scheduled for local delivery in California. Federal agents sealed the package and had it sent to the Santa Ana police department, which, with the cooperation of the local Federal Express office, delivered the drugs to one J. R. Daza. The recipient obtained the package from the carrier's local office and drove to his apartment where he took the drug package inside.

While Daza was still under law enforcement observation, Charles Acevedo arrived at the apartment, entered Daza's apartment, and left after a ten-minute visit. As Acevedo headed for his automobile, police observed that he carried a brown paper bag of the same size as the marijuana shipped from Hawaii. Police observed Acevedo place the package in the trunk of a Honda and prepare to drive away. Officers stopped his car and conducted a warrantless search of the package only for what they believed was marijuana. A search of the brown bag revealed a quantity of marijuana.

Acevedo failed to have the evidence suppressed and pled guilty but reserved his right to appeal the denial of his Fourth Amendment claim that the bag had been improperly searched. The California Court of Appeal, Fourth District, reversed the trial court with the conclusion that although the police had probable cause to believe that the bag contained drugs, the bag should not have been opened without a warrant. According to the Court of Appeal, since the bag had been placed inside of the motor vehicle, a separate expectation of privacy existed under the circumstances. In addition, the Court of Appeal held that police lacked probable cause to believe that Acevedo's car itself otherwise contained contraband.

---

[121]See *Carroll v. United States,* 267 U.S. 132 (1925), where the Court permitted the stop and search of a motor vehicle where liquor was the suspected illegal cargo; however, the Court did not determine the precise limits to a search of an automobile stopped with probable cause.

The California Court of Appeal reasoned that the case was controlled by *United States v. Chadwick* (1977), where officers would have been permitted to seize a container for which probable cause existed but failed to obtain a needed warrant to open the container. The Supreme Court of California rejected the government's petition for review.

The Supreme Court of the United States granted certiorari for the purpose of clarifying search and seizure law applicable to a closed container in an automobile.

PROCEDURAL ISSUE

Where probable cause exists for the search of a container within an automobile and where there is no probable cause to search the entire vehicle, may police stop the car, seize the container, and search it without a warrant?

HELD: YES

RATIONALE

Justice Blackmun delivered the opinion of the Court.

★ ★ ★

II

★ ★ ★

In *United States v. Ross,* 456 U.S. 798, decided in 1982, we held that a warrantless search of an automobile under the *Carroll* doctrine could include a search of a container or package found inside the car when such a search was supported by probable cause....In *Ross,* therefore, we clarified the scope of the *Carroll* doctrine as properly including a "probing search" of compartments and containers within the automobile so long as the search is supported by probable cause.

In addition to this clarification, *Ross* distinguished the *Carroll* doctrine from the separate rule that governed the search of closed containers. The Court had announced this separate rule, unique to luggage and other closed packages, bags, and containers, in *United States v. Chadwick,* 433 U.S. 1 (1977). In *Chadwick,* federal narcotics agents had probable cause to believe that a 200-pound double-locked footlocker contained marijuana. The agents tracked the locker as the defendants removed it from a train and carried it through the station to a waiting car. As soon as the defendants lifted the locker into the trunk of the car, the agents arrested them, seized the locker, and searched it. In this Court, the United States did not contend that the locker's brief contact with the automobile's trunk sufficed to make the *Carroll* doctrine applicable. Rather, the United States urged that the search of movable luggage could be considered analogous to the search of an automobile. 433 U.S., at 11–12. The Court rejected this argument because, it reasoned, a person expects more privacy in his luggage and personal effects than he does in his automobile.

In *Arkansas v. Sanders,* 442 U.S. 753 (1979), the Court extended *Chadwick*'s rule to apply to a suitcase actually being transported in the trunk of a car. In *Sanders,* the police had probable cause to believe a suitcase contained marijuana. They watched as the defendant placed the suitcase in the trunk of a taxi and was driven away. The police pursued the taxi for several blocks, stopped, found the suitcase in the trunk, and searched it. Although the Court had applied the *Carroll* doctrine to searches of integral parts of the automobile itself (indeed, in *Carroll,* contraband whiskey was in the upholstery of the seats, *see* 267 U.S., at 136), it did not extend the doctrine to the warrantless search of personal luggage "merely because it was located in an automobile lawfully stopped by the police." Again, the *Sanders* majority stressed the heightened privacy expectation in personal luggage and concluded that the presence of luggage in an automobile did not diminish the owner's expectation of privacy in his personal items.

In *Ross,* the Court endeavored to distinguish between *Carroll,* which governed the *Ross* automobile search, and *Chadwick,* which governed the *Sanders* automobile search. It held that the *Carroll* doctrine covered searches of automobiles when the police had probable cause to search an entire vehicle but that the *Chadwick* doctrine governed searches of luggage when the officers had probable cause to search only a container within the vehicle. Thus, in a *Ross* situation, the police could conduct a reasonable search under the Fourth Amendment without obtaining a warrant, whereas in a *Sanders* situation, the police had to obtain a warrant before they searched.

★ ★ ★

III

★ ★ ★

The Court in *Ross* rejected *Chadwick*'s distinction between containers and cars....It also recognized that it was arguable that the same exigent circumstances that permit a warrantless search of an automobile would justify the warrantless search of a movable container. In deference to the rule of *Chadwick* and *Sanders,* however, the Court put that question to one side....We now must decide the question deferred in *Ross:* whether the Fourth Amendment requires the police to obtain a warrant to open the sack in a movable vehicle simply because they lack probable cause to search the entire car. We conclude that it does not.

IV

★ ★ ★

The line between probable cause to search a vehicle and probable cause to search a package in that vehicle is not always clear, and separate rules that govern the two objects to be searched may enable the police to broaden their power to make warrantless searches and disserve privacy interests....At the moment when officers stop an automobile, it may be less than clear whether they suspect with a high degree of certainty that the vehicle contains drugs in a bag or simply contains drugs. If the police know that they may open a bag only if they are actually searching the entire car, they may search more extensively than they otherwise would in order to establish the general probable cause required by *Ross.*

★ ★ ★

To the extent that the *Chadwick-Sanders* rule protects privacy, its protection is minimal. Law enforcement officers may seize a container and hold it until they obtain a search warrant. *Chadwick,* 433 U.S. at 13.

> Since the police, by hypothesis, have probable cause to seize the property, we can assume that a warrant will be routinely forthcoming in the overwhelming majority of cases.

And the police often will be able to search containers without a warrant, despite the *Chadwick-Sanders* rule, as a search incident to a lawful arrest. In *New York v. Belton,* 453 U.S. 454 (1981), the Court said:

> [W]e hold that when a policeman has made a lawful custodial arrest of the occupant of an automobile, he may, as a contemporaneous incident of that arrest, search the passenger compartment of that automobile.

It follows from this conclusion that the police may also examine the contents of any containers found within the passenger compartment. *Id.,* at 460.

★ ★ ★

In light of the minimal protection to privacy afforded by the *Chadwick-Sanders* rule, and our serious doubt whether that rule substantially serves privacy interests, we now hold that the Fourth Amendment does not compel a separate treatment for an automobile search that extends only to a container within the vehicle.

V

★ ★ ★

Sanders was explicitly undermined in *Ross,* 456 U.S., at 824, and the existence of the dual regimes for automobile searches that uncover containers has proved as confusing as the *Chadwick* and *Sanders* dissenters predicted. We conclude that it is better to adopt one clear-cut rule to govern automobile searches and eliminate the warrant requirement for closed containers set forth in *Sanders.*

VI

★ ★ ★

In the case before us, the police had probable cause to believe that the paper bag in the automobile's trunk contained marijuana. That probable cause now allows a warrantless search of the paper bag. The facts in the record reveal that the police did not have probable cause to believe that contraband was hidden in any other part of the automobile and a search of the entire vehicle would have been without probable cause and unreasonable under the Fourth Amendment.

★ ★ ★

Until today, this Court has drawn a curious line between the search of an automobile that coincidentally turns up a container and the search of a container that coincidentally turns up in an automobile. The protections of the Fourth Amendment must not turn on such coincidences. We therefore interpret *Carroll* as providing one rule to govern all automobile searches. The police may search an automobile and the containers within it where they have probable cause to believe contraband or evidence is contained.

The judgment of the California Court of Appeal is reversed and the case is remanded to that court for further proceedings not inconsistent with this opinion.

It is so ordered.

COMMENTS, NOTES, AND QUESTIONS

1. Had Acevedo exited the apartment as he did but kept walking down the street and never entered a motor vehicle, could police have stopped and warrantlessly searched him and his baggage? Why or why not? How would you argue this? Can one expect a reduced level of privacy in automobiles? Is this the real teaching of *United States v. Ross*? One could argue that an inconsistency exists if, given probable cause, Acevedo and his container could not have been searched without a warrant had he walked down the street but could have been searched where he, as he did in this case, placed it inside his automobile. Should the Fourth Amendment expectation of privacy in a container depend on whether one is in an automobile or merely walking on the public street? Is there a logical distinction between the expectation of privacy while walking and driving a motor vehicle?

2. *Acevedo* teaches that police may search any container *within a motor vehicle* without a warrant provided probable cause exists to search the automobile for objects that police reasonably believe could be within the container. Similarly, police may not search containers that by their nature could not conceal the object of the search. For example, a stolen computer monitor could not reasonably be hidden within an automobile glove box, and where that object is the goal, looking inside the glove box would not constitute a reasonable search.

CASE 4.7

Drug Interdiction Roadblocks Unreasonable under Fourth Amendment

Indianapolis v. Edmond
Supreme Court of the United States
531 U.S. 32 (2000)

FACTS

The city of Indianapolis initiated a program operated by police which involved the use of roadblocks in particular locations within the city for the purposes of discovering individuals who might be trafficking in or using drugs or who were visibly impaired as drivers. There was no requirement that any particular driver be suspected of drug involvement. The police stopped a predetermined number of vehicles and then allowed all traffic to proceed while the stopped cars were processed. At each of the roadblock locations, police were stationed so that each automobile which was stopped would have one officer approach and ask for a driver's license and registration card. Each driver was told that he or she had been stopped at a drug checkpoint at which time the officer visibly looked over the automobile's interior and a drug sniffing dog walked around the outside of each vehicle. No vehicle was stopped out of sequence and no further search could be conducted unless the individual consented or particularized suspicion concerning drug use or possession developed. The checkpoints were operated generally during the daylight hours and had lighted signs displaying the message: "NARCOTICS CHECKPOINT ___ MILE AHEAD, NARCOTICS K-9 IN USE, BE PREPARED TO STOP."

Since James Edmond and others had been stopped at a narcotics checkpoint and believed that their rights under the Constitution had been violated, they filed a lawsuit on behalf of themselves and the class of all motorists who had been stopped or might be stopped under the program at the Indianapolis drug checkpoints. Edmond and the others claimed that the roadblocks violated the Fourth Amendment of the United States Constitution because they constituted an unreasonable stop and search due to lack of individualized suspicion. The federal district court denied their request for a preliminary injunction but the Court of Appeals reversed and the Supreme Court of the United States granted certiorari.

PROCEDURAL ISSUE

Consistent with the Fourth Amendment, may police officers set up roadblocks where the primary purpose was to check motorists for visible signs of drug use or possession where there has been no individualized suspicion directed toward the automobile or the driver?

HELD: NO

RATIONALE

Justice O'Connor delivered the opinion of the Court.

★ ★ ★

II

The Fourth Amendment requires that searches and seizures be reasonable. A search or seizure is ordinarily unreasonable in the absence of individualized suspicion of wrongdoing. *Chandler v. Miller,* 520 U.S. 305, 308 (1997). While such suspicion is not an "irreducible" component of reasonableness, *[United States v.] Martinez-Fuerte,* 428 U.S. at 561, we have recognized only limited circumstances in which the usual rule does not apply. For example, we have upheld certain regimes of suspicionless searches where the program was designed to serve "special needs, beyond the normal need for law enforcement." See, e.g., *Vernonia School Dist. 47J v. Acton,* 515 U.S. 646 (1995) (random drug testing of student athletes); *[National] Treasury Employees [Union] v. Von Raab,* 489 U.S. 656 (1989) (drug tests for United States Customs Service employees seeking transfer or promotion to certain positions); *Skinner v. Railway Labor Executives' Assn.,* 489 U.S. 602 (1989) (drug and alcohol tests for railway employees involved in train accidents or found to be in violation of particular safety regulations).

★ ★ ★

We have also upheld brief, suspicionless seizures of motorists at a fixed Border Patrol checkpoint designed to intercept illegal aliens, *Martinez-Fuerte, supra,* and at a sobriety checkpoint aimed at removing drunk drivers from the road, *Michigan Dept. of State Police v. Sitz,* 496 U.S. 444 (1990). In addition, in *Delaware v. Prouse,* 440 U.S. 648, 663 (1979), we suggested that a similar type of roadblock with the purpose of verifying drivers' licenses and vehicle registrations would be permissible. In none of these cases, however, did we indicate approval of a checkpoint program whose primary purpose was to detect evidence of ordinary criminal wrongdoing.

★ ★ ★

In *[Michigan v.] Sitz,* we evaluated the constitutionality of a Michigan highway sobriety checkpoint program. The *Sitz* checkpoint involved brief suspicionless stops of motorists so that police officers could detect signs of intoxication and remove impaired drivers from the road. 496 U.S. at 447–448. Motorists who exhibited signs of intoxication were diverted for a license and registration check and, if warranted, further sobriety tests. This checkpoint program was clearly aimed at reducing the immediate hazard posed by the presence of drunk drivers on the highways, and there was an obvious connection between the imperative of highway safety and the law enforcement practice at issue. The gravity of the drunk driving problem and the magnitude of the State's interest in getting drunk drivers off the road weighed heavily in our determination that the program was constitutional.

★ ★ ★

III

It is well established that a vehicle stop at a highway checkpoint effectuates a seizure within the meaning of the Fourth Amendment. See, *e.g., Sitz, supra,* at 450. The fact that officers walk a narcotics-detection dog around the exterior of each car at the Indianapolis checkpoints does not transform the seizure into a search. Just as in *Place,* an exterior sniff of an automobile does not require entry into the car, and is not designed to disclose any information other than the presence or absence of narcotics. Like the dog sniff in *Place,* a sniff by a dog[122] that simply walks around a car is "much less intrusive than a typical search." Rather, what principally distinguishes these checkpoints from those we have previously approved is their primary purpose.

★ ★ ★

We have never approved a checkpoint program whose primary purpose was to detect evidence of ordinary criminal wrongdoing. Rather, our checkpoint cases have recognized only limited exceptions to the general rule that a seizure must be accompanied by some measure of individualized suspicion. We suggested in *Prouse* that we would not credit the "general interest in crime control" as justification for a regime of suspicionless stops. Consistent with this suggestion, each of the checkpoint programs that we have approved[123] was designed primarily to serve

---

[122]In *United States v. Place,* 462 U.S. 696 (1983), the Court, among other things, held that a sniff by a drug dog is not a search under the Fourth Amendment.

[123]The Court has approved brief stops in a variety of contexts where there was no individualized suspicion. For example, in *Michigan v. Sitz,* 496 U.S. 444 (1990), the Court approved brief suspicionless stops of motorists so that police officers could detect signs of intoxication and remove impaired drivers from the road. In *United States v. Martinez-Fuerte,* 428 U.S. 543 (1976), the Court approved

purposes closely related to the problems of policing the border or the necessity of ensuring roadway safety. Because the primary purpose of the Indianapolis narcotics checkpoint program is to uncover evidence of ordinary criminal wrongdoing, the program contravenes the Fourth Amendment.

Petitioners propose several ways in which the narcotics detection purpose of the instant checkpoint program may instead resemble the primary purposes of the checkpoints in *Sitz* and *Martinez-Fuerte*. Petitioners state that the checkpoints in those cases had the same ultimate purpose of arresting those suspected of committing crimes. Securing the border and apprehending drunk drivers are, of course, law enforcement activities, and law enforcement officers employ arrests and criminal prosecutions in pursuit of these goals. If we were to rest the case at this high level of generality, there would be little check on the ability of the authorities to construct roadblocks for almost any conceivable law enforcement purpose. Without drawing the line at roadblocks designed primarily to serve the general interest in crime control, the Fourth Amendment would do little to prevent such intrusions from becoming a routine part of American life.

★ ★ ★

The primary purpose of the Indianapolis narcotics checkpoints is in the end to advance "the general interest in crime control," *Prouse*, 440 U.S. at 659, n. 18. We decline to suspend the usual requirement of individualized suspicion where the police seek to employ a checkpoint primarily for the ordinary enterprise of investigating crimes. We cannot sanction stops justified only by the generalized and ever-present possibility that interrogation and inspection may reveal that any given motorist has committed some crime.

★ ★ ★

Because the primary purpose of the Indianapolis checkpoint program is ultimately indistinguishable from the general interest in crime control, the checkpoints violate the Fourth Amendment. The judgment of the Court of Appeals is accordingly affirmed.

It is so ordered.

COMMENTS, NOTES, AND QUESTIONS

1. Would the *Edmond* Court be likely to approve a stop and visual search plan where the ostensible reason was to interdict alcohol-impaired drivers, while secondarily looking for evidence of drug possession or use? If police followed the approved course of action from *Michigan v. Sitz,* would it seem that so long as police were primarily looking for alcohol-impaired drivers, the secondary purpose of drug interdiction would be permissible? Could the police, at an alcohol road check, have a drug-sniffing dog walk around some of the cars? Would such a practice stand a good chance of finding support in the Supreme Court based on what *Edmond* held and the legal reasoning? Why or why not?

2. Normally, the Fourth Amendment, as interpreted, requires individual suspicion prior to any action being taken by a governmental law enforcement agent. Is the drunk-driving phenomenon sufficiently serious that we need to give up some freedoms under the Constitution to combat the scourge of alcohol-impaired drivers? If this diminution of freedom is done in the name of safety, why not allow police to do random drug checks on automobile drivers? In the name of safety and reasonableness, we could require a drug screen at the time of renewal of driver's licenses without any individualized suspicion. Would that make our roads safer? Would we get to the point where police might be able to ask where a person was going? Or what he or she planned to do that evening? It seems like the *Edmond* Court was attempting to draw a line on suspicionless searches beyond which it might not be willing to venture in the future.

CASE 4.8

Consent Searches Tested by the Totality of the Circumstances Test

Schneckloth v. Bustamonte
Supreme Court of the United States
412 U.S. 218 (1973)

FACTS

Early one morning, in Sunnyvale, California, at approximately 2:40 A.M., Officer James Rand stopped an automobile

---

immigration stops without any suspicion at fixed sites one hundred miles from the border. However, in *Delaware v. Prouse,* 440 U.S. 648 (1979), the Court refused to approve a suspicionless stop of a lone motorist to check driving documents.

being operated with improper safety equipment. Several men were inside the vehicle, among them Joe Gonzales, Joe Alcala, and Robert Bustamonte. When Gonzalez, who had been driving, could not produce any identification, Officer Rand requested identification from any of the others. Alcala proved to be the only one who produced a driver's license and volunteered the fact that the auto belonged to his brother.

When Officer Rand requested permission to search the vehicle, Alcala quickly consented. He opened the trunk in a spirit of cooperation. Inside the passenger compartment, the searching officers uncovered three stolen checks which police linked to the defendant, Robert Bustamonte. Prior to the discovery of the checks, no person was under arrest and no one was threatened with adverse consequences.

Bustamonte[124] alleged that consent to search the vehicle had not been properly given since Alcala did not know that he had the right to refuse consent. The trial court held that the search had been valid since consent had been properly requested and granted. As a result, the trial court convicted Bustamonte of unlawfully possessing a stolen check.

In affirming the conviction, the California Court of Appeal held that the state had met its burden of proving that valid consent was given by Alcala. The Court characterized the consent as having been given freely "without coercion or submission to authority."

Initial efforts at obtaining a writ of *habeas corpus* did not bear fruit, but the Court of Appeals for the Ninth Circuit reversed the District Court's denial of *habeas corpus.* It held that Alcala *must* have known that his consent could have been withheld and in the absence of this knowledge, consent to search the automobile was invalid. The Supreme Court of the United States granted certiorari.

PROCEDURAL ISSUE

In order to properly give consent to a search, must the person who has dominion and control over the property know that there is a legal right to refuse to grant consent?

HELD: NO

RATIONALE

Mr. Justice Stewart delivered the opinion of the Court.

★ ★ ★

The precise question in this case, then, is what must the state prove to demonstrate that a consent was "voluntarily" given. Both state and federal courts have reviewed the search involved in the case before us. The Court of Appeals for the Ninth Circuit concluded that it is an essential part of the State's initial burden to prove that a person knows he has a right to refuse consent. The California courts have followed the rule that voluntariness is a question of fact to be determined from the totality of all the circumstances, and that the state of a defendant's knowledge is only one factor to be taken into account in assessing the voluntariness of a consent.

A

The most extensive judicial exposition of the meaning of "voluntariness" has been developed in those cases in which the Court has had to determine the "voluntariness" of a defendant's confession for purposes of the Fourteenth Amendment. Almost 40 years ago, in *Brown v. Mississippi,* 297 U.S. 278, the Court held that a criminal conviction based upon a confession obtained by brutality and violence was constitutionally invalid under the Due Process Clause of the Fourteenth Amendment. In some 30 different cases decided during the era that intervened between *Brown* and *Escobedo v. Illinois,* 378 U.S. 478, 84 S.Ct. 1758, 12 L.Ed.2d 977, the Court was faced with the necessity of determining whether in fact the confession in issue has been "voluntarily" given. It is to that body of case law to which we turn for initial guidance on the meaning of "voluntariness" in the present context.

Those cases yield no talismanic definition of "voluntariness," mechanically applicable to the host of situations where the question has arisen. "The notion of 'voluntariness,'" Mr. Justice Frankfurter once wrote, "is itself an amphibian."

Rather, "voluntariness" has reflected an accommodation of the complex of values implicated in police

---

[124]Under more recent court decisions, Bustamonte probably would not have possessed any expectation of privacy under *Rakas v. Illinois,* 439 U.S. 128 (1978), and would not have been allowed to argue the merits of consent, since he could not show that his personal rights had been violated by searching the motor vehicle owned by another person.

questioning of a suspect. At one end of the spectrum, is the acknowledged need for police questioning as a tool for the effective enforcement of criminal laws. Without such investigation, those who were innocent might be falsely accused, those who were guilty might wholly escape prosecution, and many crimes would go unsolved. In short, the security of all would be diminished. [Citation omitted.] At the other end of the spectrum, is the set of values reflecting society's deeply felt belief that the criminal law cannot be used as an instrument of unfairness, and that the possibility of unfair and even brutal police tactics poses a real and serious threat to civilized notions of justice.

★ ★ ★

In determining whether a defendant's will was overborne in a particular case, the Court has assessed the totality of all the surrounding circumstances—both the characteristics of the accused and the details of the interrogation. Some of the factors taken into account have included the youth of the accused, his lack of education, or his low intelligence, the lack of any advice to the accused of his constitutional rights, the length of detention, the repeated and prolonged nature of the questioning, and the use of physical punishment such as the deprivation of food or sleep. [Citations omitted.] In all of these cases, the Court determined the factual circumstances surrounding the confession, assessed the psychological impact on the accused, and evaluated the legal significance of how the accused reacted.

The significant fact about all of these decisions is that none of them turned on the presence or absence of a single controlling criterion; each reflected a careful scrutiny of all the surrounding circumstances. In none of them did the Court rule that the Due Process Clause required the prosecution to prove as part of its initial burden that the defendant knew he had a right to refuse to answer the questions that were put. While the state of the accused's mind, and the failure of the police to advise the accused of his rights, were certainly factors to be evaluated in assessing the "voluntariness" of an accused's responses, they were not in and of themselves determinative.

★ ★ ★

B

Similar considerations lead us to agree with the courts of California that the question whether a consent to a

search was in fact "voluntary" or was the product of duress or coercion, express, or implied, is a question of fact to be determined from the totality of all the circumstances. While knowledge of the right to refuse consent is one factor to be taken into account, the government need not establish such knowledge as the *sine qua non* of an effective consent.

★ ★ ★

Consequently, we cannot accept the position of the Court of Appeals in this case that proof of knowledge of the right to refuse consent is a necessary prerequisite to demonstrating a "voluntary" consent. Rather it is only by analyzing all the circumstances of an individual consent that it can be ascertained whether in fact it was voluntary or coerced. It is this careful sifting of the unique facts and circumstances of each case that is evidenced in our prior decisions involving consent searches.

★ ★ ★

In short, neither this Court's prior cases, nor the traditional definition of "voluntariness" requires proof of knowledge of a right to refuse as the *sine qua non* of an effective consent to a search.

★ ★ ★

In this case there is no evidence of any inherently coercive tactics—either from the nature of the police questioning or the environment in which it took place. Indeed, since consent searches will normally occur on a person's own familiar territory, the spectre of incommunicado police interrogation in some remote station house is simply inapposite. There is no reason to believe, under circumstances such as are present here, that the response to a policeman's question is presumptively coerced; and there is, therefore, no reason to reject the traditional test for determining the voluntariness of a person's response.

★ ★ ★

E

Our decision today is a narrow one. We hold only that when the subject of a search is not in custody and the State attempts to justify a search on the basis of his consent, the Fourth and Fourteenth Amendments require that it demonstrate that the consent was in fact voluntarily given, and not the result of duress or coercion, express or implied. Voluntariness is a question of fact to be determined from all circumstances, and while the subject's knowledge of a right to refuse is a factor to be taken into account, the prosecution is not required to demonstrate such knowledge as a prerequisite to establishing a voluntary consent.

[Judgment reversed.]

COMMENTS, NOTES, AND QUESTIONS

1. Do you think Alcala felt free to cooperate with the officers or to attempt to hinder their search of his brother's automobile? What would the average person have felt about cooperating under these circumstances? What if the men did not speak English very well? Would this affect the decision to grant consent? Is the middle of the night the time to appear less than cooperative with law enforcement officers? Consent to search may excuse the requirement of probable cause and, in some contexts, the procurement of a warrant. Under the consent theory, the totality of the circumstances test has been developed to determine whether a person has given consent freely and voluntarily. The factors to be considered include the level of education and general intelligence of the consenting party, the coerciveness of the circumstances, whether the individual was under arrest, whether the person knew about the right to refuse to grant consent, whether the police indicated a search would be conducted anyway, and whether police falsely stated that they possessed a warrant. Although these factors are not exclusive, they demonstrate the usual considerations that courts use in determining whether consent was lawfully given.

2. Was Alcala the proper person to give consent? Was it his absent brother who owned the vehicle? Was Alcala the person who actually possessed dominion over and control of the car even though he was not the driver? Generally, the only person who can complain about an alleged illegal search and seizure is the person who had an expectation of privacy, and that person may be the one with dominion and control or the owner of the vehicle. The *Schneckloth* Court rendered its decision without particular concern about which person was the individual who had an expectation of privacy within the automobile. Subsequent to *Schneckloth,* in *Rakas v. Illinois,* 439 U.S. 128 (1978), the Court held that social guests as passengers in an automobile generally possess no expectation

of privacy within the car because neither passenger had any ownership or possessory interest in the automobile. See *Rakas v. Illinois,* 439 U.S. 128 (1978). If a person has no expectation of privacy, there is no Fourth Amendment issue to litigate because that person had no standing to complain about a search concerning another person's property.

3. In the context of a hotel or motel, which person has dominion and control over a hotel room? Would the front desk official be in control sufficiently to consent to allowing police inside the rented guest rooms? Does the housekeeper have dominion and control, since that person can control a great deal of what happens within the house? Since consent to search must be voluntary and must come from the proper person, the individual who has dominion and control over the property is the one from whom consent must be acquired. Hotel owners and managers may not consent to search the rooms of guests on the theory that they do not possess shared dominion and control over the premises rented by the guest. *Stoner v. California,* 376 U.S. 483 (1964). Once the guest has vacated the premises, the dominion and control revert to the manager, who is then a proper person to grant voluntary consent.

4. There may be times when police in good faith believe that they are obtaining consent to search from the proper party [the one with dominion and control] but are simply mistaken or have been deceived. In *Illinois v. Rodriguez,* 497 U.S. 177 (1990), the former girlfriend of the defendant used her key to admit officers to the interior of the Rodriguez apartment. The girlfriend had moved out several weeks prior to admitting the officers and did not possess shared dominion and control of the apartment, but she did not volunteer this information to the officers. From all appearances to the officers, the former girlfriend, who possessed a key, seemed to be a proper person to allow them to enter the apartment under a consent theory. The Supreme Court of the United States ultimately upheld the legality of the search and seizure using the doctrine of apparent authority. From all appearances, with nothing to negate it, the former girlfriend appeared to share dominion and control and wanted to allow police inside the apartment to arrest the defendant. Where the police operate in good faith and believe that a proper person, with apparent authority over the property, has given consent to a search, the search is lawful under the Fourth Amendment. Valid consent to search may be offered by one who has shared dominion and control over the property, according to the general rule.

5. What is the procedure where a police officer lies to a person in charge of property with a view to inducing consent? Does a lie destroy otherwise good consent? Should the consent be considered "good"? If law enforcement officers lie in order to induce a person to give consent, the general rule is that the lie destroys the consent purportedly given. The theory seems to be that where police are intentionally untruthful to a consenting party, they remove the chance that the consent has been voluntarily offered. In *Bumper v. North Carolina,* 391 U.S. 543 (1968), police lied to the grandmother of the suspect and told her, falsely, that they had a warrant to search her home. She told officers to come ahead and search. In overturning the validity of the search, Justice Stewart for the Court stated:

> When a law enforcement officer claims authority to search a home under a warrant, he announces in effect that the occupant has no right to resist the search. The situation is instinct with coercion—albeit colorably lawful coercion. Where there is coercion, there cannot be consent. *Bumper v. North Carolina,* 391 U.S. 543 at 550 (1968).

An outright lie or clear deception by agents of the state or federal government destroys consent to search under the Fourth Amendment, as a general rule.

CASE 4.9

Search and Seizure: The Plain View Doctrine

Horton v. California
Supreme Court of the United States
496 U.S. 128 (1990)

FACTS

A California trial court convicted petitioner Horton of an armed robbery involving the treasurer of the San Jose Coin Club. As the victim, Wallaker, entered his garage, two masked men, one armed with an Uzi submachine gun, attacked him. One of the robbers used an electrical "stun gun" which rendered the victim unable to resist. As the robbers carried on a fairly open conversation between themselves, they bound and handcuffed Wallaker. The victim recognized petitioner Horton's distinctive voice while another witness observed the robbers leaving the scene of the crime and was able to add some corroboration to the identification. Additional

evidence disclosed that Horton had gained knowledge that Wallaker possessed a large quantity of cash and jewelry because Horton had attended a coin show where Wallaker had done business.

After making an initial investigation, police obtained a warrant to search Horton's residence for the proceeds of the robbery. The affidavit for the search warrant described weapons as well as proceeds of the robbery as being objects of the proposed search, but the warrant mentioned only robbery proceeds including three specifically described rings. During the execution of the warrant, police seized an Uzi submachine gun, a .38-caliber revolver, two "stun guns," a handcuff key, and several other items. The officer conducting the search admitted searching not only for the rings but for other evidence connecting Horton to the crime. Some of the seized evidence was not discovered "inadvertently" since police expected to find some of the seized materials.

Following Horton's allegation that the warrant had been defective since it did not mention firearms and the police fully expected to find guns, the trial court refused to suppress the evidence taken from Horton's home. After a jury convicted Horton, he appealed with no success to the California Court of Appeals. Subsequently, the Supreme Court of California denied review.

Since the application of the plain view exception to the warrant requirement had been construed by the California courts to not require inadvertence in discovery under the plain view doctrine, the Supreme Court of the United States granted certiorari.

PROCEDURAL ISSUE

Is warrantless seizure of criminal evidence in plain view prohibited by the Fourth Amendment if the discovery of the evidence was expected even though the item was not listed on a search warrant?

HELD: NO

RATIONALE

Justice Stevens delivered the opinion of the Court.

In this case we revisit an issue that was considered, but not conclusively resolved, in *Coolidge v. New Hampshire,* 403 U.S. 443 (1971): Whether the warrantless search of evidence of crime in plain view is prohibited by the Fourth Amendment if the discovery of the evidence was not inadvertent. We conclude that even though inadvertence is a characteristic of most legitimate "plain view" seizures, it is not a necessary condition.

I

★ ★ ★

The criteria that generally guide "plain view" seizures were set forth in *Coolidge v. New Hampshire,* 403 U.S. 443 (1971). The Court held that the seizure of two automobiles parked in plain view on the defendant's driveway in the course of arresting the defendant violate the Fourth Amendment. Accordingly, particles of gun powder that had been subsequently found in vacuum sweepings from one of the cars could not be introduced in evidence against the defendant. The State endeavored to justify the seizure of the automobiles, and their subsequent search at the police station, on four different grounds, including the "plain view" doctrine. The scope of that doctrine as it had developed in earlier cases was fairly summarized in these three paragraphs from Justice Stewart's opinion:

> It is well established that under certain circumstances the police may seize evidence in plain view without a warrant. But it is important to keep in mind that, in the vast majority of cases, *any* evidence seized by the police will be in plain view, at least at the moment of seizure. The problem with the 'plain view' doctrine has been to identify the circumstances in which plain view has legal significance rather than being simply the normal concomitant of any search, legal or illegal.

★ ★ ★

Justice Stewart then described the two limitations on the doctrine that he found implicit in its rationale: First, "that plain view *alone* is never enough to justify the warrantless seizure of evidence," and second, "that the discovery of evidence in plain view must be inadvertent."

★ ★ ★

It is, of course, an essential predicate to any valid warrantless seizure of incriminating evidence that the officer did not violate the Fourth Amendment in arriving at the place from which the evidence could be plainly viewed. There are, moreover, two additional conditions that must be satisfied to justify the warrantless seizure. First, not only must the item be in plain view, its incriminating character must also be "immediately apparent." Thus, in *Coolidge,* the cars were obviously in plain view, but their probative value remained uncertain until after the interiors were swept and examined microscopically. Second, not only must the officer be lawfully located in a place from which the object can be plainly seen, but he or she must also have a lawful right of access to the object itself....In all events, we are satisfied that the absence of inadvertence was not essential to the Court's rejection of the State's "plain view" argument in *Coolidge.*

III

Justice Stewart concluded that the inadvertence requirement was necessary to avoid a violation of the express constitutional requirement that a valid warrant must particularly describe the things to be seized. He explained:

> The rationale of the exception to the warrant requirement, as just stated, is that a plain-view seizure will not turn an initially valid (and therefore limited) search into a "general" one, while the inconvenience of procuring a warrant to cover an inadvertent discovery is great. But where the discovery is anticipated, where the police know in advance the location of the evidence and intend to seize it, the situation is altogether different. The requirement of a warrant to seize imposes no inconvenience whatever, or at least none which is constitutionally cognizable in a legal system that regards warrantless searches as "per se unreasonable" in the absence of "exigent circumstances."
>
> If the initial intrusion is bottomed upon a warrant that fails to mention a particular object, though the police know its location and intent to seize it, then there is a violation of the express constitutional requirement of "Warrants...particularly describing...[the] things to be seized." 403 U.S., at 469–471.

We find two flaws in this reasoning. First, evenhanded law enforcement is best achieved by the application of objective standards of conduct, rather than standards that depend upon the subjective state of mind of the officer. The fact that an officer is interested in an item of evidence and fully expects to find it in the course of a search should not invalidate its seizure if the search is confined in area and duration by the terms of a warrant or a valid exception to the warrant requirement.

★ ★ ★

Second, the suggestion that the inadvertence requirement is necessary to prevent the police from conducting general searches, or from converting specific warrants into general warrants, is not persuasive because that interest is already served by the requirements that no warrant issue unless it "particularly describ[es] the place to be searched and the persons or things to be seized," see *Maryland v. Garrison,* 480 U.S. 79, 84 (1987); and that a warrantless search be circumscribed by the exigencies which justify its initiation. See, *e.g., Maryland v. Buie,* 494 U.S. 325, 332–334 (1990); *Mincey v. Arizona,* 437 U.S. 385, 393 (1978). Scrupulous adherence to these requirements serves the interests in limiting the area and duration of the search that the inadvertence requirement inadequately protects. Once those commands have been satisfied and the officer has a lawful right of access, however, no additional Fourth Amendment interest is furthered by requiring that the discovery of evidence be inadvertent.

[Affirmed.]

COMMENTS, NOTES, AND QUESTIONS

1. Is it important that an officer not violate the Fourth Amendment in arriving at the location from which the incriminating evidence can be viewed? Could a police officer go inside a home without a warrant if the officer observed a marijuana plant through a glass apartment window in plain view? Why or why not? Consider a situation in which an officer was inside a home on a domestic violence call and opened a bathroom medicine chest to see prescription medicine bottles but moved the bottle to see if the name on the bottle matched that of one of the occupants of the home. Would this be a plain view search? Why or why not? See *Arizona v. Hicks,* 480 U.S. 321 (1987), for a suggested answer.

2. Would it be proper for police to seize what appeared to be marijuana under the following circumstances? An officer responding to a domestic disturbance in a backyard observed what appeared to be marijuana growing in a greenhouse attached to the home next door. May the officer break into the greenhouse and seize the offending plants without a warrant where the officer has probable cause? Does the fact that the plants are in plain view help? Would this constitute an emergency that relieves the officer from having to obtain a warrant?

3. The legal concept of the "plain view" doctrine is that the use of the doctrine does not involve a search in the traditional sense. The officer merely must lawfully occupy a physical position from which he or she develops probable cause to seize the property. The relationship of the evidence to crime must be clear, such as a finding of drugs, property involved in the crime, or other contraband. The property is immediately seizable, since it would be unreasonable to expect or require an officer to leave and obtain a warrant.

Special Problem Searches: Administrative, Inventory, School, Airport, and Work Searches

Chapter Outline

Key Terms

Administrative probable cause
Administrative search: business
Administrative search: home
Airport passenger search
Closely (heavily) regulated industry
Emergency administrative search
Functional equivalent of international border
International border search

Inventory search: motor vehicle
Inventory search: personal property
Inventory search policy
Private employer search
Reasonable basis to suspect
Reduced expectation of privacy: juveniles
Suspicionless public school search
Suspicionless workplace search

1. INTRODUCTION TO ADMINISTRATIVE, INVENTORY, SCHOOL, AIRPORT, AND WORK SEARCHES

In a variety of contexts, local, state, and federal governmental agencies possess informational needs that can be met by searches that do not necessarily have as their primary goal the discovery of criminal activity. The Fourth Amendment to the Constitution grants to individuals the right to be free from unreasonable searches and seizures, not to be free from all searches and seizures. It follows from this that a government may be relatively free to conduct any type of search so long as it is deemed to be reasonable under the circumstances. For example, when necessary to implement social programs and to structure public policy, governments may conduct searches and request information in ways that do not offend the Fourth Amendment. In a variety of contexts, some searches have been described as "special needs" searches where a branch of government is attempting to promote a policy, promote social interests, protect property and society, or accomplish a variety of goals expected of governments. However, in pursuing some special needs searches, where Fourth Amendment interests are clearly implicated, the nature of particular searches may dictate the use of warrants.

Special needs searches include administrative searches covering a wide variety of topics, including searches of houses for zoning compliance, scrutiny of ordinary businesses for fire and safety issues, and searches of closely regulated industries. Some of the special needs searches may require warrants; others do not because of the nature of the search or the need for immediacy. Searches of closely regulated industries and businesses may not require a search warrant and may not require probable cause due to the fact that conducting these businesses requires a relinquishment of some Fourth Amendment protections. In all cases of administrative searches, emergency or exigent circumstances will excuse the procurement of the warrant that might have otherwise been necessary.

Inventory searches occur when a governmental agency must take custody of personal property for which it retains a level of responsibility for safekeeping. Where an individual has been arrested and police take control of an automobile, it may be reasonable to impound the vehicle to keep it from harm and other damage. In addition, the contents of the automobile may contain valuables for which a police agency might have responsibility. It is generally considered reasonable, so long as the law enforcement agency has an inventory search policy and routinely follows the directives in that policy, to conduct an inventory of the automobile to assure the security of any of its contents. If by some chance evidence of criminality appears, such evidence will usually be admissible in court. An inventory search may also be applied to personal property taken from an arrestee such as a purse, wallet, backpack, or similar item. Once again, it is generally considered reasonable to catalog the contents of these items and to secure them until they are ready to be delivered to the individual from whom they were taken. Paramount justifications for inventory search include the protection of property, the protection of police from dangerous items or ordinance, and the protection of police against false claims of loss while the property is not in the owner's possession.

The protection of schoolchildren provides the justification for a variety of school-based special needs searches of both student property and the student personally. A large percentage of legal cases involving searches of school-age children concern drug use and sale within the context of the public schools. While it has been held by the United States Supreme Court that children possess Fourth Amendment rights, case law is also very clear that children do not enjoy the exact same Fourth Amendment rights as adults. Courts on many levels have approved the search of persons, purses, backpacks, and lockers for items that offend the criminal law and/or for evidence that school rules have been broken. In many instances, individual suspicion that a particular student has transgressed the law or violated school rules may allow search of that student and/or his or her possessions. In other contexts involving secondary school athletes and students involved in extracurricular activities, suspicionless drug testing has been approved as meeting the reasonableness standard under the Fourth Amendment.

Special needs searches include workplace searches of individuals, whether conducted by a private employer or a state or federal government agency. In some cases, the government agency requires that employees desiring transfers or promotions submit to a drug screening test despite the absence of any individualized suspicion. In the context of private employers who may be required by the federal government or a state government to conduct drug searches of their employees, suspicionless testing has been approved. The general rationale involves the weighing of the employees' expectation of privacy against the significant needs of the government for a drug-free workplace and for the private employer who must meet government-mandated drug testing guidelines. In situations where a government employee may be required to carry a firearm and/or deal with drug interdiction, suspicionless testing has been mandated. Federal regulations require that operators of instrumentalities of interstate commerce, such as railroads, be subject to drug testing following an accident involving a specified level of property damage. As a general rule, many of these workplace drug testing searches have been upheld as reasonable under the Fourth Amendment.

Various types of searches involving airline passengers, crew, and other workers have received court approval under the category of special needs searches. For the past several decades, persons wishing to board domestic commercial airliners have been forced to choose between submitting to a personal and baggage search prior to boarding or finding alternate means of transportation. Searches of passenger baggage, both carry-on and checked, have been based on either a consent theory or an administrative search basis. Following the events of September 11, 2001, extensive new types and levels of airport searches have either been initiated or loom on the horizon, including deeper personal screening and enhanced chemical and hazardous material screening.

International border searches may be considered within the special needs search category because the requirements of national sovereignty allow extreme scrutiny over items entering or leaving the United States. As a means of enforcing the international boundary, persons crossing a border of the United States possess diminished Fourth Amendment rights and may be searched for any reason without a showing of probable cause. Searches at an international border and its functional equivalent, an international airport, are generally subject to identical rules concerning searches. As one moves inland from a border, Fourth Amendment rights begin to have full application. Permanent stations along the major highways leading to and from the border allow government agents to scrutinize traffic passing through the choke point and to stop individuals where evidence appears that the person may not be entitled to be in the United States. Roving patrols near the border have been allowed to make stops based on reasonable suspicion that a person, a person's possessions, or a vehicle's content offends the law. In conducting a special needs stop and search, federal border officials possess much leeway in their activity, but their overall conduct inside the United States remains subject to the Fourth Amendment concept of reasonableness.

Some types of special needs searches are not covered in this chapter. Parolees and probationers, as a condition of their release, can be required to submit to searches based on a lower standard than that traditionally required by the Fourth Amendment. Persons in prisons have reduced expectations of privacy and are subject to search at any time. Special needs searches mentioned in this chapter are, therefore, not exclusive, and a variety of others exist that are beyond the scope of this book.

2. ADMINISTRATIVE SEARCHES

The states and the federal government are empowered with the authority to promote the general welfare, public health, and safety. This power frequently has been called the "police" power and is used not in its traditional law enforcement fashion but to denote a government's power to promote and ensure the common good of society. The Fourth Amendment limitation against unreasonable searches and seizures has been held to apply to commercial structures used in business and industry. The expectation of privacy in commercial operations includes protection against criminal investigatory searches and also applies to searches designed to implement and enforce social regulatory schemes.[125] These social objectives range from protecting water supplies, to preventing conditions that could cause a conflagration, to ensuring worker safety in commerce, industry, and transportation. If a governmental administrative search encompasses a secondary desire to procure evidence of criminal activity, such search is generally valid so long as the facts and circumstances justify a proper administrative search. However, when the searching individual may have the authority to conduct both administrative searches and criminal investigative searches, care must be exercised to assure that an administrative search has not been conducted by reliance on or exercise of law enforcement powers.[126] While the Supreme Court has not had occasion to rule on significant new challenges to administrative searches in recent years, the principles pertaining to these searches are fairly well known, and most of the parameters have been probed by litigants.

---

[125]*New York v. Burger,* 482 U.S. 691, 699 (1987).
[126]A Massachusetts court held that a police officer acting like an administrative searcher, who did not have criminal probable cause, illegally searched the subject's tack room where the subject stored leather horse harnesses and saddles. The cocaine he discovered should have been excluded from evidence, since the officer had crossed over from conducting an administrative search to executing a criminal search, which required a warrant or a substitute for a warrant. See *Commonwealth v. Rosenthal,* 52 Mass. App. Ct. 707; 755 N.E.2d 817 (2001).

3. ADMINISTRATIVE SEARCHES OF ORDINARY BUSINESSES AND INDUSTRIES

Fourth Amendment expectations of privacy in business or commercial settings differ from those expected in a personal residence or in an automobile in the sense that there is a reduced level of privacy that society is prepared to recognize as reasonable. Businesses invite customers to visit parts of their premises, and manufacturing entities sometimes have thousands of employees who enter the physical plant each day. Many commercial operations are subject by law to certain inspections for health and safety so that the operators understand that agents of the government will enter the property on occasion. These factors do not, however, mean that a warrant to inspect or search will not be required; most operators of businesses can choose to require governmental inspectors to possess warrants[127] prior to gaining admission. The fact that a business entity has the right to insist on a warrant in most cases, however, does not mean that most businesses will require a warrant prior to governmental entry for inspection.

4. ADMINISTRATIVE SEARCHES OF CLOSELY REGULATED INDUSTRIES

While most businesses may be searched only with a warrant, absent consent, one category of commerce is subject to inspection without warrant. Businesses or industries classified as closely regulated industries possess a diminished expectation of privacy over all or some of their operations. A primary example of a closely regulated industry is the manufacture, transport, and sale of intoxicating spirits. In *Colonnade Catering Corporation v. United States,*[128] the Court noted that in England and its colonies, which later became the United States, inspectors were permitted to enter brewing houses and similar establishments upon request and without a warrant. Subsequent federal law allowed officials, without a warrant, to enter and inspect distilling premises and those of companies that imported spirits. The sale and disposition of firearms, while not traditionally regulated as pervasively as alcohol, has been held to be an example of a closely regulated industry. In *United States v. Biswell,*[129] the Court allowed as reasonable under the Fourth Amendment a warrantless inspection of a federally licensed firearm dealer under the theory that the law authorizing the inspection would constitute only a limited threat to the pawnshop operator's expectation of privacy. The *Biswell* Court noted:

> When a dealer chooses to engage in this pervasively regulated business and to accept a federal license, he does so with the knowledge that his business records, firearms, and ammunition will be subject to effective inspection. 406 U.S. 311, 316 (1972).

The general rule that has emerged appears to indicate that persons and corporate entities engaged in closely regulated businesses or industries possess a reduced level of Fourth Amendment protections.

---

[127]See *Marshall v. Barlow's Inc.,* 436 U.S. 307 (1978).
[128]397 U.S. 72 (1970).
[129]406 U.S. 311 (1972).

5. ORDINARY COMMERCIAL SEARCH: WARRANT REQUIRED

Although some businesses might seem to fall into the category of closely regulated industries because of federal or state safety requirements, not every business need submit to warrantless inspections. For example, in *Marshall v. Barlow's, Inc.,* 436 U.S. 307 (1978), federal inspectors attempted to make a warrantless inspection of Barlow's company, an electrical and plumbing business. Barlow refused to allow the Occupational Safety and Health Administration (OSHA) inspector into private areas of the firm and sued the federal government seeking injunctive relief from warrantless OSHA inspections. The trial court held that a warrant for the type of search involved here was necessary, absent consent, under the Fourth Amendment and that the OSHA statutory authorization for warrantless inspection was unconstitutional. Barlow may have had an expectation of privacy in his business that was reduced somewhat by virtue of inviting employees onto his property. According to the *Barlow's* Court:

> The owner of a business has not, by the necessary utilization of employees in his operation, thrown open the areas where employees alone are permitted to the warrantless scrutiny of Government agents. *Barlow's* at 315.

The Court proved unwilling to allow governmental inspection of businesses in the absence of warrant or consent where the businesses were not traditionally pervasively regulated under traditional and long-standing legislative formulations. Precisely what causes a business to be known as a closely regulated industry may be discerned on a case-by-case basis. Coal mining has been found to fit the pattern,[130] as have businesses dealing in firearms[131] and alcohol.[132] While the list is not exhaustive of the types of businesses covered under close regulation, it is arguable that as enhanced governmental regulation occurs, more businesses and industries may come under the description of being closely regulated industries.

6. ADMINISTRATIVE SEARCHES OF HOMES: NO WARRANT ORIGINALLY REQUIRED

An appropriate starting point in the consideration of administrative searches of residences and private homes is *Frank v. Maryland,*[133] where the Supreme Court upheld a criminal conviction that resulted from the refusal by a dwelling's occupier to permit a warrantless inspection of private residential premises. Prompted by a citizen complaint, the government desired to conduct a warrantless inspection to ascertain whether a public nuisance involving rats existed. When the occupier persisted in refusing to allow warrantless admission, an arrest for refusal to allow an inspection followed. The city code provided as follows:

> Whenever the Commissioner of Health shall have cause to suspect that a nuisance exists in any house, cellar, or enclosure, he may demand entry therein in the day

---

[130]*Donovan v. Dewey,* 452 U.S. 594 (1981).
[131]*United States v. Biswell,* 406 U.S. 311 (1972).
[132]*Colonnade Catering Corporation v. United States,* 397 U.S. 72 (1970).
[133]359 U.S. 360 (1959).

time, and if the owner or occupier shall refuse or delay to open the same and admit a free examination, he shall forfeit and pay for every such refusal the sum of Twenty Dollars. § 120 of Art. 12 of the Baltimore City Code. *Frank v. Maryland* at 361.

A trial court found Frank guilty of violating the Baltimore health code. When the case arrived at the Supreme Court of the United States, the Court upheld the statute authorizing a warrantless arrest[134] for refusing to allow the inspectors access to the home. It noted that there was a long history of warrantless housing-type inspections, and modern requirements of health and sanitation dictate that due process has not been violated by the provision for warrantless admission to a private home upon a complaint.

The lesson of *Frank* indicated that warrantless searches of private premises for administrative purposes did not require a warrant and that a refusal to allow entry might be followed by criminal legal proceedings. The only method to determine whether a governmental agent could lawfully enter involved risking a criminal prosecution. The *Frank* Court felt that the Fourth Amendment was designed to have primary effect when criminal investigations were involved. Consequently, the Court held that the privacy interests under *Frank* "touch[ed] at most upon the periphery of the important interests safeguarded by the Fourteenth Amendment's protection against official intrusion."[135] For those reasons, as an exception to the usual requirements of a warrant, no warrant was required to conduct a residential inspection.

7. A CHANGE IN REQUIREMENTS: SEARCHES OF PRIVATE PREMISES REQUIRE WARRANTS

The Supreme Court indicated a significant change in direction when it decided *Camara v. Municipal Court* (see Case 5.1).[136] A housing inspector repeatedly had been refused entrance to private premises following a complaint that the commercial leasehold was being used for private residential purposes. Camara sued the district court in Superior Court for a writ of prohibition of enforcement of the municipal code but had no success in the California court system. The *Camara* Court held that the interests at stake when the government desired to enforce zoning restrictions were different than when the Court decided *Frank v. Maryland*. Instead of believing that privacy interests being protected were peripheral to the Fourth Amendment protections, the *Camara* Court determined that the privacy interests were quite a bit more important than was believed in *Frank*. Warrantless administrative searches cannot be justified, according to the Court, on the grounds that they make minimal demands on occupants. The Court stated:

> [W]e hold that administrative searches of the kind at issue here are significant intrusions upon the interests protected by the Fourth Amendment, that such searches, when authorized and conducted without a warrant procedure, lack the traditional safeguards which the Fourth Amendment guarantees to the individual,

---

[134]At this time, the Fourth Amendment had not yet been incorporated into the Due Process Clause of the Fourteenth Amendment, so *Frank* was argued under due process protected by the Fourteenth Amendment. See *Mapp v. Ohio*, 367 U.S. 643 (1961).

[135]*Frank v. Maryland*, 359 U.S. 360, 367 (1959).

[136]387 U.S. 523 (1967).

and that the reasons put forth in *Frank v. Maryland* and in other cases for upholding these warrantless searches are insufficient to justify so substantial a weakening
of the Fourth Amendment's protections. *Camara v. Municipal Court*, 387 U.S. 523
at 534.

The *Camara* Court allowed a "watered-down" version of probable cause to be sufficient for procuring an administrative warrant. Clearly, criminal probable cause
would be a difficult standard to meet in the administrative setting, so the Court indicated that administrative inspections must meet a special standard of probable
cause fitting this type of intrusion. According to the Court:

> "[P]robable cause" to issue a warrant to inspect must exist if reasonable legislative
> or administrative standards for conducting an area inspection are satisfied with re-
> spect to a particular dwelling. Such standards, which will vary with the municipal
> program being enforced, may be based upon the passage of time, the nature of the
> building (e.g., a multi-family apartment house), or the condition of the entire area,
> but they will not necessarily depend upon specific knowledge of the condition of
> the particular dwelling. *Camara v. Municipal Court,* 387 U.S. 523 at 538.

In a later case, Justice O'Connor echoed the standards for administrative probable
cause and the issuance of an administrative warrant when she stated:

> [T]he appropriate standard for administrative searches is not probable cause in its
> traditional meaning. Instead, an administrative warrant can be obtained if there is a
> showing that reasonable legislative or administrative standards for conducting an
> inspection are satisfied. *O'Connor v. Ortega,* 480 U.S. 709, 723 (1987).

The administrative probable cause criterion, while using the identical language
of criminal probable cause, in practice has proven to be a lower standard and fairly
easy to meet. Administrative probable cause may mature due to complaints by citizens, employees within an industry, or labor unions, or by observations derived from
routine governmental activities. When courts are faced with a request for an administrative warrant, they must weigh the governmental need to search against the reasonable expectation of privacy and will normally issue warrants, practically as a
mere formality.

As is the case with traditional searches under the Fourth Amendment, exceptions to the administrative warrant exist. The clearest case arises when the occupier
of premises gives a free and voluntary consent for the administrative search. The
standards for judging whether the property occupier has rendered valid consent are
arguably cloudy, but better judgment requires that the "totality of the circumstances" test, as illustrated in *Schneckloth v. Bustamonte,*[137] be used as a clear benchmark. Under the *Schneckloth* standard of the "totality of the circumstances" for

---

[137]412 U.S. 218 (1973). In determining whether a free and voluntary consent has been given under the "totality of the circumstances"
test, a variety of factors have been considered. The factors "taken into account have included the youth of the accused, *e.g., Haley v.
Ohio,* 332 U.S. 596; his lack of education, *e.g., Payne v. Arkansas,* 356 U.S. 560; or his low intelligence, *e.g., Fikes v. Alabama,* 352 U.S.
191; the lack of any advice to the accused of his constitutional rights, *e.g., Davis v. North Carolina,* 384 U.S. 737; the length of detention, *e.g., Chambers v. Florida, supra;* the repeated and prolonged nature of the questioning, *e.g., Ashcraft v. Tennessee,* 322 U.S. 143; and
the use of physical punishment such as the deprivation of food or sleep, *e.g., Reck v. Pate,* 367 U.S. 433." *Schneckloth* at 226.

determining voluntariness, the government need not have to prove that the person possessed knowledge of the right to refuse granting of consent.

In addition to the consent theory, exigent circumstances or emergency situations permit warrantless administrative searches and seizures. The *Camara* Court clearly contemplated continued used of emergency administrative searches when it observed:

> ...[N]othing we say today is intended to foreclose prompt inspections, even without a warrant, that the law has traditionally upheld in emergency situations. *Camara v. Municipal Court,* 387 U.S. 523, 539.

Demonstrative of this principle, the Court noted with approval searches and seizures of unwholesome food, compulsory smallpox vaccination, health quarantine, and summary destruction of tubercular cattle.

8. ADMINISTRATIVE SEARCHES: REASONABLE UNDER THE FOURTH AMENDMENT

To summarize, administrative searches trigger Fourth Amendment concerns and, in the absence of consent or other exception, generally require warrants based on probable cause. The quantum of proof necessary to constitute administrative probable cause has been reduced to the point that extreme specificity concerning either the reasons for the search or the precise place to be searched proves to be an easy burden to meet. The relaxed standards under probable cause are justified, since the administrative search is directed not toward the uncovering of criminal wrongdoing but toward the furthering of health, safety, and welfare regulations of municipalities, the states, and the federal government.

9. INVENTORY SEARCHES: PROBABLE CAUSE NOT REQUIRED

An inventory search is a special type of search under the Fourth Amendment because it does not require, as its basis, the finding of probable cause. The inventory search is considered reasonable in the absence of probable cause due to the fact that other rationales beyond finding evidence of crime support its use. When property lawfully comes into the hands of law enforcement personnel, they are under a duty of safekeeping for the property until it is returned to the rightful possessor. As is often the case, property comes to the police within different types of containers. A purse or backpack may contain valuable personal property; a car may hold hidden treasures or stolen property; and these types of personal property may hide harmful ordinance, noxious gases, or other dangerous items. Once a person and property come under the dominion and control of the police, it is reasonable under the Fourth Amendment that the property be inventoried, cataloged, and securely stored. During this process, if additional evidence of the possessor's criminality becomes evident, generally this evidence may be used in a criminal trial. Since the police are not looking for evidence of crime, but inadvertently stumble upon it while conducting a reasonable inventory, there should be no constitutional impediment to its use. The inventory search occurs most frequently when motor vehicles are involved or where individuals have been arrested while in possession of personal property and accoutrements.

10. VEHICLE INVENTORY SEARCHES

Some vehicle searches may follow valid arrests of the driver or passenger using the theory of search incident to arrest,[138] and other warrantless searches may be justified under an inventory search theory. The inventory search[139] stands on a different footing and is designed to protect the property of the arrestee from loss and the police from false claims of loss, as well as protect the police and property custodians from any dangerous substance or ordinance that might be contained within a motor vehicle. Inventory searches have been approved in several cases, including *South Dakota v. Opperman*[140] and *Colorado v. Bertine,*[141] where the search parameters were directed by a written policy (see Case 5.3). Where motor vehicles have been lawfully impounded, the Court approved the use of inventory searches as reasonable responses even in the absence of probable cause.

In *Opperman,* the defendant had parked his car in a place where it was unlawful to do so, and in due course police had it towed to an impound lot. Since the automobile contained some personal items, the officer who noticed the valuables had the car unlocked and initiated an inventory using a standard inventory form pursuant to the department's normal procedure. The officer discovered some marijuana in addition to some valuables. While the trial court refused to suppress the criminal evidence because it considered the search reasonable, the Supreme Court of Colorado reversed the conviction, concluding that the evidence had been obtained in violation of the Fourth Amendment prohibition against unreasonable searches and seizures. The Supreme Court of the United States reversed and upheld as reasonable the inventory search as regulated by the police department's policy.[142]

According to the Court, the police procedures followed in *Opperman* did not involve an unreasonable search in violation of the Fourth Amendment. The Court noted that there is a diminished expectation of privacy in a motor vehicle and that police departments for many years have possessed inventory policies that are followed when securing valuables taken into custody. The Court noted:

> When vehicles are impounded, local police departments generally follow a routine practice of securing and inventorying the automobiles' contents. These procedures developed in response to three distinct needs: the protection of the owner's property while it remains in police custody; the protection of the police against claims or disputes over lost or stolen property; and the protection of the

---

[138]For examples of searches incident to arrest of drivers of motor vehicles, see *United States v. Robinson,* 414 U.S. 218 (1973), and *Gustafson v. Florida,* 414 U.S. 260 (1973).

[139]An inventory search may be conducted after an automobile has been lawfully impounded, as occurred in *Florida v. White,* 526 U.S. 559 (1999), where the officers, conducting a routine inventory search, discovered illegal drugs within the automobile.

[140]428 U.S. 364 (1976).

[141]479 U.S. 367 (1987).

[142]*South Dakota v. Opperman,* 428 U.S. 364, 375 (1976).

police from potential danger. The practice has been viewed as essential to respond to incidents of theft or vandalism. [Internal citations omitted.] *Opperman* at 369.

The *Opperman* Court approved the concept of the inventory search, which had been used by many police departments in many states. The principle was followed in *Colorado v. Bertine*,[143] where a police officer arrested a driver for driving under the influence of alcohol. While waiting for a tow truck, and in accordance with local procedures, the backup officer inventoried the van's contents.[144] He opened a closed backpack in which he found containers that held controlled substances, cocaine paraphernalia, and a large amount of cash. The officer was acting in good faith and attempting to follow his department's policy under the circumstances. The Supreme Court upheld the admission into evidence in *Bertine* because the police were operating their inventory search in an objectively reasonable manner for the purpose of protecting valuables and protecting police officers from harm.[145]

11. INVENTORY SEARCHES OF MOTOR VEHICLES: WRITTEN POLICY REQUIRED

An inventory search of a motor vehicle requires that the police agency have and follow an inventory search policy. In the absence of a policy regulating this process, individual officers would have unlimited discretion so that a particular inventory search could evolve into a ruse for conducting a general search. The policy regulating inventory searches must be designed to produce an inventory rather than permitting the inventory officer so much latitude that no standards exist.

Consistent with other vehicle inventory search cases is the case *Florida v. Wells*,[146] where an arrested driver gave police permission to open the trunk of his impounded car. An inventory search of the car revealed marijuana within a suitcase. The *Wells* Court approved the state court decision holding that the evidence should have been suppressed on the ground that the Florida Highway Patrol possessed no governing standards covering the opening of closed containers found within motor vehicles. In the absence of an inventory policy, the officer could search wherever he desired, which could turn an inventory search into a general snooping without any purpose or rationale. Without the policy, a search based on an inventory theory is deemed unreasonable, and the evidence seized will generally be excluded from court. The *Wells* Court ruled that the evidence of drug possession should have been excluded from Wells' trial.

Under the vehicle inventory theory, to perform a valid search requires that the particular law enforcement agency have a clear inventory search policy that police routinely follow. The policy must contain general guidelines for police practice and can allow a police officer some discretion concerning the scope of the search. Situations that may be fatal to inventory searches are the absence of an inventory policy, a failure to routinely follow the policy, or a policy that gives the inventory officer virtually unbridled discretion in the scope of the search.

---

[143]479 U.S. 367 (1987).
[144]Ibid. at 369.
[145]Ibid. at 376.
[146]495 U.S. 1 (1990).

12. INVENTORY SEARCHES OF PERSONAL PROPERTY

Whereas inventory searches usually develop where police have lawfully impounded a motor vehicle, the legal principle is not so limited. The principle has been applied to search the effects of an arrestee who was in the process of being booked into jail following his arrest. In *Illinois v. Lafayette,*[147] a police officer responding to a dispatch about a disturbance at a movie theater found Lafayette involved in an altercation with the manager (see Case 5.2). The officer arrested Lafayette for disturbing the peace, handcuffed him, and took him to the police station along with a purse-type shoulder bag. Subsequent to arriving at the police station, Lafayette was required to empty his pockets and shoulder bag, which revealed some tobacco. The booking officer discovered some amphetamine pills inside the shoulder bag. The officer had looked over the bag and the other materials as a result of the department's standard procedure to inventory everything brought to the jail by a person under arrest.

The trial court ordered suppression of the drug evidence recovered from the shoulder bag because it rejected the theory that the station house search could be justified as a search incident to arrest. Since the search had not happened contemporaneously with the arrest, it could not qualify as a search incident to an arrest. A state appellate court determined that the evidence should have been suppressed under Fourth Amendment principles because a greater privacy interest existed in personal items like purses and bags; therefore, the station house procedure could not qualify as a valid inventory search. The Supreme Court granted certiorari and reversed the state court. As the *Lafayette* Court stated the issue:

> The question here is whether, consistent with the Fourth Amendment, it is reasonable for police to search the personal effects of a person under lawful arrest as part of the routine administrative procedure at a police station house incident to booking and jailing the suspect. *Lafayette* at 644.

According to the Court, since an inventory search is merely an incidental administrative step during the booking process that follows arrest, it constitutes a reasonable search under the Fourth Amendment. In determining whether or not Lafayette's rights under the Fourth Amendment were violated, the Court found it necessary to balance the intrusion on the rights of the arrestee against any legitimate governmental interests. The arrestee would rather have personal property remain unsearched and undisturbed to protect his privacy. On the other hand, it is not unheard of that individuals working within police departments have stolen property belonging to arrested persons. Sometimes arrestees make false claims about lost property. Arrested persons have also been known to injure themselves and other inmates or police with belts, knives, drugs, or other items brought into jail. Dangerous instrumentalities, including bladed weapons and chemical weapons, have been discovered within innocent-looking articles taken from arrested persons. When one weighs the interest of privacy of the individual against the needs and desires of the government, the inescapable conclusion is that it is quite appropriate to conduct inventory searches of personal property under the

---

[147]462 U.S. 604 (1983).

circumstances, and such searches appear to be reasonable under the Fourth Amendment[148] according to the *Lafayette* Court.

13. SCHOOL SEARCHES MUST BE BASED ON FOURTH AMENDMENT REASONABLENESS

The Fourth Amendment has been held applicable in cases where officials at public schools conduct searches, and where law enforcement officials conduct searches whether the school is public or private. Children as well as adults have rights under the Fourth Amendment, but their rights have been deemed to be more limited than those enjoyed by adults. Searches of children in school may fall into a variety of categories, since the goals of school officials differ according to the program being implemented. The goal of a search may be to discover recreational pharmaceuticals in a student's locker, purse, or backpack; other types of searches may be much more intrusive, such as where the school system desires to ensure that student leaders and athletes remain drug-free. The standards for reasonable suspicion[149] will normally be a prerequisite to a search of the personal property of the public school student, but in many cases there will be no individualized suspicion prior to a urine test for an athlete. Depending on how student lockers are assigned, a student may or may not have an expectation of privacy in the locker itself. If at the time of the assignment it is made clear to the student that there will be no relinquishment of authority over the interior of the locker, he or she may have no expectation of privacy unless there is a container within the locker, such as a personal backpack. On the other hand, if the locker has been granted to or rented to the student as a private place to store school-related items, the student may retain an expectation of privacy under the Fourth Amendment. It must be noted that if school authorities allow a drug-sniffing dog under the control of the police to walk down school hallways, this approach does not constitute a search[150] because the animal is detecting the odors that are outside of a particular locker.

In an early test of the Fourth Amendment involving public school students, the Court held that a student could be searched by school officials (government employees) where there were reasonable grounds for believing that the student's possessions violated either a school rule or the law.[151] In *New Jersey v. T.L.O.*,[152] a student had been under suspicion for smoking tobacco in the school rest room (see Case 5.4). A principal eventually searched the student's purse on the theory that she possessed tobacco; that search did disclose tobacco, and a later, deeper search revealed marijuana, rolling paper, money, and a customer list. Following juvenile proceedings, the case was eventually heard by the Supreme Court of the United States to determine whether the search was reasonable under the circumstances.

---

[148]*Illinois v. Lafayette,* 462 U.S. 604, 648 (1983).
[149]See *New Jersey v. T.L.O.,* 469 U.S. 325 (1985).
[150]A "sniff test" by a trained narcotics dog is not considered to be a search within the meaning of the Fourth Amendment because it does not require physical intrusion of the object being sniffed, and it does not expose anything other than the contraband items. *United States v. Place,* 462 U.S. 696, 706–707 (1983).
[151]See *New Jersey v. T.L.O.,* 469 U.S. 325 (1985).
[152]Ibid.

The *T.L.O.* Court suggested a two-step approach that would consider, first, whether the search was justified at its inception and, second, whether the search as actually conducted was reasonably related in scope to the circumstances that justified the interference in the first place. Since there had been a credible accusation that the student had been smoking in the rest room, the school official possessed sufficient suspicion to conduct a search of the student's purse. The items that were initially disclosed suggested the need for a deeper inquiry. The results that come from this case include the concept that school officials need not obtain a warrant before searching a student, and that the search of a student by a school official will be justified where there are reasonable grounds for suspecting that the search will turn up evidence that the student has transgressed either the law or the rules of the school. Reasonable suspicion or reasonable grounds appear to be synonymous terms supporting the threshold of public school searches.

14. PUBLIC SCHOOL DRUG SEARCHES: DRUG TESTING OF ATHLETES

In a case involving no individualized suspicion, a school system decided to implement drug tests for all students who participated in interscholastic athletics.[153] In Oregon, the Vernonia School District 47J determined that all athletes desiring to participate in a sport must submit to a drug test at the beginning of the season before playing his or her respective sport. At a subsequent time, all athletes were to have their names placed in a pool from which 10 percent of them would be selected for random drug testing on the day of the drawing. In no case was there to be a requirement of individualized suspicion of drug use prior to testing. When one student's parents refused to consent to drug screening, the school prohibited him from participating in sports. The family filed suit, alleging a violation of the Fourth Amendment as applied to the states through the Fourteenth Amendment's Due Process Clause.

When the case reached the Supreme Court in *Vernonia School District 47J v. Acton,*[154] the Court first determined that personal drug screening constituted a search under the Fourth Amendment (see Case 5.5). The Court then had to determine whether the school district was operating in a reasonable fashion with respect to the drug tests by balancing the expectation of privacy of the students against the needs of the school system. According to the Court, drug use had expanded within the school system, and students had become more unruly. In addition, it was believed that allowing participation in sports by students who were under the influence of drugs could result in increased injuries or even death. The *Acton* Court considered that public school students have some reduced expectation of privacy because they can be required to be vaccinated and to take school physicals prior to admission. The Court also looked at the privacy measures built in to the drug tests so that the urine could be collected without the teacher actually watching the student produce it. The Court considered the need to reduce drug usage and

---

[153] *Vernonia School Dist. 47J v. Acton,* 515 U.S. 646 (1995).
[154] Ibid.

the reasonable attempts by the school under this policy to have drug-free athletes. On balance, the *Acton* Court concluded that the school district's policy was reasonable under the Fourth Amendment.[155] While public school students do possess a reasonable expectation of privacy, that privacy can be reduced where students wish to play sports, an activity that places them in a role model position. Students who do not wish to play sports generally are under no duty to submit to any sort of drug screen or test.

15. PUBLIC SCHOOL DRUG SEARCHES: SUSPICIONLESS TESTING OF NONATHLETES

Following *Acton,* public school districts had the authority to screen sports participants for drug use and abuse. In a later decision, the Court approved an extension of *Acton* to all middle and high school students whose districts required a drug test prior to engaging in any extracurricular activity. The Tecumseh, Oklahoma, School District adopted a drug policy that required students who were interested in participating in extracurricular activities to consent to urinalysis. The actual practice of the school district had been to test all the athletes engaging in competitive sports, but the policy allowed the district to test other individuals involved in extracurricular activities. Pursuant to the drug testing policy, covered students were required to take a drug test prior to initiating an extracurricular activity; the school district mandated that students submit to random drug testing while participating in that activity; and covered students had to agree to be tested at any time upon facts that created a reasonable suspicion of drug use.

In *Board of Education v. Earls,*[156] several students and their parents brought a legal action against the school district under 42 U.S.C. Sec. 1983 alleging that their civil rights had been violated by the drug testing policy and that the policy violated their rights under the Fourth Amendment (see Case 5.6). The students argued that, while it might be reasonable to test school athletes, as in *Acton,* it was not reasonable to require suspicionless testing for other activities when the school district had failed to identify any special need or problem common to students engaged in nonathletic extracurricular activities. The federal district court found for the school district because the judge felt that there was a certain history of drug abuse in the school system that created a legitimate cause for concern and could be effectively addressed by testing the students involved in extracurricular activities. The Court of Appeals for the Tenth Circuit reversed because it believed that the school district failed to show that a serious drug problem existed among nonathletes engaged in extracurricular activities. The Supreme Court granted certiorari to consider the reasonableness of testing such students under the circumstances.

The Supreme Court, in *Earls,* cited *Delaware v. Prouse*[157] and noted that it generally determines the reasonableness of a search and seizure by balancing the nature

---

[155] *Vernonia School District 47J v. Acton,* 515 U.S. 646, 665 (1995).

[156] 536 U.S. 822 (2002).

[157] 440 U.S. 648 (1978). According to the *Prouse* Court, "[T]he permissibility of a particular law enforcement practice is judged by balancing its intrusion on the individual's Fourth Amendment interests against its promotion of legitimate governmental interests." *Prouse* at 654.

of the intrusion against the individual's privacy with the promotion of reasonable government interests, but that the Fourth Amendment does not always require an individual level of suspicion. The respondent schoolchildren argued that they possessed a stronger interest in privacy than athletes because they did not have to disrobe in front of fellow participants. This argument did not have much effect on the majority of the Court, which observed that undressing in close proximity to fellow students is a frequent part of some nonathletic extracurricular activities and that any related distinction was not a cornerstone of the Court's decision in *Acton*.[158] Additionally, the Court noted that the sole outcome of a failed drug test involved a limitation on that student's participation in extracurricular activities. Justice Thomas, writing for the Court, stated, "Given the minimally intrusive nature of the sample collection and the limited uses to which the test results are put, we conclude that the invasion of students' privacy is not significant."[159] The Court essentially found that a school system's interest in assuring a safe and drug-free educational experience outweighed an individual student's Fourth Amendment right to privacy. Consequently, the *Earls* Court reversed the court of appeals by rejecting its view that the Fourth Amendment prohibited drug testing under the circumstances; it also upheld the right of a school district to require consent to submit to a drug test as a prerequisite for participation in extracurricular activities.

When *Acton* and *Earls* are considered together, public schools may initiate drug testing policies covering every student who steps forward to become involved in any optional school activity. The drug policy need not focus on individual suspicion in requiring testing and may appropriately involve random decisions on which students to subject to a test. These tests are, arguably, based somewhat on consent of the parent or guardian and consent of the student, since a prior agreement to submit to the drug testing program remains an essential precursor to participation in an extracurricular activity. The Court has approved drug testing as a reasonable approach, consistent with the Fourth Amendment, to the perceived national problem of drug abuse by schoolchildren. As of the current state of jurisprudence, unconsented drug screening of all public school children does not appear reasonable under the Fourth Amendment.

16. GOVERNMENT SEARCHES IN THE WORKPLACE

While diminished expectations of privacy may inure to schoolchildren, the same reduced constitutional expectations have not traditionally applied to adults in the workplace. In recent years, to implement national policies to assure a drug-free workplace, both the private sector and governments at various levels have created plans and developed other programs to prevent drug-using prospective employees from being hired and to remove drug-using employees from service. As a general rule, the private sector is not regulated by the rules dictated by the Fourth Amendment. The same cannot be said for governmental employers, whether state or federal,

---

[158] *Vernonia School District 47J v. Acton*, 515 U.S. 646 (1995).
[159] *Board of Education v. Earls*, 536 U.S. 822, 834 (2002).

because the Fourth Amendment has full impact on governments and adults generally have full Fourth Amendment rights. In order for a government program involving searches and seizures to pass constitutional muster, the search program must be reasonable given the circumstances. In evaluating the constitutionality of governmental personnel workplace searches, courts tend to indulge in a weighing process whereby the interests of individuals are balanced against the needs of the governmental employer. If a plan involving search and seizure for government employees is to gain judicial approval, courts must determine that the search or seizure contemplated is objectively reasonable.

In an early case involving suspicionless employee searches by the federal government, *National Treasury Employees Union v. Von Raab,*[160] the Customs Service, which assists in enforcing drug laws involving smuggling, embarked upon a plan requiring urine tests of selected employees seeking transfer or promotion to positions having a direct involvement in drug interdiction or requiring the employee to carry a firearm or to deal with classified material. The results of the testing were not to be used in criminal prosecutions, but adverse results could affect employment and curtail opportunities for advancement. The labor union representing some of the employees filed suit alleging that the drug tests required for employees violated the guarantees of the Fourth Amendment against unlawful searches and seizures. The *Von Raab* Court considered the interests at stake and determined a warrant procedure was not a constitutional requirement. The Court evaluated the needs of the government and balanced those needs against the loss of privacy of the employees, concluding that the equities favored the government. The testing program contained general parameters to alert employees when testing might occur and to guide the testing process to ensure that reasonable standards would be met. The government position appeared to gain added justification when the Court noted that a warrant procedure in this area would dissipate precious government assets. According to the Court, it is reasonable for employees who apply for promotion to particular positions to be tested for drug use in the absence of a requirement of probable cause or some level of individualized suspicion. From the thrust of the *Von Raab* decision, it is clear that governmental units may conduct drug tests on less than individualized suspicion so long as the government makes the case that its operations require drug-free employees due to the sensitive nature of their position of employment.

17. GOVERNMENT-MANDATED PRIVATE EMPLOYER SEARCHES

Whereas *Von Raab* directly involved governmental workplace searches, the federal government decided to pursue additional searches where private employers were required by the government to conduct drug tests on employees under certain conditions. The Federal Railroad Safety Act of 1970 authorized the secretary of transportation to set standards for all areas of railroad safety. Pursuant to this authority and because there had been some drug- or alcohol-related accidents, the secretary

---

[160]489 U.S. 656 (1989).

promulgated regulations that required certain railroad employees of private companies to be tested for drugs or alcohol subsequent to reportable major train accidents. The regulations mandated that both blood and urine samples would be required to meet the goals of the drug testing program. Employees who refused to provide the required blood or urine samples were not eligible to work in their particular positions for nine months, but individual employees could request a hearing concerning the merits of the refusal to give the requested samples of body fluids. If an employee declined to give a blood sample, the regulations allowed the railroad corporation to presume drug impairment. All the drug tests were to be administered in the absence of probable cause to believe that an employee was under the influence of drugs or alcohol.

The Railway Labor Executives' Association and various of its member labor organizations brought suit because they believed that required searches and seizures on less than probable cause constituted a violation of railroad employees' rights under the Fourth Amendment.[161] The trial court granted summary judgment for the government, but the court of appeals reversed on the authority that the Fourth Amendment required individualized suspicion prior to drug or alcohol testing. The Supreme Court of the United States accepted the case and reinstated the trial court decision in favor of the government.

The Court determined that the Fourth Amendment did have application to railroad workers who might be detained and required, for all practical purposes, to give a blood or urine sample. Although railroad workers are, for the most part, private employees, the Court determined that since the government required the use of drug tests, the railroads were acting in the position of the government, and for that reason the workers possessed Fourth Amendment protections. According to the Court, when intrusions are made into the body for the purposes of gathering body fluids, such conduct constitutes a search. The next aspect of the case that the Court was required to consider involved a determination of whether such intrusion could be deemed reasonable under the circumstances. The *Skinner* Court analyzed the practicalities of the situation and determined that a warrant system would not be feasible in this context because in the length of time it would take to procure a warrant to search body fluids, much of the evidence would be carried away from the body in the normal elimination process. The Court also determined that any requirement of individualized suspicion would frustrate the goals of determining drug or alcohol impairment. The *Skinner* Court held:

> We conclude that the compelling Government interests served by the FRA's [Federal Railroad Administration's] regulations would be significantly hindered if railroads were required to point to specific facts giving rise to a reasonable suspicion of impairment before testing a given employee. In view of our conclusion that, on the present record, the toxicological testing contemplated by the regulations is not an undue infringement on the justifiable expectations of privacy of covered employees, the Government's compelling interests outweigh privacy concerns. *Skinner v. Railway Labor Executives' Association,* 489 U.S. 602, 633 (1989) (see Case 5.7).

[161]See *Skinner v. Railway Labor Executives' Assn.,* 489 U.S. 602 (1989).

The essence of the decision turns on the fact that safety in railroad operations is of such paramount importance to the government, to business, and to everyone in general that a search of those employees constitutes a reasonable approach under the Fourth Amendment even in the absence of individualized suspicion and without a warrant. The principle of this case may easily be taken to other areas of transportation, as well as to other businesses where there has been extensive federal government regulation.

18. AIRPORT SEARCHES: GENERALLY FOUNDED ON THEORY OF CONSENT

For the past several decades, airplane hijacking and terrorist activity have dictated that persons boarding scheduled commercial aircraft within and departing from or to the United States be subjected to searches. In promoting aviation safety, the searches involved personal passenger screening complete with searches of checked baggage and carry-on luggage. The routine searching of luggage and of passengers has been upheld as reasonable under the circumstances. As Judge Friendly noted in upholding the constitutionality of airline passenger searches:

> When the risk is the jeopardy to hundreds of human lives and millions of dollars of property inherent in the pirating or blowing up of a large airplane, that danger alone meets the test of reasonableness, so long as the search is conducted in good faith for the purpose of preventing hijacking or like damage, and with reasonable scope, and the passenger has been given advance notice of his liability to such a search, so that he can avoid it by choosing not to travel by air. *United States v. Edwards,* 498 F.2d 496, 500 (CA2 1974).

Similarly, the Ninth Circuit in *United States v. Davis* held that airport security measures must meet the standard of reasonableness requirements under the Fourth Amendment. The court noted:

> An airport screening search is reasonable if: (1) it is no more extensive or intensive than necessary, in light of current technology, to detect weapons or explosives; (2) it is confined in good faith to that purpose; and (3) passengers may avoid the search by electing not to fly. 482 F.2d 893, 913 (CA9 1973).

Until recent changes in federal law,[162] much airport scrutiny and most passenger searches were conducted by employees of the airlines following federal directives. For the foreseeable future, once the recent federal law has been fully implemented, searches of airline passengers and flight crews will be conducted by employees of the federal government and a few contract screeners in small airports. When private companies conducted the screening mandated by the federal government, it was possible to view the searches as being conducted by private

---

[162]On November 19, 2001, President Bush signed the Aviation and Transportation Security Act, which established a new Transportation Security Administration under the control of the Department of Transportation. The Transportation Security Administration presently has authority for searching and screening of airline passengers and passenger property in the United States. In a few airports, companies under contract with the Transportation Security Administration conduct passenger screening. See Public Law 107-71, 107th Congress.

nongovernmental corporations, which, arguably, would not implicate the Fourth Amendment. The better view involves conceding that the Fourth Amendment has application because the federal government mandated passenger screening. However, each search may be deemed as consensual, since a person can avoid any search by deciding not to board an aircraft. Once a person gives consent by placing bags or carry-on luggage on the screening devices, generally the consent cannot be withdrawn. With the recent federal government takeover of passenger screening and baggage searching, an administrative search or consent theory should remain a valid justification for upholding reasonable airport searches.

With the present policy of screening airport passengers as they enter boarding concourses and with the posting of written notices that all baggage, personal effects, and persons are subject to search at any time after a person passes a certain point in the airport concourse, these searches fall under a consent theory or an administrative search rationale[163] under the Fourth Amendment. Passengers who have entered the airport but have not passed beyond security screening will generally not be deemed to have consented to give up their Fourth Amendment rights. Consent may be obtained by placing visible warnings to all persons who might enter an airport that their entry and transit beyond a particular point signifies consent to search by governmental agents. Airport security and search and seizure implications will undoubtedly be further litigated in the years to come as significant changes and alterations in Fourth Amendment jurisprudence evolve.

19. BORDER SEARCHES: SOVEREIGNTY AND THE FOURTH AMENDMENT

Searches by governmental agents at the international borders of the United States are deemed to be reasonable because the federal government has the right to control the items that leave or enter the nation. These searches, which may occur at the border or its functional equivalent, do not require probable cause or reasonable suspicion, and a warrant is not necessary. It overstates the case to say that nobody has any Fourth Amendment rights at the border, but it is rather close. Obviously, a strip search may not be conducted in a public place near the border, and body cavity searches will require some additional justification. While most border crossings and searches are rather swift, the duration of detention may be lengthy where there is suspicion that a person is a smuggler. In *United States v. Montoya de Hernandez,*[164] the subject was detained for about sixteen hours as a suspected alimentary canal drug smuggler. Suspicion arose due to the nature of her current travel plans and past travel patterns, all of which pointed to her as being a probable drug smuggler. Medical personnel eventually assisted in retrieving cocaine during a rectal search pursuant to a warrant.

In addition to actual border searches, the federal government may set up fairly fixed checkpoints on roads leading to and from the border areas. At these locations, vehicles moving through the area are subjected to an intermediate level of scrutiny.

---

[163]See *United States v. de los Santos Ferrer,* 999 F.2d 7, 9 (1st Cir. 1993), where passenger airport searches were characterized as being administrative searches conducted for limited and exigent purposes.
[164]473 U.S. 531 (1985).

The officers may ask routine questions of the occupants and evaluate their responses to determine if additional inquiries should be pursued. The questioning at the checkpoints may be conducted in the absence of any individualized suspicion of any occupant of a motor vehicle, but to conduct an additional and more intrusive search requires probable cause or some other legal justification.

Since fixed borders and fixed checkpoints on major highways can easily be by-passed by determined individuals, courts have deemed reasonable the practice of using roving patrols and stops by federal officials.[165] However, where governmental officials patrol border areas, the officers may stop vehicles only if they possess specific articulable facts and couple those facts with rational inferences therefrom, giving rise to reasonable suspicion that the vehicles may contain illegal aliens[166] or contraband items. Subsequent to a stop, federal officials may ask the driver and any passengers about their citizenship and whether the individuals are in the United States lawfully. Any additional detention or deeper search beyond the plain view requires either consent or probable cause to search.

The standard of reasonable suspicion sufficient to stop vehicles near the border was originally borrowed from the stop and frisk line of cases beginning with *Terry v. Ohio*.[167] The Supreme Court reaffirmed this legal theory in 2002 in *United States v. Arvizu*,[168] a case in which a border patrol agent developed reasonable suspicion to believe that Arvizu was engaged in illegal trafficking in drugs. According to the Court, when an officer engages in the process of making a determination of reasonable suspicion, the officer should consider the totality of the circumstances in reaching a conclusion. Arvizu, the driver of a minivan, was making every effort to avoid any officer by driving back roads in a remote part of southeastern Arizona, specifically avoiding all checkpoints. Border patrol agents moved so as to intercept the suspicious vehicle. As Arvizu passed the officer's vehicle positioned on the side of the road, he did not react to the officer the way local people usually did, which seemed odd. Instead of waving, the driver's posture was stiff and he clearly avoided looking at the officer's vehicle. The children, riding in the heavily loaded minivan, had their feet on top of some cargo where their feet should have been. Since the driver took a route typical of a person who wished to avoid the Immigration Service officers in the area, the officer could look at the totality of the circumstances to conclude that reasonable basis to suspect criminal activity existed. This justified the initial stop of the vehicle in *Arvizu*.

20. BORDER SEARCH SUMMARY

When a person crosses the international border leading to or from the United States, no suspicion is required to conduct a search of the person or his or her belongings. More intimate personal searches involving body cavity searches will require probable cause and a court order. At permanent checkpoints, officers may stop

---

[165]See *United States v. Brignoni-Ponce,* 422 U.S. 873 (1975).
[166]*Almeida-Sanchez v. United States,* 413 U.S. 266 (1973).
[167]392 U.S. 1 (1968).
[168]534 U.S. 266 (2002).

vehicles in the absence of individualized suspicion and visually observe the occupants of the vehicle. Only where probable cause matures, consent is granted, or some other theory allows a search may a search of a vehicle or of a person be considered lawful. Where the government observes suspicious individuals at some distance from the border, probable cause will allow a stop and search, but a vehicle may be stopped on less than probable cause, using the stop and frisk standard of reasonable basis to suspect criminal activity.

MAJOR CASES

CASE 5.1

Warrants Generally Required for Administrative Searches

Camara v. Municipal Court
Supreme Court of the United States
387 U.S. 523 (1967)

FACTS

Following the receipt of a complaint, an inspector of the San Francisco Division of Housing Inspection attempted to enter the first floor of an apartment building on which apartment living was not allowed. The building manager had informed the inspector that the appellant was using the street level premises as a personal place of residence in contravention of the building's occupancy permit. When the inspector confronted Camara with a request to inspect the premises, he refused to permit the inspection unless the housing inspector possessed a search warrant.

Acting on the same complaint, the building inspector returned to attempt a search without a warrant and requested admission to the building, to which Camara maintained his original position. Following local protocol, the inspector caused a citation to be mailed requesting Mr. Camara to appear at the district attorney's office. When the appellant ignored this request, two inspectors visited appellant a third time to inform him of his duty under Section 503 of the municipal code.

> Sec. 503. RIGHT TO ENTER BUILDING. Authorized employees of the City departments or City agencies, so far as may be necessary for the performance of their duties, shall, upon presentation of proper credentials, have the right to enter, at reasonable times, any building, structure, or premises in the City to perform any duty imposed upon them by the Municipal Code.

When Camara refused to permit the two inspectors to enter the premises, prosecutors filed a complaint charging him with refusing to permit a lawful warrantless inspection of his premises in violation of Section 503. Camara brought an action in Superior Court alleging that he had been charged criminally for violating the San Francisco Housing Code by refusing to permit a warrantless search of his residence. He requested that the Superior Court issue a writ of prohibition to the criminal court because the authorization of warrantless searches permitted by the ordinance was unconstitutional on its face. The Superior Court refused, a position which continued through the California state system resulting in a writ of certiorari being issued by the Supreme Court of the United States.

PROCEDURAL ISSUE

Consistent with the Fourth Amendment, and absent an emergency or other exception to the warrant requirement, may the occupier of real property require that a government possess a warrant permitting entry where the purpose is an administrative search?

HELD: YES

RATIONALE

Mr. Justice White delivered the opinion of the Court.

★ ★ ★

I

★ ★ ★

In *Frank v. State of Maryland,* this Court upheld the conviction of one who refused to permit a warrantless inspection of private premises for the purposes of locating and abating a suspected public nuisance....the *Frank [v. Maryland]* opinion has generally been interpreted as carving out an additional exception to the rule that [warrants are generally required for searches under the Fourth Amendment].

To the *Frank* majority, municipal fire, health, and housing inspection programs touch at most upon the periphery of the important interests safeguarded by the Fourteenth Amendment's protection against official intrusions,

359 U.S. at 367, because the inspections are merely to determine whether physical conditions exist which do not comply with minimum standards prescribed in local regulatory ordinances.

We may agree that a routine inspection of the physical condition of private property is a less hostile intrusion than the typical policeman's search for the fruits and instrumentalities of crime. For this reason alone, Frank differed from the great bulk of Fourth Amendment cases which have been considered by this Court. But we cannot agree that the Fourth Amendment interests at stake in these inspection cases are merely "peripheral." It is surely anomalous to say that the individual and his private property are fully protected by the Fourth Amendment only when the individual is suspected of criminal behavior. For instance, even the most law-abiding citizen has a very tangible interest in limiting the circumstances under which the sanctity of his home may be broken by official authority, for the possibility of criminal entry under the guise of official sanction is a serious threat to personal and family security. And even accepting Frank's rather remarkable premise, inspections of the kind we are here considering do, in fact, jeopardize "self-protection" interests of the property owner. Like most regulatory laws, fire, health, and housing codes are enforced by criminal processes. In some cities, discovery of a violation by the inspector leads to a criminal complaint. Even in cities where discovery of a violation produces only an administrative compliance order, refusal to comply is a criminal offense, and the fact of compliance is verified by a second inspection, again without a warrant. Finally, as this case demonstrates, refusal to permit an inspection is itself a crime, punishable by fine or even by jail sentence.

The *Frank* majority suggested, and appellee reasserts, two other justifications for permitting administrative health and safety inspections without a warrant. First, it is argued that these inspections are "designed to make the least possible demand on the individual occupant." The ordinances authorizing inspections are hedged with safeguards, and at any rate the inspector's particular decision to enter must comply with the constitutional standard of reasonableness even if he may enter without a warrant. In addition, the argument proceeds, the warrant process could not function effectively in this field. The decision to inspect an entire municipal area is based upon legislative or administrative assessment of broad factors such as the area's age and condition. Unless the magistrate is to review such policy matters, he must issue a "rubber stamp" warrant which provides no protection at all to the property owner.

In our opinion, these arguments unduly discount the purposes behind the warrant machinery contemplated by the Fourth Amendment. Under the present system when the inspector demands entry the occupant has no way of knowing whether enforcement of the municipal code involved requires inspection of his premises, no way of knowing the lawful limits of the inspector's power to search, and no way of knowing whether the inspector himself is acting under proper authorization. These are questions which may be reviewed by a neutral magistrate without any reassessment of the basic agency decision to canvass an area. Yet only by refusing entry and risking a criminal conviction can the occupant at present challenge the inspector's decision to search. And even if the occupant possesses sufficient fortitude to take this risk, as appellant did here, he may never learn any more about the reason for the inspection than that the law generally allows housing inspectors to gain entry. The practical effect of this system is to leave the occupant subject to the discretion of the official in the field. This is precisely the discretion to invade private property which we have consistently circumscribed by a requirement that a disinterested party warrant the need to search.

The final justification suggested for warrantless administrative searches is that the public interest demands such a rule: it is vigorously argued that the health and safety of entire urban populations is dependent upon enforcement of minimum fire, housing, and sanitation standards, and that the only effective means of enforcing such code is by routine systematized inspection of all physical structures. [However], the question is not...whether these inspections may be made, but whether they may be made without a warrant....

It has nowhere been urged that fire, health, and housing code inspection programs could not achieve their goals within the confines of a reasonable search warrant requirement. Thus, we do not find the public need argument dispositive.

In summary, we hold that administrative searches of the kind at issue here are significant intrusions upon the interests protected by the Fourth Amendment, that such searches when authorized and conducted without a warrant procedure lack the traditional safeguards which the Fourth Amendment guarantees to the individual....Because of the nature of the municipal programs under consideration, however, these conclusions must be the beginning, not the end, of our inquiry. The *Frank* majority gave recognition to the unique character of these inspection programs by refusing to require search warrants; to reject that disposition does not justify ignoring the question whether some other accommodation between public need and individual rights is essential.

II

The Fourth Amendment provides that, "no Warrants shall issue but upon probable cause." Borrowing from more typical Fourth Amendment cases, appellant argues not only that code enforcement inspection programs must be circumscribed by a warrant procedure, but also that warrants should issue only when the inspector possesses probable cause to believe that a particular dwelling contains violations of the minimum standards prescribed by the code being enforced. We disagree.

Unlike the search pursuant to a criminal investigation, the inspection programs at issue here are aimed at securing city-wide compliance with minimum physical standards for private property. The primary governmental interest at stake is to prevent even the unintentional development of conditions which are hazardous to public health and safety. Because fires and epidemics may ravage large urban areas, because unsightly conditions adversely affect the economic values of neighboring structures, numerous courts have upheld the police power of municipalities to impose and enforce such minimum standards even upon existing structures. In determining whether a particular inspection is reasonable—and thus in determining whether there is probable cause to issue a warrant for that inspection—the need for the inspection must be weighed in terms of these reasonable goals of code enforcement.

There is unanimous agreement among those most familiar with this field that the only effective way to seek universal compliance with the minimum standards required by municipal codes is through routine periodic inspections of all structures. It is here that the probable cause debate is focused, for the agency's decision to conduct an area inspection is unavoidably based on its appraisal of conditions in the area as a whole, not on its knowledge of conditions in each particular building. Appellee contends that, if the probable cause standard urged by appellant is adopted, the area inspection will be eliminated as a means of seeking compliance with code standards and the reasonable goals of code enforcement will be dealt a crushing blow.

In meeting this contention, appellant argues first, that his probable cause standard would not jeopardize

area inspection programs because only a minute portion of the population will refuse to consent to such inspections and second, that individual privacy in any event should be given preference to the public interest in conducting such inspections. The first argument, even if true, is irrelevant to the question whether the area inspection is reasonable within the meaning of the Fourth Amendment. The second argument is in effect an assertion that the area inspection is an unreasonable search. Unfortunately, there can be no ready test for determining reasonableness other than by balancing the need to search against the invasion which the search entails. But we think that a number of persuasive factors combine to support the reasonableness of code enforcement area inspections. First, such programs have a long history of judicial and public acceptance. Second, the public interest demands that all dangerous conditions be prevented or abated, yet it is doubtful that any other canvassing technique would achieve acceptable results. Many such conditions—faulty wiring is an obvious example—are not observable from outside the building and indeed may not be apparent to the inexpert occupant himself. Finally because the inspections are neither personal in nature nor aimed at the discovery of evidence of crime they involve a relatively limited invasion of the urban citizen's privacy.

★ ★ ★

Having concluded that the area inspection is a "reasonable" search of private property within the meaning of the Fourth Amendment, it is obvious that "probable cause" to issue a warrant to inspect must exist if reasonable legislative or administrative standards for conducting an area inspection are satisfied with respect to a particular dwelling. Such standards, which will vary with the municipal program being enforced, may be based upon the passage of time, the nature of the building (e.g., a multifamily apartment house) or the condition of the entire area, but they do not necessarily depend upon specific knowledge of the condition of the particular dwelling. It has been suggested that so to vary the probable cause test from the standard applied in criminal cases would be to authorize a "synthetic search warrant" and thereby, to lessen the overall protections of the Fourth Amendment. But we do not agree. The warrant procedure is designed to guarantee that a decision to search private property is justified by a reasonable governmental interest. But reasonableness is still the ultimate standard. If a valid public interest justifies the intrusion contemplated, then there is probable cause to issue a suitably restricted search warrant.... [The use of this procedure] neither endangers time-honored doctrines applicable to criminal investigations nor makes a nullity of the probable cause requirement in this area. It merely gives full recognition to the competing public and private interests here at stake....

III

Since our holding emphasizes the controlling standard of reasonableness nothing we say today is intended to foreclose prompt inspections, even without a warrant, that the law has traditionally upheld in emergency situations. [Citations omitted. The deleted citations refer to cases dealing with particular emergency situations: seizure of unwholesome food, compulsory smallpox vaccination, health quarantine, and summary destruction of tubercular cattle.] On the other hand, in the case of most routine area inspections, there is no compelling urgency to inspect at a particular time or on a particular day. Moreover, most citizens allow inspections of their property without a warrant. Thus, as a practical matter and in light of the Fourth Amendment's requirement that a warrant specify the property to be searched, it seems likely that warrants should normally be sought only after entry is refused unless there has been a citizen complaint or there is other satisfactory reason for securing immediate entry.

★ ★ ★

The judgment is vacated, and the case is remanded for further proceedings not inconsistent with this opinion.

It is so ordered.

COMMENTS, NOTES, AND QUESTIONS

1. Should a warrant be required to inspect a commercial property? Would a warrant be necessary in the private areas of a warehouse not open to the public? Do business operators have an expectation of privacy in their buildings, papers, and effects? Did the Fourth Amendment exempt from coverage all persons engaged in commercial activities? For answers, consider *See v. City of Seattle,* 387 U.S. 541 (1967). In *See,* the Court required that inspectors procure a warrant to gain entry to a commercial warehouse. According to the Court's rationale, See had been improperly convicted of violating a local ordinance that made it a crime to refuse a warrantless entry of a fire inspector. The words of the ordinance empowered fire inspectors to conduct routine inspections

without probable cause and without possession of a warrant. The *See* Court held that "administrative entry, without consent, upon the portions of commercial premises which are not open to the public may only be compelled through prosecution or physical force within the framework of a warrant procedure." *See* at 546. *See* extended similar *Camara* residential protection under the Fourth Amendment to business and business buildings.

2. How may administrative probable cause be developed? How does the *Camara* Court suggest? Must it come from governmental observation, or can administrative probable cause come from tips offered by informants and disgruntled employees? Specific complaints of an informant, such as occurred in *Camara,* may develop probable cause in a manner similar to criminal probable cause. Does the level of believability of administrative probable cause have to be as believable as the level necessary to demonstrate criminal probable cause? According to *See,* the level of certainty and believability required of a citizen or informant needed to produce administrative probable cause is a lower standard than necessary for criminal probable cause. Administrative probable cause, though it goes by the same term as criminal probable cause, may exist with significantly lower levels of proof. Should the levels of proof be so different? Since the Fourth Amendment made no distinction between criminal and administrative probable cause, did the framers of the Fourth Amendment intend such a distinction in probable cause? Why or why not?

3. Must commercial searches under the auspices of the Occupational Safety and Health Administration (OSHA) be based on both a warrant and probable cause? An OSHA search has administrative aspects, but violations that are uncovered can lead to monetary fines based on what a search revealed. In *Marshall v. Barlow's, Inc.,* 436 U.S. 307 (1978), a routine OSHA inspection program caused the administrative agency to determine to warrantlessly inspect the electrical and plumbing services business owned by Barlow. The government desired to inspect the nonpublic work areas in places of employment covered by OSHA, but the management refused because the OSHA inspectors did not have a search warrant. In construing the Fourth Amendment as requiring probable cause, the Court specified the standards that must be met to mature OSHA probable cause inspections. As the Court noted:

A warrant showing that a specific business has been chosen for an OSHA search on the basis of a general administrative plan for the enforcement of the Act derived from neutral sources such as the dispersion of employees in various types of industries across a given area, and the desired frequency of searches in any of the lesser divisions of the area would serve to protect an employer's Fourth Amendment rights. *Barlow's* at 321.

In OSHA-type searches, an inspection of businesses and industries has often been justified under a "worst first" standard in which the commercial enterprises that have the most hazardous records are selected for administrative inspections ahead of businesses that have compiled a better safety record.

4. Do some businesses or industries possess a lower expectation of privacy in conducting operations than do other entities? Are some undertakings so dangerous that governmental inspection may be undertaken in the absence of probable cause because an inspection is reasonable under the circumstances? Administrative searches of "heavily regulated industries" or "closely regulated industries" are justified in the absence of a warrant because the state or federal government has consistently and pervasively regulated the manner of the business practice. Thus, the entrepreneur has a diminished expectation of privacy if he or she initiates business in the area.

> The greater latitude to conduct warrantless inspections of commercial property reflects the fact that the expectation of privacy that the owner of commercial property enjoys in such property differs significantly from the sanctity accorded an individual's home, and that this privacy interest may, in certain circumstances, be adequately protected by regulatory schemes authorizing warrantless inspections. *Donovan v. Dewey,* 452 U.S. 594, at 598, 599 (1981).

Representative examples of heavily regulated industries include firearm sales and manufacturing, horse racing, liquor manufacturing and sales, mineral extraction through mining, pharmacies, nursing homes, and explosives manufacturing. See *Donovan v. Dewey,* 452 U.S. 594 (1981).

5. An example of an industry that did not qualify as a heavily regulated or pervasively regulated industry involved the making of goat cheese in Virginia. Pursuant to the law in the Commonwealth of Virginia, pervasively regulated industries may be subject to warrantless administrative searches where the state has a substantial interest in regulating the industry, where the regulation of the industry reasonably serves the state's interest, and where warrantless searches are necessary to achieve the state's interests. To

meet due process standards, the language of the statute covering pervasively regulated businesses reasonably informed the operators that warrantless searches may be routine. Statutory time and place limitations also applied. A woman filed suit for a declaratory judgment concerning Virginia's assertion that the making of goat cheese at her home and on her small farm constituted a heavily or pervasively regulated industry subject to warrantless searches. The court found no basis for holding that a goat cheese operation on a small farm qualified as a pervasively regulated industry and enjoined the government from attempting to make any future warrantless searches of the operation. The circuit court judge ruled that there was no administrative search exception for goat cheese making under the circumstances. See *Solem v. Courter,* 57 Va. Cir. 143 (2001).

6. In the absence of a warrant, governmental inspectors are not permitted, as a general rule, to force open the building in which they wish to make an inspection. In *Colonnade Catering Corporation v. United States,* 397 U.S. 72 (1970), the federal statute, 26 U.S.C. § 5146(b), allowed a search of licensed facilities that served and stored intoxicating liquors. Failure to allow the search was punishable by a fine only. In *Colonnade Catering,* federal agents broke into the storage area without statutory authority. This breaking and search was held to have been unreasonable without a warrant because the federal agents were not empowered to break and possessed no warrant. The statute not only must grant power to search but must grant the right to forcibly make the search. Failure to follow the law resulted in the exclusion of evidence because of the illegal search.

CASE 5.2

Inventory Search Following Arrest Requires No Warrant or Probable Cause

Illinois v. Lafayette
Supreme Court of the United States
462 U.S. 640 (1983)

FACTS

Lafayette became involved in an oral dispute in an altercation with the theater manager where he was disturbing the peace at the Town Cinema in Kankakee, Illinois. Police took respondent into custody for disturbing the peace, handcuffed him, and transported him to the police station. Lafayette carried a purse-type shoulder bag on the trip to the station. The booking officer at the station conducted an inventory search of all of Lafayette's personal possessions within his purse. The inventory/search revealed some cigarettes removed by Lafayette from the bag and the officer found some amphetamine tablets within the packaging normally surrounding cigarettes. The presence of the drugs resulted in a charge of violating the Illinois Controlled Substance Act.

In an attempt to keep the drugs from being used against him, Lafayette filed a motion to suppress the amphetamine tablets on the ground that the search of his shoulder bag at the station house did not constitute a valid search. His theory argued that the search of the bag could not be justified as incident to a lawful arrest and did not fall under the theory of a valid inventory search.

The inventory/search officer, Mietzner, testified that he did not expect to find drugs when he examined the defendant's possessions and he noted that it was standard policy to inventory everything at the time a person was being booked. In response to a question, the officer conceded that the shoulder bag was small enough to have been placed in a larger inventory bag and secured in that manner. After the close of Officer Mietzner's testimony and after the state raised the justification that the search was valid as an inventory search or as a delayed search incident to arrest, the trial court disagreed and ordered suppression of the evidence.

The Illinois Appellate Court agreed with Lafayette's contentions and affirmed the trial court order. The court held that the station house search of the shoulder bag did not constitute either a valid search incident to arrest or a valid inventory search of Lafayette's possessions. It noted that the state's interests could have been met in a less intrusive manner by sealing the shoulder bag without looking through its contents. The Illinois Supreme Court declined to review the case and the Supreme Court of the United States granted certiorari.

PROCEDURAL ISSUE

In the absence of probable cause to search and consistent with the Fourth Amendment, may police reasonably search the personal effects of a person under lawful arrest as part of the routine administrative procedure at a police station house incident to booking and jailing the suspect, as long as the inventory procedure follows standard police practice?

HELD: YES

RATIONALE

Chief Justice Burger delivered the opinion of the Court.

★ ★ ★

II

[T]he justification for [inventory] searches does not rest on probable cause, and hence the absence of a warrant is immaterial to the reasonableness of the search. Indeed, we have previously established that the inventory search constitutes a well-defined exception to the warrant requirement. See *South Dakota v. Opperman, supra* [428 U.S. 364 (1976)]. The Illinois court and respondent rely on *United States v. Chadwick,* 433 U.S. 1 (1977), and *Arkansas v. Sanders,* 442 U.S. 753 (1979); in the former, we noted that "probable cause to search is irrelevant" in inventory searches and went on to state:

> This is so because the salutary functions of a warrant simply have no application in that context; the constitutional reasonableness of inventory searches must be determined on other bases. *Id.,* 433 U.S., at 10 n. 5.

A so-called inventory search is not an independent legal concept but rather an incidental administrative step following arrest and preceding incarceration. To determine whether the search of respondent's shoulder bag was unreasonable we must "balanc[e] its intrusion on the individual's Fourth Amendment interests against its promotion of legitimate governmental interests." *Delaware v. Prouse,* 440 U.S. 648, 654 (1979).

In order to see an inventory search in proper perspective, it is necessary to study the evolution of interests along the continuum from arrest to incarceration. We have held that immediately upon arrest an officer may lawfully search the person of an arrestee, *United States v. Robinson,* 414 U.S. 218 (1973); he may also search the area within the arrestee's immediate control, *Chimel v. California,* 395 U.S. 752 (1969). We explained the basis for this doctrine in *United States v. Robinson, supra,* where we said:

> A police officer's determination as to how and where to search the person of a suspect whom he has arrested is necessarily a quick *ad hoc* judgment which the Fourth Amendment does not require to be broken down in each instance into an analysis of each step in the search. The authority to search the person incident to a lawful custodial arrest, while based upon the need to disarm and to discover evidence, does not depend

on what a court may later decide was the probability in a particular arrest situation that weapons or evidence would in fact be found upon the person of the suspect. A custodial arrest of a suspect based on probable cause is a reasonable intrusion under the Fourth Amendment; that intrusion being lawful, a search incident to the arrest requires no additional justification. *It is the fact of the lawful arrest which establishes the authority to search,* and we hold that in the case of a lawful custodial arrest *a full search of the person is not only an exception to the warrant requirement of the Fourth Amendment, but is also a "reasonable" search under that Amendment.* 414 U.S., at 235 (emphasis added).

An arrested person is not invariably taken to a police station or confined; if an arrestee is taken to the police station, that is no more than a continuation of the custody inherent in the arrest status. Nonetheless, the factors justifying a search of the person and personal effects of an arrestee upon reaching a police station but prior to being placed in confinement are somewhat different from the factors justifying an immediate search at the time and place of arrest.

The governmental interests underlying a stationhouse search of the arrestee's person and possessions may in some circumstances be even greater than those supporting a search immediately following arrest. Consequently, the scope of a stationhouse search will often vary from that made at the time of arrest. Police conduct that would be impractical or unreasonable—or embarrassingly intrusive—on the street can more readily—and privately—be performed at the station....

At the stationhouse, it is entirely proper for police to remove and list or inventory property found on the person or in the possession of an arrested person who is to be jailed. A range of governmental interests support an inventory process. It is not unheard of for persons employed in police activities to steal property taken from arrested persons; similarly, arrested persons have been known to make false claims regarding what was taken from their possession at the stationhouse. A standardized procedure for making a list or inventory as soon as reasonable after reaching the stationhouse not only deters false claims but also inhibits theft or careless handling of articles taken from the arrested person. Arrested persons have also been known to injure themselves—or others—with belts, knives, drugs or other items on their person while being detained. Dangerous instrumentalities—such as razor blades, bombs, or weapons—can be concealed in innocent-looking articles taken from the arrestee's possession. The bare recital of these mundane

realities justifies reasonable measures by police to limit these risks—either while the items are in police possession or at the time they are returned to the arrestee upon his release....In short, every consideration of orderly police administration benefiting both police and the public points toward the appropriateness of the examination of respondent's shoulder bag prior to his incarceration.

★ ★ ★

The Illinois court held that the search of respondent's shoulder bag was unreasonable because "preservation of the defendant's property and protection of the police from claims of lost or stolen property, could have been achieved in a less intrusive manner."...

The reasonableness of any particular governmental activity does not necessarily or invariably turn on the existence of alternative "less intrusive" means. In *Cady v. Dombrowski,* 413 U.S. 433 (1973), for example, we upheld the search of the trunk of a car to find a revolver suspected of being there. We rejected the contention that the public could equally well have been protected by the posting of a guard over the automobile. In language equally applicable to this case, we held, "[t]he fact that the protection of the public might, in the abstract, have been accomplished by 'less intrusive' means does not, by itself, render the search unreasonable."

★ ★ ★

[W]e hold that it is not "unreasonable" for police, as part of the routine procedure incident to incarcerating an arrested person, to search any container or article in his possession, in accordance with established inventory procedures.

The judgment of the Illinois Appellate Court is reversed and the case is remanded for proceedings not inconsistent with this opinion.

COMMENTS, NOTES, AND QUESTIONS

1. Does the *Lafayette* Court indicate that an inventory search at the station house may be more compelling and reasonable than a search on the street following an arrest? Why would a search of a person at the station house, where the police presence is pervasive, be more necessary than a search incident to an arrest? What could the purse or backpack hold when it is brought to the police station? Drugs? Explosives? Other dangerous objects? If no inventory were taken of some individuals and their possessions,

police could conceivably have protective custody of recreational pharmaceuticals during a criminal case and then unknowingly return them to a drug dealer upon release from custody. The irony of such a situation is that it makes the police safekeepers of a drug dealer's inventory.

2. How could an inventory search at the police station help police beyond avoiding harmful ordinance being introduced? What does the *Lafayette* Court say about safeguarding valuables that may come into police custody? Does that theory make an inventory search reasonable? Consider the situation where a seller in raw diamonds engages in disorderly conduct with a person on the street. If police arrest the diamond dealer, it might be unreasonable not to take an inventory of his or her wares. Could an inventory search reduce a subsequent claim of loss of goods by the diamond dealer?

3. In *Lafayette,* had the police decided to search the backpack at the point of arrest, what theories would have been permissible to justify the search? Search incident to lawful arrest? How far could the inventory search theory go? Is there any place that would have been off limits to search if the search were based on the theory of search incident to lawful arrest? What if the backpack were searched two days later on an inventory theory? Should that hold up in court? Why or why not?

4. Could an inventory search theory be used to justify searches for which probable cause to search failed to exist? In Lafayette's case, there was no probable cause to believe that his backpack contained contraband. In the absence of the arrest, no legal theory permitted the search of the backpack/purse, and Lafayette could have gone on his way. This would have been true if the officer had merely issued a citation to Lafayette and terminated the encounter in that manner. The officer possessed some discretion concerning whether to arrest, but once that decision had been made, the inventory theory allowed a significant search.

CASE 5.3

Written Inventory Search Policy Mandatory: Some Discretion on Scope Permitted

Colorado v. Bertine
Supreme Court of the United States
479 U.S. 367 (1987)

FACTS

A Boulder, Colorado, police officer possessing probable cause arrested Bertine for operating a motor vehicle under the influence of alcohol. The officer called for a tow truck to remove Mr. Bertine's motor vehicle and pursuant to a written policy, proceeded to conduct an immediate inventory search of the contents of the motor vehicle. The policy required that the officer follow standard procedures for impounding vehicles and mandated that a detailed inventory involving the opening of containers be conducted, which required the listing of all contents. Inside the vehicle, the officer discovered a backpack which contained various controlled substances, money, and cocaine paraphernalia. The officer did not have probable cause to search the motor vehicle and its contents at the time of the inventory. The search conducted by the officer followed local police department requirements which required a detailed inspection and inventory of all impounded vehicles but gave the officer on the scene discretion concerning whether to impound a vehicle.

Although the search was "somewhat slipshod" in the manner in which it was conducted, the trial court held that neither the inventory search policy nor the inventory search violated the dictates of the Fourth Amendment. Interestingly, the trial court held that the inventory search as conducted in this case *violated relevant portions of the State of Colorado constitution.* With a slight twist in legal theory, the Supreme Court of Colorado upheld the trial court decision but based the affirmation and the exclusion of evidence on the Fourth Amendment rather than on the Colorado state constitution. The Supreme Court of the United States granted Colorado's petition for a writ of certiorari.

PROCEDURAL QUESTION

Consistent with the Fourth Amendment, where police officers have some limited discretion pursuant to a departmental inventory search policy of either conducting an inventory search of an impounded vehicle and its contents or not impounding the vehicle, does such discretion leave the inventory search policy without sufficient standards?

HELD: NO

RATIONALE

Chief Justice Rehnquist delivered the opinion of the Court.

★ ★ ★

[A]n inventory search may be "reasonable" under the Fourth Amendment even though it is not conducted pursuant to warrant based upon probable cause. In *[South Dakota v.] Opperman* [428 U.S. 364 (1976)], this Court assessed the reasonableness of an inventory search of the glove compartment in an abandoned automobile impounded by the police. We found that inventory procedures serve to protect an owner's property while it is in the custody of the police, to insure against claims of lost, stolen, or vandalized property, and to guard the police from danger.

★ ★ ★

In our more recent decision, *[Illinois v.] Lafayette* [462 U.S. 640 (1983)], a police officer conducted an inventory search of the contents of a shoulder bag in the possession of an individual being taken into custody. In deciding whether this search was reasonable, we recognized that the search served legitimate governmental interests similar to those identified in *Opperman*. We determined that those interests outweighed the individual's Fourth Amendment interests and upheld the search.

★ ★ ★

In the present case, as in *Opperman* and *Lafayette,* there was no showing that the police, who were following standardized procedures, acted in bad faith or for the sole purpose of investigation. In addition, the governmental interests justifying the inventory searches in *Opperman* and *Lafayette* are nearly the same as those which obtain here. In each case, the police were potentially responsible for the property taken into their custody. By securing the property, the police protected the property from unauthorized interference. Knowledge of the precise nature of the property helped guard against claims of theft, vandalism, or negligence. Such knowledge also helped to avert any danger to police or others that may have been posed by the property.

★ ★ ★

The Supreme Court of Colorado also expressed the view that the search in this case was unreasonable because Bertine's van was towed to a secure, lighted facility and because Bertine himself could have been offered the opportunity to make other arrangements for the safekeeping of his property. But the security of the storage facility does not completely eliminate the need for inventorying; the police may still wish to protect themselves or the owners of the lot against false claims of theft or dangerous instrumentalities.

★ ★ ★

Bertine finally argues that the inventory search of his van was unconstitutional because departmental regulations gave the police officers discretion to choose between impounding his van and parking and locking it in a public parking place. The Supreme Court of Colorado did not rely on this argument in reaching its conclusion, and we reject it. Nothing in *Opperman* or *Lafayette* prohibits the exercise of police discretion so long as that discretion is exercised according to standard criteria and on the basis of something other than suspicion of evidence of criminal activity. Here, the discretion afforded the Boulder police was exercised in light of standardized criteria, related to the feasibility and appropriateness of parking and locking a vehicle rather than impounding it. There was no showing that the police chose to impound Bertine's van in order to investigate suspected criminal activity.

While both *Opperman* and *Lafayette* are distinguishable from the present case on their facts, we think that the principles enunciated in those cases govern the present one. The judgment of the Supreme Court of Colorado is therefore

Reversed.

COMMENTS, NOTES, AND QUESTIONS

1. Inventory searches of lawfully impounded automobiles received clear judicial approval in *South Dakota v. Opperman,* 428 U.S. 364 (1976). In *Opperman,* police towed a motor vehicle that had articles of personal property clearly visible within the car. No probable cause existed to believe the automobile contained any substance that offended the law. An officer, in the process of taking inventory, observed some drugs in the glove compartment. The Court upheld the seizure of the drugs on the theory that the officer had been engaged in a caretaking search of a lawfully impounded vehicle and such search was not unreasonable under the Fourth Amendment. Note carefully that the Court in *Florida v. Wells,* 495 U.S. 1 (1990), required that police inventory searches be conducted under a written policy, a requirement that the police actually followed in the *Opperman* search. The validity of the inventory policy followed in *Opperman* was not litigated by the *Opperman* defendant.

2. Could an inventory search be used as a pretext to conduct a search for which probable cause did not exist? In *Whren v. United States,* 517 U.S. 806 (1996), the Court noted that it did not desire to entertain Fourth Amendment challenges based on the actual motivations of individual officers and held that subjective intentions play no role in ordinary, probable cause Fourth Amendment analysis. In *Arkansas v. Sullivan,* 532 U.S. 769 (2001), the Court clearly upheld the *Whren* principle that if there is a lawful reason to stop or seize, it does not matter what ulterior motive or alleged pretext motivates the officer. What if an officer possessed discretion concerning whether or not to tow a car and chose towing, since such course of conduct would permit a search? Would that invalidate the search? Under *Bertine,* the discretion or pretext under *Sullivan* does not invalidate the search. Should such a search be upheld?

CASE 5.4

Public School Student Searches: A Lower Level of Constitutional Protection

New Jersey v. T.L.O.
Supreme Court of the United States
469 U.S. 325 (1985)

FACTS

After encountering two female students smoking tobacco in the restroom of a high school, the school official took the pair for disciplinary processing to the assistant vice principal, Mr. Choplick. One of the detained students, Ms. T.L.O., denied smoking and indicated that she did not use tobacco products. Then Mr. Choplick asked to see her purse, which he promptly opened, and conducted a brief search.

The purse proved to contain cigarettes and rolling papers which the assistant vice principal knew were often associated with the use of marijuana. Since he suspected that the purse might contain additional contraband, he conducted a full search of the student's purse. This second search produced some marijuana, a pipe, some baggies, some money, and a customer list. Ms. T.L.O. eventually confessed to her drug dealing to the police and admitted that she sold to her high school friends. In due course, the state prosecutor brought juvenile delinquency proceedings against Ms. T.L.O.

Upon the advice of counsel, Ms. T.L.O. filed a motion to suppress her confession on the legal ground that it had been obtained by an unlawful first search conducted by the assistant vice principal. The court rejected the motion to suppress and it adjudicated Ms. T.L.O. as delinquent by virtue of her marijuana possession. As part of the adjudication of delinquency, the juvenile judge ordered her to serve a one-year term of probation.

Ms. T.L.O. perfected her appeal to the New Jersey Supreme Court, where it ruled in her favor and ordered suppression of the evidence. The prosecution appealed the case to the Supreme Court of the United States, which granted a writ of certiorari.

PROCEDURAL ISSUE

Prior to conducting a search under the Fourth Amendment, must a public-school officer possess reasonable grounds for suspecting that a student has or is violating one of the school's rules or the criminal law?

HELD: YES

RATIONALE

Mr. Justice White delivered the opinion of the Court.

★ ★ ★

II

In determining whether the search at issue in this case violated the Fourth Amendment, we are faced initially with the question whether that Amendment's prohibition on unreasonable searches and seizures applies to searches conducted by public school officials. We hold that it does.

It is now beyond dispute that

> the Federal Constitution, by virtue of the Fourteenth Amendment, prohibits unreasonable searches and seizures by state officers. *Elkins v. United States,* 364 U.S. 206, 213 (1960).

Equally indisputable is the proposition that the Fourteenth Amendment protects the rights of students against encroachment by public school officials:

> The Fourteenth Amendment, as now applied to the States, protects the citizen against the State itself and all of its creatures—Boards of Education not excepted.

★ ★ ★

It may well be true that the evil toward which the Fourth Amendment was primarily directed was the resurrection of the pre-Revolutionary practice of using general warrants or "writs of assistance" to authorize searches for contraband by officers of the Crown. But this Court has never limited the Amendment's prohibition on unreasonable searches and seizures to operations conducted by the police. Rather, the Court has long spoken of the Fourth Amendment's strictures as restraints imposed upon "governmental action"—that is, "upon the activities of sovereign authority." Accordingly, we have held the Fourth Amendment applicable to the activities of civil as well as criminal authorities: building inspectors, see *Camara v. Municipal Court,* 387 U.S. 523, 528 (1967), Occupational Safety and Health Act inspectors, see *Marshall v. Barlow's, Inc.,* 436 U.S. 307, 312–313 (1978), and even firemen entering privately owned premises to battle a fire, see *Michigan v. Tyler,* 436 U.S. 499, 506 (1978), are all subject to the restraints imposed by the Fourth Amendment. As we observed in *Camara v. Municipal Court, supra,*

> [t]he basic purpose of this Amendment, as recognized in countless decisions of this Court, is to safeguard the privacy and security of individuals against arbitrary invasions by governmental officials. 387 U.S. at 528.

★ ★ ★

We have held school officials subject to the commands of the First Amendment, see *Tinker v. Des Moines Independent Community School District,* 393 U.S. 503 (1969), and the Due Process Clause of the Fourteenth Amendment. If school authorities are state actors for purposes of the constitutional guarantees of freedom of expression and due process, it is difficult to understand why they should be deemed to be exercising parental rather than public authority when conducting searches of their students. More generally, the Court has recognized that "the concept of parental delegation" as a source of school authority is not entirely "consonant with compulsory education laws." Today's public school officials do not merely exercise authority voluntarily conferred on them by individual parents; rather, they act in furtherance of publicly mandated educational and disciplinary policies. See, e.g., the opinion in *State ex rel. T.L.O.,* 94 N.J. at 343, 463 A.2d at 934, 940, describing the New Jersey statutes regulating school disciplinary policies and establishing the authority of school officials over their students. In carrying out searches and other disciplinary functions pursuant to such policies, school officials act as representatives of the State, not merely as surrogates for the parents, and they cannot claim the parents' immunity from the strictures of the Fourth Amendment.

III

To hold that the Fourth Amendment applies to searches conducted by school authorities is only to begin the inquiry into the standards governing such searches. Although the underlying command of the Fourth Amendment is always that searches and seizures be reasonable, what is reasonable depends on the context within which a search takes place. The determination of the standard of reasonableness governing any specific class of searches requires "balancing the need to search against the invasion which the search entails." *Camara v. Municipal Court, supra,* at 536–537. On one side of the balance are arrayed the individual's legitimate expectations of privacy and personal security; on the other, the government's need for effective methods to deal with breaches of public order.

★ ★ ★

The State of New Jersey has argued that, because of the pervasive supervision to which children in the schools are necessarily subject, a child has virtually no legitimate expectation of privacy in articles of personal property "unnecessarily" carried into a school. This argument has two factual premises: (1) the fundamental incompatibility of expectations of privacy with the maintenance of a sound educational environment; and (2) the minimal interest of the child in bringing any items of personal property into the school. Both premises are severely flawed.

★ ★ ★

We have recently recognized that the need to maintain order in a prison is such that prisoners retain no legitimate expectations of privacy in their cells, but it goes almost without saying that "[t]he prisoner and the schoolchild stand in wholly different circumstances, separated by the harsh facts of criminal conviction and incarceration." *Ingraham v. Wright, supra,* at 669. We are not yet ready to hold that the schools and the prisons need be equated for purposes of the Fourth Amendment.

Nor does the State's suggestion that children have no legitimate need to bring personal property into the schools seem well anchored in reality. Students at a minimum must bring to school not only the supplies needed for their studies, but also keys, money, and the necessaries of personal hygiene and grooming. In addition, students may carry on their persons or in purses or wallets such nondisruptive yet highly personal items as photographs, letters, and diaries. Finally, students may have perfectly legitimate reasons to carry with them articles of property needed in connection with extracurricular or recreational activities. In short, schoolchildren may find it necessary to carry with them a variety of legitimate, noncontraband items, and there is no reason to conclude that they have necessarily waived all rights to privacy in such items merely by bringing them onto school grounds.

★ ★ ★

Against the child's interest in privacy must be set the substantial interest of teachers and administrators in maintaining discipline in the classroom and on school grounds. Maintaining order in the classroom has never been easy, but in recent years, school disorder has often taken particularly ugly forms: drug use and violent crime in the schools have become major social problems.

★ ★ ★

How, then, should we strike the balance between the schoolchild's legitimate expectations of privacy and the school's equally legitimate need to maintain an environment in which learning can take place? It is evident that the school setting requires some easing of the restrictions to which searches by public authorities are ordinarily subject. The warrant requirement, in particular, is unsuited to the school environment: requiring a teacher to obtain a warrant before searching a child suspected of an infraction of school rules (or of the criminal law) would unduly interfere with the maintenance of the swift and informal disciplinary procedures needed in the schools. Just as we have in other cases dispensed with the warrant requirement when "the burden of obtaining a warrant is likely to frustrate the governmental purpose behind the search," *Camara v. Municipal Court,* 387 U.S. at 532–533, we hold today that school officials need not obtain a warrant before searching a student who is under their authority.

The school setting also requires some modification of the level of suspicion of illicit activity needed to justify a search. Ordinarily, a search—even one that may permissibly be carried out without a warrant—must be based upon "probable cause" to believe that a violation of the law has occurred. However, "probable cause" is not an irreducible requirement of a valid search. The fundamental command of the Fourth Amendment is that searches and seizures be reasonable, and although

> both the concept of probable cause and the requirement of a warrant bear on the reasonableness of a search,…in certain limited circumstances neither is required. *Almeida-Sanchez v. United States,* 413 U.S. 266, 277 (1973).

We join the majority of courts that have examined this issue in concluding that the accommodation of the privacy interests of schoolchildren with the substantial need of teachers and administrators for freedom to maintain order in the schools does not require strict adherence to the requirement that searches be based on probable cause to believe that the subject of the search has violated or is violating the law. Rather, the legality of a search of a student should depend simply on the reasonableness, under all the circumstances, of the search. Determining the reasonableness of any search involves a twofold inquiry: first, one must consider "whether the… action was justified at its inception," *Terry v. Ohio,* 392 U.S. at 20; second, one must determine whether the search as actually conducted "was reasonably related in scope to the circumstances which justified the interference in the first place," ibid. Under ordinary circumstances, a search of a student by a teacher or other school official will be "justified at its inception" when there are reasonable grounds for suspecting that the search will turn up evidence that the student has violated or is violating either the law or the rules of the school. Such a search will be permissible in its scope when the measures adopted are reasonably related to the objectives of the search and not excessively intrusive in light of the age and sex of the student and the nature of the infraction.

There remains the question of the legality of the search in this case. We recognize that the "reasonable grounds" standard applied by the New Jersey Supreme Court in its consideration of this question is not substantially different from the standard that we have adopted today. Nonetheless, we believe that the New Jersey court's application of that standard to strike down the search of T.L.O.'s purse reflects a somewhat crabbed notion of reasonableness. Our review of the facts surrounding the search leads us to conclude that the search was in no sense unreasonable for Fourth Amendment purposes.

The incident that gave rise to this case actually involved two separate searches, with the first—the search for cigarettes—providing the suspicion that gave rise to the second—the search for marihuana. Although it is the fruits of the second search that are at issue here, the validity of the search for marihuana must depend on the reasonableness of the initial search for cigarettes, as there would have been no reason to suspect that T.L.O. possessed marihuana had the first search not taken place. Accordingly, it is to the search for cigarettes that we first turn our attention.

★ ★ ★

Thus, if Mr. Choplick in fact had a reasonable suspicion that T.L.O. had cigarettes in her purse, the search was justified despite the fact that the cigarettes, if found, would constitute "mere evidence" of a violation.

★ ★ ★

Our conclusion that Mr. Choplick's decision to open T.L.O.'s purse was reasonable brings us to the question of the further search for marihuana once the pack of cigarettes was located. The suspicion upon which the search for marihuana was founded was provided when Mr. Choplick observed a package of rolling papers in the purse as he removed the pack of cigarettes. Although T.L.O. does not dispute the reasonableness of Mr. Choplick's belief that the rolling papers indicated the presence of marihuana, she does contend that the scope of the search Mr. Choplick conducted exceeded permissible bounds when he seized and read certain letters that implicated T.L.O. in drug dealing. This argument, too, is unpersuasive. The discovery of the rolling papers concededly gave rise to a reasonable suspicion that T.L.O. was carrying marihuana as well as cigarettes in her purse. This suspicion justified further exploration of T.L.O.'s purse, which turned up more evidence of drug-related activities: a pipe, a number of plastic bags of the type commonly used to store marihuana, a small quantity of marihuana, and a fairly substantial amount of money. Under these circumstances, it was not unreasonable to extend the search to a separate zippered compartment of the purse; and when a search of that compartment revealed an index card containing a list of "people who owe me money" as well as two letters, the inference that T.L.O. was involved in marihuana trafficking was substantial enough to justify Mr. Choplick in examining the letters to determine whether they contained any further evidence. In short, we cannot conclude that the search for marihuana was unreasonable in any respect.

Because the search resulting in the discovery of the evidence of marihuana dealing by T.L.O. was reasonable,

the New Jersey Supreme Court's decision to exclude that evidence from T.L.O.'s juvenile delinquency proceedings on Fourth Amendment grounds was erroneous. Accordingly, the judgment of the Supreme Court of New Jersey is

Reversed.

COMMENTS, NOTES, AND QUESTIONS

1. If this frequently quoted statement that students do not "shed their constitutional rights…at the schoolhouse gate," *Tinker v. Des Moines Independent Community School District,* 393 U.S. 503, 506 (1969), is true, has the Court in *T.L.O.* offered secondary students a bit less protection than adults? Reasonable suspicion seems to be a lower standard than probable cause. Is it? It could be argued that such a standard seems to be similar to the legal precursor for a valid stop and frisk. See *Terry v. Ohio,* 392 U.S. 1 (1968).

2. The principal did not need to procure a warrant for a search of the student's purse. Should we require warrants for some school searches? Drug-sniffing dogs, which may be brought through schools and their grounds to sniff lockers or cars in a student parking lot, are not conducting searches. See *United States v. Place,* 462 U.S. 696, 707 (1983). Why not? Could school administrators search through each student's bag upon entry to school each day? Would it take some individualized suspicion like we had in *T.L.O.?* Note that students are in a different position than airline travelers because they must attend school under compulsory attendance laws.

CASE 5.5

Scheduled and Random Drug Tests for Student Athletes

Vernonia School Dist. 47J v. Acton
Supreme Court of the United States
515 U.S. 646 (1995)

FACTS

The Vernonia School District 47J made a determination that drug use and related problems were beginning to create harm to the students in their district and resolved to take affirmative steps to combat the threat. The school board decided that athletes who desired to participate in any particular sport must all submit to a drug test at the beginning of the season. According to the Student Athlete

Drug Policy, students wishing to play sports were required to sign a form consenting to the testing and had to obtain the written consent of their parents to play sports and to be tested. The athlete who passed the initial drug screen could initiate participation in the sport but was subject to random drug tests throughout the particular season. All athletes were to have their names placed in a lottery from which ten percent of the athletes would be selected for random drug testing on the day of the drawing. There was no requirement of individualized suspicion of drug use prior to testing.

One student who desired to play had parents who refused to consent to drug screening. The school prohibited him from participating in sports unless his parents cooperated with the drug testing program. The family filed suit alleging that the suspicionless drug testing constituted a violation of the Fourth Amendment as applied to the states through the Fourteenth Amendment's Due Process Clause.

After filing suit in federal district court, the trial court rejected the claims, after due consideration, but the Court of Appeals reversed the lower court, holding that the policy on drug testing violated the Fourth Amendment as applied to the States. The Supreme Court granted certiorari to decide whether this violates the Fourth and Fourteenth Amendments to the United States Constitution.

PROCEDURAL ISSUE

Where a public school district desires to implement consent-based student drug tests of athletes, regardless of suspicion of drug use, does that policy violate the Fourth Amendment's proscription against unreasonable searches and seizures?

HELD: NO

RATIONALE

Mr. Justice Scalia delivered the opinion of the Court.

★ ★ ★

II

The Fourth Amendment to the United States Constitution provides that the Federal Government shall not violate "[t]he right of the people to be secure in their persons, houses, papers, and effects, against unreasonable searches and seizures...." We have held that the Fourteenth Amendment extends this constitutional guarantee to searches and seizures by state officers, *Elkins v. United States,* 364 U.S. 206, 213 (1960), including public school officials, *New Jersey v. T.L.O.,* 469 U.S. 325, 336–337 (1985). In *Skinner v. Railway Labor Executives' Assn.,* 489 U.S. 602, 617 (1989), we held that state-compelled collection and testing of urine, such as that required by the Student Athlete Drug Policy, constitutes a "search" subject to the demands of the Fourth Amendment. See also *[National] Treasury Employees [Union] v. Von Raab,* 489 U.S. 656, 665 (1989).

As the text of the Fourth Amendment indicates, the ultimate measure of the constitutionality of a governmental search is "reasonableness." At least in a case such as this, where there was no clear practice, either approving or disapproving the type of search at issue at the time the constitutional provision was enacted, whether a particular search meets the reasonableness standard

> is judged by balancing its intrusion on the individual's Fourth Amendment interests against its promotion of legitimate governmental interests. *Skinner, supra,* at 619 (quoting *Delaware v. Prouse,* 440 U.S. 648, 654 (1979)).

Where a search is undertaken by law enforcement officials to discover evidence of criminal wrongdoing, this Court has said that reasonableness generally requires the obtaining of a judicial warrant, *Skinner, supra,* at 619. Warrants cannot be issued, of course, without the showing of probable cause required by the Warrant Clause. But a warrant is not required to establish the reasonableness of all government searches; and when a warrant is not required (and the Warrant Clause therefore not applicable), probable cause is not invariably required either. A search unsupported by probable cause can be constitutional, we have said, "when special needs, beyond the normal need for law enforcement, make the warrant and probable-cause requirement impracticable." *Griffin v. Wisconsin,* 483 U.S. 868, 873 (1987) (internal quotation marks omitted).

We have found such "special needs" to exist in the public school context. There, the warrant requirement "would unduly interfere with the maintenance of the swift and informal disciplinary procedures [that are] needed," and "strict adherence to the requirement that searches be based upon probable cause" would undercut "the substantial need of teachers and administrators for freedom to maintain order in the schools." The school search we approved in *T.L.O.,* while not based on probable cause, was based on individualized suspicion of wrongdoing. As we explicitly acknowledged, however, "'the Fourth Amendment imposes no irreducible requirement of such suspicion,'" *id.* at 342, n. 8 (quoting *United States v. Martinez-Fuerte,* 428 U.S. 543, 560–561 (1976)).

★ ★ ★

Fourth Amendment rights, no less than First and Fourteenth Amendment rights, are different in public schools than elsewhere; the "reasonableness" inquiry cannot disregard the schools' custodial and tutelary responsibility for children. For their own good and that of their classmates, public school children are routinely required to submit to various physical examinations, and to be vaccinated against various diseases.

★ ★ ★

Legitimate privacy expectations are even less with regard to student athletes. School sports are not for the bashful. They require "suiting up" before each practice or event, and showering and changing afterwards. Public school locker rooms, the usual sites for these activities, are not notable for the privacy they afford.

★ ★ ★

There is an additional respect in which school athletes have a reduced expectation of privacy. By choosing to "go out for the team," they voluntarily subject themselves to a degree of regulation even higher than that imposed on students generally. In Vernonia's public schools, they must submit to a pre-season physical exam,…they must acquire adequate insurance coverage or sign an insurance waiver, maintain a minimum grade point average, and comply with any

> rules of conduct, dress, training hours and related matters as may be established for each sport by the head coach and athletic director with the principal's approval. Record, Exh. 2, p. 30, ¶ 8.

Somewhat like adults who choose to participate in a "closely regulated industry," students who voluntarily participate in school athletics have reason to expect intrusions upon normal rights and privileges, including privacy. See *Skinner,* 489 U.S. at 627; *United States v. Biswell,* 406 U.S. 311, 316 (1972).

★ ★ ★

That the nature of the concern [over drug use by children] is important—indeed, perhaps compelling—can

hardly be doubted. Deterring drug use by our Nation's schoolchildren is at least as important as enhancing efficient enforcement of the Nation's laws against the importation of drugs, which was the governmental concern in *Von Raab, supra,* at 668, or deterring drug use by engineers and trainmen, which was the governmental concern in *Skinner, supra,* at 628.

★ ★ ★

As to the efficacy of this means for addressing the problem: it seems to us self-evident that a drug problem largely fueled by the "role model" effect of athletes' drug use, and of particular danger to athletes, is effectively addressed by making sure that athletes do not use drugs.

★ ★ ★

VI

Taking into account all the factors we have considered above—the decreased expectation of privacy, the relative unobtrusiveness of the search, and the severity of the need met by the search—we conclude Vernonia's Policy is reasonable, and hence constitutional.

★ ★ ★

We therefore vacate the judgment, and remand the case to the Court of Appeals for further proceedings consistent with this opinion.

It is so ordered.

COMMENTS, NOTES, AND QUESTIONS

1. It could be argued that since children do not have all the rights of adults, the Court is continuing to interpret the Fourth Amendment in a different fashion for children than for adults. This practice was noted in *New Jersey v. T.L.O.,* 469 U.S. 325 (1985), where a student in a school could be searched on less than traditional probable cause. Should children have diminished legal protections under the Constitution? They may have reduced responsibility within the juvenile justice system. With the greater opportunity to certify juveniles as adults and where some prosecutors make the transfer call, should juvenile rights be the same as those for adults? Why or why not?

2. In *Acton,* in dicta, the Court took great pains to inform legislators and regulatory agencies that a blanket suspicionless drug testing policy in all contexts might raise constitutional issues.

> We caution against the assumption that suspicionless drug testing will readily pass constitutional muster in other contexts. The most significant element in this case is the first we discussed: that the Policy was undertaken in furtherance of the government's responsibilities, under a public school system, as guardian and tutor of children entrusted to its care. *Vernonia School Dist. 47J v. Acton,* 515 U.S. 646, 665 (1995).

While these words were not necessary to the *Acton* decision, the Court undertook some effort to send a message that suspicionless searches might have some limits. For example, what limits might the Court place on testing of all students who eat in the school cafeteria? Would there be a better chance if a school just tested children who were transported to school on buses? What would be some of the arguments for and against suspicionless testing of schoolchildren in these hypothetical cases?

CASE 5.6

Public School Drug Testing: No Individual Suspicion Required for Competitive School Activities

Board of Education v. Earls, No. 01-332 (2002)
Supreme Court of the United States
536 U.S. 822 (2002)

FACTS

The Tecumseh, Oklahoma, School District adopted a policy which required all middle and high school students to consent to urinalysis drug testing in order to participate in any extracurricular activity. In actual practice, the school board did not apply drug testing except for competitive extracurricular activities sponsored by the state sanctioning body. Several high school students who objected to the drug-testing policy filed suit in a federal district court alleging that under 42 U.S.C. Sec. 1983 they were eligible for equitable relief and they contended that the policy violated their rights guaranteed by the Fourth Amendment.

The district court believed that the case, *Vernonia School Dist. 47J v. Acton,* 515 U.S. 646 (1995), controlled because of similarities in the drug testing policy. In *Vernonia,*

the Supreme Court of the United States upheld the drug testing of school athletes in the absence of any individual suspicion. Thus, the district court granted summary judgment in favor of the Tecumseh, Oklahoma, School District. The student plaintiffs appealed to the Court of Appeal for the Tenth Circuit, which disagreed with the lower court and found in favor of the students, holding that the drug testing policy violated the Fourth Amendment. According to the Court of Appeal, a school district must demonstrate some identifiable drug abuse before imposing a suspicionless drug testing program. The Court held that the Tecumseh, Oklahoma, School District had failed to show that its children possessed a drug problem among students participating in the competitive extracurricular activities offered by the school system.

The Supreme Court of the United States granted the school district's petition for certiorari.

PROCEDURAL QUESTION

Does the school district policy of requiring student consent for suspicionless drug testing of all students who wish to participate in extracurricular competitive activities violate the Fourth Amendment prohibition against unreasonable searches and seizures?

HELD: NO

RATIONALE

Justice Thomas delivered the opinion of the Court.

★ ★ ★

II

The Fourth Amendment to the United States Constitution protects "[t]he right of the people to be secure in their persons, houses, papers, and effects, against unreasonable searches and seizures." Searches by public school officials, such as the collection of urine samples, implicate Fourth Amendment interests. See *Vernonia* [*School Dist. v. Acton,* 515 U.S. 646], at 652; *cf. New Jersey v. T.L.O.,* 469 U.S. 325, 334 (1985). We must therefore review the School District's Policy for "reasonableness," which is the touchstone of the constitutionality of a governmental search.

★ ★ ★

Given that the School District's Policy is not in any way related to the conduct of criminal investigations, respondents [the students] do not contend that the School District requires probable cause before testing students for drug use. Respondents instead argue that drug testing must be based at least on some level of individualized suspicion. It is true that we generally determine the reasonableness of a search by balancing the nature of the intrusion on the individual's privacy against the promotion of legitimate governmental interests. But we have long held that "the Fourth Amendment imposes no irreducible requirement of [individualized] suspicion." *United States v. Martinez-Fuerte,* 428 U.S. 543, 561 (1976).

> [I]n certain limited circumstances, the Government's need to discover such latent or hidden conditions, or to prevent their development, is sufficiently compelling to justify the intrusion on privacy entailed by conducting such searches without any measure of individualized suspicion. *Von Raab, supra,* at 668.

Therefore, in the context of safety and administrative regulations, a search unsupported by probable cause may be reasonable "when 'special needs, beyond the normal need for law enforcement, make the warrant and probable-cause requirement impracticable.'" *Griffin v. Wisconsin,* 483 U.S. 868, 873 (1987).

Significantly, this Court has previously held that "special needs" inhere in the public school context. See *Vernonia, supra,* at 653; *T.L.O., supra,* at 339–340. While schoolchildren do not shed their constitutional rights when they enter the schoolhouse, see *Tinker v. Des Moines Independent Community School Dist.,* 393 U.S. 503, 506 (1969),

> Fourth Amendment rights...are different in public schools than elsewhere; the "reasonableness" inquiry cannot disregard the schools' custodial and tutelary responsibility for children. *Vernonia, supra,* at 656.

In particular, a finding of individualized suspicion may not be necessary when a school conducts drug testing.

In *Vernonia,* this Court held that the suspicionless drug testing of athletes was constitutional. The Court, however, did not simply authorize all school drug testing, but rather conducted a fact-specific balancing of the intrusion on the children's Fourth Amendment rights against the promotion of legitimate governmental interests. Applying the principles of *Vernonia* to the somewhat different facts of this case, we conclude that Tecumseh's Policy is also constitutional.

A

We first consider the nature of the privacy interest allegedly compromised by the drug testing. As in *Vernonia,* the context of the public school environment serves as the backdrop for the analysis of the privacy interest at stake and the reasonableness of the drug testing policy in general. ("Central...is the fact that the subjects of the Policy are (1) children, who (2) have been committed to the temporary custody of the State as schoolmaster"); ("The most significant element in this case is the first we discussed: that the Policy was undertaken in furtherance of the government's responsibilities, under a public school system, as guardian and tutor of children entrusted to its care"); ("[W]hen the government acts as guardian and tutor the relevant question is whether the search is one that a reasonable guardian and tutor might undertake").

A student's privacy interest is limited in a public school environment where the State is responsible for maintaining discipline, health, and safety. Schoolchildren are routinely required to submit to physical examinations and vaccinations against disease. Securing order in the school environment sometimes requires that students be subjected to greater controls than those appropriate for adults. See *T.L.O., supra,* at 350 (Powell, J., concurring) ("Without first establishing discipline and maintaining order, teachers cannot begin to educate their students. And apart from education, the school has the obligation to protect pupils from mistreatment by other children, and also to protect teachers themselves from violence by the few students whose conduct in recent years has prompted national concern").

Respondents argue that because children participating in nonathletic extracurricular activities are not subject to regular physicals and communal undress, they have a stronger expectation of privacy than the athletes tested in Vernonia. See Brief for Respondents 18–20. This distinction, however, was not essential to our decision in Vernonia, which depended primarily upon the school's custodial responsibility and authority.

In any event, students who participate in competitive extracurricular activities voluntarily subject themselves to many of the same intrusions on their privacy as do athletes. Some of these clubs and activities require occasional off-campus travel and communal undress. All of them have their own rules and requirements for participating students that do not apply to the student body as a whole. For example, each of the competitive extracurricular activities governed by the Policy must abide by the rules of the Oklahoma Secondary Schools Activities Association, and a faculty sponsor monitors the students for compliance with the various rules dictated by the clubs and activities. This regulation of extracurricular activities further diminishes the expectation of privacy among schoolchildren. *Cf. Vernonia, supra,* at 657 ("Somewhat like adults who choose to participate in a closely regulated industry, students who voluntarily participate in school athletics have reason to expect intrusions upon normal rights and privileges, including privacy." (internal quotation marks omitted.)) We therefore conclude that the students affected by this Policy have a limited expectation of privacy.

B

Next, we consider the character of the intrusion imposed by the Policy. Urination is "an excretory function traditionally shielded by great privacy." *Skinner,* 489 U.S. at 626. But the "degree of intrusion" on one's privacy caused by collecting a urine sample "depends upon the manner in which production of the urine sample is monitored." *Vernonia, supra,* at 658.

Under the Policy, a faculty monitor waits outside the closed restroom stall for the student to produce a sample and must listen for the normal sounds of urination in order to guard against tampered specimens and to insure an accurate chain of custody. The monitor then pours the sample into two bottles that are sealed and placed into a mailing pouch along with a consent form signed by the student. This procedure is virtually identical to that reviewed in *Vernonia,* except that it additionally protects privacy by allowing male students to produce their samples behind a closed stall. Given that we considered the method of collection in *Vernonia* a "negligible" intrusion, 515 U.S. at 658, the method here is even less problematic.

★ ★ ★

Moreover, the test results are not turned over to any law enforcement authority. Nor do the test results here lead to the imposition of discipline or have any academic consequences. Rather, the only consequence of a failed drug test is to limit the student's privilege of participating in extracurricular activities. Indeed, a student may test positive for drugs twice and still be allowed to participate in extracurricular activities.

★ ★ ★

Given the minimally intrusive nature of the sample collection and the limited uses to which the test results

are put, we conclude that the invasion of students' privacy is not significant.

C

Finally, this Court must consider the nature and immediacy of the government's concerns and the efficacy of the Policy in meeting them. This Court has already articulated in detail the importance of the governmental concern in preventing drug use by schoolchildren. The drug abuse problem among our Nation's youth has hardly abated since *Vernonia* was decided in 1995. In fact, evidence suggests that it has only grown worse. As in *Vernonia,*

> the necessity for the State to act is magnified by the fact that this evil is being visited not just upon individuals at large, but upon children for whom it has undertaken a special responsibility of care and direction. *Id.* at 662.

The health and safety risks identified in *Vernonia* apply with equal force to Tecumseh's children. Indeed, the nationwide drug epidemic makes the war against drugs a pressing concern in every school.

Additionally, the School District in this case has presented specific evidence of drug use at Tecumseh schools. Teachers testified that they had seen students who appeared to be under the influence of drugs and that they had heard students speaking openly about using drugs.

★ ★ ★

Given the nationwide epidemic of drug use and the evidence of increased drug use in Tecumseh schools, it was entirely reasonable for the School District to enact this particular drug testing policy.

We also reject respondents' argument that drug testing must presumptively be based upon an individualized reasonable suspicion of wrongdoing because such a testing regime would be less intrusive. In this context, the Fourth Amendment does not require a finding of individualized suspicion and we decline to impose such a requirement on schools attempting to prevent and detect drug use by students.

★ ★ ★

Finally, we find that testing students who participate in extracurricular activities is a reasonably effective means of addressing the School District's legitimate concerns in preventing, deterring, and detecting drug use. While in *Vernonia* there might have been a closer fit between the testing of athletes and the trial court's finding that the drug problem was "fueled by the 'role model' effect of athletes' drug use," such a finding was not essential to the holding. *Vernonia* did not require the school to test the group of students most likely to use drugs, but rather considered the constitutionality of the program in the context of the public school's custodial responsibilities. Evaluating the Policy in this context, we conclude that the drug testing of Tecumseh students who participate in extracurricular activities effectively serves the School District's interest in protecting the safety and health of its students.

III

Within the limits of the Fourth Amendment, local school boards must assess the desirability of drug testing schoolchildren. In upholding the constitutionality of the Policy, we express no opinion as to its wisdom. Rather, we hold only that Tecumseh's Policy is a reasonable means of furthering the School District's important interest in preventing and deterring drug use among its schoolchildren. Accordingly, we reverse the judgment of the Court of Appeals.

It is so ordered.

COMMENTS, NOTES, AND QUESTIONS

1. Why did the *Earls* Court think that the drug testing policy was reasonable? Did the fact that the school district had a special responsibility of care and safety toward all students have an impact on the reasonableness of the drug searches? How important is the fact that students must "step forward" by engaging in extracurricular activities in order for drug screening to be required? There may be a clear element of voluntary consent involved here, but the Court did not address that issue. All students may avoid drug testing by not becoming involved in activities beyond the classroom.

2. From your reading of the instant case, how clear is it that secondary public school students possess significant Fourth Amendment rights? How different are the rights for adults and secondary public school students under the Fourth Amendment? From a public policy perspective, could the fact that secondary school children possess a lesser level of legal protection because of their status teach a wrong lesson that one's rights might depend on one's position in society? Why or why not?

3. From your reading of this case and prior cases, do you think that the Supreme Court of the United States would allow the drug testing of every single student, even those who participated in nothing other than attending required school classes? Why or why not? Why did the *Earls* Court not require individualized suspicion as a standard for drug testing? Why would this approach not be practical?

4. According to the *Earls* Court, citing *Tinker v. Des Moines Independent Community School Dist.,* 393 U.S. 503, 506 (1969), "schoolchildren do not shed their constitutional rights when they enter the schoolhouse." Consistent with the *Earls* decision, could a public school teacher decide to search the purses of every female student? What level of suspicion would the teacher need so that such a search would be reasonable? Note that *Earls* allows a search without any individual suspicion. Assume that a secondary teacher had some information that one student possessed marijuana, but there was no reason to suspect any particular student. Consistent with the Fourth Amendment, could the teacher search every student for possession of drugs? Why or why not?

CASE 5.7

Workplace Searches in the Absence of Individualized Suspicion

Skinner v. Railway Labor Executives' Association
Supreme Court of the United States
489 U.S. 602 (1989)

FACTS

The Secretary of Transportation was granted power under the Federal Railroad Safety Act of 1970 to prescribe the necessary safety rules and regulations for all areas of railroad safety. Pursuant to that statute, the Secretary made a finding that alcohol and drug abuse by railway employees posed an ongoing threat to railway safety. Following the confines of the law, the Secretary instituted regulations that permitted blood and urine tests for employees who are on the job when specified railway events and accidents occur. In addition, the Federal Railroad Administration [FRA] adopted regulations that would allow railroad companies to administer breath and urine tests to employees who violate specified safety rules, even in the absence of an accident. Also, the railroads were prohibited from bargaining with employees to dispense with some of the tests. These blood, urine, and breath tests were to be administered without any individualized showing or suspicion of alcohol or drug impairment. Essentially, individual probable cause for the tests was not a requirement. If an employee refused to participate in the tests, the job that the individual had been performing could not be performed by that employee for nine months.

In the case at bar, the specific portions of the regulations required toxicological testing of blood and urine following every "major train accident" and after all "impact accidents" involving a reportable human injury. The railroad was to provide transportation for all involved crew members to an independent medical facility. The results of the tests were to be given to the employees involved and an employee who refused to take the tests could not perform specific regulated work for nine months.

The respondents, the Railway Labor Executives' Association and several labor unions, brought suit to enjoin the Federal Railroad Administration's regulation on Fourth Amendment (and other) grounds.

The federal district court granted summary judgment on behalf of the petitioner railroad employee organizations, but the Court of Appeals for the Ninth Circuit reversed the trial court. The theory behind the reversal of the district court concerned the exigencies of accident situations which required swift testing without the requirement of a warrant. In addition, the Court of Appeals held that "accommodation of railroad employees' privacy interest with the significant safety concerns of the government does not require adherence to a probable cause requirement." The Court of Appeals did require that the government have particularized suspicion prior to testing any railroad employee.

The Supreme Court granted certiorari to consider whether the regulations invalidated by the Court of Appeals violate privacy rights under the Fourth Amendment.

PROCEDURAL ISSUE

Where governmental regulations require testing of certain employee body fluids and breath without either probable cause or particularized suspicion in an industry where impairment by drugs may have catastrophic consequences, does such a search violate the Fourth Amendment?

HELD: NO

RATIONALE

Justice Kennedy delivered the opinion of the Court.

★ ★ ★

We granted the Government's petition for a writ of certiorari to consider whether the regulations invalidated by the Court of Appeals violate the Fourth Amendment. We now reverse.

★ ★ ★

Our precedents teach that where, as here, the Government seeks to obtain physical evidence from a person, the Fourth Amendment may be relevant at several levels. See, *e.g., United States v. Dionisio,* 410 U.S. 1, 8 (1973). The initial detention necessary to procure the evidence may be a seizure of the person, *Cupp v. Murphy,* 412 U.S. 291, 294–295 (1973); *Davis v. Mississippi,* 394 U.S. 721, 726–727 (1969), if the detention amounts to a meaningful interference with his freedom of movement. *INS v. Delgado,* 466 U.S. 210, 215 (1984).

★ ★ ★

We have long recognized that a "compelled intrusio[n] into the body for blood to be analyzed for alcohol content" must be deemed a Fourth Amendment search. See *Schmerber v. California,* 384 U.S. 757, 767–768 (1966).

★ ★ ★

Unlike the blood-testing procedure at issue in *Schmerber,* the procedures prescribed by the FRA regulations for collecting and testing urine samples do not entail a surgical intrusion into the body. It is not disputed, however, that chemical analysis of urine, like that of blood, can reveal a host of private medical facts about an employee, including whether she is epileptic, pregnant, or diabetic. Nor can it be disputed that the process of collecting the sample to be tested, which may in some cases involve visual or aural monitoring of the act of urination, itself implicates privacy interests.

★ ★ ★

To hold that the Fourth Amendment is applicable to the drug and alcohol testing prescribed by the FRA regulations is only to begin the inquiry into the standards governing such intrusions.

★ ★ ★

The Government's interest in regulating the conduct of railroad employees to ensure safety, like its supervision of probationers or regulated industries, or its operation of a government office, school, or prison, "likewise presents 'special needs' beyond normal law enforcement that may justify departures from the usual warrant and probable-cause requirements." *Griffin v. Wisconsin,* 483 U.S., at 875.

★ ★ ★

An essential purpose of a warrant requirement is to protect privacy interests by assuring citizens subject to a search or seizure that such intrusions are not the random or arbitrary acts of government agents. A warrant assures the citizen that the intrusion is authorized by law, and that it is narrowly limited in its objectives and scope. [Citations omitted.] A warrant also provides the detached scrutiny of a neutral magistrate, and thus ensures an objective determination whether an intrusion is justified in any given case. See *United States v. Chadwick, supra,* 433 U.S., at 9. In the present context, however, a warrant would do little to further these aims. Both the circumstances justifying toxicological testing and the permissible limits of such intrusions are defined narrowly and specifically in the regulations that authorize them, and doubtless are well known to covered employees.

★ ★ ★

By and large, intrusions on privacy under the FRA regulations are limited. To the extent transportation and like restrictions are necessary to procure the requisite blood, breath, and urine samples for testing, this interference alone is minimal given the employment context in which it takes place.

★ ★ ★

The breath tests authorized by Subpart D of the regulations are even less intrusive than the blood tests prescribed by Subpart C. Unlike blood tests, breath tests do not require piercing the skin and may be conducted safely outside a hospital environment and with a minimum of inconvenience or embarrassment. Further, breath tests reveal the level of alcohol in the employee's bloodstream and nothing more.

★ ★ ★

A more difficult question is presented by urine tests. Like breath tests, urine tests are not invasive of the body and, under the regulations, may not be used as an occasion

for inquiring into private facts unrelated to alcohol or drug use. We recognize, however, that the procedures for collecting the necessary samples, which require employees to perform an excretory function traditionally shielded by great privacy, raise concerns not implicated by blood or breath tests. While we would not characterize these additional privacy concerns as minimal in most contexts, we note that the regulations endeavor to reduce the intrusiveness of the collection process. The regulations do not require that samples be furnished under the direct observation of a monitor, despite the desirability of such a procedure to ensure the integrity of the sample.

★ ★ ★

We do not suggest, of course, that the interest in bodily security enjoyed by those employed in a regulated industry must always be considered minimal. Here, however, the covered employees have long been a principal focus of regulatory concern. As the dissenting judge below noted:

> "[t]he reason is obvious. An idle locomotive, sitting in the roundhouse, is harmless. It becomes lethal when operated negligently by persons who are under the influence of alcohol or drugs." 839 F.2d, at 593.

Though some of the privacy interests implicated by the toxicological testing at issue reasonably might be viewed as significant in other contexts, logic and history show that a diminished expectation of privacy attaches to information relating to the physical condition of covered employees and to this reasonable means of procuring such information. We conclude, therefore, that the testing procedures contemplated by Subparts C and D pose only limited threats to the justifiable expectations of privacy of covered employees. By contrast, the government interest in testing without a showing of individualized suspicion is compelling. Employees subject to the tests discharge duties fraught with such risks of injury to others that even a momentary lapse of attention can have disastrous consequences.

★ ★ ★

We conclude that the compelling government interests served by the FRA's regulations would be significantly hindered if railroads were required to point to specific facts giving rise to a reasonable suspicion of impairment before testing a given employee. In view of our conclusion that, on the present record, the toxicological testing contemplated by the regulations is not an undue infringement on the justifiable expectations of privacy of covered employees, the Government's compelling interests outweigh privacy concerns.

★ ★ ★

Alcohol and drug tests conducted in reliance on the authority of Subpart D cannot be viewed as private action outside the reach of the Fourth Amendment. Because the testing procedures mandated or authorized by Subparts C and D effect searches of the person, they must meet the Fourth Amendment's reasonableness requirement. In light of the limited discretion exercised by the railroad employers under the regulations, the surpassing safety interests served by toxicological tests in this context, and the diminished expectation of privacy that attaches to information pertaining to the fitness of covered employees, we believe that it is reasonable to conduct such tests in the absence of a warrant or reasonable suspicion that any particular employee may be impaired. We hold that the alcohol and drug tests contemplated by

Subparts C and D of the FRA's regulations are reasonable within the meaning of the Fourth Amendment.

The judgment of the Court of Appeals is accordingly reversed.

COMMENTS, NOTES, AND QUESTIONS

1. The Court seems to be saying that because the testing rules were promulgated, that fact alone reduces the expectation of privacy that an employee would otherwise have possessed. Would a rule allowing business searches on less than probable cause be justified merely because the rule had been promulgated? Why or why not?

2. The Court balances the compelling interest of the government in drug testing without probable cause or individualized suspicion against the Fourth Amendment expectation of privacy. Does the text of the Fourth Amendment suggest a balancing of interests? Could balancing of interests be covered by the contention that such drug tests are merely "reasonable" searches under the Fourth Amendment?

Principles of the Exclusionary Rule: Remedies and Exceptions to Constitutional Violations

Chapter Outline

Key Terms

Bivens remedy
Concept of standing
Derivative evidence
Doctrine of attenuation
Exclusionary rule
Fourth Amendment
Fruit of the poisonous tree doctrine

Good faith exception
Independent source rule
Motion to suppress
Rule of inevitable discovery
Silver platter doctrine
Vicarious standing
Writs of assistance

1. INTRODUCTION TO REMEDIES FOR FOURTH AMENDMENT VIOLATIONS

The Constitution of the United States provides for a democratic form of government, details the basic organization of the government, and guarantees a variety of personal rights to individual persons. The federal government must follow its own rules when it interacts with persons within its jurisdiction. Law-abiding citizens are to be left alone by governmental agents, and criminals are to be apprehended by law-abiding law enforcement agents. When the law enforcers transgress a law or constitutional provision in their effort to discover, capture, or prosecute suspected violators of criminal laws, the proper approach to confronting one lawbreaker dealing with another lawbreaker poses some interesting questions concerning the method of adjusting the competing equities. In his dissenting opinion in *Olmstead v. United States*,[169] Justice Brandeis offered a forceful and frequently quoted answer to the proper approach the government should take:

> In a government of laws, existence of the government will be imperilled if it fails to observe the law scrupulously. Our Government is the potent, the omnipresent teacher. For good or for ill, it teaches the whole people by its example. Crime is contagious. If the Government becomes a lawbreaker, it breeds contempt for law; it invites every man to become a law unto himself; it invites anarchy. To declare that in the administration of the criminal law the end justifies the means—to declare that the Government may commit crimes in order to secure the conviction of a private criminal—would bring terrible retribution.

In *Mapp v. Ohio*,[170] Justice Clark echoed the thoughts of Justice Brandeis: "Nothing can destroy a government more quickly than its failure to observe its own laws, or worse, its disregard of the charter of its own existence." Alternatively, should we just look the other way when law enforcement officials violate the law in an effort to promote a greater good? Or should we wonder how a society maintains its moral leadership when its own agents fail to respect and follow the basic law under which society is organized? Should we allow the wronged party to sue the wrongdoing public official?[171] The current approach involves excluding the evidence illegally obtained and, in effect, placing the suspect and the government in the same position, legally and evidentially, that they would have occupied had the government agent not violated the law. The exclusion of illegally seized evidence has some exceptions based on logic, need, and common sense.

2. VIOLATION OF THE FOURTH AMENDMENT AND THE EXCLUSION OF EVIDENCE

Consistent with present judicial construction of the Fourth Amendment and consistent with the case law interpreting the amendment, evidence that has been illegally seized by either a state or the federal government may be suppressed from

[169]277 U.S. 438, 485 (1928).
[170]367 U.S. 643, 659 (1961).
[171]See *Bivens v. Six Unknown Named Agents,* 403 U.S. 388 (1971), where the Court created a civil cause of action against federal employees who acted illegally in searching an apartment.

prosecutorial introduction in a criminal trial. Suppression from evidence as a remedy for a governmental violation of the Fourth Amendment may seem to be a rather drastic measure, since the accused individual may go free as a result of the blunder of a police officer. In essence, one wrongdoer goes free because another wrongdoer has violated the supreme law of the land. Arguably, to allow the use of evidence that has been illegally seized against a person who had a right of privacy concerning that property would mean that the Fourth Amendment would have little force and almost no effect and would become close to a nullity. In opposition to this theory of exclusion is the thought that the evidence should be admissible against the accused wrongdoer if we will allow the wrongdoer a remedy of suit against the law enforcement official[172] who had violated the rights of the accused individual. In the absence of either the exclusion of evidence or the availability of a suit against the offending officer, law enforcement officials might have little incentive to respect the requirements of the Fourth Amendment. The trial exclusion of evidence illegally seized appears to be the Fourth Amendment remedy of choice for the present time.

3. THE FOURTH AMENDMENT: IMPLEMENTATION PRIOR TO 1914

Prior to 1914, the Fourth Amendment had faced judicial interpretation and scrutiny in several court cases. Among these was the case of *Boyd v. United States,* decided by the United States Supreme Court in 1886, in which the compulsory production of private papers was in question. Justice Bradley looked to the origin and intent of the Framers of the Fourth Amendment to discern the amendment's meaning and scope.[173] He recalled the lessons of history, which were more recent to him than to us, in which the British government, prior to the American Revolution, had empowered its agents to use general search warrants called writs of assistance. In many of the American colonies, British agents were issued what amounted to blank search warrants that allowed the search of private houses for personal items, personal documents and effects, and other evidence that would be used in court to convict the possessor. The colonists had protested the use of these blanket warrants in a variety of ways but to little or no avail prior to the Revolutionary War. In response to the writs of assistance and other abuses of privacy, the prohibition against unreasonable searches and seizures was grafted into the Constitution in the form of the Bill of Rights so that Americans would not have to fear that the practice of unlimited intrusion into private areas might creep back into national law enforcement practice.

Over the years since 1791, when the Bill of Rights was ratified by the required number of states, federal law enforcement practice has not always complied with what was believed to be dictated by the Fourth Amendment. Initially there existed no particular remedy against federal agents when violations of the Fourth Amendment occurred, except on a case-by-case basis. Where a defendant successfully argued that personal constitutional rights had been violated, he or she might have

---

[172]See Chief Justice Berger's dissent in *Bivens v. Six Unknown Named Agents,* 403 U.S. 388, 421 (1971), where he proposed a variety of remedies for Fourth Amendment violations while allowing the use of the illegally seized evidence against the person whose rights had been violated.

[173]See *Boyd v. United States,* 116 U.S. 616, 625 (1886).

some modicum of success in having a conviction reversed based on illegal law enforcement activity.[174]

Justice Day, in *Weeks v. United States,* referred to the opinion of Justice Bradley[175] in explaining the original motivation and intent of the Framers of the Fourth Amendment.

> [I]t took its origin in the determination of the framers of the Amendments to the Federal Constitution to provide for that instrument a Bill of Rights, securing to the American people, among other things, those safeguards which had grown up in England to protect the people from unreasonable searches and seizures, such as were permitted under the general warrants issued under authority of the government, by which there had been invasions of the home and privacy of the citizens, and the seizure of their private papers in support of charges, real or imaginary, made against them. Such practices had also received sanction under warrants and seizures under the so-called writs of assistance, issued in the American colonies. *See* 2 Watson, Const. 1414 *et seq.* Resistance to these practices had established the principle which was enacted into the fundamental law in the Fourth Amendment, that a man's house was his castle, and not to be invaded by any general authority to search and seize his goods and papers. *Weeks v. United States,* 232 U.S. 383, 390 (1914).

The Supreme Court in *Boyd v. United States* granted a new trial where the federal government had forced the defendant to provide evidence from his private place of business in the absence of a search warrant. The *Boyd* Court did not fashion a rule of exclusion of evidence illegally seized or procured, but the use of such illegally seized evidence was deemed to create reversible error in Boyd's case. At the time *Boyd* was decided, it appeared that the Court was moving toward developing an exclusion rule that would help enforce the Fourth Amendment, but it was not, at that time, willing to take such a step.

4. THE EXCLUSIONARY RULE: ENFORCING THE FOURTH AMENDMENT

By 1914, the Court appeared to reconsider the legality of admitting evidence in federal courts where the evidence had been illegally seized. In the case of *Weeks v. United States,* the defendant's personal residence had been entered by local police officers and a United States marshal. Both the police and the federal agent had seized evidence, which they wished to use against Weeks in a criminal gambling case. No warrant was used by any of the law enforcement agents involved in the search for evidence, and Weeks had not been present to grant any consent for the entry. Prior to trial and consistent with the practice at the time, Weeks had requested the return of the documents that the federal government sought to use against him. The motion for the return of the evidence had been denied, and Weeks had been convicted partly based on evidence illegally taken from his residence.

With his appeal properly before the United States Supreme Court, Weeks contended that the Fourth Amendment to the Constitution prohibited the United

---

[174]See *Boyd v. United States,* 116 U.S. 616 (1886).
[175]*Boyd* at 625, 626.

States marshal from making the seizure and that his conviction should be reversed. After reviewing some of the history that motivated the adoption of the Fourth Amendment and after looking at the conduct of the federal agent, Justice Day, writing for the *Weeks* Court, stated:

> We therefore reach the conclusion that the letters in question were taken from the house of the accused by an official of the United States, acting under color of his office, in direct violation of the constitutional rights of the defendant; that, having made a seasonable application for their return, which was heard and passed upon by the court, there was involved in the order refusing the application a denial of the constitutional rights of the accused, and that the court should have restored these letters to the accused. In holding them and permitting their use upon the trial, we think prejudicial error was committed. *Weeks v. United States,* 232 U.S. 383, 398 (1914).

The action of the *Weeks* Court had the effect of telling federal law enforcement agents that if seizures of evidence were to be made in the future, they must be in compliance with the Fourth Amendment or the evidence would not be admitted in federal courts. Consistent with the *Weeks* case, if evidence illegally seized by federal agents managed to be admitted in court against defendants whose rights have been violated, upon appeal the convictions could be reversed. The ruling applied only to federal law enforcement officials and not to state officials, who were not limited in their conduct by the Fourth Amendment.[176] Interestingly enough, if federal law enforcement officials violated the Fourth Amendment in seizing evidence against a defendant, they could take the evidence to a state prosecutor, who was not limited by the Fourth Amendment, and the evidence could be used for prosecution under state law.[177]

5. SUPPRESSION OF ILLEGALLY SEIZED EVIDENCE

While the literal language of the Fourth Amendment protects people against unreasonable searches and seizures conducted by governmental agents, once a violation has occurred, there is no way to reverse the wrong. Since the defendant cannot be restored to the status quo prior to the search, a process that puts the defendant nearly in the same position as he or she would have been but for the illegality would appear to be an appropriate approach. However, since the Fourth Amendment is not self-enforcing, and its text fails to provide any remedy for a governmental violation, the remedy of evidentiary exclusion is the proper procedure to pursue. Cases decided prior to 1914 rarely addressed concerns related to a remedy because the evidence illegally seized was frequently excluded on other constitutional grounds.[178]

---

[176]The Fourth Amendment was originally intended by its Framers and adopters to limit the federal government and was not designed to have any application so as to affect state law enforcement practice. The Fourth Amendment was incorporated into the Due Process Clause of the Fourteenth Amendment in *Mapp v. Ohio,* 367 U.S. 643 (1961).

[177]This assumes that the evidence illegally seized by federal agents under the Fourth Amendment would tend to support a violation of state law.

[178]See *Boyd v. United States,* 116 U.S. 616 (1886).

Where the government has illegally seized evidence, current practice permits the aggrieved party to file a motion to suppress the evidence from introduction in court against that party or person. Usually the wronged party files a pretrial motion to suppress the evidence with a request to have the property returned to the defendant. A hearing is held to determine whether the defendant has a personal legal basis to complain about a violation of Fourth Amendment rights. A judge must make a determination whether, under the circumstances, the government actually violated the constitutional rights of the defendant and decide the remedy to be applied. If the judge agrees with the defendant, the evidence will be ruled inadmissible for use to prove guilt;[179] where the judge believes that no violation occurred, the evidence will be admissible unless excluded by the substantive rules of evidence.

6. BASIS FOR THE EXCLUSIONARY RULE

The philosophy underpinning the exclusionary rule is predicated on the belief that if the courts were to permit the use of illegally seized evidence, they would be condoning, and perhaps even become indirect participants in, Fourth Amendment transgressions. To maintain judicial propriety, courts should not sanction Fourth Amendment illegality by allowing prosecutors to introduce the fruits of illegal searches conducted by police agencies. In addition, when the incentive for law enforcement officials to violate the amendment is removed, future illegal seizures should be deterred and reduced. As Justice O'Connor explained the rationale, "The purpose of the Fourth Amendment exclusionary rule is to deter unreasonable searches, no matter how probative their fruits."[180] Although the exclusionary rule may assist an individual defendant's case, the Court has recognized that it is not a personal constitutional right, since it does not redress the injury suffered through the illegal search or seizure and does not place the injured party in the same position as if the illegality had not transpired; the damage to the constitutional right has already occurred.[181]

Although the Fourth Amendment and the exclusionary rule clearly apply to federal criminal practice, the same cannot be said for searches and seizures occurring outside the territorial jurisdiction of the United States. When American agents conduct searches, seizures, and/or arrests in foreign countries, the Fourth Amendment and the exclusionary rule will not prevent the introduction of the evidence against the target in an American courtroom. According to the Court, there is no evidence that the drafters of the Fourth Amendment intended it to have extraterritorial effect or to be applied to foreign nationals or their property when located in foreign territory.[182]

---

[179]Illegally obtained evidence may be used for impeachment purposes where the defendant takes the witness stand and offers evidence contradictory to known but illegally seized evidence. In *Walder v. United States,* 347 U.S. 62 (1954), heroin had been illegally seized from the defendant, who denied that he ever had possession or ever sold drugs. The *Walder* Court approved the use for impeachment purposes of the evidence seized illegally in violation of the defendant's Fourth Amendment rights. Similarly, in *Harris v. New York,* 401 U.S. 222 (1971), the Court approved the use of a statement illegally taken in violation of *Miranda* principles to be used to impeach a defendant who told a story different from the version offered in violation of *Miranda.*

[180]*Oregon v. Elstad,* 470 U.S. 298 (1985).

[181]*Withrow v. Williams,* 507 U.S. 680, 686 (1993).

[182]See *United States v. Verdugo-Urquidez,* 494 U.S. 259 (1990).

7. CHALLENGE TO THE EXCLUSIONARY RULE: THE SILVER PLATTER DOCTRINE

The Court designed the exclusionary rule to limit federal law enforcement officials. State and local police, however, remained free to search and seize, and prosecutors continued to use such evidence without any federal limitation. As Justice Blackmun noted,

> In *Weeks,* it was held, however, that the Fourth Amendment did not apply to state officers, and, therefore, that material seized unconstitutionally by a state officer could be admitted in a federal criminal proceeding. *United States v. Janis,* 428 U.S. 433, 444 (1976).

In actual practice, state officials conducted searches that would have been considered illegal if carried out by federal officials and then transferred the evidence to federal prosecutors, who did not hesitate to use the evidence. Such evidence was considered admissible in federal courts, since no federal official had violated the Fourth Amendment, and neither the Fourth Amendment nor the exclusionary rule applied to state officials. This practice of evidence transfer, known as the "silver platter doctrine," was in regular use until the Court struck it down. The Court held that evidence obtained by state law enforcement agents as the result of unreasonable searches and seizures in the absence of the involvement of federal officers must be excluded from evidentiary use against a federal defendant who makes an appropriate objection.[183]

8. APPLICATION OF THE EXCLUSIONARY RULE TO STATE CRIMINAL PROCEDURE

State criminal practice moved to conformity with the federal standard when the *Weeks* exclusionary rule was held to apply to the states in *Mapp v. Ohio* (see Case 6.1).[184] The Court determined that the constitutional guarantees of the Fourth Amendment were incorporated into the Due Process Clause of the Fourteenth Amendment, and thus required state criminal procedure to follow the federal model. With a view toward enforcing the Fourth Amendment, the *Mapp* Court thought it necessary to make the *Weeks*-based exclusionary rule applicable against the states. The net effect of *Mapp* was to make state and federal Fourth Amendment practice subject to the same limitations with respect to search and seizure.

9. EXCLUSION OF DERIVATIVE EVIDENCE

Law enforcement investigations often lead in unusual directions and produce evidence of criminal activity other than that which was originally anticipated. When police follow the path suggested by evidence that has been illegally seized or

---

[183]*Elkins v. United States,* 364 U.S. 206 (1960).
[184]367 U.S. 643 (1961).

wrongfully discovered, exploiting that evidence may create admissibility problems for the prosecutor. The Supreme Court expanded the sweep of the exclusionary rule to require suppression of evidence derived from illegally obtained secondary evidence when the prosecutor's plan involved admitting it against one who had an expectation of privacy. As explained by the *Nix* Court:

> The doctrine requiring courts to suppress evidence as the tainted "fruit" of unlawful governmental conduct had its genesis in *Silverthorne Lumber Co. v. United States,* 251 U.S. 385 (1920); there, the Court held that the exclusionary rule applies not only to the illegally obtained evidence itself, but also to other incriminating evidence derived from the primary evidence. *Nix v. Williams,* 467 U.S. 431, 441 (1984).

In *Wong Sun v. United States,*[185] the Court reaffirmed the principle of tainted derivative evidence exclusion when it voted to exclude evidence that law enforcement officials had obtained by exploiting an initial Fourth Amendment violation (see Case 6.2). Officers were led to a secondary evidence location by evidence that originally was illegally discovered. The Court held that the evidence in the second location would never have been discovered "but for" the agent's initial violation of the defendant's rights under the Fourth Amendment. The *Wong Sun* "fruit of the poisonous tree doctrine" permits a defendant to exclude evidence seized from locations where the defendant possessed no constitutional expectation of privacy.

In *Wong Sun,* police illegally entered a defendant's residence in the absence of probable cause and without a warrant of any kind. No incriminating physical evidence surfaced from that original search. However, the defendant gave oral evidence that implicated a second defendant and produced narcotic drugs from the home of the second defendant. The second defendant gave oral evidence and possessed drugs that implicated the first defendant in drug use and possession. Ultimately, the *Wong Sun* Court held that the first defendant could suppress evidence taken from a search of the second defendant's home, since the original illegality at the first defendant's home led to the discovery of the contraband at the second location. At first blush this may appear to do violence to the Court's oft-repeated principle that Fourth Amendment rights are personal and cannot be asserted vicariously. Upon closer scrutiny, the evidence in *Wong Sun* was discovered by exploiting the original illegal entry to the defendant's home. But for the original illegality, no evidence against the first defendant would have been discovered.

The result of expanding the *Mapp* holding in *Wong Sun* to exclude derivative evidence from use in court to prove guilt served to enhance respect for the Fourth Amendment by removing more of the incentive to conduct illegal searches and seizures. Following *Wong Sun,* both evidence illegally seized and evidence discovered by virtue of exploiting information learned from an illegal entry will not be acceptable in court if offered against one whose rights were initially violated.

---

[185]371 U.S. 471 (1963).

10. MAJOR EXCEPTIONS TO THE EXCLUSIONARY RULE

Although supportive of defendant rights, the "fruit of the poisonous tree doctrine" derived from *Wong Sun v. United States*[186] has not seen complete favor with subsequent justices on the Supreme Court. Over the years since *Wong Sun,* the Court has recognized three legal theories that limit the exclusionary effect. The independent source rule of *Segura v. United States*[187] and of *Murray v. United States,*[188] the rule of inevitable discovery demonstrated by *Nix v. Williams,*[189] and the doctrine of attenuation described in *Wong Sun* all permit prosecutorial use of evidence illegally seized. In these exceptional situations, the justices of the Supreme Court believed strict application of the exclusionary rule would not have significantly altered the conduct or practice of law enforcement officials because the deterrent effect on police operations was viewed as marginal or nonexistent. Where there is an absence of, or a limited, deterrent effect, the rationale of the exclusionary rule is not enhanced, and courts generally refuse to suppress the evidence.

11. EXCLUSIONARY RULE EXCEPTION: THE INDEPENDENT SOURCE RULE

In cases where police have run afoul of the Fourth Amendment, but where an alternative or parallel, but legal, method of discovery of evidence exists, courts generally do not exclude the evidence.[190] The independent source rule allows trial court introduction of evidence obtained or discovered during, or as a consequence of, an illegal search and seizure, so long as the evidence was later obtained independently from proper law enforcement activity untainted by the initial illegality. In *Murray v. United States,*[191] law enforcement officials conducted an illegal search that produced evidence of criminal activities (see Case 6.3). Evidence sufficient to prove probable cause to search existed prior to the illegal entry and search and came from lawful sources. Since the illegally obtained information was not used as part of the foundation for probable cause and was not included on the affidavit for a search warrant, the subsequent warrant-based search was not invalidated on Fourth Amendment grounds.

In an earlier case prior to *Murray, Segura v. United States,*[192] the Court approved the admissibility of evidence derived from an independent source. *Segura* involved police officers who entered a private apartment and conducted a protective sweep following an arrest of one of the occupants. No warrant or other exception allowed the entry into the premises. In the process of conducting the sweep, the officers observed, in plain view, various drug paraphernalia. Two officers remained in the apartment awaiting a warrant being procured by others, but, because of various delays, the search warrant was not issued until some nineteen hours after the initial incursion.

---

[186]371 U.S. 471 (1963).
[187]468 U.S. 796 (1984).
[188]487 U.S. 533 (1988).
[189]467 U.S. 431 (1984).
[190]See *Silverthorne Lumber Co., Inc. v. United States,* 251 U.S. 385 (1920).
[191]487 U.S. 533 (1988).
[192]468 U.S. 796 (1984).

In executing the search warrant, the agents discovered additional drugs and records of narcotics transactions. These items were seized, together with those observed during the security check. The trial court suppressed all the evidence, and the court of appeals held that the evidence discovered in plain view on the initial entry must be suppressed, but the evidence seized during the execution of the warrant-based search should have been admitted. The court of appeals agreed with the federal trial court that the initial warrantless entry and the limited security sweep were not justified by exigent circumstances and were therefore illegal.

The Supreme Court of the United States reversed on the theory that some of the drug evidence would have eventually been seized in a lawful manner. The *Segura* Court held the opinion that the drugs and other items not observed during the initial entry but first discovered by the agents the day after the first entry, under an admittedly valid search warrant, should have been admitted because an independent source for probable cause existed. According to Chief Justice Burger:

> None of the information on which the warrant was secured was derived from or related in any way to the initial entry into petitioners' apartment; the information came from sources wholly unconnected with the entry, and was known to the agents well before the initial entry. No information obtained during the initial entry or occupation of the apartment was needed or used by the agents to secure the warrant. It is therefore beyond dispute that the information possessed by the agents before they entered the apartment constituted an independent source for the discovery and seizure of the evidence now challenged. *Segura* at 814 (1984).

So long as sufficient untainted evidence supports the existence of probable cause, warrants obtained in situations where the government has committed illegal activities will not result in the fruits of the searches being suppressed. In essence, where the evidence observed during an initial illegal search has not been used to produce probable cause to issue a warrant, and separate information proves that probable cause can be established by an independent source untainted by any illegality, courts generally uphold the validity of warrants so issued. The independent source rule may be applied where police possess two avenues or sources of obtaining evidence, one of which is illegal and the other legal. Where the two avenues are not connected, the evidence may be deemed to have an independent source and should be ruled as admissible. Therefore, there is no reason to exclude evidence that has a lawful and independent source because law enforcement officials followed a lawful method of discovery.

12. EXCLUSIONARY RULE EXCEPTION: THE RULE OF INEVITABLE DISCOVERY

Courts have recognized an additional exception to the *Mapp* exclusionary rule and the *Wong Sun* fruits of the poisonous tree doctrine, called the "rule of inevitable discovery." Under this theory, where law enforcement officers find evidence through illegal means but would have discovered the same evidence through legal means, the evidence should not be excluded from use at trial. According to the Court in *Nix v. Williams,* 467 U.S. 431 (1984), "Exclusion of physical evidence that would inevitably have been discovered adds nothing to either the integrity or fairness of a criminal trial" (see Case 6.4). In a situation involving a clear case of inevitable discovery, the police would have obtained the evidence if no illegality had taken place, and to exclude the evidence would place the police and prosecution in a worse position than if no Fourth Amendment transgression occurred. In the *Nix* case, information needed to find a murder victim's body was given to police by virtue of a violation of the *Miranda* principles. Police would have eventually discovered the victim's body fairly soon because they planned to search the very area that contained the body. Under this theory, the government must show that the contested evidence *actually* would have been discovered within a reasonable time.

In a clear demonstration of the rule of inevitable discovery in actual practice, police arrested a woman after observing her performing an oral sex act for money in a public place. Subsequent to the arrest, police officers retrieved the woman's purse from the vehicle of her customer and subjected it to a warrantless search, which revealed a crack cocaine pipe containing residue. The trial court ordered the suppression of the evidence taken from the purse, since there was no probable cause to search the person and no exigent circumstances were present to justify the intrusion. The trial court rejected the rule of inevitable discovery on the theory that the cocaine evidence was not derivative but was direct evidence to which the rule of inevitable discovery should not be applied. The court of appeals reversed the trial court decision, on the grounds that the pipe inevitably would have been discovered during routine booking procedures at the local jail. While the trial court was correct that a search of the purse was not based on probable cause, the search could have been justified as being incident to a lawful arrest or under the inventory search theory, either of which would have permitted the introduction of the evidence under the rule of inevitable discovery.[193]

13. EXCLUSIONARY RULE EXCEPTION: THE DOCTRINE OF ATTENUATION

Another aspect of *Wong Sun v. United States* involved the doctrine of attenuation, which seemed to have its genesis in the case of *Nardone v. United States*.[194] Under this doctrine, where the evidence has been illegally seized, the prosecution may argue that although the evidence was obtained in violation of the Constitution, it has been "purged" of its taint because sufficient time and/or events have transpired since the search or discovery. As the Court explained in *United States v. Crews:*

> In the typical "fruit of the poisonous tree" case, however, the challenged evidence was acquired by the police after some initial Fourth Amendment violation, and the question before the court is whether the chain of causation proceeding from the unlawful conduct has become so attenuated or has been interrupted by some intervening circumstance so as to remove the "taint" imposed upon that evidence by the original illegality. 445 U.S. 463, 471 (1980).

---

[193]*Ohio v. Sincell,* 2002 Ohio 1783; 2002 Ohio App. LEXIS 1656 (2002).
[194]308 U.S. 338 (1939).

In *Wong Sun,* two of the defendants returned following pretrial release to attempt to make a plea bargain with the police.[195] Several days had passed since the illegal searches and seizures; thus, the defendants had had sufficient time to make an independent assessment concerning the merits of confessing to the police. Wong Sun had been released on his own recognizance subsequent to his arraignment and had returned to speak with police voluntarily several days later to make the virtual confession. The *Wong Sun* Court held that the obtaining of the confession evidence was sufficiently separated (attenuated) from the illegality of the original police conduct as to not have been prompted or intimately influenced by the earlier illegal search and was, therefore, not excludable on Fourth Amendment grounds.

14. EXCLUSIONARY RULE EXCEPTION: THE GOOD FAITH EXCEPTION

Where police officers act in objective good faith in following the directives of a warrant, the Court has recognized the desirability of an exception to the application of the exclusionary rule. In the companion cases of *United States v. Leon*[196] and *Massachusetts v. Sheppard,*[197] the Court adopted the "good faith" exception to the exclusionary rule. The two cases involved errors made by judges in issuing legally defective search warrants wherein the mistakes were not readily apparent to police officers. Proper procedure had been followed by the officers, who were not in a position to question the legality of the warrants issued by the judicial officials. In both cases, the officers executing the warrants acted in objective good faith. Since the purpose of the exclusionary rule was to deter illegal police conduct and not to alter judicial behavior, where police act in "good faith," the exclusionary rule cannot have its deterrent effect. In situations where the rationale of the rule is not enhanced, the reason for the remedy of exclusion disappears and the evidence should be admitted to court. Secondarily, the Court noted that there was no evidence to suggest that the judges or magistrates ignore or attempt to subvert the Fourth Amendment. The Court could perceive no basis for believing that evidence excluded pursuant to a defective warrant would have a significant deterrent effect on judicial officials. In essence, the Court held that since the exclusionary rule was originally designed to alter police conduct, courts should not use it to punish errors of judges and magistrates.

As a general rule, courts that follow the good faith exception to the exclusionary rule do not apply it where the magistrate or judge who issued the search warrant was misled by the police officers who made the warrant application; where the judge abandoned the judicial function and clearly failed to follow the law; where the recitation of probable cause warranted no reasonable belief in probable cause; and where the warrant appeared so facially deficient that no reasonable officer could presume it was valid.[198] A federal court of appeals upheld a trial court determination that applied the good-faith exception to the exclusionary rule where the

---

[195]They seemed unaware that they should have been discussing a plea bargain with the prosecutor rather than the police.
[196]468 U.S. 897 (1984).
[197]468 U.S. 981 (1984).
[198]*United States v. Martin,* 297 F.3d 1308, 1313 (2002).

court concluded that police officers had operated in good faith. In making an investigation of a crack lab, police had conducted surveillance of a crack producer, pulled his trash from a multifamily apartment, found cocaine residue in the trash, and talked to persons who stated that the subject was "cooking up" quantities of crack. In addition, police investigated the subject's prior criminal history, which showed earlier drug convictions. The defendant contended that the officer involved in the task force should have known of the deficiencies in the affidavit, since he had been so instrumental in procuring the warrant. The trash pulls were not clearly linked to the defendant, and some of the information was stale, but the court concluded that, even though probable cause did not exist, police reliance on the warrant was objectively reasonable because the affidavit was not so lacking in indicators of probable cause that it would suggest that the officer's belief in the validity of the warrant was unreasonable. The court of appeals affirmed the trial court decision allowing the admission of the evidence; it noted that two confidential sources were used and independently corroborated, and the detective tried to obtain sufficient evidence to produce current probable cause to search. The court of appeals held that a reasonable officer would have believed that when the judge issued the particular search warrant under these facts, it was a valid warrant.[199]

In a slightly different type of case, the good-faith exception has been applied to permit property forfeiture where real property had been used to grow marijuana. Under the law as it existed, police appropriately scanned the defendant's home and discovered a heat pattern consistent with cannabis cultivation. The officers used this information to procure a search warrant, the execution of which revealed a marijuana horticulture operation within the home. Subsequent to the search, the Supreme Court decided *Kyllo v. United States,* 533 U.S. 27 (2001), which held that thermal scanning of a private home by police without a warrant constituted an unreasonable search. Since the original search had been reasonably believed to be legal but was later declared illegal under the Fourth Amendment in *Kyllo,* the police could not have anticipated how the Supreme Court would rule. When the federal government wanted to receive the house in a civil forfeiture action, the defendant contended that the prosecutor should not be permitted to introduce evidence of drug operations, since the government obtained the knowledge of cultivation by an illegal search. The court of appeals held that the good faith of the officers in conducting the original thermal imaging search operated to allow the introduction of the marijuana-growing operation, which supported a forfeiture of the home to the federal government.[200]

15. LIMITATIONS ON THE EXCLUSIONARY RULE: PAROLE REVOCATION HEARINGS

Evidence illegally seized under the Fourth Amendment does not have to be excluded from every legal proceeding. In parole revocation hearings, the rule of exclusion has no application because its use would be incompatible with such hearings' traditionally

---

[199]*United States v. Robinson,* 2003 U.S. App. LEXIS 13770 (2003).
[200]*United States v. 15324 County Highway East,* 332 F.3d 1070 (2003).

nonadversarial posture. Additionally, the application of the rule of exclusion would produce only incremental extra deterrence on law enforcement officials. In *Pennsylvania v. Scott,*[201] evidence of weapons possession had been seized from the parolee's home by parole officers who conducted a warrantless raid. The search of the home followed receipt of information which indicated that Scott had been in violation of conditions of his parole. During a parole revocation hearing, Scott complained that his rights had been violated by a warrantless search of his home, and he objected to the introduction of weapon evidence on the theory that the search transgressed Fourth Amendment requirements. In rejecting Scott's complaint, Justice Thomas noted that the exclusionary rule was not mandated by the Constitution and that it should be applied only where the deterrence benefits outweighed the costs to society that the rule exacted when applied.[202] According to Justice Thomas, parole revocation hearings did not meet the test for applying the rule. As he noted in *Scott:*

> The deterrence benefits of the exclusionary rule would not outweigh these costs. As the Supreme Court of Pennsylvania recognized, application of the exclusionary rule to parole revocation proceedings would have little deterrent effect upon an officer who is unaware that the subject of his search is a parolee. In that situation, the officer will likely be searching for evidence of criminal conduct with an eye toward the introduction of the evidence at a criminal trial. The likelihood that illegally obtained evidence will be excluded from trial provides deterrence against Fourth Amendment violations, and the remote possibility that the subject is a parolee and that the evidence may be admitted at a parole revocation proceeding surely has little, if any, effect on the officer's incentives. 524 U.S. 357, 367 (1998).

Justice Thomas's opinion reflected the philosophy of refusing to apply the exclusionary rule where its deterrent effects appear almost nonexistent. Minimal deterrent effect on officer conduct should exist in any case where the searched individual was not known by the law enforcement agent to be a parolee. The officer would most likely follow the Fourth Amendment, since he or she would want to produce a prosecutable case. In the *Scott* parole revocation situation, however, the parole officers searched the residence of Scott with full knowledge that there was no warrant and probably believed that he could make no official complaint. The sole deterrent effect in *Scott* would come from compliance with the rules under which parole officers operated.

16. LIMITATIONS ON THE EXCLUSIONARY RULE: OTHER CONTEXTS

The Supreme Court has held that the exclusionary rule does not have to be applied in situations where its deterrent value would have little or no significant effect. As Justice O'Connor stated, "Where the rule's deterrent effect is likely to be marginal, or where its application offends other values central to our system of constitutional governance or the judicial process, we have declined to extend the

---

[201]524 U.S. 357 (1998).
[202]*Scott* at 363.

rule to that context."[203] The application of the exclusionary rule is excused where a police officer reasonably relied on a warrant to search when the warrant was later ruled invalid for reasons unrelated to law enforcement.[204] Courts do not have to apply the rule when a defendant attempts to assert a third party's Fourth Amendment rights in an effort to exclude evidence that did not violate the defendant's constitutional rights.[205] In a case where a police officer relied on a statute that purported to give rights to search which were later deemed unconstitutional, the fruits of the search did not have to be excluded, since the officer had reasonably relied upon the constitutionality of the statute.[206] A party to a criminal case may use evidence illegally obtained to impeach a defendant without inviting the application of the exclusionary rule.[207] As Justice Brennan phrased the principle, "The impeachment exception to the exclusionary rule permits the prosecution in a criminal proceeding to introduce illegally obtained evidence to impeach the defendant's own testimony."[208] In a similar vein, the Fourth Amendment's exclusionary rule does not mandate suppression of evidence seized in the absence of probable cause where the erroneous finding of probable cause resulted from clerical errors of court employees.[209] The Court rejected an invitation to apply the Fourth Amendment and its exclusionary rule in a manner that would exclude grand jury consideration of testimony based on illegally seized evidence.[210]

17. ALTERNATIVE REMEDIES TO FOURTH AMENDMENT VIOLATIONS: THE *BIVENS* CIVIL SUIT

Where an individual has been subjected to an illegal search and seizure and that person is to be tried for a criminal offense, the exclusionary rule offers a remedy that attempts to put the aggrieved individual in a similar situation as he or she would have been in had the illegal search not occurred. However, the exclusionary rule offers no remedy to an individual who has been allegedly a victim of an illegal search and/or seizure but is not a defendant in a criminal case. Since there is no evidence to suppress and no criminal case to be tried, the aggrieved individual must look to other avenues for redress.

In *Bivens v. Six Unknown Named Agents,*[211] employees of the Federal Bureau of Narcotics entered Bivens' apartment without a warrant, in the absence of probable cause, and without the use of any recognized exception under the Fourth Amendment. The federal officers arrested Bivens for alleged narcotics violations that were

---

[203]*Duckworth v. Eagan,* 492 U.S. 195, 208 (1989).
[204]*United States v. Leon,* 468 U.S. 897, 920–922 (1984).
[205]*Alderman v. United States,* 394 U.S. 165, 174–175 (1969).
[206]*Illinois v. Krull,* 480 U.S. 340, 349–350 (1987).
[207]*Walder v. United States,* 347 U.S. 62, 65 (1954). A similar principle allows the impeachment of statements taken in violation of *Miranda v. Arizona,* 384 U.S. 436 (1966). See *Harris v. New York,* 401 U.S. 222 (1971).
[208]*James v. Illinois,* 493 U.S. 307, 308–309 (1990).
[209]In *Arizona v. Evans,* 514 U.S. 1 (1995), a police officer conducted a search following an arrest when the arrest involved "bad" probable cause due to the failure of a clerk to properly remove a warrant notice from a computer system used by police.
[210]*United States v. Calandra,* 414 U.S. 338, 349 (1974).
[211]403 U.S. 388 (1971).

without foundation. The agents manacled the petitioner in front of his wife and children, threatened to arrest the entire family, and completely searched the apartment. When no criminal case had been brought against him for a period of time, Bivens brought suit for damages in federal court, alleging that the illegal search and seizure caused him mental suffering, humiliation, and embarrassment. The legal difficulty with Mr. Bivens' suit was that federal law did not give him a clear cause of action against the agents. Ultimately this case reached the Supreme Court of United States, which judicially created a cause of action that allowed the suit to proceed. According to Justice Brennan, part of the rationale for allowing a suit against the officers for damages for legal wrongs was not an unusual theory.

> That damages may be obtained for injuries consequent upon a violation of the Fourth Amendment by federal officials should hardly seem a surprising proposition. Historically, damages have been regarded as the ordinary remedy for an invasion of personal interests in liberty. *Bivens* at 395.

Following the *Bivens* case,[212] individuals against whom federal agents have conducted illegal searches and seizures possess a remedy in federal court to sue for damages based on the violation of the Fourth Amendment. Thus, where the exclusionary rule offers no legal remedy for alleged federal government misconduct, a direct suit against the officers may be the only remedy available.

18. LIMITS TO USE OF THE EXCLUSIONARY RULE: THE CONCEPT OF STANDING

Any person who wishes to suppress evidence alleged to have been illegally seized in violation of the Fourth Amendment must demonstrate that the government has violated some personal expectation of privacy. As Justice Kennedy explained the concept, "Fourth Amendment rights are personal, and when a person objects to the search of a place and invokes the exclusionary rule, he or she must have the requisite connection to that place."[213] The right of privacy may be demonstrated by proof that the defendant had a possessory interest in the searched property, that the accused was legally occupying the premises, or that proof of possession of the seized evidence was crucial to proof of guilt. The government must have seized the evidence from a place where the defendant personally had a right to privacy which society generally recognizes as reasonable. Only where the evidence is sought to be used against the one asserting the privacy right does that individual have standing to suppress the evidence. Having standing does not ensure suppression of the evidence, however; it only allows that individual the opportunity to argue that the evidence should be excluded based on a violation of the Fourth Amendment. Assuming proof

---

[212]In *Correctional Services Corporation v. Malesko,* 534 U.S. 61 (2001), the Court noted that it had extended the reach and rationale of *Bivens* on two occasions. In both cases, the Court extended the *Bivens* rationale to provide a cause of action against individual governmental officers who have allegedly acted unconstitutionally. In *Carlson v. Green,* 446 U.S. 14 (1980), the Court permitted the survivor of a deceased federal prisoner to maintain a civil damage suit against federal officers due to unconstitutional conduct, and it allowed a suit where there was no alternative remedy at law for a congressional employee who had allegedly been the victim of discrimination by a United States congressman in *Davis v. Passman,* 442 U.S. 228 (1971).
[213]*Minnesota v. Carter,* 525 U.S. 83, 100 (1998), Justice Kennedy, concurring.

of standing can successfully be made, a trial court will permit a defendant to argue that his personal Fourth Amendment rights were violated, but the right to argue does not ensure success in suppressing the evidence.

In a case involving standing, *Rakas v. Illinois,*[214] the Court held that a mere guest riding in a passenger car had no expectation of privacy in the automobile, since he did not assert that he was either an owner or a lessee of the vehicle (see Case 6.5). Since Rakas lacked a sufficient connection to the automobile, the trial court properly refused to entertain his motion to suppress on the theory that he lacked standing. The one individual who could have demonstrated standing would have been the owner, but the owner would have possessed standing to suppress evidence *only* if he or she were accused of criminal activities. The owner of the car could not attempt to suppress evidence sought to be used against a third person with no expectation of privacy in the motor vehicle, since Fourth Amendment rights are personal and cannot be asserted vicariously.

The *Rakas* case called into serious question the rule of automatic standing from *Jones v. United States.*[215] Under *Jones,* standing was considered automatic where the defendant had been charged with a crime involving possession or was legitimately on the premises (an apartment). In *United States v. Salvucci,*[216] the Court overruled the rule of automatic standing in *Jones* by deciding that something more than "legitimately on the premises" was required to demonstrate standing. The *Salvucci* Court noted that the reason for automatic standing had ceased to exist because, in the period between *Jones* and *Salvucci,* the Court had determined that a defendant could admit possession for Fourth Amendment purposes and not have that admission used against him or her at a trial for possession of the article.[217] According to the *Rakas* Court, a prosecutor could claim that a defendant possessed the seized article criminally but did not have sufficient possession of the article to have been subjected to a Fourth Amendment violation.

19. VICARIOUS STANDING NOT PERMITTED

Following the *Salvucci* decision, a person who wishes to suppress evidence alleged to have been illegally seized must detail precisely how his or her personal Fourth Amendment rights have been violated. Generally, a defendant must be able to demonstrate a significant proprietary or possessory interest in the property in order to demonstrate sufficient standing. A person has no standing to suppress evidence where a third party's premises have been illegally searched, since that person could have possessed no legitimate expectation of privacy at a third party's home.

However, even where a proprietary or significant possessory interest has not been proven, permission to use a room may prove sufficient to enable a defendant to successfully demonstrate standing. In *Minnesota v. Olson,*[218] the legitimate occupier

---

[214]439 U.S. 128 (1978).
[215]362 U.S. 257 (1960).
[216]448 U.S. 83 (1980).
[217]See *Simmons v. United States,* 390 U.S. 377 (1968).
[218]495 U.S. 91 (1990).

of an apartment had permitted Olson to stay in one of the rooms (see Case 6.6). Olson did not pay rent or have a key, but an understanding between him and the occupant allowed him to stay in the apartment. The *Olson* Court noted that from the view of an overnight guest, "he seeks shelter in another's home precisely because it provides him with privacy." Since Olson's expectation of privacy was rooted in common understandings that are recognized by our society, the Court decided that he possessed standing to argue.

The Court distinguished *Olson* from a different Minnesota case where the defendants were legitimately on the premises with the consent of the lessee but had not stayed a night and did not plan an overnight visit. In *Minnesota v. Carter,*[219] the defendants were bagging cocaine in a private apartment when, pursuant to an informant's tip, a police officer observed them by looking through parted curtains (see Case 6.7). While police sought a search warrant, Carter and another man left the property but were stopped in their automobile by police. A subsequent search revealed a firearm and a quantity of cocaine within the car.

Prior to trial, Carter and the other defendants filed a motion to suppress all evidence obtained from the later search of the apartment and the automobile, as well as to suppress several incriminating statements made by defendants to police following their arrest. The legal theory offered by the defendants' attorney contended that the initial police observation of their drug activities through the curtain was an unreasonable search in violation of the Fourth Amendment and that all evidence obtained directly or derivatively as a result of this search was inadmissible as fruit of the poisonous tree. The trial court held that the police officer had not conducted an illegal search, in connection with Carter and his accomplices, by looking in the window, and that since the two defendants were not overnight social guests, they had no standing to complain about a search and seizure within the apartment. When the case reached the Supreme Court of Minnesota, it reversed the lower court and held that Carter and the others had standing under the Fourth Amendment because they had a legitimate expectation of privacy. Therefore, since standing had been established, the Court determined that privacy existed in an apartment to do both legal and illegal activity and that the officer's observation of this illegal activity violated the two defendants' expectation of privacy under the Fourth Amendment.

In an opinion written by Chief Justice Rehnquist, the Court reversed the opinion of the Minnesota Supreme Court because it had followed a legal theory that had been obsolete for twenty years. Chief Justice Rehnquist noted that an overnight guest in a house may have a Fourth Amendment expectation of privacy but that a person legitimately on the premises for a brief time for commercial purposes does not enjoy the same expectation of privacy. According to Rehnquist, while the apartment was a dwelling place for the usual occupant, it was, for Carter and his drug-selling conspirator, simply a place to do business, which would not support a legitimate expectation of privacy under the Fourth Amendment.[220]

---

[219]525 U.S. 83 (1998).

[220]According to Chief Justice Rehnquist, the purely commercial nature of the transaction, the relatively short period of time on the premises, and the lack of any previous connection between Carter and his friend and the householder all lead us to conclude that

Thus, in *Olson,* the Court upheld the existence of a Fourth Amendment expectation of privacy because the defendant not only was legitimately on the premises but also had permission to spend the night, which gave him what society recognizes as some level of privacy as a social guest. In Carter's case, the defendant and his associates were merely using the premises of the occupant for commercial purpose for a brief time. Such activity was deemed to be quite different from being an overnight social guest in a friend's home; because of this difference, according to Chief Justice Rehnquist, Carter and his companion had no standing to even argue about a violation of privacy under the Fourth Amendment.

In addition to legitimate expectations of privacy, aggrieved parties may allege standing due to the relationship between them and the seized property. The attempt to create standing does not frequently bring success, as demonstrated by *United States v. Padilla,*[221] where members of a criminal conspiracy involved in drug trafficking attempted to allege that they had an expectation of privacy by virtue of being managers in the criminal enterprise. Law enforcement officials had seized an automobile involved in the transportation of illegal drugs at a time when the leaders of the operation were not present with the vehicle. The drug kingpins' attempt to create or allege standing under the Fourth Amendment ran aground when they could demonstrate no personal expectation of privacy that had been violated by federal officials.

20. SUMMARY

Violations of the Constitution that result in illegally seized evidence may permit the person against whom the evidence is sought to have it suppressed. The individual wishing to exclude the evidence from trial must be the person whose constitutional rights have been violated. While most evidence that is the subject of suppression is alleged to have been illegally seized by virtue of a Fourth Amendment violation, similar rules of exclusion apply to other violations of the Constitution that produce evidence. The theory of the exclusionary rule contemplates that by removing the law enforcement incentive to violate the United States Constitution and the Fourth Amendment, in particular, federal and state officials will be less likely to transgress the dictates of the law because such conduct produces no prosecution benefit. Where the exclusionary rule does not have the effect of deterring law enforcement conduct, the rule is less likely to be applied. The good faith exception, the rule of inevitable discovery, the rule of attenuation, and the independent source rule are examples of situations in which police conduct would not have been altered; for that reason, the exclusionary rule is generally not applied so as to exclude evidence from trial.

Carter's situation is closer to that of one simply permitted on the premises. The Court held that any search that may have occurred did not violate their Fourth Amendment rights. 525 U.S. 83, 91 (1998).
[221]508 U.S. 77 (1993).

MAJOR CASES

CASE 6.1

Genesis of the Exclusionary Rule for State Courts

Mapp v. Ohio
Supreme Court of the United States
367 U.S. 643 (1961)

FACTS

The appellant, Miss Mapp, was convicted of knowingly having in her possession and under her control some lewd and lascivious books, pictures, and photographs in violation of an Ohio statute. The evidence, which aided in her conviction, was taken by police officers, and as the Ohio Supreme Court admitted, was secured during the execution of an illegal search and seizure.

Miss Mapp lived alone with her fifteen-year-old daughter in a second-floor apartment in Cleveland. In the early afternoon of May 23, 1957, three policemen arrived at the home and rang the doorbell. When they were asked the purpose of their visit, the police officers stated that they wanted to talk to her, but they would not disclose to her the topic of their inquiry while they remained on the street. In reality, the police had information that a person who had been involved in a recent bombing was present in the home and that there was a large amount of gambling paraphernalia stored within.

Following a telephone consultation with her attorney, Miss Mapp informed the police that she would admit them only if they produced a search warrant. The officers did not force an entry, but kept the home under observation for the next three hours.

After more officers arrived several hours later, the police attempted and effectuated an entry by breaking the glass to a rear door. When the appellant asked to see a search warrant, an officer waved a piece of paper, purporting to be a search warrant. Miss Mapp promptly grabbed the paper and placed it to her bosom for safekeeping. The officers, after a brief physical struggle, retrieved it, handcuffed her, and took her upstairs, where she was forced to sit on her own bed. The arrival of Mapp's attorney did nothing to aid the situation since the police would not allow him to enter the home.

The search covered her dresser, a chest of drawers, a closet, and other areas of the bedroom. Police looked through her photo album and personal papers. The search continued through the rest of the second floor, including the other bedroom, the kitchen, and the dinette. A search of the basement revealed a trunk that contained the obscene materials upon which this conviction rested.

Over proper objection, at Miss Mapp's trial, the prosecution introduced no evidence of a search warrant and the judge permitted the introduction of the evidence secured by the search. Ms. Mapp was convicted by virtue of the evidence seized from her home.

The Ohio Supreme Court affirmed the conviction with the rationale that the evidence had not been taken from her person by the use of brutal or offensive physical force sufficient to offend a sense of justice.

PROCEDURAL ISSUE

Should the guarantees of the Fourth Amendment be incorporated into the Due Process Clause of the Fourteenth Amendment and the exclusionary rule of *Weeks v. United States* be extended to prohibit the use of illegally seized evidence in state criminal prosecutions?

HELD: YES

RATIONALE

Mr. Justice Clark delivered the opinion of the Court.

★ ★ ★

I

★ ★ ★

[I]n *Weeks v. United States,* (1914) 232 U.S. 383, at pages 391–392, [the Court] stated that:

> "The Fourth Amendment...put the courts of the United States and Federal officials, in the exercise of their power and authority, under limitations and restraints [and]...forever secure[d] the people, their persons, houses, papers, and effects, against all unreasonable searches and seizures under the guise of law...and the duty of giving to it force and effect is obligatory upon all entrusted under our Federal system with the enforcement of the laws."

Specifically dealing with the use of the evidence unconstitutionally seized, the Court concluded:

> "If letters and private documents can thus be seized and held and used in evidence against a citizen accused

of an offense, the protection of the Fourth Amendment declaring his right to be secure against such searches and seizures is of no value, and, so far as those thus placed are concerned, might as well be stricken from the Constitution…"

Finally, the Court in that case clearly stated that the use of the seized evidence involved "a denial of the constitutional rights of the accused."

★ ★ ★

This Court has ever since required of federal law officers a strict adherence to that command which this Court has held to be a clear, specific, and constitutionally required—even if judicially implied—deterrent safeguard without insistence upon which the Fourth Amendment would have been reduced to "a form of words."

★ ★ ★

II

In 1949,…this Court, in *Wolf v. Colorado,* 328 U.S. 25 (1949),…[considered] the effect of the Fourth Amendment upon the States through the operation of the Due Process Clause of the Fourteenth Amendment. It said:

"[W]e have no hesitation in saying that were a State affirmatively to sanction such police incursion to privacy it would run counter to the guaranty of the Fourteenth Amendment."

★ ★ ★

[The Supreme Court in *Wolf* declined to apply the *Weeks* exclusionary rule to state criminal prosecutions involving violation of Fourth Amendment principles.]

★ ★ ★

The Court in *Wolf* first stated that "[t]he contrariety of views of the States" on the adoption of the exclusionary rule of *Weeks* was "particularly impressive" (at p. 29); and, in this connection, that it could not "brush aside the experience of the States which deem the incidence of such conduct by the police too slight to call for a deterrent remedy…by overriding the [States'] relevant rules of evidence." At pp. 31-32.

While in 1949, prior to the *Wolf* case, almost two-thirds of the States were opposed to the use of the exclusionary rule, now despite the *Wolf* case, more than half of

those since passing upon it…have…adopted or adhere to the *Weeks* rule. [Citations omitted.] Significantly, among those now following the rule is California, which, according to its highest court, was "compelled to reach that conclusion because other remedies have completely failed to secure compliance with the constitutional provision.…" *People v. Cahan,* 1955, 44 Cal.2d 434, 445, 282 P.2d 905. In connection with this California case, we note that the second basis elaborated in *Wolf* in support of its failure to enforce the exclusionary rule against the States was that "other means of protection" have been afforded the right of privacy (partially protected by the Fourth and Fourteenth Amendments). 338 U.S., at page 30. The experience of California that other remedies have been worthless and futile is buttressed by the experience of other States. The obvious futility of relegating the Fourth Amendment to the protection of other remedies has, moreover, been recognized by this Court since *Wolf.* See *Irvine v. California,* 347 U.S. 128, 137 (1954).

III

The Court incorporated the Fourth Amendment into the Due Process Clause of the Fourteenth Amendment and adopted the exclusionary rule to enforce it.

★ ★ ★

IV

Since the Fourth Amendment's right of privacy has been declared enforceable against the States through the Due Process Clause of the Fourteenth, it is enforceable against them by the same sanction of exclusion as is used against the Federal Government. Were it otherwise, then just as without the *Weeks* rule the assurance against unreasonable federal searches and seizures would be a "form of words," valueless and undeserving of mention.

★ ★ ★

V

★ ★ ★

There are those who say, as did Justice (then Judge) Cardozo, that, under our constitutional exclusionary doctrine, "[t]he criminal is to go free because the constable has blundered." *People v. Defore,* 242 N.Y. at 21, 150 N.E. at 587. In some cases, this will undoubtedly be the result. But, as was said in *Elkins,* "there is another consideration—the imperative of judicial integrity." 364 U.S. at 222. The criminal goes free, if he must, but it is the law that sets him free. Nothing can destroy a government more quickly than its failure to observe its own laws, or worse, its disregard of the charter of its own existence.

★ ★ ★

Having once recognized that the right of privacy embodied in the Fourth Amendment is enforceable against the States, and that the right to be secure against rude invasions by state officers, is therefore, constitutional in origin, we can no longer permit that right to remain an empty promise. Because it is enforceable in the same manner and to like effect as other basic rights secured by the Due Process Clause, we can no longer permit it to be revocable at the whim of any police officer who, in the name of law enforcement itself, chooses to suspend its enjoyment. Our decision…gives to the individual no more than that which the Constitution guarantees him, to the police officer no less than that to which honest law enforcement is entitled, and, to the courts, that judicial integrity so necessary in the true administration of justice.

The judgment of the Supreme Court of Ohio is reversed and the cause remanded for further proceedings not inconsistent with this opinion.

Reversed and remanded.

COMMENTS, NOTES, AND QUESTIONS

1. In *Weeks v. United States,* 232 U.S. 383 (1914), mentioned in the *Mapp* case, the Supreme Court held that, in a federal prosecution, the Fourth Amendment barred the use of evidence secured through an illegal federal search and seizure. This rule of exclusion was not derived from the explicit requirements of the Fourth Amendment and was not based on legislation passed by Congress designed to enforce the Constitution. Was the development of the exclusionary rule essential or desirable to enforce the Fourth Amendment? Were there alternative

ways of enforcement that could have been effective? What would some of these theories involve?

2. Prior to deciding *Mapp,* the Court in *Wolf v. Colorado,* 338 U.S. 25 (1949), determined that the rule of *Weeks* would not be extended to state cases in the same way the exclusionary rule removed evidence from federal prosecutions. Why did the *Mapp* Court suddenly discover that the *Weeks* rationale, which it had earlier rejected in *Wolf v. Colorado* and *Rochin v. California,*[222] now should be applied to the states? Did the Court hold the view that the other means of private enforcement of the exclusionary rule had proven inadequate since *Wolf*?

3. Having determined that the Fourth Amendment applied to state activity, and that the exclusionary rule limited admissibility of illegally seized evidence in state cases, does the exclusionary rule now apply with the same force and effect to the states as it had been applied to federal criminal prosecutions since *Weeks*? Does the Court in *Mapp* say this?

4. How does the exclusionary rule apply to the states, since the original intent of the Fourth Amendment limited the activities only of the federal government? The Supreme Court adopted what some scholars call the "selective incorporation doctrine." Under this judicial theory, the justices consider various guarantees of the Bill of Rights to be so fundamental to liberty that the Due Process Clause of the Fourteenth Amendment must include some of the guarantees within its protections. On a case-by-case basis, a particular right has been "incorporated" into the Due Process Clause and, thereafter, applies to limit state criminal procedural practice. In *Mapp,* the Court felt that alternative remedies to violations of the Fourth Amendment by state officials had not ensured respect for the requirements of the amendment,[223] so alternative methods of enforcement were required.

5. Should the Fourth Amendment and the exclusionary rule generally have any application outside the territorial jurisdiction of the United States? It appears that the Framers of the Fourth Amendment did not contemplate extending its protections to other nations and especially to foreign citizens residing in their respective home nations or

---

[222]342 U.S. 165 (1952). In *Rochin,* the police had illegally broken into the defendant's home and choked him after he swallowed some narcotics. Police removed Rochin to a hospital, where he was forced to vomit the remains of the drugs. A trial court admitted the evidence against him, but the conviction was reversed by the Supreme Court as violative of due process rather than determining that the Fourth Amendment and the exclusionary rule should be applied to the states. Adopting the exclusionary rule for state cases did not happen until *Mapp v. Ohio* in 1961.

[223]While the Supreme Court was not willing, initially, to hold that the Fourth Amendment and its exclusionary rule should be applied to state activity, California had adopted the exclusionary rule as a matter of state law in 1955. See *People v. Cahan,* 44 Cal.2d 434, 282 P.2d 905.

to their property. The Supreme Court held that a search of a Mexican national's home in Mexico by Drug Enforcement Administration (DEA) agents did not require a warrant from a United States court. The Court noted that a warrant from the United States would have no lawful effect in Mexico. Aliens do enjoy certain constitutional rights, but those rights are not required to be applied in their own nation. In *United States v. Verdugo-Urquidez,* 494 U.S. 259 (1990), the Court refused to suppress evidence seized in Mexico without a warrant because the history, text, and practice of the Fourth Amendment fail to indicate that extraterritorial coverage of the amendment was intended.

CASE 6.2

Exclusion of Derivative Evidence: The Fruit of the Poisonous Tree Doctrine

Wong Sun v. United States
Supreme Court of the United States
371 U.S. 471 (1963)

FACTS

James Toy and Wong Sun, a.k.a. "Sea Dog," were convicted in the Federal District Court for the Northern District of California for the knowing transportation and concealment of illegally imported heroin.

Following several weeks of surveillance of Hom Way, police arrested him and uncovered heroin in his personal possession. Hom Way told the officers that he recently purchased the drug from "Blackie Toy" who lived on Leavenworth Street in San Francisco. Police cruised the thirty-block length of the street until they discovered "Oye's Laundry" at six in the morning.

After denying entry to plainclothes officers who had appeared and requested possession of their nonexistent laundry, Toy slammed the door and fled to the rear of the laundry/home. The federal narcotics agents followed Toy into his home against his will and cornered him in his bedroom. Immediately prior to Toy's flight, the officers had identified themselves as federal agents. The bedroom at the rear of the laundry was subjected to a warrantless search and Toy subjected to a similar search and arrest.

While the search produced no evidence of illegality, Toy promptly denied that he had any narcotics but implicated one "Johnny." Toy dutifully led the officers to the home of Johnny Yee and told the agents that they had smoked heroin the previous night.

A warrantless entry of Johnny Yee's place of residence produced less than an ounce of heroin. Just as Toy was willing to talk, so was Yee. Johnny Yee implicated Toy in heroin possession and Wong Sun as his supplier. A subsequent search of Wong Sun's residence uncovered no additional heroin.

Petitioners James Toy and Johnny Yee were arraigned almost immediately and released the same day. Wong Sun secured his release a day later. Several days later, Toy, Yee, and Wong Sun appeared at the police station and voluntarily submitted to interrogation by agents who prepared a statement summarizing the information obtained from each. Each man offered what amounted to a confession of guilt. Neither Toy nor Wong Sun would sign the statements, but Wong Sun admitted the accuracy of his statement.

At the trial Johnny Yee, who was to be a government witness, repudiated his earlier unsigned statement and invoked his Fifth Amendment privilege against self-incrimination. The government offered in evidence Toy's initial statements, the heroin found at Yee's home, Toy's unsigned statement, and Wong Sun's unsigned statement. Toy alleged that his initial statements and all the evidence which was derived therefrom should be excluded from evidence due to the Fourth Amendment violation which occurred as his home was illegally entered. The District Court rejected his argument and allowed the admission of the evidence that led to the conviction of Toy and Wong Sun.

The Court of Appeals affirmed and the Supreme Court granted certiorari.

PROCEDURAL ISSUE

Where evidence has been seized in violation of an individual's rights under the Fourth Amendment, must that evidence and any derivative evidence be excluded from the prosecutor's use for purposes of proving guilt?

HELD: YES

RATIONALE

Mr. Justice Brennan delivered the opinion of the Court.

★ ★ ★

We believe that significant differences between the cases of the two petitioners require separate discussion of each. We shall first consider the case of petitioner Toy.

I

The Court of Appeals found there was neither reasonable grounds nor probable cause for Toy's arrest. Giving due weight to that finding, we think it is amply justified by the facts clearly shown on this record. It is basic that an arrest with or without a warrant must stand upon firmer ground than mere suspicion, though the arresting officer need not have in hand evidence which would suffice to convict. The quantum of information which constitutes probable cause—evidence which would "warrant a man of reasonable caution in the belief" that a felony has been committed [citation omitted]—must be measured by the facts of the particular case.

★ ★ ★

The threshold question in this case, therefore, is whether the officers could, on the information which impelled them to act, have procured a warrant for the arrest of Toy. We think that no warrant would have issued on evidence then available.

★ ★ ★

Thus we conclude that the Court of Appeals' findings that the officers' uninvited entry into Toy's living quarters was unlawful and that the bedroom arrest which followed was likewise unlawful, was fully justified on the evidence. It remains to be seen what consequences flow from this conclusion.

II

It is conceded that Toy's declarations in his bedroom are to be excluded if they are held to be "fruits" of the agents' unlawful action.

★ ★ ★

The exclusionary rule has traditionally barred from trial physical, tangible materials obtained either during or as a direct result of an unlawful invasion. It follows from our holding in *Silverman v. United States*, 365 U.S. 505, that the Fourth Amendment may protect against the overhearing of verbal statements as well as against the more traditional seizure of "papers and effects." Similarly, testimony as to matters observed during an unlawful invasion has been excluded in order to enforce the basic constitutional policies. Thus, verbal evidence which derives so immediately from an unlawful entry and an unauthorized arrest as the officers' action in the present case is no less the "fruit" of official illegality than the more common tangible fruits of the unwarranted intrusion.

★ ★ ★

The government argues that Toy's statements to the officers in his bedroom, although closely consequent upon the invasion which we hold unlawful, were nevertheless admissible because they resulted from "an intervening independent act of a free will." This contention, however, takes insufficient account of the circumstances. Six or seven officers had broken the door and followed on Toy's heels into the bedroom where his wife and child were sleeping. He had been almost immediately handcuffed and arrested. Under such circumstances it is unreasonable to infer that Toy's response was sufficiently an act of free will to purge the primary taint of the unlawful invasion.

The Government also contends that Toy's declarations should be admissible because they were ostensibly exculpatory, rather than incriminating. There are two answers to this argument. First, the statements soon turned out to be incriminating, for they led directly to the evidence which implicated Toy. Second, when circumstances are shown such as those which induced these declarations, it is immaterial whether the declarations be termed "exculpatory." [Footnote omitted.] Thus, we find no substantial reason to omit Toy's declarations from the protection of the exclusionary rule.

III

We now consider whether the exclusion of Toy's declarations requires also the exclusion of the narcotics taken from Yee, to which those declarations led the police. The prosecutor candidly told the trial court that "we wouldn't have found those drugs except that Mr. Toy helped us to." Hence this is not the case envisioned by this Court where the exclusionary rule has no application because the Government learned of the evidence "from an independent source," *Silverthorne Lumber Co. v. United States*, 251 U.S. 385; nor is this a case in which the connection between the lawless conduct of the police and the discovery of the challenged evidence has "become so attenuated as to dissipate the taint." *Nardone v. United States*, 308 U.S. 338, 341. We need not hold that all evidence is "fruit of the poisonous tree" simply because it would not have come to light but for the illegal actions of the police. Rather, the more apt question in such a case is

> whether, granting establishment of the primary illegality, the evidence to which instant objection is made has been come at by exploitation of that illegality or instead by means sufficiently distinguishable to be purged of the primary taint. Maguire, *Evidence of Guilt,* 221 (1959).

We think it clear that the narcotics were "come at by the exploitation of that illegality" and hence that they may not be used against Toy.

IV

It remains only to consider Toy's unsigned statement. We need not decide whether, in light of the fact that Toy was free on his own recognizance when he made the statement, that statement was a fruit of the illegal arrest. [Citation omitted.] Since we have concluded that his declarations in the bedroom and the narcotics surrendered by Yee should not have been admitted in evidence against him, the only proofs remaining to sustain his conviction are his and Wong Sun's unsigned statements. Without scrutinizing the contents of Toy's ambiguous recitals, we conclude that no reference to Toy in Wong Sun's statement constitutes admission by Toy. We arrive at this conclusion upon two clear lines of decisions which converge to require it. One line of our decisions establishes that criminal confessions and admissions of guilt require extrinsic corroboration; the other line of precedents holds that an out-of-court declaration made after arrest may not be used at trial against one of the declarant's partners in crime.

It is a settled principle of the administration of criminal justice in the federal courts that a conviction must rest upon firmer ground than the uncorroborated admission or confession of the accused.

★ ★ ★

The import of our previous holdings is that a co-conspirator's hearsay statements may be admitted against the accused for no purpose whatever, unless made during and in furtherance of the conspiracy. Thus, as to Toy, the only possible source of corroboration is removed and his conviction must be set aside for lack of competent evidence to support it.

V

We now turn to the case of the other petitioner, Wong Sun. We have no occasion to disagree with the finding of the Court of Appeals that his arrest, also, was without probable cause or reasonable grounds. At all events no evidentiary consequences turn upon that question. For Wong Sun's unsigned confession was not the fruit of that arrest, and was therefore properly admitted at trial. On the evidence that Wong Sun had been released on his own recognizance after a lawful arraignment, and had returned voluntarily several days later to make the statement, we hold that the connection between the arrest and the statement had "become so attenuated as to dissipate the taint." *Nardone v. United States,* 308 U.S. 338, 341. The fact that the statement was unsigned, whatever bearing this may have upon its weight and credibility, does not render it inadmissible; Wong Sun understood and adopted its substances, though he could not comprehend the English words. The petitioner has never suggested any impropriety in the interrogation itself which would require the exclusion of this statement.

We must then consider the admissibility of the narcotics surrendered by Yee. Our holding, *supra,* that this ounce of heroin was inadmissible against Toy does not compel a like result with respect to Wong Sun. The exclusion of the narcotics as to Toy was required solely by their tainted relationship to information unlawfully obtained from Toy, and not by any official impropriety connected with their surrender by Yee. The seizure of this heroin invaded no right of privacy of person or premises which would entitle Wong Sun to object to its use at his trial.

★ ★ ★

However, for the reasons that Wong Sun's statement was incompetent to corroborate Toy's admissions contained in Toy's own statement, any references to Wong Sun in Toy's statement were incompetent to corroborate Wong Sun's admissions. Thus, the only competent source of corroboration for Wong Sun's statement was the heroin itself. We cannot be certain, however, on this state of the record, that the trial judge may not also have considered the contents of Toy's statement as a source of corroboration.

★ ★ ★

We intimate no view one way or the other as to whether the trial judge might have found in the narcotics alone sufficient evidence to corroborate Wong Sun's admissions that he delivered heroin to Yee and smoked heroin at Yee's house around the date in question.

★ ★ ★

We therefore hold that petitioner Wong Sun is also entitled to a new trial. [Jimmy Toy also received a new trial.]

Judgment of Court of Appeals reversed and case remanded to the District Court.

COMMENTS, NOTES, AND QUESTIONS

1. This case, *Wong Sun,* must be considered in the context of *Mapp v. Ohio* and is both a significant affirmation and an extension of the reach of the exclusionary rule. Under *Mapp,* evidence that had been directly seized due to the illegal nature of the search under the Fourth Amendment would be excluded from evidence during the prosecution's case. The *Mapp* case did not address derivative evidence and how it was to be handled. The *Wong Sun* case answers the question that *Mapp* did not need to address, since all the evidence was found inside the Mapp house. Following the *Mapp* decision, evidence that has been obtained by virtue of exploiting an original illegality will be excluded from trial, as a general rule. Thus, when *Mapp* and *Wong Sun* are read together, illegally seized evidence and derivative evidence that would not have been uncovered except for the original illegality will be similarly excluded.

2. The *Wong Sun* Court required that the victim of the Fourth Amendment violation possess an expectation of privacy in the area initially searched. Only if there was a legitimate expectation of privacy and if a violation of that right of privacy produced a direct or indirect link to incriminating evidence would the "fruit of the poisonous tree" doctrine have application. This principle is known as possessing "standing" to complain; without it, one cannot successfully suppress evidence. Could Wong Sun have possessed any expectation of privacy at Johnny Yee's home, under the circumstances of this case? Why or why not? Could you change the facts so that Wong Sun would clearly have some expectation of privacy at Johnny Yee's home?

3. Consider whether the following derivative evidence would be admissible against defendant Baker. Police discovered evidence of cocaine trafficking in the car possessed by Abel, as well as evidence in the same car that Baker was also involved in the drug dealing. Should Baker be able to argue about suppressing the evidence taken (even illegally) from the car of Abel? Could Baker have an expectation of privacy in a car in the possession of another person? Does *Wong Sun* help provide an answer? See also *Rakas v. Illinois,* 439 U.S. 128 (1978), for additional information on the concept of standing to suppress.

CASE 6.3

Seized Evidence Admissible: The Independent Source Rule

Murray v. United States
Supreme Court of the United States
487 U.S. 533 (1988)

FACTS

Murray, the petitioner, and Carter were convicted in a federal district court for conspiracy to possess and distribute marijuana contrary to federal law. A portion of the incriminating trial evidence came from the execution of a search warrant for which the probable cause had been based on independent sources of evidence.

In gathering information concerning marijuana trafficking, federal narcotics officers conducted surveillance on a warehouse that was believed to be the site of significant drug activity. The officers observed Murray and Carter driving vehicles into, and later out of, the warehouse. When the vehicles and the petitioners later left, the agents observed a tractor-trailer rig with a large dark container inside. Several agents illegally forced their way into the warehouse and observed in plain view numerous burlap-wrapped bales. Other federal officers followed the petitioners and observed them giving control of their respective vehicles to other persons. Agents properly stopped the new drivers and lawfully seized the vehicles. Subsequent searches of the vehicles revealed quantities of marijuana. The officers left the warehouse without disturbing the contents and did not return until they possessed a search warrant.

In the affidavit for the warehouse search warrant, the officers included no mention of their previous illegal entry or what that illegal search disclosed. Probable cause was not based on information obtained illegally by the government but on lawfully gathered information sufficient to support probable cause to search. Pursuant to the warrant, federal agents seized approximately 270 bales of marijuana and a customer list.

The District Court denied respondent's motion to suppress the evidence and the First Circuit Court of Appeals affirmed. The Supreme Court granted certiorari.

PROCEDURAL ISSUE

Where police unlawfully enter premises and observe illegal activity and subsequently obtain and execute a search warrant which was not based on the observations of the illegal activities but on independent, untainted evidence, has the evidence been properly seized pursuant to the warrant and is it admissible in court?

HELD: YES

RATIONALE

Justice Scalia delivered the opinion of the Court.

In *Segura v. United States,* 468 U.S. 796 (1984), we held that police officers' illegal entry upon private premises did not require suppression of evidence subsequently discovered on the basis of information wholly unconnected with the initial entry. In these consolidated cases we are faced with the question whether again, assuming evidence obtained pursuant to an independently obtained search warrant, the portion of such evidence that had been observed in plain view at the time of a prior illegal entry must be suppressed.

I

★ ★ ★

II

★ ★ ★

Almost simultaneously with our development of the exclusionary rule, in the first quarter of this century, we also announced what has come to be known as the "independent source" doctrine. See *Silverthorne Lumber Co. v. United States,* 251 U.S. 385, 392 (1920). That doctrine, which has been applied to evidence acquired not only through Fourth Amendment violations but also through Fifth and Sixth Amendment violations, has recently been described as follows:

> [T]he interest of society in deterring unlawful police conduct and the public interest in having juries receive all probative evidence of a crime are properly

balanced by putting the police in the same, not a *worse,* position that they would have been in if no police error or misconduct had occurred.... When the challenged evidence has an independent source, exclusion of such evidence would put the police in a worse position than they would have been in absent any error or violation. *Nix v. Williams,* 467 U.S. 431, 443 (1984)[.]

The dispute here is over the scope of this doctrine. Petitioners contend that it applies only to evidence obtained for the first time during an independent lawful search. The Government argues that it applies also to evidence initially discovered during, or as a consequence of, an unlawful search, but later obtained independently from activities untainted by the initial illegality. We think the Government's view has better support in both precedent and policy.

Our cases have used the concept of "independent source" in a more general and a more specific sense. The more general sense identifies all evidence acquired in a fashion untainted by the illegal evidence-gathering activity. Thus, where an unlawful entry has given investigators knowledge of facts x and y, but fact z has been learned by other means, fact z can be said to be admissible because derived from an "independent source." This is how we used the term in *Segura v. United States,* 468 U.S. 796 (1984).

★ ★ ★

The original use of the term, however, and its more important use for purposes of this case, was more specific. It was originally applied in the exclusionary rule context, by Justice Holmes, with reference to that particular category of evidence acquired by an untainted search *which is identical to the evidence unlawfully acquired*—that is, in the example just given, to knowledge of facts x and y derived from an independent source:

> The essence of a provision forbidding the acquisition of evidence in a certain way is that not merely evidence so acquired shall not be used before the Court but that it shall not be used at all. Of course this does not mean that the facts thus obtained become sacred and inaccessible. If knowledge of them is gained from an independent source they may be proved like any others. *Silverthorne Lumber, supra,* at 392.

★ ★ ★

Petitioners' asserted policy basis for excluding evidence which is initially discovered during an illegal search, but is subsequently acquired through an independent and lawful source, is that a contrary rule will remove all deterrence to, and indeed positively encourage, unlawful police searches. As petitioners see the incentives, law enforcement officers will routinely enter without a warrant to make sure that what they expect to be on the premises is in fact there. If it is not, they will have spared themselves the time and trouble of getting a warrant; if it is, they can get the warrant and use the evidence despite the unlawful entry. We see the incentives differently. An officer with probable cause sufficient to obtain a search warrant would be foolish to enter the premises first in an unlawful manner. By doing so, he would risk suppression of all evidence on the premises, both seen and unseen, since his action would add to the normal burden of convincing a magistrate that there is probable cause the much more onerous burden of convincing a trial court that no information gained from the illegal entry affected either the law enforcement officers' decision to seek a warrant or the magistrate's decision to grant it. Nor would the officer *without* sufficient probable cause to obtain a search warrant have any added incentive to conduct an unlawful entry, since whatever he finds cannot be used to establish probable cause before a magistrate.

★ ★ ★

III

To apply what we have said to the present case: Knowledge that the marijuana was in the warehouse was assuredly acquired at the time of the unlawful entry. But it was also acquired at the time for entry pursuant to the warrant, and if that later acquisition was not the result of the earlier entry there is no reason why the independent source doctrine should not apply. Invoking the exclusionary rule would put the police (and society) not in the *same* position they would have occupied if no violation occurred, but in a *worse* one. See *Nix v. Williams*, 467 U.S., at 443.

We think this is also true with respect to the tangible evidence, the bales of marijuana.... The independent source doctrine does not rest upon such metaphysical analysis, but upon the policy that, while the government should not profit from its illegal activity, neither should it be placed in a worse position than it would otherwise have occupied. So long as a later, lawful seizure is generally independent of an earlier, tainted one (which may well be difficult to establish where the seized goods are kept in the police's possession) there is no reason why the independent source doctrine should not apply.

The ultimate question, therefore, is whether the search pursuant to warrant was in fact a genuinely independent source of the information and tangible evidence at issue here. This would not have been the case if the agents' decision to seek the warrant was prompted by what they had seen during the initial entry, or if information obtained during that entry was presented to the Magistrate and affected his decision to issue the warrant. On this point the Court of Appeals said the following:

> [W]e can be absolutely certain that the warrantless entry in no way contributed in the slightest either to the issuance of a warrant or to the discovery of the evidence during the lawful search that occurred pursuant to the warrant.

★ ★ ★

This is as clear a case as can be imagined where the discovery of the contraband in plain view was totally irrelevant to the later securing of a warrant and the successful search that ensued. As there was no causal link whatever between the illegal entry and the discovery of the challenged evidence, we find no error in the court's refusal to suppress. *United States v. Moscatiello*, 771 F.2d, at 603, 604.

★ ★ ★

Accordingly, we vacate the judgements and remand these cases to the Court of Appeals with instructions that it remand to the District Court for determination whether the warrant-authorized search of the warehouse was an independent source of the challenged evidence in the sense we have described.

It is so ordered.

COMMENTS, NOTES, AND QUESTIONS

1. Would the result in *Murray* have been the same if the defendants could have demonstrated that evidence necessary to the establishment of probable cause could only have been derived from the initial illegal entry to the premises? What are the reasons for your conclusion? As a matter of good law enforcement, should we allow police officers to violate the Fourth Amendment without any penalty when it fails to produce admissible evidence? Are there dangers when police officers conduct themselves in

the manner of burglars? Could a home or office occupier think police were intruders and deal with them on that basis?

2. Does the *Murray* decision encourage police officers to make illegal entries to discover evidence and to use that evidence as a basis for obtaining a warrant? Why or why not? Would officers use an illegal entry to verify information to be sure of the accuracy of other information, which would then be included on the affidavit for a search warrant? Would this approach work? The argument could be made that police could make illegal entries and, where police find nothing that offends the law, merely leave and not pursue the matter further. However, what if the officer finds evidence of criminality and is precluded from using that evidence as a basis or partial basis for probable cause? How could probable cause be established independently?

CASE 6.4

Admission of Illegally Seized Evidence: The Rule of Inevitable Discovery

Nix v. Williams
Supreme Court of the United States
467 U.S. 431 (1984)

FACTS

On Christmas Eve, a teenager observed defendant Williams carrying a large bundle wrapped in a blanket from which two skinny white legs protruded. Police discovered other evidence connecting Williams to the crime, and a warrant for his arrest was properly issued. After additional investigation, police believed that the girl's body must be located between Des Moines, Iowa, and a rest stop along the local interstate highway.

Following an investigation, police arrested Williams in Davenport, Iowa, and was transported back to Des Moines. Police agreed not to interrogate the defendant until he could speak with his counsel at Des Moines. Concurrent with Williams' return to police custody, other officers were conducting an extensive search for the girl's body. The search encompassed the area where the body was actually located, but the girl's remains had not been discovered when Williams' return trip began.

At the initiation of the return trip, one of the custodial officers began a conversation with Williams in which he directed his attention to the task of finding the girl's remains. The officer said:

I want to give you something to think about while we're traveling down the road. . . . Number one, I want you to observe the weather conditions, it's raining, it's sleeting, it's freezing, driving is very treacherous, visibility is poor, it's going to be dark early this evening. They are predicting several inches of snow for tonight, and I feel that you yourself are the only person that knows where this little girl's body is, that you yourself have only been there once, and if you get a snow on top of it you yourself may be unable to find it. And since we will be going right past the area on the way into Des Moines, I feel that we could stop and locate the body, that the parents of this little girl should be entitled to a Christian burial for the little girl who was snatched away from them on Christmas Eve and murdered. And I feel we should stop and locate it on the way in rather than waiting until morning and trying to come back out after a snow storm and possibly not being able to find it at all. *Brewer v. Williams,* 430 U.S. 387 (1977).

The officer concluded his speaking to Williams with an admonition that Williams not answer the officer and that he think about what the officer had said. The officer noted that they would be driving near the town where the police believed the body was located.

Following some inquiries by the defendant related to other evidence in the case, Williams spontaneously and without immediate prompting agreed to direct the officers to the girl's remains. Police ceased their search for the body and the defendant showed the officers where he had left the body. The place of discovery was in an area which the police would have eventually searched and made the same discovery, but at a later time.

At Williams' second murder trial for the death of the little girl, the government did not introduce evidence that defendant had directed police to the body. The trial court admitted other evidence, including the condition of the body and the results of medical and chemical tests. The court permitted the use of evidence related to the corpse on the theory that police would have inevitably discovered the same evidence within a short time. The jury found Williams guilty of first-degree murder and he appealed.

The Supreme Court of Iowa affirmed the conviction and held that an independent source rule existed as an exception to the *Mapp* exclusionary rule. The Court held that there must be proof that police did not act in bad faith for the purpose of discovering the evidence and that the challenged evidence would have been discovered by lawful means. The Court rejected Williams' contention that the evidence should have been excluded as the "fruit" of the poisonous tree under *Wong-Sun v. United States,* 371 U.S. 471. Williams pursued his federal remedies by applying for a writ of habeas corpus.

The Supreme Court of the United States granted certiorari.

PROCEDURAL ISSUE

Where evidence, which inevitably would have been lawfully seized or discovered by law enforcement officials, has been obtained more immediately as the result of a violation of the constitutional rights of an arrestee, should a trial court exclude such evidence from admission in court?

HELD: NO

RATIONALE

Chief Justice Burger delivered the opinion of the Court.

We granted certiorari to consider whether, at respondent Williams' second murder trial in state court, evidence pertaining to the discovery and condition of the victim's body was properly admitted on the ground that it would ultimately or inevitably have been discovered even if no violation of any constitutional or statutory provision had taken place.

I

★ ★ ★

II

A

The Iowa Supreme Court correctly stated that the "vast majority" of all courts, both state and federal, recognize an inevitable discovery exception to the exclusionary rule. We are now urged to adopt and apply the so-called ultimate or inevitable discovery exception to the exclusionary rule.

Williams contends that evidence of the body's location and condition is "fruit of the poisonous tree," *i.e.,* the "fruit" or product of Detective Leaming's plea to help the child's parents give her "a Christian burial," which this Court had already held equated to interrogation. He contends that admitting the challenged evidence violated the

Sixth Amendment [right to counsel] whether it would have been inevitably discovered or not. Williams also contends that, if the inevitable discovery doctrine is constitutionally permissible, it must include a threshold showing of police good faith.

B

★ ★ ★

Wong Sun v. United States, 371 U.S. 471 (1963), extended the exclusionary rule to evidence that was the indirect product or "fruit" of unlawful police conduct, but there again the Court emphasized that evidence that has been illegally obtained need not always be suppressed, stating:

> We need not hold that all evidence is 'fruit of the poisonous tree' simply because it would not have come to light *but for the illegal actions* of the police. Rather, the more apt question in such a case is
>
> > whether, granting establishment of the primary illegality, the evidence to which instant objection is made has been come at by exploitation of that illegality or instead by means sufficiently distinguishable to be purged of the primary taint. *Id.,* at 487–488 (emphasis added) (quoting J. Maguire, *Evidence of Guilt* 221 (1959)).

★ ★ ★

The core rationale consistently advanced by this Court for extending the exclusionary rule to evidence that is the fruit of unlawful police conduct has been that this admittedly drastic and socially costly course is needed to deter police from violations of constitutional and statutory protections. This Court has accepted the argument that the way to ensure such protections is to exclude evidence seized as a result of such violations notwithstanding the high social cost of letting persons obviously guilty go unpunished for their crimes. On this rationale, the prosecution is not to be put in a better position than it would have been in if no illegality had transpired.

By contrast, the derivative evidence analysis ensures that the prosecution is not put in a worse position simply because of some earlier police error or misconduct. The independent source doctrine allows admission of evidence that has been discovered by means wholly independent of any constitutional violation.

★ ★ ★

When the challenged evidence has an independent source, exclusion of such evidence would put the police in a worse position than they would have been in absent any error or violation. There is a functional similarity between these two doctrines in that exclusion of evidence that would inevitably have been discovered would also put the government in a worse position, because the police would have obtained that evidence if no misconduct had taken place. Thus, while the independent source exception would not justify admission of evidence in this case, its rationale is wholly consistent with and justifies our adoption of the ultimate or inevitable discovery exception to the exclusionary rule.

★ ★ ★

Exclusion of physical evidence that would inevitably have been discovered adds nothing to either the integrity or fairness of a criminal trial.

★ ★ ★

The search had commenced at approximately 10 a.m. and moved westward through Poweshiek County into Jasper County. At approximately 3 p.m., after Williams had volunteered to cooperate with the police, Detective Leaming, who was in the police car with Williams, sent word to Ruxlow and the other Special Agent directing the search to meet him at the Grinnell truck stop and the search was suspended at that time. Ruxlow also stated that he was "under the impression that there was a possibility" that Williams would lead them to the child's body at that time. The search was not resumed once it was learned that Williams had led the police to the body, which was found two and one-half miles from where the search had stopped in what would have been the easternmost grid to be search in Polk County. There was testimony that it would have taken an additional three to five hours to discover the body if the search had continued; the body was found near a culvert, one of the kinds of places the teams had been specifically directed to search.

On this record it is clear that the search parties were approaching the actual location of the body, and we are satisfied, along with three courts earlier, that the volunteer search teams would have resumed the search had Williams not earlier led the police to the body and the body inevitably would have been found. The evidence asserted by Williams as newly discovered, *i.e.,* certain

photographs of the body and deposition testimony of Agent Ruxlow made in connection with the federal habeas proceeding, does not demonstrate that the material facts were inadequately developed in the suppression hearing in state court or that Williams was denied a full, fair, and adequate opportunity to present all relevant facts at the suppression hearing.

The judgment of the Court of Appeals is reversed, and the case is remanded for further proceedings consistent with this opinion.

It is so ordered.

COMMENTS, NOTES, AND QUESTIONS

1. A legal requirement for the government to prevail in cases of alleged "inevitably discoverable" evidence, according to the *Nix* Court, dictated that the prosecution prove by a preponderance of the evidence that the questioned evidence would eventually have been discovered by lawful means. If the burden of proof can be met, evidence initially obtained from unlawful government conduct may be introduced during the prosecution's case in chief where there is proof of a future lawful discovery. Do you think it was clearly inevitable that in this case the body would have been discovered in the normal course of events? Why or why not? Would police misconduct be better deterred if the illegal conduct caused the evidence to be excluded? Would police be on notice to more carefully observe the law? Or would exclusion of evidence in a case similar to *Nix* have very little deterrent effect in most cases?

2. While the *Nix* decision is binding on federal courts, state courts remain free to reject (based on state law or state judicial interpretation) the rule of inevitable discovery as an exception to the exclusionary rule. Iowa or any other state could decide that the burden of proof on the prosecution should be by clear and convincing evidence or could reject the concept of inevitable discovery altogether. If the prosecutor had to prove by clear and convincing evidence that the illegally discovered evidence would have been discovered by lawful means, would this result in more careful police work? Why or why not?

3. Although the *Nix* decision focused on a violation of the Sixth Amendment right to counsel and the related violation of the requirements of *Miranda v. Arizona,* 384 U.S. 436 (1966), the principle of inevitable discovery is fairly applicable whenever government agents obtain evidence in violation of the defendant's constitutional rights that has a second and lawful source involving inevitable discovery.

CASE 6.5

Standing to Suppress Evidence Requires Violation of Personal Rights

Rakas v. Illinois
Supreme Court of the United States
439 U.S. 128 (1978)

FACTS

Rakas and King were convicted of armed robbery of clothing store employees. A police description of the getaway automobile alerted other officers to the fact of the robbery and escape of the felons. After the automobile carrying Rakas had been stopped, the subsequent search of the car revealed a box of shells and a sawed-off rifle. Neither Rakas nor King owned the automobile, and neither ever asserted that he owned the rifle or shells seized.

The trial court refused to consider the motion to suppress the evidence seized from the car on the ground that Rakas was merely a guest passenger in the automobile of a friend and lacked legal standing to contest the constitutionality of the search. The basis for the conclusion that Rakas had asserted no Fourth Amendment expectation of privacy in the vehicle directly related to his lack of declared ownership or possession of the car, rifle, or shells.

The trial court admitted the evidence from the car against Rakas and both he and King were convicted. The Appellate Court of Illinois affirmed the conviction. The Illinois Supreme Court refused to hear the case and the Supreme Court granted certiorari.

PROCEDURAL ISSUE

Where an automobile search has been conducted and the accused made no claim to ownership or possession of the auto or the incriminating evidence within, does such a person have standing under the Fourth Amendment to contest the legality of the search?

HELD: NO

RATIONALE

Mr. Justice Rehnquist delivered the opinion of the Court.

★ ★ ★

II

Petitioners first urge us to relax or broaden the rule of standing enunciated in *Jones v. United States,* 362 U.S. 257 (1960), so that any criminal defendant at whom a search was "directed" would have standing to contest the legality of that search and object to the admission at trial of evidence obtained as a result of the search. Alternatively petitioners argue that they have standing to object to the search under *Jones* because they were "legitimately on [the] premises" at the time of the search.

The concept of standing discussed in *Jones* focuses on whether the person seeking to challenge the legality of a search as a basis for suppressing evidence was himself the "victim" of the search and seizure. *Id.,* at 261. Adoption of the so-called "target" theory advanced by petitioners would, in effect, permit a defendant to assert that a violation of the Fourth Amendment rights of a third party entitled him to have evidence suppressed at his trial.

★ ★ ★

A

We decline to extend the rule of standing in Fourth Amendment cases in the manner suggested by petitioners. As we stated in *Alderman v. United States,* 394 U.S. 165, 174 (1969), "Fourth Amendment rights are personal rights which, like some other constitutional rights, may not be vicariously asserted." [Citations omitted.] A person who is aggrieved by an illegal search and seizure only through the introduction of damaging evidence secured by a search of a third person's premises or property has not had any of his Fourth Amendment rights infringed. And since the exclusionary rule is an attempt to effectuate the guarantee of the Fourth Amendment, *United States v. Calandra,* 414 U.S. 338, 347 (1974), it is proper to permit only defendants whose Fourth Amendment rights have been violated to benefit from the rule's protections.

★ ★ ★

In support of their target theory, petitioners rely on the following quotation from *Jones:*

> In order to qualify as a 'person aggrieved by an unlawful search and seizure' one must have been a victim of a search or seizure, *one against whom the search was directed,* as distinguished from one who claims prejudice only through the use of evidence gathered as a consequence of a search or seizure directed at someone else. 362 U.S., at 261 (emphasis added).

They also rely on *Bumper v. North Carolina*, 391 U.S. 543, 548, n. 11 (1968), and *United States v. Jeffers*, 342 U.S. 48 (1951).

★ ★ ★

In *Jones*, the Court set forth two alternative holdings: It established a rule of "automatic" standing to contest an allegedly illegal search where the same possession needed to establish standing is an essential element of the offense charged; and second it stated that "anyone legitimately on premises where a search occurs may challenge its legality by way of a motion to suppress." 362 U.S., at 264, 267. Had the Court intended to adopt the target theory now put forth by petitioners, neither of the above two holdings would have been necessary since Jones was the "target" of the police search in that case. Nor does *United States v. Jeffers, supra,* or *Bumper v. North Carolina, supra,* support the target theory. Standing in *Jeffers* was based on the property seized. Similarly, in *Bumper,* the defendant had a substantial possessory interest in both the house searched [Bumper lived in the home with his grandmother] and the rifle seized. 391 U.S., at 548 n.11, 88 S.Ct., at 1791.

In *Alderman v. United States,* Mr. Justice Fortas, in a concurring and dissenting opinion, argued that the Court should "include within the category of those who may object to the introduction of illegal evidence 'one against whom the search was directed.'" 394 U.S., at 206–209.

★ ★ ★

The Court's opinion in *Alderman* counseled against [Justice Fortas's view of] such an extension of the exclusionary rule:

> The deterrent values of preventing the incrimination of those whose rights the police have violated have been considered sufficient to justify the suppression of probative evidence even though the case against the defendant is weakened or destroyed. We adhere to that judgment. But we are not convinced that the additional benefits of extending the exclusionary rule to other defendants would justify further encroachment upon the public interest in prosecuting those accused of crime and having them acquitted or convicted on the basis of all the evidence which exposes the truth. *Id.,* at 174–175.

Each time the exclusionary rule is applied it exacts a substantial social cost for the vindication of Fourth Amendment rights. Relevant and reliable evidence is kept from the trier of fact and the search for truth at trial is deflected. Since our cases generally have held that one whose Fourth Amendment rights are violated may successfully suppress evidence obtained in the course of an illegal search and seizure, misgivings as to the benefit of enlarging the class of persons who may invoke that rule are properly considered when deciding whether to expand standing to assert Fourth Amendment violations.

B

★ ★ ★

We can think of no decided cases of this Court that would have come out differently had we concluded, as we do now, that the type of standing requirement discussed in *Jones* and reaffirmed today is more properly subsumed under substantive Fourth Amendment doctrine. Rigorous application of the principle that the rights secured by this Amendment are personal, in place of a notion of "standing," will produce no additional situations in which evidence must be excluded. The inquiry under either approach is the same. But we think the better analysis forthrightly focuses on the extent of a particular defendant's rights under the Fourth Amendment, rather than of any theoretically separate, but invariably intertwined concept of standing....

It should be emphasized that nothing we say here casts the least doubt on cases which recognize that, as a general proposition, the issue of standing involves two inquiries: first, whether the proponent of a particular legal right has alleged "injury in fact," and, second, whether the proponent is asserting his own legal rights and interests rather than basing his claim for relief upon the rights of third parties. But this Court's long history of insistence that Fourth Amendment rights are personal in nature has already answered many of these traditional standing inquiries, and we think that definition of those rights is more properly placed within the purview of substantive Fourth Amendment law than within that of standing.

Analyzed in these terms, the question is whether the challenged search or seizure violated the Fourth Amendment rights of a criminal defendant who seeks to exclude the evidence obtained during it. That inquiry in turn requires a determination of whether the disputed search and seizure has infringed an interest of the defendant which the Fourth Amendment was designed to protect.

★ ★ ★

C

Here, petitioners who were passengers occupying a car which they neither owned nor leased, seek to analogize their position to that of the defendant in *Jones v. United States*. In *Jones,* petitioner was present at the time of the search of an apartment which was owned by a friend. The friend had given Jones permission to use the apartment and a key to it, with which Jones had admitted himself on the day of the search. He had a suit and shirt at the apartment and had slept there "maybe the night," but his home was elsewhere. At the time of the search, Jones was the only occupant of the apartment because the lessee was away for a period of several days. Under these circumstances, this Court stated that while one wrongfully on the premises could not move to suppress evidence obtained as a result of searching them, "anyone legitimately on premises where a search occurs may challenge its legality." Petitioners argue that their occupancy of the automobile in question was comparable to that of Jones in the apartment and that they therefore have standing to contest the legality of the search—or as we have rephrased the inquiry, that they, like Jones, had their Fourth Amendment rights violated by the search.

We do not question the conclusion in *Jones* that the defendant in that case suffered a violation of his personal Fourth Amendment rights if the search in question was unlawful. Nonetheless, we believe that the phrase "legitimately on premises" coined in *Jones* creates too broad a gauge for measurement of Fourth Amendment rights. For example, applied literally, this statement would permit a casual visitor who has never seen, or been permitted to visit, the basement of another's house to object to a search of the basement if the visitor happened to be in the kitchen of the house at the time of the search. Likewise, a casual visitor who walks into a house one minute before a search of the house commences and leaves one minute after the search ends would be able to contest the legality of the search. The first visitor would have absolutely no interest or legitimate expectation of privacy in the basement, the second would have none in the house, and it advances no purpose served by the Fourth Amendment to permit either of them to object to the lawfulness of the search.

We think that *Jones* on its facts merely stands for the unremarkable proposition that a person can have a legally sufficient interest in a place other than his own home so that the Fourth Amendment protects him from unreasonable governmental intrusion into the place.

★ ★ ★

D

Judged by the foregoing analysis, petitioners' claims must fail. They asserted neither a property nor a possessory interest in the automobile, nor an interest in the property seized. And as we have previously indicated, the fact that they were "legitimately on [the] premises" in the sense that they were in the car with the permission of its owner is not determinative of whether they had a legitimate expectation of privacy in the particular areas of the automobile searched. It is unnecessary for us to decide here whether the same expectations of privacy are warranted in a car as would be justified in a dwelling place in analogous circumstances. We have on numerous occasions pointed out that cars are not to be treated identically with houses or apartments for Fourth Amendment purposes. [Citations omitted.] But here petitioners' claim is one which would fail even in an analogous situation in a dwelling place, since they made no showing that they had any legitimate expectation of privacy in the glove compartment or area under the seat of the car in which they were merely passengers. Like the trunk of an automobile, these are areas in which a passenger *qua* passenger simply would not normally have a legitimate expectation of privacy.

★ ★ ★

III

The Illinois courts were therefore correct in concluding that it was unnecessary to decide whether the search of the car might have violated the rights secured to someone else by the Fourth and Fourteenth Amendments to the United States Constitution. Since it did not violate any rights of these petitioners, their judgment of conviction is affirmed.

COMMENTS, NOTES, AND QUESTIONS

1. Since Rakas was "legitimately on the premises" of the vehicle with the getaway driver's permission, why was he not treated the same way as the Court treated Jones in *Jones v. United States*? If Rakas has been allowed to contest the alleged illegal stop and search, would such a principle help enforce extra respect for the Fourth Amendment? Would such a policy incur needless social costs in an effort to assure a reduction in Fourth Amendment violations?

2. Consider the case in which a woman carried a man's drugs in her purse and police required her to empty her purse, revealing all the drugs. Assume that the police had no right under the circumstances to require the woman

to dump her purse. After emptying her purse, the woman told the man to take his possessions off the table, and he complied. Since the man claimed the drugs when placed on the table, can he argue that the drugs should be suppressed at his trial for drug possession? Why or why not? Was the woman's expectation of privacy violated? What expectation of privacy did the man have for possessions in the woman's purse? Does the *Rakas* case give you any help to get the drugs suppressed? Why or why not? Assume that the woman's Fourth Amendment rights were violated. Can she attempt to suppress the drugs if the government wants to prosecute her for possession of the man's drugs? Should she be successful? See *Rawlings v. Kentucky,* 448 U.S. 98 (1980), for a suggested answer.

3. Although *Rakas* involved a search of a motor vehicle, the majority opinion attempted to cast doubt on the continued validity of the "automatic standing" rule of *Jones v. United States,* 362 U.S. 257 (1960). *Jones* essentially held that anyone who had been charged with a crime that required proof of possession of evidence seized or who was legitimately on the premises had standing to contest the search. In *United States v. Salvucci,* 448 U.S. 83 (1980), the Court took the position, foreshadowed in *Rakas,* that *Jones* and its "automatic standing" rule should be overruled. The *Salvucci* Court stressed that the replacement for the old "automatic standing" rule was the "legitimate expectation of privacy" test. No bar exists that prohibits a state court to continue to follow the *Jones* rule of "automatic standing" as a matter of state criminal procedure.

4. The *Rakas* Court noted that the issue of standing to suppress evidence unconstitutionally seized requires a two-step analysis. The first step requires that the proponent of the particular right must actually allege and prove an injury to personal constitutional rights; the second demands that the proponent show that he or she is asserting personal legal rights and interests rather than basing the claim for relief on the rights of third parties. In other words, the question is whether the challenged search or seizure violated the rights of the criminal defendant who seeks to suppress the evidence or violated the rights of some third party. Assume that the driver in *Rakas* owned the vehicle and that some drugs were discovered within the console of the car. Should she be able to argue concerning whether the drugs should be suppressed if the government wants to offer them in court against her? Do you think she would win her suppression case? How is she is a different position than Rakas?

CASE 6.6

Legitimately on the Premises: Almost a Return to Jones v. United States

Minnesota v. Olson
Supreme Court of the United States
495 U.S. 91 (1990)

FACTS

Police suspected respondent Olson of being the driver of the getaway car used in a robbery-murder, and they developed probable cause to stop an automobile thought to contain Olson and a friend. Police captured one of the men, but the other subject, Olson, escaped. Evidence within the automobile indicated that the other felon might be a Rob or Roger Olson located at a particular address. Initially, police could not locate Olson, but an informant told police that Olson had admitted to her that he had been the driver in the robbery. The informant also gave information that Olson had been staying in a duplex with the informant, but that Olson officially lived elsewhere.

Police surrounded the duplex when Olson was believed to be within the structure. Without seeking permission to enter and with weapons drawn, officers discovered Olson in a closet. Following his arrest, he made incriminating statements.

The trial court refused to suppress Olson's statements as the fruit of an unlawful seizure and he was convicted of murder, robbery, and assault. The Minnesota Supreme Court reversed the convictions on the ground that Olson had a sufficient interest in the home to challenge the legality of the warrantless arrest. The Supreme Court of the United States granted the State's petition for certiorari.

PROCEDURAL QUESTION

Where police make a nonemergency, warrantless, nonconsensual entry into a home with probable cause to arrest, where the subject has been and continues to be a guest, does such conduct violate the arrestee's expectation of privacy under the Fourth Amendment?

HELD: YES

RATIONALE

Justice White delivered the opinion of the Court.

★ ★ ★

II

It was held in *Payton v. New York,* 445 U.S. 573 (1980), that a suspect should not be arrested in his house without an arrest warrant, even though there is probable cause to arrest him. The purpose of the decision was not to protect the person of the suspect but to protect his home from entry in the absence of a magistrate's finding of probable cause. In this case, the court below held that Olson's warrantless arrest was illegal because he had a sufficient connection with the premises to be treated like a householder. The State challenges that conclusion.

Since the decision in *Katz v. United States,* 389 U.S. 347 (1967), it has been the law that

> capacity to claim the protection of the Fourth Amendment depends…upon whether the person who claims the protection of the Amendment has a legitimate expectation of privacy in the invaded place. *Rakas v. Illinois,* 439 U.S. 128, 143 (1978).

A subjective expectation of privacy is legitimate if it is "'one that society is prepared to recognize as "reasonable,"'" *id.,* at 143–144, n. 12, quoting *Katz, supra,* at 361 (Harlan, J., concurring).

★ ★ ★

As recognized by the Minnesota Supreme Court, the facts of this case are similar to those in *Jones v. United States,* 362 U.S. 257 (1960). In *Jones,* the defendant was arrested in a friend's apartment during the execution of a search warrant and sought to challenge the warrant as not supported by probable cause.

> [Jones] testified that the apartment belonged to a friend, Evans, who had given him the use of it, and a key, with which [Jones] had admitted himself on the day of the arrest. On cross-examination [Jones] testified that he had a suit and shirt at the apartment, that his home was elsewhere, that he paid nothing for the use of the apartment, that Evans had let him use it 'as a friend,' that he had slept there 'maybe a night,' and that at the time of the search Evans had been away in Philadelphia for about five days.

The Court ruled that Jones could challenge the search of the apartment because he was "legitimately on [the] premises," *id.,* at 267. Although the "legitimately on [the] premises" standard was rejected in *Rakas* as too broad, 439 U.S., at 142–148, the *Rakas* Court explicitly reaffirmed the factual holding in *Jones:*

We do not question the conclusion in *Jones* that the defendant in that case suffered a violation of his personal Fourth Amendment rights if the search in question was unlawful…

> We think that *Jones* on its facts merely stands for the unremarkable proposition that a person can have a legally sufficient interest in a place other than his own home so that the Fourth Amendment protects him from unreasonable governmental intrusion into that place. 439 U.S., at 141–142.

Rakas thus recognized that, as an overnight guest, Jones was much more than just legitimately on the premises.

The distinctions relied on by the State between this case and *Jones* are not legally determinative. The State emphasizes that in this case Olson was never left alone in the duplex or given a key, whereas in *Jones* the owner of the apartment was away and Jones had a key with which he could come and go and admit and exclude others.

★ ★ ★

We do not understand *Rakas,* however, to hold that an overnight guest can never have a legitimate expectation of privacy except when his host is away and he has a key or that only when those facts are present may an overnight guest assert the "unremarkable proposition" that a person may have a sufficient interest in a place other than his home to enable him to be free in that place from unreasonable searches and seizures.

To hold that an overnight guest has a legitimate expectation of privacy in his host's home merely recognizes the everyday expectations of privacy that we all share. Staying overnight in another's home is a longstanding social custom that serves functions recognized as valuable by society. We stay in others' homes when we travel to a strange city for business or pleasure, when we visit our parents, children, or more distant relatives out of town, when we are in between jobs or homes, or when we house-sit for a friend. We will all be hosts and we will all be guests many times in our lives. From either perspective, we think that society recognizes that a houseguest has a legitimate expectation of privacy in his host's home.

From the overnight guest's perspective, he seeks shelter in another's home precisely because it provides him with privacy, a place where he and his possessions will not be disturbed by anyone but his host and those his host allows inside.

★ ★ ★

Because respondent's expectation of privacy in the Bergstrom home was rooted in "understandings that are recognized and permitted by society," *Rakas* at 144, n. 12, it was legitimate, and respondent can claim the protection of the Fourth Amendment.

★ ★ ★

III

★ ★ ★

IV

We therefore affirm the judgment of the Minnesota Supreme Court.

COMMENTS, NOTES, AND QUESTIONS

1. Consider *Olson* in light of *Rakas v. Illinois,* which held that a guest did not have an expectation of privacy in an automobile in which he was riding. Does *Olson* overrule or cast doubt on *Rakas?* Could the difference be explained by noting the level of privacy expected in an automobile as compared with a home?

2. In *Jones v. United States,* mentioned in *Olson,* the defendant, who was a guest at a friend's apartment, was permitted to contest a search and seizure on the grounds that he was more than an overnight guest. Jones was, at least, legitimately on the premises, but was that a sufficient reason to allow him to claim an expectation of privacy in the apartment belonging to another? What connection to the apartment of another is necessary for a person to possess Fourth Amendment rights? Would it be important that a person asserting an expectation of privacy in the apartment of another had slept overnight on the premises? Could the sleepover be the deciding factor? Why or why not?

3. Do hotel and motel guests have expectations of privacy? Hotel housekeepers are routinely allowed to enter when the guest is away, and the manager possesses a pass key. Should the fact that some third parties may be permitted to enter a hotel room defeat an expectation of privacy? See *Stoner v. California,* 376 U.S. 483 (1964). According to *Olson:*

> A subjective expectation of privacy is legitimate if it is "'one that society is prepared to recognize as "reasonable,"'" *id.,* at 143–144, n. 12, quoting *Katz, supra,* at 361 (Harlan, J., concurring). *Olson* at 496.

Is whatever society is prepared to recognize as reasonable what the Court is prepared to decide is reasonable?

4. Since a home occupier has the right to exclude anyone from the home or to allow anyone or everyone inside the home, could one argue that a guest has no expectation of privacy, since the home occupier could invite the police to enter at any time? Does it matter that social custom concerning house guests contemplates a threshold level of privacy?

CASE 6.7

Legitimately on the Premises: Insufficient by Itself to Acquire Standing

Minnesota v. Carter
Supreme Court of the United States
525 U.S. 83 (1998)

FACTS

Pursuant to a tip, a police officer peered through a window where a gap in the curtains allowed him to see inside an apartment. The officer observed Carter and an associate in the process of bagging a white powder which could have been cocaine. Subsequent tests revealed that the two men were in fact dividing up cocaine powder into smaller quantities. Before warrants could be prepared, Carter and his associates left the premises, entered an automobile, and proceeded to drive away. Police officers stopped the car, and when Mr. Carter and his associate exited, police observed a black zippered pouch and a firearm. Police arrested Carter, his business associate, Johns, and another individual, Kimberly Thompson, and also conducted a warrantless search of the apartment. The results of the search revealed a cocaine powder residue and plastic baggies used to package the cocaine. Mr. Carter and Mr. Johns were not residents of the apartment but had arranged to use it for a brief time, and both men lived at other locations. Carter paid for the use of the apartment with some complimentary cocaine for its occupant.

Following charges being lodged against Carter and Johns, they filed a motion to suppress the drug evidence as well as some post-arrest statements which they had made to the police which were incriminating in nature. Through counsel, they contended that the first officer's observations and the subsequent warrantless search by that officer and others of the apartment occurred in violation of their personal Fourth Amendment rights. The trial court rejected their allegations and held that they had no expectation of privacy within the apartment because they were not overnight guests, among other reasons. The Court of

Appeals ruled that Carter and his associate did not have standing because they were only using the apartment as a business location on a temporary basis, but the Supreme Court of Minnesota reversed the Court of Appeals and ruled that Mr. Carter and his associates had standing because they possessed a legitimate expectation of privacy on the premises. In addition, the Supreme Court of Minnesota held that the officer's initial observations were unreasonable under the Fourth Amendment. The Supreme Court of the United States granted certiorari.

PROCEDURAL ISSUE

Where an individual with no possessory interest in an apartment pays the residents of the apartment for temporary use so that drugs may be repackaged on a one-time basis, does that individual possess an expectation of privacy in the apartment as construed under the Fourth Amendment?

HELD: NO

RATIONALE

Chief Justice Rehnquist delivered the opinion of the Court.

★ ★ ★

The Fourth Amendment guarantees:

The right of the people to be secure in their persons, houses, papers, and effects, against unreasonable searches and seizures shall not be violated, and no Warrants shall issue but upon probable cause, supported by Oath or affirmation and particularly describing the place to be searched and the persons or things to be seized.

The Amendment protects persons against unreasonable searches of "their persons [and] houses," and thus indicates that the Fourth Amendment is a personal right that must be invoked by an individual. See *Katz v. United States*, 389 U.S. 347, 351 (1967) ("[T]he Fourth Amendment protects people, not places"). But the extent to which the Fourth Amendment protects people may depend upon where those people are. We have held that

capacity to claim the protection of the Fourth Amendment depends…upon whether the person who claims the protection of the Amendment has a legitimate expectation of privacy in the invaded place.

Rakas, supra, at 143. See also *Rawlings v. Kentucky,* 448 U.S. 98, 106 (1980).

The text of the Amendment suggests that its protections extend only to people in "their" houses. But we have held that, in some circumstances, a person may have a legitimate expectation of privacy in the house of someone else. In *Minnesota v. Olson,* 495 U.S. 91 (1990), for example, we decided that an overnight guest in a house had the sort of expectation of privacy that the Fourth Amendment protects. We said:

To hold that an overnight guest has a legitimate expectation of privacy in his host's home merely recognizes the everyday expectations of privacy that we all share. Staying overnight in another's home is a longstanding social custom that serves functions recognized as valuable by society. We stay in others' homes when we travel to a strange city for business or pleasure, we visit our parents, children, or more distant relatives out of town, when we are in between jobs, or homes, or when we house-sit for a friend....

From the overnight guest's perspective, he seeks shelter in another's home precisely because it provides him with privacy, a place where he and his possessions will not be disturbed by anyone but his host and those his host allows inside. We are at our most vulnerable when we are asleep because we cannot monitor our own safety or the security of our belongings. It is for this reason that, although we may spend all day in public places, when we cannot sleep in our own home, we seek out another private place to sleep, whether it be a hotel room or the home of a friend. *Id.* at 98–99.

★ ★ ★

Respondents here were obviously not overnight guests, but were essentially present for a business transaction, and were only in the home a matter of hours. There is no suggestion that they had a previous relationship with Thompson [the legitimate occupier of the apartment], or that there was any other purpose to their visit. Nor was there anything similar to the overnight guest relationship in *Olson* to suggest a degree of acceptance into the household. While the apartment was a dwelling place for Thompson, it was, for these respondents, simply a place to do business.

Property used for commercial purposes is treated differently for Fourth Amendment purposes than residential property. "An expectation of privacy in commercial premises, however, is different from, and indeed less than, a similar expectation in an individual's home." *New York v. Burger,* 482 U.S. 691, 700 (1987). And while it was a "home" in which respondents were present, it was not their home. Similarly, the Court has held that, in some circumstances, a worker can claim Fourth Amendment protection over his own workplace. See, e.g., *O'Connor v. Ortega,* 480 U.S. 709 (1987). But there is no indication that respondents in this case had nearly as significant a connection to Thompson's apartment as the worker in *O'Connor* had to his own private office. See *id.* at 716–717.

If we regard the overnight guest in *Minnesota v. Olson* as typifying those who may claim the protection of the Fourth Amendment in the home of another, and one merely "legitimately on the premises" as typifying those who may not do so, the present case is obviously somewhere in between. But the purely commercial nature of the transaction engaged in here, the relatively short period of time on the premises, and the lack of any previous connection between respondents and the householder all lead us to conclude that respondents' situation is closer to that of one simply permitted on the premises. We therefore hold that any search which may have occurred did not violate their Fourth Amendment rights.

Because we conclude that respondents had no legitimate expectation of privacy in the apartment, we need not decide whether the police officer's observation constituted a "search." The judgment of the Supreme Court of Minnesota is accordingly reversed, and the cause is remanded for proceedings not inconsistent with this opinion.

It is so ordered.

COMMENTS, NOTES, AND QUESTIONS

1. "It has long been the rule that a defendant can urge the suppression of evidence obtained in violation of the Fourth Amendment only if that defendant demonstrates that his Fourth Amendment rights were violated by the challenged search or seizure." *United States v. Padilla,* 508 U.S. 77 (1993). While the *Carter* Court focused on Carter's legitimate privacy expectations, did the people who originally rented the apartment have an expectation of privacy so that they could argue that their rights had been violated when the police entered without a warrant? Could Carter have the usual occupiers of the apartment try to suppress the evidence for him? Why or why not? Consider the leading case on vicarious standing, *Alderman v. United States,* 394 U.S. 165 (1969).

What legal theory might prevent the occupiers from suppressing the evidence in Carter's trial? Would law enforcement officers develop a greater respect for the exclusionary rule if anyone against whom the illegally seized evidence was directed could suppress that evidence? The marginal increase in effectiveness would be offset by the criminal justice and social costs of allowing more criminals to evade conviction. Would this trade-off be appropriate? Why or why not?

2. Although Carter and his associates were not operating a traditional commercial establishment, was their expectation of privacy reduced because they were engaged in business? Do you think that the type of business should make any difference concerning Fourth Amendment rights? Why or why not? If one considers the level of privacy expected by social guests, Carter and his business partners did not seem to be like friends and guests who had been invited over for the weekend or other extended period of time. Could it be argued that if the police officer had to manually part the curtains, which those in the apartment had specifically drawn together, such conduct would constitute an unreasonable search and seizure even though these were semicommercial transactions? Since the Court found an insufficient expectation of privacy for Carter in the home of another, it found that Carter possessed no standing to argue the legitimacy of the search and seizure. Carter occupied a similar legal position to that found by Mr. Rakas in *Rakas v. Illinois,* 439 U.S. 128 (1978), where he was merely a social guest in his girlfriend's automobile.

3. As was noted in *Carter,* expectations of privacy in commercial establishments may be reduced. According to *New York v. Berger,* 482 U.S. 691 (1987), where the owner's privacy interests may be reduced and the government interests in regulating particular businesses are concomitantly heightened, even a warrantless inspection of commercial premises, if it meets certain criteria, is reasonable within the meaning of the Fourth Amendment. For example, if a business owner operates a closely regulated industry or business, the expectation of privacy is substantially reduced to where searches without warrants may be permissible. Closely regulated businesses have included automobile junkyards in *New York v. Berger;* liquor sales in *Colonnade Catering v. United States,* 397 U.S. 72 (1970); pawnshop operations where firearms were sold in *United States v. Biswell,* 406 U.S. 311 (1972); and mining operations in *Donovan v. Dewey,* 452 U.S. 594 (1981).

CHAPTER 7

Miranda *Principles: Fifth and Sixth Amendment Influences on Police Practice*

Chapter Outline

1. Introduction to *Miranda* Warnings
2. The Basis for the Warnings
3. The Road to *Miranda*
4. The Case of *Miranda v. Arizona*
5. Prerequisites for *Miranda* Warnings
6. Substance of the Warnings
7. Delivering the *Miranda* Warnings
8. When *Miranda* Warnings Are Required: The Triggering Events
9. When Interrogation Must Cease
10. Necessary Condition for *Miranda* Warnings: Custody
11. Necessary Condition for *Miranda* Warnings: Interrogation
12. *Miranda* Interrogation: The Functional Equivalent
13. Exigent Circumstance Exception to *Miranda* Interrogation
14. Right to Counsel under *Miranda* Is Personal to Arrestee
15. Procedure for Waiver of *Miranda* Protection
16. Congressional Challenge to the *Miranda* Warnings
17. *Miranda* Warnings: Required by the Constitution
18. *Miranda* Summary
19. Major Cases
    - Case 7.1: *Miranda* Warnings: Genesis of the Rule and Proper Practice
    - Case 7.2: The Functional Equivalent of Interrogation
    - Case 7.3: Judicial Remedy for *Miranda* Violation
    - Case 7.4: *Miranda* Warnings: Legal Requirements under the United States Constitution

Key Terms

Constitutional requirement for warning
Custody
Emergency exception
Functional equivalent of interrogation
Impeachment use of *Miranda*
Interrogation
Miranda warning

Misdemeanor warning
Necessary conditions for warning
Public safety exception
Right to counsel
Right to remain silent
Separate offense interrogation
Waiver

1. INTRODUCTION TO *MIRANDA* WARNINGS

Under our adversarial system of criminal justice, a defendant generally need not offer evidence that might help prove the government's case. The Fifth Amendment privilege against self-incrimination allows an accused to remain silent, and, in support of this right, the teaching of *Miranda v. Arizona,* 384 U.S. 436 (1966), requires that police advise a person in custody that he or she does not have an affirmative duty to speak with representatives of the government and that he or she may remain silent. Whether an accused has been charged in state or federal court, he or she has no obligation to assist the prosecution. Many individuals who become defendants are unaware of the right to remain silent and are similarly ignorant of other important constitutional rights possessed by persons under United States jurisdiction. As a result of constitutional requirements and from a concern that trained police officers might overcome an individual's reluctance to speak with police, judicial decisions have required law enforcement agents to offer a minimum measure of legal advice to those who come into police custody and for whom the police wish to interrogate. The legal advice should be calculated to alert an arrestee not only that he or she has the right of silence and the right to consult with an attorney but that legal counsel will be made available free of charge to those who might have difficulty hiring an attorney. The warnings must be administered in a manner the arrestee can understand, and *Miranda* must be given whether the suspect is in custody for a felony or misdemeanor.

2. THE BASIS FOR THE WARNINGS

Under the Constitution of the United States, Amendment Five,[224] no person can be required to become a "witness against himself" unless the person freely and voluntarily makes the decision to testify or otherwise offer adverse evidence. If an individual is ignorant of the right or is overreached by law enforcement officials, the right may be lost. Prior to 1966, officers could bring pressure to bear on a person in custody to tell police the facts in criminal cases, and arrestees often confessed due to overwhelming pressure. According to *Miranda v. Arizona,*[225] police violence and the "third degree" flourished in numerous places in the 1930s and in some places thereafter (see Case 7.1).

Reportedly, some police resorted to physical brutality, beating, hanging, and protracted isolation from friends and relatives to obtain confessions.[226] Such activity, designed to make a person confess and become a witness against him- or herself, transgressed the guarantee of the Fifth Amendment.[227]

---

[224]Amendment Five: "No person...shall be *compelled in any criminal case to be a witness against himself,* nor be deprived of life, liberty, or property, without due process of law;..." (emphasis added).

[225]385 U.S. 436 (1966).

[226]See *Brown v. Mississippi,* 297 U.S. 278 (1936), for an especially egregious case of in-custody interrogation that totally transgressed any constitutional boundary, even though at that time the Fifth Amendment did not apply against the states, and the Court decided the case on due process grounds of the Fourteenth Amendment.

[227]The Fifth Amendment did not originally apply against the states but only limited the federal government. Following *Malloy v. Hogan,* 378 U.S. 1 (1964), the amendment had the same effect on the states. As Justice Brennan stated in the lead opinion, "We hold

Originally, the Fifth Amendment limited federal law enforcement practice and had no application against the states. While many state constitutions offered identical protections from compelled testimonial self-incrimination, state courts did not always enforce the guarantee equitably in criminal prosecutions. When the Supreme Court decided *Malloy v. Hogan,*[228] state and federal criminal procedure became identical with respect to protections against self-incrimination under the Fifth Amendment. *Malloy* determined that the Fifth Amendment's privilege against self-incrimination was incorporated into the Due Process Clause of the Fourteenth Amendment and was enforceable against the states. Police practices developed that partially undercut the self-incrimination guarantee by careful use of psychology and other methods that produced confessions without physical violence or threat. Police manuals of the pre-*Miranda* era taught psychological tactics that could break down a suspect's will to resist, such as keeping the arrestee isolated in unfamiliar surroundings, having the officers alone with the individual and in total control, appearing to want only specific details, since guilt was to be assumed, and giving the arrestee logical reasons for having committed the crime. Although not everyone succumbed to these practices, for many people, the totality of police tactics had the effect of "wearing them down" to the point that some even confessed to crimes they had not committed.

3. THE ROAD TO *MIRANDA*

An example of the problems surrounding police interrogation is provided by the case of *Escobedo v. Illinois,* 378 U.S. 478 (1964), where Mr. Escobedo had been arrested and interrogated for a homicide. His attorney succeeded in having him released, but police rearrested him and kept him away from family, friends, and his attorney. His attorney arrived at the police station and observed Mr. Escobedo but was prevented from talking to him despite Escobedo's clear, repeated requests. At no time was Escobedo warned about his right under the Constitution to remain silent. During the interrogation he remained handcuffed in a standing position, and he stated that he was nervous, upset, and agitated, since he had not slept well for more than a week. A Spanish-speaking officer played Escobedo against another suspect and told him that he could go home if he implicated the other suspect in the crime. After Escobedo noted some involvement in the homicide, officers moved to obtain the details that implicated him further.

Escobedo alleged that his right to remain silent under the Fifth Amendment and his right to an attorney under the Sixth Amendment had been violated by techniques the police used. When the Supreme Court decided the case, it ruled in Escobedo's favor and held that where an investigation is no longer a general inquiry into an unsolved crime but has begun to focus on a particular suspect; where the suspect has been taken into police custody and the police carry out a process of interrogations that lends itself to eliciting incriminating statements;

---

today that the Fifth Amendment's exception from compulsory self-incrimination is also protected by the Fourteenth Amendment against abridgment by the States."
[228]378 U.S. 1 (1964).

where the suspect has requested and been denied an opportunity to consult with his lawyer; and where the police have not effectively warned the suspect of his or her absolute constitutional right to remain silent, the accused has been denied "the assistance of counsel" in violation of the Sixth Amendment. In *Escobedo v. Illinois,*[229] the Court held that no statement elicited by the police during the interrogation should have been used against him at his criminal trial. The Court stopped short of requiring that police affirmatively warn all persons interrogated while in custody of their constitutional rights, but that appeared to be the direction in which it was moving.

4. THE CASE OF *MIRANDA V. ARIZONA*

In *Miranda v. Arizona,*[230] the police took Ernesto Miranda into custody, kept him in an unfamiliar atmosphere, and subjected him to traditional police practices designed to get him to confess to the crime for which he had been arrested. Miranda, who had some mental problems, had been described as an indigent Mexican and as a seriously disturbed individual with pronounced sexual fantasies. None of the police practices involved overt physical coercion, disingenuous psychological games, or unusual tricks to gain a confession. However, the police *did not* inform Miranda that he had a right to remain silent and that he possessed a privilege against self-incrimination, that he could have an attorney to advise him, and that if he was too poor to pay for legal advice, the assistance of legal counsel would be free of charge. The *Miranda* Court felt that the presence of counsel, in Miranda's case, would have provided the adequate protection necessary to make the police interrogation conform to the dictates of the privilege against self-incrimination. Counsel's presence with Miranda would have ensured that statements made in the government-controlled interrogation atmosphere were not the product of compulsion.

In deciding *Miranda,* the Court resorted to "rule-making" by holding that an individual held for interrogation must be clearly informed by police that he or she has the right to consult with a lawyer and to be represented by the lawyer during interrogation. The person must be told that anything he or she says can be used as evidence. The Court noted that the warning under *Miranda* was an absolute prerequisite to interrogation.[231] According to the Court, it would not accept any circumstantial evidence that the person may have been aware of the right against self-incrimination. The Court believed that only through such a warning would there be ascertainable assurance that an accused would be aware of this right. Following the *Miranda* decision, if an individual indicates that the

---

[229]378 U.S. 478 (1964).
[230]384 U.S. 436 (1966).
[231]The Court required that the warning be given to everyone who was subject to custodial interrogation. In *Miranda v. Arizona,* 384 U.S. at 468, the Court stated, "[A] warning is an absolute prerequisite in overcoming the inherent pressures of the interrogation atmosphere. It is not just the subnormal or woefully ignorant who succumb to an interrogator's imprecations, whether implied or expressly stated, that the interrogation will continue until a confession is obtained or that silence in the face of accusation is itself damning, and will bode ill when presented to a jury." And at 384 U.S. 471, 472, the *Miranda* Court stated, "No amount of circumstantial evidence that the person may have been aware of this right will suffice to stand in its stead."

assistance of counsel is desired before any interrogation occurs, the police cannot rationally ignore or deny this request on the basis that the individual does not have or cannot afford a retained attorney. After the warnings have been given, when an arrestee indicates that he or she would like to remain silent, or at any time indicates that he or she wants to remain silent thereafter, or requests the assistance of legal counsel, according to the *Miranda* Court, interrogation must cease immediately.

5. PREREQUISITES FOR *MIRANDA* WARNINGS

Subsequent to the Court's *Miranda* decision, all law enforcement agencies were required to carefully advise every detainee of the constitutional rights under the Fifth and Sixth Amendments at any time the police contemplated questioning a person in custody. While the original *Miranda* case dealt with a felony, a later decision[232] extended the right to be apprised of constitutional rights to misdemeanant detainees for whom interrogation was desired.

In *Berkemer v. McCarty,*[233] police had made a traffic stop for suspicion of misdemeanor driving under the influence of alcohol or drugs. While McCarty was in custody, police questioned him concerning the details of his offense in hopes of obtaining evidence to be used against him. At no point in this sequence of events did the police inform McCarty that he had a right to remain silent, to consult with an attorney, and to have an attorney appointed for him if he could not afford one. McCarty offered incriminating evidence, which the prosecutor introduced against him in court. The *McCarty* Court held that the *Miranda* warnings had to be given to misdemeanor suspects in custody who the police wished to interrogate. Following *McCarty, Miranda* warnings must be given to all individuals prior to custodial interrogation, whether the offense investigated is a felony or a misdemeanor and regardless of the educational level or legal understanding of the arrestee. The warnings need not be offered if interrogation is not contemplated or in situations where custody does not exist at the time the question is uttered.

6. SUBSTANCE OF THE WARNINGS

According to the *Miranda* Court, several warnings must be given to a person who is in custody and who police officers would like to interrogate. The individual must be first informed in clear and unequivocal terms that he or she has the right to remain silent. Without this information, the person in custody might be unaware of the legal right not to speak. This warning seems to be an absolute prerequisite to overcoming the inherent pressure to talk that accompanies the interrogation atmosphere of an arrest. Second, the individual must be told that anything that is communicated to police may be used against him or her in a court of law. This advice is necessary to create awareness not only of the right to silence but also of the consequences

---

[232]468 U.S. 420 (1984).
[233]Ibid.

of deciding to forgo it by speaking to law enforcement personnel. Third, the arrestee must be informed of the right to consult with an attorney; otherwise, the circumstances surrounding an in-custody interrogation can often overcome the will of an individual who has only been told about the right to remain silent and of the potential use of information if he or she chooses to speak. With the assistance of an attorney there is much less likelihood that the police will attempt any level of coercion, and if any does occur, the attorney may testify about that fact. Fourth, the police must inform the arrestee that if he or she cannot afford an attorney, one will be appointed prior to any questioning. The information concerning free legal advice may prove to be very important for many individuals. In the absence of this knowledge, an arrestee might otherwise understand that a right to legal counsel exists only if one can afford to pay for the service. If these four basic warnings are not properly offered by law enforcement personnel to an individual who has been subjected to custodial interrogation, any evidence that the individual might convey, though offered voluntarily under traditional analysis, will be excluded from the prosecution's case in chief.

7. DELIVERING THE *MIRANDA* WARNINGS

In an effort to properly comply with the *Miranda* requirements, police officers often resort to a reading of the warnings from a printed form or card. Problems arise when officers administer the warnings in less than perfect order or, in some cases, with less than textbook clarity.[234] As a matter of routine practice, many police departments follow the oral warning with a written warning containing a check sheet to be signed by the person in custody. The sheet indicates whether the person understood the advisement of rights, desired to waive the warnings or to take advantage of them, wished to remain silent, and/or desired to consult with an attorney.

One of the difficulties with reading the *Miranda* warnings involves the circumstances under which they are typically administered. An oral warning sometimes must be given during an unsettled street scene or a domestic disturbance, situations that are less than ideal for conveying information. Although there must be a fairly clear administration of the warnings, some deviation from the original language has been upheld as appropriate. In *Duckworth v. Eagan*,[235] the Supreme Court approved a warning[236] given in a confusing manner in which the officer stated that the arrestee had the right to an attorney if and when he went to court. The warning first indicated that there was the right to counsel but then removed the essence of the guarantee when the arrestee was told that the police had no way to give him an attorney. Even

---

[234]A rigid reading of the warnings as suggested in *Miranda* is not absolutely required to meet the warning requirements. In *California v. Prysock,* 453 U.S. 355 (1981), the Court held that *Miranda* warnings need not be a virtual incantation of the precise language contained in the original opinion.

[235]492 U.S. 195 (1989).

[236]The marginally defective warning approved by the Court as minimally adequate in *Duckworth v. Eagan,* 492 U.S. 195 at 198 (1989), did not add to the clarity of how the warnings should be administered. The *Duckworth* warning is as follows: "You have the

though the language was less than a model of clarity and could imply that an attorney was not available immediately, the Court held that it met the minimum standards under *Miranda*.

8. WHEN *MIRANDA* WARNINGS ARE REQUIRED: THE TRIGGERING EVENTS

As a general rule, law enforcement officials possess no affirmative duty to warn any person of constitutional rights until the officer places the individual in custody and intends to initiate questioning. Thus, the triggering factors that give rise to the necessity of offering the *Miranda* warnings are governmental custody coupled with interrogation. As a general rule, if custody exists and interrogation occurs, any statement made by the subject prior to the administration of proper warnings cannot be admitted in evidence against defendant for proof of guilt. For example, in *Oregon v. Elstad*,[237] prior to giving the proper warnings, police lawfully arrested Elstad, asked an incriminating question, and received a response (see Case 7.3). Elstad's immediate answer, including the incriminating statements, was suppressed from his trial.

Some evidence taken in violation of *Miranda* may have utility for impeachment purposes if the defendant were to offer testimony from the witness stand that directly conflicted with earlier non-*Mirandized* statements.[238] In such a situation, the prosecution may introduce the illegally obtained statements solely to attempt to impeach the defendant and not for proof of guilt.

Once the warnings have been properly administered, the subject may choose to assert the rights under *Miranda* or may decide to waive the rights to silence and/or counsel. A waiver may be oral, written, or both, but the essence of a waiver is that the arrestee understands the significance of the rights being relinquished and the consequences that may flow from that decision. If the arrestee has been taken to a police station, the written waiver is most commonly used; a street waiver typically takes an oral form.

9. WHEN INTERROGATION MUST CEASE

During the encounter with police, if the arrestee indicates in any manner and at any time that there is no further desire to be interrogated, the police inquiry must

---

right to remain silent. Anything you say can be used against you in court. You have a right to talk to a lawyer for advice before we ask you any questions, and to have him with you during questioning. You have this right to the advice and presence of a lawyer even if you cannot afford to hire one. *We have no way of giving you a lawyer, but one will be appointed for you, if you wish, if and when you go to court.* If you wish to answer questions now without a lawyer present, you have the right to stop answering questions at any time. You also have the right to stop answering at any time until you've talked to a lawyer" (emphasis added). The *Duckworth* Court noted that the warning actually given touched all the bases required by Miranda, since the subject had been substantially given a warning that alerted him to his rights to silence, counsel, and the effects if he chose to speak. So long as the warnings offered contain the essentials of the right to silence and the right to counsel (free if the subject is indigent), the *Miranda* requirements have been satisfied.

[237]470 U.S. 298 (1985).
[238]See *Harris v. New York,* 401 U.S. 222 (1971).

immediately cease, according to the Court in *Edwards v. Arizona.*[239] The police are not allowed to try to change the mind of the arrestee; they must respect the right to silence until he or she has consulted an attorney and indicates a desire to speak to the police. In *Edwards,* the defendant asserted his right to speak with an attorney, and the initial interrogation ended. The next morning, when two detectives arrived at the jail, the detention officer in charge told Edwards that he "had" to speak with officers who wanted to talk to him. Eventually, Edwards implicated himself in criminal activities. The Court held that the admission into evidence of Edwards' confession given to the two detectives violated his rights under the Fifth and Fourteenth Amendments as construed in *Miranda v. Arizona.* According to *Miranda,* if the accused indicates a wish to remain silent, the interrogation must cease; if he requests counsel, the interrogation must cease until an attorney is present. The Court decided that where an accused has expressed the desire to deal with the police only through counsel, he or she is not subject to further interrogation by the authorities until counsel has been made available, unless the arrestee personally initiates further communication, exchanges, or conversations with the law enforcement officers.

Interrogation with custody has been permitted where an arrestee has not requested an attorney and has not clearly noted his or her desire to remain silent, or where the arrestee has made an ambiguous reference to counsel insufficient to invoke the prohibition against further questioning. Nothing in *Edwards* requires the furnishing of counsel to a suspect who consents to answer questions without the assistance of a lawyer. Where an arrestee indicated only a desire to stand on the Fifth Amendment privilege against self-incrimination and has not requested to speak with a lawyer, police may inquire if he or she wants to answer questions after they have waited a significant amount of time. Police must inquire concerning crimes *unrelated to the crime for which the person is in custody,* and police must offer the *Miranda* warnings a second time.[240]

Even where police attempt to question an arrestee about additional crimes *unrelated* to the reason for initial custody and the arrestee has previously invoked the right to counsel protections under *Miranda,* such questioning runs afoul of *Arizona v. Roberson.*[241] In *Roberson,* the arrestee indicated that he did not wish to speak with police and wanted an attorney. Three days later, while the defendant was still in custody, a different police officer approached him, advised him of his rights, and obtained a confession for a crime for which Roberson was not then under arrest. Since Roberson had indicated that he wished to speak only to a lawyer and not to police, that wish should have been respected under the *Edwards* rule. The *Roberson* Court held that the confession for the second crime should have been excluded from admission at his trial for the second offense.

However, when the arrestee has not refused to speak with police or asserted his or her right to silence and has not requested to speak with an attorney but has been

---

[239]451 U.S. 477 (1981).
[240]*Michigan v. Moseley,* 423 U.S. 96 at 106, 107 (1975).
[241]486 U.S. 675 (1988).

to court on different charges, police may ask if the arrestee is willing to waive *Miranda* rights and speak with police concerning criminal matters unrelated to the reason the defendant was in court. An accused's invocation of his or her Sixth Amendment right to counsel during a judicial proceeding does not constitute an invocation of the *Miranda*-derived right to counsel emanating from the Fifth Amendment's guarantee against compelled self-incrimination.[242] Under these circumstances, the *Edwards* rule does not apply.

Since *Miranda* warnings are necessary only where both custody *and* interrogation are present, if police merely make an arrest with no immediate design of interrogation, there is no absolute need to offer *Miranda* warnings. Similarly, where a question directed to a person clearly not in custody might elicit an incriminating response, no *Miranda* warning is essential, since the person is free to leave and free to disregard the question. Some situations involving both custody and interrogation do not require a *Miranda* warning where the element of coercion does not exist. If, for example, the police place a plainclothes officer with an arrestee within a jail cell and the arrestee is unaware that the person with whom he or she is speaking is a police officer, no *Miranda* warnings are necessary provided the plainclothes officer does not actually question the arrestee about the crime for which he or she is in custody.[243]

In *Perkins,* police placed an undercover officer in a cell with Perkins, who was incarcerated on charges unrelated to homicide. The undercover officer engaged in small talk and banter until the two men began to talk of their criminal careers. Perkins made damaging admissions about a homicide, which he readily admitted committing. According to the Court, the prosecution could use Perkins' admissions against him because there was no chance of coercion or overreaching by the government, since Perkins was unaware of the status of his cellmate. The *Perkins* Court held that "an undercover law enforcement officer posing as a fellow inmate need not give *Miranda* warnings to an incarcerated suspect before asking questions that may elicit an incriminating response."[244]

10. NECESSARY CONDITION FOR *MIRANDA* WARNINGS: CUSTODY

To determine when *Miranda* warnings become mandatory, an understanding of the legal definition of custody proves essential. Although the concept of custody would appear to be quite clear, court definitions have failed to provide a complete model of clarity.[245] In *Miranda,* the Court considered custody to exist when the individual had been restrained of his freedom of movement in any significant manner or otherwise deprived of freedom of action in any significant way. While a formal arrest clearly meets this standard, other situations with murky fact patterns fail to offer a

---

[242]See *McNeil v. Wisconsin,* 501 U.S. 171 (1991).

[243]See *Illinois v. Perkins,* 496 U.S. 292 (1990).

[244]*Perkins* at 300.

[245]Custody, for *Miranda* purposes, has not been deemed to occur when a traffic stop has been made, even though the driver is not free to leave and is under the control of the police officer. *Berkemer v. McCarty,* 468 U.S. 420 (1984). Stopping a car is a Fourth Amendment "seizure," but the driver is not considered in custody according to *Delaware v. Prouse,* 440 U.S. 648 (1979).

bright line for determination. In *California v. Beheler*,[246] a suspect with information about a homicide had responded to a police invitation to discuss the matter at the station house. At the interview and prior to offering any *Miranda* warning, police informed Beheler that they believed he had been involved in the crime. During the discussion, Beheler admitted his presence and some participation in the homicide, at which point the police informed him of his *Miranda* rights. Although Beheler was released without charge at that time, he contended that he had been in actual custody at the time of his inculpatory statements. The Court ultimately stated that as "a determination of whether a suspect is 'in custody' for purposes of receiving *Miranda* protection, the ultimate inquiry is simply whether there is a 'formal arrest or restraint on freedom of movement.'"[247] Applying this standard, Beheler was not in custody when he voluntarily met with and spoke to the investigators. The key to *Beheler* may have been the fact that he was freely permitted to leave at the end of the questioning, indicating a lack of custody.

In another case with similar but not identical facts, when federal agents notified an elderly suspect that they would like to discuss some matters with him, the suspect suggested that they talk in a conference room that he controlled. The federal agents rejected the conference room location and insisted on driving with the suspect to the local FBI headquarters. Once inside the government conference room, they failed to tell the subject that he was not under arrest and that he was free to leave at any time. The interview lasted approximately four hours, during which the government agents failed to give the suspect breaks from the discussion even to call his wife, as was his custom due to ill health. The officers did not want him to call home because it might have interfered with the interview. When the agents were satisfied by what they had learned and ended the discussions, the subject wanted to drive himself home, but officers accompanied him to his office and on the trip to his home. The trial court ordered suppression of the evidence discovered from the interview on the ground that, under the circumstances, no reasonable person would have felt free to have ended the interview and walked out the door. According to the judge, the *Miranda* warnings should have been given because the suspect had been interrogated while in custody.[248]

While an arrest accompanied with the use of handcuffs while the subject is in complete control of an officer would indicate that custody exists, other situations similar to *Beheler* may not be so clear, even when the individual freely leaves the police station following an interview. In *Thompson v. Keohane*,[249] police asked a murder suspect to voluntarily come to the station to answer some questions. Thompson was not given any *Miranda* warnings, and he was told he was free to leave at any time

---

[246]463 U.S. 1121 (1983).

[247]*California v. Beheler*, 464 U.S. 1121 at 1125 (1983). In a case similar to *Beheler, Oregon v. Mathiason*, 429 U.S. 492 (1977), the subject agreed to meet with police at the patrol office. After they informed him that he was a suspect in a burglary and falsely told him that his fingerprints were found at the scene, Mathiason confessed but was not held at that time. The Supreme Court held in *Mathiason* that "a noncustodial situation is not converted to one in which *Miranda* applies simply because a reviewing court concludes that, even in the absence of any formal arrest or restraint on freedom of movement, the questioning took place in a 'coercive environment.'" 429 U.S. at 495.

[248]*United States v. Fisher*, 215 F. Supp. 2d 1212, 1216, 1217 (2002).

[249]516 U.S. 99 (1995).

while or after talking with police. Police told him that he was a suspect in a murder, and Thompson subsequently admitted killing his ex-wife. He was allowed to leave the station because he was not under arrest. Following his conviction for murder, he contended that he had been in custody during the interrogation and that his confession should have been excluded from evidence because his rights under *Miranda* had been violated. According to the *Thompson* Court, for custody purposes,

> Two discrete inquiries are essential to the determination: first, what were the circumstances surrounding the interrogation; and second, given those circumstances, would a reasonable person have felt he or she was not at liberty to terminate the interrogation and leave. *Thompson* at 112.

Most individuals would consider themselves in custody following a confession to murder, and most police officers would not allow such a person to leave the police station, but Thompson appeared not to be in custody, and *Miranda* may not have been required.[250]

In some situations, an individual may believe that the police have taken custody when, in fact, they have made no such decision.[251] In such a case, "a person who honestly but unreasonably believes he is in custody is subject to the same coercive pressures as one whose belief is reasonable; this suggests that such persons also are entitled to warnings."[252] Alternatively, a detainee may feel free to leave when, in reality, police would not permit the individual to leave if an attempt were to be made. Another view of when custody exists focuses on the point in time when a reasonable officer would believe that custody has been taken of the individual, but this view does not appear to be the controlling opinion.

11. NECESSARY CONDITION FOR *MIRANDA* WARNINGS: INTERROGATION

The second factor to be considered in determining whether *Miranda* warnings need to be administered concerns the question of whether police officers have initiated interrogation. Most interrogation takes the form of the officer asking direct questions and the arrestee answering, refusing to answer, or being evasive in the response. While the existence of interrogation can generally be discerned from the conduct of the participants, the act of interrogation may not always be composed of interrogatory sentences. Subtle communication may disguise a question, making it appear as a declarative sentence where the pressure is on the subject to make a response. If, in the presence of the arrestee, police officers talk among themselves about the case at hand and make derogatory remarks about the crime, the suspect, or the manner in which the crime was committed, the arrestee may be prompted or feel obligated to say something that could be incriminating. If a response was

---

[250]The Court in *Thompson* sent the case back to the lower courts for a determination of whether, under the two-step test, outlined earlier here, Thompson was really in custody. 516 U.S. 99 at 117 (1995).

[251]See *Oregon v. Mathiason,* 429 U.S. 492 (1977), where the defendant had been invited to the police station for discussions concerning a burglary. The police initially told Mathiason that he was not under arrest and allowed him to leave the station following his interview, where he made inculpatory statements. The Court held that Mathiason was not in custody or otherwise deprived of his freedom of action in any significant way, and it approved the trial court's admission of his police station statement.

[252]*Oregon v. Mathiason,* 429 U.S. 492, 496 (1977), Justice Marshall, dissenting.

reasonably expected by police under the circumstances, many courts will hold that the act of speaking in the presence of the arrestee constituted the functional equivalent of interrogation and a violation of the principles of *Miranda*.

12. *MIRANDA* INTERROGATION: THE FUNCTIONAL EQUIVALENT

Interrogation may take many different forms and may be so subtle that the one being interrogated may not always be aware that questioning is actually happening. In *Rhode Island v. Innis,*[253] the Court held that the term *interrogation,* for *Miranda* purposes, not only includes direct and unequivocal questions but also encompasses "any words or actions on the part of the police (other than those normally attendant to arrest and custody) that the police should know are reasonably likely to elicit an incriminating response from the suspect" (see Case 7.2).[254] In *Innis,* the police officers were talking to themselves but in front of an arrestee concerning the missing firearm belonging to the arrestee. One of the officers stated that there were quite a few handicapped children running around and playing near the crime scene because a school for such children was located nearby. The officer noted, "God forbid one of them might find a weapon with shells and they might hurt themselves."[255] Innis told the officers to turn the car around and that he would show them the location of the gun. A practice that the police reasonably should know is likely to motivate a suspect to make an incriminating response possesses the same legal effect as overt interrogation. In the *Innis* case, the Court clearly indicated that the definition of interrogation focuses on the reasonable intentions of the police rather than on the individual in custody. For example, if two police officers were to speak with each other in front of an arrestee and comment that if one of them had been arrested, he certainly would have denied guilt or explained his innocence, courts would likely hold that the arrestee had been interrogated under *Miranda.* However, merely asking a subject prior to a pat-down whether he had any sharp objects that could hurt the officer does not constitute custodial interrogation under *Miranda,* even if it produces incriminating verbal or physical evidence. Since the officers' question serves the noncriminal purpose of officer safety, it falls squarely within the class of questions that typically accompany arrest and custody.[256] Police conduct constitutes interrogation or its functional equivalent where it is intended to motivate an arrestee to initiate conversation that the police desire to hear.[257]

Private, nongovernmental questioning and conversation do not implicate the protective warnings of *Miranda.* Interrogation did not occur where a wife, in the

---

[253] 446 U.S. 291 (1980).

[254] *Innis* at 301.

[255] Ibid. at 316.

[256] *Oregon v. Cunningham,* 179 Ore. App. 498; 40 P.3d 535 (2002).

[257] Not all unwarned custodial interrogation by police will be suppressed from introduction at trial. Questions asked of an arrestee that are for record-keeping purposes, that are routine booking questions, and that request biographical data necessary for booking or pre-trial purposes are exempt from exclusion under *Miranda.* See *Pennsylvania v. Muniz,* 496 U.S. 582 at 601 (1990). Also consider *New York v. Quarles,* 467 U.S. 649 (1984), which permitted an emergency interrogation from which evidence was not suppressed. Illegally seized evidence under *Miranda* may be used for impeachment purposes in some situations, according to *New York v. Harris,* 401 U.S. 222 (1971).

presence of an officer, was allowed to speak with her husband who was under arrest for murder of their son. In *Arizona v. Mauro,*[258] police had arrested Mauro following his confession to the murder of his own son. Subsequent to receiving his *Miranda* warnings, he told the officers he did not wish to speak further until he had seen an attorney. With some reluctance, police allowed his wife to speak with Mauro in the presence of a police officer and in full view of an operating tape recorder. The information on the audio recording was properly admitted at his murder trial despite Mauro's contention that the tape recording constituted custodial interrogation. Although the police might have expected that some incriminating information might be elicited between husband and wife, the police officers were not conducting an interrogation, even though they openly recorded the conversation. The Court refused to follow language from *Innis* where the Court stated that interrogation includes a "practice that the police should know is reasonably likely to evoke an incriminating response from a suspect."[259] Crucial to the Court's decision in *Mauro* was the fact that the police did not conduct the interrogation; Mauro's spouse questioned him about his role in the death of their son.

13. EXIGENT CIRCUMSTANCE EXCEPTION TO *MIRANDA* INTERROGATION

Although the Court initially required that *Miranda* warnings be offered in every situation in which law enforcement officials desired to conduct custodial interrogation of an arrestee, the Court recognized a public safety or emergency exception. In *New York v. Quarles,*[260] the officer had reason, based on a complaint, to believe that the arrestee had hidden a loaded gun in a store near the officer, which could have been used to harm the officer or the public. Presumably, the arrestee could have lunged to gain dominion and control of the gun, or a confederate could have acquired it and attempted to harm the officer or frustrate the arrest. Under the circumstances, the *Quarles* Court held that the officer was free to inquire about the weapon prior to offering any *Miranda* warning and that the prosecution was permitted to introduce both the weapon and the oral answers against the defendant. In contrast to the usual requirements, due to the emergency situation, the *Quarles* Court permitted the admission of the words and the gun despite the absence of *Miranda* warnings prior to custodial interrogation.

Under *Quarles,* the rule emerged that where an immediate danger to the safety of the public or a police officer appeared to exist, police can delay offering the *Miranda* warnings and may question the suspect in an effort to alleviate the imminent danger. The questions asked of a subject should be directed toward discovery of a dangerous weapon and must be reasonably directed to ending a police or public danger rather than focused on the collection of evidence. Emergencies could conceivably include the location of explosives, the location of a kidnapping victim, discovery of poisons directed at the public, or other terror-type situations in which time is crucial to life and health. The exact limits of the public safety exception to

[258]481 U.S. 520 (1987).
[259]*Innis* at 301.
[260]467 U.S. 649 (1984).

Miranda have not been fully developed in state and federal litigation, and the Supreme Court of the United States has not accepted a second case concerning the doctrine. Since the number of public safety exception cases remains small, the full development of this doctrine will be a long time coming. Notwithstanding the failure to offer the *Miranda* warnings where the public safety exception has application, verbal and physical evidence obtained by delaying the *Miranda* warnings will be admissible at trial against an arrestee and will not normally be subject to evidentiary exclusion.

A New Jersey court reviewed the requirements of a public safety emergency and found that the doctrine had some limitations. In *New Jersey v. Stephenson,*[261] police had been called to a motel room occupied by a single person who had been reported threatening others with a firearm. When the subject allowed police to enter the motel room, they patted him down, with negative results. One of the officers asked about the location of the gun, which prompted obvious nervous demeanor on the part of the subject. The officers noted that the subject appeared to be looking for a way to leave the motel room. At this point the officers handcuffed him but told him that he was not under arrest. When the officers told him that they would get a warrant to search the room, the suspect gestured toward a dresser and stated that a gun was inside. Upon finding the gun, the police placed him under arrest and advised him of his *Miranda* rights. The court of appeals held that the public safety exception under the *Quarles* case did not apply to a situation where the public was in no immediate danger and the police faced no unusual danger, since they had the situation well under control. The appeals court rejected the admission of the firearm into evidence, since the court felt that the police were in the process of gathering information for a prosecution instead of acting to protect themselves or the public from an immediate danger.[262]

14. RIGHT TO COUNSEL UNDER *MIRANDA* IS PERSONAL TO ARRESTEE

The *Miranda*-derived right to counsel is personal to the accused and cannot be asserted by a family member or even the arrestee's attorney. In *Moran v. Burbine,*[263] the police arrested Burbine on a burglary charge but quickly focused on him as a possible homicide suspect wanted in another jurisdiction. Burbine's sister, who was unaware that police had Burbine under suspicion for murder, arranged for a public defender to render legal assistance for her brother on the burglary charge. When the attorney phoned the police, they informed her that Burbine would not be interrogated on the burglary charge that evening. Significantly, the police did not tell the attorney that another jurisdiction's law enforcement officials were planning to question Burbine on the homicide. Burbine did not know that he was represented by counsel.

---

[261]350 N.J. Super 517; 796 A.2d 274 (2002).
[262]See *Minnesota v. Caldwell,* 639 N.W.2d 64 (2002), where a gun was admitted under the public safety exception, since it was believed to be in a public place. See also *Allen v. Roe,* 305 F.3d 1046 (9th Cir. 2002), where the court approved the admission of a firearm believed to be located in a public area when officers questioned the suspect prior to offering *Miranda* warnings.
[263]475 U.S. 412 (1986).

When the police from the second jurisdiction orally gave him new *Miranda* warnings, Burbine waived his rights and also signed three written warning acknowledgments. Subsequently Burbine signed three incriminating statements admitting to the murder. Burbine was unaware of his sister's efforts to retain counsel and of the attorney's telephone call to police, but at no time did he request an attorney.

Following his conviction for murder, Burbine appealed, contending that his rights under *Miranda* and his right to due process had been violated by the police practice. The Supreme Court held that police deception of the defendant's attorney—by not telling her that her client was a homicide suspect and by actively misinforming her that her client would not be interrogated that evening—did not violate the protections of *Miranda*. Similarly, when the police did not inform the suspect that his attorney wished to speak with him, such subterfuge did not affect the voluntariness of his statements to police or alter his lack of desire to have an attorney present. The *Burbine* Court held that the trial court ruled correctly by allowing the confessions into evidence and that Burbine had waived his right to counsel and his Fifth Amendment privilege against self-incrimination. Requiring police to inform an arrestee that an attorney wishes to consult with him or her would create an inappropriate shift in the careful balance struck in *Miranda* between the needs of law enforcement and the constitutional protections accruing to the accused.

The *Burbine* Court clearly held that the constitutional rights enforced by *Miranda* are personal to the accused and cannot be asserted by a family member, an attorney, or any other individual.

15. PROCEDURE FOR WAIVER OF *MIRANDA* PROTECTION

In order to relinquish the protections offered by *Miranda,* an individual may indicate the decision to waive *Miranda* rights by an oral statement, a written statement, or both, or by other unambiguous conduct. In *Miranda v. Arizona,* the Court held that a suspect's waiver of the Fifth Amendment privilege against self-incrimination is valid only if it is made voluntarily, knowingly, and intelligently. In determining the standards for a *Miranda* waiver, the Court in *Moran v. Burbine* held that a two-step approach was required:

> First, the relinquishment of the right must have been voluntary in the sense that it was the product of a free and deliberate choice, rather than intimidation, coercion, or deception. Second, the waiver must have been made with a full awareness of both the nature of the right being abandoned and the consequences of the decision to abandon it. 475 U.S. 412, at 421 (1975).

Waivers are not effective unless there are both particular and systemic assurances that the coercive pressures of custody were not the inducing cause. In determining whether a defendant has chosen to give up his *Miranda* rights, courts look to all the attendant circumstances. A waiver may exist where the arrestee initiated the conversation with police or requested that an officer come to the cell and speak with the arrestee, or where the arrestee confessed without any intervention by police. For example, in *Colorado v. Connelly,* 479 U.S. 157 (1986), Connelly walked up to a police officer and confessed to murder; after being advised of his *Miranda* warnings and indicating that he understood them, he stated that he still wished to talk about the murder. The Court approved Connelly's waiver by affirmative conduct and by voluntary consent. The Court did not suggest that the officer should have stopped Connelly and warned him under *Miranda* before allowing him to continue his confession to murder.

Typically, investigators prefer to obtain a written statement of waiver, but during the initial phases of an investigation such practice may prove difficult, and the lack of a written waiver is not fatal to admissibility.[264] For example, if an arrestee purportedly makes a valid waiver and subsequently denies so doing, a heavy burden of proof rests with the government to demonstrate that the decision to waive the constitutional rights was made knowingly and intelligently.[265]

A waiver of the *Miranda* warnings may be implied rather than expressed in many contexts. If an arrestee fails to state that he or she is waving his or her rights but does so by words and/or conduct and begins talking to police, sometimes asking officers questions and generally engaging them in conversation, a waiver under *Miranda* may exist. As a general rule, a valid waiver cannot be inferred from the silence of an arrestee after warnings are given or deduced from the fact that the arrestee eventually offered a confession. As the Court stated in *Carnley v. Cochran:*

> Presuming waiver from a silent record is impermissible. The record must show, or there must be an allegation and evidence which show, that an accused was offered counsel but intelligently and understandingly rejected the offer. Anything less is not waiver. 369 U.S. 506, 516 (1962).

Moreover, where in-custody interrogation is involved, there is no room for the contention that the privilege is waived if the individual answers some questions or gives some information on his own prior to invoking his right to remain silent when interrogated. In most cases, if law enforcement officers did not violate an arrestee's constitutional rights or practice coercion, an individual's personal motivation to waive the protections of *Miranda* to make an admission or a confession does not create an involuntary confession. A confession has not been received in violation of *Miranda* and is not considered coerced even if it has been prompted by a mental illness,[266] a desire to please family members, or an overwhelming religious experience.[267] On issues of alleged waiver of *Miranda* rights, the prosecution has the burden of proof by a preponderance of the evidence.[268]

---

[264]According to the Court in *North Carolina v. Butler,* 441 U.S. 369 (1979), the absence of a written *Miranda* waiver of rights is not necessarily determinative of waiver. As the Butler Court stated, "An express written or oral statement of waiver of the right to remain silent or of the right to counsel is usually strong proof of the validity of that waiver, but is not inevitably either necessary or sufficient to establish waiver."

[265]Ibid.

[266]See *Colorado v. Connelly,* 479 U.S. 157 (1986).

[267]Ibid.

[268]Ibid.

16. CONGRESSIONAL CHALLENGE TO THE *MIRANDA* WARNINGS

From the initial decision in *Miranda v. Arizona,* members of Congress, among others, were neither happy with the result nor willing to allow a guilty person to go free because of a defective warning provided by a police officer. In the wake of that decision, Congress enacted 18 U.S.C. § 3501,[269] which provided that the admissibility of such statements taken in violation of the *Miranda* warnings should turn only on whether they were voluntarily made and not be thrown out of court because of a defective *Miranda* warning. Under Section 3501, the Congress directed federal courts to determine if the confession or other inculpatory statements were voluntarily made, taking into consideration the time when the suspect made a confession, whether the suspect had been warned of the use of his or her statement, whether the individual had been made aware of the right to counsel, and whether counsel was present when the statement was made. According to congressional intent, if the statement or confession were made voluntarily, then such evidence should be admitted in federal courts. In other words, the evidence should be admitted if voluntarily offered where there was an absence of coerciveness. The design of Congress was to override the Court's decision in *Miranda v. Arizona* and replace it with traditional voluntariness of confession standard[270] rather than follow *Miranda's* conclusive presumption of coerciveness and exclusion where the warnings had not been given properly.

17. *MIRANDA* WARNINGS: REQUIRED BY THE CONSTITUTION

In *Dickerson v. United States,* 530 U.S. 428 (2000), the Supreme Court determined that the case of *Miranda v. Arizona* was of constitutional dimension and could not be overturned by an act of Congress (see Case 7.4). Until the definitive answer of *Dickerson,* the statute purporting to supersede *Miranda* was ignored by every trial court in the years following its enactment. *Dickerson* affirmed the belief that the federal statute was of no real consequence and was actually unconstitutional.

In a case involving an alleged bank robbery, one Dickerson had been interrogated at an FBI field office, at which time he was in custody and had not received the traditional *Miranda* warnings. He filed a motion to suppress his statements, and the trial court granted the motion. This pretrial decision was appealed by the United States to the Court of Appeals for the Fourth Circuit. That court reversed the trial court decision and concluded that despite the lack of *Miranda* warning, the

---

[269] 18 U.S.C. § 3501 provides, among other things, that: "(a) In any criminal prosecution brought by the United States or by the District of Columbia, a confession shall be admissible in evidence if it is voluntarily given. Before such confession is received in evidence, the trial judge shall, out of the presence of the jury, determine any issue as to voluntariness. If the trial judge determines that the confession was voluntarily made it shall be admitted in evidence and the trial judge shall permit the jury to hear relevant evidence on the issue of voluntariness and shall instruct the jury to give such weight to the confession as the jury feels it deserves under all the circumstances."

[270] The Supreme Court agreed with the Court of Appeals for the Fourth Circuit that the Congress intended to overrule *Miranda*. In *Dickerson v. United States,* 530 U.S. 428 at 436 (2000), the Court noted, "Given § 3501's express designation of voluntariness as the touchstone of admissibility, its omission of any warning requirement, and the instruction for trial courts to consider a nonexclusive list of factors relevant to the circumstances of a confession, we agree with the Court of Appeals that Congress intended by its enactment to overrule *Miranda*."

statements should be admitted against Dickerson, since his statements had been voluntarily given consistent with 18 U.S.C. § 3501. The court of appeals based its decision on a determination that Section 3501 superseded the decision of *Miranda v. Arizona* and that the *Miranda* decision was not of constitutional dimension and, therefore, could be overruled by an act of Congress.[271]

When the Supreme Court decided to hear the case, it noted that it possessed supervisory authority over the federal courts, and it could use that authority to prescribe rules of evidence and procedure that are binding in federal tribunals. The Court observed that Congress may not supersede court decisions interpreting and applying the Constitution, and that the case turned on whether the *Miranda* decision announced a constitutional rule or merely served as an example of the Court's exercise of its supervisory authority to regulate the admission of evidence in federal courts. The Supreme Court held that since *Miranda* and its companion cases applied the *Miranda* warnings to state courts and that the Court has no general supervisory authority over state courts, and that since the United States Supreme Court's authority over state courts is limited to enforcing the commands of the United States Constitution, the *Miranda* decision must have been of constitutional dimension. According to the *Dickerson* Court, the *Miranda* decision and its requirements could not be overturned by an act of Congress because the Supreme Court had announced a rule of procedure required by the United States Constitution when it decided the case of *Miranda v. Arizona*. Thus the congressional attempt to overturn the rule of *Miranda* and substitute it with a traditional standard of voluntariness ended with a stronger reaffirmation of the principles and practice that have grown up around the case of *Miranda v. Arizona*.

18. *MIRANDA* SUMMARY

Although every person is presumed to know the law, when a person is arrested and becomes subject to interrogation, this presumption no longer applies, and law enforcement officers must present warnings to those in custody. The warnings were believed necessary so that law enforcement agents would be less likely to overcome or overreach the will of the person in police custody. The warnings must convey that the individual has a right to remain silent and a right to an attorney, and that if the individual chooses to speak with police, anything said may be used against him or her in a court of law. If a person wishes to speak and later decides not to speak further, the request will be respected. If the person in custody would like to speak with an attorney, one will be made available before any questioning and will be available without cost if the person cannot afford legal representation. While there may be questions concerning precisely when a person enters police custody and questions of precisely what constitutes interrogation, where both custody and interrogation are present, the *Miranda* warnings must be offered to the individual or any evidence obtained will not be affirmatively admissible against the arrestee. Where a person in custody wishes to exercise the right of silence, the right to consult legal

---

[271]*Dickerson v. United States,* 166 F.3d 667 (4th Cir.1999).

counsel, or both, interrogation must cease until the individual, by conduct, indicates that he or she wishes to speak further. Failure to respect the constitutional rights of the arrestee will result in excludable evidence. An exception to the *Miranda* warnings exists in the context of an emergency where safety of the officer or other individuals nearby may be compromised if the warnings are given prior to immediate interrogation.

MAJOR CASES

CASE 7.1

Miranda *Warnings: Genesis of the Rule and Proper Practice*

Miranda v. Arizona
Supreme Court of the United States
384 U.S. 436 (1966)

FACTS

Phoenix police arrested Ernesto Miranda at his home on March 13, 1963, and removed him to the police station. After the complaining witness identified Miranda, police questioned him for two hours. Miranda and the police emerged from the room with a signed confession in which Miranda acknowledged that he had voluntarily confessed with complete knowledge that his statement could be used against him in court.

Miranda's attorney objected to the admission of his confession on the ground that the confession was obtained in violation of Miranda's Fifth Amendment right to remain silent. The officers recounted Miranda's confession and related the specifics under which it had been obtained. The trial court admitted the confession into evidence over Miranda's continued objection. The trial court found Miranda guilty of kidnapping and rape, and the court sentenced him to twenty to thirty years on each count with the sentences to be served concurrently.

The Supreme Court of Arizona held that none of Miranda's constitutional rights had been violated and affirmed his conviction. The court relied heavily on the admitted fact that Miranda had not specifically requested the assistance of counsel.

PROCEDURAL ISSUE

Where police desire to interrogate an arrestee, must police warn the subject of the right to remain silent under the Fifth Amendment and of the right to have the assistance of counsel under the Sixth Amendment prior to beginning any interrogation?

HELD: YES

RATIONALE

Mr. Chief Justice Warren delivered the opinion of the Court.

Our holding will be spelled out with some specificity in the pages which follow but briefly stated it is this: the prosecution may not use statements, whether exculpatory or inculpatory, stemming from custodial interrogation of the defendant unless it demonstrates the use of procedural safeguards effective to secure the privilege against self-incrimination. By custodial interrogation, we mean questioning initiated by law enforcement officers after a person has been taken into custody or otherwise deprived of his freedom of action in any significant way. As for the procedural safeguards to be employed, unless other fully effective means are devised to inform accused persons of their right of silence and to assure a continuous opportunity to exercise it, the following measures are required. Prior to any questioning, the person must be warned that he has a right to remain silent, that any statement he does make may be used as evidence against him, and that he has a right to the presence of an attorney, either retained or appointed. The defendant may waive effectuation of these rights, provided the waiver is made voluntarily, knowingly and intelligently. If, however, he indicates in any manner and at any stage of the process that he wishes to consult with an attorney before speaking there can be no questioning. Likewise, if the individual is alone and indicates in any manner that he does not wish to be interrogated, the police may not question him. The mere fact that he may have answered some questions or volunteered some statements on his own does not deprive him of the right to refrain from answering any further inquiries until he has consulted with an attorney and thereafter consents to be questioned.

I

The constitutional issue we decide in each of these cases[272] is the admissibility of statements obtained from a defendant questioned while in custody or otherwise deprived of his freedom of action in any significant way. In each, the defendant was questioned by police officers, detectives, or a prosecuting attorney in a room in which he was cut off from the outside world. In none of these cases was the defendant given a full and effective warning of his rights at the outset of the interrogation process. In all the cases, the questioning elicited oral admission, and in three of them, signed statements as well which were admitted at their trials. They all thus share salient features—incommunicado interrogation of individuals in a police-dominated atmosphere, resulting in self-incriminating statements without full warnings of constitutional rights.

An understanding of the nature and setting of this in-custody interrogation is essential to our decisions today. The difficulty in depicting what transpires at such interrogations stems from the fact that in this country they have largely taken place incommunicado. From extensive factual studies undertaken in the early 1930's, including the famous *Wickersham Report to Congress by a Presidential Commission,* it is clear that police violence and the "third degree" flourished at that time. In a series of cases decided by this Court long after these studies, the police resorted to physical brutality—beating, hanging, whipping—and to sustained and protracted questioning incommunicado in order to extort confessions. The Commission on Civil Rights in 1961 found much evidence to indicate that "some policemen still resort to physical force to obtain confessions," 1961 *Comm'n on Civil Rights Rep. Justice,* pt. 5, 17. The use of physical brutality and violence is not, unfortunately, relegated to the past or to any part of the country. Only recently in Kings County, New York, the police brutally beat, kicked and placed lighted cigarette butts on the back of a potential witness under interrogation for the purpose of securing a statement incriminating a third party.

The examples given above are undoubtedly the exception now, but they are sufficiently widespread to be the object of concern. Unless a proper limitation upon custodial interrogation is achieved—such as these decisions will advance—there can be no assurance that practices of this nature will be eradicated in the foreseeable future.

★ ★ ★

In the cases before us today…we concern ourselves primarily with this interrogation atmosphere and the evils it can bring. In No. 759, *Miranda v. Arizona,* the police arrested the defendant and took him to a special interrogation room where they secured a confession.

★ ★ ★

In [Mr. Miranda's case], we might not find the defendant's statement to have been involuntary in traditional terms. Our concern for adequate safeguards to protect precious Fifth Amendment rights is, of course, not lessened in the slightest.

★ ★ ★

II

★ ★ ★

The question in these cases is whether the [Fifth Amendment] privilege is applicable during a period of custodial interrogation.

★ ★ ★

This question, in fact, could have been taken as settled in federal courts almost 70 years ago, when, in *Bram v. United States,* 168 U.S. 532, 542,…(1897), this Court held:

> In criminal trials, in the courts of the United States, wherever a question arises whether a confession is incompetent because not voluntary, the issue is controlled by that portion of the Fifth Amendment . . . commanding that no person "shall be compelled in any criminal case to be a witness against himself."

★ ★ ★

III

Today, then, there can be no doubt that the Fifth Amendment privilege is available outside of criminal court proceedings and serves to protect persons in all settings in which their freedom of action is curtailed in any significant way from being compelled to incriminate themselves. We have concluded that without proper safeguards

---

[272]The Court consolidated four similarly postured cases that presented claims that confessions were inadmissible because of lack of counsel or lack of warnings concerning counsel and silence.

the process of in-custody interrogation of persons suspected or accused of crime contained inherently compelling pressures which work to undermine the individual's will to resist and to compel him to speak where he would not otherwise do so freely. In order to combat these pressures and to permit a full opportunity to exercise the privilege against self-incrimination, the accused must be adequately and effectively apprised of his rights and the exercise of those rights must be fully honored.

★ ★ ★

At the outset, if a person in custody is to be subjected to interrogation, he must first be informed in clear and unequivocal terms that he has the right to remain silent. For those unaware of the privilege, the warning is needed simply to make them aware of it—the threshold requirement for an intelligent decision as to its exercise. More important, such a warning is an absolute prerequisite in overcoming the inherent pressures of the interrogation atmosphere. It is not just the subnormal or woefully ignorant who succumb to an interrogatory's imprecations, whether implied or expressly stated, that the interrogation will continue until a confession is obtained or that silence in the fact of accusation is itself damning and will bode ill when presented to a jury. Further, the warning will show the individual that his interrogators are prepared to recognize his privilege should he choose to exercise it.

★ ★ ★

The warning of the right to remain silent must be accompanied by the explanation that anything said can and will be used against the individual in court. This warning is needed in order to make him aware not only of the privilege, but also of the consequences of forgoing it. It is only through an awareness of these consequences that there can be any assurance of real understanding and intelligent exercise of the privilege. Moreover, this warning may serve to make the individual more acutely aware that he is faced with a phase of the adversary system—that he is not in the presence of persons acting solely in his interest.

The circumstances surrounding in-custody interrogation can operate very quickly to overbear the will of one merely made aware of his privilege by his interrogators. Therefore, the right to have counsel present at the interrogation is indispensable to the protection of the Fifth Amendment privilege under the system we delineate today.

★ ★ ★

Accordingly we hold that an individual held for interrogation must be clearly informed that he has the right to consult with a lawyer and to have the lawyer with him during interrogation under the system for protecting the privilege we delineate today. As with warnings of the right to remain silent and that anything stated can be used in evidence against him, this warning is an absolute prerequisite to interrogation. No amount of circumstantial evidence that the person may have been aware of this right will suffice to stand in its stead. Only through such a warning is there ascertainable assurance that the accused was aware of this right.

If an individual indicates that he wishes the assistance of counsel before any interrogation occurs, the authorities cannot rationally ignore or deny his request on the basis that the individual does not have or cannot afford a retained attorney. The financial ability of the individual has no relationship to the scope of the rights involved here. The privilege against self-incrimination secured by the Constitution applies to all individuals.

★ ★ ★

In order to fully apprise a person interrogated of the extent of his rights under this system, then, it is necessary to warn him not only that he has the right to consult with an attorney, but also that if he is indigent a lawyer will be appointed to represent him. Without this additional warning, the admonition of the right to consult with counsel would often be understood as meaning only that he can consult with a lawyer if he has one or has the funds to obtain one. The warning of a right to counsel would be hollow if not couched in terms that would convey to the indigent—the person most often subjected to interrogation—the knowledge that he too has a right to have counsel present. As with the warnings of the right to remain silent and of the general right to counsel, only by effective and express explanation to the indigent of this right can there be assurance that he was truly in a position to exercise it.

Once warnings have been given, the subsequent procedure is clear. If the individual indicates in any manner, at any time prior to or during questioning, that he wishes to remain silent, the interrogation must cease. At this point he has shown that he intends to exercise his

Fifth Amendment privilege; any statement taken after the person invokes his privilege cannot be other than the product of compulsion, subtle or otherwise. Without the right to cut off questioning, the setting of in-custody interrogation operates on the individual to overcome free choice in producing a statement after the privilege has been once invoked. If the individual states that he wants an attorney, the interrogation must cease until an attorney is present. At that time, the individual must have an opportunity to confer with the attorney and to have him present during any subsequent questioning. If the individual cannot obtain an attorney and he indicates that he wants one before speaking to police, they must respect his decision to remain silent.

★ ★ ★

An express statement that the individual is willing to make a statement and does not want an attorney, followed closely by a statement, could constitute a waiver. But a valid waiver will not be presumed simply from the silence of the accused after warnings are given or simply from the fact that a confession was in fact eventually obtained. A statement we made in *Carnley v. Cochran,* 369 U.S. 506, 516 (1962), is applicable here:

> Presuming waiver from a silent record is impermissible. The record must show, or there must be an allegation and evidence which show, that an accused was offered counsel but intelligently and understandingly rejected the offer. Anything less is not waiver.

Moreover, where in-custody interrogation is involved, there is no room for the contention that the privilege is waived if the individual answers some questions or gives some information on his own prior to invoking his right to remain silent when interrogated.

★ ★ ★

The warnings required and the waiver necessary in accordance with our opinion today are, in the absence of a fully effective equivalent, prerequisites to the admissibility of any statement made by a defendant. No distinction can be drawn between statements which are direct confessions and statements which amount to "admissions" of part or all of an offense. The privilege against self-incrimination protects the individual from being compelled to incriminate himself in any manner; it does not distinguish degrees of incrimination. Similarly, for precisely the same reason, no distinction may be drawn between inculpatory statements and statements alleged to be merely "exculpatory."

★ ★ ★

The principles announced today deal with the protection which must be given to the privilege against self-incrimination when the individual is first subjected to police interrogation while in custody at the station or otherwise deprived of his freedom of action in any significant way. It is at this point that our adversary system of criminal proceedings commences, distinguishing itself at the outset from the inquisitorial system recognized in some countries. Under the system of warnings we delineate today or under any other system which may be devised and found effective, the safeguards to be erected about the privileges must come into play at this point.

Our decision is not intended to hamper the traditional function of police officers in investigating crime. When an individual is in custody on probable cause, the police may, of course, seek out evidence in the field to be used at trial against him. Such investigation may include inquiry of persons not under restraint. General on-the-scene questioning as to facts surrounding a crime or other general questioning of citizens in the fact-finding process is not affected by our holding. It is an act of responsible citizenship for individuals to give whatever information they may have to aid in law enforcement. In such situations the compelling atmosphere inherent in the process of in-custody interrogation is not necessarily present.

In dealing with statements obtained through interrogation, we do not purport to find all confessions inadmissible. Confessions remain a proper element in law enforcement. Any statement given freely and voluntarily without any compelling influences is, of course, admissible in evidence. The fundamental import of the privilege while an individual is in custody is not whether he is allowed to talk to the police without the benefit of warnings and counsel, but whether he can be interrogated. There is no requirement that police stop a person who enters a police station and states that he wishes to confess to a crime, or a person who calls the police to offer a confession or any other statement he desires to make. Volunteered statements of any kind are not barred by the Fifth Amendment and their admissibility is not affected by our holding today.

To summarize, we hold that, when an individual is taken into custody or otherwise deprived of his freedom by the authorities in any significant way and is subjected to questioning, the privilege against self-incrimination is jeopardized. Procedural safeguards must be employed to protect the privilege, and unless other fully effective means are adopted to notify the person of his right of silence and to assure that the exercise of the right will be scrupulously honored, the following measures are required. He must be warned prior to any questioning that he has the right to remain silent, that anything he says can be used against him in a court of law, that he has the right to the presence of an attorney, and that, if he cannot afford an attorney one will be appointed for him prior to any questioning if he so desires. Opportunity to exercise these rights must be afforded to him throughout the interrogation. After such warnings have been given, and such opportunity afforded him, the individual may knowingly and intelligently waive these rights and agree to answer questions or make a statement. But unless and until such warnings and waiver are demonstrated by the prosecution at trial, no evidence obtained as a result of interrogation can be used against him.

IV

★ ★ ★

V

★ ★ ★

Therefore, in accordance with the foregoing, the judgment of the Supreme Court of Arizona…[is] reversed.

It is so ordered.

COMMENTS, NOTES, AND QUESTIONS

1. In *Miranda,* the Court had a concern that interrogation might involve police overreaching of persons being questioned. Does the Court seem to place an insurmountable barrier to a prosecutor ever demonstrating that a particular interrogation was not coercive and the subject offered a voluntary and free confession or admission in the absence of offering the warnings? According to the *Miranda* Court, "a warning is an absolute prerequisite in overcoming the inherent pressures of the interrogation atmosphere." Does this close the door on a prosecutor arguing that a confession was voluntarily given where the

Miranda warning was not offered, or is there another way to show voluntariness?

2. In *Miranda,* the Court noted that the rules for custodial interrogation did not include any change from prior practice when an arrestee volunteered statements. The Court clarified that the admissibility of gratuitous statements offered to the police remained unaffected by the *Miranda* decision. If a person were to speak to an officer and offer a confession to a murder, would the officer have to stop the confession and warn the person under *Miranda* prior to hearing the confession? Why or why not? Assume that an individual arrived at a police station and immediately began confessing his involvement in a bank robbery or a homicide. Clearly, at some point, the officer would not allow the person to leave. Could the officer merely listen to the confession without offering a *Miranda* warning? If the officer were to ask a substantive question concerning the bank robbery, would the question transgress the dictates of *Miranda*? Why or why not? See *Colorado v. Connelly,* 479 U.S. 157 (1986).

3. The precise point at which a person enters into police custody proves clear in most arrests, but it may be somewhat ambiguous in other contexts. In *Dunaway v. New York,* 442 U.S. 2000 (1979), the police decided to "pick up" Dunaway without probable cause and without his consent. Dunaway arrived at the police station, where, following *Miranda* warnings, the police proceeded to interrogate him on a homicide case. Dunaway would have been forcibly restrained if he had attempted to leave the police station, and during his interrogation, he was never told that he was free to leave. Dunaway waived counsel and eventually made statements and drew sketches that incriminated him in the homicide. Under such circumstances, was Dunaway in custody for *Miranda* purposes? How important would it be that he believed that he was not free to leave? Should this be determinative for *Miranda* purposes? Or is the crucial factor for custody purposes the fact that the police would not have allowed him to leave?

4. Custody should be a clear-cut legal concept, but at times it can seem somewhat ambiguous. In *Thompson v. Keohane,* 516 U.S. 99 (1995), Thompson was subjected to a two-hour interrogation by several Alaska state troopers at their headquarters. Thompson's ex-wife had been missing for a while, and the police had been notified of a suspicious death of a woman. The police had invited Thompson to come to headquarters and discuss the case, but they did not tell him that he was a prime suspect. Thompson was told that he was free to leave at any time. Informing Thompson that execution of a

search warrant was under way at his home, and that his truck was about to be searched pursuant to another warrant, the troopers asked questions that invited a confession. Thompson eventually told troopers that he had killed his former wife. The police permitted Thompson to leave police headquarters but impounded his truck for a search. Following his conviction for first-degree murder, he appealed, contending that he had been subjected to custodial interrogation in violation of *Miranda*. To determine the issue of custody, the Court decided that two discrete questions must be answered. First, what were the circumstances surrounding the interrogation; and, second, given those circumstances, would a reasonable person have felt he or she was not at liberty to terminate the interrogation and leave? Due to other related issues, the Court sent the case back for review under these standards.

Under the circumstances, would a reasonable person have felt free to go prior to confessing to murder? What about after confessing to murder? Did the fact that the police allowed him to leave influence your decision? Could the police have allowed Thompson to leave the station so that they would have created a reduced chance of having him make a *Miranda* argument?

CASE 7.2

The Functional Equivalent of Interrogation

Rhode Island v. Innis
Supreme Court of the United States
446 U.S. 291 (1980)

FACTS

Following a dispatch to pick up a fare, a Providence, Rhode Island, taxicab driver disappeared. His body was discovered a few days later in a shallow grave with a fatal shotgun wound to the head. A day after the body had been discovered, another taxicab driver reported that he had been robbed at gunpoint by a man wielding a sawed-off shotgun. While waiting to give an official statement, the driver noticed a photograph of Mr. Innis on the mug board of the police station and told police that Innis was the robber. The driver also picked a photograph of Mr. Innis from a photographic lineup. The police began to concentrate the search in the area in which the robbery of the taxicab driver occurred.

A police officer discovered Mr. Innis walking on the public street, placed him under arrest, and read him the standard *Miranda* warnings. While the two men waited in the patrol car for other police officers to arrive, the arresting officer did not converse with the respondent other than to respond to Innis' request for a cigarette. Subsequently, a police captain read the *Miranda* warnings to Mr. Innis a second time. Innis indicated that he wished to speak with an attorney, so the police began to transport the arrestee to the police station.

The officer in charge assigned three officers to transport Innis to the central station. They placed Innis in the vehicle and the police captain then instructed the officers not to question Innis or intimidate or coerce him in any way. En route to the jail, two officers conversed about what a tragedy it would be if one of the children from the handicapped children's school happened to find a loaded shotgun. While Patrolman Williams said nothing, Gleckman spoke in the presence of Innis and noted that it would be too bad if a little girl would pick up the gun.

Patrolman Gleckman later testified at Innis's trial:

> A. At this point, I was talking back and forth with Patrolman McKenna stating that I frequent this area while on patrol [and that, because a school for handicapped children is located nearby] there's a lot of handicapped children running around in this area, and God forbid one of them might find a weapon with shells and they might hurt themselves. App. 43–44.

Officer Gleckman also indicated that, in the conversation with Officer McKenna, he intimated that it would be a tragedy if some little girl would find the gun and accidentally kill herself.

The third officer, Williams, did not join the conversation, but Mr. Innis interrupted the conversation of Officers McKenna and Gleckman and told them that he would reveal where he had hidden the missing shotgun if they would return to the scene of his arrest. Upon arrival, the police captain, who was still on the arrest scene, again read the *Miranda* rights to Mr. Innis who again indicated that he still understood them. Innis noted that he wanted to show the police the gun because of the danger to the handicapped school children. He led the police to a nearby field, where he pointed out the shotgun under some rocks by the side of the road.

The prosecutor introduced the shotgun as evidence after the trial court refused Innis' efforts to suppress the shotgun under *Miranda*. Following the return of a guilty verdict, Innis filed a successful appeal based on the alleged *Miranda* violation. The Rhode Island Supreme Court agreed with his contention concerning the

Miranda violation and reversed his conviction. The Court held that from the moment that Innis had invoked his right to counsel, all questioning between any officer in the police cruiser and Innis should have ceased. According to the Court, the police officers in the vehicle had "interrogated" the respondent without a valid waiver of his right to counsel when they spoke in front of him. The Rhode Island Supreme Court believed that Innis had been subjected to "subtle coercion" that was the functional equivalent of interrogation.

The Supreme Court of the United States granted certiorari to address the meaning of "interrogation" under *Miranda v. Arizona,* 440 U.S. 934.

PROCEDURAL ISSUE

Where police officers discuss an arrestee's case where the arrestee can hear the police and where the officers' conversation has not been specially tailored to motivate or coerce the arrestee to speak on the facts of the case, does such conduct by police officers constitute the functional equivalent of interrogation under *Miranda*?

HELD: NO

RATIONALE

Mr. Justice Stewart delivered the opinion of the Court.

★ ★ ★

II

In its *Miranda* opinion, the Court concluded that in the context of "custodial interrogation" certain procedural safeguards are necessary to protect a defendant's Fifth and Fourteenth Amendment privilege against compulsory self-incrimination....

The court in the *Miranda* opinion...outlined in some detail the consequences that would result if a defendant sought to invoke those procedural safeguards. With regard to the right to the presence of counsel, the Court noted:

> Once warnings have been given, the subsequent procedure is clear.... If the individual states that he wants an attorney, the interrogation must cease until an attorney is present. At that time, the individual must have an opportunity to confer with the attorney and to have him present during any subsequent questioning. If the individual cannot obtain an attorney

and he indicates that he wants one before speaking to police, they must respect his decision to remain silent. *Id.* At 473–474.

In the present case, the parties are in agreement that the respondent was fully informed of his *Miranda* rights, and that he invoked his *Miranda* right to counsel when he told Captain Leyden that he wished to consult with a lawyer. It is also uncontested that the respondent was "in custody" while being transported to the police station.

The issue, therefore, is whether the respondent was "interrogated" by the police officers in violation of the respondent's undisputed right under *Miranda* to remain silent until he had consulted with a lawyer. In resolving this issue, we first define the term "interrogation" under *Miranda* before turning to a consideration of the facts of this case.

A

The starting point for defining "interrogation" in this context is, of course, the Court's *Miranda* opinion. There the Court observed that,

> [b]y custodial interrogation, we mean *questioning* initiated by law enforcement officers after a person has been taken into custody or otherwise deprived of his freedom of action in any significant way. *Id.* At 44 (emphasis added).

This passage and other references throughout the opinion to "questioning" might suggest that the *Miranda* rules were to apply only to those police interrogation practices that involve express questioning of a defendant while in custody.

We do not, however, construe the *Miranda* opinion so narrowly. The concern of the Court in *Miranda* was that the "interrogation environment" created by the interplay of interrogation and custody would "subjugate the individual to the will of his examiner," and thereby undermine the privilege against compulsory self-incrimination.

★ ★ ★

The Court in *Miranda* also included in its survey of interrogation practices the use of psychological ploys, such as to "postulate" "the guilt of the subject," to "minimize the moral seriousness of the offense," and "to cast blame on the victim or on society." It is clear that these techniques of persuasion, no less than express questioning, were thought, in a custodial setting, to amount to interrogation.

★ ★ ★

It is clear therefore that the special procedural safeguards outlined in *Miranda* are required not where a suspect is simply taken into custody, but rather where a suspect in custody is subjected to interrogation. "Interrogation," as conceptualized in the *Miranda* opinion, must reflect a measure of compulsion above and beyond that inherent in custody itself.

We conclude that the *Miranda* safeguards come into play whenever a person in custody is subjected to either express questioning or its functional equivalent. That is to say, the term "interrogation" under *Miranda* refers not only to express questioning, but also to any words or actions on the part of the police (other than those normally attendant to arrest and custody) that the police should know are reasonably likely to elicit an incriminating response from the suspect. The latter portion of this definition focuses primarily upon the perceptions of the suspect, rather than the intent of the police. This focus reflects the fact that the *Miranda* safeguards were designed to vest a suspect in custody with an added measure of protection against coercive police practices, without regard to objective proof of the underlying intent of the police. A practice that the police should know is reasonably likely to evoke an incriminating response from a suspect thus amounts to interrogation. But since the police surely cannot be held accountable for the unforeseeable results of their words or actions, the definition of interrogation can extend only to words or actions on the part of police officers that they *should have known* were reasonably likely to elicit an incriminating response.

B

Turning to the facts of the present case, we conclude that the respondent was not "interrogated" within the meaning of *Miranda*. It is undisputed that the first prong of the definition of "interrogation" was not satisfied, for the conversation between Patrolmen Gleckman and McKenna included no express questioning of the respondent. Rather, that conversation was, at least in form, nothing more than a dialogue between the two officers to which no response from the respondent was invited.

Moreover, it cannot be fairly concluded that the respondent was subjected to the "functional equivalent" of questioning. It cannot be said, in short, that Patrolmen Gleckman and McKenna should have known that their conversation was reasonably likely to elicit an incriminating response from the respondent. There is nothing in the record to suggest that the officers were aware that the respondent was peculiarly susceptible to an appeal to his

conscience concerning the safety of handicapped children. Nor is there anything in the record to suggest that the police knew that the respondent was unusually disoriented or upset at the time of his arrest.

The case thus boils down to whether, in the context of a brief conversation, the officers should have known that the respondent would suddenly be moved to make a self-incriminating response. Given the fact that the entire conversation appears to have consisted of no more than a few off-hand remarks, we cannot say that the officers should have known that it was reasonably likely that Innis would so respond. This is not a case where the police carried on a lengthy harangue in the presence of the suspect. Nor does the record support the respondent's contention that, under the circumstances, the officers' comments were particularly "evocative." It is our view, therefore, that the respondent was not subjected by the police to words or actions that the police should have known were reasonably likely to elicit an incriminating response from him.

★ ★ ★

For the reasons stated, the judgment of the Supreme Court of Rhode Island is vacated, and the case is remanded to that court for further proceedings not inconsistent with this opinion.

It is so ordered.

COMMENTS, NOTES, AND QUESTIONS

1. Were the officers really interrogating Mr. Innis? Does it defy common sense for the *Innis* Court to say that the police conduct did not amount to interrogation? In determining what conduct by police could be construed as questioning or its functional equivalent, on what factors did the Innis Court seemed to focus? On the intent of the police officers? Or on the effects upon the arrestee? Was the Court concerned about the conduct of the officers? The *Innis* court stressed that the test of whether police officers intended their speech to constitute interrogation turned on whether a reasonable person would realize that his or her speech would be likely to produce an incriminating response from the person in custody. Do you agree with the Court that the officers were not interrogating Innis? Why or why not? Could you formulate a case example where the officers' conduct would be construed as the functional equivalent of interrogation?

2. Should the prohibition against custodial interrogation cover the situation where police allow family members to ask questions of a relative in custody? The Court in *Arizona v. Mauro,* 481 U.S. 520 (1987), allowed police to listen to conversations between the defendant and his wife without running afoul of *Miranda.* In *Mauro,* Mrs. Mauro asked if she could speak to her husband, who was under arrest for killing their son. One of the officers was reluctant to allow the meeting, but after Mrs. Mauro insisted, he subsequently allowed her to talk with her husband. Mrs. Mauro spoke with the defendant in the presence of a police officer who had a tape recorder running on a table in view of the defendant and his wife. There was a high probability that the police suspected that the pair would discuss the homicide. Defense counsel argued that the police conduct should be construed as the functional equivalent of interrogation under the *Innis* Court's definition of custodial interrogation:

> [A]ny words or *actions* on the part of the police (other than those normally attendant to arrest and custody) that the police should know are reasonably likely to elicit an incriminating response from the suspect. *Innis* at 527.

Under such circumstances, the *Mauro* Court held that the defendant's statements were made to his wife and were not made in response to police-initiated questions; therefore, they were not considered to be the product of an improper custodial interrogation. The situation could not be considered coercive because it did not involve any psychological ploys to get an arrestee to speak, and the arrestee knew that police were listening. Do you agree with the *Mauro* Court's interpretation of the *Innis* definition of interrogation? Why or why not? One could argue that when a wife talks to her accused husband, who has been arrested for the murder of their son, something incriminating might be offered!

3. Emergency situations allow police to ask some custodial questions before offering the *Miranda* warnings. An immediate warning can be excused in cases of emergency or where the safety of the public or police officers could be endangered if *Miranda* were administered prior to initial questioning. See *New York v. Quarles,* 467 U.S. 649 (1984). What fact patterns or other factors should qualify as emergency circumstances that would excuse the initial *Miranda* warning? An Ohio court noted:

> In order to establish the need for the exception, the state must demonstrate that 1) there was an objectively reasonable need to protect the police or the public, 2) from an immediate danger, 3) associated with a weapon, and that 4) the questions asked were related to that danger and reasonably necessary to secure public safety. This analysis is to be conducted on a case by case basis. *Ohio v. Prim,* 134 Ohio App. 3d 142, 154; 730 N.E.2d 455, 463 (1999).

Should an emergency exception apply only where death or serious bodily injury might occur? Should danger to property constitute an emergency? What if it were a large, unoccupied building? Should an arrestee's rights under *Miranda* change in an emergency? Why or why not? Are there higher values being protected by the police when they question someone during an emergency?

4. A practice that the police should understand would be likely to provoke an incriminating response from an arrestee amounts to custodial interrogation. Should it matter if the police know that a person has particular vulnerabilities and exploit those weaknesses to get a person to incriminate him- or herself? Would it matter that the suspect had indicated a desire to talk to his or her lawyer before speaking to anyone else? Should such conduct on the part of police who have a person in custody be considered interrogation? In *Brewer v. Williams,* 430 U.S. 387 (1977), an officer who knew a mental patient was deeply religious did not interrogate in the usual sense. He played upon the sensitivities of the arrestee to get the prisoner to tell him where a murdered girl's body was located in order to give her a Christian burial. The Supreme Court held this approach to constitute the functional equivalent of interrogation under *Miranda.*

CASE 7.3

Judicial Remedy for **Miranda** *Violation*

Oregon v. Elstad
Supreme Court of the United States
470 U.S. 298 (1985)

FACTS

A police informant notified police that Michael Elstad had intimate involvement in a residential burglary where $150,000 in property and art objects had been taken. Police secured a warrant for the arrest of eighteen-year-old Elstad, who lived with his parents. Upon arrival at the Elstad residence, police notified Elstad's mother of their purpose and she led them to his bedroom. The officers did not tell Elstad that he was under arrest at the moment they first spoke to him. Since young Elstad was not fully clothed, one of the officers remained with him while he dressed and the other officer spoke with Mrs. Elstad in the kitchen.

No *Miranda* warning had been given while the police officer was with young Elstad in the bedroom and still had not been administered when the two walked to the living room. Officer Burke later testified:

> I sat down with Mr. Elstad and I asked him if he was aware of why Detective McAllister and myself were there to talk with him. He stated no, he had no idea why we were there. I then asked him if he knew a person by the name of Gross, and he said yes, he did, and also added that he heard that there was a robbery at the Gross house. And at that point, I told Mr. Elstad that I felt he was involved in that, and he looked at me and stated, "Yes, I was there."

The officers then escorted Elstad to the back of the patrol car where the police placed him inside for transport to the Polk County Sheriff's Office. Deputy Sheriff McAllister read the *Miranda* warnings to Elstad from a printed card about an hour after arriving at the sheriff's building. Elstad stated that he understood his rights, and, having these rights in mind, wished to speak with the officers. Elstad gave a full confession, explaining that he had known that the house was not occupied and had been paid to lead several acquaintances to the residence and show them how to gain entry through a defective sliding glass door.

Prior to his bench trial, Elstad attempted to have the oral and written confessions suppressed as a violation of his rights under *Miranda*. He contended that the statement he made in response to questioning at his house "let the cat out of the bag" and tainted the subsequent confession as "fruit of the poisonous tree."[273] Essentially, Elstad contended that the unwarned statement at his home prompted his confession at the police station and should be suppressed since he would not have confessed if the police had not unlawfully questioned him at his home. The judge ruled that the statement, "I was there," had to be excluded due to the obvious *Miranda* violation, but the voluntary written confession would be admitted into evidence since it had not been tainted by the living room conversation. The judge rejected Elstad's argument that

the stationhouse confession was the "fruit of the poisonous tree" of an earlier violation of *Miranda*.

The Oregon Court of Appeals reversed Elstad's burglary conviction on the theory that the signed voluntary confession was rendered inadmissible due to initial improper custodial interrogation in the family living room in violation of the principles of *Miranda*. The illegal admission at his home, the Court believed, prompted Elstad to confess at the police station as the "fruit of the poisonous tree." The Supreme Court of Oregon declined to review the case. The Supreme Court of the United States granted certiorari.

PROCEDURAL ISSUE

Does the self-incrimination clause of the Fifth Amendment require the suppression of a free and voluntary confession, made after proper *Miranda* warnings and a valid waiver of rights, where the police had obtained an earlier voluntary but unwarned admission from the defendant?

HELD: NO

RATIONALE

Justice O'Connor delivered the opinion of the Court.

★ ★ ★

II

The arguments advanced in favor of suppression of respondent's confession rely heavily on metaphor. One metaphor, familiar from the Fourth Amendment context, would require that respondent's confession, regardless of its integrity, voluntariness, and probative value, be suppressed as the "tainted fruit of the poisonous tree" of the *Miranda* violation. A second metaphor questions whether a confession can be truly voluntary once the "cat is out of the bag." Taken out of context, each of these metaphors can be misleading. They should not be used to obscure fundamental differences between the role of the Fourth Amendment exclusionary rule and the function of *Miranda* in guarding against the prosecutorial use of compelled statements as prohibited by the Fifth Amendment. The Oregon court assumed and respondent here contends that a failure to administer *Miranda* warnings necessarily

---

[273]See *Wong Sun v. United States,* 361 U.S. 461 (1963), where the first violation of the Constitution (illegal search) led to discovery of additional evidence by virtue of exploiting the original illegality. The *Wong Sun* Court held that the evidence from both constitutional violations should be excluded from trial.

breeds the same consequences as police infringement of a constitutional right, so that evidence uncovered following an unwarned statement must be suppressed as "fruit of the poisonous tree." We believe this view misconstrues the nature of the protections afforded by *Miranda* warnings and therefore misreads the consequences of police failure to supply them.

★ ★ ★

The Court in *Miranda* requires suppression of many statements that would have been admissible under traditional due process analysis by presuming that statements made while in custody and without adequate warnings were protected by the Fifth Amendment. The Fifth Amendment, of course, is not concerned with nontestimonial evidence. *See Schmerber v. California* (1966) (defendant may be compelled to supply blood samples). Nor is it concerned with moral and psychological pressures to confess emanating from sources other than official coercion. Voluntary statements "remain a proper element in law enforcement."

> "Indeed, far from being prohibited by the Constitution, admissions of guilt by wrongdoers, if not coerced, are inherently desirable....Absent some officially coerced self-accusation, the Fifth Amendment privilege is not violated by even the most damning admissions." *United States v. Washington,* 431 U.S. 181, 187 (1977).

★ ★ ★

Respondent's contention that his confession was tainted by the earlier failure of the police to provide *Miranda* warnings and must be excluded as "fruit of the poisonous tree" assumes the existence of a constitutional violation.[274] This figure of speech is drawn from *Wong Sun v. United States* (1963), in which the Court held that evidence and witnesses discovered as a result of a search in violation of the Fourth Amendment must be excluded from evidence. The *Wong Sun* doctrine applies as well when the fruit of the Fourth Amendment violation is a confession. It is settled law that a confession obtained through custodial interrogation after an illegal arrest should be excluded unless intervening events break the causal connection between the illegal arrest and the confession so that the confession is sufficiently an act of free will to purge the primary taint.

...[A] procedural *Miranda* violation differs in significant respects from violations of the Fourth Amendment, which have traditionally mandated a broad application of the "fruits" doctrine. The purpose of the Fourth Amendment exclusionary rule is to deter unreasonable searches, no matter how probative their fruits....Where a Fourth Amendment violation "taints" the confession, a finding of voluntariness for the purposes of the Fifth Amendment is merely a threshold requirement in determining whether the confession may be admitted in evidence. Beyond this, the prosecution must show a sufficient break in events to undermine the inference that the confession was caused by the Fourth Amendment violation.

★ ★ ★

The *Miranda* exclusionary rule, however, serves the Fifth Amendment and sweeps more broadly than the Fifth Amendment itself. It may be triggered even in the absence of a Fifth Amendment violation. The Fifth Amendment prohibits use by the prosecution in its case in chief only of compelled testimony. Failure to administer *Miranda* warnings creates a presumption of compulsion. Consequently, unwarned statements that are otherwise voluntary within the meaning of the Fifth Amendment must nevertheless be excluded from evidence under *Miranda*. Thus, in the individual case, *Miranda*'s preventive medicine provides a remedy even to the defendant who has suffered no identifiable constitutional harm.

---

[274]*Wong Sun v. United States,* 371 U.S. 471 (1963), held, inter alia, that where a person's Fourth Amendment rights have been violated by police, evidence obtained directly or indirectly from exploitation of the illegal search or seizure cannot be introduced to prove guilt at a criminal trial. This principle involved an extension of *Mapp v. Ohio,* 367 U.S. 643 (1961) (which excluded evidence illegally seized by police from state trials) to evidence that can be called derivative of the original wrongdoing by law enforcement agents. The police are not permitted to benefit from wrongdoing and are placed in the same evidentiary position as if no wrongdoing had occurred. Note that *Mapp* and *Wong Sun* involved violations of the United States Constitution, not transgressions of a prophylactic or remedial legal rule developed by the Court like the *Miranda* warnings. The waters get more murky since in *Dickerson v. United States,* 530 U.S. 428 (2000), the Court held that the *Miranda* warnings were of constitutional dimension and were required by the Constitution. The *Dickerson* case may require the Court to revisit *Elstad* in the future because such conduct may violate the Constitution.

In *Michigan v. Tucker,* 417 U.S. 433 (1974), the Court was asked to extend the *Wong Sun* fruits doctrine to suppress the testimony of a witness for the prosecution whose identity was discovered as the result of a statement taken from the accused without benefit of full *Miranda* warnings. As in respondent's case, the breach of the *Miranda* procedures in *Tucker* involved no actual compulsion. The Court concluded that the unwarned questioning

> "did not abridge respondent's constitutional privilege...but departed only from the prophylactic standards later laid down by this Court in *Miranda* to safeguard that privilege."

Since there was no actual infringement of the suspect's constitutional rights, the case was not controlled by the doctrine expressed in *Wong Sun* that fruits of a constitutional violation must be suppressed. In deciding "how sweeping the judicially imposed consequences" of a failure to administer *Miranda* warnings should be, the *Tucker* Court noted that neither the general goal of deterring improper police conduct nor the Fifth Amendment goal of assuring trustworthy evidence would be served by suppression of the witness' testimony. The unwarned confession must, of course, be suppressed, but the Court ruled that introduction of the third-party witness' testimony did not violate Tucker's Fifth Amendment rights.

We believe that this reasoning applies with equal force when the alleged "fruit" of a noncoercive *Miranda* violation is neither a witness nor an article of evidence but the accused's own voluntary testimony. As in *Tucker,* the absence of any coercion or improper tactics undercuts the twin rationales—trustworthiness and deterrence—for a broader rule. Once warned, the suspect is free to exercise his own volition in deciding whether or not to make a statement to the authorities. The Court has often noted: "'[A] living witness is not to be mechanically equated with the proffer of inanimate evidentiary objects illegally seized. . . . [T]he living witness is an individual human personality whose attributes of will, perception, memory and *volition* interact to determine what testimony he will give.'" *United States v. Ceccolini,* 435 U.S. 268, 277 (1978) (emphasis added) (quoting from *Smith v. United States,* 117 U.S. App. D.C. 1, 3-4, 324 F.2d 879, 881-882 (1963) (Burger, J.) [footnotes omitted], cert. denied, 377 U.S. 954 (1964)).

★ ★ ★

When a prior statement is actually coerced, the time that passes between confessions, the change in place of interrogations, and the change in identity of the interrogators all bear on whether that coercion has carried over into the second confession. The failure of police to administer *Miranda* warnings does not mean that the statements received have actually been coerced, but only that courts will presume the privilege against compulsory self-incrimination has not been intelligently exercised.

B

★ ★ ★

The Oregon court nevertheless identified a subtle form of lingering compulsion, the psychological impact of the suspect's conviction that he has let the cat out of the bag and, in so doing, has sealed his own fate. But endowing the psychological effects of *voluntary* unwarned admissions with constitutional implications would, practically speaking, disable the police from obtaining the suspect's informed cooperation even when the official coercion proscribed by the Fifth Amendment played no part in either his warned or unwarned confessions. As the Court remarked in *[United States v.] Bayer:*

> [A]fter an accused has once let the cat out of the bag by confessing, no matter what the inducement, he is never thereafter free of the psychological and practical disadvantages of having confessed. He can never get the cat back in the bag. The secret is out for good. In such a sense, a later confession may always be looked upon as fruit of the first. But this Court has never gone so far as to hold that making a confession under circumstances which preclude its use, perpetually disables the confessor from making a usable one after those conditions have been removed. 331 U.S., at 540–541 [1947].

★ ★ ★

This Court has never held that the psychological impact of voluntary disclosure of a guilty secret qualifies as state compulsion or compromised the voluntariness of a subsequent informed waiver. The Oregon court, by adopting this expansive view of Fifth Amendment compulsion, effectively immunizes a suspect who responds to pre-*Miranda* warning questions from the consequences of his subsequent informed waiver of the privilege of remaining silent. This immunity comes at a high cost to legitimate law enforcement activity, while adding little desirable protection to the individual's interest in not being compelled to testify against himself. When neither the initial nor the subsequent admission is coerced, little justification exists for permitting the highly probative evidence of a voluntary confession to be irretrievably lost to the factfinder.

★ ★ ★

III

Though belated, the reading of respondent's rights was undeniably complete. McAllister testified that he read the *Miranda* warnings aloud from a printed card and recorded Elstad's responses. There is no question that respondent knowingly and voluntarily waived his right to remain silent before he described his participation in the burglary. It is also beyond dispute that respondent's earlier remark was voluntary, within the meaning of the Fifth Amendment. Neither the environment nor the manner of either "interrogation" was coercive. The initial conversation took place at midday, in the living room area of respondent's own home, with his mother in the kitchen area, a few steps away. Although in retrospect the officers testified that respondent was then in custody, at the time he made his statement he had not been informed that he was under arrest.

★ ★ ★

Respondent, however, has argued that he was unable to give a fully informed waiver of his rights because he was unaware that his prior statement could not be used against him. Respondent suggests that Deputy McAllister, to cure this deficiency, should have added an additional warning to those given him at the Sheriff's office. Such a requirement is neither practicable nor constitutionally necessary. In many cases, a breach of *Miranda* procedures may not be identified as such until long after full *Miranda* warnings are administered and a valid confession obtained.

★ ★ ★

IV

When police ask questions of a suspect in custody without administering the required warnings, *Miranda* dictates that the answers received be presumed compelled and that they be excluded from evidence at trial in the State's case in chief. The Court has carefully adhered to this principle,

permitting a narrow exception only where pressing public safety concerns demanded. The Court today in no way retreats from the bright line rule of *Miranda*. We do not imply that good faith excuses a failure to administer *Miranda* warnings; nor do we condone inherently coercive police tactics or methods offensive to due process that render the initial admission involuntary and undermine the suspect's will to invoke his rights once they are read to him. A handful of courts have, however, applied our precedents relating to confessions obtained under coercive circumstance to situations involving wholly voluntary admissions, requiring a passage of time or break in events before a second, fully warned statement can be deemed voluntary. Far from establishing a rigid rule, we direct courts to avoid one; there is no warrant for presuming coercive effect where the suspect's initial inculpatory statement, though technically in violation of *Miranda,* was voluntary. The relevant inquiry is whether, in fact, the second statement was also voluntarily made. As in any such inquiry, the finder of fact must examine the surrounding circumstances and the entire course of police conduct with respect to the suspect in evaluating the voluntariness of his statements. The fact that a suspect chooses to speak after being informed of his rights is, of course, highly probative. We find that the dictates of *Miranda* and the goals of the Fifth Amendment proscription against use of compelled testimony are fully satisfied in the circumstances of this case by barring use of the unwarned statement in the case in chief. No further purpose is served by imputing "taint" to subsequent statements obtained pursuant to a voluntary and knowing waiver. We hold today that a suspect who has once responded to unwarned yet uncoercive questioning is not thereby disabled from waiving his rights and confessing after he has been given the requisite *Miranda* warnings.

The judgment of the Court of Appeals of Oregon is reversed, and the case is remanded for further proceedings not inconsistent with this opinion.

It is so ordered.

Justice Brennan, with whom Justice Marshall joins, dissenting.

The Self-Incrimination Clause of the Fifth Amendment guarantees every individual that, if taken into official custody, he shall be informed of important constitutional rights and be given the opportunity knowingly and voluntarily to waive those rights before being interrogated about suspected wrongdoing. *Miranda v. Arizona,* 384 U.S.

436 (1966). This guarantee embodies our society's conviction that: "no system of criminal justice can, or should, survive if it comes to depend for its continued effectiveness on the citizens' abdication through unawareness of their constitutional rights." *Escobedo v. Illinois,* 378 U.S. 478, 490 (1964).

Even while purporting to reaffirm these constitutional guarantees, the Court has engaged of late in a studied campaign to strip the *Miranda* decision piecemeal and to undermine the rights *Miranda* sought to secure.

COMMENTS, NOTES, AND QUESTIONS

1. The *Elstad* Court recognized a distinction between the exclusion of evidence under the principles of *Miranda* and the exclusion of evidence following a governmental violation of the United States Constitution. The opinion developed the concept that the same government act could violate the principles of *Miranda* without *always* violating the Fifth, Fourth, or Fourteenth Amendments. Where the governmental conduct transgresses *Miranda,* evidence obtained by virtue of the *Miranda* violation will be suppressed from use at trial to prove guilt. If law enforcement officers have not created a violation of constitutional dimension, there is no occasion to apply the "fruit of the poisonous tree" exclusion of evidence doctrine of *Wong Sun v. United States,* 371 U.S. 471 (1963). The Court held that Elstad's rights under *Miranda* were violated by the interrogation in the family living room and that evidence obtained due to the violation was properly suppressed from use at his trial, but once Elstad was properly warned under *Miranda,* all evidence subsequently volunteered was properly admissible in court against him.

2. Does Elstad's confession at the police station after he made the admission that he had been involved in the burglary make sense even after he was properly warned under *Miranda*? Is it possible that he did not understand the *Miranda* warnings and the significance of confessing to the police? Was the "cat out of the bag,"[275] according to logic, and thus Elstad could not take back the admission offered in the living room? Would most people conclude that they might as well tell the whole story, since part of it was already known to the police? Did the prosecution benefit from the botched *Miranda* warning? If so, how?

3. In the *Elstad* case, assume that the officer who waited while Elstad dressed had grabbed him in a headlock and asked him if he was involved in the neighborhood burglary. What if Elstad had admitted to involvement only after the officer twisted his neck to the point where Elstad felt pain? This conduct would violate the Fifth Amendment privilege against self-incrimination. Would a *Miranda* warning, given in the living room minutes later, have cured the constitutional violation in the bedroom if Elstad admitted involvement a second time when not under physical stress? Would Elstad's station house confession following a new station house *Miranda* warning still be the product of the Fifth Amendment violation in the bedroom? Why or why not?

4. Were the objections of the dissenters clear when they contended that the Fifth Amendment requires every individual to be informed of constitutional rights upon custody? Or does the teaching of *Miranda* require that level of information? *Elstad*'s central teaching seems to be that it is possible to violate the principles of *Miranda* without violating the Fifth Amendment privilege against self-incrimination. On this premise, Elstad's constitutional rights were not violated because the officer in the bedroom and in the living room did not coerce Elstad to do anything. If Elstad's Fifth Amendment rights were violated, the derivative evidence (the confession at the police station) would have to have been excluded as well.

5. Can some interrogation precede the offering of the *Miranda* warnings? Could you imagine a case where Miranda warnings need not be given prior to official interrogation while the arrestee was in custody? Consider *Illinois v. Perkins,* 496 U.S. 292 (1990), where police placed an undercover agent, Parisi, in a jail cellblock with Perkins, who was incarcerated on aggravated robbery charges *unrelated* to the murder that Parisi was investigating. During casual jail banter, Parisi asked Perkins if he had ever killed anyone and received an affirmative answer complete with significant inculpatory details. Undercover officer Parisi did not offer any *Miranda* warning to Perkins when he asked questions inside the jail.

After careful consideration, the trial court ordered Perkins's jailhouse confession to Parisi suppressed from use at trial, and the appellate court in Illinois affirmed. The Supreme Court of the United States had a different

---

[275]The "cat out of the bag" theory mentioned in *Elstad* may be familiar to most people. The theory is that when one places a cat in a paper bag as a matter of child's play, the first time is fairly easy. On the second occasion, after the cat has escaped from the bag from the first time, placing the cat inside the bag is a much more daunting task. In Elstad's situation, once he told the officer that he had been at the burglary scene, he could never get those words back in his mouth and would think that he had sealed his fate.

opinion and reversed the Illinois courts. According to the *Perkins* Court:

> *Miranda* was not meant to protect suspects from boasting about their criminal activities in front of persons whom they believe to be their cellmates. This case is illustrative. Respondent had no reason to feel that undercover agent Parisi had any legal authority to force him to answer questions or that Parisi could affect respondent's future treatment. Respondent viewed the cellmate-agent as an equal, and showed no hint of being intimidated by the atmosphere of the jail. In recounting the details of the Stephenson murder, respondent was motivated solely by the desire to impress his fellow inmates. He spoke at his own peril. *Illinois v. Perkins,* 496 U.S. 292, 298 (1990).

Even though custodial interrogation by governmental agents occurred, the Court held that *Miranda* was not triggered because there could be no intimidation by police when the individual (Parisi) was not believed to be working for the prosecution. Should the police offer *Miranda* warnings in such a situation, since custody and interrogation exist at the same time? Do you agree with the Court that there could be no intimidation in a jail setting? Why or why not?

CASE 7.4

Miranda *Warnings: Legal Requirements under the United States Constitution*

Dickerson v. United States
Supreme Court of the United States
530 U.S. 428 (2000)

FACTS

Subsequent to the decision of *Miranda v. Arizona,* law enforcement officials were required to read to persons in custody warnings against self-incrimination and to advise concerning the availability of the right to counsel. A breach of the warning process followed by incriminating statements resulted in the voluntary statements being excluded for proof of guilt in state and federal criminal trials. Displeased with the *Miranda* warning requirement, Congress enacted 18 U.S.C. § 3501 which, in essence, made the admissibility of statements taken in violation of the *Miranda* warnings turn solely on whether they were made freely and voluntarily under traditional understandings of the words.

Dickerson, under indictment for bank robbery and allied crimes, filed a petition to suppress incriminating statements he made following a custodial, non-*Mirandized* interrogation. The trial court granted his motion and ruled that his statements would be excluded from trial; the prosecution appealed to the Court of Appeal for the Fourth Circuit, citing the requirements of 18 U.S.C. § 3501. In reversing the trial court, the Court of Appeal conceded that petitioner had not received proper *Miranda* warnings, but held that Section 3501 was satisfied because his statement was voluntary and not the product of duress. It concluded that *Miranda* was not a constitutionally required holding, and that Congress could by statute have the final say on the admissibility question by overruling the Supreme Court by statutory law.

PROCEDURAL ISSUE

Was the original decision of *Miranda v. Arizona* mandating, inter alia, warnings of the rights of silence and of counsel, of constitutional dimension required by the United States Constitution and, therefore, not susceptible of being overturned by legislation passed by the United States Congress?

HELD: YES

RATIONALE

Chief Justice Rehnquist delivered the opinion of the Court.

★ ★ ★

In *Miranda,* we noted that the advent of modern custodial police interrogation brought with it an increased concern about confessions obtained by coercion. Because custodial police interrogation, by its very nature, isolates and pressures the individual, we stated that,

> [e]ven without employing brutality, the "third degree" or [other] specific stratagems,...custodial interrogation exacts a heavy toll on individual liberty and trades on the weakness of individuals. *Id.* at 455.

We concluded that the coercion inherent in custodial interrogation blurs the line between voluntary and involuntary statements, and thus heightens the risk that an individual will not be "accorded his privilege under the Fifth Amendment...not to be compelled to incriminate himself." Accordingly, we laid down "concrete constitutional guidelines for law enforcement agencies and courts to follow." Those guidelines established that the admissibility in evidence of any statement given during custodial interrogation of a suspect would depend on whether the police provided the suspect with four warnings. These warnings (which have come to be known colloquially as "*Miranda* rights") are:

> a suspect has the right to remain silent, that anything he says can be used against him in a court of law, that he has the right to the presence of an attorney, and that if he cannot afford an attorney one will be appointed for him prior to any questioning if he so desires. *Id.* at 479.

Two years after *Miranda* was decided, Congress enacted Sec. 3501. That section provides, in relevant part:

> (a) In any criminal prosecution brought by the United States or by the District of Columbia, a confession…shall be admissible in evidence if it is voluntarily given. Before such confession is received in evidence, the trial judge shall, out of the presence of the jury, determine any issue as to voluntariness. If the trial judge determines that the confession was voluntarily made it shall be admitted in evidence and the trial judge shall permit the jury to hear relevant evidence on the issue of voluntariness and shall instruct the jury to give such weight to the confession as the jury feels it deserves under all the circumstances.
>
> (b) The trial judge in determining the issue of voluntariness shall take into consideration all the circumstances surrounding the giving of the confession, including (1) the time elapsing between arrest and arraignment of the defendant making the confession, if it was made after arrest and before arraignment, (2) whether such defendant knew the nature of the offense with which he was charged or of which he was suspected at the time of making the confession, (3) whether or not such defendant was advised or knew that he was not required to make any statement and that any such statement could be used against him, (4) whether or not such defendant had been advised prior to questioning of his right to the assistance of counsel; and (5) whether or not such defendant was without the assistance of counsel when questioned and when giving such confession.

The presence or absence of any of the above-mentioned factors to be taken into consideration by the judge need not be conclusive on the issue of voluntariness of the confession.

Given Sec. 3501's express designation of voluntariness as the touchstone of admissibility, its omission of any warning requirement, and the instruction for trial courts to consider a nonexclusive list of factors relevant to the circumstances of a confession, we agree with the Court of Appeals that Congress intended by its enactment to overrule *Miranda*.…Because of the obvious conflict between our decision in *Miranda* and Sec. 3501, we must address whether Congress has constitutional authority to thus supersede *Miranda*. If Congress has such authority, Sec. 3501's "totality of the circumstances" approach must prevail over *Miranda*'s requirement of warnings; if not, that section must yield to *Miranda*'s more specific requirements.

★ ★ ★

Congress may not legislatively supersede our decisions interpreting and applying the Constitution. This case therefore turns on whether the *Miranda* Court announced a constitutional rule or merely exercised its supervisory authority to regulate evidence in the absence of congressional direction. Recognizing this point, the Court of Appeals surveyed *Miranda* and its progeny to determine the constitutional status of the *Miranda* decision. 166 F.3d at 687–692. Relying on the fact that we have created several exceptions to *Miranda*'s warnings requirement and that we have repeatedly referred to the *Miranda* warnings as "prophylactic," *New York v. Quarles,* 467 U.S. 649, 653 (1984), and "not themselves rights protected by the Constitution," *Michigan v. Tucker,* 417 U.S. 433, 444 (1974), the Court of Appeals concluded that the protections announced in *Miranda* are not constitutionally required.

We disagree with the Court of Appeals' conclusion, although we concede that there is language in some of our opinions that supports the view taken by that court. But first and foremost of the factors on the other side—that *Miranda* is a constitutional decision—is that both *Miranda* and two of its companion cases applied the rule to proceedings in state courts—to wit, Arizona, California, and New York. Since that time, we have consistently applied *Miranda*'s rule to prosecutions arising in state courts. It is beyond dispute that we do not hold a supervisory power over the courts of the several States.

The *Miranda* opinion itself begins by stating that the Court granted certiorari

> to explore some facets of the problems…of applying the privilege against self-incrimination to in-custody interrogation, and to give concrete *constitutional guidelines for law enforcement agencies and courts to follow.* 384 U.S. at 441–442 (emphasis added).

In fact, the majority opinion is replete with statements indicating that the majority thought it was announcing a constitutional rule. Indeed, the Court's ultimate conclusion was that the unwarned confessions obtained in the four cases before the Court in *Miranda* "were obtained from the defendant under circumstances that did not meet constitutional standards for protection of the privilege."

Additional support for our conclusion that *Miranda* is constitutionally based is found in the *Miranda* Court's invitation for legislative action to protect the constitutional right against coerced self-incrimination. After discussing the "compelling pressures" inherent in custodial police interrogation, the *Miranda* Court concluded that,

> [i]n order to combat these pressures and to permit a full opportunity to exercise the privilege against self-incrimination, the accused must be adequately and effectively appraised of his rights and the exercise of those rights must be fully honored. (Citations omitted.)

★ ★ ★

The Court of Appeals also relied on the fact that we have, after our *Miranda* decision, made exceptions from its rule in cases such as *New York v. Quarles,* 467 U.S. 649 (1984), and *Harris v. New York,* 401 U.S. 222 (1971). See 166 F.3d at 672, 689–691. But we have also broadened the application of the *Miranda* doctrine in cases such as *Doyle v. Ohio,* 426 U.S. 610 (1976), and *Arizona v. Roberson,* 486 U.S. 675 (1988). These decisions illustrate the principle—not that *Miranda* is not a constitutional rule—but that no constitutional rule is immutable. No court laying down a general rule can possibly foresee the various circumstances in which counsel will seek to apply it, and the sort of modifications represented by these cases are as much a normal part of constitutional law as the original decision.

[The Court noted that it might not decide the *Miranda* case the same way as it originally did, but that the principle of *stare decisis* militates against overruling *Miranda* now. The Court noted that a deviation from an established line of cases requires a special justification, which did not exist in this case.]

★ ★ ★

We do not think there is such justification for overruling *Miranda*. *Miranda* has become embedded in routine police practice to the point where the warnings have become part of our national culture. See *Mitchell v. United States,* 526 U.S. 314, 331–332 (1999) (Scalia, J., dissenting) (stating that the fact that a rule has found "'wide acceptance

in the legal culture' " is "adequate reason not to overrule" it). While we have overruled our precedents when subsequent cases have undermined their doctrinal underpinnings,…we do not believe that this has happened to the *Miranda* decision. If anything, our subsequent cases have reduced the impact of the *Miranda* rule on legitimate law enforcement while reaffirming the decision's core ruling that unwarned statements may not be used as evidence in the prosecution's case in chief.

The disadvantage of the *Miranda* rule is that statements which may be by no means involuntary, made by a defendant who is aware of his "rights," may nonetheless be excluded and a guilty defendant go free as a result. But experience suggests that the "totality of the circumstances" test which Sec. 3501 seeks to revive is more difficult than *Miranda* for law enforcement officers to conform to, and for courts to apply in a consistent manner.…The requirement that *Miranda* warnings be given does not, of course, dispense with the voluntariness inquiry. But, as we said in *Berkemer v. McCarty,* 468 U.S. 420 (1984),

> [c]ases in which a defendant can make a colorable argument that a self-incriminating statement was "compelled" despite the fact that the law enforcement authorities adhered to the dictates of *Miranda* are rare. *Id.* at 433, n. 20.

In sum, we conclude that *Miranda* announced a constitutional rule that Congress may not supersede legislatively. Following the rule of *stare decisis,* we decline to overrule *Miranda* ourselves. The judgment of the Court of Appeals is therefore

Reversed.

Justice Scalia, with whom Justice Thomas joins, dissenting.

Those to whom judicial decisions are an unconnected series of judgments that produce either favored or disfavored results will doubtless greet today's decision as a paragon of moderation, since it declines to overrule *Miranda v. Arizona,* 384 U.S. 436 (1966). Those who understand the judicial process will appreciate that today's decision is not a reaffirmation of *Miranda,* but a radical revision of the most significant element of *Miranda:* the rationale that gives it a permanent place in our jurisprudence.

Marbury v. Madison, 1 Cranch 137 (1803), held that an Act of Congress will not be enforced by the courts if what it prescribes violates the Constitution of the United States. That was the basis on which *Miranda* was decided.

One will search today's opinion in vain, however, for a statement (surely simple enough to make) that what 18 U.S.C. Sec. 3501 prescribes—the use at trial of a voluntary confession, even when a *Miranda* warning or its equivalent has failed to be given—violates the Constitution. The reason the statement does not appear is not only (and perhaps not so much) that it would be absurd, inasmuch as Sec. 3501 excludes from trial precisely what the Constitution excludes from trial, viz., compelled confessions; but also that Justices whose votes are needed to compose today's majority are on record as believing that a violation of *Miranda* is not a violation of the Constitution. [Citations omitted.] And so, to justify today's agreed-upon result, the Court must adopt a significant *new,* if not entirely comprehensible, principle of constitutional law. As the Court chooses to describe that principle, statutes of Congress can be disregarded, not only when what they prescribe violates the Constitution, but when what they prescribe contradicts a decision of this Court that "announced a constitutional rule," ante at 7. As I shall discuss in some detail, the only thing that can possibly mean in the context of this case is that this Court has the power, not merely to apply the Constitution but to expand it, imposing what it regards as useful "prophylactic" restrictions upon Congress and the States. That is an immense and frightening antidemocratic power, and it does not exist.

It takes only a small step to bring today's opinion out of the realm of power-judging and into the mainstream of legal reasoning: the Court need only go beyond its carefully couched iterations that "*Miranda* is a constitutional decision," ante at 438, that "*Miranda* is constitutionally based," ante at 440, that *Miranda* has "constitutional underpinnings," ante at 440, n. 5, and come out and say quite clearly: "We reaffirm today that custodial interrogation that is not preceded by *Miranda* warnings or their equivalent violates the Constitution of the United States." It cannot say that, because a majority of the Court does not believe it. The Court therefore acts in plain violation of the Constitution when it denies effect to this Act of Congress.

COMMENTS, NOTES, AND QUESTIONS

1. If a decision of the Supreme Court has as its basis the interpretation of the Constitution, the Congress cannot tell the Court that a different meaning must be used. The Supreme Court is the final arbiter of what the Constitution means and what it may require. Do the arguments offered by the majority convince you that this case was of constitutional dimension? At first blush, since it in-

volved a state criminal procedure practice and the Court does not have any supervisory powers over state courts, the original case must have been of constitutional dimension or it would not have been decided as it was.

2. Is the *Dickerson* case an example of a situation in which the Court majority did not want to disturb fairly settled practice (*Miranda* warnings) by plunging into uncharted legal waters? As Justice Rehnquist noted in the majority opinion:

> Whether or not we would agree with *Miranda*'s reasoning and its resulting rule were we addressing the issue in the first instance, the principles of *stare decisis* weigh heavily against overruling it now. See, *e.g., Rhode Island v. Innis,* 446 U.S. 291, 304 (1980) (Burger, C.J., concurring in judgment) ("The meaning of *Miranda* has become reasonably clear and law enforcement practices have adjusted to its strictures; I would neither overrule *Miranda,* disparage it, nor extend it at this late date"). *Dickerson,* 530 U.S. 428, 543.

Law enforcement agencies and personnel have become comfortable with the requirements of *Miranda* warnings, and the Court may not have wanted to change the standard on interrogation to a general voluntariness standard that would breed future litigation.

Where in the Constitution is the result in *Miranda v. Arizona* suggested or dictated? Justice Scalia, in his dissent in *Dickerson,* raises the issue concerning the existence of constitutional authority for requiring *Miranda* warnings. If such warnings are not constitutionally dictated, presumably Congress may legislate for federal courts and regulate the admission of evidence in the federal judicial system. However, acts of Congress will not be enforced by the Court if the act and what it requires is deemed to conflict with the United States Constitution. As a general proposition of law, if the result of a federal court decision is not mandated by the Constitution, Congress can override nonconstitutional decisions of the Court. What is the best argument that the original *Miranda* decision was required to be decided the way it was by the Constitution? Justice Scalia noted, "One will search today's opinion in vain, however, for a statement (surely simple enough to make) that what 18 U.S.C. § 3501 [the statute attempting to overrule *Miranda*] prescribes—the use at trial of a voluntary confession, even when a *Miranda* warning or its equivalent has failed to be given—violates the Constitution." Does he have a point? Can he successfully be refuted? What arguments would you offer?

Confession and the Privilege against Self-Incrimination

Chapter Outline

Key Terms

Adverse prosecutorial comment
Blood alcohol tests
Due Process Clause of Fourteenth Amendment
Fifth Amendment privilege
Impeachment use of confession
Involuntary confession
Nontestimonial evidence
Physical compulsion

Right assertable against government
Testimonial evidence
Totality of the circumstances test
Transactional immunity
Use immunity
Voluntary confession
Waiver of privilege

1. INTRODUCTION TO THE FIFTH AMENDMENT PRIVILEGE

Amendment Five

No person shall be…compelled in any criminal case to be a witness against himself…

The Fifth Amendment provides a guarantee that a person shall not have to offer assistance in making a conviction by becoming a witness against him- or herself, but case law has determined that an individual may have to offer nontestimonial evidence that may have the effect of assisting the government in the case against that individual. Although originally not intended to limit the states, the Fifth Amendment has been held to apply to state criminal practice through the Due Process Clause of the Fourteenth Amendment. The Fifth Amendment helps assure reliability and truthfulness of evidence, since compelled evidence may be based on coercion and lack of free will and be motivated to remove or end coercion or torture. Since the amendment guarantees that a person shall not have to self-incriminate, the prohibition against use of coerced evidence helps to enforce that right not to be overreached into giving damaging evidence. Where testimonial evidence has been obtained in violation of the Fifth Amendment, it will be excluded from use at trial, a fact that removes any police incentive to obtain such evidence in violation of the Constitution. In addition to removing physical or psychological motivations to coerce a defendant, the Fifth Amendment forces the prosecution to obtain damaging evidence from sources external to the defendant in order to obtain a conviction.

2. ORIGINAL INTENT AND THE FIFTH AMENDMENT

As originally contemplated by the Framers of the Bill of Rights, the Fifth Amendment privilege against self-incrimination[276] allowed a person to refuse to divulge any evidence that could assist the federal government in prosecuting that individual. It was not clear whether the privilege merely prevented words from being extracted from the individual or whether other means of obtaining information of an incriminating nature might be included within the protection. Justice Thomas suggested that the Fifth Amendment may have originally possessed a broader meaning than that currently in vogue with the Supreme Court. In his concurring opinion in *United States v. Hubbell,* he noted:

> The Fifth Amendment provides that "[n]o person…shall be compelled in any criminal case to be a witness against himself." The key word at issue in this case is "witness." The Court's opinion, relying on prior cases, essentially defines "witness" as a person who provides testimony, and thus restricts the Fifth Amendment's ban to only those communications "that are 'testimonial' in character." Ante at 34. None of this Court's cases, however, has undertaken an analysis of the meaning of the term at the time of the founding. A review of that period reveals substantial support for the view that the term "witness" meant a person who gives or furnishes evidence, a broader meaning than that which our case law currently ascribes to the term. 530 U.S. 27, 49–50 (2000).

---

[276]Amendment Five: "*No person… shall be compelled in any criminal case to be a witness against himself,* nor be deprived of life, liberty, or property, without due process of law; nor shall private property be taken for public use, without just compensation" (emphasis added).

Although, according to Justice Thomas, the Framers of the Fifth Amendment may have intended to include a prohibition against general production of incriminating evidence, case law and recent precedent have restricted the privilege to cover only testimonial evidence, as a general rule. Since the Fifth Amendment originally applied only against the federal government, the protection against self-incrimination had application only when the federal government attempted to require an individual to give incriminating information. As originally conceived, the Fifth Amendment failed to offer any protection to a person when a state official requested documentary or physical evidence of an incriminating nature. Prior to a 1964 case,[277] protection from self-incrimination in state courts depended upon state constitutional law, state statutory law, and state judicial interpretations of that law and was completely independent of federal law.

3. PRIVILEGE AGAINST SELF-INCRIMINATION: EXCLUDABLE EVIDENCE

Evidence obtained in violation of the Fifth Amendment is generally excluded from affirmative use in criminal trials. Since a person need not serve as a "witness against himself," judicial construction illuminating and explaining the phrase proves crucial. The privilege provides protection for an accused from being required to actually testify against him- or herself as a witness or otherwise give evidence that is testimonial or communicative in nature. According to the Court in *Doe v. United States:*

> [I]n order to be testimonial, an accused's communication must itself, explicitly or implicitly, relate a factual assertion or disclose information. Only then is a person compelled to be a "witness" against himself. *Doe v. United States,* 487 U.S. 201, 210 (1988).

A state violates the privilege against self-incrimination when it obtains evidence against a defendant through efforts that force the defendant to divulge adverse information. The privilege is violated where a state gains evidence by

> the cruel, simple expedient of compelling it from his own mouth....In sum, the privilege is fulfilled only when the person is guaranteed the right "to remain silent unless he chooses to speak in the unfettered exercise of his own will." *Miranda v. Arizona,* 384 U.S. 436, 460 (1966).

And in *Culombe v. Connecticut,* the Court suggested the proper inquiry for determining the voluntariness of a confession:

> Is the confession the product of an essentially free and unconstrained choice by its maker? If it is, if he has willed to confess, it may be used against him. If it is not, if his will has been overborne and his capacity for self-determination critically impaired, the use of his confession offends due process. 367 U.S. 568, 602 (1961).

---

[277]See *Malloy v. Hogan,* 378 U.S. 1 (1964), where the Court held that the Fifth Amendment privilege against self-incrimination should be applied to state criminal prosecutions through the Due Process Clause of the Fourteenth Amendment.

The essence of the privilege is that if a person wishes to testify, it should be due to the personal decision of the defendant, freely made and not motivated by mental or physical coercion on behalf of the government. There is a requirement that a government "which proposes to convict and punish an individual produce the evidence against him by the independent labor of its officers"[278] rather than devise a method of extracting the appropriate evidence personally from a defendant by overreaching his or her mind and will.

4. THE FOURTEENTH AMENDMENT ALTERATIONS

Following the Civil War, the United States adopted the Fourteenth Amendment (1868), which, among other things, required that the states grant procedural due process to all persons.[279] In a nutshell, procedural due process requires that the state governments treat all individuals with fundamental fairness. The Framers of this Amendment did not envision that it might encompass most of the guarantees of the first eight amendments. Similarly, the precise extent of fundamental fairness included in due process was not delineated in the amendment, but the concept has been amplified and described more fully by court decisions subsequent to its adoption.

5. REQUIRED PRODUCTION OF NONTESTIMONIAL EVIDENCE AND THE FIFTH AMENDMENT

While involuntary confessions should not be admitted in court,[280] the government may compel the production of other types of evidence that, though not testimonial, helps the prosecution gain convictions. The privilege against self-incrimination protects a defendant from being compelled to testify against him- or herself or otherwise provide the prosecution with evidence of a testimonial or communicative nature, but not from being compelled by the state to produce real or physical evidence. To be testimonial, the communication must, explicitly or implicitly, relate a factual assertion or disclose similar information.

The Fifth Amendment does not insulate an individual from being forced to divulge business records when the person is a mere custodian. In *Bellis v. United States*,[281] the Court noted:

---

[278]*Culombe v. Connecticut*, 367 U.S. 568, 581–582 (1961).

[279]Amendment Fourteen: "...nor shall any State *deprive any person of life, liberty, or property, without due process of law*; nor deny to any person within its jurisdiction the equal protection of the laws" (emphasis added).

[280]In *Arizona v. Fulminante*, 499 U.S. 279 (1991), where an involuntary confession had been introduced against Fulminante, the Court held that a coerced confession admitted in court would not automatically result in a reversal and new trial. The resolution of a case involving a coerced confession should turn on an evaluation of the "harmless error" standard that would reverse a conviction unless it could be said beyond a reasonable doubt that the outcome would not be different without the admission of the coerced confession. The Court reversed Fulminante's conviction. See also *Chapman v. California*, 386 U.S. 18 (1967), where the Court rejected the position "that all federal constitutional errors in the course of a criminal trial require reversal. We held that the Fifth Amendment violation of prosecutorial comment upon the defendant's failure to testify would not require reversal of the conviction if the State could show 'beyond a reasonable doubt that the error complained of did not contribute to the verdict obtained.'" 386 U.S. at 24.

[281]417 U.S. 85 (1974).

It has long been established, of course, that the Fifth Amendment privilege against compulsory self-incrimination protects an individual from compelled production of his personal papers and effects as well as compelled oral testimony. In *Boyd v. United States,* 116 U.S. 616 (1886), we held that "any forcible and compulsory extortion of a man's own testimony or of his private papers to be used as evidence to convict him of crime" would violate the Fifth Amendment privilege. *Id.* at 630; see also *id.* at 633–635; *Wilson v. United States,* 221 U.S. 361, 377 (1911).

However, in *Bellis,* the custodian of the records for a law firm could not successfully invoke a personal Fifth Amendment privilege against incrimination in common law firm records, since they were not his personal papers but collective papers of the firm and had to be divulged when requested by a federal grand jury.

In *Schmerber v. California,*[282] the Court upheld the introduction of evidence of intoxication taken from a suspected alcohol-impaired driver by a doctor at the request of a police officer (see Case 8.1). The motorist contended that the use of his blood violated his Fifth Amendment privilege against self-incrimination because it effectively made him a witness against himself, but the Court rejected that argument. According to the Court, the Fifth Amendment provides protection to an accused "only from being compelled to testify against himself, or otherwise provide the State with evidence of a testimonial or communicative nature." According to *Schmerber:*

> [B]oth federal and state courts have usually held that it [Fifth Amendment privilege against self-incrimination] offers no protection against compulsion to submit to fingerprinting, photographing, or measurements, to write or speak for identification, to appear in court, to stand, to assume a stance, to walk, or to make a particular gesture. The distinction which has emerged, often expressed in different ways, is that the privilege is a bar against compelling "communications" or "testimony," but that compulsion which makes a suspect or accused the source of "real or physical evidence" does not violate it. *Schmerber v. California,* 384 U.S. at 764 (1966).

Justice Stevens noted in *United States v. Hubbell* that Justice Holmes had concluded that there existed a significant difference between using duress to compel testimony from a witness and requiring that person to engage in activity that could lead to incrimination.[283] In essence, the *Schmerber* Court held that mere physical evidence, though it may communicate information, is not considered testimonial and is not prohibited under the Fifth Amendment.

The *Schmerber* Court was on solid ground with an earlier case, *Holt v. United States,*[284] where Justice Holmes dismissed an argument that the Fifth Amendment privilege against self-incrimination would be violated by requiring a defendant to put on an article of clothing for identification purposes. Justice Holmes noted that

> the prohibition of compelling a man in a criminal court to be witness against himself is a prohibition of the use of physical or moral compulsion to extort communications from him, not an exclusion of his body as evidence when it may be material. 218 U.S. at 252.

[282]384 U.S. 757 (1966).
[283]530 U.S. 27, 35–36 (2000).
[284]218 U.S. 245 (1910).

The wearing of clothing, while it could harm a defendant's case, was not considered "testimonial" and thus did not constitute a violation of the Fifth Amendment.

In a case in which the legal theory was consistent with *Schmerber,* the Supreme Court held that the Fifth Amendment did not offer protection to a grand jury witness who had been ordered to give a voice sample for comparison purposes. In *United States v. Dionisio,*[285] a trial court mandated that Dionisio make a voice recording for use by the prosecutor in a grand jury proceeding. Dionisio refused on the ground, among others, that to offer a sample of his voice would violate his Fifth Amendment privilege against self-incrimination because the sample might be used against him in a criminal prosecution. The *Dionisio* Court rejected his Fifth Amendment argument with the conclusion that prior cases have uniformly rejected the contention that the compelled display of identifiable physical characteristics infringes on the privilege against compelled testimonial self-incrimination.

Consistent with case law, the prosecution may force a person to exhibit his or her body and the extent of his or her motor skills while under suspicion for driving under the influence of alcohol. In *Pennsylvania v. Muniz,*[286] police videotaped a motorist attempting to perform various diagnostic tests for intoxication and later used the video in court in an attempt to demonstrate impairment. The Court approved the introduction of portions of the recording that revealed only the physical manner in which his speech was constructed and demonstrated the defendant's lack of muscular coordination without revealing any testimonial components of those responses.

6. ASSERTION OF THE PRIVILEGE AGAINST SELF-INCRIMINATION

The privilege against self-incrimination has been determined to benefit only real human beings and does not apply to corporations or other artificial business entities. Where a witness offers testimony that would tend to incriminate, he or she may not retroactively assert the privilege so as to render the previously offered testimony useless; the privilege has been deemed to have been waived by conduct. The privilege is personal to the person who asserts it, and it generally cannot be asserted by one person on behalf of another. An individual who is asked or has been subpoenaed to give evidence against another individual may not invoke the first individual's Fifth Amendment privilege to prevent giving evidence against the other person. A defendant who is awaiting sentencing may assert the privilege if called to testify against a second individual, since that evidence might adversely affect the sentence ultimately imposed.[287] Because the Fifth Amendment does not apply outside of the United States, as a general rule, an individual may not successfully invoke the privilege not to testify when that evidence might tend to incriminate the individual solely in a foreign nation.[288]

---

[285] 410 U.S. 1 (1973).
[286] 496 U.S. 582 (1990).
[287] *Estelle v. Smith,* 451 U.S. 454, 463 (1981).
[288] *United States v. Balsys,* 524 U.S. 666 (1998).

7. PRIVILEGE AGAINST SELF-INCRIMINATION ASSERTABLE IN A VARIETY OF CONTEXTS

While the privilege against self-incrimination is often viewed as being available only at a criminal trial, the application of the privilege is not so limited, and its assertion may properly occur in a variety of contexts. The privilege may be asserted anytime a police officer asks questions of an individual, whether or not that person is in custody. A person may refuse to testify on Fifth Amendment grounds when called as a witness in a grand jury proceeding where the answers might tend to incriminate the witness. Since legislative bodies have power to compel witness attendance, if an individual is asked a question for which the answer might be incriminating, refusal under the Fifth Amendment has been held to be appropriate. In essence, anytime a government or its agents demand or request that an individual offer evidence of a testimonial nature that might either directly incriminate or indirectly lead to other evidence that would incriminate, any person may refuse to testify on Fifth Amendment grounds.[289]

8. PROSECUTION COMMENT ON DEFENDANT'S USE OF FIFTH AMENDMENT

When a defendant does not offer evidence but probably has such knowledge, he or she may be relying on the Fifth Amendment privilege. A failure to explain evidence or to personally present a defense cannot be rendered especially costly by allowing a prosecutor to adversely comment on the failure of the defendant to take the witness stand. To allow a prosecutor to comment on a defendant's use of the Fifth Amendment would render the privilege against self-incrimination somewhat illusory. In *Griffin v. California*,[290] the defendant chose not to testify in his capital murder trial, and the judge instructed the jury not to draw any inference of guilt or innocence from this failure. The prosecutor reminded the jury that the defendant knew things that he was not telling the jury and invited the jury to consider the failure to testify against the defendant. The Supreme Court reversed the conviction with the observation that the Fifth Amendment forbids adverse comment by the prosecution on the accused's silence and instructions from the judge concerning the silence of the accused that indicate that silence may be evidence of guilt.

9. AN EQUIVALENT SUBSTITUTE FOR THE FIFTH AMENDMENT PRIVILEGE: IMMUNITY

Where a prosecutor determines that the importance of obtaining evidence or testimony to assist in one prosecution outweighs the loss that accrues to society when a different guilty party goes free, a grant of immunity to that individual may be appropriate. In such a case, the prosecution may require a person to give evidence that might tend to convict or to be a link in a chain of evidence that might result in a successful prosecution. In order to successfully require an individual to offer evidence that might provide a link toward a conviction, the prosecution must offer

---

[289]If either use immunity or transactional immunity has been accorded to the witness at a grand jury session, legislative hearing, or similar proceeding, no Fifth Amendment privilege remains, and the witness must testify in response to questions.
[290]380 U.S. 609 (1965).

some type of immunity. The level or scope of the immunity must be coextensive with the protections offered by the privilege against self-incrimination. As a general rule, use immunity is the minimal level of immunity that replaces the same level of protection originally offered by the Fifth Amendment's privilege against self-incrimination. As Chief Justice Rehnquist noted in *Braswell v. United States,* "Testimony obtained pursuant to a grant of statutory use immunity may be used neither directly nor derivatively."[291] Use immunity means that the prosecution will not take evidence offered by a witness or defendant and use it affirmatively against the individual and will not use the evidence as a link in a chain to discover additional evidence related to the original evidence. Since this level of immunity merely replaces the guarantee under the Fifth Amendment with an equal level of protection, once it is given, the prosecution may require the witness to answer questions that could otherwise be barred by the assertion of the privilege against self-incrimination.[292]

10. WAIVER OF THE FIFTH AMENDMENT PRIVILEGE

Like most constitutional rights, the Fifth Amendment privilege against self-incrimination is a waivable right, and a waiver is effective provided it is properly accomplished. The most obvious waiver of the Fifth Amendment privilege occurs in the context of the *Miranda* warning where the individual either orally or in writing agrees to talk with police and understands that what he or she says may be used in a court of law. A defendant may waive the privilege by voluntarily taking the witness stand at the trial, where the witness testifies fully and is subject to cross-examination.[293] A waiver of the Fifth Amendment privilege may occur where a defendant seeks out a police officer and freely offers a confession to criminal activity, provided the defendant's waiver has been made voluntarily, knowingly, and intelligently.[294]

The concept that a waiver of the Fifth Amendment privilege must have been made "voluntarily, knowingly, and intelligently" does not mean that a defendant understands every legal nuance and effect of the decision to waive the privilege. For example, in *Connecticut v. Barrett,* the arrestee indicated a willingness to talk about his crimes with police but did not want to make any written statement.[295] According to the Supreme Court, the *Barrett* trial court held that the arrestee's decision was a voluntary waiver of constitutional protections and that there was no evidence of threats, trickery, or other overreaching on the part of police. Waiver will generally be a question of fact to be resolved during pretrial legal proceedings, subject to appeal following conviction.

In determining whether a defendant has properly waived the Fifth Amendment privilege against self-incrimination and has voluntarily given a confession, courts often evaluate the voluntariness of the statement by the use of a test that considers

---

[291]487 U.S. 99, 117 (1988).
[292]See *Kastigar v. United States,* 406 U.S. 441 (1972).
[293]*Powell v. Texas,* 492 U.S. 680, 684 (1989).
[294]See *Colorado v. Spring,* 479 U.S. 564, 572 (1987).
[295]479 U.S. 523, 527 (1987).

the totality of the circumstances.[296] When deciding the admissibility of a confession, courts often consider the subject's age, education, and level of sobriety; the circumstances of the *Miranda* warning; the subject's prior experience with police and the criminal justice system; the length and circumstances of any interrogation; threats made by officials, if any; promises made; and any other factors that could produce an involuntary confession.[297]

In one case involving an allegation of the use of an involuntary confession, the defendant had been charged with assault of his minor child. According to police, following *Miranda* warnings, the defendant waived his Fifth Amendment privilege against self-incrimination and admitted to committing the assault. As part of his argument against use of his confession, he contended that his statements had been taken involuntarily, since at the time they were given he was suffering from the effects of lack of sleep and was not thinking clearly due to the influence of recent marijuana use. The trial court had admitted the confession into evidence following a pretrial hearing. According to the reviewing court, the defendant's age and education did not contribute to an involuntary confession, and a psychological evaluation demonstrated a normal understanding of social situations. The court rejected the defendant's contention of involuntariness even though he alleged that he was unable to understand his *Miranda* rights because he was of low-average intelligence and had completed only six years of formal education. In negating one of the defendant's contentions, a prosecution expert offered evidence that the defendant's cognitive functioning was not significantly impaired by either marijuana or lack of sleep. In support of a voluntary waiver, the court noted that the defendant had prior criminal justice experience, since he had been arrested on other occasions and seemed to understand what he faced in the present situation. The reviewing court evaluated the manner of the interrogation and concluded that the length, tactics, and methods employed by the police were not likely to produce and did not produce an involuntary confession. According to the appellate court, giving due consideration to all the factors, the trial court was correct in allowing it to be admitted against the defendant.[298] While each case is determined on its unique fact pattern, most courts consider all relevant information under a totality of the circumstances test to determine whether a defendant's Fifth Amendment right not to self-incriminate has been violated.

Waiver of the Fifth Amendment privilege against self-incrimination in one context may not constitute a waiver of the privilege for all jurisdictions and for all potential causes of action. In a Minnesota case, a witness pled guilty to murder and testified against another defendant, waiving her Fifth Amendment privilege at the trial. When the state wanted her to testify against a different defendant in the same criminal case, she refused, and the trial court held her in contempt of court. The judge took the position that the earlier testimony indicated a waiver of her privilege concerning the case and her involvement in it. The refusing witness feared a possibility of a federal prosecution and based her refusal to testify on the ground that she

---

[296]*Montana v. Loh,* 275 Mont. 460, 475; 914 P.2d 592, 601 (1996).
[297]*Montana v. Campbell,* 278 Mont. 236; 924 P.2d 1304, 1307, 1308 (1996).
[298]*Montana v. Hoffman,* 314 Mont. 155, 162, 163; 64 P.3d 1013, 1018 (2003).

had remaining concerns about criminal liability. The court of appeal agreed that where the courts of one jurisdiction attempt to compel testimony from a witness that could be used by a different jurisdiction in a subsequent proceeding, the witness possesses a Fifth Amendment privilege that can be asserted, even if it has been waived in an earlier proceeding.[299]

11. CONFESSION PRACTICE PRIOR TO THE WARREN COURT REVOLUTION

In an old case involving state racial discrimination and brutality, *Brown v. Mississippi,*[300] the Court determined that brutal beatings directed and conducted by a state cannot be used to coerce a confession from a defendant without violating the defendant's right to due process of law under the Fourteenth Amendment (see Case 8.2). In *Brown,* the suspects were subjected to extensive physical torture, including hanging and repeated whipping, to the point that they made involuntary confessions to law enforcement officials. Since the free will of the defendants had been broken by torture, there were two reasons not to admit their confessions. First of all, no one could be sure that the confessions were true and accurate, since the defendants had been coerced into offering them; second, fundamental fairness prohibited the use of the confessions due to the methods used to extract them. The lesson of *Brown* suggested that where the defendant's free exercise of discretion in giving a confession has been eliminated, the resulting confession, whether truthful or not, cannot be used against the defendant. In a state court, any confession extracted from a defendant, even if truthful, should not be introduced in evidence, since the process of extraction failed to comport with the fundamental fairness required under due process of law. While *Brown* was not decided on Fifth Amendment grounds because the amendment had not then been deemed to apply to state government actions, the basis for excluding the use of coerced confessions can be traced to the rationale behind the privilege against self-incrimination.

Demonstrative of the due process principle prohibiting the use of involuntary confessions is the case of *Payne v. Arkansas,* 356 U.S. 560 (1958), where a retarded man had been convicted in an Arkansas state court of first-degree murder. Over his objection at his trial, the prosecution introduced a confession, which the defendant alleged had been improperly taken. He had been arrested and placed in a cell for two days without access to friends, family, or legal counsel; he had been given very little food during a forty-hour period; and a mob had gathered outside the jail. The defendant confessed after being told that the chief of police would try to keep the mob from coming and getting him if he would tell the police the whole story. Several police officers entered the room with a court reporter, and several local businessmen were present when the defendant gave his confession.

According to the *Payne* Court, the use in a state criminal trial of a defendant's confession obtained by coercion, whether physical or mental, has been forbidden under decisions interpreting the Fourteenth Amendment. The confession was

---

[299]See *In re Contempt of Ecklund,* 636 N.W.2d 585, 589, 590 (2001). For a case with the same outcome based on a similar legal rationale, see also *Martin v. Flanagan,* 259 Conn. 487; 789 A.2d 979 (2001).
[300]297 U.S. 278 (1936).

motivated by the defendant's fear that a mob might end his life and that law enforcement might do little or nothing to prevent it unless he cooperated by offering an acceptable confession. The Court found that torture of either the mind or body can affect free will, since the will is influenced as much by fear as by force. Upon a finding of involuntariness of the confession, the Supreme Court reversed the conviction on due process grounds.

During the years in which the Court adjudicated coerced confession cases prior to determining that the self-incrimination clause of the Fifth Amendment applied to the states, due process proved to be the constitutional vehicle of choice. As court membership changed over the years and as novel constitutional changes became accepted, the court moved toward incorporating various parts of the Bill of Rights into the Due Process Clause of the Fourteenth Amendment. In various cases, arguments were made that suggested that due process must include an exclusion of evidence if illegally seized, a prohibition against double jeopardy, and a right to a grand jury indictment in a serious state case, among others. Some rights arguably might be essential to criminal justice, while others might be desirable but not absolutely essential. Over the years, the Court evaluated those rights and incorporated most, though not all, of the rights from the first eight amendments into the Fourteenth Amendment and made them applicable to the states.

12. EVOLUTION OF INTERROGATION AND CONFESSION UNDER THE WARREN COURT

Following *Brown* and *Payne*, the Court decided *Malloy v. Hogan*,[301] where it held that the privilege against self-incrimination contained within the Fifth Amendment should provide protection against a state that was seeking to force an individual to give criminal evidence against himself. In *Malloy*, the previously convicted defendant had been called to testify before a referee concerning his gambling and other activities, which he refused to do on grounds that the answers might tend to incriminate him. Since the Fifth Amendment offered him no protection, at that time, he was committed to jail until he would agree to testify. Following the denial of his state court application for a writ of habeas corpus, the case eventually reached the Supreme Court. According to the holding of the *Malloy* Court, "[T]he Fourteenth Amendment guaranteed the petitioner the protection of the Fifth Amendment's privilege against self-incrimination."[302] The Due Process Clause operated as if the federal Fifth Amendment privilege against self-incrimination had been written within the words "due process."

The *Malloy* Court determined that in enforcing the concept of due process in state cases, the Fifth Amendment privilege against self-incrimination must be read as part and parcel of the Fourteenth Amendment's guarantee of due process. Therefore, in meeting the constitutional requirement of voluntariness under a "totality of the circumstances" test, an admissible confession must be the result of the defendant's free and voluntary decision, unfettered by coercion, whether physical or mental.

---

[301]378 U.S. 1 (1964).
[302]*Malloy* at 3.

Factors that courts consider in making a determination concerning whether a particular confession has been properly offered involve the treatment of the individual by law enforcement officials. The length of the time of interrogation and manner of questioning, including rest periods for food, personal essentials, and sleep, are considered in deciding a question of the voluntariness of a confession. The number of interrogators who have repeatedly "worked" on the defendant in an effort to "whipsaw" him or her into an untenable position must also be weighed. Age, level of education, intelligence, and emotional health are additional elements that must be considered in specific cases to determine whether a particular individual has made a proper confession.

13. MODERN EVOLUTION OF INTERROGATION AND CONFESSION

The process of defining the scope of the privilege against self-incrimination involved numerous court cases and did not proceed in a completely orderly manner. Clearly, any concept of due process must include a prohibition of physical and mental torture designed to break a person's will to produce a coerced confession. In a case in which the plaintiff claimed a violation of civil rights based on an alleged Fifth Amendment violation, the Court determined that where an officer, in the absence of *Miranda* warnings, was merely asking questions of a severely injured suspect while he was receiving hospital treatment, such conduct did not constitute a violation of the Fifth Amendment. The suspect was never prosecuted, and his incriminating statements were never used against him. There was no evidence that the officer was trying to coerce the suspect. According to the Court, the suspect "was no more compelled to be a witness against himself than an immunized witness is forced to testify on pain of contempt."[303] In addition, jurisprudence has determined that the privilege against self-incrimination is not violated by the use of many traditional identification procedures, such as being forced to stand in a lineup, to wear a particular piece of clothing, to utter the words allegedly spoken by the criminal, to make a voice recording, and to give blood, hair, or fingernail samples.[304] Although such identification procedures may communicate potentially incriminating evidence, courts have determined that the processes are not communicative in a testimonial nature and, therefore, are not regulated or prohibited by the Fifth Amendment privilege.

14. PERSONAL MOTIVATIONS FOR CONFESSION IRRELEVANT

Under current interpretation, if an arrestee decides to make a confession, internal personal motivations are generally not factors to take into consideration where the law enforcement personnel have not improperly created the stimulus to confess. In *Colorado v. Connelly*,[305] the defendant approached a police officer and confessed to

---

[303]*Chavez v. Martinez,* 538 U.S. 760 (2003).
[304]See, generally, *Schmerber v. California,* 384 U.S. 757 (1966).
[305]479 U.S. 157 (1986).

a homicide (see Case 8.4). While the confession appeared to be the result of a personal decision, an existing mental illness created the motivation to confess.[306] According to the defendant's doctor, the mental disease produced "voices" that told the defendant either to make a confession or to commit suicide. Connelly may not have possessed an entirely free will whether or not to make a confession and may have confessed due to personal internal motivations. Since the police dealt with him properly, warned him under *Miranda,* and did not otherwise motivate him to offer a confession, whatever personal motivation Connelly may have possessed had no effect on police conduct. *Connelly* stands for the proposition that so long as police do not illegally coerce physically or otherwise mentally motivate an individual to confess, the confession will not be excludable under grounds of a Fifth Amendment violation.

15. INVOLUNTARY CONFESSION NOT AVAILABLE FOR PROOF OF GUILT

An involuntary confession is not admissible against a defendant in a state court by virtue of the Due Process Clause of the Fourteenth Amendment.[307] Similarly, an involuntary confession should be excluded from a federal criminal trial based on the Fifth Amendment's Due Process Clause. To determine whether a confession has been voluntarily offered or involuntarily extracted, courts must examine the totality of the circumstances.[308] A trial court might consider the physical condition under which an arrestee has been held; the age of the defendant; whether the defendant has seen friends or family; and whether the arrestee consulted with an attorney and received sufficient sleep, food, water, and access to toilet facilities. It would be essential to determine whether threats of harm have been made and whether physical harm has occurred to the arrestee. Upon the evaluation of the factors under the totality of the circumstances test, a trial judge should render a ruling concerning the admissibility of the confession.

If the evidence shows that a confession has been made freely, voluntarily, and without duress, compulsion, or coercion, it should be admitted against the defendant. Where a court makes a determination that a confession has been involuntarily taken, the court should refuse to allow the introduction of that confession in evidence. From an appellate perspective, once an involuntary confession has been admitted for consideration as evidence in a trial court, analysis under the harmless error rule determines the resolution of the appeal. Under this standard, if an appellate court determines that the use of the involuntary confession had no effect on the

---

[306]When Connelly spoke with police, he denied any drug use or that he had been drinking. Connelly did mention that in the past he had been a mental patient in several mental hospitals. Connelly told police that his conscience had been bothering him following the homicide.

[307]See *Arizona v. Fulminante,* 499 U.S. 279 (1991).

[308]In making a determination under the totality of the circumstances test, Justice Stewart in *Schneckloth v. Bustamonte,* 412 U.S. 218, 226 (1973), offered some suggestions of factors the Court has considered in past cases. "Some of the factors taken into account have included the youth of the accused, *e.g., Haley v. Ohio,* 332 U.S. 596; his lack of education, *e.g., Payne v. Arkansas,* 356 U.S. 560; or his low intelligence, *e.g., Fikes v. Alabama,* 352 U.S. 191; the lack of any advice to the accused of his constitutional rights, *e.g., Davis v. North Carolina,* 384 U.S. 737; the length of detention, *e.g., Chambers v. Florida* [309 U.S. 227]; the repeated and prolonged nature of the questioning, *e.g., Ashcraft v. Tennessee,* 322 U.S. 143; and the use of physical punishment such as the deprivation of food or sleep, *e.g., Reck v. Pate,* 367 U.S. 433.

outcome of the case, the resulting conviction will not be disturbed. On the other hand, if an appellate court cannot say that, beyond a reasonable doubt, the admission of the involuntary confession had no effect on the outcome, then the criminal case should be reversed.[309]

In *Arizona v. Fulminante,* 499 U.S. 279 (1991), the prosecution used the defendant's confession against him in a murder prosecution (see Case 8.3). The defendant was serving time in a federal prison but was having a rough time of it because it was rumored among the other prisoners that he was a child murderer. Another federal prisoner, working with police, offered to protect Fulminante if he could hear the whole story about the killing of the child. In exchange for security within prison, Fulminante confessed to the government's agent and subsequently to the government agent's wife. The state prosecutor used the prison confession against Fulminante in a successful state murder prosecution. On appeal, the Supreme Court reversed the conviction since the coerced confession should not have been introduced in court because the manner in which it was obtained violated the Due Process Clause of the Fourteenth Amendment, and the Court held that the harmless error standard had not been met.

16. INVOLUNTARY CONFESSION NOT AVAILABLE FOR IMPEACHMENT

An involuntary confession, while illegally obtained, cannot be used for impeachment purposes. Assume that a defendant has given a confession that has been determined to have been obtained by virtue of physical or mental coercion. There is no way to discern whether the coerced confession possessed any reliability or truth. In addition, there is also a desire that the police must obey the law while enforcing the law, and that our society and culture might well be undermined as much from illegal police investigatory tools as from criminals themselves.[310] We might exclude an illegally obtained confession from the case in chief of the prosecution on federal constitutional grounds, but we also would have to exclude it from use as impeachment evidence because we have no way of determining its truthfulness. A confession obtained in violation of the Constitution stands on different grounds than one taken after a defective *Miranda* warning, since the confession following *Miranda* may well be truthful but inadmissible only on *Miranda* grounds.

17. VIOLATION OF *MIRANDA:* USE OF CONFESSION FOR IMPEACHMENT PURPOSES

The Fifth Amendment privilege against self-incrimination cannot be fully understood without reference to the landmark case, *Miranda v. Arizona.*[311] The Court in *Miranda* held that anytime a person is in law enforcement custody and an officer intends to conduct any interrogation, the arrestee must be told of the right to speak with counsel prior to questioning, that there exists no requirement that the

---

[309]*Arizona v. Fulminante,* 499 U.S. 279 (1991).
[310]See *Blackburn v. Alabama,* 361 U.S. 199, 206 (1960).
[311]394 U.S. 436 (1966).

individual speak with the officer, and that anything the person does say may be used against him or her in a court of law. If the dictates of *Miranda* are not met, the evidence thereby obtained will not be admissible in court for purposes of proving guilt. The exclusion is virtually absolute despite the strong chance that any statement offered was given without violation of the Fifth Amendment privilege against self-incrimination. As the *Miranda* Court noted, the warnings were required and a waiver of rights necessary as a prerequisite to the admission of any statement made by a person in custody. The *Miranda* prohibition does not depend on proof of a Fifth Amendment violation; the evidence is excluded because of the chance that the statement was not voluntarily offered by the arrestee.

Where a confession has been taken in violation of *Miranda,* but not under duress or coercion, the confession can be used for impeachment purposes,[312] so long as there is no allegation of involuntariness. Impeachment use of a "bad" *Miranda* confession may be admissible in a case where a defendant has taken the witness stand and offered a story that is materially inconsistent from the original. The confession presumably will offer accurate evidence, since it has been given by the subject's free decision and is excludable from the prosecution's case only due to the *Miranda* violation. If impeachment use of voluntary confessions taken in violation of *Miranda* were not permitted, the shield provided by *Miranda* would be altered into a license to commit defense perjury.[313] In such a case the defendant would possess little worry that earlier contrary evidence from the defendant's own mouth might be used to impeach.

MAJOR CASES

CASE 8.1

Extraction of Body Fluids: No Violation of Fifth Amendment Privilege

Schmerber v. California
Supreme Court of the United States
384 U.S. 757 (1966)

FACTS

A police officer arrested Schmerber at a hospital while he was receiving treatment for injuries suffered in an accident involving the automobile that he had been driving. At the direction of a police officer, a hospital doctor took a blood sample from petitioner's body at the hospital. The chemical analysis of his blood revealed a blood alcohol level which was indicative of intoxication. The report of his blood alcohol level was admitted in evidence at his

trial. The Los Angeles Municipal Court convicted petitioner Schmerber of driving an automobile while under the influence of alcohol.

At the trial, Schmerber's attorney objected to trial court use of the analysis of the blood evidence on the ground that the blood had been withdrawn despite his refusal to consent to the test. Through counsel, Schmerber contended that the withdrawal of the blood and the acceptance of the analysis as evidence denied him the exercise of his constitutional rights against self-incrimination under the Fifth Amendment and his rights under several different provisions of the United States Constitution. The Appellate Department of the California Superior Court rejected these contentions and affirmed the conviction. The Supreme Court of the United States granted certiorari to consider the constitutional arguments offered by Mr. Schmerber.

PROCEDURAL QUESTION

Does the medically appropriate extraction of bodily fluids from a person against the will of the individual and the

---

[312]See *Harris v. New York,* 401 U.S. 222, 225 (1971).
[313]Ibid. at 226.

subsequent use of the evidence against that person violate the Fifth Amendment privilege against self-incrimination?

HELD: NO

RATIONALE

Mr. Justice Brennan delivered the opinion of the Court.

★ ★ ★

I

The Due Process Clause Claim

Breithaupt [*v. Abram,* 352 U.S. 432 (1957)] was also a case in which police officers caused blood to be withdrawn from the driver of an automobile involved in an accident, and in which there was ample justification for the officer's conclusion that the driver was under the influence of alcohol. There, as here, the extraction was made by a physician in a simple, medically acceptable manner in a hospital environment. There, however, the driver was unconscious at the time the blood was withdrawn, and hence had no opportunity to object to the procedure. We affirmed the conviction there resulting from the use of the test in evidence, holding that, under such circumstances, the withdrawal did not offend "that 'sense of justice' of which we spoke in *Rochin v. California,* 342 U.S. 165." 352 U.S. at 435.[314] *Breithaupt* thus requires the rejection of petitioner's due process argument, and nothing in the circumstances of this case or in supervening events persuades us that this aspect of *Breithaupt* should be overruled.

II

The Privilege against Self-Incrimination Claim

Breithaupt [*v. Abram,* 352 U.S. 432] summarily rejected an argument that the withdrawal of blood and the admission of the analysis report involved in that state case violated the Fifth Amendment privilege of any person not to "be compelled in any criminal case to be a witness against himself," citing *Twining v. New Jersey,* 211 U.S. 78. But that case, holding that the protections of the Fourteenth Amendment do not embrace this Fifth Amendment privilege, has been succeeded by *Malloy v. Hogan,* 378 U.S. 1, 8. We there held that "[t]he Fourteenth Amendment secures against state invasion the same privilege that the Fifth Amendment guarantees against federal infringement—the right of a person to remain silent unless he choose to speak in the unfettered exercise of his own will, and to suffer no penalty…for such silence." We therefore must now decide whether the withdrawal of the blood and admission in evidence of the analysis involved in this case violated petitioner's privilege. We hold that the privilege protects an accused only from being compelled to testify against himself, or otherwise provide the State with evidence of a testimonial or communicative nature, and that the withdrawal of blood and use of the analysis in question in this case did not involve compulsion to these ends.

It could not be denied that in requiring petitioner to submit to the withdrawal and chemical analysis of his blood, the State compelled him to submit to an attempt to discover evidence that might be used to prosecute him for a criminal offense. He submitted only after the police officer rejected his objection and directed the physician to proceed. The officer's direction to the physician to administer the test over petitioner's objection constituted compulsion for the purpose of the privilege. The critical question, then, is whether petitioner was thus compelled "to be a witness against himself."

If the scope of the privilege coincided with the complex of values it help to protect, we might be obliged to conclude that the privilege was violated. In *Miranda v. Arizona, ante,* at 460, the Court said of the interests protected by the privilege: "All these policies point to one overriding thought: the constitutional foundation underlying the privilege is the respect a government—state or federal—must accord to the dignity and integrity of its citizens. To maintain a 'fair state-individual balance,' to require the government 'to shoulder the entire load'…to respect the inviolability of the human personality, our accusatory system of criminal justice demands that the government seeking to punish an individual produce the evidence against him by its own independent labors, rather than by the cruel, simple expedient of compelling

---

[314]In *Rochin,* police officers warrantlessly searched the stomach of the defendant by having a doctor force an emetic into his stomach so that the officers could collect some drugs when the defendant vomited. The conviction was reversed on due process grounds under the Fourteenth Amendment because the *Rochin* Court found that the forced pumping of the arrestee's stomach offended due process by the use of conduct that shocked the conscience and violated the parameters of civilized conduct. See *Rochin* at 172–173.

it from his own mouth." The withdrawal of blood necessarily involves puncturing the skin for extraction, and the percent by weight of alcohol in that blood, as established by chemical analysis, is evidence of criminal guilt. Compelled submission fails on one view to respect the "inviolability of the human personality." Moreover, since it enables the State to rely on evidence forced from the accused, the compulsion violates at least one meaning of the requirement that the State procure the evidence against an accused "by its own independent labors."

As the passage in *Miranda* implicitly recognizes, however, the privilege has never been given the full scope which the values it helps to protect suggest. History and a long line of authorities in lower courts have consistently limited its protection to situations in which the State seeks to submerge those values by obtaining the evidence against an accused through "the cruel, simple expedient of compelling it from his own mouth....In sum, the privilege is fulfilled only when the person is guaranteed the right 'to remain silent unless he chooses to speak in the unfettered exercise of his own will.'" *Ibid.*

★ ★ ★

It is clear that the protection of the [Fifth Amendment] privilege [against self-incrimination] reaches an accused's communications, whatever form they might take, and the compulsion of responses which are also communications, for example, compliance with a subpoena to produce one's papers. *Boyd v. United States,* 116 U.S. 616. On the other hand, both federal and state courts have usually held that it offers no protection against compulsion to submit to fingerprinting, photographing, or measurements, to write or speak for identification, to appear in court, to stand, to assume a stance, to walk, or to make a particular gesture. The distinction which has emerged, often expressed in different ways, is that the privilege is a bar against compelling "communications" or "testimony," but that compulsion which makes a suspect or accused the source of "real or physical evidence" does not violate it.

★ ★ ★

In the present case...not even a shadow of testimonial compulsion upon or enforced communication by the accused was involved either in the extraction or in the chemical analysis. Petitioner's testimonial capacities were in no way implicated; indeed, his participation, except as a donor, was irrelevant to the results of the test, which depend on

chemical analysis and on that alone. Since the blood test evidence, although an incriminating product of compulsion, was neither petitioner's testimony nor evidence relating to some communicative act or writing by the petitioner, it was not inadmissible on [Fifth Amendment] privilege grounds.

★ ★ ★

Affirmed.

Mr. Justice Black with whom Mr. Justice Douglas joins, dissenting.

I would reverse petitioner's conviction. I agree with the Court that the Fourteenth Amendment made applicable to the States the Fifth Amendment's provision that "no person...shall be compelled in any criminal case to be a witness, against himself...." But I disagree with the Court's holding that California did not violate petitioner's constitutional right against self-incrimination when it compelled him, against his will, to allow a doctor to puncture his blood vessels in order to extract a sample of blood and analyze it for alcoholic content, and then used that analysis of evidence to convict petitioner of a crime.

The Court admits that:

> the State compelled [petitioner] to submit to an attempt to discover evidence [in his blood] that might be [and was] used to prosecute him for a criminal offense.

To reach the conclusion that compelling a person to give his blood to help the State convict him is not equivalent to compelling him to be a witness against himself strikes me as quite an extraordinary feat. The Court, however, overcomes what had seemed to me to be an insuperable obstacle to its conclusion by holding that

> ...the privilege protects an accused only from being compelled to testify against himself, or otherwise provide the State with evidence of a testimonial or communicative nature, and that the withdrawal of blood and use of the analysis in question in this case did not involve compulsion to these ends. (Footnote omitted.)

I cannot agree that this distinction and reasoning of the Court justify denying petitioner his Bill of Rights' guarantee that he must not be compelled to be a witness against himself.

COMMENTS, NOTES, AND QUESTIONS

1. When a person does not want to assist in offering evidence that might contribute to his or her own conviction, it seems as if the person is being required to offer "testimony" against him- or herself. Why does the *Schmerber* Court indicate that the Fifth Amendment privilege would not be violated in such a situation? Do you agree with the Court's reasoning? What would you argue in opposition to the Court's position?

2. If blood samples do not violate the privilege against self-incrimination, could a court require a person to make a voice recording for use by the prosecution? Would a voice recording be a bit more like actual testimony against oneself? Requiring a suspect to offer a voice sample would seem to be a potential link in a chain of evidence leading to conviction. One might argue that making a recording is providing testimony. Is it? In *United States v. Dionisio,* 410 U.S. 1 (1973), a trial court ordered Dionisio to make a voice recording for use by the prosecutor in a grand jury investigation. Dionisio refused on the ground, among others, that to offer a sample of his voice would violate his Fifth Amendment privilege against self-incrimination because the sample might be used against him in a criminal prosecution. The Supreme Court rejected Dionisio's Fifth Amendment argument with the conclusion that prior cases have uniformly rejected the contention that the compelled display of identifiable physical characteristics infringes on the privilege against compelled testimonial self-incrimination.

3. Handwriting samples could be incriminating, but would they be considered "testimonial" in nature? Should handwriting samples be treated like voice samples? The Court, in *Gilbert v. California,* 388 U.S. 263 (1967), determined that the required giving of a handwriting sample did not violate the Fifth Amendment privilege against self-incrimination, since the character or quality of one's written communication, in contrast to its content, is merely an identifying physical characteristic.

4. Uttering words offered by the real criminal and exhibiting one's physical appearance do not create a violation of any Fifth Amendment claim, according to the Court in *United States v. Wade,* 388 U.S. 218 (1967). In *Wade,* the Court approved a trial court order that required Wade to appear in a physical lineup and to utter the words used by a robbery suspect. A person's appearance may assist in providing the prosecution with incriminating evidence, but appearance is not the same as requiring incriminating testimony from the individual.

5. Under *Schmerber* and numerous other cases, it has become clear that physical attributes such as fingerprints, weight, height, tone of speech, manner of handwriting, walk, general body stance, content of blood or other bodily fluids, and general appearance are not testimonially communicative and, as such, are not subject to Fifth Amendment privilege self-incrimination claims. While performing a particular act may provide nontestimonial incriminating evidence, a criminal suspect may be compelled to put on a shirt, *Holt v. United States,* 218 U.S. 245 (1910); to provide a blood sample, *Schmerber,* or a handwriting example, *Gilbert v. California,* 388 U.S. 263 (1967); to make a recording of his voice, *United States v. Wade,* 388 U.S. 218 (1967); or to read text that was recorded for grand jury use, *United States v. Dionisio,* 410 U.S. 1 (1973). The act of exhibiting such physical characteristics is not the same as a sworn communication by a witness that relates either express or implied assertions of fact or belief. However, since all physical characteristics may assist in the process of conviction in a particular case, should the use of these attributes by the prosecution be covered by the Fifth Amendment? Why or why not? How would you construct your argument? Consider the contention of Justice Thomas, who argued that the original intent of the Fifth Amendment may have covered such items in his concurrence in *United States v. Hubbell,* 530 U.S. 27 (2000).

6. According to the Court, the drawing of a blood sample from Schmerber did not involve any forced testimonial communication. However, the intrusion of the hospital staff to extract the sample of blood implicated Fourth Amendment issues, which require that the officer have probable cause for the search of the blood. The evanescent nature of alcohol in the blood effectively created the emergency that excused the failure to obtain a search warrant prior to making the intrusion into Schmerber's body.

CASE 8.2

Torture-Based Confessions Violate Due Process

Brown v. Mississippi
Supreme Court of the United States
297 U.S. 278 (1936)

FACTS

Brown and two other African-Americans were indicted for murder on April 4, 1934, and pled not guilty at their arraignment. The court immediately appointed counsel for their trial defense, because the trial was scheduled for the next day. Following a two-day trial, at which the defendants' confessions were introduced against them, the jury found the men guilty of murder and sentenced them to death.

At trial and on appeal, the defendants alleged that the method by which police obtained the confession violated the Due Process Clause of the Fourteenth Amendment guaranteeing fundamentally fair treatment and the Fifth Amendment protection against compulsory self-incrimination.

One of the defendants, Ellington, was asked to accompany an officer to the home of the deceased where a group of white men had gathered. Upon an accusation of guilt and his denial, the defendant was hanged by a rope from a tree. He protested his innocence when the rope was loosened, but the men hanged him a second time and no confession followed. Even after being tied to a tree and whipped, Ellington maintained his innocence as he walked home.

Several days later, the deputy arrested Ellington and took him out of the state to Alabama where officers whipped him again. Following threats of whipping until he confessed, Ellington agreed to make a full confession as the deputy sheriff would dictate. The trial court allowed this coerced confession to be introduced against the defendant.

The two other defendants, Brown and Shields, were made to strip in their jail cells, placed over the backs of chairs, and whipped until their backs were cut to pieces. The same officer who tortured Brown indicated to the two defendants that the whippings would continue until they confessed. Brown and Shields confessed to the murder and were warned of dire consequences if they should ever change their story.

The next day, two sheriffs, one from the county in which the killing occurred and one from the county of the jail, in the company of numerous other persons, went to the jail to hear the "free and voluntary" confessions repeated by the three defendants. Although the defendants repudiated their confessions in open court, the court permitted the prosecution to introduce the tortured confessions into evidence. Aside from the confessions, there was no evidence sufficient to warrant the submission of the case to the jury.

Upon appeal through the Mississippi state court system, the Supreme Court of Mississippi refused to grant the petitioners any relief. The Supreme Court of the United States granted certiorari.

PROCEDURAL ISSUE

Where defendants have been physically tortured under police and/or mob direction, does the introduction of subsequent coerced confession against defendants violate the Due Process Clause of the Fourteenth Amendment?

HELD: YES

RATIONALE

Mr. Chief Justice Hughes delivered the opinion of the Court.

★ ★ ★

1. The State stresses the statement in *Twining v. New Jersey,* 211 U.S. 78, 114, that "exemption from compulsory self-incrimination in the courts of the States is not secured by any part of the Federal Constitution," and the statement in *Snyder v. Massachusetts,* 291 U.S. 97, 105, that "the privilege against self-incrimination may be withdrawn and the accused put upon the stand as a witness for the State." But the question of the right of the State to withdraw the privilege against self-incrimination is not here involved. The compulsion to which the quoted statements refer is that of the processes of justice by which the accused may be called as a witness and required to testify. Compulsion by torture to extort a confession is a different matter.

The State is free to regulate the procedure of its courts in accordance with its own conceptions of policy, unless in so doing it "offends some principle of justice so rooted in the traditions and conscience of our people as to be ranked as fundamental." *Snyder v. Massachusetts, supra; Rogers v. Peck,* 199 U.S. 425, 434....It may dispense with indictment by a grand jury and substitute complaint or information. *Walker v. Sauvinet,* 92 U.S. 90; *Hurtado v. California,* 110 U.S. 516; *Snyder v. Massachusetts, supra.* But the freedom of the State in establishing its policy is the freedom of constitutional government and is limited by the requirement of due process of law....[Even if a state could dispense with trial by jury], it does not follow that it may substitute trial by ordeal. The rack and torture chamber may not be substituted for the witness stand. The State may not permit an accused to be hurried to conviction under mob domination—where the whole proceeding is but a mask—without supplying corrective process. *Moore v. Dempsey,* 261 U.S. 86, 91. The State may not deny to the accused the aid of counsel. *Powell v. Alabama,* 287 U.S. 45. Nor may a State, through the action of its officers, contrive a conviction through the pretense of a trial which in truth is "but used as a means of depriving a defendant of liberty through a deliberate deception of court and jury by the presentation of testimony known to be perjured." *Mooney v. Holohan,* 294 U.S. 103, 112. And the trial equally is a mere pretense where the state authorities have contrived a conviction resting solely upon confessions obtained by violence. The due process clause requires

> that state action, whether through one agency or another, shall be consistent with the fundamental principles of liberty and justice which lie at the base of all our civil and political institutions. *Hebert v. Louisiana,* 272 U.S. 312, 316.

It would be difficult to conceive of methods more revolting to the sense of justice than those taken to procure the confessions of these petitioners, and the use of the confessions thus obtained as the basis for conviction and sentence was a clear denial of due process.

2. It is in this view that the further contention of the State must be considered. That contention rests upon the failure of counsel for the accused, who had objected to the admissibility of the confessions, to move for their exclusion after they had been introduced and the fact of coercion had been proved. It is a contention which proceeds upon a misconception of the nature of petitioner's complaint. That complaint is not of the commission of mere error, but of a wrong so fundamental that it made the whole proceeding a mere pretense of a trial and rendered the conviction and sentence wholly void. We are not concerned with a mere question of state practice, or whether counsel assigned to petitioners were competent or mistakenly assumed that their first objections were sufficient. In an earlier case the Supreme Court of the State had recognized the duty of the court to supply corrective process where due process of law had been denied. In *Fisher v. State,* 145 Miss. 116, 134; 110 So. 361, 365, the court said: "Coercing the supposed state's criminals into confessions and using such confessions so coerced from them against them in trials has been the curse of all countries. It was the chief inequity, the crowning infamy of the Star Chamber, and the Inquisition, and other similar institutions. The constitution recognized the evils that lay behind these practices and prohibited them in this country.… The duty of maintaining constitutional rights of a person on trial for his life rises above mere rules of procedure and wherever the court is clearly satisfied that such violations exist, it will refuse to sanction such violations and will apply the corrective."

In the instant case, the trial court was fully advised by the undisputed evidence of the way in which the confessions had been procured. The trial court knew that there was no other evidence upon which conviction and sentence could be based. Yet it proceeded to permit conviction and to pronounce sentence. The conviction and sentence were void for want of the essential elements of due process, and the proceeding thus vitiated could be challenged in any appropriate manner. *Mooney v. Holohan, supra.* It was challenged before the Supreme Court of the State by the express invocation of the Fourteenth Amendment. That court entertained the challenge, considered the federal question thus presented, but declined to enforce petitioners' constitutional right. The court thus denied a federal right fully established and specially set up and claimed and the judgment must be

Reversed.

COMMENTS, NOTES, AND QUESTIONS

1. The *Brown* Court decided the case on the basis of the Due Process Clause of the Fourteenth Amendment, which requires the states to treat individuals with fundamental fairness when applying legal procedures, including the taking of confessions. The reasoning and approach of *Brown* are fairly transferrable to the rationale behind the Court's decision in *Malloy v. Hogan,* 378 U.S. 1; 84 S.Ct. 1489 (1964). There the Court held that the Fifth Amendment prohibition against compelled testimonial self-incrimination was incorporated into the Due Process Clause of the Fourteenth Amendment as a limitation on state criminal practice. In effect, the Court determined that fundamentally fair treatment included the right not to incriminate oneself. *Malloy* held that any time a question concerning the voluntariness of a confession arose in either a state or federal court, resolution of the issue was to be controlled by the self-incrimination portion of the Fifth Amendment. Once judicially brought to bear against the states, the Fifth Amendment privilege against self-incrimination had the same application in a state case as if the trial were a federal trial.

2. In *Payne v. Arkansas,* 356 U.S. 560 (1958), a retarded nineteen-year-old African American with a fifth-grade education was convicted in an Arkansas court of first-degree murder and sentenced to death. At his trial, over his objection, a confession was admitted into evidence and shown by undisputed evidence to have been obtained by significant coercion. Police had arrested Payne without a warrant, and he was never taken before a magistrate or advised of his right to remain silent or to have counsel, as required by state law. After being held

incommunicado for three days without counsel, adviser, or friend, and with very little food, he confessed after being told by the chief of police that some people were coming to get (kill) him, and that, if he would tell the truth, the chief probably would keep them from coming into the jail to get him. The Supreme Court of the United States reversed the conviction and held that the confession obtained in this fashion was not properly admissible; Payne's due process rights under the Fourteenth Amendment had been violated because there had been no expression of a free and voluntary choice to make a confession.

3. In determining whether a confession has been given freely and voluntarily, courts typically look to see if the defendant's will was overborne by the circumstances. Factors to consider include both the characteristics of the accused and the details of the interrogation under a totality of the circumstances test. See *Schneckloth v. Bustamonte,* 412 U.S. 218 (1973). Some of the factors the Court has taken into account in the past have included the youth of the accused, *Haley v. Ohio,* 332 U.S. 596 (1948); lack of education, *Payne v. Arkansas,* 356 U.S. 560 (1958); low intelligence, *Fikes v. Alabama,* 352 U.S. 191 (1957); the lack of any advice to the accused regarding his constitutional rights, *Davis v. North Carolina,* 384 U.S. 737 (1966); the length of detention, *Chambers v. Florida,* 309 U.S. 227 (1940); the repeated and prolonged nature of the questioning, *Ashcraft v. Tennessee,* 322 U.S. 143 (1944); and the use of physical punishment such as the deprivation of food or sleep, *Reck v. Pate,* 367 U.S. 433 (1961). The Court in *Culombe v. Connecticut,* 367 U.S. 568 (1961), phrased a test for voluntariness of a confession as follows:

> The ultimate test remains that which has been the only clearly established test in Anglo-American courts for two hundred years: the test of voluntariness. Is the confession the product of an essentially free and unconstrained choice by its maker? If it is, if he has willed to confess, it may be used against him. If it is not, if his will has been overborne and his capacity for self-determination critically impaired, the use of his confession offends due process.

4. In *South Dakota v. Neville,* 459 U.S. 553 (1983), the defendant attempted to prevent a prosecutor's comment on the defendant's failure to take a Breathalyzer test following an arrest for driving while intoxicated. The South Dakota courts granted Neville's motion to suppress, and the prosecution appealed to the Supreme Court. According to the Supreme Court, the admission into evidence of a defendant's refusal to submit to a blood

alcohol test would not have violated Neville's Fifth Amendment privilege against self-incrimination. According to the Court, a refusal to take such a test, after a police officer has lawfully requested it, is not an act coerced by the officer, and thus is not protected by the Fifth Amendment privilege against self-incrimination as applied to the states through the Due Process Clause of the Fourteenth Amendment.

5. Suppose that a person walked over to a uniformed police officer and wanted to talk about a homicide. The individual appeared to be under some stress and a bit agitated but continued to speak of the homicide while offering his confession of guilt. Would the officer be taking an involuntary confession if he or she merely listened attentively? Should the officer warn the person that what he was saying might be used against him in a court of law? Would the fact that the individual has mental problems create a situation where the confession would be regarded as involuntary? Why or why not? Under the circumstances, could it be said that the officer was coercing the individual? See *Colorado v. Connelly,* 479 U.S. 157 (1986), Case 8.4. As a general rule, gratuitously offered confessions are generally admissible. Personal motivations, so long as not related to law enforcement conduct, do not usually cause a confession to be considered involuntary under due process analysis. While mental problems may have motivated a person to confess to a police officer, if there was no pressure placed by the officer to confess, arguably due process has not been violated.

CASE 8.3

Subtly Coerced Confessions by Government Agent Not Admissible

Arizona v. Fulminante
Supreme Court of the United States
499 U.S. 279 (1991)

FACTS

After Fulminante's eleven-year-old stepdaughter was murdered in Arizona, he emerged as a prime suspect in her murder due to a series of inconsistent statements he made to police and to the effect of other evidence. Even when the victim's body was discovered, police remained unable to develop sufficient evidence to successfully prosecute Mr. Fulminante for the homicide of his stepdaughter.

Later, a federal court convicted Fulminante on an unrelated crime and he served time in a federal correctional facility. During this incarceration, some inmates began to give him a rough time because of the rumor that he was a child murderer and rapist/molester. Sarivola, an inmate and a former police officer working undercover for the Federal Bureau of Investigation, pretended to befriend Fulminante and offered "protection" from other inmates on the condition that Fulminante tell Sarivola the complete story of the child killing. After Fulminante admitted his sexual assault of the victim, he confessed to murder and then related to Sarivola significant details concerning the girl's death.

Following Fulminante's release from prison, for unknown reasons, he repeated the substance of his original confession to Sarivola's future wife, Donna. Both this admission to homicide and the earlier prison confession were introduced at Fulminante's subsequent trial for the murder of his stepdaughter. The prosecution obtained a capital conviction and a death penalty for Fulminante.

In his appeal, defendant contended that the first confession had been coerced and, therefore, its use at trial violated his rights to due process under the Fifth and Fourteenth Amendments. The Arizona Supreme Court originally ruled that although the first confession was coerced, its introduction in evidence constituted harmless error due to the overwhelming strength of the state's case. Upon reconsideration, the Arizona court reversed defendant's conviction and overruled its prior decision holding that the harmless error standard should not apply to coerced confessions. The Supreme Court of the United States granted certiorari to resolved differing interpretations among the states and federal courts.

PROCEDURAL ISSUE

Where a confession has been illegally coerced from a suspect by a police operative in violation of the Fifth Amendment and admitted in evidence against the accused, on appellate review, should courts apply the harmless error analysis concerning the admissibility of the confession?

HELD: YES

RATIONALE

Mr. Justice White delivered the opinion of the Court.

★ ★ ★

Because of differing views in the state and federal courts over whether the admission at trial of a coerced confession is subject to a harmless-error analysis, we granted the State's petition for certiorari, 494 U.S. (1990). Although a majority of this Court finds that such a confession is subject to a harmless-error analysis, for the reasons set forth below, we affirm the judgment of the Arizona court.

II

We deal first with the State's contention that the court below erred in holding Fulminante's confession to have been coerced. The State argues that it is the totality of the circumstances that determines whether Fulminante's confession was coerced, cf. *Schneckloth v. Bustamonte,* 412 U.S. 218, 226 (1973), but contends that rather than apply this standard, the Arizona court applied a "but for" test, under which the court found that but for the promise given by Sarivola, Fulminante would not have confessed.

★ ★ ★

In applying the totality of the circumstances test was to determine that the confession to Sarivola was coerced, the Arizona Supreme Court focused on a number of relevant facts. First, the court noted that "because [Fulminante] was an alleged child murderer, he was in danger of physical harm at the hands of other inmates." In addition, Sarivola was aware that Fulminante had been receiving "'rough treatment from the guys.'"

★ ★ ★

Although the question is a close one, we agree with the Arizona Supreme Court's conclusion that Fulminante's confession was coerced. The Arizona Supreme Court found a credible threat of physical violence unless Fulminante confessed. Our cases have made clear that a finding of coercion need not depend upon actual violence by a government agent; a credible threat is sufficient.

★ ★ ★

III

Four of us, Justices Marshall, Blackmun, Stevens, and myself, would affirm the judgment of the Arizona Supreme Court on the ground that the harmless-error rule is inapplicable to erroneously admitted coerced confessions. We thus disagree with the Justices who have a contrary view.

The majority today abandons what until now the Court has regarded as the

> axiomatic [proposition] that a defendant in a criminal case is deprived of due process of law if his conviction is founded, in whole or in part, upon an involuntary confession, without regard for the truth or falsity of the confession, *Rogers v. Richmond,* 365 U.S. 534, and even though there is ample evidence aside from the confession to support the conviction. [Citations omitted.]

The Court has repeatedly stressed that the view that the admission of a coerced confession can be harmless error because of the other evidence to support the verdict is "an impermissible doctrine," *Lynumn v. Illinois,* 372 U.S. 528, 537 (1963); for "the admission in evidence, over objection, of the coerced confession vitiates the judgment because it violates the Due Process Clause of the Fourteenth Amendment."

★ ★ ★

Today, a majority of the Court, without any justification…overrules this vast body of precedent without a word and in so doing dislodges one of the fundamental tenets of our criminal justice system.

In extending to coerced confessions the harmless error rule of *Chapman v. California,* 386 U.S. 18 (1967), the majority declared that because the Court has applied that analysis to numerous other "trial errors," there is no reason that it should not apply to an error of this nature as well. The four of us remain convinced, however, that we should abide by our cases that have refused to apply the harmless error rule to coerced confessions, for a coerced confession is fundamentally different from other types of erroneously admitted evidence to which the rule has been applied. Indeed, as the majority concedes, *Chapman* itself recognized that prior cases "have indicated that there are some constitutional rights so basic to a fair trial that their infraction can *never* be treated as harmless error," and it placed in that category the constitutional rule against using a defendant's coerced confession against him at his criminal trial.

★ ★ ★

A defendant's confession is "probably the most probative and damaging evidence that can be admitted against him," *Cruz v. New York,* 481 U.S. 186, 195 (1987)

(White, J., dissenting), so damaging that a jury should not be expected to ignore it even if told to do so, and because in any event it is impossible to know what credit and weight the jury gave to the confession. Concededly, this reason is insufficient to justify a *per se* bar to the use of *any* confession. Thus, *Milton v. Wainwright,* 407 U.S. 371 (1972), applied harmless-error analysis to confession obtained and introduced in circumstances that violated the defendant's Sixth Amendment right to counsel. Similarly, the Courts of Appeals have held that the introduction of incriminating statements taken from defendants in violation of *Miranda v. Arizona,* 384 U.S. 436 (1966), is subject to treatment as harmless error.

Nevertheless, in declaring that it is

> impossible to create a meaningful distinction between confessions elicited in violation of the Sixth Amendment and those in violation of the Fourteenth Amendment, *post* at 312 (opinion of Rehnquist, C. J.),

the majority overlooks the obvious. Neither *Milton v. Wainwright* nor any of the other cases upon which the majority relies involved a defendant's *coerced* confession, nor were there present in these cases the distinctive reasons underlying the exclusion of coerced incriminating statements of the defendant. First, some coerced confessions may be untrustworthy. *Jackson v. Denno,* 378 U.S., at 385–386; *Spano v. New York,* 360 U.S., at 320. Consequently, admission of coerced confession may distort the truth-seeking function of the trial upon which the majority focuses. More importantly, however, the use of coerced confessions, "whether true or false," is forbidden

> because the methods used to extract them offend an underlying principle in the enforcement of our criminal law: that ours is an accusatorial and not an inquisitorial system—a system in which the State must establish guilt by evidence independently and freely secured and may not by coercion prove its charge against an accused out of his own mouth, *Rogers v. Richmond,* 365 U.S., at 540–541.

★ ★ ★

The search for truth is indeed central to our system of justice, but "certain constitutional rights are not, and should not be, subject to harmless-error analysis because those rights protect important values that are unrelated to the truth-seeking function of the trial." *Rose v. Clark,* 478 U.S., at 587. The right of a defendant not to have his coerced confession used against him is among those rights, for using a coerced confession "abort[s] the basic trial process" and "render[s] a trial fundamentally unfair." *Id.*, at 577, 578, n. 6.

For the foregoing reasons the four of us would adhere to the consistent line of authority that has recognized as a basic tenet of our criminal justice system, before and after both *Miranda* and *Chapman,* the prohibition against using a defendant's coerced confession against him at his criminal trial.

IV

Since five Justices have determined that harmless error analysis applies to coerced confessions, it becomes necessary to evaluate under that ruling the admissibility of Fulminante's confession to Sarivola. *Chapman v. California,* 386 U.S., at 24, made clear that "before a federal constitutional error can be held harmless, the court must be able to declare a belief that was harmless beyond a reasonable doubt." The Court has the power to review the record *de novo* in order to determine an error's harmlessness. In so doing, it must be determined whether the State has met its burden of demonstrating that the admission of the confession to Sarivola did not contribute to Fulminante's conviction. Five of us are of the view that the State has not carried its burden and accordingly affirm the judgment of the court below reversing petitioner's conviction.

A confession is like no other evidence. Indeed,

> the defendant's own confession is probably the most probative and damaging evidence that can be admitted against him.…[T]he admissions of a defendant come from the actor himself, the most knowledgeable and unimpeachable source of information about his past conduct. Certainly, confessions have profound impact on the jury, so much so that we may justifiably doubt its ability to put them out of mind even if told to do so. *Bruton v. United States,* 391 U.S. at 139–140 (White, J., dissenting).

★ ★ ★

While some statements by a defendant may concern isolated aspects of the crime or may be incriminating only when linked to other evidence, a full confession in which the defendant discloses the motive for and means of the crime may tempt the jury to rely upon that evidence alone in reaching its decision. In the case of a coerced confession such as that given by Fulminante to Sarivola, the risk that the confession is unreliable, coupled with the profound impact that the confession has upon the jury, requires a reviewing court to exercise extreme caution before determining that the admission of the confession at trial was harmless.

★ ★ ★

Our review of the record leads us to conclude that the State has failed to meet its burden of establishing, beyond a reasonable doubt, that the admission of Fulminante's confession to Anthony Sarivola was harmless error. Three considerations compel this result.

First, the transcript discloses that both the trial court and the State recognized that a successful prosecution depended on the jury believing the two confessions. Absent the confessions, it is unlikely that Fulminante would have been prosecuted at all, because the physical evidence would have been insufficient to convict.

★ ★ ★

Second, the jury's assessment of the confession to Donna Sarivola could easily have depended in large part on the presence of the confession to Anthony Sarivola. Absent the admission at trial of the first confession, the jurors might have found Donna Sarivola's story unbelievable.

★ ★ ★

Third, the admission of the first confession led to the admission of other evidence prejudicial to Fulminante. For example, the State introduced evidence that Fulminante knew of Sarivola's connections with organized crime in an attempt to explain why Fulminante would have been motivated to confess to Sarivola in seeking protection. Absent the confession, this evidence would have had no relevance and would have been inadmissible at trial.

★ ★ ★

Finally, although our concern here is with the effect of the erroneous admission of the confession on Fulminante's conviction, it is clear that the presence of the confession also influenced the sentencing phase of the trial. Under Arizona law, the trial judge is the sentencer. Ariz. Rev. Stat. 13-703(B) (1989).

★ ★ ★

Although the sentencing judge might have reached the same conclusions even without the confession to Anthony Sarivola, it is impossible to say so beyond a reasonable doubt. Furthermore, the judge's assessment of Donna Sarivola's credibility, and hence the reliability of the second confession, might well have been influenced by the corroborative effect of the erroneously admitted first confession. Indeed, the fact that the sentencing judge focused on the similarities between the two confessions in determining that they were reliable suggests that either of the confessions alone, even when considered with all the other evidence, would have been insufficient to permit the judge to find an aggravating circumstance beyond a reasonable doubt as a requisite prelude to imposing the death penalty.

Because a majority of the Court has determined that Fulminante's confession to Anthony Sarivola was coerced and because a majority has determined that admitting this confession was not harmless beyond a reasonable doubt, we agree with the Arizona Supreme Court's conclusion that Fulminante is entitled to a new trial at which the confession is not admitted. Accordingly the judgment of the Arizona Supreme Court is

Affirmed.

Chief Justice Rehnquist, with whom Justice O'Connor joins, Justice Kennedy and Justice Souter join as to Parts I and II, and Justice Scalia joins as to Parts II and III, delivering the opinion of the Court as to Part II, and dissenting as to Parts I and III.

The Court today properly concludes that the admission of an "involuntary" confession at trial is subject to harmless error analysis. Nonetheless, the independent review of the record which we are required to make shows that respondent Fulminante's confession was not in fact involuntary. And even if the confession were deemed to be involuntary, the evidence offered at trial, including a second, untainted confession by Fulminante, supports the conclusion that any error was certainly harmless.

★ ★ ★

II

Since this Court's landmark decision in *Chapman v. California,* 386 U.S. 18 (1967), in which we adopted the general rule that a constitutional error does not automatically require reversal of a conviction, the Court has applied harmless error analysis to a wide range of errors and has recognized that most constitutional errors can be harmless.

★ ★ ★

The admission of an involuntary confession is a "trial error," similar in both degree and kind to the erroneous admission of other types of evidence. The evidentiary impact of an involuntary confession, and its effect upon the composition of the record, is indistinguishable from that of a confession obtained in violation of the Sixth Amendment—of evidence seized in violation of the Fourth Amendment—or of a prosecutor's improper comment of a defendant's silence at trial in violation of the Fifth Amendment. When reviewing the erroneous admission of an involuntary confession, the appellate court, as it does with the admission of other forms of improperly admitted evidence, simply reviews the remainder of the evidence against the defendant to determine whether the admission of the confession was harmless beyond a reasonable doubt.

★ ★ ★

Of course an involuntary confession may have a more dramatic effect on the course of a trial than do other trial errors—in particular cases it may be devastating to a defendant—but this simply means that a reviewing court will conclude in such a case that its admission was not harmless error; it is not a reason for eschewing the harmless error test entirely.

III

I would agree with the finding of the Supreme Court of Arizona in its initial opinion—in which it believed harmless-error analysis was applicable to the admission of involuntary confessions—that the admission of Fulminante's confession was harmless.

NOTES, COMMENTS, AND QUESTIONS

1. In *Fulminante,* was the pressure to confess created by the government or by other inmates not working in concert with the government? Should that fact matter? Would Fulminante's confession have been considered involuntary if a private citizen not working for the government had offered him protection in exchange for his story? Would the confession have been any less voluntary if it had been extracted by a private citizen rather than a government informant? Why or why not? Should this factor matter? Where a confession has been determined to have been involuntarily given, should we have concerns about its accuracy? Should that be a reason to exclude it? What would constitute a good argument for exclusion?

2. Prior to *Fulminante,* in cases where coerced confessions had allegedly been used in evidence, courts tended to reverse convictions once they had determined that a

particular confession had been coerced. What could have been the rationale for automatic reversal of convictions based partly on coerced confessions? Are you sure that a coerced confession is a truthful statement of what occurred? Why or why not?

3. *Fulminante* reaffirmed the test for determining whether the trial use of a coerced confession should require a reversal. In *Chapman v. California,* 386 U.S. 18 (1967), mentioned in *Fulminante,* the Court held that the "harmless error" rule should apply in cases involving a federal constitutional error:

> "…we hold, as we now do, that, before a federal constitutional error can be held harmless, the court must be able to declare a belief that it was harmless beyond a reasonable doubt." 386 U.S. 18, 24.

When a reviewing court can state with certainty that the particular admission of an involuntary confession did not affect the result of a case, a reversal is not mandated. However, if the reviewing court has a reasonable doubt that the confession may have influenced a finder of fact, a reversal is appropriate.

4. Does a police officer violate the Fifth Amendment privilege against self-incrimination by conducting an allegedly coercive interrogation of an injured suspect in the absence of offering any *Miranda* warning where the evidence received was never used against the suspect? In *Chavez v. Martinez,* 538 U.S. 760 (2003), police officers engaged in a struggle with Martinez during which Martinez obtained one officer's service weapon but was ultimately subdued, leaving Martinez blind and paralyzed. At the hospital, Chavez, a police officer, without interfering with the delivery of medical care, interrogated Martinez intermittently during the time Martinez obtained emergency hospital treatment and received incriminating evidence that potentially could have been used against Martinez. Subsequently, Martinez filed a civil rights suit against Chavez, alleging that the officer's acts in interrogating him violated federal law and the Fifth Amendment prohibition that he should not be compelled in a criminal case to offer evidence against himself. The Supreme Court noted that Martinez was incorrect, since the Fifth Amendment requires that a defendant have been required to testify against himself in a criminal case, which never happened since no charges were ever filed. The *Chavez* Court explained that although law enforcement conduct prior to trial might impair the privilege against self-incrimination, no constitutional violation occurs until the information is used against a defendant at trial. Thus,

Martinez was never made a witness against himself, and his Fifth Amendment rights were not violated.

CASE 8.4

Private Motivations Do Not Render Confession Involuntary

Colorado v. Connelly
Supreme Court of the United States
479 U.S. 157 (1986)

FACTS

Connelly approached a uniformed off-duty Denver police officer, Patrick Anderson, and stated that he had committed a murder and indicated a desire to discuss the situation. The officer advised Connelly of his right under *Miranda* to remain silent and informed him that anything he said could be used against him in court. Connelly indicated that he had come all the way from Boston to confess to the murder and that he understood his rights and wanted to talk. When Officer Anderson asked if Connelly had been drinking or taking drugs, Mr. Connelly replied in the negative but added that he had previously been admitted as a mental patient in several hospitals.

Subsequent to a second warning of the right to remain silent and the arrival of a homicide detective, the officer warned Connelly for the third time. Connelly indicated that he was the person responsible for the murder of Mary Ann Junta, a young girl who had been killed in Denver. Connelly was taken to headquarters, told his story to another officer, and led the police to the location of the homicide. During the entire encounter with officers and during the confessions, Connelly appeared clear headed and normal in all respects.

Connelly began giving confused answers during an interview with a public defender. He noted that "voices" had told him to return to Denver and the "voices" had directed his confession. Convinced that the confessions were involuntary due to the defendant's mental state, the public defender filed a motion to suppress the confessions as not being freely and voluntarily given.

At a motion to suppress hearing, a psychiatrist testified that Connelly suffered from schizophrenia and was in a psychotic state the day prior to the confession. Such diagnosis indicated that the disease interfered with respondent's volitional abilities and impaired his capacity to make free and rational choices.

The trial court ordered that the statements to police be suppressed because they had been given involuntarily. The state Supreme Court agreed and held that the correct test for admissibility was "whether the statements are 'the product of a rational intellect and a free will.'" According to the court, the capacity for proper judgment and free choice may be overcome by mental illness as well as other factors. The Supreme Court of the United States granted certiorari.

PROCEDURAL QUESTION

Where a person with a history of mental illness confesses to a police officer following an appropriate warning of his Fifth Amendment privilege against self-incrimination, must the confession be suppressed as involuntarily given where the police have not coerced the individual in any way?

HELD: NO

RATIONALE

Chief Justice Rehnquist delivered the opinion of the Court.

★ ★ ★

II

The Due Process Clause of the Fourteenth Amendment provides that no State shall "deprive any person of life, liberty, or property, without due process of law." Just last Term, in *Miller v. Fenton,* 474 U.S. 104 (1985), we held that by virtue of the Due Process Clause

certain interrogation techniques, either in isolation or as applied to the unique characteristics of a particular suspect, are so offensive to a civilized system of justice that they must be condemned."

Indeed, coercive government misconduct was the catalyst for this Court's seminal confession case, *Brown v. Mississippi,* 297 U.S. 278 (1936). In that case, police officers extracted confessions from the accused through brutal torture. The Court had little difficulty concluding that even though the Fifth Amendment did not at that time apply to the States, the actions of the police were "revolting to the sense of justice." *Id.,* at 286. The Court has retained this due process focus, even after holding, in *Malloy v. Hogan,* 378 U.S. 1 (1964), that the Fifth Amendment privilege against compulsory self-incrimination applies to the States.

Thus the cases considered by this Court over the 50 years since *Brown v. Mississippi* have focused upon the crucial element of police overreaching. While each confession case has turned on its own set of factors justifying the conclusion that police conduct was oppressive, all have contained a substantial element of coercive police conduct. Absent police conduct causally related to the confession, there is simply no basis for concluding that any state actor has deprived a criminal defendant of due process of law. Respondent correctly notes that as interrogators have turned to more subtle forms of psychological persuasion, courts have found the mental condition of the defendant a more significant factor in the "voluntariness" calculus. See *Spano v. New York,* 360 U.S. 315 (1959). But this fact does not justify a conclusion that a defendant's mental condition, by itself and apart from its relation to official coercion, should ever dispose of the inquiry into constitutional "voluntariness."

Respondent relies on *Blackburn v. Alabama,* 361 U.S. 199 (1960), and *Townsend v. Sain,* 372 U.S. 293 (1963), for the proposition that the "deficient mental condition of the defendants in those cases was sufficient to render their confessions involuntary." But respondent's reading of *Blackburn* and *Townsend* ignores the integral element of police overreaching present in both cases. In *Blackburn,* the Court found that the petitioner was probably insane at the time of his confession and the police learned during the interrogation that he had a history of mental problems. The police exploited this weakness with coercive tactics: "the eight- to nine-hour sustained interrogation in a tiny room which was upon occasion literally filled with police officers; the absence of Blackburn's friends, relatives, or legal counsel; [and] the composition of the confession by the Deputy Sheriff rather than by Blackburn." 361 U.S., at 207–208. These tactics supported a finding that the confession was involuntary. Indeed, the Court specifically condemned police activity that "wrings a confession out of an accused against his will." *Townsend* presented a similar instance of police wrongdoing. In that case, a police physician had given Townsend a drug with truth-serum properties.

The subsequent confession, obtained by officers who knew that Townsend had been given drugs, was held involuntary. These two cases demonstrate that while mental condition is surely relevant to an individual's susceptibility to police coercion, mere examination of the confessant's state of mind can never conclude the due process inquiry.

Our "involuntary confession" jurisprudence is entirely consistent with the settled law requiring some sort of "state action" to support a claim of violation of the

Due Process Clause of the Fourteenth Amendment. The Colorado trial court, of course, found that the police committed no wrongful acts, and that finding has been neither challenged by respondent nor disturbed by the Supreme Court of Colorado. The latter court, however, concluded that sufficient state action was present by virtue of the admission of the confession into evidence in a court of the State. 702 P.2d, at 728–729.

The difficulty with the approach of the Supreme Court of Colorado is that it fails to recognize the essential link between coercive activity of the State, on the one hand, and a resulting confession by a defendant, on the other. The flaw in [Connelly's] constitutional argument is that it would expand our previous line of "voluntariness" cases into a far-ranging requirement that courts must divine a defendant's motivation for speaking or acting as he did even though there be no claim that governmental conduct coerced his decision.

The most outrageous behavior by a private party seeking to secure evidence against a defendant does not make that evidence inadmissible under the Due Process Clause. We have also observed that "[j]urists and scholars uniformly have recognized that the exclusionary rule imposes a substantial cost on the societal interest in law enforcement by its proscription of what concededly is relevant evidence." Moreover, suppressing respondent's statements would serve absolutely no purpose in enforcing constitutional guarantees. The purpose of excluding evidence seized in violation of the Constitution is to substantially deter future violations of the Constitution. See *United States v. Leon,* 468 U.S. 897 (1984). Only if we were to establish a brand new constitutional right—the right of a criminal defendant to confess to his crime only when totally rational and properly motivated—could respondent's present claim be sustained.

We have previously cautioned against expanding "currently applicable exclusionary rules by erecting additional barriers to placing truthful and probative evidence before state juries...." *Lego v. Twomey,* 404 U.S. 477, 488–489 (1972). We abide by that counsel now. "[T]he central purpose of a criminal trial is to decide the factual question of the defendant's guilt or innocence," *Delaware v. Van Arsdall,* 475 U.S. 673, 681 (1986), and while we have previously held that exclusion of evidence may be necessary to protect constitutional guarantees, both the necessity for the collateral inquiry and the exclusion of evidence deflect a criminal trial from its basic purpose. Respondent would now have us require sweeping inquiries into the state of mind of a criminal defendant who has confessed, inquiries quite divorced from any co-

ercion brought to bear on the defendant by the State. We think the Constitution rightly leaves this sort of inquiry to be resolved by state laws governing the admission of evidence and erects no standard of its own in this area. A statement rendered by one in the condition of respondent might be proved to be quite unreliable, but this is a matter to be governed by the evidentiary laws of the forum, see, e.g., Fed. Rule Evid. 601, and not by the Due Process Clause of the Fourteenth Amendment. "The aim of the requirement of due process is not to exclude presumptively false evidence, but to prevent fundamental unfairness in the use of evidence, whether true or false." *Lisenba v. California,* 314 U.S. 219, 236 (1941).

We hold that coercive police activity is a necessary predicate to the finding that a confession is not "voluntary" within the meaning of the Due Process Clause of the Fourteenth Amendment. We also conclude that the taking of respondent's statements, and their admission into evidence, constitute no violation of that Clause.

III

A

The Supreme Court of Colorado went on to affirm the trial court's ruling that respondent's later statements made while in custody should be suppressed because respondent had not waived his right to consult an attorney and his right to remain silent. That court held that the State must bear its burden of proving waiver of these *Miranda* rights by "clear and convincing evidence." 702 P.2d, at 729. Although we have stated in passing that the State bears a "heavy" burden in proving waiver, *Miranda v. Arizona,* 384 U.S., at 475, we have never upheld that the "clear and convincing evidence" standard is the appropriate one.

In *Lego v. Twomey, supra,* this Court upheld a procedure in which the State established the [legal standard for the] voluntariness of a confession by no more than a preponderance of the evidence. We upheld it for two reasons. First, the voluntariness determination has nothing to do with the reliability of jury verdicts; rather, it is designed to determine the presence of police coercion. Thus, voluntariness is irrelevant to the presence or absence of the elements of a crime, which must be proved beyond a reasonable doubt. See *In re Winship,* 397 U.S. 358 (1970). Second, we rejected Lego's assertion that a high burden of proof was required to serve the values protected by the exclusionary rule. We surveyed the various reasons for excluding evidence, including a violation of the requirements of *Miranda v. Arizona, supra,* and we stated that "[i]n each instance, and without regard to its probative value, evidence is kept from the trier of guilt or innocence for reasons wholly apart from enhancing the reliability of verdicts." *Lego v. Twomey,* 404 U.S., at 488....

We now reaffirm our holding in *Lego:* Whenever the State bears the burden of proof in a motion to suppress a statement that the defendant claims was obtained in violation of our *Miranda* doctrine, the State need prove waiver only by a preponderance of the evidence. See *Nix v. Williams,* 467 U.S. 431, 444, and n.5 (1984). [Citation omitted.] "[T]he controlling burden of proof at suppression hearings should impose no greater burden than proof by a preponderance of the evidence..."

★ ★ ★

B

★ ★ ★

Respondent urges this Court to adopt his "free will" rationale, and to find an attempted waiver invalid whenever the defendant feels compelled to waive his rights by reason of any compulsion, even if the compulsion does not flow from the police....Respondent's perception of coercion flowing from the "voice of God," however important or significant such a perception may be in other disciplines, is a matter to which the United States Constitution does not speak.

IV

The judgment of the Supreme Court of Colorado is accordingly reversed, and the cause is remanded for further proceedings not inconsistent with this opinion.

It is so ordered.

COMMENTS, NOTES, AND QUESTIONS

1. In *Lego v. Twomey,* 404 U.S. 477 (1972), mentioned in the principal case, the Court held that the minimum standard required of the prosecution where it must establish the voluntariness of a confession is by the preponderance of the evidence. Since the voluntary standard looks to see what the police have done, it is not particularly concerned with the motivations of the arrestee but whether the police have engaged in coercive tactics or other unfair activities. Thus, in the *Connelly* case, the prosecution needed to prove that it was more likely than not that Connelly had voluntarily confessed to the murder without being subjected to coercion of the police.

2. As a practical matter, has a confession been voluntarily offered where psychological problems motivate a person to confess when he or she would not have done so in the absence of mental problems? The answer is that an individual may have a variety of motives, but so long as police coerciveness is not a factor, the reason a person offers a confession is generally not material. What if an individual confessed but did not possess a free will due to mental disease or defect? Is such a confession admissible against the maker? Would the *Connelly* Court have decided the case differently if Connelly had been under the influence of alcohol or drugs? Why or why not? Would the confession have been admitted if it were coerced by the threat of physical harm from a person or persons unconnected with the police? As a judge, would you have reason to question the reliability of the confession in that situation?

Identification Procedures: Constitutional Considerations

Chapter Outline

Key Terms

Due process requirements
Eyewitness identification
Fifth Amendment privilege at lineup
Identification: the *Neil* five-factors test
Improper steering
Individual show-up
Lineup

No right to counsel: photographic array
Photographic array
Right to counsel: limitations
Right to counsel: postarrest limitations
Right to counsel: postindictment
Right to counsel: postinformation
Suggestiveness at lineup

1. IDENTIFICATION PROCEDURES: INTRODUCTION

Attempts to screen the potentially guilty from the rest of society have been a problem of long standing without absolutely clear solutions that guarantee accuracy with reasonable certainty. Although a variety of methods of identification are available, a witness identification of the human body with a focus on the face has been a traditional avenue to discriminate the guilty from the innocent. We make discriminations on identity based on gender, race, skin color, eye color, height, and weight, as well as the tone of voice and linguistic characteristics. The use of fingerprinting, blood-typing, and DNA matching has been added to the traditional ways of discerning identity. Newer types of biometric measures are just now making their way to the forefront of identity screening. Measuring and identifying the blood vessel patterns on the human retina and using mathematical ratios and formulas to measure the face and head are among the most modern methods of what is claimed to be foolproof identification. Some of the newest methods will eventually become widely used in the law enforcement community, but even though the technology may be quite accurate, the expense of such advanced scientific measures may limit their application in the near term. The admissibility of scientific identity testing, assuming that the data have been obtained with due concern for appropriate criminal procedure, generally rests more with the law of evidence than with substantive criminal procedure.[315]

2. RIGHT TO COUNSEL AND DUE PROCESS CONCERNS

In most instances, traditional witness identification, with procedures based on fairly settled law, will be the path followed by most police departments and prosecutors. Most of the larger issues concerning identification procedures have been litigated years ago to the point that prosecutors, the defense bar, and the law enforcement community have fairly clear directives concerning the appropriateness of specific procedures. Issues surrounding the right to counsel during lineup procedures under the Sixth Amendment remain clear and are not subject to much dispute. The appropriateness and practice of conducting preindictment and preinformation interrogation in the absence of legal counsel are well known. Due process concerns involving suggestiveness or steering have been detailed in a variety of court cases so that there is a fairly clear certainty, if proper procedures are followed, that a criminal case will not be reversed for errors in this area. However, an appellate court should reverse a conviction based partially or wholly on eyewitness identification where the pretrial identification procedure "was so impermissibly suggestive as to give rise to a very substantial likelihood of irreparable misidentification."[316]

The legal standards involving identification procedures have seen little activity in the United States Supreme Court over the last several years, and there is no indication that future major changes are likely to be forthcoming. Commentators have criticized the identification process as creating potential for error in too many cases,[317] but judges and courts have not proven to be particularly amenable to change even when faced with scientific studies challenging the correctness or reliability of eyewitness identification.

---

[315]See, for example, *People v. Venegas,* 74 Cal. Rptr. 2d 262 (1998), where the Supreme Court of California considered the admissibility of DNA (deoxyribonucleic acid) testing under the rules of evidence and prior case law.

[316]*Simmons v. United States,* 390 U.S. 377, 384 (1968).

[317]See, for example, "Miscarriages of Justice and the Constitution," 2 Buff. Crim. L. R (1999), by Donald A. Dripps, and "Learning from Our Mistakes: A Criminal Justice Commission to Study Wrongful Convictions," 38 Cal. W. L. Rev. 333 (2002), by Keith A. Findley.

Proper identification of criminal suspects involves an inquiry concerning whether the suspect possesses a right to counsel and whether the identification procedure meets the standards of due process. Although the identification of a suspect may be one step toward a conviction, the Fifth Amendment privilege against compelled testimonial self-incrimination has been held not to be implicated when a witness views a suspect. Some suspects may refuse to participate in a lineup because identification may provide a step toward an eventual guilty verdict, but there is no constitutional basis for a suspect to refuse to participate in a lineup. In *United States v. Wade,* the defendant contended that by forcing him to take part in an in-person lineup, the government violated his Fifth Amendment privilege against self-incrimination (see Case 9.1).[318] The *Wade* Court rejected the suggestion by noting that the Fifth Amendment privilege protects a defendant from being required to testify against him- or herself and not from exhibiting him- or herself to potential eyewitnesses.[319]

Consistent with due process considerations, identification procedures include showing a single suspect to a witness, conducting a traditional lineup, having a witness look through the "mug book" or a computer-generated modern version, and conducting a photographic array of suspects. In all the identification processes, there must be no "steering" of the witness with a view to identifying a particular person as the criminal.

3. RIGHT TO COUNSEL UNDER THE SIXTH AMENDMENT

Court decisions have held that suspects may be entitled to the Sixth Amendment right to the assistance of legal counsel when a lineup is being conducted by law enforcement agents. Past decisions indicate that legal counsel is required at all "critical stages" of the criminal justice process where substantial rights of an accused may be compromised. Some identifications occur in the absence of counsel but under circumstances that have court approval. A failure to follow the rules and regulations developed through case law may culminate in a conviction ultimately being overturned or in the refusal of a court to allow a witness to offer an identification. The most clear-cut situation where the right to counsel exists occurs when there is a postindictment or postinformation in-person lineup. According to the Court in *United States v. Wade,*[320] when an arrestee has been formally charged with a crime, an in-person lineup constitutes a critical stage of the criminal justice process during which the suspect has a constitutional right to the assistance of counsel. In *Wade,* the Court quoted one commentator who observed:

> [t]he influence of improper suggestion upon identifying witnesses probably accounts for more miscarriages of justice than any other single factor—perhaps it is responsible for more such errors than all other factors combined. Wall, *Eyewitness Identification in Criminal Cases* 26.

---

[318]*United States v. Wade,* 388 U.S. 218 (1967).
[319]Ibid. at 221.
[320]Ibid. at 218.

Justice Brennan indicated concern with eyewitness identification procedures when he cautioned in *Wade* at 229:

> Suggestion can be created intentionally or unintentionally in many subtle ways. And the dangers for the suspect are particularly grave when the witness' opportunity for observation was insubstantial, and thus his susceptibility to suggestion the greatest.

Brennan continued to emphasize his concern for requiring reliable eyewitness identification procedures when he quoted from a legal encyclopedia:

> [i]t is a matter of common experience that, once a witness has picked out the accused at the line-up, he is not likely to go back on his word later on, so that, in practice, the issue of identity may (in the absence of other relevant evidence) for all practical purposes be determined there and then, before the trial. Williams Hammelmann, Identification Parades, Part I, [1963] Crim.L.Rev. 479, 482. *Wade* at 229.

The *Wade* Court indicated that in many cases the witness identification of a suspect as the guilty party may effectively conclude a criminal case and seal the fate of the accused, whether guilty or not. Once an eyewitness has selected a particular person as the guilty party and the government has taken clear steps to prosecute, the eyewitness is unlikely to recant the identification at a later time due to personal and institutional pressures.

According to the *Wade* Court, a major factor in the miscarriage of justice has traditionally been the degree of suggestion inherent in the manner in which the government presents the arrestee to the witness for the purpose of identification. Writing for the majority, Justice Brennan cited cases of questionable identification procedures in which one suspect had been identified by a witness where the suspect was the only person of oriental heritage in the lineup, a case where a tall suspect had been placed with short participants, and where a young suspect had been placed in a lineup array with older men.[321] Suggestive identification procedures create the potential for impermissibly "steering" eyewitnesses toward identifying a particular suspect, producing a due process violation.

The *Wade* case determined that the Sixth Amendment right to counsel extends to a person under an indictment or otherwise formally charged[322] with a criminal offense who is placed in an in-person lineup. An attorney may offer corrective suggestions concerning lineup procedures that will assist the police in conducting a proper identification. Naturally, law enforcement personnel have no interest in identifying the wrong person and should cooperate with an arrestee's counsel. In the absence of counsel, a variety of wrongs could occur, and the suspect would be powerless to contest their occurrence even if the arrestee became aware of them.

---

[321]Justice Brennan, in *United States v. Wade,* 388 U.S. 218, 232 (1967), at n.17, quoting Wall, *Eye-Witness Identification in Criminal Cases* 53, a commentator who had compiled a list of fact patterns illustrating the potentials for abuse in identification procedures.

[322]The concept of formal charge does not include an arrest for federal constitutional purposes on the theory that the government has not made a clear decision on prosecution. See *Kirby v. Illinois,* 406 U.S. 682 (1972).

Witnesses may be unaware of subtle steering in the making of an identification, and the suspect might be completely ignorant of undue suggestiveness in whatever form it might take. Other lineup participants possess no particular interest in protesting an improper lineup, since they are not targets of the identification procedure. Thus, where a suspect is represented by counsel and errors in procedure appear about to develop, the attorney may request that corrective measures be taken prior to the occurrence of irreparable misidentification.[323]

In a companion case to *Wade, Gilbert v. California,* the defendant had been required to participate in a postindictment in-person lineup without the presence of his attorney. Because there were so many witnesses to the alleged crimes of Gilbert, the lineup proceedings occurred in an auditorium with bright lights shining on the participants so that they could not observe the witnesses. Nearly one hundred witnesses gathered in the auditorium, where presumably they were able to talk with each other and observe identifications made by fellow witnesses. During the guilt phase of his capital murder trial, Gilbert sought to elicit confirmation from some of these eyewitnesses that they had made earlier identifications of him at the auditorium lineup, thus indicating that the identification procedure occurred without his attorney being present. The *Gilbert* Court vacated the sentence of death, since it held:

> The admission of the in-court identifications without first determining that they were not tainted by the illegal lineup but were of independent origin was constitutional error. *United States v. Wade, supra.* We there held that a post-indictment pretrial lineup at which the accused is exhibited to identifying witnesses is a critical stage of the criminal prosecution; that police conduct of such a lineup without notice to, and in the absence of, his counsel denies the accused his Sixth Amendment right to counsel and calls in question the admissibility at trial of the in-court identifications of the accused by witnesses who attended the lineup. *Gilbert* at 273.

From the *Wade* and *Gilbert* cases, a clear rule has emerged that postindictment or postinformation in-person lineups require the presence of counsel, absent waiver, or the evidence concerning the lineup will, at a minimum, be excluded from trial.

4. RIGHT TO COUNSEL DURING IDENTIFICATION: LIMITATIONS

A reading of the *Wade* and *Gilbert* cases would seem to indicate that the Supreme Court of the United States was moving in the direction of mandating the presence of counsel at all identification procedures. It could be argued that counsel would have to be supplied for every individual arrested by police if any witness identification process was contemplated. However, the Court backed away from the *Wade* holding a bit when it determined that the Sixth Amendment right to

---

[323]One could argue that in a photographic array, the same vices that legal counsel should prevent by being present in a postindictment, postinformation lineup could easily happen with no one present to complain.

counsel during the identification process does not apply in every conceivable context. In *Kirby v. Illinois,*[324] the Court required that formal adversarial proceedings beyond a bare arrest have to be initiated before the right to counsel matured at witness identification procedure. The defendants in *Kirby* had been arrested for robbery but had not been formally charged. While Kirby was in custody, police allowed the victim to enter a holding room and make an identification by merely observing Kirby and another defendant, who were the lone occupants. According to the Court, Kirby and his companion had no right to counsel for purposes of identification, since they had not been indicted, had not had an information filed against them, were not being arraigned or subjected to a preliminary hearing, and were not facing a clear decision by the state to prosecute. The rule that emerged requires the presence of counsel when an information has been filed or an indictment returned, but no right to counsel exists for a person who has been merely arrested and who police want to subject to an identification process.

5. PHOTOGRAPHIC ARRAYS: NO SIXTH AMENDMENT RIGHT TO COUNSEL

The use of a still photographic array for identification purposes, even where the subject has been indicted or a prosecution has otherwise been initiated, does not require the presence of counsel, according to *United States v. Ash.*[325] According to the Court, an arrestee or defendant has no Sixth Amendment right to counsel at a photographic array, no matter when it occurs, because the procedure is not one at which the accused requires "aid in coping with legal problems or assistance in meeting his adversary."[326] Were legal counsel required at each and every photo array, as a practical matter, an attorney would have to participate every time a witness looked at a mug book or computer display of photographs, even if the target was on the run and had never been captured. In the pretrial context, the attorney's role is to assist the defendant in dealing with legal questions and to suggest solutions where unfair practices or conditions appear. Where a defendant is not present, as in a police presentation of a photographic array to eyewitnesses, "no possibility arises that the accused might be misled by his lack of familiarity with the law or overpowered by his professional adversary."[327] Since a photographic array does not involve an actual defendant-witness confrontation similar to a trial, the assistance of an attorney is not constitutionally mandated. However, impermissible "steering," suggestive photograph selection, or the repeated presence of only the suspect's picture in a series of photographic arrays collectively remain as potential problems for an accused for which a remedy may prove illusory.

In dealing with photographic arrays, the Supreme Court was not willing to further extend the right to counsel under the Sixth Amendment, even though potential prejudice to a particular defendant might arise due to improper conduct of law enforcement officials. The Court noted that photographic identifications were not

---

[324]406 U.S. 682 (1972).
[325]413 U.S. 300 (1973).
[326]Ibid. at 313.
[327]Ibid. at 317.

the only part of a criminal prosecution where an unfair prosecutor might fail to follow due process requirements. According to Justice Blackmun, writing for the Court in *Ash:*

> Evidence favorable to the accused may be withheld; testimony of witnesses may be manipulated; the results of laboratory tests may be contrived. In many ways, the prosecutor, by accident or by design, may improperly subvert the trial. The primary safeguard against abuses of this kind is the ethical responsibility of the prosecutor, who, as so often has been said, may "strike hard blows," but not "foul ones." *Berger v. United States,* 295 U.S. 78, 88 (1935); *Brady v. Maryland,* 373 U.S. 83, 87–88 (1963). If that safeguard fails, review remains available under due process standards. See *Giglio v. United States,* 405 U.S. 150 (1972). *Ash* at 320.

The Court trusted that most prosecutors would properly follow the law, and in cases where the prosecution failed to accord due process to a defendant at a nonadversarial photographic array, a defendant's legal counsel should be able to ferret out the wrongdoing and ultimately achieve justice. However, a practical problem, never addressed by the Court, exists where the wrongdoing never becomes apparent through pretrial discovery or from cross-examination during trial, instead remaining hidden to wreak its unconstitutional wrong on an unknowing defendant's case.

6. DUE PROCESS CONCERNS: SUGGESTIVENESS OF IDENTIFICATION

Consistent with due process considerations, all identification procedures should be constructed in a neutral manner with a view to producing a reliable and accurate identification. Where impermissible steering, directing, or suggesting transpires, the accuracy of the result comes into question. While a witness ideally may be offered several choices of photographs or of several persons in a lineup, on occasions a formal lineup or photographic array is impractical and other techniques must be substituted. Sometimes a suspect quickly enters police custody, virtually at the crime scene, and is subjected to a return to the scene for an immediate identification or exclusion from further police interest. If a victim cannot travel to the location of the suspect, the suspect may be brought to the victim without violating the suspect's due process rights or the right to counsel. However, such a procedure becomes improper where adversarial proceedings have been initiated and the defendant has appeared at a preliminary hearing without counsel. An identification by a witness who observed the defendant alone at the preliminary hearing should have been excluded from the subsequent trial due to the violation not of due process but of the Sixth Amendment right to counsel.[328]

Exigent or emergency circumstances permit identification by witnesses where practical necessities dictate the rapid use of creative identification procedures despite the risks of suggestiveness. In *Stovall v. Denno,*[329] police brought an arrested homicide suspect to the hospital bedside of a victim whose health was in a precarious state (see Case 9.2). The victim was permitted to identify the unrepresented suspect

---

[328]See *Moore v. Illinois,* 434 U.S. 220 (1977).
[329]388 U.S. 293 (1967).

as the killer of her husband, despite the suggestiveness inherent in the one-on-one encounter. According to the *Stovall* Court, such practice was appropriate under the circumstances of the case: a sole suspect, a critically injured victim, and a need for identification. The teaching of *Stovall* illustrates that there are identifications in which counsel need not be present and the use of a formal lineup is not required so long as there is no significant chance of irreparable misidentification of the suspect.

Improper suggestiveness may violate the Due Process Clause of the Fourteenth Amendment in a situation where successive lineups were conducted and where the only common individual to all of them happened to be the defendant. In *Foster v. California*,[330] the defendant was initially placed in a lineup that contained three men. The defendant was nearly six feet tall, and the other two men in the lineup were significantly shorter, a fact that gave rise to an impermissible steering argument. One of the eyewitnesses to the case said that he "thought" Foster was one of the guilty men but was not positive. After speaking to Foster and hearing his voice, the eyewitness was not any more secure in his identification, even after meeting with him one-on-one in a room. A week or so later, the police arranged for the eyewitness to view another lineup involving five men. Foster was the only person in the second lineup who had appeared in the first lineup. The witness made a certain identification of Foster following the second lineup. The *Foster* Court reversed and remanded the case. According to *Foster*, successive positioning in repeated lineups clearly violated due process and could not be lawfully conducted as a general rule. In many respects, the result in *Foster* was required if the Court followed its prior *Wade* decision because *Wade* had held that lineups constitute a critical stage of the criminal justice process and that judged by the totality of the circumstances, an identification procedure cannot be allowed to stand where the procedures were unnecessarily suggestive and conducive to irreparable mistaken identification.

7. ACCURATE EYEWITNESS IDENTIFICATION: THE *NEIL* FIVE-FACTORS TEST

Whether or not counsel is required, the identification process must produce reliable and reasonably accurate identification. In an effort to determine the appropriate standard for proper eyewitness identification procedures, the Court clarified *Stovall v. Denno* by adopting a more specific test in *Neil v. Biggers* (see Case 9.3).[331] In developing the "totality of the circumstances" test, the Court listed five factors as a guideline to measure whether a particular identification process comported with due process and eliminated any significant chance of irreparable misidentification. When considering a claim involving an alleged improper identification, courts must consider the opportunity of the witness to view the criminal at the time of the crime, the witness's degree of attention, the accuracy of the witness's original description of the criminal, the level of certainty demonstrated by the witness at the time of the confrontation, and the length of time that had passed between the crime scene identification and the confrontation. A proper analysis by a trial court of these

---

[330]394 U.S. 440 (1969).
[331]409 U.S. 188 (1972).

factors, called the "totality of the circumstances test," should result in only proper eyewitness identifications being admitted to evidence by trial court judges.

In *Neil v. Biggers,* officers paraded a suspect past the complaining victim in a rape case. Previously, the victim-witness had looked at mug books and photographs and had attended in-person lineups for about six months and had identified no one. When she walked past the suspect in a hallway, she indicated that she was very sure he was the perpetrator. At the crime scene, she had a good opportunity to see his face and body and paid close attention during the crime, and her original description proved quite accurate. The six-month delay was viewed as the weakest part of her identification but did not destroy it because of her level of certainty. The *Neil* Court approved the courtroom use of eyewitness identification of the suspect even though he was not represented by counsel at the time of his identification. Consistent with *Kirby,* since the suspect had not been formally charged with a crime, he did not possess the right to counsel at the time of his identification by the victim.

The *Neil* eyewitness identification test may be applied to virtually any type of identification process, from an in-person lineup to the use of a photographic array. An interesting and somewhat suggestive procedure occurred in *Manson v. Brathwaite,*[332] where a trained police officer observed a drug dealer during an undercover narcotics purchase (see Case 9.4). Subsequently, the officer described the suspected drug dealer to a fellow officer in such detail that the fellow officer believed he knew the identity of the suspect. The second officer obtained a photograph of the suspected drug dealer and placed it on the original officer's desk. When the undercover officer looked at the photograph, he instantly recognized the drug suspect. At the time of the viewing of the photograph, the suspect did not have counsel and was not under arrest.

The Supreme Court upheld the identification of Brathwaite by the undercover officer by using the five-factors test of *Neil v. Biggers* and concluded that, under the circumstances, such a procedure did not violate due process. The officer had been trained in observation of suspects, especially concerning details relating to identification. He had a fairly clear view of the suspect, and little time had transpired between the original view and the identification. The officer was sure of his identification, and the suspect description matched the description originally offered by the officer.

Many states have adopted the *Neil v. Biggers* five-factors test or some slight variation for evaluating eyewitness identification issues. Kansas follows its own test, which incorporates some of the *Neil* case and adds some slightly different considerations. According to a Kansas case, the factors used to determine eyewitness identification are as follows:

(1) The opportunity of the witness to view the actor during the event; (2) the witness's degree of attention to the actor at the time of the event; (3) the witness's capacity to observe the event, including his or her physical and mental acuity; (4) whether the witness's identification was made spontaneously and remained consistent thereafter, or whether it was the product of suggestion; and (5) the nature of the event being observed and the likelihood that the witness would perceive, remember

---

[332]432 U.S. 98 (1977).

and relate it correctly. This last area includes such factors as whether the event was an ordinary one in the mind of the observer during the time it was observed, and whether the race of the actor was the same as the observer's. *Kansas v. Long,* 721 P.2d 483 at 493 (1986).

In a recent Kansas case, a trial court used the test for eyewitness identification to determine whether an accused robber had been identified consistent with fundamental fairness. In the robbery, the perpetrator entered the store with a bandanna over his lower face, acted as if he had a firearm up his sleeve, and threatened the clerk. The robber was face-to-face with the clerk, who looked away only long enough to retrieve the money. The robber immediately left the scene and removed the bandanna as he entered his car. Within minutes, the police captured a man who matched the description and had the clerk identify him. Following admission of the eyewitness identification at trial and his conviction, the defendant appealed, alleging a violation of due process involving an alleged misidentification offered at trial by the clerk-victim. The appellate court considered the degree of attention offered by the clerk and noted that the eyewitness was completely focused on the robber, the clerk's ability to perceive the robber was unimpeded, and the two were in close proximity. The appellate court felt that the clerk properly described the appearance of the robber. The victim offered information concerning the robber's sideburns, which he could see under the bandanna, and the victim's description of the robber, especially his height, was quite accurate. The appellate court noted with approval that the trial court properly considered whether the event was ordinary to the witness and whether the race of the perpetrator was the same as that of the witness. An armed robbery, according to the court, was not an ordinary event to the store clerk, so that facts surrounding the event should have been memorable to the victim. When the appellate court considered all the factors, it affirmed the conviction, since it determined that there was little likelihood of misidentification by the convenience store clerk.[333] This type of trial and appellate court analysis serves to prevent misidentification of defendants by meeting due process standards under both state and federal constitutions.

8. CURRENT APPLICATION OF IDENTIFICATION PROCEDURES

Since for several years the Supreme Court of the United States has not heard a major case that altered the due process requirements of eyewitness identification, the general framework involving the right to counsel and to due process remains relatively settled law. Demonstrative of generally accepted identification process is a case from the Court of Appeals for the Seventh Circuit, *United States v. Traeger,*[334] where the defendant alleged that his identification in a bank robbery case contained constitutional errors.

In *Traeger,* the defendant contended that a bank teller's identification of him as the robber should have been suppressed. At the crime scene, the teller had an excellent

[333]*Kansas v. Hunt,* 69 P.3d 571, 577 (2003).
[334]289 F.3d 461 (2002).

view of the robber and made a certain identification three weeks following the crime. According to Traeger, his constitutional right to due process had been violated because the lineup, as composed, was unduly suggestive. The defendant was much taller and much more robust than the other men in the lineup, a fact, he alleged, that made him stand out from the others. The identification process occurred three weeks after the robbery, with all the participants dressed in traditional jail orange jumpsuits. In the beginning stages of the lineup, all the men were seated, which disguised height differentials, but subsequently, the men were asked to stand one by one. Since the defendant was by far the largest of the participants, he contended that the lineup procedure was unduly suggestive. The Court of Appeals noted that it normally engaged in a two-step process in evaluating such a claim:

> First, we ask whether the defendant established that the identification procedure was unnecessarily suggestive. If it was, we ask whether, under the totality of the circumstances, the identification was reliable despite the suggestive procedures. In determining the reliability of an identification, we consider five factors: (1) the witness' opportunity to view the criminal at the time of the crime, (2) the witness' degree of attention, (3) the accuracy of the witness' prior description of the criminal, (4) the level of certainty that the witness demonstrated at the time of the confrontation, and (5) the time elapsed between the crime and the confrontation. *See Cossel v. Miller,* 229 F.3d 649, 655 (7th Cir. 2000) (citing *Neil v. Biggers,* 409 U.S. 188, 199–200, 34 L. Ed. 2d 401, 93 S. Ct. 375 (1972)). *Traeger* at 474.

In reviewing the material facts, the *Traeger* Court determined, from viewing photographs of the lineup, that even though the defendant was much larger in stature and more robust than the other participants, the differences were not so great as to create an unduly suggestive lineup. The court also found that the bank teller had ample opportunity to view the robber while she was getting money from her drawer and that her level of attention appeared to have been elevated by the fact that she was the victim of a robbery. She accurately described Traeger as an individual who was in his midthirties, "who was 6'3" tall, weighed 300 to 350 pounds, was unshaven, and wore a blond ponytail."[335] The Court rejected the defense argument concerning unfair suggestiveness because Traeger wore an ankle strap restraint during the lineup. The barely visible plastic ankle restraint would not be recognizable as a restraint unless one were intimately acquainted with the criminal justice system, and there was no evidence that the bank teller focused on Traeger's feet at the lineup.[336]

Ultimately, the Court of Appeals rejected defendant Traeger's complaints based on the alleged improper identification procedures because the Court followed the suggestions offered by the Supreme Court in *Neil v. Biggers,* mentioned previously. While most state courts have followed the principles suggested in *Neil* and reconfirmed by the Court in *Manson v. Brathwaite*[337] when deciding identification issues, some states have determined to pursue a more in-depth evaluation and may reject identifications, based on state case law. States are free to offer greater procedural

---

[335]Ibid.
[336]Ibid.
[337]432 U.S. 98 (1977).

safeguards and follow more stringent concepts of due process concerning identification and to reject procedures that would pass muster under the minimal federal constitutional standards.[338]

9. SUMMARY: ADMISSIBILITY OF IDENTIFICATION AT TRIAL

Where the identification meets constitutional standards, the eyewitness may offer identification evidence from the witness stand. In the event that problems such as a failure to provide counsel at a postindictment lineup or where undue suggestiveness transpired during a lineup, the witness may be prevented from making an in-court identification. At a minimum, the witness will be prohibited from making any mention of the improper lineup. If improper suggestiveness or other illegal procedure occurred, courts are required to determine whether the witness is testifying from the original observation, not bolstered by the illegal observation at the lineup. Addressing this issue, the Court in *United States v. Wade* noted, "We do not think this disposition can be justified without first giving the Government the opportunity to establish by clear and convincing evidence that the in-court identifications were based upon observations of the suspect other than the lineup identification."[339] If a trial court determines that the identification proffered by the witness has been influenced or tainted by the illegal procedure, the witness's testimony relative to identity must be excluded. Under the circumstances, the level of certainty of the witness may have been buttressed by the power of suggestion or by repeatedly seeing the suspect in successive lineups to the point that the witness may actually be offering testimony not from the crime scene identification but from the lineup itself.

Generally, the prosecution is permitted to attempt to establish by clear and convincing evidence that the eyewitness identification was based on observations of the defendant at other locations and not based primarily on a lineup tainted with due process problems. The government must prove that the witness's memory has not been influenced by an illegal lineup and that the identification emanated from appropriate observations. If the prosecution meets the burden of proof, the witness is permitted to offer evidence concerning identity.

If an issue of tainted identification reaches an appellate court, the task is similar to the process followed by a trial court. The appellate court must determine whether the in-court identification had an independent source and was permissibly admitted at trial. If it did not have an independent source, the reviewing court must evaluate whether the introduction of the evidence constituted harmless error beyond a reasonable doubt.[340]

---

[338]For some alternative state approaches to identification problems that generally offer additional protections to defendants, see *Commonwealth v. Henderson,* 411 Mass. 309 (1991); *State v. Ramirez,* 817 P.2d 774 (Utah 1991); *People v. Adams,* 53 N.Y.2d 241 (1981).
[339]*United States v. Wade,* 388 U.S. 218, 240 (1967).
[340]Ibid. at 242.

MAJOR CASES

CASE 9.1

In-Person Lineups Constitute a Critical Stage of Criminal Prosecution

United States v. Wade
Supreme Court of the United States
388 U.S. 218 (1967)

FACTS

A man wearing a strip of tape on each side of his face robbed a federally insured bank in Eustance, Texas. Six months later, a grand jury indicted Wade and police arrested him. Wade had counsel appointed, and the police subjected him to an in-person lineup. This identification procedure was conducted in the absence of any notice to Wade's appointed counsel and resulted in his identification as the bank robber by two bank employees. Unfortunately for Wade, the employees later identified Wade as the robber in open court.

At trial, counsel for defendant made a motion that the eyewitness's identification in court be stricken due to the violation of Wade's right to counsel at the in-person lineup. The trial court overruled the motion and Wade's robbery conviction resulted.

The Court of Appeals reversed the verdict on the theory that holding a lineup in the absence of the defendant's court-appointed attorney violated the defendant's Sixth Amendment right to counsel. It ordered a retrial at which the in-court identification evidence was to be excluded. The Supreme Court of the United States granted certiorari.

PROCEDURAL ISSUE

Where a person has been formally charged[341] with a particular crime, does an in-person lineup constitute a critical stage of the criminal justice process so that the person has the Sixth Amendment right to have counsel present?

HELD: YES

RATIONALE

Mr. Justice Brennan delivered the opinion of the Court.

★ ★ ★

III

The Government characterizes the lineup as a mere preparatory step in the gathering of the prosecution's evidence, not different—for Sixth Amendment purposes—from various other preparatory steps, such as systematized or scientific analyzing of the accused's fingerprints, blood sample, clothing, hair, and the like. We think there are differences which preclude such stages being characterized as critical stages at which the accused has the right to the presence of his counsel.

★ ★ ★

IV

[T]he confrontation compelled by the State between the accused and the victim or witnesses to a crime to elicit identification evidence is peculiarly riddled with innumerable dangers and variable factors which might seriously, even crucially, derogate from a fair trial. The vagaries of eyewitness identification are well-known; the annals of criminal law are rife with instances of mistaken identification. Mr. Justice Frankfurter once said:

> What is the worth of identification testimony even when uncontradicted? The identification of strangers is proverbially untrustworthy. The hazards of such testimony are established by a formidable number of instances in the records of English and American trials. These instances are recent—not due to the brutalities of ancient criminal procedure. *The Case of Sacco and Vanzetti* 30 (1927).

A major factor contributing to the high incidence of miscarriage of justice from mistaken identification has been the degree of suggestion inherent in the manner in which the prosecution presents the suspect to witnesses for pretrial identification. A commentator has observed that

---

[341]The term *formally charged* means that the defendant has been indicted or that an information has been filed against the defendant. A mere arrest does not, by itself, indicate a formal charge as interpreted by the Supreme Court of the United States. Some states have determined, as a matter of state law, that the arrest is the triggering event giving rise to the right to counsel.

[t]he influence of improper suggestion upon identifying witnesses probably accounts for more miscarriages of justice than any other single factor—perhaps it is responsible for more such errors than all other factors combined. Wall, *Eye-Witness Identification in Criminal Cases* 26.

Suggestion can be created intentionally or unintentionally in many subtle ways. And the dangers for the suspect are particularly grave when the witness' opportunity for observation was insubstantial, and thus his susceptibility to suggestion the greatest.

Moreover,

"[i]t is a matter of common experience that, once a witness has picked out the accused at the line-up, he is not likely to go back on his word later on, so that in practice the issue of identity may (in the absence of other relevant evidence) for all practical purposes be determined there and then, before the trial."

The pretrial confrontation for purpose of identification may take the form of a lineup, also known as an "identification parade" or "showup," as in the present case, or presentation of the suspect alone to the witness, as in *Stovall v. Denno, supra.* It is obvious that risks of suggestion attend either form of confrontation and increase the dangers inhering in eyewitness identification. But as is the case with secret interrogation, there is serious difficulty in depicting what transpires at lineups and other forms of identification confrontations. "Privacy results in secrecy and this in turn results in a gap in our knowledge as to what in fact goes on. . . ." *Miranda v. State of Arizona, supra,* 384 U.S. at 448. For the same reasons, the defense can seldom reconstruct the manner and mode of lineup identification for judge or jury at trial. Those participating in a lineup with the accused may often be police officers; in any event, the participants' names are rarely recorded or divulged at trial. The impediments to an objective observation are increased when the victim is the witness. Lineups are prevalent in rape and robbery prosecutions and present a particular hazard that a victim's understandable outrage may excite vengeful or spiteful motives. In any event, neither witnesses not lineup participants are apt to be alert for conditions prejudicial to the suspect. And if they were, it would likely be of scant benefit to the suspect, since neither witnesses nor lineup participants are likely to be schooled in the detection of suggestive influences. Improper influences may go undetected by a suspect, guilty or not, who experiences the emotional tension which we might expect in one being confronted with potential accusers. Even when he does observe abuse, if he has a criminal record, he may be reluctant to take the stand and open up the admission of prior convictions. Moreover, any protestations by the suspect of the fairness of the lineup made at trial are likely to be in vain; the jury's choice is between the accused's unsupported version and that of the police officers present. In short, the accused's inability effectively to reconstruct at trial any unfairness that occurred at the lineup may deprive him of his only opportunity meaningfully to attack the credibility of the witness' courtroom identification.

What facts have been disclosed in specific cases about the conduct of pretrial confrontations for identification illustrate both the potential for substantial prejudice to the accused at that stage and the need for its revelation at trial. A commentator provides some striking examples:

"In a Canadian case . . . the defendant had been picked out of a lineup of six men, of which he was the only Oriental. In other cases, a black-haired suspect was placed among a group of light-haired persons, tall suspects have been made to stand with short non-suspects, and, in a case where the perpetrator of the crime was known to be a youth, a suspect under twenty was placed in a lineup with five other persons, all of whom were forty or over."

Similarly, state reports, in the course of describing prior identification admitted as evidence of guilt, reveal numerous instances of suggestive procedures, for example, that all in the lineup but the suspect were known to the identifying witness, that the other participants in a lineup were grossly dissimilar in appearance to the suspect, that only the suspect was required to wear distinctive clothing which the culprit allegedly wore, that the witness is told by the police that they have caught the culprit after which the defendant is brought before the witness alone or is viewed in jail, that the suspect is pointed out before or during a lineup, and that the participants in the lineup are asked to try on an article of clothing which fits only the suspect.

The potential for improper influence is illustrated by the circumstances, insofar as they appear, surrounding the prior identifications in the three cases we decide today. In the present case, the testimony of the identifying witnesses elicited on cross-examination revealed that those witnesses were taken to the courthouse and seated in the courtroom to await assembly of the lineup. The courtroom faced on a hallway observable to the witnesses through an open door. The cashier testified that she saw Wade "standing in the hall" within sight of an FBI agent. Five or six other prisoners later appeared in the hall. The vice president testified that he saw a person in the hall in the custody of the agent who "resembled the person that we identified as the one that had entered the bank."

★ ★ ★

Since it appears that here is grave potential for prejudice, intentional or not, in the pretrial lineup, which may not be capable of reconstruction at trial, and since presence of counsel itself can often avert prejudice and assure a meaningful confrontation at trial, there can be little doubt that for Wade the postindictment lineup was a critical stage of the prosecution at which he was "as much entitled to such aid [of counsel] . . . as at the trial itself." *Powell v. Alabama,* 287 U.S. 45, at 57. Thus both Wade and his counsel should have been notified of the impending lineup, and counsel's presence should have been a requisite to conduct of the lineup, absent an "intelligent waiver." See *Carnley v. Cochran,* 369 U.S. 506. No substantial countervailing policy considerations have been advanced against the requirement of the presence of counsel. Concern is expressed that the requirement will forestall prompt identifications and result in obstruction of the confrontations. As for the first, we note that in the two cases in which the right to counsel is today held to apply, counsel had already been appointed and no argument is made in either case that notice to counsel would have prejudicially delayed the confrontations. Moreover, we leave open the question whether the presence of substitute counsel might not suffice where notification and presence of the suspect's own counsel would result in prejudicial delay. And to refuse to recognize the right to counsel for fear that counsel will obstruct the course of justice is contrary to the basic assumptions upon which this Court has operated in Sixth Amendment cases.

In our view counsel can hardly impede legitimate law enforcement; on the contrary, for the reasons expressed, law enforcement may be assisted by preventing the infiltration of taint in the prosecution's identification evidence. That result cannot help the guilty avoid conviction but can only help assure that the right man had been brought to justice.

★ ★ ★

V

We come now to the question whether the denial of Wade's motion to strike the courtroom identification by the bank witnesses at trial because of the absence of his counsel at the lineup required, as the Court of Appeals held, the grant of a new trial at which such evidence is to be excluded. We do not think this disposition can be justified without first giving the Government the opportunity to establish by clear and convincing evidence that the in-court identifications were based upon observations of the suspect other than the lineup identification.

A rule limited solely to the exclusion of testimony concerning identification at the lineup itself, without regard to admissibility of the courtroom identification, would render the right to counsel an empty one. The lineup is most often used, as in the present case, to crystallize the witnesses' identification of the defendant for future reference. We have already noted that the lineup identification will have that effect. The State may then rest upon the witnesses' unequivocal courtroom identification, and not mention the pretrial identification as part of the State's case at trial. Counsel is then in the predicament in which Wade's counsel found himself—realizing that possible unfairness at the lineup may be the sole means of attack upon the unequivocal courtroom identification, and having to probe in the dark in an attempt to discover and reveal unfairness, while bolstering the government witness' courtroom identification by bringing out and dwelling upon his prior identification.

★ ★ ★

On the record now before us we cannot make the determination whether the in-court identifications had an independent origin. This was not an issue at trial, although there is some evidence relevant to a determination. That inquiry is most properly made in the District Court. We therefore think the appropriate procedure to be followed is to vacate the conviction pending a hearing to determine whether the in-court identifications had an independent source, or whether, in any event, the introduction of the evidence was harmless error, *Chapman v. State of California,* 386 U.S. 18, and for the District Court to reinstate the conviction or order a new trial, as may be proper.

Judgment of Court of Appeals vacated and case remanded with direction.

COMMENTS, NOTES, AND QUESTIONS

1. Would you see a problem where multiple witnesses were permitted to make an identification of one defendant while each witness could hear the other make an identification? Would the power of suggestion create an impermissible potential for misidentification? How should a lineup be conducted, consistent with fundamental fairness, when large numbers of witnesses need to attend? In *Gilbert v. California*, 388 U.S. 263 (1967), an auditorium of up to a hundred witnesses to crimes allegedly committed by the defendant assembled together in the presence of each other. The witnesses spoke to each other concerning identity of various suspects, and some witnesses requested to see some of the lineup participants more than once. The witnesses were allowed to identify the number of the suspect which each thought was a guilty party in front of the other witnesses. Among the due process problems was a chance that an unsure witness would identify the defendant after hearing and seeing other witnesses make positive identifications. The *Gilbert* Court held that the use of such an identification process violates the due process rights of a suspect, since the chances for misidentification are greatly and impermissibly enhanced.

2. Could it be said that an arrest is really the initiation of a criminal prosecution and that, following arrest, counsel should be available to a criminal defendant? Or is it only when an indictment has been returned or an information filed that the adverse positions of the parties become solidified so that counsel at a lineup should be required? What if police procure an arrest warrant? Could this act be construed as the formal initiation of a prosecution for which counsel at an in-person lineup should be permitted? Following the opinion in *Wade,* the thrust of the case would give rise to the implication that, in the future, an attorney might be required in all confrontations between suspects and eyewitnesses. In the years between the *Wade* and *Gilbert* cases and the decision in *Kirby v. Illinois,* the activist nature of the Supreme Court appeared to temper a bit. *Wade* and *Gilbert* indicated that a defendant possessed the right to counsel at a postindictment in-person lineup, and it would not have been too much of a stretch, constitutionally, to require counsel for all postarrest identification processes. What about a person subjected to a lineup prior to the return of an indictment or the filing of an information? Additional extension of the

right to counsel did not come to pass as the Court refused to go further in that direction in *Kirby v. Illinois,* 406 U.S. 682 (1972). In *Kirby,* the Court determined that an attorney was not constitutionally required if the identification procedure occurred after arrest but prior to indictment or the filing of an information.

3. If police have a suspect appear in a series of lineups and confrontations, and an unsure eyewitness gradually gains certainty in making an identification, would this procedure violate due process? Should it? Would a witness who observed the same person in successive lineups have an identification consciously or unconsciously enhanced in memory so as to make a positive recognition at a later date? In *Foster v. California,* 394 U.S. 440 (1969), an eyewitness to an armed robbery indicated a tentative identification of Foster as one of the perpetrators but was ultimately unsure. Later, Foster was taken to a room with the witness and placed in a position to have the witness observe him. The witness remained unsure of making an identification. After a week passed, police again exhibited Foster to the witness in a traditional lineup, with the result that the witness made a completely certain identification of Foster. The Court held that this identification practice was unnecessarily suggestive and likely to result in an irreparable mistaken identification. In *Foster,* the witness could have become so familiar with the defendant, by observing him in successive lineups, that the witness honestly believed that the identification came from the original crime scene observation.

4. Do opportunities for steering, suggestion, and other mischief occur at photographic lineups or arrays? How would a defense counsel be able to offer assistance to a defendant when police show a series of photographs to witnesses? Should the photographic array proceeding be videotaped for preservation of any due process violations? According to *United States v. Ash,* 413 U.S. 300 (1973), the right to counsel does not extended to require the presence of counsel at a photographic array or other viewing of photographs. In *Ash,* the prosecutor showed eyewitnesses photographs of Ash and another suspect in an effort to determine whether the witnesses would be able to make identifications at trial. The Court proved unwilling to extend the right to counsel to include a prosecutor's pretrial interviews with witnesses.[342] According to the Court, "[s]ince the accused himself is not present at the time of the photographic display, and asserts no right to be present, no possibility arises that the accused might be misled by his

---

[342]In *Patterson v. Illinois,* 487 U.S. 285 at 298 (1988), Justice White, writing for the Court, indicated continued approval of the *Ash* result that no right to counsel attached to "postindictment photographic display identification," since the accused does not have to deal with complicated legal problems at that stage of the proceeding.

lack of familiarity with the law." Despite the lack of a right to counsel, the defendant may be able to argue that a violation of due process has occurred if impermissible "steering" transpired while the witness viewed the photographs. How could a defendant find out what happened at a photographic lineup to make a due process violation argument when neither the defendant nor the defense attorney was permitted to be present?

CASE 9.2

One-Person Show-Up Does Not Violate Due Process

Stovall v. Denno
Supreme Court of the United States
388 U.S. 293 (1967)

FACTS

During the murder of Dr. Behrendt, his wife had engaged the knife-wielding assailant in an effort to save her husband's life. When the attacker turned his attention to her, she had a good opportunity for viewing her assailant. Although she was critically wounded by repeated stabbing, she gave a description of the attacker. During the homicide investigation, police collected a shirt from the kitchen floor and keys in a pocket which they traced to the defendant. One day later, Stovall was in custody for the death of Dr. Behrendt and for the attack on his wife.

Because of her serious knife wounds, Mrs. Behrendt was hospitalized for surgery in order to save her life. The police arranged with her doctor to bring Stovall to her hospital bedside for the purposes of identification. Mrs. Behrendt had survived surgery, but was not in good shape and her ability to live was in some doubt. So far as was known, she was clear-headed and not under the influence of drugs which would cloud her judgement. The defendant entered the hospital room handcuffed to a police officer who asked if Mrs. Behrendt recognized Stovall as the man who was the assailant of her husband and of herself. She readily identified him both by appearance and by a voice sample which the police required that the defendant offer at her bedside.

At the trial, Mrs. Behrendt readily made another identification of defendant in open court. She had originally

seen him at the crime scene and then again in the hospital room. Stovall "claimed that, among other constitutional rights allegedly denied him at his trial, the admission of Mrs. Behrendt's identification testimony violated his rights under the Fifth, Sixth, and Fourteenth Amendments because he had been compelled to submit to the hospital room confrontation without the help of counsel and under circumstances which unfairly focused the witness' attention on him as the man believed by the police to be the guilty person."[343] The trial court rejected his contentions and the court proceeding resulted in a conviction for capital murder for which the defendant received the death penalty.

Since his appellate efforts proved unsuccessful in the New York state court system, he filed a motion for a writ of *habeas corpus* in the proper federal district court. Among other legal arguments, Stovall alleged that his rights under the Sixth Amendment right to counsel had been violated and that the government of New York had violated his rights to due process under the Fourteenth Amendment. His Sixth Amendment right had been transgressed, he alleged, because he had been compelled to participate in the hospital room identification/confrontation without being represented by legal counsel. In addition, the circumstances under which he had been identified unfairly focused the witness's attention on him as the man believed by the police to be guilty of the attacks. The district court rejected his arguments as did the court of appeals. The Supreme Court granted certiorari.

PROCEDURAL ISSUE

When a crime scene witness might not live to testify and where police conduct a one-person show-up in a hospital room for purposes of identification with an arrestee who has not been indicted, does such conduct violate due process under the Fourteenth Amendment?

HELD: NO

RATIONALE

Mr. Justice Brennan delivered the opinion of the Court.

This federal habeas corpus proceeding attacks collaterally a state criminal conviction for the same alleged

---

[343] *Stovall* at 295, 296.

constitutional errors in the admission of allegedly tainted identification evidence that were before us on direct review of the convictions involved in *United States v. Wade* [388 U.S. 218] and *Gilbert v. California* [388 U.S. 263].

★ ★ ★

Wade and *Gilbert* fashion exclusionary rules to deter law enforcement authorities from exhibiting an accused to witnesses before trial for identification purposes without notice to and in the absence of counsel. A conviction which rests on a mistaken identification is a gross miscarriage of justice. The *Wade* and *Gilbert* rules are aimed at minimizing that possibility by preventing the unfairness at the pretrial confrontation that experience has proved can occur and assuring meaningful examination of the identification witness' testimony at trial.

★ ★ ★

We have outlined in *Wade* the dangers and unfairness inherent in confrontations for identification. The possibility of unfairness at that point is great, both because of the manner in which confrontations are frequently conducted and because of the likelihood that the accused will often be precluded from reconstructing what occurred and thereby from obtaining a full hearing on the identification issue at trial. The presence of counsel will significantly promote fairness at the confrontation and a full hearing at trial on the issue of identification. We have, therefore, concluded that the confrontation is a "critical stage," and that counsel is required at all confrontations. It must be recognized, however, that, unlike cases in which counsel is absent at trial or on appeal, it may confidently be assumed that confrontations for identification can be, and often have been, conducted in the absence of counsel with scrupulous fairness and without prejudice to the accused at trial. Therefore, while we feel that the exclusionary rules set forth in *Wade* and *Gilbert* are justified by the need to assure the integrity and reliability of our system of justice, they undoubtedly will affect cases in which no unfairness will be present.

[The Court also determined that *Wade* and *Gilbert* would not be retroactive so as to reach conduct which had occurred prior to the date of those decisions. The Court had a concern that retroactivity would wreak havoc in the criminal justice system and chose not to follow that path.]

★ ★ ★

II

We turn now to the question whether petitioner, although not entitled to the application of *Wade* and *Gilbert* to his case, is entitled to relief on his claim that, in any event, the confrontation conducted in this case was so unnecessarily suggestive and conducive to irreparable mistaken identification that he was denied due process of law.... The practice of showing suspects singly to persons for the purpose of identification, and not as part of a line-up, has been widely condemned. However, a claimed violation of due process of law in the conduct of a confrontation depends on the totality of the circumstances surrounding it, and the record in the present case reveals that the showing of Stovall to Mrs. Behrendt in an immediate hospital confrontation was imperative. The Court of Appeals, en banc, stated, 355 F.2d at 735,

> Here was the only person in the world who could possibly exonerate Stovall. Her words, and only her words, "He is not the man," could have resulted in freedom for Stovall. The hospital was not far distant from the courthouse and jail. No one knew how long Mrs. Behrendt might live. Faced with the responsibility of identifying the attacker, with the need for immediate action and with the knowledge that Mrs. Behrendt could not visit the jail, the police followed the only feasible procedure and took Stovall to the hospital room. Under these circumstances, the usual police station line-up, which Stovall now argues he should have had, was out of the question.

The judgment of the Court of Appeals is affirmed.

It is so ordered.

COMMENTS, NOTES, AND QUESTIONS

1. What about the defendant's argument in *Stovall* that, since the eyewitness had only one person to pick or not pick, the situation involved an unfair chance of misidentification? Would the witness believe that the police would go through the effort of bringing a truly innocent person for her viewing? Is the Supreme Court persuasive when it talks of the witness as being the only person who could exonerate Stovall? Until she identified him, did he really need "clearing" of a crime? Could you have devised a better method of nonsuggestive identification? Would a photographic array have worked? Why or why not? Is the chance of misidentification reduced by

the fact that police required Stovall to give a voice sample for the victim to consider?[344]

2. In the instant case, among other legal arguments, the defendant contended that his Fifth Amendment privilege against self-incrimination had been violated by showing his person to the eyewitness. A positive identification could most assuredly assist police as a link in evidence that could result in his conviction. In *United States v. Wade,* the court held, among other things, that the use of lineup, properly conducted, would not violate the Fifth Amendment privilege against self-incrimination. Citing *Schmerber v. California,* 384 U.S. 757, 761, the Court held that the privilege protects an accused only from being compelled to testify against himself or to otherwise provide the state with evidence of a testimonial or communicative nature that could be used as substantive evidence against the individual. Should being forced to show one's person to a victim be considered as self-incrimination? Or is it more like a simple physical fact involving no actual communication?

3. Through counsel, Mr. Stovall argued that the *Wade* and *Gilbert* cases should be made retroactive; if this occurred, Stovall arguably would have been entitled to counsel at the hospital confrontation/identification. Since he had not been represented at the hospital, he could argue that the identification should have been ruled inadmissible at the trial court level. Interestingly, in *Stovall,* the Court stated:

> The presence of counsel will significantly promote fairness at the confrontation and a full hearing at trial on the issue of identification. We have, therefore, concluded that the confrontation is a "critical stage," and that counsel is required at all confrontations. *Stovall* at 298.

If the Court really meant what it said, should it not have determined that Stovall needed counsel to assist in preventing erroneous misidentification by the witness?

The *Stovall* Court backed away from any retroactive application of the right to counsel for Stovall when it noted:

> We hold that *Wade* and *Gilbert* affect only those cases and all future cases which involve confrontations for identification purposes conducted in the absence of

counsel after this date. The rulings of *Wade* and *Gilbert* are therefore inapplicable in the present case. We think also that, on the facts of this case, petitioner was not deprived of due process of law in violation of the Fourteenth Amendment. *Stovall* at 296.

4. Consider a case in which a woman had been attacked by a man wearing a ski mask under circumstances that appeared to indicate attempted rape. She never saw him well enough to identify him visually, but she had ample opportunity to talk with him and try to get him to go to her home instead of continuing the attack in her vehicle. The attacker fled when some motion-activated lights were illuminated. Police and the victim had reason to think that the perpetrator might be a man who lived two doors away, so police interrogated this neighbor while they tape-recorded his voice. The police played the tape—which contained only the voices of the police officers and the defendant—for the victim. No other comparisons were available, and the police told the victim that the voice was that of the suspect. The woman identified the voice as belonging to her attacker. Should this voice identification be admitted in court against the man who lived two doors down the street? Is there a chance of misidentification under the circumstances? How would you rule if you were the judge? Why? Review the outcome in a real case that was the basis for this scenario; see *Michigan v. Williams,* 244 Mich. App. 533; 624 N.W.2d 575 (2001).

CASE 9.3

Five-Factors Test to Determine Reliable Eyewitness Identification

Neil v. Biggers
Supreme Court of the United States
409 U.S. 188 (1972)

FACTS

A Tennessee trial court convicted Biggers of rape based on the victim's visual and voice identification of him. According to the victim, the rape began at her home where the victim initially managed to observe the attacker's face

---

[344]Giving a voice sample does not violate the Fifth Amendment privilege against self-incrimination. "[B]oth federal and state courts have usually held that it [Fifth Amendment] offers no protection against compulsion to submit to fingerprinting, photographing, or measurements, to write or speak for identification, to appear in court, to stand, to assume a stance, to walk, or to make a particular gesture." *Schmerber v. California,* 384 U.S. 757, 764 (1966).

as it was illuminated from the light of her kitchen and again when the perpetrator took her across a field under a full moon. On at least two occasions, she was face to face with her attacker with an excellent opportunity to observe his facial features and other details relative to identity. The victim initially described her assailant as being between sixteen and eighteen years old and between five feet ten inches and six feet tall, as weighing between one hundred eighty and two hundred pounds, and as having a dark brown complexion. The victim's initial description offered to police clearly matched the defendant in every detail.

Police attempted to construct a proper lineup, but were unable to find sufficient numbers of similarly featured individuals. Police permitted the victim to observe the defendant as she walked past the suspect. She described the rapist as being fat and flabby with a youthful voice and smooth skin. Only after the police had Biggers speak did the victim identify him as the fellow who had raped her. In order to obtain a voice identification and at the victim's request, the police required Biggers to say "shut up or I'll kill you." Upon seeing Biggers and after hearing his voice, her identification of him as the perpetrator proved instantaneous and positive. She testified that it was petitioner's voice that "was the first thing that made me think it was the boy."[345] At that point, she made a certain and unambiguous identification of the defendant as the rapist.

During the seven months between the rape and her identification of the defendant, the victim had looked at countless mug shots, viewed suspects in her own home, and observed many in-person lineups and photographic arrays, but had never identified any suspect.

The trial court jury convicted Biggers of rape and he had no success with direct appellate review. A petition for a writ of *habeas corpus* was granted by a federal district court and affirmed by the Court of Appeals for the Sixth Circuit. The Supreme Court of the United States granted certiorari.

PROCEDURAL ISSUE

Where a rape victim has been permitted to walk past the arrestee, where the victim made a positive identification based on visual inspection and after hearing a voice sample, does such a suggestive identification process, in the absence of a standard lineup or photographic array, violate a defendant's right to due process under the Fourteenth Amendment?

HELD: NO

RATIONALE

Mr. Justice Powell delivered the opinion of the Court.

★ ★ ★

III

We have considered on four occasions the scope of due process protection against the admission of evidence deriving from suggestive identification procedures. In *Stovall v. Denno,* 388 U.S. 293 (1967), the Court held that the defendant could claim that "the confrontation conducted…was so unnecessarily suggestive and conducive to irreparable mistaken identification that he was denied due process of law." *Id.,* at 301–302. This, we held, must be determined "on the totality of the circumstances." We went on to find that on the facts of the case then before us, due process was not violated, emphasizing that the critical condition of the injured witness justified a showup in her hospital room. At trial, the witness, whose view of the suspect at the time of the crime was brief, testified to the out-of-court identification, as did several police officers present in her hospital room, and also made an in-court identification.

Subsequently, in a case where the witnesses made in-court identifications arguably stemming from previous exposure to a suggestive photographic array, the Court restated the governing test:

> "[W]e hold that each case must be considered on its own facts, and that convictions based on eye-witness identification at trial following a pretrial identification by photograph will be set aside on that ground only if the photographic identification procedure was so impermissibly suggestive as to give rise to a very substantial likelihood of irreparable misidentification." *Simmons v. United States,* 390 U.S. 377, 384 (1968).

Again we found the identification procedure to be supportable, relying both on the need for prompt utilization of other investigative leads and on the likelihood that the photographic identifications were reliable, the witnesses

---

[345] *Biggers v. Tennessee,* 390 U.S. 404, 406 (1968).

having viewed the bank robbers for periods of up to five minutes under good lighting conditions at the time of the robbery.

The only case to date in which the Court has found identification procedures to be violative of due process is *Foster v. California,* 394 U.S. 440, 442 (1969). There, the witness failed to identify Foster the first time he confronted him, despite a suggestive lineup. The police then arranged a showup, at which the witness could make only a tentative identification. Ultimately, at yet another confrontation, this time a lineup, the witness was able to muster a definite identification. We held all of the identifications inadmissible, observing that the identifications were "all but inevitable" under the circumstances. *Id.,* at 443.

Some general guidelines emerge from these cases as to the relationship between suggestiveness and misidentification. It is, first of all, apparent that the primary evil to be avoided is "a very substantial likelihood of irreparable misidentification." *Simmons v. United States,* 390 U.S., at 384. While the phrase was coined as a standard for determining whether an in-court identification would be admissible in the wake of a suggestive out-of-court identification, with the deletion of "irreparable" it serves equally well as a standard for the admissibility of testimony concerning the out-of-court identification itself. It is the likelihood of misidentification which violates a defendant's right to due process, and it is this which was the basis of the exclusion of evidence in *Foster.* Suggestive confrontations are disapproved because they increase the likelihood of misidentification, and unnecessarily suggestive ones are condemned for the further reason that the increased chance of misidentification is gratuitous.

★ ★ ★

We turn, then, to the central question, whether under the "totality of the circumstances" the identification was reliable even though the confrontation procedure was suggestive. As indicated by our cases, *the factors to be considered in evaluating the likelihood of misidentification include the opportunity of the witness to view the criminal at the time of the crime, the witness' degree of attention, the accuracy of the witness' prior description of the criminal, the level of certainty demonstrated by the witness at the confrontation, and the length of time between the crime and the confrontation.* [Emphasis added.] Applying these factors, we disagree with the District Court's conclusion.

★ ★ ★

We find that the District Court's conclusions on the critical facts are unsupported by the record and clearly erroneous. The victim spent a considerable period of time with her assailant, up to half an hour. She was with him under adequate artificial light in her house and under a full moon outdoors, and at least twice, once in the house and later in the woods, faced him directly and intimately. She was no casual observer, but rather the victim of one of the most personally humiliating of all crimes. Her description to the police, which included the assailant's approximate age, height, weight, complexion, skin texture, build, and voice, might not have satisfied Proust but was more than ordinarily thorough. She had "no doubt" that respondent was the person who raped her. In the nature of the crime, there are rarely witnesses to a rape other than the victim, who often has a limited opportunity of observation. The victim here, a practical nurse by profession, had an unusual opportunity to observe and identify her assailant. She testified at the habeas corpus hearing that there was something about his face "I don't think I could ever forget."

There was, to be sure, a lapse of several months between the rape and the confrontation. This would be a seriously negative factor in most cases. Here, however, the testimony is undisputed that the victim made no previous identification at any of the showups, lineups, or photographic showings. Her record for reliability was thus a good one, as she had previously resisted whatever suggestiveness inheres in a showup. Weighing all the factors, we find no substantial likelihood of misidentification. The evidence was properly allowed to go to the jury.

Affirmed in part, reversed in part, and remanded.

COMMENTS, NOTES, AND QUESTIONS

1. What assistance could an attorney have provided to Mr. Biggers at the walk-by conducted in the hallway? Would there have been ways in which the police could have assisted the victim in making an identification? Would an attorney have been able to either prevent improper suggestion or to contest it in court if he or she had been present for the walk-by? Or should the police have waited until they were able to assemble a formal lineup, since the case was of such a serious nature? Could one argue that the victim had waited longer than six months to make an identification, so an

additional day or so should not have made much of a difference?

2. In *Neil v. Biggers,* did the circumstances where the victim walked past Biggers and listened to him speak make her identification of the defendant possibly an "irreparable misidentification"? Why or why not? Would the police have had her come to the station to view someone who probably did not meet her earlier description? What would most people think? Would the fact that she had looked at other people and pictures and never made any identification until the Biggers identification tell you that she is careful and would not likely make a mistake? The literature is full of stories of eyewitness misidentification resulting in miscarriages of justice.

3. The *Neil* Court adopted the test for pretrial eyewitness identification from *Simmons v. United States,* 390 U.S. 377 (1968). In *Simmons,* the Court held that a pretrial identification should be ruled improper and therefore inadmissible where the "identification procedure was so impermissibly suggestive as to give rise to a very substantial likelihood of irreparable misidentification." *Simmons,* at 384. In order to give effect to the *Simmons* test, the *Neil* Court identified five factors that should be considered in determining whether a witness has made a proper and accurate identification. While the identification in *Neil* was not a lineup in the traditional sense, the factors are to be used whenever the issue concerns a proper identification. The five factors are the opportunity of the witness to view the criminal at the time of the crime, the witness's degree of attention, the accuracy of the witness's prior description of the criminal, the level of certainty demonstrated by the witness at the confrontation, and the length of time between the crime and the confrontation. If all the factors are properly considered, the chances of "irreparable misidentification" are substantially diminished according to the theory of the Court.

4. The fact that the five factors of *Neil* have been properly considered by a trial court does not necessarily end the matter of appropriate identification. The five-factors test focuses only on the eyewitness and not the surrounding proceedings. Due process guarantees under the Fifth and Fourteenth Amendments dictate that the police conduct lineups and other identification procedures in a fundamentally fair fashion. In a given identification procedure, the process may have been inappropriate if, under the circumstances, the presence of counsel was required, or if improper steering by lineup officers transpired, or undue suggestiveness was created by the makeup or operation of the lineup.

CASE 9.4

Police Use of Preindictment and Preinformation Photos Permissible

Manson v. Brathwaite
Supreme Court of the United States
432 U.S. 98 (1977)

FACTS

While working as an undercover narcotics officer for the Connecticut State Police, Jimmy D. Glover made a planned purchase of drugs from a known narcotics dealer. Glover and an informant arrived at the dealer's apartment for the purpose of making a buy. Glover knocked on the third-floor apartment door during the late afternoon. Natural light illuminated the drug dealer's face so that Glover was able to see the man and his facial features with a great deal of clarity. As a trained officer who might have to testify in court, Glover needed to be alert for possible problems which might develop as well as be alert for his own safety. When Officer Glover requested "two things" of heroin, respondent took two ten dollar bills from Glover and disappeared within the apartment. He soon returned with two glassine bags of a powder later determined to be heroin.

After Glover left the vicinity of the purchase, he offered a detailed description of the suspect to fellow officer D'Onofrio. Since the narrative description of the unknown drug dealer offered by Glover seemed to describe a man D'Onofrio knew, he obtained a photograph which was placed on Officer Glover's desk. Approximately two days later, Glover viewed the police photo of respondent and instantly identified the picture as being a photo of respondent.

Brathwaite was charged in a two-count information with possession and sale of heroin. At his trial, defense counsel did not object to the use of the photograph or the identification process and Brathwaite was convicted. Brathwaite's appeals in the Connecticut courts proved fruitless.

Pursuing his federal habeas corpus remedy, Brathwaite alleged that admission of the identification testimony violated his right to due process of law under the Fourteenth Amendment. The district court dismissed the petition, but the Court of Appeals for the Second Circuit reversed. The Supreme Court of the United States granted certiorari to consider the identification issues.

PROCEDURAL ISSUE

Where one photograph has been used by police to compare to a mental image possessed by an officer, can such examination of the photograph be characterized as unnecessary and unduly suggestive so as to violate due process of the Fourteenth Amendment?

HELD: NO

RATIONALE

Mr. Justice Blackmun delivered the opinion of the Court.

This case presents this issue as to whether the Due Process Clause of the Fourteenth Amendment compels the exclusion, in a state criminal trial, apart from any consideration of reliability, of pretrial identification evidence obtained by a police procedure that was both suggestive and unnecessary. This Court's decisions in *Stovall v. Denno,* 388 U.S. 293 (1967), and *Neil v. Biggers,* 409 U.S. 188 (1972), are particularly implicated.

II

★ ★ ★

The Court of Appeals confirmed that the exhibition of the single photograph to Glover was "impermissibly suggestive," 527 F.2d, at 366, and felt that, in addition, "it was unnecessarily so." *Id.,* at 367. There was no emergency and little urgency. The court said that prior to the decision in *Biggers,* except in cases of harmless error, "a conviction secured as the result of admitting an identification obtained by impermissibly suggestive and unnecessary measures could not stand." *Ibid.* It noted what it felt might be opposing inferences to be drawn from passages in *Biggers,* but concluded that the case preserved the principle "requiring the exclusion of identifications resulting from 'unnecessarily suggestive confrontation'" in post-*Stovall* situations. The court also concluded that for post-*Stovall* identifications, *Biggers* had not changed the existing rule. Thus: "Evidence of an identification unnecessarily obtained by impermissibly suggestive means must be excluded under *Stovall.* No rules less stringent than these can force police administrators and prosecutors to adopt procedures that will give fair assurance against the awful risks of misidentification." 527 F.2d, at 371.

★ ★ ★

IV

★ ★ ★

Since the decision in *Biggers,* the Courts of Appeals appear to have developed at least two approaches to such evidence. The first, or per se approach, employed by the Second Circuit in the present case, focuses on the procedures employed and requires exclusion of the out-of-court identification evidence, without regard to reliability, whenever it has been obtained through unnecessarily suggested confrontation procedures. The justifications advanced are the elimination of evidence of uncertain reliability, deterrence of the police and prosecutors, and the stated "fair assurance against the awful risks of misidentification." 527 F.2d, at 371.

The second, or more lenient, approach is one that continues to rely on the totality of the circumstances. It permits the admission of the confrontation evidence if, despite the suggestive aspect, the out-of-court identification possesses certain features of reliability. Its adherents feel that the per se approach is not mandated by the Due Process Clause of the Fourteenth Amendment. This second approach, in contrast to the other, is *ad hoc,* and serves to limit the societal costs imposed by a sanction that excludes relevant evidence from consideration and evaluation by the trier of fact.

★ ★ ★

There are, of course, several interests to be considered and taken into account. The driving force behind *United States v. Wade,* 388 U.S. 218 (1967), *Gilbert v. California,* 388 U.S. 263 (1967) (right to counsel at a post-indictment line-up), and *Stovall,* all decided on the same day, was the Court's concern with the problems of eyewitness identification. Usually the witness must testify about an encounter with a total stranger under circumstances of emergency or emotional stress. The witness' recollection of the stranger can be distorted easily by the circumstances or by later actions of the police. Thus, *Wade* and its companion cases reflect the concern that the jury not hear eyewitness testimony unless that evidence has aspects of reliability.

★ ★ ★

We therefore conclude that reliability is the linchpin in determining the admissibility of identification testimony for both pre- and post-*Stovall* confrontations. The factors to be considered are set out in *Biggers*. These include the opportunity of the witness to view the criminal at the time of the crime, the witness' degree of attention, the accuracy of his prior description of the criminal, the level of certainty demonstrated at the confrontation, and the time between the crime and the confrontation. Against these factors is to be weighed the corrupting effect of the suggestive identification itself.

★ ★ ★

V

We turn, then, to the facts of this case and apply the analysis:

1. The opportunity to view. Glover testified that for two to three minutes he stood at the apartment door, within two feet of the respondent. The door opened twice, and each time the man stood at the door. The moments passed, the conversation took place, and payment was made. Glover looked directly at his vendor. It was near sunset, to be sure, but the sun had not yet set, so it was not dark or even dusk or twilight. Natural light from outside entered the hallway through a window. There was natural light, as well, from inside the apartment.

2. The degree of attention. Glover was not a casual or passing observer, as is so often the case with eyewitness identification. Trooper Glover was a trained police officer on duty—a specialized and dangerous duty—when he called at the third floor of 201 Westland in Hartford on May 5, 1970. Glover himself was a [black male] and unlikely to perceive only general features of "hundreds of Hartford black males," as the Court of Appeals stated. 527 F.2d, at 371. It is true that Glover's duty was that of ferreting out narcotics offenders and that he would be expected in his work to produce results. But it is also true that, as a specially trained, assigned, and experienced officer, he could be expected to pay scrupulous attention to detail, for he knew that subsequently he would have to find and arrest his vendor. In addition, he knew that his claimed observations would be subject later to close scrutiny and examination at any trial.

3. The accuracy of the description. Glover's description was given to D'Onofrio within minutes after the transaction. It included the vendor's race, his height, his build, the color and style of his hair, and the high cheekbone facial feature. It also included clothing the vendor wore. No claim has been made that respondent did not possess the physical characteristics so described. D'Onofrio

reacted positively at once. Two days later, when Glover was alone, he viewed the photograph D'Onofrio produced and identified its subject as the narcotics seller.

4. The witness' level of certainty. There is no dispute that the photograph in question was that of respondent. Glover, in response to a question whether the photograph was that of the person from whom he made the purchase, testified: "There is no question whatsoever." This positive assurance was repeated.

5. The time between the crime and the confrontation. Glover's description of his vendor was given to D'Onofrio within minutes of the crime. The photographic identification took place only two days later. We do not have here the passage of weeks or months between the crime and the viewing of the photograph.

These indicators of Glover's ability to make an accurate identification are hardly outweighed by the corrupting effect of the challenged identification itself. Although identifications arising from single-photograph displays may be viewed in general with suspicion, see *Simmons v. United States*, 390 U.S., at 383, we find in the instant case little pressure on the witness to acquiesce in the suggestion that such a display entails. D'Onofrio had left the photograph at Glover's office and was not present when Glover first viewed it two days after the event. There thus was little urgency and Glover could view the photograph at his leisure. And since Glover examined the photograph alone, there was no coercive pressure to make an identification arising from the presence of another. The identification was made in circumstances allowing care and reflection.

★ ★ ★

Surely, we cannot say that under all the circumstances of this case there is "a very substantial likelihood of irreparable misidentification." *Id.*, at 384. Short of that point, such evidence is for the jury to weigh. We are content to rely upon the good sense and judgment of American juries, for evidence with some element of untrustworthiness is customary grist for the jury mill.

★ ★ ★

We conclude that the criteria laid down in *Biggers* are to be applied in determining the admissibility of evidence offered by the prosecution concerning a post-*Stovall* identification, and that those criteria are satisfactorily met and complied with here.

The judgment of the Court of Appeals is reversed.

Comments, Notes, and Questions

1. Are you comfortable with due process resting on the ethical behavior of the police while conducting a photo array or the viewing of a single photo? There is no way to reconstruct the dialogue that transpired between officers when a determination of identity has been made. In addition, there probably would have been no prosecutor present to supervise a photo array to ensure that due process has been followed. Is this one area of law enforcement, since it is not adversarial, where we need to trust the good faith of the individuals involved? Should other safeguards be devised to cover photo situations where no counsel is present?

2. At some point, where police are simply using photographs as a tool of the trade, claims of due process violations by defendants may become legally frivolous. Is that close to happening here? Could you argue that Officer Glover's observation of the single photograph of Brathwaite at the police station presented a risk of misidentification by "steering" Glover to identify Brathwaite? Is it tempered by the fact that Glover has nothing to gain by arresting the wrong man while a guilty one might go free? Is that too simplistic a view? Does the process indicate that Glover's initial description of Brathwaite to his fellow officer was so complete that it prompted the officer to select the photograph of Brathwaite, proving a good identification?

3. A photographic array or even a single photograph does not require the presence of counsel even where adversary proceedings have been initiated. In *United States v. Ash,* 413 U.S. 300 (1973), the Court held that the Sixth Amendment right to counsel does not exist at photographic arrays conducted by the government, even for those under arrest at the time of the photographic array. The Court noted that the ethical responsibility of the prosecutor should serve to safeguard the integrity of the photographic identification process. Had the Court gone the other way in *Ash,* mug books and computer-generated images would have become somewhat less useful if the "target" had to be represented by counsel. Should counsel be required under the Sixth Amendment at photographic arrays? What are the arguments for each position?

The Decision to Prosecute: Indictment and Information

Chapter Outline

Key Terms

Compelled testimony
Composition of grand jury
Effect of discrimination
Fifth Amendment privilege
Grand jury secrecy: limitations
Grand jury standard: probable cause
Grand jury target
Indictment
Infamous crime

Information
Right to grand jury indictment
Secrecy of grand jury: purpose
Serious criminal case
Transactional immunity
Unlawfully seized evidence: admissible
Use immunity
Waiver of right to indictment

1. INTRODUCTION: INITIATING CRIMINAL CHARGES

A serious federal criminal prosecution must be initiated by an indictment unless a criminal target consents to having an information filed against the individual.[346] For federal prosecutions, the Fifth Amendment of the Constitution provides that "[n]o person shall be held to answer for a capital, or otherwise infamous crime, unless on a presentment or indictment of a Grand Jury," but the Supreme Court has determined that this portion of the Fifth Amendment does not require states to follow the federal practice.[347] As Chief Justice Rehnquist noted, "*Hurtado [v. California]* held that the Due Process Clause did not make applicable to the States the Fifth Amendment's requirement that all prosecutions for an infamous crime be instituted by the indictment of a grand jury."[348]

The case that Chief Justice Rehnquist referred to, *Hurtado v. California,* 110 U.S. 516 (1884), involved a defendant who had been charged and convicted of capital murder and had been sentenced to death without the benefit of a grand jury indictment (see Case 10.1). In making his appeal to the Supreme Court, he contended that the adoption of the Fourteenth Amendment and its Due Process Clause dictated that the provisions of the Fifth Amendment requiring grand jury indictments be applied to state criminal cases. The *Hurtado* Court reviewed extensive legal history of the concept of due process, from the Magna Carta through the development of the Constitution of the United States to the passage of the Fourteenth Amendment, and concluded that due process did not include the right to a grand jury indictment in a state case. The Framers of the Fourteenth Amendment did not profess to "secure to all persons in the United States the benefit of the same law and the same remedies."[349]

In contrast to state cases, federal prosecutions require grand jury indictments where the case involves a capital offense or is an infamous crime. The issue of whether the offense charged constitutes an infamous crime under the Fifth Amendment must "be determined either by the character of the punishment or by other incidents of the sentence prescribed."[350] In a later case, the Court ruled that a sentence of hard labor while incarcerated in a prison constituted an infamous punishment.[351] Under the rules governing federal criminal procedure, any offense that carries a punishment of death or calls for a term of incarceration exceeding one year must be prosecuted by indictment, except where a target waives the constitutional right to an indictment. A waiver of a grand jury indictment is not permitted for an offense carrying the death penalty; such a prosecution must be initiated by an indictment.[352] While the initial prosecution of criminal cases in many states virtually mirrors the federal formulation, the states are not bound to follow the federal model and may vary their initiation of criminal prosecutions significantly.

---

[346]See Federal Rules of Criminal Procedure 7(b) (G.P.O. 2002).

[347]See *Hurtado v. California,* 110 U.S. 516 (1884).

[348]*Albright v. Oliver,* 510 U.S. 266 (1994). And see *Apprendi v. New Jersey,* 530 U.S. 466 at 477 n.3 (2000), where Justice Stevens noted that the Fifth Amendment right to a grand jury indictment has not been construed to be applicable in state criminal cases.

[349]*Hurtado* at 535, Justice Matthews quoting Justice Bradly in *Missouri v. Lewis,* 101 U.S. 22 at 31 (1879).

[350]*Ex parte Wilson,* 114 U.S. 417, 426 (1885).

[351]See *United States v. Moreland,* 258 U.S. 433 (1922).

[352]Federal Rules of Criminal Procedure, Rule 7(a) (G.P.O. 2002).

A representative decision giving effect to the Fifth Amendment indictment requirement was *United States v. Moreland*, 258 U.S. 433 (1922) (see Case 10.2). The federal government initiated a prosecution against Moreland in the Juvenile Court for the District of Columbia for the crime of willfully neglecting or refusing to provide for the support of his minor children. A trial jury found him guilty, and the court sentenced him to imprisonment at hard labor in the workhouse for six months. Moreland appealed to the Court of Appeals, which reversed the conviction, but the government appealed to the Supreme Court. The *Moreland* Court held that a federal charge where the punishment dictated imprisonment at hard labor constituted an infamous crime, necessitating a grand jury indictment or presentment prior to the initiation of a federal prosecution.

2. THE INDICTMENT: STARTING A CRIMINAL PROSECUTION

An indictment is the written accusation returned by a grand jury following deliberation after hearing a prosecutor's evidentiary presentation. The grand jury delivers the indictment to a court of competent jurisdiction in which a person is charged with an offense against the criminal law. State practice generally follows the requirements of the federal government dictating that the indictment present a "plain, concise, and definite written statement of the essential facts,"[353] which, consistent with due process, gives a defendant fair notice of the offense charged. An indictment is generally sufficient when it gives enough facts to allow the defendant to understand the nature of the charge and to prepare a defense.

3. THE INFORMATION: STARTING A CRIMINAL PROSECUTION

Whether used in a state or federal court, generally an information initiating a serious criminal case includes "a plain, concise and definite written statement of the essential facts constituting the offense charged."[354] The information normally carries the signature of the prosecuting attorney representing the state or federal government. The intent of the information is to convey to a defendant the basic outlines of the case the government believes that it possesses against the defendant. An information should contain sufficient detail that the defendant is alerted to the activity the prosecutor believes to have been criminal. An information need not provide extensively detailed information concerning the alleged facts. It should, however, carry a clear indication of the laws the defendant is alleged to have broken. A clear statement of the facts has been deemed necessary in order to meet due process by giving fair notice to the defendant of the charges against which he or she must defend. Some states allow the prosecutor discretion to make the decision whether to proceed via indictment or information, while other state jurisdictions dictate by state law or constitution the required approach. In a state that allows a prosecutor the luxury of determining how to proceed, the prosecutor

---

[353]See ibid., Rule 7(c)(1).
[354]Ibid.

has a fairly free hand in making a decision whether to procure an indictment or file an information. California's procedure is demonstrative of states that require trial court permission or consent to initiate a criminal case by an information or to pursue an indictment,[355] but which approach to pursue remains the choice of the prosecutor.

4. GENERAL GRAND JURY PROCEDURE

The grand jury is composed of adult citizens of the jurisdiction who have been given the task of determining whether probable cause exists that a particular person or persons have committed a specific crime or crimes. The grand jury serves as a buffer to insulate persons from an overzealous government. The beauty of the grand jury system includes "the protection of citizens against unfounded criminal prosecutions"[356] because the grand jury determines the "course of its inquiry."[357] In explaining the role of a grand jury, it was noted in *United States v. Williams* that while the grand jury functions

> in the courthouse and under judicial auspices, its institutional relationship with the judicial branch has traditionally been, so to speak, at arm's length. Judges' direct involvement in the functioning of the grand jury has generally been confined to the constitutive one of calling the grand jurors together and administering their oaths of office. 504 U.S. 36, 47 (1992).

To support the investigatory role, a grand jury possesses broad powers to force witnesses to come forth and testify and to bring various items of evidence for grand jury scrutiny. A grand jury can force witnesses to provide voice samples,[358] handwriting specimens,[359] and various body samples relevant to identity, since no Fifth Amendment testimonial privilege is involved.

Once the grand jury has been empaneled, the process of investigation begins when the prosecutor individually calls a series of witnesses before the assembled body and asks questions of each witness. To obtain an indictment, the prosecutor must present sufficient evidence for the grand jury to determine that probable cause exists, but the prosecutor has no duty to provide a grand jury with exculpatory evidence in favor of the targeted individual.[360] Significantly, during the grand jury stage, the rules of evidence do not apply, so the prosecutor, as well as the grand jurors, may ask a fairly wide range of questions of the witnesses. Questions concerning hearsay, rumor, innuendo, fact, and opinion are often asked of each witness. Any individual who may be the subject of the grand jury inquiry has no constitutional

---

[355]See Cal. Const., Art. I § 14 (2001), Felony prosecutions; Arraignment. "Felonies shall be prosecuted as provided by law, either by indictment or, after examination and commitment by a magistrate, by information."
[356]*United States v. Calandra,* 414 U.S. 338, 343 (1974).
[357]Ibid.
[358]See *United States v. Dionisio,* 410 U.S. 1 (1973).
[359]See *United States v. Mara,* 410 U.S. 18 (1973).
[360]See *United States v. Williams,* 504 U.S. 36, 47 (1992).

right to appear and present any type of evidence, a case, or a defense. The target of the grand jury inquiry, the one suspected of being criminally involved, may be asked to testify, but due to the Fifth Amendment privilege against self-incrimination, any target may refuse to answer any and all questions where there is a possibility of self-incrimination. An ordinary witness may similarly refuse to answer a grand jury's inquiries if the response might produce an incriminating answer, but a grand jury witness may not refuse to answer questions if they are based on evidence illegally seized in violation of the witness's personal Fourth Amendment rights.[361] The prosecutor may choose not to call the target as a witness because the government may not want the suspect to know that legal proceedings are ongoing. If alerted to potential criminal proceedings, some targets might flee or engage in steps designed to frustrate justice. Because no judge presides over a grand jury, virtually any topic into which the prosecutor desires to inquire can be said to be generally within the competence of the grand jury.

5. SERIOUS FEDERAL PROSECUTIONS GENERALLY REQUIRE INDICTMENT

According to case law and consistent with the Fifth Amendment, the federal government must use an indictment to initiate a serious criminal case.[362] The relevant portion of the amendment provides that the federal government shall not cause a person to be "held to answer for a capital, or otherwise infamous crime, unless on a presentment or indictment of a Grand Jury." This portion of the Fifth Amendment has been effectuated by the Federal Rules of Criminal Procedure, which necessitate a grand jury indictment for crimes for which the potential punishment exceeds one year.[363] Since most rights guaranteed by the Constitution consist of waivable rights, the Federal Rules of Criminal Procedure provide for a potential defendant to waive the right to a grand jury indictment[364] and consent to having an information used to initiate a formal criminal prosecution. Proper procedure requires that the target of an investigation, after having been advised of the proposed charge and its ramifications, including advisement of appropriate legal rights, may waive the Fifth Amendment right to a grand jury indictment in open court[365] and consent to the entry of an information.

Federal grand juries are summoned as the need arises; they consist of no fewer than sixteen and no more than twenty-three members. Alternate jurors may be

---

[361] *Smith v. United States,* 423 U.S. 1303, 1306 (1975).

[362] An infamous crime has been defined as a crime punishable by death or by imprisonment in a penitentiary or at hard labor, *Ex parte Wilson,* 114 U.S. 417, 427 (1885), and *United States v. Moreland,* 258 U.S. 433 (1922).

[363] See Federal Rules of Criminal Procedure, Rule 7(a) (G.P.O. 2002): "An offense which may be punished by death shall be prosecuted by indictment. An offense which may be punished by imprisonment for a term exceeding one year or at hard labor shall be prosecuted by indictment or, if indictment is waived, it may be prosecuted by information. Any other offense may be prosecuted by indictment or by information."

[364] Ibid. Rule 7(b): "An offense which may be punished by imprisonment for a term exceeding one year or at hard labor may be prosecuted by information if the defendant, after having been advised of the nature of the charge and of the rights of the defendant, waives in open court prosecution by indictment."

[365] Ibid.

summoned by the court that empaneled the grand jury. Under Rule 6, the grand jury must vote with twelve votes in favor of indictment in order to return an indictment.[366]

The court that empaneled the grand jury appoints a foreperson and a deputy foreperson who have the power to administer oaths to witnesses and to obtain from witnesses the affirmation to tell the truth.[367] In addition, the foreperson keeps a record of the votes of the grand jurors and is required to file the record with the clerk of the court that empaneled the grand jury.

6. GRAND JURY INDICTMENT

Once a federal grand jury has heard evidence and completed deliberations, the jurors must vote to determine whether to issue an indictment or to ignore the evidence presented by refusing to indict. Similar practice is followed in state grand juries even if the total number of grand jurors is different from that in federal practice, but a simple majority vote is generally required for an indictment.

Good grand jury procedure dictates that the allegation of criminal activity contained within an indictment be concise and definite, and include the necessary and essential facts of the offense charged. According to Federal Rule of Criminal Procedure 7(c)(1): "The indictment or information shall state for each count the official or customary citation of the statute, rule, regulation or other provision of law which the defendant is alleged therein to have violated."

The requirement of specificity detailing the offense and the operative facts merely serves to meet due process standards by alerting the indicted defendant about the offenses for which a defense must be mounted or other response offered.

7. COMPOSITION OF THE GRAND JURY

As a strong general rule, a grand jury must be chosen from a pool of individuals residing in the judicial district where the criminal activity has been alleged to have transpired, and the pool of potential jurors must be representative of a fair cross section of the community. However, the *actual* grand jury chosen does not have to reflect a fair cross section of the population, and a potential defendant does not possess any right to have a grand jury that actually reflects a fair cross section of the community.[368] Individual grand jury targets who are later indicted may have procedural defenses available where improper grand jury selection has occurred. For example, where a white defendant in a state prosecution complained that black jurors had been excluded from serving as forepersons of grand juries in the district for numerous years, sufficient standing to complain was accorded to the defendant because, among other things, it involved the alleged discriminatory selection of grand jurors

---

[366]See Federal Rules of Criminal Procedure, Rule 6(f) (G.P.O. 2002).
[367]Ibid., Rule 6(c).
[368]*Castaneda v. Partida,* 430 U.S. 482, 509 (1977).

themselves,[369] including the foreperson.[370] And the Court in *Peters v. Kiff* recognized that the "exclusion of a discernible class from jury service injures not only those defendants who belong to the excluded class, but other defendants as well, in that it destroys the possibility that the jury will reflect a representative cross-section of the community."[371] Essentially, grand juries must be properly selected consistent with due process to allow the principle of fair indictments that meet constitutional muster.

8. GRAND JURY HEARS IMPROPERLY SEIZED EVIDENCE

Since the grand jury is generally concerned solely with determining probable cause, procedural and evidentiary rules that are customarily followed at trial traditionally see little application in the grand jury context. For example, the rules of evidence produce only a slight limitation on the type of hearsay, rumor, and innuendo permitted for grand jury consideration. Police officers who have interrogated individuals who have implicated other individuals may offer testimony for which the officer possessed absolutely no firsthand information. Similarly, the exclusionary rule, developed to ensure police respect for the Fourth Amendment, provides virtually no protection for a person who has personally been the victim of an illegal search and seizure and who is subsequently questioned by a grand jury concerning the illegally seized evidence.

In *United States v. Calandra,*[372] the Court refused to allow the grand jury witness, Calandra, to litigate the question of whether he had been the victim of a Fourth Amendment violation when police allegedly searched his business premises illegally. The prosecutor wanted to question Calandra at a grand jury proceeding concerning the significance and importance of loan-sharking evidence that had been seized from his place of business. Calandra alleged that the government had seized the evidence in violation of his constitutional rights under the Fourth Amendment. The *Calandra* Court noted that since a grand jury proceeding could not be characterized as an adversarial hearing in which the guilt or innocence of an accused could be determined, and since a grand jury proceeding involved only a preliminary ex parte investigation, Calandra had to answer or be held in contempt of court. According to the general rule, a witness summoned to appear and testify before a grand jury may not refuse to answer questions on the ground that they are based on evidence obtained from an unlawful search and seizure. Therefore, evidence that has been illegally seized under the Fourth Amendment may be considered by a grand jury, and the

---

[369]See *Campbell v. Louisiana,* 523 U.S. 392 (1998). It must be noted that the right to avoid discrimination in grand juror selection in a state prosecution does not depend upon any Fifth Amendment right, since that part of the Fifth Amendment does not regulate state grand jury practice. Allegations of unconstitutionality for state grand jury operations generally are regulated by the Due Process Clause of the Fourteenth Amendment.

[370]See *Campbell v. Louisiana,* 523 U.S. 392 (1998), where the Court held that a white defendant had standing to complain about racial discrimination against black citizens in the selection of a grand jury and in the selection of black grand jury foremen. In a similar fashion, a white defendant has standing to complain about the prosecutor's use of peremptory challenges to African American trial jurors based on their race. See *Powers v. Ohio,* 499 U.S. 400 (1991).

[371]407 U.S. 493, 500 (1972).

[372]414 U.S. 338 (1974).

possessor of the seized material may be forced to testify concerning the evidence.[373] By permitting the grand jury to consider virtually any shred of evidence, unencumbered by evidentiary rules or Fourth Amendment exclusions, the grand jury system operates with a minimum of judicial intervention and supervision and a maximum level of efficiency.

While the process used to initiate serious criminal cases is regulated by the United States Constitution, federal law, state laws, and state constitutions, all serious criminal prosecutions begin through the use of either an indictment or an information. The requisite level of evidence for either charging vehicle involves only the determination of probable cause to believe that a particular person has committed a specified crime. Once the decision to initiate a criminal prosecution has been made and formal steps have been taken, the case proceeds without regard as to whether its genesis occurred in an information or from an indictment.

9. WITNESSES MAY BE COMPELLED TO TESTIFY BEFORE A GRAND JURY

As a general rule, witnesses whom a prosecutor believes may have evidence to offer can be summoned before a grand jury and forced to give testimony. A requirement to give evidence is not absolute, and constitutional privileges may be asserted to prevent testimony. The invocation of the Fifth Amendment privilege against compelled testimonial self-incrimination is probably the most frequent assertion made by a potential grand jury witness, but this assertion can be overcome by a grant of immunity offered by the prosecution. Where a witness has information that does not involve the witness in personal criminality or suggest a potential criminal prosecution for the witness, the witness must testify under oath and give the requested information.

Where a witness has been subpoenaed to testify in a grand jury proceeding, it is not uncommon for the individual to have concerns about personal criminal liability and to consider using a constitutional privilege not to testify. When a witness has asserted a Fifth Amendment privilege under circumstances where the prosecutor clearly desires that the witness answer, a hearing before a judge of the jurisdiction will be held. The question that has been asked and for which an answer has been refused will be analyzed by the judge to determine whether its nature and its probable answer would tend to incriminate the witness or could provide a link in a chain of evidence that could incriminate. If the nature of the question indicates that a criminally significant answer may be forthcoming, the judge may order that the witness's assertion of the Fifth Amendment privilege has been appropriate and the witness need not answer. If the judge believes that the answer would not or could not incriminate the witness, he or she will order that the witness answer the question or questions. The prosecutor has a choice to make where the judge believes that the answer might prove incriminating. Where the possibility exists that the witness possesses valuable

---

[373]While a witness may not have a Fourth Amendment right not to testify concerning an illegally seized piece of evidence, the witness may assert a Fifth Amendment privilege against compelled testimonial self-incrimination where discussion of the evidence could tend to incriminate the witness. However, if the evidence has been seized illegally in violation of the witness's Fourth Amendment rights, it may be excluded from *trial* if witness is the defendant whose rights had been violated.

information that cannot be ascertained from any other source, under such circumstances, the prosecutor may be willing to offer immunity to the witness with the concurrence of the judge.

Witnesses subpoenaed to appear before a grand jury are frequently required to bring evidence with them.[374] Such evidence may consist of both documentary and physical evidence, and the production of such evidence may be based on less than probable cause. Witnesses may be required to testify about evidence that has been illegally obtained in violation of the Fourth Amendment.[375]

10. GRAND JURY WITNESS IMMUNITY

Any witness called before a grand jury to testify may assert a Fifth Amendment privilege against self-incrimination and refuse to testify. Such conduct is appropriate whether the witness is a target or simply an ordinary witness, but the assertion of a constitutional right or rights may not be the end of the individual's role as a witness. In the case of an individual who has been called to testify before a federal grand jury and refuses to cooperate based on an assertion of federal constitutional rights, the United States attorney may request that a federal district judge compel the witness to responsively answer questions. Once the witness has been properly accorded immunity,[376] which is coextensive with the Fifth Amendment protection, he or she must answer the questions, regardless of whether the answers might be incriminating. Essentially, the immunity offers the witness the same level of protection that had been granted by the Fifth Amendment.

Where a witness or target witness has been forced to give testimony, none of the testimony that has been compelled under court order may be used against the witness in the present inquiry or in any other criminal case.[377] In effect, this is called use immunity, since the evidence, extracted from the witness under pain of contempt of court, cannot be used directly against the witness and cannot serve as a link in a chain of facts that leads to other incriminating evidence. Essentially, what has been offered by the witness is useless to the prosecution against that witness but may be used against other individuals not covered by the grant of immunity. When the prosecutor, in conjunction with a federal district court, has conferred use immunity on a witness, the prosecutor may still prosecute the witness for any crime or crimes for which proper proof exists that is independently sourced and separate from the evidence given by the witness before the grand jury. However, where the prosecution cannot develop new evidence with clearly independent sources and appears to

---

[374]*United States v. Salameh,* 152 F.3d 88, 109 (2nd Cir. 1998), upholding a subpoena to a witness/target to bring materials to a federal grand jury investigating the first World Trade Center bombing.

[375]*United States v. Calandra,* 414 U.S. 338 (1974).

[376]Generally, two types of immunity may be offered to a potential grand jury witness who has a fear of criminal prosecution. Under use immunity, the government promises not to use the words offered by the witness against the witness, either directly or indirectly. The witness still can be prosecuted by independently sourced evidence. A broader type of immunity, transactional immunity, means that the witness will not be prosecuted for crimes covered by the grant of immunity.

[377]See 18 U.S.C. 6002 (2003).

have violated the provisions of a grant of immunity, the evidence cannot be used either to obtain an indictment or to prosecute the witness at a criminal trial.[378]

Where a state desires that a witness give evidence that may incriminate that witness, state practice generally operates in a manner similar to the federal scheme when use immunity and derivative use immunity have been conferred. For example, in a Louisiana case involving inflated prices for voting machine purchases and kickbacks, the prosecutor procured use and derivative immunity for a necessary witness who had a part in the criminal scheme. Under current Louisiana law that was in force then and remains current law,

> [n]o testimony or other information compelled under the order, or any information directly or indirectly derived from such testimony or other information, may be used against the witness in any criminal case, except a prosecution for perjury, giving a false statement or otherwise failing to comply with the order. Louisiana Code of Criminal Procedure Art. 439.1 (2003).

When the prosecution subsequently indicted the immunized witness for related crimes that the witness had revealed to the original grand jury, a Louisiana trial court quashed the indictment, since the state failed to meet its burden of proving that all the evidence used to obtain the indictment had independent sources. In upholding the trial court decision, the appellate court noted that the duty on the prosecution involved a demonstration that the sources it used to obtain evidence for the indictment were based on evidence derived from wholly independent sources. Since the burden of proof failed, the trial court properly quashed the indictment obtained in violation of the grant of use and derivative use immunity.[379]

In other states, reluctant witnesses, who may be faced with a similar compulsion to testify despite an assertion of the right against compelled self-incrimination, may fare much better than witnesses involved in an immunity scheme like that of Louisiana. For example, in Ohio, in the grand jury context, if a witness refuses to answer or produce information on the basis of an asserted privilege against self-incrimination, the trial court will compel the witness to answer if the prosecutor makes a written request that the court order a witness to do so.[380] The judge must inform the witness that by answering the question or producing information, he or she will receive immunity by not being subject to any criminal penalty based on any transaction or matter that has been the subject of the inquiry. This type of immunity, transactional immunity, offers broader protection to the reluctant witness than is offered by the federal plan or the Louisiana practice detailed earlier. It means that the Ohio witness will not be prosecuted, whereas the immunity covered in the federal practice and in Louisiana is more limited.

State practice varies widely concerning the level of immunity offered to reluctant grand jury witnesses who have asserted a privilege against self-incrimination. For example, while many states offer a broad grant of transactional immunity, the California practice mirrors the federal approach by offering use immunity. If a potential witness

---

[378]See *United States v. Hubbell,* 530 U.S. 27 (2000).

[379]*Louisiana v. Foster,* 845 So.2d 393, 401–403 (2003).

[380]See Ohio Revised Code, Ann. § 2945.44 (Anderson 2001).

refuses to answer a question or produce evidence of any other kind on the ground that he or she may be incriminated thereby in a grand jury proceeding or in any subsequent criminal proceeding, the prosecutor may ask the relevant court to hold a hearing on the merits of ordering the witness to answer.[381] The district attorney of the county must request in writing that the court order the witness to answer the prosecutor's inquiries. If the judge determines that justice requires that the witness answer, he or she issues a court order requiring the witness to answer or produce evidence.[382] The witness must comply but receives, in return, use immunity. The net effect of this type of immunity is that any testimony or other information compelled under the court's order and any information directly or indirectly obtained from the witness's testimony cannot be used against that witness in any criminal case. The California statute permits a prosecutor to request the granting of the broader protection, transactional immunity, but leaves that decision up to the prosecutor.[383]

11. GRAND JURY SECRECY

Since both state and federal grand juries meet in secret, only individuals necessary to the proceeding may be present. The grand jurors, the prosecutor(s), a witness, and a court reporter are necessary parties when evidence is being taken. Upon necessity, an interpreter may be allowed to be present. Generally, when the jurors retire to deliberate and vote concerning whether to issue an indictment or indictments, no other person may be present. Following the conclusion of the grand jury, disclosures of the nature, purpose, and evidence by any of the individuals present, other than witnesses, to other persons are prohibited. An exception exists for disclosure to necessary parties and to other governmental officials pursuant to the Federal Rules of Criminal Procedure.[384]

When an indictment has been returned by a grand jury, the Federal Rules of Criminal Procedure allow a federal judicial official to order that the existence of the indictment be kept secret to facilitate the taking of the defendant into custody. In furtherance of grand jury secrecy, various records, court orders, and evidence of witnesses called before the grand jury may be kept sealed to prevent disclosure of evidence that has been offered to the grand jury.

12. PURPOSE OF GRAND JURY SECRECY

The secrecy surrounding the grand jury serves a variety of purposes, some that are designed to make life easier for the jurors and some that benefit the prosecution. If such secrecy did not exist, there would always be the possibility that witnesses who were scheduled to appear before the grand jury would be reluctant to testify fully and completely. If grand jury secrecy were routinely breached, the grand jurors would potentially become targets for retribution and retaliation if they voted for

---

[381]Cal. Pen. Code § 1324 (2003).
[382]Ibid.
[383]Ibid.
[384]Federal Rules of Criminal Procedure, Rule 6(e)(2) (G.P.O. 2002).

an indictment. A reason often cited as a justification for general secrecy surrounding the grand jury is that it prevents potential targets of grand jury action from choosing to flee the jurisdiction.[385] Secrecy may ensure that a grand jury can meet without coercion or improper influence, may reduce the chance of witness tampering by those who may be expected to testify, and may encourage free and full disclosure by witnesses who actually testify. Secrecy prevents the harming of reputations of those individuals who are considered but never indicted. Public disclosure would otherwise permit the unindicted to suffer undeserved public opprobrium and potentially be held up to public ridicule. Although grand jury secrecy serves important interests, secrecy is not absolute and may be breached where good cause has been shown.

13. LIMITS OF GRAND JURY SECRECY

As might be reasonably expected, disclosures of grand jury testimony and information may be made by prosecution attorneys in the exercise of their duties. Members of prosecutors' offices are normally under a duty to disclose no information about grand jury testimony unless necessary to meet the duty entrusted to staff members. A judge may order grand jury information released to a defendant's attorney subsequent to a showing that a defendant may possess grounds for a motion to dismiss the indictment due to irregular matters that transpired at or during the grand jury process.[386] Grand jury information may be released pursuant to court order to prevent an injustice or miscarriage of justice in separate case. As the Supreme Court noted in *Douglas Oil v. Petrol Stops:*

> [T]he standard for determining when the traditional secrecy of the grand jury may be broken: parties seeking grand jury transcripts under Rule 6(e) must show that the material they seek is needed to avoid a possible injustice in another judicial proceeding, that the need for disclosure is greater than the need for continued secrecy, and that their request is structured to cover only material so needed. 441 U.S. 211 (1979).

Thus, the burden to prove that grand jury secrecy should be breached falls upon the party wishing to have access to the secret information; courts do not lightly allow the information to freely circulate following a release.

The most common outlet for a breach of grand jury secrecy, not involving any court ruling or breach of law, involves a witness who has testified in front of a grand jury and who makes a choice to speak publicly. Of course, only the grand jurors and the prosecutor will know if the witness who talks publicly about testimony given by that witness is recounting the same story offered to the grand jury. Such talk could undermine the basic design of the public policy, which desires secrecy, and might otherwise alert a target or subject the witness to pressure or harm. With a desire to

---

[385]See *United States v. Procter & Gamble,* 356 U.S. 677 at 681, n. 6, quoting *United States v. Rose,* 215 F.2d 617, 628–629 (CA3 1954).
[386]Federal Rules of Criminal Procedure, Rule 7(e)(3)(c) (G.P.O. 2002).

assure secrecy, many states enacted laws and rules that require witnesses who have testified to refrain from speaking about what was said within the grand jury room.[387]

The almost absolute secrecy under which a typical grand jury operates has fostered litigation on occasion. For example, under recent Florida law, a person who had testified before a grand jury was not permitted to disclose information that the individual had given to the grand jury under penalty of criminal prosecution. Florida prohibited publication, broadcasting, divulgement, or communication of any material offered to a grand jury to any other person. The witness was prohibited from knowingly causing or permitting anyone else to offer the same information to anyone else. In *Butterworth v. Smith,*[388] a reporter desired to divulge his grand jury testimony in a book that he planned to write about his experiences concerning alleged corruption of public officials. The criminal case covered by the grand jury had been resolved, and the grand jury had been disbanded and was no longer investigating the subject about which the reporter wanted to write. At the time he testified before the grand jury, the reporter was warned by the prosecutor's office personnel that he should not to reveal his testimony in any manner and that if he did disclose his testimony, such a choice could result in a criminal prosecution.

As a result of the effect of Florida law on grand jury witnesses and because he wished to write about his experiences, the reporter sued to have the Florida law declared unconstitutional as a violation of the First Amendment.[389] This was the end result in *Butterworth* when the Supreme Court decided that it should balance the reporter's asserted First Amendment rights against Florida's interests in preserving the confidentiality of its grand jury proceedings.[390] While the interests of Florida were substantial, they did not overcome the right of the individual under the First Amendment to write and speak about matters over which he possessed knowledge important to the public. Thus, the rule derived from *Butterworth* was that a witness who has testified before a grand jury could divulge to the public what he says he told the grand jury. In effect, witness secrecy has been rolled back somewhat, but it still remains strong on the grand jurors, the prosecutors, and any stenographers and court workers who attain knowledge of grand jury information. These individuals can be subject to court sanction if they reveal evidence that came before the grand jury, but witnesses may now talk openly.

14. PURSUANT TO A WAIVER, FEDERAL CHARGES MAY BE INITIATED BY AN INFORMATION

While a federal offense that is punishable by death must be initiated by a grand jury indictment, other lesser offenses may use the charging instrument known as an information. The use of a grand jury is not required where the target individual waives the Fifth

---

[387]Fla. Stat. § 905.27 (1989).

[388]494 U.S. 624 (1990).

[389]Amendment One: "Congress shall make no law...abridging the freedom of speech, or of the press..." The First Amendment has been applied to the states through the Fourteenth Amendment's Due Process Clause. See, e.g., *Miami Herald v. Tornillo,* 418 U.S. 241 (1974), and *New York Times v. Sullivan,* 376 U.S. 254 (1964). And see *Butterworth v. Smith,* 494 U.S. 624 (1990).

[390]*Butterworth* at 635.

Amendment right to an indictment and consents to the filing of an information. Since many grand jury targets are unaware of an ongoing investigation of personal criminal conduct, waiver of a grand jury indictment does not occur in the typical criminal case. However, if an investigation has flowered to the point where federal prosecutors are considering an indictment, and where a target is well aware of the nature and seriousness of the case, plea negotiations may be initiated through counsel. Where the discussions move forward to the agreement stage of a negotiated plea, a waiver of the right to a grand jury indictment may be part of a plea bargain. Prior to knowingly waiving the right to an indictment, the target individual must be informed of the nature of the expected charges and of personal constitutional rights under the circumstances. If the target waives the right to a grand jury indictment in open court, the prosecution is free to proceed against the individual by filing an information against the target.[391]

While an information possesses the operative effect of an indictment, the government may use it as the initiating step of a formal prosecution. Just as would be the case with an indictment, fair notice is required to be given to alert the defendant to the nature of the charges. It must be written clearly and precisely so as to place a defendant in a position to understand the nature of the charges against which he or she must defend. While it may include detailed accusations, an information, at a minimum, need only offer notice consistent with due process to the defendant of the charges that have been filed. Multiple counts of alleged criminal activity may be included in an information so long as they remain consistent with the parameters of the consent offered.[392]

15. FIFTH AMENDMENT GRAND JURY REQUIREMENT: INAPPLICABLE TO STATE PROSECUTIONS

Whereas the indictment clause of the Fifth Amendment, as generally construed, requires the federal government to initiate the prosecution of serious federal crimes by the use of a grand jury, the states are not so limited. Since the Supreme Court of the United States has never construed the Fifth Amendment requirement of a grand jury indictment to apply to serious state criminal cases, an accused does not possess a federal constitutional right to a grand jury indictment in a state prosecution.[393] Therefore, all states are free to grant a state-created right to a grand jury indictment for whatever class of crimes they might choose or to eliminate all use of the grand jury process.

Although there is no federal constitutional requirement that states initiate serious prosecutions by means of a grand jury indictment, where a state does employ a grand jury process, it must meet minimal standards of due process under the command of the Fourteenth Amendment. Numerous states have state constitutional requirements that place the right to a grand jury indictment on a footing similar to that for federal prosecutions.[394] Like the federal provision permitting the potential defendant to waive the right to an indictment, many state jurisdictions allow the suspect to waive the state-created right.

---

[391]See Rule 7(a), (b) (G.P.O. 2002).
[392]See, generally, Rule 7(c)(1) (G.P.O. 2002).
[393]See *Hurtado v. California,* 110 U.S. 516 (1884).
[394]See Article I, Section 10, Ohio Constitution.

As a representative example, the state of Ohio allows a felony defendant to waive the right to an indictment when done in writing and in open court. However, the Ohio Rules of Criminal Procedure do not permit a waiver of indictment in a case punishable by death or life imprisonment.[395] In contrast, the state of Washington allows prosecutions of a serious nature to be initiated by a prosecutor using an information or by the procurement of an indictment by a grand jury.[396] Washington prosecutors can choose which avenue to pursue. In California, which follows a similar legislative plan as Washington, if the prosecutor chooses to proceed by use of an information, a preliminary examination of the case against the defendant must occur and a judicial order holding the defendant to answer for the alleged crime must be entered if the facts warrant. Following this process, the information shall be issued by the prosecutor and delivered to the court.[397] In any event, probable cause to believe that a particular individual committed a specified crime is the level of proof required for a prosecutor to file an information or for a grand jury to return an indictment.

In jurisdictions that permit the initiation of serious criminal cases by information, individual state constitutions and statutes dictate the nature and form that the information takes. Typically, the information contains a concise statement that the accused has committed some specified offense against the state. It need not contain technical averments or allegations that are not essential to proof of guilt. The prosecutor prepares the information in the name of the state, but the information usually must conclude with the signature of the prosecutor or assistant prosecutor.

16. EFFECT OF DISCRIMINATION ON THE GRAND JURY

For many years following the end of the American Civil War, and lasting until fairly recently in some quarters, some African American citizens were kept from serving on juries by a variety of techniques. Some of the methods were extralegal means that led the people who selected grand jury members to rarely choose blacks citizens.[398] Literacy tests, poll tax schemes, and difficulties in voter registration prevented many African Americans from being officially eligible to vote, which, consequently, kept many from qualifying as jurors of any sort. Not only were African Americans excluded, but Mexican Americans also faced discrimination in serving on grand juries in many jurisdictions. In the 1970s, in Texas, the system for identifying prospective grand jurors involved the use of a jury commission where the nominated jurors subsequently had

---

[395]See Ohio Rules of Criminal Procedure, Crim. R. 7(A) (Anderson 2003).
[396]See Rev. Code Wash. § 10.37.015 (2000): "No person shall be held to answer in any court for an alleged crime or offense, unless upon an information filed by the prosecuting attorney, or upon an indictment by a grand jury, except in cases of misdemeanor or gross misdemeanor before a district or municipal judge, or before a court martial." The authority for using an information or using a grand jury comes from the Washington Constitution, Art. I, § 25, Prosecution by Information. "Offenses heretofore required to be prosecuted by indictment may be prosecuted by information, or by indictment, as shall be prescribed by law."
[397]Cal. Pen. Code § 739 (2001): "When a defendant has been examined and committed, as provided in Section 872, it shall be the duty of the district attorney of the county…to file in the superior court of that county…, an information against the defendant which may charge the defendant with either the offense or offenses named in the order of commitment or any offense or offenses shown by the evidence taken before the magistrate to have been committed. The information shall be in the name of the people of the State of California and subscribed by the district attorney."
[398]See *Cassell v. Texas*, 339 U.S. 282 (1950).

their qualifications screened by a court judge, with the result that Mexican American citizens often were woefully underrepresented on grand juries.[399] Where litigants could prove that racial discrimination had infected their individual cases, the Supreme Court of the United States proved motivated to redress the grievance and grant relief in the form of outright reversal of any conviction.[400]

Although racial discrimination in grand jury selection had been decried in prior cases,[401] discrimination received a new condemnation in *Vasquez v. Hillery,*[402] where a California county practiced discrimination in keeping African Americans from grand jury service (see Case 10.3). In *Hillery,* the Supreme Court reaffirmed the principle that the conviction of a defendant indicted by a grand jury from which members of his own race had been systematically excluded would not be sustained. According to the Court, racial discrimination in the grand jury could never be considered to be harmless error. The *Hillery* Court rejected the government of California's argument that racial discrimination in Hillery's case amounted to harmless error and that a subsequent fair trial cured any taint in the case attributable to the racially flawed indictment process. The Supreme Court followed the reasoning of its much earlier decision in *Strauder v. West Virginia,*[403] where it reversed a state conviction on the ground that the indictment charging the offense had been returned by a grand jury from which blacks had been excluded.

The *Hillery* Court refused even to consider whether a fair trial cured racial discrimination. The Court was not persuaded that discrimination in the grand jury had no influence on the fairness of a criminal trial that results from the actions of an illegally constituted grand jury. According to the Court, the grand jury does not determine only that probable cause exists to believe that a defendant committed a crime. The grand jury possesses the power to charge a greater offense or a lesser offense and to indict for numerous counts or a single count; it also has the power to indict for a capital offense or a noncapital offense, in its sole use of discretion based on the same set of facts. The *Hillery* Court proved determined to stay with the one remedy it believed available where racial discrimination had been proven: outright reversal. This remedy remained despite the state's contention that requiring California to retry Hillery years later imposed an unduly harsh penalty for a constitutional defect bearing no relation to the fundamental fairness of the trial. Outright reversal of any conviction based on proven racial discrimination in a grand jury remains the remedy required by the Court.[404] In essence, in this manner, the Court can demonstrate its commitment to the goal of ending official governmental discrimination, wherever it might raise its ugly head.

[399] *Castaneda v. Partida,* 430 U.S. 482, 484–485 (1977).

[400] In *McCleskey v. Kemp,* 481 U.S. 279, 309 (1987), Justice Powell, in the lead opinion, noted that because of the Court's clear concern "that the factor of race may enter the criminal justice process, we have engaged in 'unceasing efforts' to eradicate racial prejudice from our criminal justice system."

[401] See *Strauder v. West Virginia,* 100 U.S. 303 (1879).

[402] 474 U.S. 254 (1986).

[403] 100 U.S. 303 (1880).

[404] The Court definitely requires absolute reversal where racial discrimination in the grand jury context has been proven. However, where the violation was of the Fifth Amendment's protection against self-incrimination as applied to the states through the Due

Prior to *Hillery* but after *Strauder,* in *Rose v. Mitchell,*[405] the Court noted the lofty purpose for which the nation had made the commitment to end racial discrimination when it stated:

> Discrimination on account of race was the primary evil at which the Amendments adopted after the War Between the States, including the Fourteenth Amendment, were aimed. The Equal Protection Clause was central to the Fourteenth Amendment's prohibition of discriminatory action by the State: it banned most types of purposeful discrimination by the State on the basis of race in an attempt to lift the burdens placed on [African Americans] by our society. It is clear from the earliest cases applying the Equal Protection Clause in the context of racial discrimination in the selection of a grand jury that the Court, from the first, was concerned with the broad aspects of racial discrimination that the Equal Protection Clause was designed to eradicate, and with the fundamental social values the Fourteenth Amendment was adopted to protect.... *Rose* at 554–555.

17. THE DECISION TO PROSECUTE: THE CONCLUSION

While serious criminal cases may be initiated either by the use of a grand jury or by the filing of an information, not all American jurisdictions follow the same rules as the federal government and some of the states. The federal constitution and some state constitutions dictate that the norm of initiating a serious criminal prosecution must follow a grand jury indictment. Since the grand jury portion of the Fifth Amendment has not been deemed to apply to state practice, the states are free to begin serious criminal prosecutions without the use of a grand jury unless state law or the state's constitution provides a different rule.

MAJOR CASES

CASE 10.1

Indictment Not Required in State Prosecutions

Hurtado v. California
Supreme Court of the United States
110 U.S. 516 (1884)

FACTS

The version of the California penal code in force in 1882 provided that when evidence disclosed that an offense had been committed and that when probable cause existed to believe that a particular person had committed the offense, the district attorney would be required to file an information charging that person with that particular offense. Since the relevant level of proof appeared to exist, a state prosecutor filed the customary information against defendant Hurtado charging him with the capital murder of José Stuardo. Pursuant to the information, Hurtado stood trial after which the jury found him guilty of capital murder. Later, the trial court sentenced the defendant to death.

Hurtado, through counsel, argued that the verdict and penalty were void, having been obtained in violation of the defendant's right to due process of law guaranteed by the Fourteenth Amendment. Specifically, Hurtado argued that he had a constitutional right to be indicted by a

---

Process Clause of the Fourteenth Amendment, the Court does not require reversal automatically. The harmless error standard was applied in *Arizona v. Fulminante,* 497 U.S. 279 (1991), where a coerced confession had been used against Fulminante but was believed beyond a reasonable doubt not to have influenced the guilty verdict.
[405]443 U.S. 545 (1979).

grand jury rather than face trial pursuant to an information because the Fourteenth Amendment contained a clause guaranteeing due process. According to Hurtado, due process of law included the right to a grand jury indictment in his case because the Fifth Amendment right to a grand jury indictment applied to state criminal procedure. This legal position was universally rejected from the trial court to the Supreme Court of California. The Supreme Court of the United States granted certiorari to consider Hurtado's allegation that the right to a grand jury indictment was a requirement of due process under the Fourteenth Amendment.

PROCEDURAL ISSUE

In a state criminal prosecution for a capital offense, does a defendant have the right under the due process guarantee of the Fourteenth Amendment to an indictment by a grand jury?

HELD: NO

RATIONALE

Mr. Justice Matthews delivered the opinion of the Court.

★ ★ ★

[I]t is maintained on behalf of the plaintiff in error [defendant Hurtado] that the phrase "due process of law" is equivalent to "law of the land " as found in the twenty-ninth chapter of Magna Charta; that by immemorial usage it has acquired a fixed, definite, and technical meaning; that it refers to and includes, not only the general principles of public liberty and private right, which lie at the foundation of all free government, but the very institutions which, venerable by time and custom, have been tried by experience and found fit and necessary for the preservation of those principles, and which, having been the birthright and inheritance of every English subject, crossed the Atlantic with the colonists and were transplanted and established in the fundamental laws of the state; that, having been originally introduced into the Constitution of the United States as a limitation upon the powers of the government, brought into being by that instrument, it has now been added as an additional security to the individual against oppression by the states themselves; that one of these institutions is that of the grand jury, an indictment or presentment by which against the

accused in cases of alleged felonies is an essential part of due process of law, in order that he may not be harassed and destroyed by prosecutions founded only upon private malice or popular fury.

★ ★ ★

It is urged upon us, however, in argument, that the claim made in behalf of the plaintiff in error [Hurtado] is supported by the decision of this court in *Murray's Lessee v. Hoboken Land & Imp. Co.,* 18 How. 272. There, Mr. Justice Curtis, delivering the opinion of the court, after showing…that due process of law must mean something more than the actual existing law of the land, for otherwise it would be no restraint upon legislative power, proceeds as follows:

> To what principle, then, are we to resort to ascertain whether this process, enacted by Congress, is due process? To this the answer must be twofold. We must examine the Constitution itself to see whether this process be in conflict with any of its provisions. If not found to be so, we must look to those settled usages and modes of proceeding existing in the common and statute law of England before the emigration of our ancestors, and which are shown not to have been unsuited to their civil and political condition by having been acted on by them after the settlement of this country.

This, it is argued, furnishes an indispensable test of what constitutes "due process of law"; that any proceeding otherwise authorized by law, which is not thus sanctioned by usage, or which supersedes and displaces one that is, cannot be regarded due process of law.

But this inference is unwarranted. The real syllabus of the passage quoted is that a process of law which is not otherwise forbidden, must be taken to be due process of law, if it can show the sanction of settled usage both in England and in this country; but it by no means follows, that nothing else can be due process of law. The point in the case cited arose in reference to a summary proceeding, questioned that account as not due process of law. The answer was however exceptional it may be, as tested by definitions and principles or ordinary procedure, nevertheless, this, in substance, has been immemorially the actual law of the land, and, therefore, is due process of law. But to hold that such a characteristic is essential to due process of law, would be to deny every quality of the law but its age, and to render it incapable of progress or improvement. It would be to stamp upon our jurisprudence the unchangeableness attributed to the laws of the Medes and Persians.

★ ★ ★

The Constitution of the United States was ordained, it is true, by descendants of Englishmen, who inherited the traditions of English law and history; but it was made for an undefined and expanding future, and for a people gathered and to be gathered from many nations and of many tongues. And while we take just pride in the principles and institutions of the common law, we are not to forget that, in lands where other systems of jurisprudence prevail, the ideas and processes of civil justice are also not unknown. Due process of law, in spite of the absolutism of continental governments, is not alien to that code which survived the Roman Empire as the foundation of modern civilization in Europe, and which has given us that fundamental maxim of distributive justice *suum cuique tribuere*. There is nothing in Magna Charta, rightly construed as a broad charter of public right and law, which ought to exclude the best ideas of all systems and of every age, and as it was the characteristic principle of the common law to draw its inspiration from every fountain of justice, we are not to assume that the sources of its supply have been exhausted. On the contrary, we should expect that the new and various experiences of our own situation and system will mould and shape it into new and not less useful forms.

The concessions of Magna Charta were wrung from the King as guaranties against the oppressions and usurpations of his prerogative. It did not enter into the minds of the barons to provide security against their own body or in favor of the Commons by limiting the power of Parliament; so that bills of attainder, *ex post facto* laws, laws declaring forfeitures of estates, and other arbitrary acts of legislation which occur so frequently in English history were never regarded as inconsistent with the law of the land, for, notwithstanding what was attributed to Lord Coke in *Bonham's Case,* 8 Rep. 115, 118a, the omnipotence of Parliament over the common law was absolute, even against common right and reason. The actual and practical security for English liberty against legislative tyranny was the power of a free public opinion represented by the Commons.

In this country written constitutions were deemed essential to protect the rights and liberties of the people against the encroachments of power delegated to their governments, and the provisions of Magna Charta were incorporated into bills of rights. There were limitations upon all the powers of government, legislative as well as executive and judicial.

It necessarily happened, therefore, that as these broad and general maxims of liberty and justice held in our system a different place and performed a different function from their position and office in English constitutional history and law, they would receive and justify a corresponding and more comprehensive interpretation. Applied in England only as guards against executive usurpation and tyranny, here they have become bulwarks also against arbitrary legislation; but in that application, as it would be incongruous to measure and restrict them by the ancient customary English law, they must be held to guarantee, not particular forms of procedure, but the very substance of individual rights to life, liberty, and property.

★ ★ ★

In *Munn v. Illinois,* 94 U.S. 113–134, the Chief Justice, delivering the opinion of the court, said:

A person has no property, no vested interest, in any rule of the common law. That is only one of the forms of municipal law, and is no more sacred than any other. Rights of property which have been created by the common law cannot be taken away without due process; but the law itself, as a rule of conduct, may be changed at the will or even at the whim of the legislature, unless prevented by constitutional limitations. Indeed, the great office of statutes is to remedy defects in the common law as they are developed, and to adapt it to the changes of time and circumstances.

And in *Walker v. Sauvinet,* 92 U. S. 90, the court said:

A trial by jury in suits at common law pending in state courts is not, therefore, a privilege or immunity of national citizenship which the states are forbidden by the Fourteenth Amendment to abridge. A state cannot deprive a person of his property without due process of law; but this does not necessarily imply that all trials in the state courts affecting the property of persons must be by jury. This requirement of the Constitution is met if the trial is had according to the settled course of judicial proceedings. Due process of law is process according to the law of the land. This process in the states is regulated by the law of the state.

In *Kennard v. Louisiana ex rel. Morgan,* 92 U.S. 480, the question was whether a mode of trying [determining] the title to an office in which [there was] no provision for a jury, was due process of law. Its validity was affirmed. The Chief Justice, after reciting the various steps in the proceeding, said:

> From this it appears that ample provision has been made for the trial of the contestation before a court of competent jurisdiction; for bringing the party against whom the proceeding is had before the court and notifying him of the case he is required to meet; for giving him an opportunity to be heard in his defense; for the deliberation and judgment of the court; for an appeal from this judgment to the highest court of the state, and for hearing and judgment there. A mere statement of the facts carries with it a complete answer to all the constitutional objections urged against the validity of the act.

And Mr. Justice Miller, in *Davidson v. New Orleans,* 96 U.S. 97–1055, after showing the difficulty, if not the impossibility, of framing a definition of this constitutional phrase which should be "at once perspicuous, comprehensive, and satisfactory," and thence deducing the wisdom

> in the ascertaining of the intent and application of such an important phrase in the Federal Constitution, by the gradual process of judicial inclusion and exclusion, as the cases presented for decision shall require,

says, however, that:

> it is not possible to hold that a party has, without due process of law, been deprived of his property, when, as regards the issue affecting it, he has by the laws of the state fair trial in a court of justice, according to the modes of proceeding applicable to such a case. *See also Missouri v. Lewis,* 101 U.S. 22–31; *Ex parte Wall,* 107 U.S. 288–290.

We are to construe this phrase [due process of law] in the Fourteenth Amendment by the *usus loquendi* of the Constitution itself. The same words are contained in the Fifth Amendment. That article makes specific and express provision for perpetuating the institution of the grand jury, so far as relates to prosecutions for the more aggravated crimes under the laws of the United States. It declares that

> No person shall be held to answer for capital or otherwise infamous crime, unless on a presentment or indictment of a grand jury, except in cases arising in the

land or naval forces or in the militia when in actual service in time of war or public danger; nor shall any person be subject for the same offense to be twice put in jeopardy of life or limb nor shall he be compelled in any criminal cases to be a witness against himself.

It then immediately adds: "nor be deprived of life, liberty, or property without due process of law." According to a recognized canon of interpretation, especially applicable to formal and solemn instruments of constitutional law, we are forbidden to assume, without clear reason to the contrary, that any part of this most important amendment is superfluous. The natural and obvious inference is that, in the sense of the Constitution, "due process of law" was not meant or intended to include, *ex vi termini,* the institution and procedure of a grand jury in any case. The conclusion is equally irresistible, that when the same phrase was employed in the Fourteenth Amendment to restrain the action of the States, it was used in the same sense and with no greater extent; and that, if in the adoption of that amendment it had been part of its purpose to perpetuate the institution of the grand jury in all the States, it would have embodied, as did the Fifth Amendment, express declarations to that effect. Due process of law in the latter refers to that law of the land which derives its authority from the legislative power conferred upon Congress by the Constitution of the United States, exercised within the limits therein prescribed, and interpreted according to the principles of the common law. In the Fourteenth Amendment, by parity of reason, it refers to the law of the land in each state which derives its authority from the inherent and reserved powers of the state, exerted within the limits of those fundamental principles of liberty and justice which lie at the base of all our civil and political institutions, and the greatest security for which resides in the right of the people to make their own laws, and alter them at their pleasure.

> The Fourteenth Amendment [as was said by Mr. Justice Bradley in *Missouri v. Lewis,* 101 U.S. 22–31] does not profess to secure to all persons in the United States the benefit of the same laws and the same remedies. Great diversities in these respects may exist in two states separated only by an imaginary line. On one side of this line there may be a right of trial by jury, and on the other side no such right. Each state prescribes its own modes of judicial proceeding.

★ ★ ★

The supreme court of Mississippi, in a well-considered case, *Brown v. Levee Commissioners,* 50 Miss. 468, speaking of the meaning of the phrase "due process of law," says:

> The principle does not demand that the laws exist-ing at any point of time shall be irrepealable, or that any forms of remedies shall necessarily continue. It refers to certain fundamental rights which that sys-tem of jurisprudence, of which ours is a derivative, has always recognized. If any of these are disregarded in the proceedings by which a person is condemned to the loss of life, liberty, or property, then the depri-vation has not been by "due process of law."

★ ★ ★

It follows that any legal proceeding enforced by pub-lic authority whether sanctioned by age and custom, or newly devised in the discretion of the legislative power in furtherance of the general public good, which regards and preserves these principles of liberty and justice, must be held to be due process of law.

★ ★ ★

Tried by these principles, we are unable to say that the substitution for a presentment or indictment by a grand jury of the proceeding by information after exam-ination and commitment by a magistrate, certifying to the probable guilt of the defendant with the right on his part to the aid of counsel and to the cross examination of the witnesses produced for the prosecution, is not due process of law. It is, as we have seen, an ancient proceed-ing at common law, which might include every case of an offense of less grade than a felony, except misprision of treason; and in every circumstance of its administra-tion, as authorized by the statute of California, it careful-ly considers and guards the substantial interest of the prisoner. It is merely a preliminary proceeding, and can result in no final judgment, except as the consequence of a regular judicial trial, conducted precisely as in cases of indictments.

In reference to this mode of proceeding at the com-mon law, and which he says "is as ancient as the common law itself," Blackstone adds (4 Comm. 305):

> And as to those offenses in which informations were allowed as well as indictments, so long as they were confined to this high and respectable jurisdiction, and were carried on in a legal and regular course in His Majesty's Court of King's Bench, the subject had

no reason to complain. The same notice was given, the same process was issued, the same pleas we al-lowed, the same trial by jury was had, the same judg-ment was given by the same judges, as if the prosecution had originally been by indictment.

For these reasons, finding no error therein, the judg-ment of the supreme court of California is

affirmed.

COMMENTS, NOTES, AND QUESTIONS

1. California law addresses the practice of issuing of informations rather than presenting cases to grand juries. Cal. Pen. Code § 739 (2001) provides: "When a defendant has been examined and committed, as provided in Section 872, it shall be the duty of the district attorney of the county…to file in the superior court of that county… an information against the defendant which may charge the defendant with either the offense or offenses named in the order of commitment or any offense or offenses shown by the evidence taken before the magistrate to have been committed." The wording of the California statute seems fairly mandatory and has not undergone great change from Hurtado's day. According to *Hurtado,* California has no constitutional need to offer the grand jury for any offense unless the state law or constitution is changed. Would you prefer the grand jury system for all serious cases? Would a defendant gain anything from the use of a grand jury in-dictment? Would it make any difference if you were a pros-ecutor? Why or why not?

2. The prosecution in *Hurtado* involved the use of an information, but not without some judicial oversight. State practice authorized prosecutions for felonies by informa-tion subsequent to an examination and commitment by a magistrate. If the magistrate committed, the prosecutor could issue an information. Would the decision be any dif-ferent if the prosecutor could just issue the indictment without any judicial screening? Does the fact that a judicial official screened a case make a difference to a prosecutor? To a defendant? See *Lem Woon v. Oregon,* 229 U.S. 586 (1913), where a serious case could be brought on the word of the prosecutor alone. The Court stated that due process does not require the state to adopt the procedure of the grand jury, so the Court noted that it could find no ground for re-quiring a hearing prior to the filing of an information. Can a system of justice be deemed fairly operated in the absence of a grand jury? Why or why not? How did the Supreme Court of the United States analyze this issue in *Hurtado*?

CASE 10.2

Infamous Federal Crimes Require Grand Jury Indictment

United States v. Moreland
Supreme Court of the United States
258 U.S. 433 (1922)

FACTS

A juvenile court in the District of Columbia tried defendant Charles Moreland on a charge of willfully neglecting or refusing to support his two minor children. The prosecution used an information rather than a grand jury indictment to initiate the criminal proceeding. According to the statute involved, a punishment of a $500 fine or imprisonment in the District of Columbia at hard labor for not more than twelve months, or both, could be imposed upon conviction. A jury in the juvenile court in the District of Columbia found Moreland guilty and sentenced him to serve six months at hard labor at the local workhouse. The defendant filed his appeal with the Court of Appeals for the District of Columbia, wherein he renewed his allegation that the Fifth Amendment guarantees a person the right to a grand jury indictment in all federal prosecutions.

The Court of Appeals agreed with Moreland's legal analysis and reversed the conviction with instructions to the juvenile court to dismiss the complaint. Upon the prosecution's petition, the Supreme Court granted certiorari.

PROCEDURAL QUESTION

Where an accused might receive hard labor as part of punishment if convicted for a federal crime, does such possibility of hard labor indicate that the crime charged is an infamous crime for which the accused possesses a Fifth Amendment right to a grand jury indictment?

HELD: YES

RATIONALE

Mr. Justice McKenna delivered the opinion of the Court.

★ ★ ★

The Court of Appeals…considered that it was constrained to decide that the judgment was in violation of the Fifth Amendment, and, therefore, to reverse it on the authority of *Wong Wing v. United States,* 163 U.S. 228.

The United States resists both the authority and extent of that case by the citation of others, which, it asserts, modify or overrule it. A review of it, therefore, is of initial importance.

Certain statutes of the United States made it unlawful under certain circumstances for a Chinese laborer to be in the United States, and provided for his deportation by certain officers, among others, a Commissioner of a United States court. And one of them (Act of 1892 [Comp. St. Section 4318]) provided that, if a Chinese person or one of that descent was "convicted and adjudged to be not lawfully entitled to be or remain in the United States," he should "be imprisoned at hard labor for a period not exceeding one year, and thereafter removed from the United States."

Wong Wing, a Chinese person,…was arrested and taken before a Commissioner of the Circuit Court for the Eastern District of Michigan and adjudged to be unlawfully within the United States and not entitled to remain therein. It was also adjudged that he be imprisoned at hard labor at and in the Detroit House of Correction for the period of 60 days.

The court, considering the statutes, said they operated on two classes—one which came into the country with its consent; the other which came in without consent and in disregard of law—and that Congress had the constitutional power to deport both classes and to commit the enforcement of the law to executive officers.

This power of arrest by the executive officers and the power of deportation were sustained; but the punishment provided for by the act, and which was pronounced against Wong Wing, that is, imprisonment at hard labor, was decided to be a violation of the Fifth Amendment; he not having been proceeded against by presentment or indictment by a grand jury.

The court noted the argument and the cases cited and sustained the power of exclusion, but said that when Congress went further, and inflicted punishment at hard labor, it "must provide for a judicial trial to establish the guilt of the accused." And this because such punishment was infamous and prohibited by the Fifth Amendment, the conditions prescribed by the amendment not having been observed. The necessity of their observance was decided, because, to repeat, imprisonment at hard labor was an infamous punishment. In sanction of the decision, *Ex parte Wilson,* 114 U.S. 417, was cited and quoted from. The citation was in point. Both propositions were presented in that case, and both were decided upon elaborate consideration and estimate of authorities. See also, *Mackin v. United States,* 117 U.S. 348, 350, 6 S. Sup. Ct. 777.

★ ★ ★

The Wilson case was elaborate in the exposition of the law—its evolution and extent. The various punishments, or, we may say, the various imprisonments, to which infamy had been ascribed, were detailed, with citation of cases. In these were included, as certain, imprisonment in a penitentiary. But it was decided that the quality of infamy could attach to any imprisonment, if accompanied by hard labor. It was said, and it was necessary to say, in passing on Wilson's situation, that

> imprisonment at hard labor, compulsory and unpaid, is, in the strongest sense of the words, "involuntary servitude for crime," spoken of in the provision of the Ordinance of 1787 and of the Thirteenth Amendment of the Constitution, by which all other slavery was abolished.

In other words, it was declared that, if imprisonment was in any other place than a penitentiary and was to be at hard labor, the latter gave it character—that is, made it infamous and brought it within the prohibition of the Constitution.

★ ★ ★

Wong Wing's [constitutional argument] was recognized as a claim that his sentence to imprisonment at *hard labor* inflicted an infamous punishment, and hence conflicted with the Fifth and Sixth Amendments of the Constitution of the United States, he not having been presented or indicted by a grand jury.

"On the other hand," the court said,

> it is contended by the government that it has never been decided by this court that in all cases where the punishment may be confinement at hard labor, the crime is infamous, and many cases are cited from the reports of the state Supreme Courts, where the constitutionality of statutes providing for summary proceedings, without a jury trial, for the punishment by imprisonment at hard labor of vagrants and disorderly persons has been upheld.

The comment was an anticipation of some things that are urged in this case. At any rate, the contrast of contentions shows unmistakably upon what the court's decision was invoked, and while it decided, as we have seen, that the commissioner had power under the Act of 1892 to order Wong Wing deported and to sentence him to imprisonment, Congress could not legally invest the commissioner with power to make hard labor an adjunct of the imprisonment. It was, in effect, said that the adjunct made the imprisonment infamous, and beyond the power of legislation to direct, without making provision "for a judicial trial to establish the guilt of the accused." Wong Wing was therefore discharged from custody.

★ ★ ★

We have dwelt on this matter at length because we think more is involved than the power to deport aliens, or to punish them for illegal entry into the country—more than to deliver one from punishment who has defied the orders of a court, that enjoined upon him the manifest duty of supporting his minor children. It concerns the recognition and enforcement of a provision of the Constitution of the United States expressing and securing an important right. And the right, at times, must be accorded one whose conduct tempts to a straining of the law against him.

The ultimate contention of the United States is that the provision of the Act of March 23, 1906, for punishment by fine or imprisonment are [*sic*] severable, and that, therefore, it was error in the Court of Appeals in holding the act unconstitutional, and in directing the dismissal of the case, instead of sending it back for further proceedings.

The contention is untenable. It is what sentence can be imposed under the law, not what was imposed, that is the material consideration. When an accused is in danger of an infamous punishment, if convicted, he has a right to insist that he be not put upon trial, except on the accusation of a grand jury.

Judgment affirmed [upheld the Court of Appeal's reversal of conviction].

COMMENTS, NOTES, AND QUESTIONS

1. Moreland's alleged crime was considered an "infamous" crime for which a grand jury indictment was dictated by the Fifth Amendment. Why did the Court come to this conclusion? Should the hard labor

provision make the crime an infamous one? Under the circumstances of Moreland's case, do you think it was an extremely serious offense? Since the line between what constituted an "infamous" crime and those that were not so considered had to be drawn, was the *Moreland* Court simply drawing that necessary line in an arbitrary manner?

2. The prosecutor, in many states, has the option of initiating a criminal case either with a grand jury or by filing an information. If you were a prosecutor, which system would you prefer? Would it make any difference if you were a potential target of the prosecutor? Why or why not? Consider the situation if you were a prosecutor in a state with such alternatives and the son or daughter of a prominent politician had committed an act that required prosecution. Would you rather have a grand jury make the charge, or would you prefer to proceed with an information?

3. The Supreme Court of the United States has long recognized that the proper functioning of a grand jury system requires secrecy surrounding the proceedings. See *Douglas Oil Co. of California v. Petrol Stops Northwest*, 441 U.S. 211 (1979); *Butterworth v. Smith*, 494 U.S. 624 (1990); and Rule 6(e)(2) of the Federal Rules of Criminal Procedure. The Court described the secrecy standard in detail in *Douglas Oil*:

> Parties seeking grand jury transcripts under Rule 6(e) must show that the material they seek is needed to avoid a possible injustice in another judicial proceeding, that the need for disclosure is greater than the need for continued secrecy, and that their request is structured to cover only material so needed.

> It is clear from *[United States v.] Procter & Gamble* [356 U.S. 677 (1958)] and *Dennis* [*v. United States*, 384 U.S. 855 (1966)] that disclosure is appropriate only in those cases where the need for it outweighs the public interest in secrecy, and that the burden of demonstrating this balance rests upon the private party seeking disclosure. It is equally clear that as the considerations justifying secrecy become less relevant, a party asserting a need for grand jury transcripts will have a lesser burden in showing justification. In sum,...the court's duty in a case of this kind is to weigh carefully the competing interests in light of the relevant circumstances and the standards announced by this Court. And if disclosure is ordered, the court may include protective limitations on the use of the disclosed material....

4. Louisiana has a state grand jury procedure that is representative of many state rules covering grand jury secrecy. Louisiana law protects the privacy of information presented by witnesses by preventing disclosure of the substantive nature of each witness's testimony by anyone other than that witness. The law in conjunction with the state constitution (Louisiana Constitution, Art. V, § 34) provides that grand jury secrecy includes the identity of all witnesses and requires that grand jurors and other necessary functionaries keep secret witnesses' testimony, as well as all other matters occurring during grand jury meetings. A witness who has testified before the grand jury may disclose his or her testimony to an attorney for the accused, to government attorneys, or with the court (Louisiana Code of Criminal Procedure, Article 434 (2003)). Any other party who wishes to discover the substance of what transpired at a grand jury proceeding must show a compelling necessity for the materials at an adversarial hearing by presenting sufficient evidence to overcome the presumption of continued secrecy. See *Pettibone v. Belt, Sheriff*, 843 So.2d 1265 (2003). The essential nature of privacy protects those who are never indicted, helps prevent witness intimidation, and keeps targeted individuals from escaping.

5. Regardless of what state law provides, when a witness has finished testifying, the witness may tell the world what he or she offered to the grand jury in the way of testimony. Florida had a law (Fla. Stat. § 905.27) that attempted to seal the lips of grand jury witnesses forever, subject to certain exceptions. A reporter who had been a witness before a Florida grand jury challenged the law on the basis that it violated his First Amendment freedom. In *Butterworth v. Smith*, 494 U.S. 624 (1990), mentioned in the textual material for this section, the Court held that "insofar as the Florida law prohibits a grand jury witness from disclosing his own testimony after the term of the grand jury has ended, it violates the First Amendment to the United States Constitution." Following this case, it is abundantly clear that grand jury witnesses may report the nature and substance of the witnesses' personal testimony given to a grand jury.

CASE 10.3

Proven Grand Jury Racial Discrimination Creates Voidable Subsequent Conviction

Vasquez v. Hillery
Supreme Court of the United States
474 U.S. 254 (1986)

FACTS

Prior to 1962 and including 1962, the King's County, California, grand jury system had excluded African

Americans from participation in some aspects of justice administration. Specifically, African Americans had been excluded from serving on grand juries in King's County. During this time of racial discrimination, a grand jury indicted defendant-respondent Hillery, an African American, for murder. In a pretrial motion, defendant Hillery requested that the indictment be quashed on the ground that the grand jury which indicted him had been selected in a fashion which systematically excluded black citizens from participation. Following the trial court's refusal to quash the indictment, the trial court convicted the defendant at a trial at which fundamental fairness prevailed and about which Hillery made no complaint.

For the next sixteen years, Hillery unsuccessfully pursued direct appeals and collateral relief in his attempt to have his murder conviction overturned. Hillery contended that the grand jury which indicted him was not properly selected from a fair cross section of the community since members of his race had been systematically excluded from grand jury service. A month following the final California Supreme Court decision in his case, he filed a habeas corpus petition in a federal district court. The judge in the district court held that Hillery had established the existence of racial discrimination in the selection of the grand jury and granted the writ. The Court of Appeals affirmed the decision of the district court and the Supreme Court of the United States granted certiorari. The prosecution contended that the Court abandon the rule which requires the reversal of any conviction of a defendant indicted by a grand jury from which members of his own race have been systematically excluded by the government.

PROCEDURAL ISSUE

Where there has been admitted racial discrimination in the composition of a grand jury which issues an indictment, is any conviction which rests upon the improper indictment voidable?

HELD: YES

RATIONALE

Justice Marshall delivered the opinion of the Court.

The Warden of San Quentin State Prison [Vasquez] asks this Court to retire a doctrine of equal protection jurisprudence first announced in 1880. The time has come, he urges, for us to abandon the rule requiring reversal of

the conviction of any defendant indicted by a grand jury from which members of his own race were systematically excluded.

★ ★ ★

III

On the merits, petitioner [Vasquez, on behalf of the People of California] urges this Court to find that discrimination in the grand jury amounted to harmless error in this case, claiming that the evidence against respondent [Hillery] was overwhelming and that discrimination no longer infects the selection of grand juries in Kings County. Respondent's conviction after a fair trial, we are told, purged any taint attributable to the indictment process. Our acceptance of this theory would require abandonment of more than a century of consistent precedent.

In 1880, this Court reversed a state conviction on the ground that the indictment charging the offense had been issued by a grand jury from which blacks had been excluded. We reasoned that deliberate exclusion of blacks "is practically a brand upon them, affixed by the law, an assertion of their inferiority, and a stimulant to that race prejudice which is an impediment to securing to individuals of the race that equal justice which the law aims to secure to all others." *Strauder v. West Virginia,* 10 Otto 303 [100 U.S. 303], 308 (1880).

Thereafter, the Court has repeatedly rejected all arguments that a conviction may stand despite racial discrimination in the selection of the grand jury. [Citations omitted.] Only six years ago, the Court explicitly addressed the question of whether this unbroken line of case law should be reconsidered in favor of a harmless-error standard, and determined that it should not. *Rose v. Mitchell,* 443 U.S. 545 (1979). We reaffirmed our conviction that discrimination on the basis of race in the selection of grand jurors "strikes at the fundamental values of our judicial system and our society as a whole," and that the criminal defendant's right to equal protection of the laws has been denied when he is indicted by a grand jury from which members of a racial group purposefully have been excluded. *Id.,* at 556.

Petitioner argues here that requiring a State to retry a defendant, sometimes years later, imposes on it an unduly harsh penalty for a constitutional defect bearing no relation to the fundamental fairness of the trial. Yet intentional discrimination in the selection of grand jurors is a grave constitutional trespass, possible only under color of state authority, and wholly within the power of the State to prevent. Thus, the remedy we have embraced for over a century—the only effective remedy for this violation—is not disproportionate to the evil that it seeks to deter. If grand jury discrimination becomes a thing of the past, no conviction will ever again be lost on account of it.

Nor are we persuaded that discrimination in the grand jury has no effect on the fairness of the criminal trials that result from that grand jury's actions. The grand jury does not determine only that probable cause exists to believe that a defendant committed a crime, or that it does not. In the hands of the grand jury lies the power to charge a greater offense or a lesser offense; numerous counts or a single count; and perhaps most significant of all, a capital offense or a noncapital offense—all on the basis of the same facts. Moreover, "[t]he grand jury is not bound to indict in every case where a conviction can be obtained." *United States v. Ciambrone,* 601 F.2d 616, 629 (CA2 1979) (Friendly, J., dissenting). Thus, even if a grand jury's determination of probable cause is confirmed in hindsight by a conviction on the indicted offense, that confirmation in no way suggests that the discrimination did not impermissibly infect the framing of the indictment and, consequently, the nature or very existence of the proceedings to come.

When constitutional error calls into question the objectivity of those charged with bringing a defendant to judgment, a reviewing court can neither indulge a presumption of regularity nor evaluate the resulting harm. Accordingly, when the trial judge is discovered to have had some basis for rendering a biased judgment, his actual motivations are hidden from review, and we must presume that the process was impaired. See *Tumey v. Ohio,* 273 U.S. 510, 535 (1927) (reversal required when judge has financial interest in conviction, despite lack of indication that bias influenced decisions). Similarly, when a petit jury has been selected upon improper criteria or has been exposed to prejudicial publicity, we have required reversal of the conviction because the effect of the violation cannot be ascertained. See *Davis v. Georgia,* 429 U.S. 122 (1976) *(per curiam); Sheppard v. Maxwell,* 384 U.S. 333, 351–352 (1966). Like these fundamental flaws, which never have been thought harmless, discrimination in the grand jury undermines the structural integrity of the criminal tribunal itself, and is not amenable to harmless-error review.

Just as a conviction is void under the Equal Protection Clause if the prosecutor deliberately charged the defendant on account of his race, see *United States v. Batchelder,* 442 U.S. 114, 125 (1979), a conviction cannot be understood to cure the taint attributable to a charging body selected on the basis of race. Once having found discrimination in the selection of a grand jury, we simply cannot know that the need to indict would have been assessed in the same way by a grand jury properly constituted. The overriding imperative to eliminate this systemic flaw in the charging process, as well as the difficulty of assessing its effect on any given defendant, requires our continued adherence to a rule of mandatory reversal.

The opinion of the Court in *Mitchell* ably presented other justifications, based on the necessity for vindicating Fourteenth Amendment rights, supporting a policy of automatic reversal in cases of grand jury discrimination. That analysis persuasively demonstrated that the justifications retain their validity in modern times, for "114 years after the close of the War Between the States and nearly 100 years after Strauder, racial and other forms of discrimination still remain a fact of life, in the administration of justice as in our society as a whole." 443 U.S., at 558–559. The six years since *Mitchell* have given us no reason to doubt the continuing truth of that observation.

IV

★ ★ ★

The judgment of the Court of Appeals, accordingly, is affirmed.

COMMENTS, NOTES, AND QUESTIONS

1. Is it possible that, although racial discrimination existed at the grand jury stage, the defendant-respondent in *Hillery* received a fair trial on the merits and his conviction should be upheld? Would a fair trial "cure" any discrimination that occurred at the grand jury stage of the prosecution? Perhaps Hillery believed that his trial was sufficiently fair, since Booker T. Hillery did not challenge the fairness of the actual trial at any time during the appellate process, except to argue that he should not have been tried under a void indictment.

2. The state of California did not have to proceed against Hillery by the use of a grand jury indictment but could have used an information. Since no indictment was actually required, is this not truly a case of harmless error? Should the question of whether Hillery's conviction should have been reversed turn on whether the state has sufficient evidence to reindict him and try him again? Would it matter if a grand jury that mirrored the local

population at the time of indictment would have had only one black member? The odds of a random drawing could have resulted in no black individual sitting on the grand jury in any event.

3. Generally the Fifth Amendment has been interpreted to require a grand jury lawfully composed and selected in a manner that does not involve bias, racial or otherwise. Could bias based on racial discrimination, which admittedly occurred in *Hillery,* have been merely "harmless error" that did not affect the outcome of the murder trial? The majority opinion by Justice Marshall noted, "Once having found discrimination in the selection of a grand jury, we simply cannot know that the need to indict would have been assessed in the same way by a grand jury properly constituted." Do you think he was correct? Why or why not? Did Marshall neglect to consider the valid trial as "curing" the original indictment defect?

4. In *Vasquez v. Hillery,* the Court seemed to indicate that if one could prove racial discrimination within the grand jury context, a reversal would be virtually automatic. In a recent Louisiana case decided by the Fifth Circuit Court of Appeals, *Pickney v. Cain,* 2003 U.S. App. LEXIS 14566 (2003), the defendant had alleged a violation of equal protection due to racial discrimination in the selection of the grand jury foreperson. The Louisiana Supreme Court held that the defendant waived his equal protection claim based on discrimination in the selection of his grand jury foreperson because he failed to file a pretrial motion to quash the indictment. The defendant had procedurally defaulted his racial discrimination claim by not raising it properly prior to trial. According to the federal appellate court, a habeas corpus petitioner "may overcome the state procedural bar only by demonstrating (1) cause for the procedural default and actual prejudice as a result of the alleged violation of federal law or (2) that failure to consider his claims will result in a fundamental miscarriage of justice." *Smith v. Johnson,* 216 F.3d 521, 524 (5th Cir. 2000).

After reviewing the case and the strength of the evidence, the federal district court refused to grant a writ of habeas corpus because the defendant failed to establish any actual prejudice in the outcome of his case. According to the *Pickney* Court, a trial court reversal of the grand jury indictment would have served no purpose other than to have delayed the trial because there was sufficient evidence to indict the defendant a second time and send him to trial. The lesson seems to be that an allegation of racial discrimination made but not proven through a procedural default will not trigger an automatic reversal where there may have been prejudice but where the defendant would not have obtained a better outcome in any event.

Plea Bargaining and Guilty Pleas: Constitutional Standards

Chapter Outline

Key Terms

Alford plea
Arraignment
Breach of plea agreement
Collateral attack
Executory plea
Guilty plea effect
Judgment
Lesser included offense

Nolo contendere
Plea
Preliminary hearing
Prima facie case
Reservation of right to appeal
Specific performance
Straight plea
Waivable rights

1. INTRODUCTION TO PLEA BARGAINING AND GUILTY PLEAS

While many criminal cases are resolved by a formal trial, courts adjudicate far more cases through compromises known as negotiated pleas or plea bargains. When the legal positions of both sides have become fairly familiar to each other, attorneys representing each party have an opportunity to evaluate the relative strength of their opponent's case and to consider weak points that might produce an advantage. Through experience, the attorneys possess a fair sense of the likely outcome, barring surprises, and may be willing to consider negotiating an end to the criminal contest with the defendant's consent. The accused and the prosecutor may be willing to compromise so that each side gains from a plea agreement. For the prosecutor, the benefits may be a time savings and a conviction that becomes certain in a plea bargain, whereas the defendant may receive a lesser conviction for agreeing to plead without a trial. When each party perceives that it has received a sufficient benefit, compromise can terminate the case so long as a judge accepts the compromise agreement, known as the plea bargain.

2. ENTRY OF PLEA AND INITIAL NEGOTIATION

Following arrest, and subsequent to indictment or information, the defendant normally must enter a plea to the charge or charges the prosecution plans to pursue. The proceeding is frequently known as an arraignment, or initial appearance, but in some jurisdictions may be called a preliminary hearing,[406] especially if the prosecution is required to go forward with the presentation of a prima facie case. The charges are read to the defendant, who receives a copy of the indictment or information. At least two general options are available to the defendant at this point: the accused may determine that proceeding to trial on the charges is appropriate, or there is the possibility of compromising the allegations in the absence of trial through negotiations.

At an early stage in the criminal process, the defendant will generally be required to answer the charges by entering a plea of not guilty, guilty, or nolo contendere. A plea of not guilty means that the government and the defendant must begin preparations directed toward a trial on the merits unless plea negotiations are initiated early in the process.[407] If a defendant elects to enter a plea of nolo contendere, or no contest, the answer to the charges possesses most of the attributes of a guilty plea and has the same legal consequences in the criminal context. Analyzed more closely, this plea, though not directly an admission of guilt, constitutes an admission of the facts alleged in the indictment, information, or complaint. Alternatively, if the defendant decides to plead guilty to charges at a preliminary hearing, he or she generally must have been represented by counsel and have been addressed directly by the judge. The judge must make sure that the defendant is pleading voluntarily and understands

---

[406]In some jurisdictions that allow a serious prosecution to be initiated by information rather than by a grand jury indictment, a preliminary hearing may precede the filing of an information.

[407]The nolo contendere plea, in contrast to a guilty plea, cannot be used as a sword against the defendant in the event that civil litigation arises from the facts giving rise to the criminal accusations.

both the rights that he or she plans to relinquish and the legal consequences of a guilty plea to the charges. If these general requirements are met, the defendant may properly make a straight plea of guilty to the charges as alleged. In such a context, this would not be considered a plea bargain, merely a plea to the charges as stated. Where the defendant refuses to enter a plea or stands mute, the judge or magistrate will enter a not-guilty plea.

A large majority of criminal cases are resolved by legal proceedings that do not result in a traditional trial but involve discussions between the prosecution and the defense, with significant input from the defendant. When faced with a criminal case, it may be in the defendant's best interest to plead guilty to the charges and begin serving time and/or pay the fine, especially where the prosecution's case is very strong and the defense has very little with which to work. Alternatively, if the prosecution's case contains weak points with respect to admissible evidence or if the defendant has a colorable case that might result in a conviction for a lesser included offense, the prosecutor's office might be willing to accept a guilty plea to a lesser offense with the knowledge that a conviction is certain.

3. PLEA NEGOTIATIONS: PROCESS AND EFFECT

In order to foster open and complete disclosure on behalf of the defendant and the prosecution, the general rule for both state and federal plea negotiations is that discussions and disclosures of facts and circumstances may not later be used against the defendant at trial,[408] at least for purposes of positive proof of guilt. However, the right to prevent use of disclosures during plea negotiations in a federal prosecution is a waivable right and may be negotiated away.[409] Statements made by a defendant or on his or her behalf by legal counsel during plea negotiations that do not result in an agreement, as well as statements made prior to a plea offer that is later withdrawn or breached, are not admissible against a defendant in a federal criminal or federal civil proceeding.[410] Most states follow similar practice, although variances in both rules and applications do exist.

The fact that each side may desire a level of certainty concerning the charge to which the defendant may plead often provides the motivating factor in coming to an agreement. Another facet of plea bargaining that may be influenced by negotiation involves the type and length of sentence to be imposed. In many state courts and in the federal arena, it may be possible for the defendant to negotiate the length of the sentence or the maximum range of time over which the judge may impose a sentence.[411] In some jurisdictions, the counsel for the defendant and the

---

[408]In federal prosecutions, as a general rule, the plea negotiations cannot be used against the defendant if the case goes to trial. However, if the statement made during the negotiations was made under oath, it may be admissible in a subsequent perjury prosecution where a subsequent statement under oath has been made that was inconsistent with the first statement. Federal Rules of Evidence, Rule 410 (G.P.O. 2002).

[409]See *United States v. Mezzanatto,* 513 U.S. 196 (1995), where the Court approved the trial use of defendant's inconsistent statements, made during plea negotiations, for impeachment purposes at trial.

[410]Federal Rules of Evidence, Rule 410 (G.P.O. 2002).

[411]See Federal Rules of Criminal Procedure, Rule 11 (c)(1)(B) and (C) (G.P.O. 2002).

prosecutor may agree that the prosecutor will make a specific recommendation to the sentencing judge concerning the sentence and/or agree not to bring other charges.[412] Although this may not be binding on the judge, the prosecutor's recommendation will often carry significant influence, especially where the defendant has assisted the government in other prosecutions. In federal prosecutions, general sentencing guidelines will curtail, to some extent, the options a prosecutor may be able to offer to a defendant. A United States attorney may recommend a downward departure from the amount of time that federal sentencing guidelines suggest for a particular crime or crimes, but a federal district court judge is not bound by a prosecutor's recommendation for a lesser sentence. If the defense and prosecution reach a plea agreement in a federal case, the court must require the disclosure of the agreement at the time the plea is offered, and the trial court may accept or reject the agreement.

The plea-bargaining role of the judge varies depending on the jurisdiction. Federal judges are not permitted to participate in plea negotiations, but some state judges, to a degree, become involved in the determination of some of the components of a plea bargain. Some threats to fairness and justice exist when a judge becomes overly involved in plea negotiations. The Ohio Supreme Court highlighted some of these challenges presented by judicial plea bargaining. In *State v. Byrd,* the court stated:

> A judge's participation in the actual bargaining process presents a high potential for coercion. The defendant often views the judge as the final arbiter of his fate or at the very least the person in control of the important environment of the courtroom. He may be led to believe that this person considers him guilty of the crime without a chance of proving otherwise. He may infer that he will not be given a fair opportunity to present his case. Even if he wishes to go to trial, he may perceive the trial as a hopeless and dangerous exercise in futility. 63 Ohio St. 2d 288 (1980).

With these noted dangers to due process, a judge should tread very lightly when considering whether to become involved intimately in negotiating pleas with defendants and prosecutors.

In an Indiana case, *Anderson v. State,*[413] in open court, the trial judge and the defendant negotiated a plea agreement in return for a definite sentence of eleven years, even though the prosecutor was not in agreement. This process has not generally been encouraged by Indiana and other state appellate courts, but it does occur. In some cases, the trial judge may become too eager to end a case by a plea bargain. In one Indiana case where the trial judge attempted to get the defendant to agree to a plea by openly considering the extent of a harsh sentence the judge suggested he might impose if the case were eventually tried in his court, the Supreme Court of Indiana refused to approve a plea bargain negotiated in that manner.[414] Judges have some incentives to push negotiated pleas. A judge may be able to clear

---

[412]Ibid., Rule 11 (c)(1).
[413]263 Ind. 583 (1975).
[414]*Garrett v. State,* 737 N.E.2d 388 (Ind. 2000).

a docket to manageable levels by aggressively moving cases through the system, but he or she needs to be careful that justice is not sacrificed in the bargain. Similarly, judges need to remain aware that they occupy a neutral position in the criminal justice system and must not ally themselves with the prosecution, destroying judicial impartiality and justice, as well. A judge who decides not to accept a particular plea arrangement should indicate, with some rough parameters, the level of sentence or disposition he or she considers appropriate to the case, without attempting to dictate the eventual agreement by coercing the defendant.

In a different state case, *Ellis v. State,* 744 N.E.2d 425 (Ind. 2001), the prosecutor and the defense counsel had reached a rape case plea agreement that they presented to the judge (see Case 11.2). But because the judge believed that the negotiated sentence was too short, he indicated what he believed an appropriate disposition and sentence should encompass and stated that he would approve such a revised sentence. The judge also indicated that there were problems with identification evidence in the case and that he would entertain a change of venue motion. Later, the defendant accepted a revised plea bargain along the lines suggested by the trial judge. Afterward, however, Ellis appealed the plea agreement and conviction as involuntary since he had feared going to trial if he had rejected the judge's recommendations for a plea agreement. The basis for his reluctance to go to trial was his concern that he would receive a harsher sentence if he rejected the plea agreement containing some of the judge's suggestions. In rejecting Ellis' contentions, the Supreme Court of Indiana noted:

> The trial judge's response to the original plea proposal did not render Ellis' eventual guilty plea involuntary. The court did not press Ellis to plead guilty rather than to proceed to trial. Faced with a proposed sentence that fell outside the range the court considered reasonable, it merely advised the parties of the low end of that range, as guidance for any further negotiations. It did so in a way that carried no express or implied threat of punishment. The judge's agreement to entertain a request for a change of venue, and his emphasis on the unresolved DNA admissibility issue, demonstrated that he retained appropriate open-minded impartiality regarding the case. 744 N.E.2d 425 (Ind. 2001).

A trial judge may become involved only on the peripheral edges of a plea agreement and must be careful not to convey that the defendant might suffer adverse consequences if he or she rejects a plea agreement that contains some terms suggested by a judge. To avoid a reversal of an accepted plea bargain, a judge must always display an open-minded impartiality regarding the case and the way a plea agreement is accepted.

4. NEGOTIATED PLEA: BENEFITS TO THE DEFENSE AND TO THE PROSECUTION

As is the case in most contractual relationships, both sides generally believe that an adequate benefit accrues to each party, respectively, or they would not reach a mutual agreement. An accused gains a level of certainty concerning the ultimate outcome of a case, and the prosecutor benefits from the assurance of a conviction. Where one side may believe that it receives insufficient benefit, the completion of a plea bargain may prove to be impossible. In a large percentage of criminal cases, mutual satisfactory adjustments in the positions of each party permit agreement, sufficient to avoid trials on the merits.

A plea bargain should endow benefits to the accused, since it may offer a way to avoid extensive pretrial confinement, to begin serving time, and perhaps serve less time for a lower level of offense, especially if evidence can be offered against other potential defendants. As Justice Burger stated in *Santobello v. New York:*

> Disposition of charges after plea discussions is not only an essential part of the process, but a highly desirable part for many reasons. It leads to prompt and largely final disposition of most criminal cases; it avoids much of the corrosive impact of enforced idleness during pretrial confinement for those who are denied release pending trial; it protects the public from those accused persons who are prone to continue criminal conduct even while on pretrial release; and, by shortening the time between charge and disposition, it enhances whatever may be the rehabilitative prospects of the guilty when they are ultimately imprisoned. 404 U.S. 257, 261 (1971).

The defendant will often be willing to plead guilty to a lesser included offense after hearing the defense attorney explain the advantages held by the prosecutor and the challenges faced by the defense. As part of a lesser included offense, a defendant may escape a felony conviction if the plea that is negotiated falls to the level of a misdemeanor. A negotiated plea may allow the defendant to avoid some mandatory level of incarceration, as where a prosecutor agrees to drop a weapon or gun specification.

A variety of good outcomes may benefit a prosecutor who successfully concludes appropriate plea bargains with accused defendants. For prosecutors who take pride in their won-lost ratio, the certainty of a conviction at an agreed level offers an incentive to reach an agreed plea with a defendant, provided such agreement does not "give away the store." From a prosecutor's perspective, scarce governmental resources go further when potentially lengthy trials can be resolved through a proper plea bargain without the expenditure of time and treasure. The reality of limited resources may make it imperative to avoid the expenditure of both time and effort in one criminal case in order to reallocate assets to more serious or more challenging criminal prosecutions. A conviction obtained through a negotiated plea simply costs the jurisdiction much less than a case taken to conviction through the use of a jury in a court proceeding. A prosecutor can cover a larger caseload when some of the cases can be compromised without trial. To facilitate orderly dispositions of negotiated criminal cases, a prosecutor may offer to accept a defendant's plea to a lesser included offense in exchange for cooperation in the same case or for assistance in a related case.

In most criminal cases, both sides face technical challenges in dealing with the presentation of witnesses[415] and the availability and admissibility of evidence, so that the certainty of a plea agreement is often attractive to all parties. If every criminal

---

[415]A very young witness, the victim of a sexual offense, a reluctant witness, a witness with eyesight or memory problems, or a witness allied with the defense may present difficulties concerning his or her reliability or availability during a trial.

defendant demanded a formal trial to either a judge or a jury, the judicial system as presently constituted would grind to a halt due to insufficient numbers of judges, prosecutors, defense counsel, and juries and inadequate courthouse infrastructure. In a very real sense, the plea bargaining process serves as the lubricant of the justice system in the states and on the federal level.

5. GENERAL REQUIREMENTS FOR VALID PLEA AGREEMENTS

To properly accept a tendered plea agreement, the defendant must possess a rough understanding concerning the operative effects of compromising a criminal case. The defendant must be aware of some of the legal and constitutional rights that are being exchanged for the guilty plea. In *Brady v. United States,*[416] the Court quoted from the Court of Appeals for the Fifth Circuit, which detailed some of the applicable standards for a negotiated plea:

> [A] plea of guilty entered by one fully aware of the direct consequences, including the actual value of any commitments made to him by the court, prosecutor, or his own counsel, must stand unless induced by threats (or promises to discontinue improper harassment), misrepresentation (including unfulfilled or unfulfillable promises), or perhaps by promises that are by their nature improper as having no proper relationship to the prosecutor's business (e.g., bribes). *Shelton v. United States,* 246 F.2d 571, 572 n. 2 (C.A. 5th Cir. 1957) (en banc), rev'd on confession of error on other grounds, 356 U.S. 26 (1958).

If an agreement meets *Brady* standards, and under the assumption that both sides to the plea agreement will fulfill their commitments to each other, the plea will be binding when accepted by the judge.

Thus, where a negotiated plea has been freely and voluntarily negotiated, and properly accepted by a defendant, prosecution, and proper judicial official, its essence becomes binding on the parties. The conviction entered is equally valid as one taken from indictment or information through to a jury verdict that successfully survives appellate litigation. Plea agreements have the full effect as if the verdict had been rendered following a full trial on the merits. As Justice White noted in *Brady v. United States:*

> That a guilty plea is a grave and solemn act to be accepted only with care and discernment has long been recognized. Central to the plea and the foundation for entering judgment against the defendant is the defendant's admission in open court that he committed the act charged in the indictment. He thus stands as a witness against himself, and he is shielded by the Fifth Amendment from being compelled to do so—hence the minimum requirement that his plea be the voluntary expression of his own choice. But the plea is more than an admission of past conduct; it is the defendant's consent that judgment of conviction may be entered without a trial—a waiver of his right to trial before a jury or a judge. 397 U.S. 742, 748 (1970).

---

[416]397 U.S. 742, 755 (1970).

Unless there exists some unusual avenue of attack[417] or a right reserved to appeal[418] based on a particular legal theory, the entry of a plea agreement usually ends the criminal case, and the agreed-upon consequences begin to have their effect. Thus, the procedure in which plea bargains have been offered by the prosecution and accepted by the defendant, when voluntarily and intelligently made, has been approved by the Supreme Court and is not normally subject to later collateral attack.[419] However, if either side fails to perform its respective portion of the agreement, the plea bargain may fail and the case effectively be reopened, with consequences dependent on which side breached the agreement and with what effect.[420] If a court determines not to follow through with an initially accepted negotiated plea, a defendant may not have a remedy of specific performance. In a Louisiana case where a defendant had entered into a plea agreement, the judge noticed an illegal part of the agreement only after the fact of initial acceptance. The judge refused to perform the agreement, since the illegal term required the judge to sentence beyond his legal authority. The defendant failed in having an appellate court specifically enforce the illegal plea agreement.[421] On the other hand, if a defendant wishes to attack an executed plea agreement, the burden of proof rests with the defendant in establishing a breach or illegality by proof by a preponderance of the evidence.[422]

6. WAIVING OTHER CONSTITUTIONAL RIGHTS

"When a defendant pleads guilty he or she, of course, forgoes not only a fair trial, but also other accompanying constitutional guarantees."[423] In recognition of the relinquishment of numerous legal and constitutional rights, state courts usually, and federal courts almost uniformly, require the defendant to have the benefit of counsel.[424] The Sixth Amendment right to the assistance of counsel is, of course, a waivable right and is not necessarily an absolute prerequisite to the acceptance of a valid guilty plea. Among the rights that a criminal defendant waives by entering a guilty plea are the Fifth Amendment privilege against compulsory self-incrimination, the Sixth Amendment right to a trial by jury, the Sixth Amendment right to confront and cross-examine adverse witnesses, the right to complain about any alleged Fourth Amendment violations, the right to challenge the constitutionality of the

---

[417]See *Blackledge v. Allison,* 431 U.S. 63 (1977), and *Santobello v. New York,* 404 U.S. 257 (1971), where appeals concerning the guilty plea were involved.

[418]See *Bousley v. United States,* 523 U.S. 614 (1998), where the appeal following a plea agreement concerned a reservation of the right to challenge the quantity of drugs used to calculate the sentence.

[419]See *Mabry v. Johnson,* 467 U.S. 504, 508 (1984), where the Court explained that the law is "well settled that a voluntary and intelligent plea of guilty made by an accused person, who has been advised by competent counsel, may not be collaterally attacked."

[420]See, *infra,* this chapter, "Breach of the Plea Agreement: Remedies."

[421]*Louisiana v. Byrnside,* 795 So.2d 435 (2001).

[422]*United States v. Martin,* 25 F.3d 211, 217 (4th Cir. 1994).

[423]*United States v. Ruiz,* 536 U.S. 622 at 629 (2002), Justice Breyer writing for the Court.

[424]Since the Sixth Amendment right to counsel is a waivable right, a defendant could decide to forgo the protections counsel could offer, but judges are reluctant to allow the entry of a guilty plea in the absence of the advice of counsel, and a defendant would be ill-advised to proceed without the assistance of counsel.

composition or procedures of the grand jury, the right to compel testimony from witnesses, and, in most circumstances, the right of appeal.

Where a defendant has entered a guilty plea, such decision does not absolutely foreclose all possible avenues of direct or collateral attack. If the prosecution has been less than honest with the defendant or has failed to perform all of the agreement, a defendant may pursue legal remedies to gain the benefit of the bargain.[425] Similarly, where the defendant breaches the agreement by failing to perform, by failing to testify against other defendants, by lying under oath, or by not testifying truthfully or completely, the prosecution may avoid performing, cease performance if started, or avoid performing completely under the plea bargain. Some clear general limitations exist under a guilty plea in that a defendant does not waive the right to complain about the lack of subject matter jurisdiction, the Sixth Amendment allegation of ineffective assistance of counsel, and matters specifically reserved for appeal at the time of the entry of the guilty plea.

The legal effect of a voluntary and intelligently made guilty plea presumes a final and complete admission of every material allegation contained within the indictment or information. Upon entry of the plea, no triable issues remain for decision; it only remains for the court to determine the appropriate sentence and confer its imposition.

7. PRACTICE FOR ACCEPTING A GUILTY PLEA

Although all courts will, under the appropriate circumstances, accept a guilty plea tendered by a defendant, the procedures vary between the state and federal courts.[426] Rule 11 of the Federal Rules of Criminal Procedure regulates the mode in which a federal court may permit the entry of a guilty plea and the net effect of the plea on the accused. The court must personally address the defendant and inform him or her of various constitutional rights and the statutory effects of a plea of guilty. The judge must explain the penalties involved, including the mandatory minimum and statutory maximum sentence. The defendant must be able to comprehend the effect of the entry of a guilty plea. For example, in *United States v. King,* the Court of Appeal for the Ninth Circuit noted that

> before accepting a guilty plea, the court must address the defendant in open court and ensure that he understands the consequences of his plea, including the nature of the charge to which he is admitting, the mandatory minimum applicable penalty, the maximum possible penalty and the forfeiture of his right to a jury trial. 257 F.3d 1013, 1021 (9th Cir. 2001) (citing Fed. R. Crim. P. 11(c)).

In situations wherein the defendant is not represented by counsel due to waiver, the court is required to advise the defendant of this Sixth Amendment right. Further,

---

[425]See *United States v. Peglera,* 33 F.3d 412 (1994), where the Court granted specific performance to a defendant and sent the case back to the trial court for resentencing.

[426]In dissent, in *Boykin v. Alabama,* 395 U.S. 238, 245 (1969), Mr. Justice Harlan suggested that the majority was fastening "upon the States, as a matter of federal constitutional law, the rigid prophylactic requirements of Rule 11 of the Federal Rules of Criminal Procedure." While the states may not have to meet *Boykin* precisely, the requirements seem to be fairly close to what Rule 11 of the Federal Rules of Criminal Procedure dictate.

Rule 11 requires the court to convey to the defendant an understanding that he can persist in a not-guilty plea and be tried by a jury with the assistance of counsel. The judge must advise the defendant of the Fifth Amendment privilege against compelled testimonial self-incrimination and of the right to confront and cross-examine the adverse witnesses. Finally, the defendant must understand that the plea extinguishes the right to a trial by jury. In sum, the judge should believe that the defendant comprehends the nature and effect of the entry and acceptance of a guilty plea on the defendant; in the absence of a knowing, intelligent, and understanding plea, the judge should reject the guilty plea.[427]

8. ACCEPTING GUILTY PLEAS: DUE PROCESS REQUIRED

In accepting guilty pleas, to meet the dictates of due process, state courts are not constitutionally free to ignore commonsense requirements. In *Boykin v. Alabama*,[428] following a defendant's indictment and upon the advice of his legal counsel, the accused pled guilty at his arraignment to five counts of common-law robbery (see Case 11.1). So far as the record of the case demonstrated, the judge did not ask the defendant a single question concerning his plea, and the defendant did not speak to the judge or otherwise address the court. The Supreme Court of the United States held that the Alabama trial court committed plain error when the judge accepted the defendant's guilty plea without any affirmative demonstration that the plea was intelligently and voluntarily offered. The *Boykin* Court noted that since a guilty plea involves a waiver, among other rights, of the privilege against self-incrimination, of the right to a trial by jury, and of the right to confront one's accusers, a waiver of these rights cannot be presumed from a silent trial record. According to the *Boykin* Court, the trial judge must discuss the matter with the defendant in a way that demonstrates that the accused possesses full understanding of the plea that has been offered and comprehends its possible consequences. Where a trial judge follows the procedure outlined in *Boykin,* the judge creates a record that appellate courts may consider in determining whether the trial court properly accepted a guilty plea. In accord with *Boykin,* the Court in *Santobello v. New York* noted that plea bargaining required fairness when working toward an agreement between a defendant and a prosecutor.[429]

> [T]he accused pleading guilty must be counseled, absent a waiver. *Moore v. Michigan,* 355 U.S. 355 (1957). Fed. Rule Crim. Proc. 11, governing pleas in federal courts, now makes clear that the sentencing judge must develop, on the record, the factual basis for the plea, as, for example, by having the accused describe the conduct that gave rise to the charge. The plea must, of course, be voluntary and knowing and if it was induced by promises, the essence of those promises must in some way be made known. *Santobello* at 261, 262.

---

[427]A plea cannot be considered knowingly and intelligently offered unless a defendant first receives actual notice of the nature of the charge against him. *Smith v. O'Grady,* 312 U.S. 329, 334 (1941).
[428]395 U.S. 238 (1969).
[429]404 U.S. 257, 261 (1971).

Once a trial court has been satisfied that the plea was voluntarily made and has not resulted from unconstitutional threats or force, the judge may accept the plea or reject the agreement. "There is…no absolute right to have a guilty plea accepted."[430] If the court accepts the plea of guilty, the judge will inform the defendant that the judgment will reflect the agreement and the negotiated disposition of the case. State practice in accepting guilty pleas roughly mirrors the federal procedure largely as a result of *Boykin v. Alabama*.[431] In effect, the most important aspects of Rule 11 of the Federal Rules of Criminal Procedure have been adopted by the Court and made applicable to the states. For federal court plea bargains, the provisions of Rule 11 have been held to be mandatory, necessitating a reversal of a federal plea bargain where the judge failed to assure that the defendant comprehended the nature and effect of entering a guilty plea. The Court in *McCarthy v. United States*[432] held that a failure to personally address the defendant in open court created inherent prejudice requiring the vacation of the guilty plea. According to the *McCarthy* Court, a failure of the judge to undertake a direct inquiry of a defendant concerning whether the defendant understands the nature of the charge against him and is aware of the consequences of his guilty plea required a reversal of the judgement.

9. THE *ALFORD* PLEA: PLEADING GUILTY WHILE CLAIMING INNOCENCE

Although Rule 11(f) requires that federal courts shall not accept a guilty plea without making sufficient inquiry to demonstrate that a factual basis exists for the plea, the states are not similarly limited. Some states will not accept a guilty plea absent a factual basis, whereas others permit a defendant to plead guilty and profess innocence.[433] An example of the latter category of state practice is Rule 11(c) of the Ohio Rules of Criminal Procedure. Ohio's version of Rule 11 permits, with some exceptions, the receipt of a guilty plea without any express admission of the facts that underlie the plea. Consistent with the Ohio procedure under Rule 11, the Supreme Court approved the acceptance of a guilty plea in *North Carolina v. Alford*,[434] in a case where the defendant proclaimed his innocence but desired to plead guilty to escape the possibility of capital punishment (see Case 11.3). The *Alford* trial court received testimony indicative of guilt prior to accepting the guilty plea. The Court noted that other reasons besides the fact of guilt may influence a defendant to plead guilty, but that the decision on how to plead is one that must be made by the defendant. As the Supreme Court noted in *Alford*:

> [W]hile most pleas of guilty consist of both a waiver of trial and an express admission of guilt, the latter element is not a constitutional requisite to the imposition of

---

[430]*Lynch v. Overholser,* 369 U.S. 705, 719 (1962).

[431]395 U.S. 238 (1969).

[432]394 U.S. 459 (1969).

[433]See *North Carolina v. Alford,* 400 U.S. 25 (1970), where a defendant pled guilty while still alleging that he was innocent, in order to avoid a possible death sentence if he went to trial. The North Carolina courts approved of the practice, and the Supreme Court of the United States did not find constitutional fault with the procedure. This has come to be known as an *Alford* plea, but not all jurisdictions will accept such a plea where innocence is professed while the defendant is pleading guilty.

[434]400 U.S. 25 (1970).

criminal penalty. An individual accused of crime may voluntarily, knowingly, and understandingly consent to the imposition of a prison sentence even if he is unwilling or unable to admit his participation in the acts constituting the crime. *Alford* at 37.

Although many defendants plead guilty to charges as originally expressed in the indictment or information, others agree to enter a guilty plea to a different crime or, frequently, to a lesser degree of the original crime charged. A prosecutor may offer to ignore other potential crimes if a defendant will plead guilty to the crime charged. As is usually the case, the prosecutor and the defendant receive a benefit in exchange for the negotiated agreement. The government saves the time and expense of a trial with the attendant uncertainties and is guaranteed a conviction. The defendant knows, prior to the entry of the plea, that the conviction will be of the type and degree to which the parties agreed; that sentence recommendations, if any, will occur as negotiated; and that the other uncertainties normally associated with a criminal trial will have been eliminated.

10. PLEA BARGAIN: RESPONSIBILITIES FOR THE PROSECUTION AND FOR THE DEFENSE

A plea agreement between a defendant and a prosecutor has many similarities to a contract between two individuals. Each party agrees to perform certain duties in exchange for the other party meeting obligations that it has accepted.[435] The usual remedy in many state cases for violation of a plea agreement, where the plea bargain cannot be specifically enforced, is to allow the defendant to withdraw the plea and go to trial on the original charges.[436]

Generally, the defendant must perform his or her part of a plea agreement, which includes pleading guilty to the agreed crime or crimes and offering truthful information to police. It is not uncommon for an agreement to require the defendant to assist the police in conducting other related investigations. In a situation where a defendant has made material misrepresentations in negotiating a plea bargain, he or she is not entitled to the remedy of specific performance of the agreement.[437]

Following the plea agreement, the prosecution must perform its side of the bargain according to the agreement. If the trial judge accepts the performance of the defendant and agrees to the position of the prosecution, the plea bargain has been consummated and is complete. If the defendant somehow, either prior to or after the court accepts the agreement, fails to deliver promised future performance, the plea bargain fails, and the criminal prosecution starts anew. The defendant's performance under a plea bargain may include testifying against other defendants and could mandate that the recipient of a plea bargain testify a second time, where necessary, or be in breach of the original plea agreement.

---

[435]See *United States v. Hyde,* 520 U.S. 670, 677 (1997), where Chief Justice Rehnquist used the analogy to a contract in his discussion concerning a negotiated plea agreement.
[436]See *People v. Walker,* 54 Cal.3d 1013, 1026–1027 (1991).
[437]*People v. Johnson,* 10 Cal.3d 868, 873 (1974).

For example, in *Ricketts v. Adamson,*[438] the defendant originally testified against co-felons at their initial trial in fulfillment of his negotiated plea. The agreement provided that if the defendant refused to testify or should at any time testify untruthfully, the entire agreement would become null and void, and the original charge would automatically be reinstated. As part of the bargain and pursuant to the agreement, the trial court sentenced the defendant after he had testified against others pursuant to the plea bargain. However, he balked at testifying against his co-felons a second time when a retrial became necessary after the first trial verdict was overturned. The state managed to have the plea bargain conviction vacated and filed new charges against the defendant, since it viewed the original plea agreement as null and void due to a failure of complete performance. The defendant was convicted of capital murder and sentenced to death. This procedure was upheld by the Supreme Court, since the defendant knew the consequences of his failure to abide by the original plea agreement whose terms clearly stated that "in the event of respondent's breach occasioned by a refusal to testify, the parties would be returned to the *status quo ante.*" The *Ricketts* Court upheld the second conviction on the foregoing principles. The inescapable rule that emerged requires plea bargaining defendants to completely perform their duties; a failure to meet the requirements results in the benefits of the original plea agreement becoming null and void, leaving the defendant in the original position.

In contrast, if the prosecutor fails to deliver a promised future performance, the defendant may have some options regarding forcing the prosecutor to comply with the bargain.[439] Where the prosecution breaches the agreed plea, the defendant may be permitted to withdraw his or her original plea and start the prosecution from the beginning. Alternatively, the trial court may allow the prosecution to specifically perform the original agreement and enforce the terms as previously agreed.[440] In some situations, a judge may refuse to accept the plea bargain, which leaves both parties in substantially the same position they occupied prior to the negotiated agreement.

11. BREACH OF THE PLEA AGREEMENT: REMEDIES

Concerning a plea bargain wherein the prosecution failed to adhere to the negotiated agreement, the Court in *Santobello v. New York*[441] upheld the propriety of such bargain and fashioned a remedy for a prosecutorial breach of the agreement (see Case 11.4). In *Santobello,* the defendant had concluded a plea bargain with the prosecution that called for the defendant to enter a guilty plea to a lesser included offense in exchange for the prosecution's agreement to make no recommendation concerning the sentence for Mr. Santobello. The trial court judge accepted the plea bargain but deferred sentencing to a future date. Additional delays resulted in the

---

[438]483 U.S.1 (1987).
[439]See *Santobello v. New York,* 404 U.S. 257 (1971), and *Blackledge v. Allison,* 431 U.S. 63 (1977), for examples of remedies for troubled plea bargains.
[440]*Santobello,* at 263.
[441]Ibid.

sentencing hearing being conducted in front of a different judge and with a different prosecutor. The new prosecutor recommended the maximum one-year sentence and cited Santobello's past criminal record. Santobello successfully appealed the breached plea bargain, alleging that he did not get the benefit of his plea agreement. Chief Justice Burger's lead opinion agreed with Santobello's position that he did not receive what the agreement required, and that the remedy was up to the original trial-level court to decide whether to allow Santobello to withdraw his guilty plea and start the case anew or to require the prosecution to give Santobello specific performance of the agreement. In the case of granting specific performance, Santobello would be resentenced in a new proceeding, at which time the prosecution would make no recommendation concerning sentencing as per the original plea agreement.

The states and the federal government possess remedies for a defendant's breach of a plea bargain. Demonstrative of this principle is a Texas case in which a capital murder defendant pled guilty to the lesser included offense of murder. As part of the negotiated plea with the state, the agreement required the defendant to testify against other defendants in the case. When the time for trial for the other defendants arrived, the convicted defendant refused to testify against them. Ultimately, the state deemed the original plea as having been breached, which allowed Texas to reindict the defendant for capital murder and begin the whole process anew. As the court of appeals noted, "Appellant has been re-indicted for this offense, which should serve as adequate notice to Appellant that the State considers the plea agreement invalid."[442] When a defendant violates a portion of a plea agreement or otherwise materially fails to perform the provisions of the plea bargain, a state or the federal government may elect to declare the entire earlier agreement null and void and to proceed against the breaching party as if there had been no agreement from the beginning.

During plea negotiations, which are often conducted piecemeal and over the phone, an offer may be communicated that has not been cleared at the highest levels of the prosecutor's office and may be subject to review. An offer may contain errors that the prosecution wants to correct. In the interim, a defendant may have accepted the prosecutor's offer and may want the offer enforced even if the prosecutor wants to withdraw it. *Santobello* offers no guidance in such a situation, since the plea bargain there had been partially completed by performance and was not completely executory. In *Mabry v. Johnson,*[443] the Court held that when a defendant accepted an offer under a plea negotiation, such acceptance did not create any constitutional right to have the agreement specifically enforced (see Case 11.6). Indeed, in *Santobello,* the right to specific performance was not guaranteed; the Court offered specific performance as one of two proposed remedies. The *Santobello* Court further noted that where partial performance had been tendered by the entry of the guilty plea, and where the prosecution breached its promise concerning an executed plea agreement and the defendant has pled guilty, induced by a false promise, a

[442]See *Brunelle v. Texas,* 203 Tex. App. LEXIS 6652 (2003).
[443]467 U.S. 504 (1984).

reversal is required. In *Mabry,* all promises on both sides remained executory; thus a withdrawal of the plea offer by the prosecutor deprived the defendant of no constitutional right to which he had a legitimate expectation.

Despite the fact that the government must generally adhere to the terms of any plea bargain once made and partially executed, the prosecution may employ somewhat coercive-appearing tactics to initially induce the defendant to accept a plea bargain as offered. During the plea negotiation process, a defendant may appear to be under the influence of coercive behavior by the prosecution, but the Supreme Court has held that the concept of plea bargaining does not violate the Fifth Amendment even though an accused might feel considerable pressure to admit guilt to gain more lenient sentencing.[444] A prosecutor may indicate that if a plea bargain cannot be successfully negotiated he or she will invoke the habitual offender statute or prosecute under the three-strikes legislation to render a life sentence. Such tactics have generally received judicial approval. Essentially, a prosecutor would be doing nothing more than could have been done initially; the prosecutor is simply pursuing the same efforts in a different sequence. In *Bordenkircher v. Hayes,* 434 U.S. 357 (1978), the prosecutor offered a forgery defendant the opportunity to plead guilty as charged with the provision that the prosecutor would recommend a five-year sentence (see Case 11.5). The commonwealth attorney informed Hayes that the habitual offender statute would be used to impose a life sentence if he did not accept the prosecutor's offer. When Hayes rejected the plea offer and decided to go to trial, the prosecutor procured an indictment under the commonwealth's habitual offender statute and obtained an enhanced conviction carrying a life sentence. The *Bordenkircher* Court upheld the habitual offender conviction enhancement on the theory that the prosecutor did nothing that was not properly sanctioned by law. The defendant possessed alternatives to trial and simply chose not to avail himself of the opportunity to plead guilty to a specific offense and not risk encountering the habitual offender statute. In *Bordenkircher,* since the prosecutor could have brought the habitual offender indictment from the beginning and offered to drop it in exchange for a guilty plea, bringing it up to encourage a plea bargain at a later time did not offend due process or improperly attempt to coerce the defendant under the Fifth Amendment.

12. SUMMARY

In summary, while guilty pleas by defendants may be motivated by a wide variety of reasons, the constitutional consequences of a guilty plea generally involve waivers of legal rights. As a result, procedural protections have evolved to ensure that defendants are certain of the consequences of entering a plea of guilty. The plea must have been voluntarily and intelligently made, but it could have been motivated by a desire to escape the death penalty or to receive a penalty of certain duration. Countless guilty pleas are the result of plea negotiations that, in some instances, may be specifically enforceable, as in *Santobello,* whereas in other situations they may be subject to prosecutorial withdrawal so long as the bargain remains executory.

---

[444]See *McKune v. Lile,* 536 U.S. 24 at 42 (2002).

CASE 11.1

Minimum Requirements for Judicial Acceptance of a Guilty Plea

Boykin v. Alabama
Supreme Court of the United States
395 U.S. 238 (1969)

FACTS

An Alabama grand jury indicted defendant Boykin for five counts of robbery involving a series of crimes, offenses for which the death penalty could have been imposed under legal interpretations existent at that time. In one of the robberies, the perpetrator fired his gun into the ceiling of a store, while in a different robbery, the felon's gun discharged in such a fashion to cause injury to a bystander. After his arrest and prior to arraignment, the court determined that Boykin was indigent and appointed counsel to defend him. Plea negotiations began with the result that Boykin agreed to plead guilty to the five capital counts of robbery at the arraignment.

At the court hearing at which time Boykin offered his guilty plea, the trial judge asked no question of the defendant concerning his plea and did not inform Boykin of legal rights to which he was entitled and which he was relinquishing by his guilty plea. Boykin remained silent while the plea was being entered on his behalf.

The case required that the prosecutor empanel a jury, since Alabama law required a jury to determine the sentence in cases involving plea bargains. The prosecution presented the punishment phase of the case much as it would have done if the actual trial had been held. Boykin's attorney conducted cross-examination of the prosecution's witnesses but did not present any evidence that might have offered the jury a strong reason to vote to spare Boykin's life. However, there was no evidence that he had a prior criminal record. The court instructed the penalty-phase jury that it could give the defendant from 10 years to death by electrocution. The jury sentenced Boykin to death on each of the five robbery counts.

An automatic appeal was taken to the Alabama Supreme Court alleging, among other legal theories, that the trial court erred when it accepted his guilty plea without determining whether it was entered voluntarily and knowingly with an appreciation of the rights Boykin was waiving. After failing to get a favorable ruling by the Alabama Supreme Court, Boykin requested and was granted a writ of certiorari by the Supreme Court of the United States.

PROCEDURAL ISSUE

For a defendant to properly plead guilty in a criminal case, must the trial judge affirmatively show on the record that the guilty plea was knowingly and intelligently made and voluntarily and freely offered?

HELD: YES

RATIONALE

Mr. Justice Douglas delivered the opinion of the Court.

★ ★ ★

Respondent [Alabama] does not suggest that we lack jurisdiction to review the voluntary character of petitioner's guilty plea because he failed to raise that federal question below and the state court failed to pass upon it. But the question was raised on oral argument and we conclude that it is properly presented. The very Alabama statute (Ala. Code, Tit. 15, 382 (10) (1958)) that provides automatic appeal in capital cases also requires the reviewing court to comb the record for "any error prejudicial to the appellant, even though not called to our attention in brief of counsel." *Lee v. State,* 265 Ala. 623, 630, 93 So.2d 757, 763. The automatic appeal statute "is the only provision under the Plain Error doctrine of which we are aware in Alabama criminal appellate review." [Citation omitted.] In the words of the Alabama Supreme Court:

> "Perhaps it is well to note that in reviewing a death case under the automatic appeal statute, . . . we may consider any testimony that was seriously prejudicial to the rights of the appellant and may [395 U.S. 238, 242] reverse thereon, even though no lawful objection or exception was made thereto. [Citations omitted.] Our review is not limited to the matters brought to our attention in brief of counsel." *Duncan v. State,* 278 Ala. 145, 157, 176 So.2d 840, 851.

It was error, plain on the face of the record, for the trial judge to accept petitioner's guilty plea without an affirmative showing that it was intelligent and voluntary. That error, under Alabama procedure, was properly before the court below and considered explicitly by a majority of the justices and is properly before us on review.

A plea of guilty is more than a confession which admits that the accused did various acts; it is itself a conviction; nothing remains but to give judgment and determine punishment. Admissibility of a confession must be based on a "reliable determination on the voluntariness issue which satisfies the constitutional rights of the defendant." *Jackson v. Denno*, 378 U.S. 368. The requirement that the prosecution spread on the record the prerequisites of a valid waiver is no constitutional innovation. In *Carnley v. Cochran*, 369 U.S. [506], 516, we dealt with the problem of waiver of the right to counsel, a Sixth Amendment right. We held: "Presuming waiver from a silent record is impermissible. The record must show, or there must be an allegation and evidence which show, that an accused was offered counsel but intelligently and understandingly rejected the offer. Anything less is not waiver."

We think that the same standard must be applied to determining whether a guilty plea is voluntarily made. For, as we have said, a plea of guilty is more than an admission of conduct; it is a conviction. Ignorance, lack of comprehension, coercion, terror, inducements, subtle or blatant threats might be a perfect cover-up of unconstitutionality. The question of an effective waiver of a federal constitutional right in a proceeding is of course governed by federal standards. *Douglas v. Alabama*, 380 U.S. 415, 422.

Several federal constitutional rights are involved in a waiver that takes place when a plea of guilty is entered in a state criminal trial. First, is the privilege against compulsory self-incrimination guaranteed by the Fifth Amendment and applicable to the States by reason of the Fourteenth. *Malloy v. Hogan*, 378 U.S. 1. Second, is the right to trial by jury. *Duncan v. Louisiana*, 391 U.S. 145. Third, is the right to confront one's accusers. *Pointer v. Texas*, 380 U.S. 400. We cannot presume a waiver of these three important federal rights from a silent record.

What is at stake for an accused facing death or imprisonment demands the utmost solicitude of which courts are capable in canvassing the matter with the accused to make sure he has full understanding of what the plea connotes and of its consequence. When the judge discards that function, he leaves a record inadequate for any review that may be later sought.

The three dissenting justices in the Alabama Supreme Court stated the law accurately when they concluded that there was reversible error "because the record does not disclose that the defendant voluntarily and understandingly entered his pleas of guilty." 281 Ala., at 663, 207 So.2d, at 415.

[The conviction was] Reversed.

Mr. Justice Harlan, whom Mr. Justice Black, joins, dissenting.

The Court today holds that petitioner Boykin was denied due process of law, and that his robbery convictions must be reversed outright, solely because "the record [is] inadequate to show that petitioner…intelligently and knowingly pleaded guilty." The Court thus in effect fastens upon the States, as a matter of federal constitutional law, the rigid prophylactic requirements of Rule 11 of the Federal Rules of Criminal Procedure. It does so in circumstances where the Court itself has only very recently held application of Rule 11 to be unnecessary in the federal courts. See *Halliday v. United States,* 394 U.S. 831 (1969). Moreover, the Court does all this at the behest of a petitioner who has never at any time alleged that his guilty plea was involuntary or made without knowledge of the consequences. I cannot possibly subscribe to so bizarre a result.

I

★ ★ ★

Petitioner was not sentenced immediately after the acceptance of his plea. Instead, pursuant to an Alabama statute, the court ordered that "witnesses…be examined, to ascertain the character of the offense," in the presence of a jury which would then fix petitioner's sentence. See Ala. Code, Tit. 14, 415 (1958); Tit. 15, 277. That proceeding occurred some two months after petitioner pleaded guilty. During that period, petitioner made no attempt to withdraw his plea. Petitioner was present in court with his attorney when the witnesses were examined. Petitioner heard the judge state the elements of common-law robbery and heard him announce that petitioner had pleaded guilty to that offense and might be sentenced to death. Again, petitioner made no effort to withdraw his plea.

On his appeal to the Alabama Supreme Court, petitioner did not claim that his guilty plea was made involuntarily or without full knowledge of the consequences. In fact, petitioner raised no questions at all concerning the plea. In his petition and brief in this Court, and in oral argument by counsel, petitioner has never asserted that the plea was coerced or made in ignorance of the consequences.

II

★ ★ ★

III

★ ★ ★

I would hold that petitioner Boykin is not entitled to outright reversal of his conviction simply because of the "inadequacy" of the record pertaining to his guilty plea. Further, I would not vacate the judgment below and remand for a state-court hearing on voluntariness. For even if it is assumed for the sake of argument that petitioner would be entitled to such a hearing if he had alleged that the plea was involuntary, a matter which I find it unnecessary to decide, the fact is that he has never made any such claim. Hence, I consider that petitioner's present arguments relating to his guilty plea entitle him to no federal relief.

COMMENTS, NOTES, AND QUESTIONS

1. Why did the Court believe that the defendant should understand a guilty plea and its legal effects? Could a less-than-worldly defendant be induced to plead guilty by an overworked or less-than-competent defense counsel?

2. The essence of a plea bargain requires that a defendant know what he or she has gained with the decision to forgo a formal trial. From your understanding of *Boykin,* do you think that Boykin understood the legal effect of his guilty plea? From a practical perspective, what did the defendant in *Boykin* gain by pleading guilty to five capital offenses? Anything? Would you have suggested that he plead guilty to a capital case?

3. Justice Harlan noted that Boykin did not attempt to withdraw his plea in the two months between the entry of the plea and the sentencing trial. How would a person unschooled in the law have managed that feat? Would his attorney have possessed any reason to withdraw a plea that the attorney had participated in arranging?

4. At the time Alabama sentenced Mr. Boykin to death, imposing capital punishment for crimes in which no one had lost life was fairly common. Later cases clarified and limited the types of crimes for which the death penalty could be imposed to situations where a human life had been taken. In *Coker v. Georgia,* 433 U.S. 584 (1977), the Supreme Court held that the crime of rape of an adult woman could not be punished by the death penalty because carrying out the death penalty as punishment for rape was out of proportion to the harm done. Under the present interpretation of the Eighth Amendment, covering cruel and unusual punishments, Boykin could not be given the death penalty for his criminal convictions.

CASE 11.2

Judicial Involvement: Problems in Plea Negotiation

Ellis v. Indiana
Supreme Court of Indiana
744 N.E.2d 425 (2001)

FACTS

The defendant, Ellis, pled guilty to four rapes and related crimes but appealed the judgments by alleging that his negotiated plea bargain had been involuntarily given. Following his arrest and after formal charges where lodged, Ellis and his attorney negotiated with the prosecutor and reached a plea bargain. The prosecution and the defense entered into a plea agreement that provided for concurrent terms of twenty years for the rape charges. When this arrangement was presented to the trial judge, who had a presentence report in front of him, the judge expressed concerns relative to the length of time to be served. One of the rape victims testified by relating her ordeal suffered at the hands of defendant. She expressed her disagreement with the potential short sentence while suggesting that the plea arrangement should be rejected by the court. The trial judge refused to accept the negotiated plea and made some suggestions concerning what he would consider appropriate under a renegotiated plea agreement.

The judge told the prosecutor that a plea for three of the rape cases would be appropriate if one of the rape cases went to trial. Any sentence which resulted from the trial would be served consecutively to twenty years for the negotiated rape cases. Alternatively, the judge noted that the defendant could plead guilty to the first three rape cases and serve concurrent sentences for them and plead guilty to the final rape case. The final rape case would carry a twenty year sentence that would be served consecutive to the first three concurrent sentences. The judge appeared to make every effort to demonstrate fairness and open-mindedness and did indicate that there was not a certainty that if defendant Ellis went to trial on the final rape case that it would result in a conviction. The judge noted that identification of defendant was problematic for the victim and the DNA evidence had not yet been analyzed to indicate the identity of the attacker.

Defendant Ellis was well aware that he faced potential sentences of over three hundred years if convicted on all counts for all the rape allegations. With this staggering number of years ahead of him, the defendant negotiated a guilty plea in which the first three rape cases would have concurrent sentences with the final rape having a consecutive sentence of twenty years. Altogether, the defendant pled guilty to four rapes with an aggregate sentence of forty years. After the judge advised the defendant of his constitutional rights, the rights that he was waiving, and after establishing a factual basis for the plea, the trial judge accepted this agreement and Ellis entered his guilty plea.

In postconviction petitions for relief to the Court of Appeals, the defendant argued that the judge's original comments in rejecting the first plea bargain made his second plea agreement involuntary in nature. Ellis alleged that he felt pressured into accepting the prosecutor's second offer because of his fear of receiving a longer sentence if he went to trial. He also expressed some concern about getting a fair trial if he rejected the prosecution's second offer. The Court of Appeals rejected Ellis' allegations and he perfected his appeal to the Supreme Court of Indiana.

PROCEDURAL ISSUE

Where a trial judge refused to accept a plea agreement offered by the prosecution and accepted by the defendant, where the judge offered some carefully neutral suggestions, does such a practice render a subsequent plea agreement, incorporating the judge's concerns, involuntary under due process standards?

HELD: NO

RATIONALE

Shepard, Chief Justice[, delivered the opinion of the court].

★ ★ ★

Limits on Judicial Involvement in Plea Agreements

A defendant's guilty plea must be voluntary. *White v. State,* 497 N.E.2d 893 (Ind. 1986). The trial judge has a duty to assure that this is so, and also to impose a sentence

that fits both the crime and the offender. Judicial participation in plea bargaining therefore presents special cause for concern. As the Ohio Supreme Court warned in *State v. Byrd,* 63 Ohio St. 2d 288, 407 N.E.2d 1384, 1387 (Ohio 1980):

> A judge's participation in the actual bargaining process presents a high potential for coercion. The defendant often views the judge as the final arbiter of his fate or at the very least the person in control of the important environment of the courtroom. He may be led to believe that this person considers him guilty of the crime without a chance of proving otherwise. He may infer that he will not be given a fair opportunity to present his case. Even if he wishes to go to trial, he may perceive the trial as a hopeless and dangerous exercise in futility.

Our own modern examination of the judicial role in bargained cases commenced with *Anderson v. State,* 263 Ind. 583 (1975). There, the trial judge and Anderson negotiated an agreement for a plea in return for an executed sentence of eleven years, over the apparent opposition of the prosecutor. The judge openly acknowledged his role, saying: "The Court accepts the plea of guilty with the plea bargaining done by the Court. Show that in your record, so it[']s not the Prosecutor's fault, it's not the Sheriff's fault, I'll take the blame for it."

This Court took a dim view of the idea that the judge and the defendant would negotiate a disposition. While concluding that such bargaining did not render a plea involuntary as a matter of law, we observed that the analysis of the facts and circumstances of such an event occurs "from the perspective that judicial participation in plea bargaining is highly suspect." *Id.* at 587. A judge's primary responsibility is to maintain the integrity of the legal system by personifying evenhanded justice, recognizing that the judge's considerable sentencing power may strongly influence the accused. Id. (citation omitted).

The sentencing judge in this case, of course, was hardly negotiating one-on-one with the defendant as the trial judge had done in *Anderson.*

Rather, the court followed a standard path for entertaining a bargain submitted by the parties. The judge ordered a presentence report and had it before him on the date set for sentencing. He heard testimony by the victim, the arguments of counsel, and so on. This was in accordance with the provisions of our statute governing entry of judgment and sentencing, Ind. Code Ann. 35-38-1 (West 1998). The Code contemplates that the court will approve the plea agreement and sentence in accordance with it or reject the agreement and move the case along towards trial or a different proposed agreement. See, *e.g.,* Ind. Code Ann. 35-35-3-3 (West 2000).

Cases following *Anderson* provide insight into when judicial involvement does or does not go too far. In *Williams v. State,* 449 N.E.2d 1080 (Ind. 1983), after the defendant pled guilty, the court observed that he was fortunate to have worked out an agreement because a jury likely would have convicted him of kidnapping, which would have carried a life sentence. The defendant later withdrew his plea with the court's permission but then re-entered it after his co-defendant agreed to testify against him. The court again told the defendant how fortunate he was to have avoided almost certain conviction and a life sentence.

In affirming denial of Williams' post-conviction voluntariness claim, we distinguished *Anderson* by noting that the trial court did not participate in the negotiations. *Id.* at 1083. Further, the record in *Williams* "commanded an inference" that the guilty plea to a lesser offense was based on the strength of the evidence and not on the judge's comments.

By contrast, we concluded that a judge had gone too far in the very recent case of *Garrett v. State,* 737 N.E.2d 388 (Ind. 2000). The trial judge pressed Garrett at length to plead guilty by emphasizing the potential sentence and ultimately declaring, "I'm telling you, if it's me and you get found guilty with this record you'll get the [maximum] eighty years." The judge went on to ask, in a disparaging manner, what defense Garrett planned to present. We refused to condone either the query and comments on Garrett's defense or the "depth of the court's inquiry regarding Garrett's decision to go to trial." We also disapproved the court's statement of its sentencing intentions as "clearly inappropriate."

Ellis' circumstances are more akin to *Williams* than to either *Anderson* or *Garrett.* Unlike in *Anderson,* where the trial court actually took credit for conducting the negotiation, the court here merely responded to a proposed agreement that had been previously negotiated by the parties without any involvement by the court.

Unlike *Garrett,* the court here did not pressure Ellis to enter or even consider a guilty plea. Indeed, one of the two alternatives the judge suggested involved trial on one set of charges. Nor did the court here threaten or otherwise express any intent to impose an especially harsh sentence if Ellis opted to proceed to trial. In further contrast to *Garrett,* the court did not disparage Ellis' proposed defense. In fact, the judge pointed out in Ellis' presence that

the State's case relied on DNA evidence that might or might not be admissible at trial.

Here, as in *Williams,* the court reacted to a proposed plea only after it was negotiated by the parties and presented to the court as a mutual agreement. The court did not engage in any "unnecessary and unwise" "editorializing." *Williams,* 449 N.E.2d at 1083. The parties here proposed an agreement that the court, exercising its discretion, declined to accept. Rather than sending the parties away to guess again at what might pass muster in some judicial version of hide-the-ball, the court indicated that the proposal was too lenient and offered two alternatives that it would deem acceptable, given the nature of the charges and what the court already knew from the presentence report and the hearing.

While judicial involvement in plea negotiations can certainly go too far, a complete prohibition on judicial comment regarding a proposed plea agreement would create a separate set of problems. When a court exercises its discretion to reject a plea agreement, it is in both parties' interests that the court explain its reasons. See *United States v. Rodriguez,* 197 F.3d 156, 158 (5th Cir. 1999) (noting that federal district courts may express their reasons for rejecting plea agreements). If a proposal falls outside the range of what the court regards as reasonable, it will be helpful to the parties to know whether the court found the proposal too lenient or too harsh, so that they may re-negotiate if both choose to do so. This Court sometimes follows such a practice when it sits as a court of first instance in hearing attorney discipline cases. See, *e.g., Matter of Haecker,* 664 N.E.2d 1176 (Ind. 1996) (parties informed that bargained sanction was too lenient; later agreement with greater sanction approved).

★ ★ ★

...[A] court may offer guidance as to what sentence it might find marginally acceptable, taking into account a presentence report prepared by the probation department. The message must not, of course, carry any express or implied threat that the defendant may be denied a fair trial or punished by a severe sentence if he or she declines to plead guilty. *Matter of Cox,* 680 N.E.2d 528, 529–30 (Ind. 1997) (judge disciplined for telling defendant that those who demand jury trial and get convicted receive higher sentences).

The trial judge's response to the original plea proposal did not render Ellis' eventual guilty plea involuntary. The court did not press Ellis to plead guilty rather than to proceed to trial. Faced with a proposed sentence that fell outside the range the court considered reasonable, it merely advised the parties of the low end of that range, as guidance for any further negotiations. It did so in a way that carried no express or implied threat of punishment. The judge's agreement to entertain a request for a change of venue, and his emphasis on the unresolved DNA admissibility issue, demonstrated that he retained appropriate open-minded impartiality regarding the case.

After his initial plea was rejected, Ellis had two months to consider his alternatives with the advice of counsel. The court again fully apprised Ellis of his rights and the consequences of his revised plea. Ellis asserted on the record that his plea decision was free and voluntary. We agree that it was.

We affirm the denial of post-conviction relief.

Dickson, Sullivan, Boehm, and Rucker, JJ., concur.

COMMENTS, NOTES, AND QUESTIONS

1. Should a judge remain entirely outside of the plea bargaining negotiation? Did the *Ellis* trial judge intervene, or did he merely make a suggestion concerning what he might approve? Can you tell the difference? Why or why not? This case emphasized the often forgotten role of the judge in plea bargaining; the judge must not serve as a rubber stamp for whatever offer a prosecutor might wish to put forth, and at the same time, the judge must attempt to ensure that justice is served by any negotiated plea that gains judicial approval.

2. How much can a judge accomplish in rejecting a plea bargain without seeming to prejudge the case on the merits? A subtle coercion may be happening when a judge refuses to approve a plea agreement and sends it back to the prosecutor and defendant to renegotiate. To obtain the most favorable outcome, does the defendant risk judicial anger or other adverse response by negotiating close to where the judge indicated he or she would not approve? If the prosecutor adopts the substance of the judge's suggestions (as happened in *Ellis*), is the judge really doing the ultimate plea bargaining?

3. How close is the *Ellis* case to *Anderson v. State,* 263 Ind. 583 (1975), mentioned within *Ellis,* where it appeared that the trial judge negotiated the agreement from the bench? Are there significant differences between *Anderson* and *Ellis*? If so, what are they? Do you think the defendant in *Anderson v. State* would have felt free to become a "hard" bargainer with a judge? Would a defendant feel somewhat intimidated if no agreement had been reached and be concerned that the judge might not be

impartial if the case went to trial? When the judge becomes a party to the plea negotiation, the defendant may well develop the opinion that the judge "already thinks I'm guilty." Such an attitude fails to make a defendant feel that his or her fate is in the hands of a neutral and detached judicial official.

CASE 11.3

Guilty Plea Acceptable Where Innocence Professed

North Carolina v. Alford
Supreme Court of the United States
400 U.S. 25 (1970)

FACTS

North Carolina indicted Alford for the capital offense of first-degree murder and the trial court assigned counsel to him for the purpose of preparing a defense to avoid the death penalty. Since numerous witnesses existed who would substantiate his innocence, Mr. Alford persisted in his plea of innocence. His attorney conducted an investigation into the testimony the witnesses were prepared to offer, but the proffered evidence proved rather damaging to the defense. Faced with the prospect that the testimony of these witnesses would have indicated guilt rather then innocence, Alford's counsel recommended that Alford accept a plea bargain and plead guilty to second-degree murder with the certainty that the death penalty could not be inflicted.

Pursuant to counsel's advice, Alford accepted the prosecutor's offer and pled guilty to second-degree murder after three witnesses for the government offered damaging testimony that was strongly indicative of guilt. Alford took the witness stand and testified that he was innocent but was pleading guilty because of his fear of the death penalty. Defense counsel elicited the facts that the plea was knowingly and intelligently made. The trial court sentenced Alford to the maximum penalty of thirty years imprisonment.

When Alford's direct postconviction relief in the state court system failed, he applied for a writ of habeas corpus in a federal district court. His efforts bore fruit when the Fourth Circuit Court of Appeals determined that he had been denied effective assistance of counsel prior to the entry of his guilty plea. According to the Court of Appeals, the lack of competent counsel to assist in his legal defense rendered his guilty plea involuntary. North Carolina appealed the reversal of the trial court's verdict and the Supreme Court granted certiorari.

PROCEDURAL ISSUE

Although proclaiming innocence but pleading guilty to a serious offense upon advice of counsel and in the face of a strong prosecution case, is the guilty plea coerced and therefore involuntarily made?

HELD: NO

RATIONALE

Mr. Justice White delivered the opinion of the Court.

★ ★ ★

We held in *Brady v. United States,* 397 U.S. 742 (1970), that a plea of guilty which would not have been entered except for the defendant's desire to avoid a possible death penalty and to limit the maximum penalty to life imprisonment or a term of years was not for that reason compelled within the meaning of the Fifth Amendment. *Jackson [v. United States,* 390 U.S. 570 (1968)] established no new test for determining the validity of guilty pleas. The standard was and remains whether the plea represents a voluntary and intelligent choice among the alternative courses of action open to the defendant. See *Boykin v. Alabama,* 395 U.S. 238, 242 (1969); [Other citations omitted]. That he would not have pleaded except for the opportunity to limit the possible penalty does not necessarily demonstrate that the plea would be to the defendant's advantage....

★ ★ ★

Ordinarily, a judgment of conviction resting on a plea of guilty is justified by the defendant's admission that he committed the crime charged against him and his consent that judgment be entered without a trial of any kind. The plea usually subsumes both elements, and justifiably so, even though there is no separate, express admission by the defendant that he committed the particular acts claimed to constitute the crime charged in the indictment. Here Alford entered his plea but accompanied it with the statement that he had not shot the victim.

If Alford's statements were to be credited as sincere assertions of his innocence, there obviously existed a factual and legal dispute between him and the State. Without

more, it might be argued that the conviction entered on his guilty plea was invalid, since his assertion of innocence negatived any admission of guilt, which, as we observed last Term in *Brady,* is normally "[c]entral to the plea and the foundation for entering judgment against the defendant...." 397 U.S., at 748.

In addition to Alford's statement, however, the court had heard an account of the events on the night of the murder, including information from Alford's acquaintances that he had departed from his home with his gun stating his intention to kill and that he had later declared that he had carried out his intention. Nor had Alford wavered in his desire to have the trial court determine his guilt without a jury trial. Although denying the charge against him, he nevertheless preferred the dispute between him and the State to be settled by the judge in the context of a guilty plea proceeding rather than by a formal trial. Thereupon, with the State's telling evidence and Alford's denial before it, [400 U.S. 33] the trial court proceeded to convict and sentence Alford for second-degree murder.

State and lower federal courts are divided upon whether a guilty plea can be accepted when it is accompanied by protestations of innocence and hence contains only a waiver of trial but no admission of guilt. Some courts, giving expression to the principle that "our law only authorizes a conviction where guilt is shown," *Harris v. State,* 76 Tex.Cr.R. 126, 131 (1915), require that trial judges reject such pleas. [Other citations omitted.] But others have concluded that they should not "force any defense on a defendant in a criminal case," particularly when advancement of the defense might "end in disaster...." *Tremblay v. Overholser,* 199 F.Supp. 569, 570 (DC 1961). They have argued that, since "guilt, or the degree of guilt, is at times uncertain and elusive,"

> [a]n accused, though believing in or entertaining doubts respecting his innocence, might reasonably conclude a jury would be convinced of his guilt and that he would fare better in the sentence by pleading guilty....*McCoy v. United States,* 124 U.S.App.D.C. 177, 179, 363 F.2d 306, 308 (1966).

★ ★ ★

Thus, while most pleas of guilty consist of both a waiver of trial and an express admission of guilt, the latter element is not a constitutional requisite to the imposition of criminal penalty. An individual accused of crime may voluntarily, knowingly, and understandingly consent even if he is unwilling or unable to admit his participation in the acts constituting the crime.

Nor can we perceive any material difference between a plea that refuses to admit commission of the criminal act and a plea containing a protestation of innocence when, as in the instant case, a defendant intelligently concludes that his interests require entry of a guilty plea and the record before the judge contains strong evidence of actual guilt. Here the State had a strong case of first-degree murder against Alford. Whether he realized or disbelieved his guilt, he insisted on his plea because in his view he had absolutely nothing to gain by a trial and much to gain by pleading. Because of the overwhelming evidence against him, a trial was precisely what neither Alford nor his attorney desired. Confronted with the choice between a trial for first-degree murder, on the one hand, and a plea of guilty to second-degree murder, on the other, Alford quite reasonably chose the latter and thereby limited the maximum penalty to a 30-year term. When his plea is viewed in light of the evidence against him, which substantially negated his claim of innocence and which further provided a means by which the judge could test whether the plea was being intelligently entered,…, its validity cannot be seriously questioned. In view of the strong factual basis for the plea demonstrated by the State and Alford's clearly expressed desire to enter it despite his professed belief in his innocence, we hold that the trial judge did not commit constitutional error in accepting it.

★ ★ ★

The Court of Appeals for the Fourth Circuit was in error to find Alford's plea of guilty invalid because it was made to avoid the possibility of the death penalty. That court's judgment directing the issuance of the writ of habeas corpus is vacated, and the case is remanded to the Court of Appeals for further proceedings consistent with this opinion.

It is so ordered.

COMMENTS, NOTES, AND QUESTIONS

1. In a plea agreement, the defendant is required to admit responsibility for every element of the crime and that he or she is the culpable party. What is to be gained by continuing to profess innocence following an entry of a guilty plea? Should that render a plea invalid where it appears that the government and the defendant have unresolved issues

of fact and law between them? Why would Alford continue to profess his innocence when he was still willing to plead guilty to murder? Do you believe that an innocent person would plead guilty to a murder for which the individual had no connection in order to avoid the possibility of receiving the death penalty? Was Alford's guilty plea really involuntary by "coercion" and fear of the death penalty? If you had been the judge, would you have felt Alford's plea was really voluntary?

2. *North Carolina v. Alford* stands for the proposition that a defendant may have the luxury of denying, both inside and outside of court, that he or she committed the crime and, yet, enter a guilty plea that implicitly admits complete responsibility for the crime. Generally, a judge would not be bound to accept such a plea, since the admission of guilt proves somewhat ambiguous concerning guilt. A judge would not be required to accept an ambiguous guilty plea since there is no federal constitutional right to plead guilty to any particular crime. If the judge in *Alford* had refused to accept the guilty plea, what course of action would you have advised Mr. Alford to have pursued? Would you have suggested that he plead guilty to be sure of saving his life? What could be gained by going to trial against strong adverse evidence?

CASE 11.4

Remedy for Breached Plea Bargain

Santobello v. New York
Supreme Court of the United States
404 U.S. 257 (1971)

FACTS

A grand jury in New York returned two felony indictments against Santobello in which it alleged that he had been promoting gambling and accused him of possession of gambling records. The defendant's attorney and the prosecutor subsequently concluded a plea bargain that resulted in Santobello agreeing to plead guilty to a lesser included offense involving the possession of gambling records. Although the maximum sentence upon conviction was one year in prison, the plea bargain required the prosecutor to make no recommendation whatsoever concerning the sentencing proceeding.

When the time came for the defendant to enter his plea, he properly appeared before the court, represented that the plea was voluntary, and admitted his guilt to the lesser included offense. The judge delayed imposition of sentence due to the absence of a presentence report.

Approximately three months passed without further action by the court. In the interim period, Santobello retained new legal counsel who possessed a different evaluation of the merits of Santobello's case. The new attorney immediately filed a motion to withdraw the guilty plea and alleged that since some of the state's evidence had been obtained in violation of Santobello's Fourth Amendment rights, the defendant wanted to litigate the search and seizure issues. The motion was not immediately resolved and the case was continued until January 1970.

Santobello appeared at his sentencing hearing before a different judge because the original judge had retired. After rejecting defendant's renewed motions for withdrawal of his guilty plea and for suppression of illegally seized evidence, the judge listened to the replacement prosecutor recommend the maximum one-year sentence. Since this recommendation was contrary to the plea agreement, Santobello's counsel argued that the plea agreement was broken by the prosecution. The new prosecutor noted that no notation existed in his records relative to sentence recommendation. The sentencing judge refused to entertain the defendant's objections to the sentence recommendation. He felt that the maximum sentence was appropriate and would not have imposed a different sentence regardless of the recommendation or lack of recommendation by the prosecution.

The Supreme Court of New York, Appellate Division approved the proceedings of the trial court and New York's highest court refused to hear the appeal. The Supreme Court of the United States granted certiorari.

PROCEDURAL ISSUE

Where the basis for a plea bargain rests on material promises made by the prosecution, must the defendant be guaranteed either that those promises will be fulfilled (where the defendant would benefit from the agreement) or that, should the promises go unfulfilled, he or she will be permitted to withdraw the guilty plea?

HELD: YES

RATIONALE

Mr. Chief Justice Burger delivered the opinion of the Court.

★ ★ ★

This record represents another example of an unfortunate lapse in orderly prosecutorial procedures, in part, no doubt, because of the enormous increase in the workload of the often understaffed prosecutor's offices. The heavy workload may well explain these episodes, but it does not excuse them. The disposition of criminal charges by agreement between the prosecutor and the accused, sometimes loosely called "plea bargaining," is an essential component of the administration of justice. Properly administered, it is to be encouraged. If every criminal charge were subjected to a full-scale trial, the States and the Federal Government would need to multiply by many times the number of judges and court facilities.

Disposition of charges after plea discussions is not only an essential part of the process but a highly desirable part for many reasons. It leads to prompt and largely final disposition of most criminal cases; it avoids much of the corrosive impact of enforced idleness during pretrial confinement for those who are denied release pending trial; it protects the public from those accused persons who are prone to continue criminal conduct even while on pretrial release; and, by shortening the time between charge and disposition, it enhances whatever may be the rehabilitative prospects of the guilty when they are ultimately imprisoned. See *Brady v. United States,* 397 U.S. 742, 751–752 (1970).

However, all of these considerations presuppose fairness in securing agreement between an accused and a prosecutor. It is now clear, for example, that the accused pleading guilty must be counseled, absent a waiver. *Moore v. Michigan,* 355 U.S. 155 (1957). Fed. Rule Crim. Proc. 11, governing pleas in federal courts, now makes clear that the sentencing judge must develop, on the record, the factual basis for the plea, as, for example, by having the accused describe the conduct that gave rise to the charge. The plea must, of course, be voluntary and knowing, and if it was induced by promises, the essence of those promises must in some way be made known. There is, of course, no absolute right to have a guilty plea accepted. *Lynch v. Overholser,* 369 U.S. 705, 719 (1962); Fed. Rule Crim. Proc. 11. A court may reject a plea in exercise of sound judicial discretion.

This phase of the process of criminal justice, and the adjudicative element inherent in accepting a plea of guilty, must be attended by safeguards to insure the defendant what is reasonably due in the circumstances. Those circumstances will vary, but a constant factor is that when a plea rests in any significant degree on a promise or agreement of the prosecutor, so that it can be said to be part of the inducement or consideration, such promise must be fulfilled.

On this record, petitioner "bargained" and negotiated for a particular plea in order to secure dismissal of more serious charges, but also *on condition that no sentence recommendation would be made by the prosecutor.* [Emphasis added.] It is now conceded that the promise to abstain from a recommendation was made, and at this stage the prosecution is not in a good position to argue that its inadvertent breach or agreement is immaterial. The staff lawyers in a prosecutor's office have the burden of "letting the left hand know what the right hand is doing" or has done. That the breach of agreement was inadvertent does not lessen its impact.

We need not reach the question whether the sentencing judge would or would not have been influenced had he known all the details of the negotiations for the plea. He stated that the prosecutor's recommendation did not influence him and we have no reason to doubt that. Nevertheless, we conclude that the interest of justice and appropriate recognition of the duties of prosecution in relation to promises made in the negotiation of pleas of guilty will be best served by remanding the case to the state courts for further consideration. The ultimate relief to which petitioner is entitled we leave to the discretion of the state court, which is in a better position to decide whether the circumstances of this case require only that there be specific performance of the agreement of the plea, in which case petitioner should be resentenced by a different judge, or whether, in the view of the state court, the circumstances require granting the relief sought by petitioner, i.e., the opportunity to withdraw his plea of guilty. We emphasize that this is in no sense to question the fairness of the sentencing judge; the fault here rests on the prosecutor.…

The judgment is vacated and the case is remanded.

★ ★ ★

Mr. Justice Marshall, with whom Mr. Justice Brennan and Mr. Justice Stewart join, concurring in part and dissenting in part.

I agree with much of the majority's opinion, but conclude that petitioner must be permitted to withdraw his guilty plea. This is the relief petitioner requested and, on the facts set out by the majority, it is a form of relief to which he is entitled.

There is no need to belabor the fact that the constitution guarantees to all criminal defendants the right to a trial by judge or jury, or, put another way, the "right not to plead guilty," *United States v. Jackson,* 390 U.S. 570, 581 (1968). This and other federal rights may be waived through a guilty plea, but such waivers are not lightly presumed and, in fact, are viewed with the "utmost solicitude." *Boykin v. Alabama,* 395 U.S. 238, 243 (1969). Given this, I believe that where the defendant presents a reason for vacating his plea and the government has not relied on the plea to its disadvantage, the plea may be vacated and the right to trial regained at least where the motion to vacate is made prior to sentence and judgment. In other words, in such circumstances I would not deem the earlier plea to have irrevocably waived the defendant's federal constitutional right to a trial.

COMMENTS, NOTES, AND QUESTIONS

1. As a general rule, where one party to a contract breaches an important part of the contract, the other party can treat the contract as broken and is no longer bound by its terms. If the prosecution breaches a plea bargain contract, should the defendant be released from performing under it? Should the remedy be up to the innocent, nonbreaching party? According to *Santobello,* with whom does the decision rest when the determination must be made concerning whether to grant specific performance of the plea agreement or to allow a withdrawal of the plea? Should the defendant have the option when the government has breached the plea agreement? Why or why not?

2. When the prosecution fails to carry through on its recommendation for leniency at sentencing, the sentence can be overturned and the defendant resentenced, giving the defendant the benefit of the plea agreement. In *United States v. Barnes,* 278 F.3d 644 (2002), the defendant and the government concluded a plea bargain, which included a provision that the government recommend that Barnes be sentenced at the low end of the federal sentencing guidelines. The plea had been accepted by the trial judge, but sentence had not been passed at that time. In open court, the judge and the defendant had discussed the sentencing at the entry of the plea, but the government failed to restate the sentencing recommendations at the actual sentencing hearing. The Sixth Circuit recognized *Santobello* as precedent and held:

> Because we hold that Defendant's substantial rights were affected by the government's failure to adhere to the letter of the plea agreement by expressly recommending that Defendant be sentenced at the low end of the guidelines at sentencing, which affected the integrity of the judicial proceeding, we vacate Defendant's sentence and remand for resentencing before a different district court judge, while intending no criticism to the sentencing judge here. *Barnes* at 649.

Even though the actual sentence that will be imposed at the resentencing may not vary at all from the sentence originally given, the defendant has bargained for the prosecutor's recommendation, which must be performed to give full effect to the negotiated plea bargain. Does this process seem a bit of a waste of judicial, prosecutorial, and defense time and money? Why? Should the vacating of a sentence be measured by a harmless error standard? What if the outcome is virtually certain to remain unchanged, even when the government's breach is considered? How should this issue be argued? Read the dissent by looking up the *Barnes* case. 278 F.3d 644; 2002 U.S. App. LEXIS 1230 (6th Cir. 2002).

3. What happens if the defendant breaches the plea agreement? Can the government specifically enforce the plea bargain? What if the defendant will not cooperate as the government believes he or she should? In *Ricketts v. Adamson,* 483 U.S.1 (1987), a defendant had his plea agreement voided by his failure to testify against the original defendants when a second trial proved to be essential. The court held that the defendant possessed an obligation to testify as many times as was necessary and that since he breached the bargain, no bargain remained. Could the *Ricketts* defendant have negotiated, as a provision in the original plea agreement, that he would only have to testify at one trial and not a second one? Would a prosecutor have agreed to this provision? What if the defendant's testimony was crucial to the conviction of the co-felons? What would you offer the defendant if you were the prosecutor and needed the testimony?

4. In federal prosecutions, the judge cannot participate in any discussions between the prosecutor and the defendant concerning the plea bargain. However, once an agreement has been reached, according to Rule 11 of the Federal Rules of Criminal Procedure, the court must personally address the defendant to determine whether the plea offered has been tendered voluntarily and intelligently. Specifically, the court must discern that the defendant understands the nature of the charges, the potential penalty, the fact that a guilty plea waives specified other constitutional rights, including the right to a trial, and that the defendant has the right to plead not guilty. In a case mentioned in the introduction to this material, *McCarthy v. United States,* 394 U.S. 459 (1969), the Supreme Court reversed the defendant's conviction on the ground that the failure of the trial judge to address the defendant personally in open court created inherent prejudice to defendant McCarthy. The Court felt that Rule 11 of the Federal Rules of Criminal Procedure dictated that the judge direct inquiry to a defendant who is pleading guilty concerning whether the defendant understood the nature of the charge against him and possessed an awareness of the consequences of the plea. Failure to address the defendant created reversible error.

5. State courts must comply with basic constitutional standards and meet state requirements in accepting guilty pleas, but they need not offer every conceivable procedural protection. In *Britt v. Smith,* 274 Ga. 611; 556 S.E.2d 435 (2001), a defendant, who unambiguously had admitted responsibility and pled guilty to murder to avoid a chance at receiving the death penalty, contended in a habeas corpus petition that his plea was not voluntarily given, since the trial court had failed to comply with Georgia procedure for accepting guilty pleas. According to the Georgia Supreme Court, a state trial court rule "requires a trial court to inform a criminal defendant on the record that he will waive certain enumerated rights by pleading guilty. Apparently, the trial judge, in accepting the guilty plea, failed to totally comply with a Georgia rule of court to advise the defendant of every right that he was relinquishing due to his guilty plea. However, that Rule is not a [Georgia] constitutional provision, and habeas corpus relief is not available unless [the defendant] suffered a substantial denial of his federal or state constitutional rights." *Britt* at 613. So long as a defendant's plea was offered knowingly and voluntarily and he was informed of his waiver of the right to a trial by jury and the privilege against self-incrimination, and that he had the right to confront his accusers if he wished, no error sufficient to cause a court to issue a writ of habeas corpus existed. The requirements of notice concerning trial by jury, self-incrimination, and confrontation addressed by the trial judge to the defendant in a guilty plea are generally believed to be required by *Boykin v. Alabama,* 395 U.S. 238 (1969).

CASE 11.5

Threats of Enhanced Charges May Lawfully Induce Plea Agreement

Bordendircher v. Hayes
Supreme Court of the United States
434 U.S. 357 (1978)

FACTS

Following a grand jury indictment on a charge of uttering a forged instrument, Paul Hayes faced a potential two to ten years of incarceration. Subsequently, Hayes, his attorney, and the Commonwealth Attorney met to discuss the possibility of a negotiated plea. The Commonwealth Attorney offered a sentence recommendation of five years incarceration in return for a guilty plea to the indictment. When Hayes appeared to reject the offer and indicated that he would stand trial and take his chances on a lower verdict, the Commonwealth Attorney stated that if the defendant Hayes rejected the prosecution's offer of the negotiated plea, the Commonwealth Attorney would procure an additional indictment pursuant to Kentucky's recidivist statute and Hayes would face a greatly enhanced sentence as a habitual offender.

Under the law of the Commonwealth of Kentucky, a person who has been convicted of three felonies faced the possibility of life in prison, consistent with the recidivist statute. Hayes had two prior felony convictions and, if convicted on the uttering charge, would qualify for a life sentence. As the Commonwealth Attorney phrased it, he wanted Hayes to plead guilty to "save the court the inconvenience and necessity of a trial." Hayes refused the tendered offer to plead guilty, whereupon, a grand jury indicted him for an additional offense under the habitual offender statute.

A jury trial resulted in Hayes' conviction of uttering a forged instrument and, upon a separate finding that Hayes had two prior felonies, the jury convicted him under the habitual offender statute and gave him a life sentence. The Kentucky Court of Appeals dismissed Hayes' constitutional objections to the life sentence and upheld the prosecutor's decision to pursue the habitual offender penalty as the legitimate use of prosecutorial pressure in the context of a plea bargaining situation. The Federal District Court refused to issue a writ of habeas corpus but the Court of Appeals for the Sixth Circuit reversed the judgment. The Court felt that the prosecutor had violated the principles of *Blackledge v. Perry,* 417 U.S. 21, which granted defendants protection from the vindictive exercise of prosecutorial discretion. The Supreme Court granted certiorari.

PROCEDURAL ISSUE

Does a state prosecutor violate the rights of an indicted defendant under the Due Process Clause of the Fourteenth Amendment when, with the express purpose of inducing a guilty plea, the prosecutor carries out a threat made during plea negotiations to procure a second indictment against the accused on more serious charges if he does not plead guilty to the offense with which he was originally charged?

HELD: NO

RATIONALE

Mr. Justice Stewart delivered the opinion of the Court.

★ ★ ★

III

We have recently had occasion to observe:

> Whatever might be the situation in an ideal world, the fact is that the guilty plea and the often concomitant plea bargain are important components of this country's criminal justice system. Properly administered, they can benefit all concerned. *Blackledge v. Allison,* 431 U.S. 63, 71.

The open acknowledgment of this previously clandestine practice has led this Court to recognize the importance of counsel during plea negotiations, *Brady v. United States,* 397 U.S. 742, 758, the need for a public record indicating that a plea was knowingly and voluntarily made, *Boykin v. Alabama,* 395 U.S. 238, 242, and the requirement that a prosecutor's plea-bargaining promise must be kept, *Santobello v. New York,* 404 U.S. 257, 262. The decision of the Court of Appeals in the present case, however, did not deal with considerations such as these, but held that the substance of the plea offer itself violated the limitations imposed by the Due Process Clause of the Fourteenth Amendment. [Citation omitted.] For the reasons that follow, we have concluded that the Court of Appeals was mistaken in so ruling.

IV

This Court held in *North Carolina v. Pearce,* 395 U.S. 711, 725, that the Due Process Clause of the Fourteenth Amendment "requires that vindictiveness against a defendant for having successfully attacked his first conviction must play no part in the sentence he receives after a new trial." The same principle was later applied to prohibit a prosecutor from reindicting a convicted misdemeanant on a felony charge after the defendant had invoked an appellate remedy, since in this situation there was also a "realistic likelihood of 'vindictiveness.'" *Blackledge v. Perry,* 417 U.S., at 27.

In those cases the Court was dealing with the State's unilateral imposition of a penalty upon a defendant who had chosen to exercise a legal right to attack his original conviction—a situation very different from the give-and-take negotiation common in plea bargaining between the prosecution and defense, which arguably possess relatively equal bargaining power. *Parker v. North Carolina,* 397 U.S. 790, 809 (opinion of Brennan, J.).

The Court has emphasized that the due process violation in cases such as *Pearce* and *Perry* lay not in the possibility that a defendant might be deterred from the exercise of a legal right, see *Colten v. Kentucky,* 407 U.S. 104; *Chaffin v. Stynchcombe,* 412 U.S. 17, but rather in the danger that the State might be retaliating against the accused for lawfully attacking his conviction. See *Blackledge v. Perry, supra* at 26–28.

★ ★ ★

While confronting a defendant with the risk of more severe punishment clearly may have a "discouraging effect on the defendant's assertion of his trial rights, the imposition of these difficult choices [is] an inevitable"—and permissible—"attribute of any legitimate system which tolerates and encourages the negotiation of pleas." [Citation omitted.] It follows that, by tolerating and encouraging the negotiation of pleas, this Court has necessarily accepted as constitutionally legitimate the simple reality that the prosecutor's interest at the bargaining table is to persuade the defendant to forgo his right to plead not guilty.

It is not disputed here that Hayes was properly chargeable under the recidivist statute, since he had in fact been convicted of two previous felonies. In our system, so long as the prosecutor has probable cause to believe that the accused committed an offense defined by statute, the decision whether or not to prosecute, and what charge to file or bring before a grand jury, generally rests entirely in his discretion.

★ ★ ★

There is no doubt that the breadth of discretion that our country's legal system vests in prosecuting attorneys carries with it the potential for both individual and institutional abuse. And broad though that discretion may be, there are undoubtedly constitutional limits upon its exercise. We hold only that the course of conduct engaged in by the prosecutor in this case, which no more than openly presented the defendant with the unpleasant alternative of forgoing trial or facing charges on which he was plainly subject to prosecution, did not violate the Due Process Clause of the Fourteenth Amendment.

Accordingly, the judgment of the Court of Appeals is reversed.

Mr. Justice Blackmun, with whom Mr. Justice Brennan and Mr. Justice Marshall join, dissenting.

★ ★ ★

The Court now says, however, that this concern with vindictivenss is of no import in the present case, despite the difference between five years in prison and a life sentence, because we are here concerned with plea bargaining where there is give-and-take negotiation, and where, it is said, *ante,* at 363, "there is no such element of punishment or retaliation so long as the accused is free to accept or reject the prosecution's offer." Yet in this case vindictiveness is present to the same extent as it was thought to be in *Pearce* and in *Perry;* the prosecutor here admitted...that the sole reason for the new indictment was to discourage the respondent from exercising his right to a trial.

★ ★ ★

Prosecutorial vindictiveness in any context is still prosecutorial vindictiveness. The Due Process Clause should protect an accused against it, however it asserts itself. The Court of Appeals rightly so held, and I would affirm the judgment.

★ ★ ★

COMMENTS, NOTES, AND QUESTIONS

1. Was the *Bordenkircher* prosecutor being vindictive toward the defendant, Hayes, by elevating the charges to include the habitual offender enhancement just because Hayes refused to accept a plea offer? Why or why not? Could the prosecutor have charged Mr. Hayes with the enhanced charges from the start? Would this process have seemed more fair if the prosecutor had started negotiations with the harshest possible crimes on the table and then offered to reduce some in exchange for some level of guilty plea? The same result might have been reached, but arguably, it would have appeared to be more appropriate.

2. In *Bordenkircher,* the argument could be made that the prosecutor may threaten the defendant with various prosecutions, which were not going to be pursued, in an effort to induce a plea bargain. So long as the prosecutor

follows a legal path, regardless of the motive, the government may threaten to pursue additional criminal counts in an effort to convince the defendant to plead guilty to the current criminal charges. Do you perceive any limitations on the prosecutor? There may be some boundaries to what a prosecutor may use to circumscribe a defendant's options. In *Blackledge v. Perry*, 417 U.S. 21 (1974), the Court granted a defendant some protection from the vindictive exercise of prosecutorial discretion. In *Blackledge*, the Court permitted a collateral attack on the conviction where the defendant had initially been charged with a misdemeanor and exercised his right to have a trial de novo. Prior to the new trial, the prosecutor elevated the misdemeanor charge to a felony stemming from the original operative facts. In striking down the elevation of the charge on due process grounds, the Court noted that the defendant was entitled to the de novo without fear that the prosecutor would "get even" for his exercise of a legal right. Does *Blackledge* survive *Bordenkircher*? *Blackledge* was decided prior to *Bordenkircher*.

3. Should initial plea negotiations be conditioned on giving up some legal rights before the prosecutor will even talk substantively with an accused? If a rule of procedure for a particular jurisdiction states that preliminary negotiation discussions cannot be used against a defendant, why should a defendant have to give anything up prior to discussions with a prosecutor? Does a prosecutor's precondition of waiver of some rights indicate overreaching and abuse of powers that a prosecutor most assuredly possesses?

In actual practice, federal prosecutors may require that defendants give up some rights as a precursor to entering into plea negotiations or other cooperation with the government. As a general rule, plea negotiations and related conversations may not be used against a defendant in the event that a negotiated plea does not end the case according to Rule 11(e)(6) of the Federal Rules of Criminal Procedure. In *United States v. Mezzanatto*, 513 U.S. 196 (1995), the prosecution told the defendant that he would have to be completely truthful in their discussions concerning the criminal case. As part of the preliminary agreement, the prosecutor told Mezzanatto that he would have to agree that any statements he made during the meeting could be used to impeach any contradictory testimony he might give at trial if the case actually went to trial. Mezzanatto agreed to waive his rights under Rule 11(e)(6), but apparently he was not always truthful with the prosecutor in all respects. When the case went to trial, the prosecutor used some of the statements made by Mezzanatto for impeachment purposes, harming Mezzanatto's case.

On his successful initial appeal, Mezzanatto contended that the particular rule of criminal procedure could not be waived because that process was not within Congress's contemplation. Writing for the Court, Justice Thomas noted that the mere possibility that the prosecutor might abuse bargaining power by requesting a waiver under Rule 11(e)(6) was not sufficient to reverse the defendant's conviction. The rules governing federal criminal procedure were enacted with the presumption that the legal rights are subject to waiver by free and voluntary agreement of the contending parties. Justice Thomas observed that plea bargaining involves some hard choices and exerts pressure on defendants to plead guilty and give up some constitutional rights, but that is not reason enough to presume unfairness on the part of federal prosecutors. The *Mezzanatto* Court reinstated the original conviction that had been reversed by the Court of Appeal for the Ninth Circuit.

CASE 11.6

Executory Plea Bargain May Be Withdrawn by Prosecution

Mabry v. Johnson
Supreme Court of the United States
467 U.S. 504 (1984)

FACTS

The defendant-respondent George Johnson and two companions were in the process of burglarizing an occupied dwelling on May 22, 1970, when the residents unexpectedly returned. In the ensuing firefight, the opposing parties exchanged gunshots with the result that the daughter of the occupier of the home lost her life and her father was wounded.

The defendant stood trial for burglary, assault, and murder and was convicted of all three crimes. Following an appeal, the Arkansas Supreme Court set aside the murder conviction. The prosecutor's office and defendant, through counsel, entered into plea negotiations. Defendant remained in custody for the other convictions.

During the second pretrial stage, the prosecutor had offered to permit defendant to plead guilty to the charge of being an accessory after the fact to a murder charge under the felony-murder theory with a recommended 21-year sentence to be served *concurrently* with the burglary and assault sentence. After consultation with defendant, the plan appeared acceptable, so the attorney for defendant communicated the acceptance to the prosecutor. Before any action in court had been taken, the prosecutor withdrew the original offer and substituted an alternative offer of the same guilty plea, but with a sentence of 21 years *consecutive* to the present sentence that Johnson was already serving.

Additional negotiations proved fruitless and Johnson's trial followed, but the judge declared a mistrial due to some irregularities. Prior to the second trial, defendant decided to accept the prosecutor's second offer with the consecutive sentence but the prosecutor told him that the offer was no longer on the table. Johnson initiated state remedies designed to enforce the state's first offer. This effort failed because Johnson could not establish that he had detrimentally relied on the prosecutor's first proposed plea agreement, and so had no right to enforce it.

After exhausting all his state remedies on direct appeal, defendant filed a petition for a writ of habeas corpus with the proper federal district court. Ultimately, the Court of Appeals was persuaded of the merits of the case and reversed the district court decision, dismissing the petition. The Court of Appeals for the Eighth Circuit reversed the District Court because it determined that fairness and due process precluded the prosecutor from withdrawing an offer of a plea that had been accepted. The Supreme Court granted certiorari.

PROCEDURAL ISSUE

When a plea bargain remains executory, does the acceptance of a prosecutor's offer of the negotiated plea have the effect of creating a constitutional right to have the bargain specifically enforced where the prosecutor later attempts to withdraw the offer?

HELD: NO

RATIONALE

Justice Stevens delivered the opinion of the Court.

★ ★ ★

A plea bargain standing alone is without constitutional significance; in itself it is a mere executory agreement which, until embodied in the judgment of a court, does not deprive an accused of liberty or any other constitutionally protected interest. It is the ensuing guilty plea that implicates the Constitution. Only after respondent

pleaded guilty was he convicted, and it is that conviction which gave rise to the deprivation of respondent's liberty at issue here.

It is well-settled that a voluntary and intelligent plea of guilty made by an accused person, who has been advised by competent counsel, may not be collaterally attacked. It is also well-settled that plea agreements are consistent with the requirements of voluntariness and intelligence—because each side may obtain advantages when a guilty plea is exchanged for sentencing concessions, the agreement is no less voluntary than any other bargained-for exchange. It is only when the consensual character of the plea is called into question that the validity of a guilty plea may be impaired. In *Brady v. United States,* 397 U.S. 742 [at 755] (1970), we stated the applicable standard:

> [A] plea of guilty entered by one fully aware of the direct consequences, including the actual value of any commitments made to him by the court, prosecutor, or his own counsel, must stand unless induced by threats (or promises to discontinue improper harassment), misrepresentation (including unfulfilled or unfulfillable promises), or perhaps by promises that are, by their nature, improper as having no proper relationship to the prosecutor's business (e.g., bribes). [Citations omitted.]

Thus, only when it develops that the defendant was not fairly apprised of its consequences can his plea be challenged under the Due Process Clause. *Santobello v. New York,* 404 U.S. 257 (1971), illustrates the point. We began by acknowledging that the conditions for a valid plea

> presuppose fairness in securing agreement between an accused and a prosecutor.... The plea must, of course, be voluntary and knowing and if it was induced by promises, the essence of those promises must in some way be made known. *Id.,* at 261–262.

It follows that when the prosecution breaches its promise with respect to an executed plea agreement, the defendant pleads guilty on a false premise, and hence his conviction cannot stand:

> [W]hen a plea rests in any significant degree on a promise or agreement of the prosecutor, so that it can be said to be part of the inducement or consideration, such promise must be fulfilled. *Id.,* at 262.

Santobello [v. New York] demonstrates why respondent may not successfully attack his plea of guilty. Respondent's plea was in no sense induced by the prosecutor's withdrawn offer; unlike Santobello, who pleaded guilty thinking he had bargained for a specific prosecutorial sentencing recommendation which was not ultimately made, at the time respondent pleaded guilty he knew the prosecution would recommend a 21-year consecutive sentence. Respondent does not challenge the District Court's finding that he pleaded guilty with the advice of competent counsel and with full awareness of the consequences—he knew that the prosecutor would recommend and that the judge could impose the sentence now under attack. Respondent's plea was thus in no sense the product of governmental deception; it rested on no "unfulfilled promise" and fully satisfied the test for voluntariness and intelligence.

Thus, because it did not impair the voluntariness or intelligence of his guilty plea, respondent's inability to enforce the prosecutor's offer is without constitutional significance.

★ ★ ★

The judgment of the Court of Appeals is reversed.

COMMENTS, NOTES, AND QUESTIONS

1. Would you have suggested that a defendant accept the first offer by the prosecution? Why or why not? Is the first offer worth anything? According to *Mabry,* does the written or oral acceptance of a prosecutor's plea offer really mean anything? Is it enforceable? Should it be? Why would a prosecutor withdraw a plea offer once it had been communicated to the defense? Could you conceive of powerful reasons for a prosecutor to retract an offer even after its terms have been presented to the defendant?

2. Should a plea bargain made by a defendant who has been properly advised by competent counsel be subject to collateral attack? Why should the defendant be permitted to go back on his or her word? Would this process allow a defendant to plead guilty and later hope to obtain a trial when evidence has become less strong? Would there ever be reasons why a plea bargain should be subject to a collateral attack? What if the defendant had incompetent legal counsel who suggested accepting a negotiated plea when a valid defense could have been used? Should that defendant be permitted to attack a conviction rendered upon such a faulty plea bargain?

3. Why would a prosecutor withdraw a plea offer once it was made? If a prosecutor can withdraw an offer of a negotiated plea after acceptance by the defendant, should the prosecutor be permitted to withdraw a plea bargain after a judge has accepted the plea? Why not allow the latter if the former procedure is permissible? Has the defendant relied to his detriment in the case of a plea bargain that a court has accepted?

Pretrial Criminal Procedure: Preliminary Hearing, Bail, Right to Counsel, Speedy Trial, Double Jeopardy, and Collateral Estoppel

Chapter Outline

Key Terms

1. PRETRIAL CRIMINAL PROCEDURE: THE INITIAL STEPS TOWARD PROSECUTION

When the investigation conducted by a police department or other law enforcement agency reaches the stage where sufficient evidence has been gathered that a criminal prosecution is either possible or likely, the focus shifts, to a degree, from the police department to the prosecutor's office. Typically, members of the prosecutor's office review the evidence presented by the police department with a view to determining whether a prosecutable case exists. Where a police investigation demonstrates that proof beyond a reasonable doubt may be possible, the prosecution needs to determine whether it is the type of case that should be pursued. Due consideration must be given to the priorities of the prosecutor's office, and the individual prosecutor must take into account the finite resources possessed by the government to determine whether the case should be brought forward to court and vigorously pursued.

While it is a given that police agencies desire the prosecution of cases they have presented to the prosecutor's office, it is possible, if not probable, that the agendas of these two law enforcement functionaries may diverge in approach and priority. Virtually every case possesses some drawback or problem that when presented in a courtroom may result in an acquittal or some other disposition. Where a case has strengths, coupled with significant weaknesses, the prosecutor may consider entering into plea negotiations, leading to a guilty plea of a lesser included offense, or in some cases a diversion to an alternate type of resolution.

Cases presented to the prosecutor's office may contain a variety of challenges, issues, and pretrial and trial problems that need to be resolved prior to making a decision to pursue a particular case. If a case presents Fourth Amendment search and seizure issues, the prosecutor's office must carefully analyze the legal position and the probable chances of prevailing in a pretrial motion to suppress.[445] For some cases the outcome of a motion to suppress may drive the decision of whether to continue the prosecution or instead drop the case. Where no search and seizure issues appear, there may still be Miranda[446] or Fifth Amendment[447] issues to be resolved prior to trial, or at least a clear evaluation of the odds of prevailing when the issues are litigated in pretrial motions to suppress. If the police allegedly have used a lineup defectively[448] or have resorted to alternative identification processes that have created legal problems,[449] definitive prosecutorial decisions may well have to await resolution of the identification issues in a case where the prosecution has been initiated. Some defendants may be in a position to raise strong arguments concerning a Sixth Amendment or a statutory right to a speedy trial.[450] Constitutional Sixth Amendment speedy trial allegations must be taken seriously because the remedy is a dismissal of the case with the inability to bring it at a later time, no matter how much additional investigation may be conducted. In a small number of cases

---

[445]See *Mapp v. Ohio,* 367 U.S. 643 (1961).
[446]See *Miranda v. Arizona,* 384 U.S. 436 (1966).
[447]See *United States v. Ruiz,* 536 U.S. 622 (2002), and *Schmerber v. California,* 384 U.S. 757 (1966).
[448]See *Gilbert v. California,* 388 U.S. 263 (1967).
[449]See *Neil v. Biggers,* 409 U.S. 188 (1972).
[450]See *Barker v. Wingo,* 407 U.S. 514 (1972).

a defendant may raise the issue of prior jeopardy, a constitutional challenge that should be resolved prior to trial. Collateral double jeopardy issues may exist in complicated cases[451] or where a retrial is being contemplated following a reversal of the conviction upon appeal. Concerns about whether a witness or a defendant may possess some level of immunity from prosecution must be evaluated prior to coming to a conclusion regarding prosecution. Where a case cries out for prosecution but contains significant evidentiary challenges, the prosecutor's office may return to the police agency and request an additional investigatory effort. There may be questions of the defendant's competency at the time of the act and/or at the projected time of the trial. In such a case, the decision to move forward with prosecution may await a report based on a psychiatric examination. In evaluating a case, prosecution witnesses play a crucial role, which the government must consider. Because witnesses possess varying degrees of believability, credibility factors must be assessed when deciding whether to bring the case to trial.

2. DUTIES OF THE PROSECUTION: FIRST STEPS

Accused individuals enter the criminal justice system from a variety of avenues. Many people are booked into a jail based on a police officer's determination that probable cause to arrest existed at the time the individual was taken into custody. Probable cause has been determined to exist if, at the time the arrest was made, "the facts and circumstances within their [police officers'] knowledge and of which they had reasonably trustworthy information were sufficient to warrant a prudent man in believing" a crime had been committed.[452] Other individuals enter police detention by virtue of an arrest warrant that was issued by a judicial official and executed by police. A few of the individuals in this second category enter custody by virtue of a grand jury determination that probable cause existed to believe a crime has been committed. If custody exists due to a grand jury indictment or by the issuance of an arrest warrant by a judge or magistrate, probable cause has been appropriately determined. However, because police officers are engaged in the often competitive enterprise of ferreting out crime[453] and because they are not neutral and detached judicial officials, if a person has been taken into custody on a police officer's determination of probable cause, case law requires a second opinion in this matter. Under such circumstances, a judge or other person in judicial office must listen to evidence giving rise to probable cause and offer a concurring determination that probable cause to arrest exists.[454] The general rule, derived from case law, is that a person can be kept in custody only forty-eight hours unless there has been a judicial determination of probable cause.[455] At a bare minimum, when a person has been arrested

---

[451]See *Ashe v. Swenson*, 397 U.S. 436 (1970).

[452]*Beck v. Ohio*, 379 U.S. 89, 91 (1964).

[453]See *Johnson v. United States*, 333 U.S. 10, 14 (1948), for the apparent origination of this phrase.

[454]According to the Court, the Fourth Amendment dictates that the government seek a judicial determination of probable cause as a prerequisite to extended restraint of liberty following arrest where the arrest is made upon a determination of a police officer.

[455]*County of Riverside v. McLaughlin*, 500 U.S. 44 (1991), determined that a probable cause hearing should be conducted within forty-eight hours subsequent to the initiation of custody in the absence of indictment or an arrest warrant. See also *Gerstein v. Pugh*, 420 U.S. 103 (1975).

without a warrant and not pursuant to a grand jury indictment, the prosecution must present evidence sufficient to establish probable cause at a hearing held within the forty-eight-hour period. This need not be an adversarial hearing, and the defendant has no right to be present or to have his or her attorney present. The prosecutor must establish probable cause to believe that the individual committed the alleged crime or crimes. This hearing is sometimes called the first hearing; it also may be labeled a probable cause only hearing where probable cause is the sole issue to be decided by the judicial official.

The next stage in the criminal justice process may involve a court hearing called an arraignment. Some jurisdictions merge the probable cause only hearing into this hearing, at which time additional other legal business will be considered beyond the determination of probable cause. If probable cause cannot be established, the defendant will generally be free to leave custody pending further investigation or a grand jury indictment. At the arraignment, the charges will be read to the defendant, and a copy of the complaint, information, or indictment will be furnished. The judge may appoint an attorney, if the defendant does not already have a retained attorney.[456] Additionally, the judge may request that the defendant enter a plea, but this is not a universal rule in every court at this point in the process. Where a plea is required under local practice, and, most assuredly, if the defendant does not have an attorney, a plea of not guilty will be entered on behalf of the defendant. Felony bail may be initially determined during this hearing, where the defendant is represented by legal counsel and the attorney can make arguments concerning the granting of bail and the amount of bail.

3. THE PRELIMINARY HEARING

Although a preliminary hearing is not a required step under the Constitution of the United States, many states use it as an additional screening device for criminal cases, especially where a grand jury has not returned an indictment or a grand jury is not expected be used. Some states dispense with a preliminary hearing completely where a grand jury has returned an indictment[457] because the probable cause determination has been made previously by the grand jury. As is the case in many legal proceedings, the statutory right to a preliminary hearing is a waivable right, and an informed defendant may dispense with this legal procedure.[458] Unlike a probable cause only hearing, the preliminary hearing is adversarial and permits the confrontation and cross-examination of prosecution witnesses by the defendant. As a general rule, states follow the rules of evidence at preliminary hearings.[459] Where a state chooses to use the preliminary hearing, it must grant a defendant the

[456]A right to counsel does exist at the arraignment, but it is at this stage that the counsel frequently is appointed. In *McNeil v. Wisconsin,* 501 U.S. 171 (1991), the Court noted that right to counsel "does not attach until a prosecution is commenced, that is, at or after the initiation of adversary judicial criminal proceedings—whether by way of formal charge, preliminary hearing, indictment, information, or *arraignment*" (emphasis added).
[457]See Ohio Rules of Criminal Procedure, Crim. R. 5(B)(1). Anderson 2001.
[458]See Cal. Penal Code § 860 (Mathew Bender 2003): "...a defendant represented by counsel may when brought before the magistrate as provided in Section 858 or at any time subsequent thereto, waive the right to an examination before such magistrate...."
[459]See Ohio Rules of Criminal Procedure, Crim. R. 5(B)(2). Anderson 2001.

Sixth Amendment right to counsel; where a defendant is indigent, there is a right to free counsel.[460]

The Supreme Court first recognized the right to counsel at a preliminary hearing in *Coleman v. Alabama*, 399 U.S. 1 (1970) (see Case 12.1). In *Coleman*, the defendants had been granted a preliminary hearing in an assault with intent to commit murder prosecution, but the indigent defendants were not represented by counsel. In deciding the case, the Court noted that an accused requires the guidance of counsel in every step of a criminal prosecution and that the Sixth Amendment right to counsel extends beyond the actual trial. The *Coleman* Court determined that a preliminary hearing constituted a critical stage of the criminal justice process, at which time the assistance of counsel was required by the federal constitution.

Consistent with the Sixth Amendment right recognized in *Coleman*, the California Penal Code provides that the defendant be allowed to have counsel during a preliminary hearing:

> The magistrate shall immediately deliver to the defendant a copy of the complaint, inform the defendant that he or she has the right to have the assistance of counsel, ask the defendant if he or she desires the assistance of counsel, and allow the defendant reasonable time to send for counsel. Cal. Penal Code § 859 (Mathew Bender 2003).

Most states allow a defendant a reasonable time in which to obtain legal counsel and will proceed with a preliminary hearing when the attorney for the defendant can be present.

As a general rule, at the beginning of a preliminary hearing, the government calls the witnesses who will be able to offer sufficient evidence to demonstrate probable cause to believe that the defendant has committed the crime or crimes for which the allegation has been made. The witnesses are subject to cross-examination by the defense, which may enable the attorney for the accused to cast sufficient doubt to destroy probable cause. In most cases, the defendant's attorney will not be successful in having the case dismissed but will be able to gather evidence about the government's theory of the case and how the prosecution will probably proceed if the case goes to trial. An additional benefit to the defendant is that the witnesses who do testify at a preliminary hearing have the effect of "freezing" their testimony, and the subsequent trial testimony must match what was given at the preliminary hearing.

Demonstrative of the general theory that the preliminary hearing shall not become a mini-trial on the merits, many jurisdictions do not allow defendants to call witnesses to rebut the general testimony placed on the record by the prosecutor or to summon witnesses in order to impeach the prosecutor's witnesses. In the interests of justice, California follows a slightly different process from the traditional preliminary hearing procedure. When the examinations of prosecution witnesses in preliminary hearings in California are complete, any witness the defendant may produce shall be sworn and examined. The limitations on defense witnesses are that

---

[460]See *Coleman v. Alabama*, 399 U.S. 1 (1970).

the magistrate shall require an offer of proof from the defense as to the testimony expected from the witness. The magistrate shall not permit the testimony of any defense witness unless the offer of proof discloses to the satisfaction of the magistrate, in his or her sound discretion, that the testimony of that witness, if believed, would be reasonably likely to establish an affirmative defense, negate an element of a crime charged, or impeach the testimony of a prosecution witness or the statement of a declarant testified to by a prosecution witness. See Cal. Penal Code § 859 (Mathew Bender 2003).

Essentially the defense witnesses would be allowed to testify if such evidence would clearly be devastating to the finding of probable cause to believe that the defendant had committed the crime or crimes.

When the preliminary hearing results in a finding by the judge or magistrate that probable cause exists, the court will order that the defendant continue to be held in custody and that the prosecutor's office take steps to continue the prosecution. In jurisdictions that are permitted to initiate serious criminal prosecutions by the use of information rather than a grand jury, the prosecutor then begins the steps that result in an information being filed by the prosecutor in the court of general jurisdiction where the case is triable.

4. BAIL ISSUES PRESENTED AT A PRELIMINARY HEARING

In many jurisdictions, once the judge or magistrate has determined that probable cause exists to hold the defendant further, the court moves to address the issue of whether to grant bail or to order pretrial detention. If an offense is subject to bail under state law, the judge must consider the relevant factors in determining what type of bail would be appropriate. Some states allow a variety of assets to be pledged to meet the required monetary amount of bail. A cash bail is sometimes required, but approved property such as stocks and bonds or real estate holdings within the court's jurisdiction are generally considered permissible types of assets. The most important factor for a judge is to set the amount of bail. In making an evaluation of the defendant and the charged crime for bail purposes, the judge may be limited by an excessive bail provision of the state's law or constitution. However, many states hold by legislation, constitution, or case law that some offenses are not bailable, so any concern of excessive bail under these circumstances does not become an issue.[461]

When a defendant is or may be entitled to bail, the defense attorney has a variety of arguments to offer concerning bail in that particular case, the amount of bail, and the conditions under which bail may be offered. A fairly extensive number of decided cases offer both the defense attorney and the counsel for the government a

---

[461]See Constitution of the State of Ohio, Article I, § 9: Bill of Rights. Most jurisdictions provide for a complete denial of bail in some cases. Demonstrative of this concept is the case of Ohio law, which does not allow bail for persons charged with capital offenses where the proof is evident or the presumption strong. Similarly, bail can be denied to a person who is charged with a felony where the proof is evident or the presumption great, and who poses a potential serious physical danger to a victim of the offense, to a witness to the offense, or to any other person or to the community. Anderson 2001.

wide range of issues to litigate concerning bail. The question of bail often arises at an arraignment or at the preliminary hearing.

5. GENERAL BAIL JURISPRUDENCE

Among other rights, the Eighth Amendment to the Constitution of the United States guarantees that "excessive bail shall not be required." A bail that has been set at an amount higher than the minimum reasonably calculated to fulfill the aims and purposes of bail may be deemed "excessive" under the Eighth Amendment. Bail allows a criminal defendant to be released from formal government custody in exchange for the payment money or the pledge of property of a value sufficient to ensure the defendant's return to court at all proper times. The rationale for conditionally releasing a person who has been accused of a crime rests on the primary consideration of the pretrial presumption of innocence.[462] Pretrial release permits the accused to freely consult with counsel, to interview and search for favorable witnesses, to assist in the preparation of an appropriate defense, and to continue gainful employment.

The assets pledged or paid as bail usually must meet state or local statutory requirements concerning type and location of the collateral as well as the value of the property. Even where sufficient property has been pledged as bail, the conditional freedom always involves the risk that a defendant might flee and fail to return when required. For this reason, if new factors become obvious or if new conditions arise in the time prior to trial, an adjustment of the amount or a reconsideration of the conditions of bail may be held at any time upon the request of either party. Offering bail is, at best, a calculated risk-weighing decision where a judge gambles that a defendant will perform consistent with the pledges and promises made in court.

Bail limitations have existed from the time of the common law, when bail was not available for all types of alleged crimes, especially the more serious offenses. Where the crime charged carries a potential life sentence or the death penalty, a judge or magistrate might refuse to set bail at any amount. Under local law or pursuant to practice, judges may deny bail where the danger to the community appears to be great, particularly in instances involving sexual crimes or drug-related offenses. The resulting situation ensures that the defendant will not flee and does not give rise to a claim of "excessive bail," since a judge denied bail completely.

While states frequently grant pretrial bail, the bail portion of the Eighth Amendment has not yet explicitly been incorporated into the Due Process Clause of the Fourteenth Amendment. Therefore, it cannot be stated with certainty whether this part of the Eighth Amendment applies to state bail practice. In any event, the states generally permit bail to be granted on terms and conditions that mirror the federal bail jurisprudence under the Eighth Amendment.[463]

In a leading case that remains good law, *Stack v. Boyle,* 342 U.S. 1 (1951), the Supreme Court determined that the factors used to set bail are subject to individual

---

[462]See *Stack v. Boyle,* 342 U.S. 1 (1951), for the rationale about setting bail amounts.

[463]Demonstrative of bail practice is the legal formulation of the state of Ohio. See the Ohio Revised Code, Section 2937.23, and Article I, Section 9, Ohio Constitution for an example of typical bail practice.

determination by taking due consideration for the personal circumstances of each person charged in federal prosecutions (see Case 12.2). Felony bail cannot be automatically set based on the charge or the past history of other persons charged with the same offense. Courts should consider the nature and circumstances of the defendant and of the crime, the strength of the evidence, the general character of the accused, and the ability of a defendant to pay for release. Bail that has been set at a greater amount than necessary to assure that the accused individual will not flee will be considered "excessive." A federal judicial official must make a unique determination for each defendant.

For state felony cases, a judicial official generally must consider numerous factors in determining the appropriate bail amount. Considerations underpinning the bail decision involve an individual analysis of the defendant's past history while under pretrial release, the defendant's ties to the local community, the defendant's work history and financial resources, the seriousness of the crime, the strength of the evidence, the potential penalty if convicted, and the likelihood that the defendant will continue criminal conduct or otherwise endanger individual members of the community. Although the primary bail consideration centers around the issue of whether the defendant will return for all required court appearances, the federal Bail Reform Act of 1984 interjected additional requirements for some federal prosecutions.[464]

6. FEDERAL BAIL PRACTICE: RECENT CONSIDERATIONS

Congress moved to correct some perceived abuses in federal bail practice, most notably the tendency of drug-trafficking defendants to post large bail amounts and flee the jurisdiction of the United States. In passing the Bail Reform Act of 1984,[465] the Congress continued most of the typical requirements for bail but changed the basic philosophy of federal bail in a few situations. The act directed federal courts specifically to look at the type of crime charged, the weight of the evidence, the defendant's physical and mental condition, any history of drug or alcohol abuse by the defendant, and the potential danger presented by the defendant toward any person and toward the community. The act changed federal bail practice in cases where the defendant was charged with specific drug offenses, a crime of violence, a life imprisonment crime, a crime for which the penalty could be greater than ten years, or where the accused had been convicted of two similar crimes within the past ten years. In these situations, the attorney for the federal government may ask for a pretrial detention order. In addition, where the federal prosecutor presents evidence that the person might flee, could present a danger to any community member, or might obstruct justice by threatening potential witnesses or jurors, bail may be denied altogether.[466]

---

[464]18 U.S.C. § 3141 *et seq.*
[465]Ibid.
[466]18 U.S.C. § 3142(e). Where a judge has conducted a hearing under the act and when the judicial official "…finds that no condition or combination of conditions will reasonably assure the appearance of the person as required and the safety of any other person and the community, he shall order the detention of the person prior to trial."

In *United States v. Salerno,*[467] the Supreme Court upheld the constitutionality of portions of the Bail Reform Act of 1984 affecting federal pretrial detention (see Case 12.3). The *Salerno* Court rejected arguments that the practice of holding some defendants in custody pending trial constituted pretrial punishment and noted that pretrial detention orders served to prevent dangers to the community, a legitimate regulatory goal. The Court stated that although the Eighth Amendment prohibited excessive bail, the language of the amendment did not address the issue of whether bail should be available in a particular case and under what circumstances bail could be denied completely.

Although the federal Bail Reform Act of 1984 contemplated that federal courts would grant bail to many persons, only two situations were recognized by the statute.[468] When a court is faced with a bail request, it may either grant release on any reasonable condition or conditions or order detention without bail. If a court grants bail, the accused is deemed released, no matter what conditions are ordered by the judge or how severe or limited the conditions of release might be. In *Reno v. Koray,*[469] the court granted the defendant presentence release to a community treatment center, where the order required that he would be confined to the physical premises of the center without permission to leave for any reason. The plain English meaning of these conditions would seem to indicate that the defendant remained in government custody rather than being free to roam abroad at his own discretion. When the defendant desired credit toward time served at the center, the *Koray* Court held that he had been released and not denied bail so that he could not apply the time toward his sentence. The lesson of the case is that a person may be "released" under conditions of bail that seem almost like being in full custody; thus a person facing a sentence might want to reconsider whether pretrial or presentence release serves an appropriate purpose where the federal prosecutor's case appears strong.

The Bail Reform Act of 1984 mandated that a federal arrestee be granted a detention hearing at his or her first appearance before a judicial official. Such hearing could be delayed up to five days at an arrestee's request or up to three days on motion by the government. At issue in *United States v. Montalvo-Murillo*[470] was the question of what remedy should be available for the arrestee if a detention hearing had been delayed longer than the federal statute permitted and delayed significantly through no fault of the arrestee (see Case 12.4). To resolve a dispute among federal courts of appeal, the Supreme Court granted certiorari to determine the remedy for failure to grant a detention hearing at the first appearance of an arrestee. The Court held that a federal court does not lose jurisdiction to make a detention determination under the Bail Reform Act even where the act has not been followed to the letter. The Court held that a court may issue a detention order even if the government has not followed the time requirements of the law. According to the *Montalvo-Murillo* Court, "Magistrates and district judges can be presumed to insist upon

---

[467] 481 U.S. 739 (1987).
[468] See 18 U.S.C. § 3585(a) and (b).
[469] 515 U.S. 50 (1995).
[470] 495 U.S. 711 (1990).

compliance with the law without the threat that we must embarrass the system by releasing a suspect certain to flee from justice."[471]

In contrast to the practice of felony bail and the litigation that accompanies it, criminal cases involving misdemeanor offenses generally do not require such detailed analysis of individual factors. Typically, alleged misdemeanors and violations of local municipal ordinances are bailable with little reference to any factor other than a local predetermined bail schedule.[472]

Regardless of whether the charged offense constitutes a felony or misdemeanor, once the amount of bail has been judicially determined, the defendant, or a person acting on behalf of the defendant, may personally pay or pledge the full amount. Not infrequently, the accused does not possess the complete bail amount or own approved values of property and must resort to using a commercial bail bondsman. Typical bond practice requires the defendant to pay 10 to 15 percent of the full bail to the bondsman in exchange for the bondsman's executing a pledge for the complete amount to the government. Bail posted through a bondsman is money that will not be returned to the defendant even if he or she fully complies with all conditions of bail.

While the issue of bail may be of extreme importance to a defendant to assist in the orderly preparation of a defense, the defendant may desire to assert other constitutional rights prior to trial. In some cases, the trial might occur too rapidly following notification of charges to allow adequate preparation; conversely, delay in getting to trial may create other problems and challenges for a defendant. Federal constitutional protections granted to all accused defendants include the Sixth Amendment right to a speedy trial; defendants also possess similar additional protections under state laws and state constitutions. Regardless of the source of the right, the guarantee of a speedy trial is a right that must be asserted prior to trial or it may be deemed to have been waived.

7. RIGHT TO A SPEEDY TRIAL: REASONABLE TIME REQUIREMENTS

The Sixth Amendment to the United States Constitution reads as follows:

> In all criminal prosecutions, the accused shall enjoy the right to a *speedy and public trial,* by an impartial jury of the State and district wherein the crime shall have been committed, which district shall have been previously ascertained by law, and to be informed of the nature and cause of the accusation; to be confronted with the witnesses against him; to have compulsory process for obtaining witnesses in his favor, and to have the assistance of counsel for his defence. (Emphasis added.)

The literal language of the Sixth Amendment states that in all prosecutions of a criminal nature, the accused has the right to a speedy trial. As a practical matter, a criminal trial may be delayed for a variety of reasons. The defendant's request for

---

[471]Ibid. at 721.
[472]See Ohio Rules of Criminal Procedure, Crim. R. 46(G). Anderson 2001. "Bond schedule. Each court shall establish a bail bond schedule covering all misdemeanors including traffic offenses, either specifically, by type, by potential penalty, or by some other reasonable method of classification."

additional time to formulate a defense, the prosecution's need to prepare its case, and the resolution of pretrial motions constitute appropriate reasons that the start of a trial may be delayed. Prior to 1967, the Sixth Amendment speedy trial right clearly applied only in federal criminal trials, but following the Court's decision in *Klopfer v. North Carolina,*[473] the right to a speedy trial became a constitutional requirement enforceable against the states through the Due Process Clause of the Fourteenth Amendment. In addition to the constitutional provision, Congress passed the Speedy Trial Act of 1974,[474] which helps move federal criminal cases to the top of trial dockets. States also have statutory speedy trial statutes designed to ensure that criminal matters generally receive expeditious resolution. In any case, a defendant has an improved chance of having a case dismissed based on a speedy trial statutory violation than on federal or state constitutional grounds; statutes are more specific concerning their provisions, making it easier to demonstrate a prosecution deficiency with legal requirements.

From a policy perspective, prompt resolution of criminal matters allows a defendant to plan for the future and allows society to make a proper disposition of the case and to move forward. Having criminal cases resolved fairly rapidly prevents a nonbailed defendant from extensive preresolution punishment and disruption or termination of employment. Additionally, a fairly quick trial allows the accused's defense to remain fairly fresh, before the memory of witnesses has had much chance to fade. A trial held within a reasonable time limits the period of public scrutiny of the defendant's affairs, which is an additional justification for a quick resolution of the defendant's legal difficulties. If there were no imperative to resolve criminal cases, a prosecutor could allow an accused to wallow in uncertainty for months or years, always wary that a prosecution could be initiated at any time.[475] Such an extended delay is not normally practiced by the prosecution, however; the government generally has the burden of proof concerning most trial issues, and delay in proceeding to trial usually works in a defendant's favor as the memory of prosecution witnesses becomes less clear with the passage of time.[476]

8. SPEEDY TRIAL STATUTES

Criminal defendants may also file pretrial motions concerning speedy trial rights based on federal law and state statutory and constitutional provisions. Typically, state and federal speedy trial statutes attempt to provide a timetable with which the prosecution must comply, subject to carefully delineated exceptions. Most statutes

---

[473]386 U.S. 213 (1967).
[474]Speedy Trial Act of 1974, 18 U.S.C. § 3161 *et seq.*
[475]The outer limit for a criminal prosecution would involve the statute of limitations. However, some states do not have a statute of limitations for all crimes, and the trend has been to lengthen the existing time limitations.
[476]"Delay is not an uncommon defense tactic. As the time between the commission of the crime and trial lengthens, witnesses may become unavailable or their memories may fade. If the witnesses support the prosecution, its case will be weakened, sometimes seriously so. And it is the prosecution which carries the burden of proof. Thus, unlike the right to counsel or the right to be free from compelled self-incrimination, deprivation of the right to speedy trial does not per se prejudice the accused's ability to defend himself." *Barker v. Wingo,* 407 U.S. 514, 521 (1972).

include provisions to prevent the release of a defendant due to a mere nonconformity with the time requirements.

Because both society and the accused possess an interest in a fairly rapid resolution of criminal cases, the state function of administering justice arguably is best served by freeing the innocent and incarcerating wrongdoers as soon as possible. Without the statutory right to a swift resolution of a criminal case, a defendant would face an uncertain future and would be forced to contend with difficulties in planning for the future, with maintaining employment, in meeting expenses of litigation, and with diminished availability of witnesses and testimony. Problems concerning availability of defense witnesses become especially acute where crispness and detail of testimony prove crucial. Further prejudice to the defendant's reputation and community standing occurs while criminal charges are pending, a factor that leads to much personal anxiety and stress. Of special concern is the prejudice suffered by a defendant who is unable to make bail and must remain incarcerated pending trial. In such a case, a speedy resolution becomes imperative.

9. SPEEDY TRIAL: WHEN THE TIME BEGINS TO RUN UNDER THE SIXTH AMENDMENT

The time aspect of the constitutional speedy trial right begins to run when a person has been arrested for a particular crime and has been either retained in custody or released on bail. The period also begins to run when a person has been indicted or has had an information filed against him or her. Only by taking one of these steps has the prosecution indicated that a criminal case has been selected for which a speedy resolution becomes meaningful. The constitutional right to a speedy trial also applies to individuals incarcerated in a foreign jurisdiction (another state) who have been indicted or had an information filed in the current state. In order not to violate the Sixth Amendment, the jurisdiction lacking custody must attempt to procure the presence of the defendant or risk a violation of the right to speedy trial. The noncustodial state may not use the excuse that unavailability is the defendant's problem where the convict is the "guest" of a foreign jurisdiction.[477]

10. TO DETERMINE WHETHER A VIOLATION EXISTS: THE FOUR-FACTORS TEST

To determine whether the federal constitutional right to a speedy trial has been violated, courts should look to four factors as described by the Court in *Barker v. Wingo* (see Case 12.5).[478] According to the *Barker* Court, attention should be directed to consideration of the length of the delay, the reason for the delay, the defendant's assertion or nonassertion of the right, and prejudice to the defendant. The length of the delay may prove determinative that the right has been violated. Case law seems to indicate that the passage of time *alone* will rarely prove sufficient to

---

[477]See *Smith v. Hooey,* 393 U.S. 374 (1969). Where a defendant has been charged in one jurisdiction while serving time in another, upon request, the noncustodial jurisdiction has a duty to attempt to obtain custody for trial or risk violating the speedy trial portion of the Sixth Amendment.
[478]407 U.S. 514, 530–531 (1972).

constitute an infraction,[479] but time, in concert with other factors, may tip the scales in the direction of a violation. In *Doggett v. United States,* the defendant had been indicted in 1980 for drug-related offenses but not arrested until late 1988, after he had been residing openly in the United States for almost six years (see Case 12.6).[480] Doggett's location could have been easily discerned except for governmental negligence. On speedy trial grounds, the *Doggett* Court overturned Doggett's conviction for drug offenses based on the length of the delay and the presence of presumed, but unproven, prejudice. Even though Doggett proved unable to present specific instances of prejudice to his case, the Court accepted the presence of prejudice by citing the extremely long wait between indictment and arrest.

The second factor mentioned in *Barker* involved the reason for the delay. Acceptable reasons include time used for psychiatric examination, defense requests for continuances, and absence or illness of necessary prosecution witnesses. Crowded court dockets and postponements purposely used or created to hinder the defense have not proven acceptable as reasons for delay. Where a defendant has requested a continuance, the right to a speedy trial has been effectively waived to the extent of the request.

The *Barker* Court noted that the assertion or failure to assert the right to a speedy trial constitutes the third factor courts must consider. While some continuances may enhance the prosecution's case, normally the defense benefits from a delay because the burden of proof rests with the government. Where the defendant remains silent and does not *assert* the right, a waiver will not conclusively be presumed, but the silence of the defendant in failing to assert the constitutional right will not materially enhance a speedy trial contention.

The final factor cited by the *Barker* Court as important to a determination of a speedy trial violation was prejudice to the defendant. Prejudice should be viewed in the light of the interests of defendants, which the speedy trial right was designed to protect. The *Barker* Court identified three such prejudicial interests: the prevention of oppressive pretrial incarceration, the diminution of anxiety and concern of the accused, and a limitation of the possibility that the defense case might be impaired.[481] Of the three, the most crucial is the third, because the inability of a defendant adequately to prepare his or her case tilts the fairness of the criminal justice system. If witnesses die or disappear during a delay, the prejudice becomes apparent. Prejudice may originate where defense witnesses are unable to recall accurately events of the distant past.

Applying the *Barker* factors to an allegation of a speedy trial violation, the top Texas criminal court in *Dragoo v. Texas,* 96 S.W.3d 308 (2003), held that a defendant's rights had not been violated. In that case, the defendant had been convicted for murder but had not been contemporaneously prosecuted for having a firearm under a disability. Three and a half years later, Texas brought the weapon under a disability

---

[479]See *Dillingham v. United States,* 423 U.S. 64 (1975), where a twenty-two-month delay between arrest and indictment and an additional twelve-month delay following indictment to trial did not constitute a violation of the Sixth Amendment right to a speedy trial. The delay alone was not sufficient to demonstrate a violation.
[480]505 U.S. 647 (1992).
[481]*Doggett v. United States,* 505 U.S. 647, 654 (1992).

case to court, although it had been filed when the prosecutor brought the murder charge. The state made no effort to get the weapons case to court, and the defendant made no demand to be tried, since he was already serving a life sentence for murder. On the day prior to trial on the weapons charge, the defendant filed a motion to dismiss on speedy trial grounds. The trial court denied the motion to dismiss the weapons charge, which prompted the defendant to pursue his legal remedies. The Texas Court of Criminal Appeals reversed the intermediate appellate court finding of a speedy trial violation. It noted that the length of the delay is a strong indicator of prejudice, but that factor diminished somewhat because there had been no demand for trial. Since the state offered no reason for the delay, such factor would weigh in favor of a violation, but the defendant offered no concrete proof concerning how the delay prejudiced his case, especially since he was incarcerated for murder for most of the period. When the Texas court weighed the *Barker* factors, it concluded that no violation of the constitutional right to a speedy trial had occurred in Dragoo's case and sent the case back to the trial court for a trial on the merits.[482]

To prevail on a federal constitutional claim of a Sixth Amendment right to a speedy trial, prejudice to the merits of a defendant's case appears to be the primary factor in winning a motion to dismiss a criminal prosecution. Sheer length of time, even in the absence of clear prejudice, may permit a trial court to find a violation, although length of time accompanied by prejudice to the merits of the case may stand the best chance of winning the motion for a defendant. Prejudice may include extensive pretrial incarceration, loss of job, stress to the defendant, or loss of witness testimony due to death or fading memory. Where a strong indication of prejudice appears and coexists in the presence of a sufficient level of the three other factors, a court may conclude that the government has violated a defendant's Sixth Amendment right to a speedy trial.

11. REMEDY FOR VIOLATION OF SIXTH AMENDMENT RIGHT TO SPEEDY TRIAL

Where the criminal defendant has prevailed on a Sixth Amendment speedy trial claim, courts have struggled to formulate an appropriate remedy. Some jurisdictions devised a method whereby a sentence would be reduced by the duration of the speedy trial violation, a remedy that ignored any prejudice to the defendant. However, the Court in *Strunk v. United States*[483] determined that the remedy must include a prejudicial dismissal of the case. Where prejudice to the defendant, such as the death of a witness, has occurred, a reduction in length of sentence would do nothing to cure that prejudice and ensure fairness in a trial involving facts from the distant past. Therefore, outright prejudicial dismissal remains the sole remedy for a violation of the Sixth Amendment right to a speedy trial. This drastic remedy creates pressure on trial courts to reject pretrial motions to dismiss and has the effect of sending speedy trial issues to appellate courts for resolution. However, it is crucial

---

[482]For another case following the *Barker v. Wingo* analysis, see *Hargrove v. Texas,* 2003 Tex. App. LEXIS 5069 (2003).
[483]412 U.S. 434 (1973).

that the issue be raised at the pretrial stage or the defendant runs a strong chance that an appellate court will rule that a waiver has occurred by virtue of failure to raise the issue in a timely manner.

12. DOUBLE JEOPARDY: A REQUIRED PRETRIAL MOTION

Along with other motions that an accused must make prior to trial is the requirement—where a prior trial may have adjudicated the case that the prosecution is attempting to bring a second time, or where the defendant faces a second punishment for a crime for which punishment jeopardy had already attached—to alert the prosecution concerning a double jeopardy claim. The constitutional prohibition against double jeopardy has been interpreted as a prohibition against a second trial for the same crime arising from one set of operative facts by the same sovereign jurisdiction and a prohibition against double punishment for the same offense. According to the Supreme Court, the double jeopardy provision offers three separate protections:

> It protects against a second prosecution for the same offense after acquittal. It protects against a second prosecution for the same offense after conviction. And it protects against multiple punishments for the same offense. *North Carolina v. Pearce,* 395 U.S. 711, 717 (1969).

Where the prosecution is unaware that it is about to transgress the constitutional prohibition, the defendant has the legal duty to make the prosecution aware of the problem prior to trial. According to the Fifth Amendment of the Constitution of the United States, "No person shall …be subject for the same offence to be twice put in jeopardy of life or limb." The Fifth Amendment prohibition against trying a criminal defendant twice for the same crime is based on the theory that the state, with all its resources, should try a defendant once and not exhaust the defendant's assets and will to resist with a series of consecutive trials. A judicial interpretation of the Fifth Amendment double jeopardy provision generally prevents imposing successive punishments for the same crime. For example, in one case, a defendant had been convicted of capital murder, but the jury could not unanimously agree on a penalty, so pursuant to state law, the judge sentenced the defendant to life in prison. When an appeals court overturned the conviction, the state planned to retry the case with death penalty specifications; the defendant contended that the judge's imposition of the life sentence effectively acquitted him of the death penalty, and to place him in jeopardy of losing life would constitute double jeopardy. The Supreme Court of the United States disagreed, saying the double jeopardy clause would not be offended, since the original jury had never acquitted him of the death penalty; it just failed to reach an agreement, constituting a hung jury that never reached a decision on the merits of the penalty. Hung juries do not prevent a retrial of either the case or the penalty.[484]

As a general rule, the contention that the prosecution may violate the defendant's rights under the double jeopardy provision of the state or federal constitution

---

[484]See *Sattazahn v. Commonwealth of Pennsylvania,* 537 U.S. 101 (2003).

must be made prior to a trial on the merits. A defendant with adequate representation who pleads guilty to gain other favorable outcomes generally waives the
right to complain on the appellate level or mount a collateral attack about an alleged double jeopardy violation.[485] However, under some circumstances and in
the interests of justice, Texas will allow a double jeopardy claim to be raised on
appeal for the first time where the undisputed facts demonstrate a clear violation
of double jeopardy on the face of the case record.[486]

13. REQUIREMENTS TO CLAIM A VIOLATION OF DOUBLE JEOPARDY

In order to successfully prevail, a defendant must have first been placed in jeopardy
prior to the claim that a subsequent prosecution runs afoul of the United States
Constitution. Jeopardy has been determined to attach when the judge begins to
hear evidence from the first witness in a bench trial[487] and when the jury is empaneled and sworn in a jury trial.[488] Pretrial motions and pretrial dismissals have not
generally been considered proceedings during which jeopardy attaches.[489] For example, if a defendant successfully obtains dismissal of an indictment on technical
grounds, a subsequent indictment and trial are not barred, since the defendant was
never placed in jeopardy. Similarly, a prosecutor could take a case to successive grand
juries if the first grand jury failed to return an indictment, without encountering
any problem concerning initial jeopardy.

Demonstrative of the concept of double jeopardy is the case of *Benton v. Maryland,* 395 U.S. 784 (1969), where the defendant had been tried for burglary and larceny (see Case 12.7). Subsequent to his jury conviction of burglary and his acquittal
of the larceny count, his convictions were reversed due to grand and trial jury irregularities. The court offered an option for re-indictment and retrial that Benton
selected. Upon his re-indictment and retrial, the jury convicted Benton of both
burglary and larceny, though the first jury had aquitted him of the latter charge.
Upon his appeal, the Supreme Court held that the Fifth Amendment provision protection against double jeopardy applied through the Due Process Clause of the
Fourteenth Amendment to limit the states. Since Benton had once been at jeopardy
for the larceny charge and had been acquitted, to try him again constituted a violation of the double jeopardy provision.

14. ALLEGING DOUBLE JEOPARDY VIOLATION: REQUIREMENT OF SAME OFFENSE

The case *United States v. Dixon*[490] demonstrates the principle that successive prosecutions must be for the same offense to qualify as a double jeopardy violation. The
Dixon Court held that the defendant had been subjected to prosecution twice for

---

[485]*Mays v. Indiana,* 790 N.E.2d 1019 (2003).
[486]*Duval v. Texas,* 59 S.W.3d 773, 776, 777 (2001).
[487]See *Downum v. United States,* 372 U.S. 734, 738 (1963).
[488]See *Crist v. Bretz,* 437 U.S. 28 (1978).
[489]See *Serfass v. United States,* 420 U.S. 377 (1975).
[490]509 U.S. 668 (1993).

the same crime where he had been released on pretrial bail and was under a court order to commit no new crimes. While free, he was arrested for drug use, a direct violation of pretrial release. At the end of a lengthy contempt of court hearing, he was found guilty of criminal contempt of court for his bail violation involving use of cocaine. When he came to trial for his drug offense committed while on bail, Dixon claimed a violation of double jeopardy because a trial court had already taken judicial action on his most recent drug offense. The Supreme Court ruled in Dixon's favor on the double jeopardy issue, since the court order to commit no new crimes and the subsequent criminal contempt conviction included the same elements as the drug charge. In effect, Dixon had been tried twice for the same criminal conduct.

15. SEPARATE OFFENSES: THE *BLOCKBURGER* TEST

Proper application of double jeopardy claims and resolution of allegations of violations of double jeopardy require that courts determine whether a course of conduct constitutes two separate crimes or whether the government is prosecuting twice for the same offense. In *Blockburger v. United States*,[491] the defendant had completed the illegal sale of a controlled substance and immediately made a second sale of the same drug to the same person, separated by only a brief interval. The defendant alleged that there was only one offense, not two separate transactions. According to the *Blockburger* Court concerning separate offenses, the sale of each quantity of drug was separated into a distinct transaction, which created a separate, though virtually identical, new offense that occurred at a different time from the first offense. Therefore, no violation of double jeopardy prohibition could be argued successfully.

Under current double jeopardy interpretation, a prohibited prosecution would follow where the government obtained a conviction or acquittal for robbery and proceeded to try the defendant for *armed* robbery arising from the same facts as the initial prosecution. The test for determining whether a second prosecution is for the "same offense" involves a consideration of whether each of the two criminal offenses under consideration requires proof of an additional fact or element that the other does not.[492] Robbery and armed robbery are examples of crimes that could not be prosecuted successively by the same sovereign if the charges arose from the same criminal act because each offense does not require proof of an element different from the other.

In an effort to generate clarity in the context of double jeopardy, the Court in *United States v. Dixon* suggested:

> In both the multiple punishment and multiple prosecution contexts, this Court has concluded that where the two offenses for which the defendant is punished or tried cannot survive the "same-elements" test, the double jeopardy bar applies. See, e.g., *Brown v. Ohio,* 432 U.S. 161, 168–169 (1977); *Blockburger v. United States,* 284 U.S. 299, 304 (1932) (multiple punishment); *Gavieres v. United States,* 220 U.S. 338,

---

[491]284 U.S. 299, 304 (1932).
[492]Ibid.

42 (1911) (successive prosecutions). The same–elements test, sometimes referred to as the "*Blockburger*" test, inquires whether each offense contains an element not contained in the other; if not, they are the "same offence" and double jeopardy bars additional punishment and successive prosecution. 509 U.S. 688, 696–697.

Where each of the acts of which a defendant stands accused contains an element different from each other, the acts will be considered separate offenses, and prosecution will not be barred by the double jeopardy clause. In the same manner, where the crimes for which an accused is to stand trial contain a unique element that the proof of the other does not require, there is no bar to being tried for each crime, since they are considered separate offenses. However, where a defendant has been charged with two separate theories of committing the same crime, such as intentional murder and felony murder of the same victim, regardless of which crime the jury convicts, the defendant may be punished only one time for the single death without running afoul of the double jeopardy clause.[493]

16. DUAL SOVEREIGNTY DOCTRINE: SUCCESSIVE PROSECUTION FOR SAME ACTS PERMITTED

Successive prosecutions are not prohibited under the Fifth Amendment double jeopardy provision where the same act or conduct violated the laws of two separate sovereign jurisdictions. As a result, citizens can be subject to the criminal laws of both the state and federal government, as well as in two separate sovereign states of the United States, for the same act or course of conduct. Therefore, under what is known as the dual sovereignty doctrine, successive prosecutions by two separate and sovereign states for the same act or acts are not prohibited by the double jeopardy provision of the Fifth Amendment. In *Heath v. Alabama*,[494] the defendant had been accused of hiring two men to kill his pregnant wife by first taking her from Alabama to Georgia, where the men killed her. Heath pled guilty to murder in Georgia. To his surprise, Alabama subsequently extradited him from Georgia and charged him with the murder of his wife. The Alabama trial court convicted Heath of the death of his wife and sentenced him to death. His double jeopardy claim failed in the Supreme Court when the Court held that Heath had committed two separate offenses by committing murder under Georgia law and murder under Alabama law. As the *Heath* Court noted:

> The dual sovereignty doctrine is founded on the common law conception of crime as an offense against the sovereignty of the government. When a defendant in a single act violates the "peace and dignity" of two sovereigns by breaking the laws of each, he has committed two distinct "offences." 474 U.S. at 88.

The crimes were described and made criminal both by the sovereign state of Georgia and by the sovereign state of Alabama. Murder in Georgia was not the same crime as murder in Alabama; the one act violated the peace and dignity of Georgia and also violated the peace and dignity of Alabama. Thus, the dual convictions were

---

[493] *Washington v. Johnson,* 113 Wn. App. 482; 54 P.3d 155 (2002).
[494] 474 U.S. 82 (1985).

appropriate, and the convictions were upheld by the Supreme Court. Proof for each crime was different, since separate statutes were violated and each homicide offense required proof of an element not found in the other crime.

The dual sovereignty doctrine applies when the separate prosecutions involve the federal government and a state in successive prosecutions. The state of Illinois properly prosecuted an alleged bank robber after he had been acquitted of federal charges stemming from his robbery of a federally insured savings and loan association. In *Bartkus v. Illinois*,[495] the trial court considered a pretrial motion to dismiss the state charges but rejected the defendant's plea of *autrefois acquit*, or prior (former) acquittal. Illinois successfully prosecuted Bartkus on robbery charges involving the same transaction that had been the subject of the failed federal prosecution. The Supreme Court approved of the successive federal and state prosecutions on the theory that each jurisdiction was sovereign and the same act constituted two separate crimes under the dual sovereignty doctrine.[496]

Following similar legal reasoning, the double jeopardy clause did not prevent a Kentucky prosecution for driving under the influence of alcohol in a case where the defendant fled from Kentucky and was apprehended by Indiana police. The Kentucky prosecution occurred following the arrest and guilty plea by the defendant to a driving under the influence charge in Indiana. Since two separate sovereigns elected to try the defendant for violation of the respective law of each state, no double jeopardy violation occurred under the circumstances.[497]

17. COLLATERAL ESTOPPEL

Even where several crimes have occurred simultaneously or almost together, successive prosecution against a defendant may be barred under the doctrine of collateral estoppel. In *Ashe v. Swenson*,[498] several men had been robbed by a person whose identity was not known to the victims. The defendant was prosecuted for the robbery of one of the victims, but the jury acquitted him due to insufficient evidence that the defendant was the robber. Subsequently, the government brought the same defendant to trial for robbing a second man on the original occasion. The evidence was similar except the issue of identity was more effectively presented, and the jury rendered a guilty verdict. The Supreme Court of the United States reversed the robbery conviction on the theory that the first jury had determined that the defendant was not proven to have been present and that the doctrine of collateral estoppel (part of the double jeopardy clause) prevented the government from requiring the defendant to litigate the issue of his identity a second time.

---

[495]359 U.S. 121 (1959).

[496]Bartkus could have been tried and convicted in the Illinois state court even if he had originally been convicted of the federal charges. Double jeopardy would not apply because of the dual sovereignty doctrine.

[497]*Commonwealth of Kentucky v. Stephenson*, 82 S.W.3d 876; 2002 Ky. LEXIS 165 (2002).

[498]397 U.S. 436 (1970).

18. DOUBLE JEOPARDY: SUMMARY

Since the protection of the Fifth Amendment's provision against double jeopardy was designed to relieve a defendant of unfair multiple trials, it must be asserted prior to the start of the second trial to be effective in preventing the second trial. Therefore, as a general rule, the assertion of the right not to be tried twice for the same crime requires that the objection be raised during the pretrial phase so the trial judge has a chance to rule on the objection to the second trial. Failure to raise the issue at the appropriate time runs a strong risk that the right has been waived. Since the prohibition against being tried twice would be lost if the defendant could not take an immediate appeal from the trial court's ruling, as a general rule, an adverse ruling on double jeopardy grounds allows an immediate appeal prior to the alleged second trial. As the Supreme Court noted in *Abney v. United States:*

> [A]spects of the guarantee's protections would be lost if the accused were forced to "run the gauntlet" a second time before an appeal could be taken; even if the accused is acquitted, or, if convicted, has his conviction ultimately reversed on double jeopardy grounds, he has still been forced to endure a trial that the Double Jeopardy Clause was designed to prohibit. Consequently, if a criminal defendant is to avoid exposure to double jeopardy, and thereby enjoy the full protection of the Clause, his double jeopardy challenge to the indictment must be reviewable before that subsequent exposure occurs. 431 U.S. 651, 662 (1977).

As a general rule, the sovereign government, whether state or federal, may not wear a defendant down by successive trials over the same events without violating the double jeopardy provision of the Fifth Amendment. However, the provision against double jeopardy does not create an absolute prohibition against successive trials. Some occasions and situations will allow second trials, such as where there has been a successful defendant appeal, a hung jury, or a lawfully declared mistrial, especially if the defendant requests the mistrial declaration.[499]

MAJOR CASES

CASE 12.1

Pretrial Right to Counsel Exists at the Preliminary Hearing

Coleman v. Alabama
Supreme Court of the United States
399 U.S. 1 (1970)

FACTS

An Alabama court convicted Coleman and some associates of assault with intent to murder a Mr. Reynolds. At the trial, Mr. Reynolds testified that he had been engaged in changing an automobile tire when three men approached him. One of the men shot Reynolds and there was evidence that Coleman put his hands on Mrs. Reynolds. As a car approached, the men ran away after one of them shot Reynolds a second time. The victims positively identified Coleman and the others as the perpetrators.

During the pretrial stage of the prosecution and at the preliminary hearing, the state of Alabama failed to furnish Coleman with legal representation to advise him of legal issues presented. Although Alabama law does not require a preliminary hearing, when one is held, a variety of defendant's rights become involved. Among the issues to be determined at an Alabama preliminary hearing are whether there is probable cause to present the case to the grand jury and whether to allow bail and in what amount

---

[499]*United States v. Newton,* 327 F.3d 17 (1st Cir. 2003).

for bailable crimes. Upon appeal, Coleman argued that Alabama's failure to provide him with appointed counsel at the preliminary hearing unconstitutionally violated the Sixth Amendment right to counsel, a "critical stage" of the prosecution.

PROCEDURAL ISSUE

Is an optional preliminary hearing, where a defendant is not required to advance any defenses and loses no potential defenses, considered a "critical stage" of the criminal justice process for which the right to counsel under the Sixth Amendment exists?

HELD: YES

RATIONALE

Mr. Justice Brennan announced the judgment of the Court and delivered the following opinion.

★ ★ ★

II

This Court has held that a person accused of a crime "requires the guiding hand of counsel at every step in the proceedings against him," *Powell v. Alabama,* 287 U.S. 45, 69 (1932), and that that constitutional principle is not limited to the presence of counsel at trial.

> It is central to that principle that in addition to counsel's presence at trial, the accused is guaranteed that he need not stand alone against the State at any stage of the prosecution, formal or informal, in court or out, where counsel's absence might derogate from the accused's right to a fair trial. *United States v. Wade, supra,* at 226.

Accordingly,

> the principle of *Powell v. Alabama* and succeeding cases requires that we scrutinize *any* pretrial confrontation of the accused to determine whether the presence of his counsel is necessary to preserve the defendant's basic right to a fair trial as affected by his right meaningfully to cross-examine the witnesses against him and have effective assistance of counsel at the trial itself. It calls upon us to analyze whether potential substantial prejudice to defendant's rights inheres in the particular confrontation and the ability of counsel to help avoid that prejudice. *Id.* at 227.

Applying this test, the Court has held that "critical stages" include the pretrial type of arraignment where certain rights may be sacrificed or lost, *Hamilton v. Alabama,* 368 U.S. 52 (1961). [Other citations omitted.] The preliminary hearing is not a required step in an Alabama prosecution. The prosecutor may seek an indictment directly from the grand jury without a preliminary hearing. *Ex parte Campbell,* 278 Ala. 114, 176 So.2d 242 (1965). The opinion of the Alabama Court of Appeals in this case instructs us that under Alabama law the sole purposes of a preliminary hearing are to determine whether there is sufficient evidence against the accused to warrant presenting his case to the grand jury, and if so to fix bail if the offense is bailable. The [Alabama] court continued:

> At the preliminary hearing…the accused is not required to advance any defenses, and failure to do so does not preclude him from availing himself of every defense he may have upon the trial of the case. Also *Pointer v. State of Texas* [380 U.S. 400 (1965)] bars the admission of testimony given at a pre-trial proceeding where the accused did not have the benefit of cross-examination by and through counsel. Thus, nothing occurring at the preliminary hearing in the absence of counsel can substantially prejudice the rights of the accused on trial. 44 Ala.App., at 433; 211 So.2d. at 921.

This Court is of course bound by this construction of the government of Alabama law. However, from the fact that in cases where the accused has no lawyer at the hearing the Alabama courts prohibit the State's use at trial of anything that occurred at the hearing, it does not follow that the Alabama preliminary hearing is not a "critical stage" of the State's criminal process. The determination whether the hearing is a "critical stage" requiring the provision of counsel depends, as noted, upon an analysis "whether potential substantial prejudice to the defendant's rights inheres in the…confrontation and the ability of counsel to help avoid that prejudice." *United States v. Wade, supra,* at 227. Plainly the guiding hand of counsel at the preliminary hearing is essential to protect the indigent accused against an erroneous or improper prosecution. First, the lawyer's skilled examination and cross-examination of witnesses may expose fatal weaknesses in the State's case, that may lead the magistrate to refuse to bind the accused over. Second, in any event, the skilled interrogation of witnesses by an experienced lawyer can fashion a vital impeachment tool for use in cross-examination of the State's witnesses at the trial, or preserve testimony favorable to the accused of a witness who does not appear at the trial. Third, trained counsel can more effectively discover the case the State has against his client and make possible the preparation of a proper defense to meet that case at the trial. Fourth, counsel can also be influential at the preliminary hearing in making effective arguments for the accused on such matters as the necessity for an early psychiatric examination or bail.

The inability of the indigent accused on his own to realize these advantages of a lawyer's assistance compels the conclusion that the Alabama preliminary hearing is a "critical stage" of the State's criminal process at which the accused is "as much entitled to such aid [of counsel]…as at the trial itself." *Powell v. Alabama, supra,* at 57.

III

There remains, then, the question of the relief to which petitioners are entitled. The trial transcript indicates that the prohibition against use by the State at trial of anything that occurred at the preliminary hearing was scrupulously observed. But on the record it cannot be said whether or not petitioners were otherwise prejudiced by the absence of counsel at the preliminary hearing. That inquiry in the first instance should more properly be made by the Alabama courts. The test to be applied is whether the denial of counsel at the preliminary hearing was harmless error under *Chapman v. California,* 368 U.S. 18 (1967). *See United States v. Wade, supra,* at 242.

We accordingly vacate the petitioner convictions and remand the case to the Alabama courts for such proceedings not inconsistent with this opinion as they may deem appropriate to determine whether such denial of counsel was harmless error and therefore whether the convictions should be reinstated or a new trial ordered.

It is so ordered.

COMMENTS, NOTES, AND QUESTIONS

1. Is failure to have counsel present at a preliminary hearing a wrong without a harm if nothing at the preliminary hearing could harm the case for Coleman? In *Coleman,* if the defendant could not lose any defense theories, how could the defendant be prejudiced by merely waiting for the later appointment of counsel? Would counsel be able to find out some of the state's theory of prosecution by requesting information during the discovery process?

2. Since Coleman did not object at his preliminary hearing, could it be argued that he waived any right to have counsel due to his silence? A failure to object may waive a double jeopardy claim or a speedy trial argument. Should this right at this stage be treated any differently? Would the average person know if a specific legal right exists at a particular stage in the legal process?

3. *Coleman* says that a defendant has a Sixth Amendment right to counsel at a preliminary hearing, and where such right was not accorded a defendant, the remedy of a new trial is available only if the case would have been decided differently by the trial court. How can a court, especially an appellate court, determine what would have happened? Is this a tough call to make? The test is called the "harmless error rule" from *Chapman v. California,* 368 U.S. 18 (1967), where if a reviewing court can say beyond a reasonable doubt that the outcome would not have been different if all rights had been given properly, there will be no reversal.

4. The right to counsel does not exist at all pretrial judicial proceedings and hearings. Where an arrest has been made without a warrant solely on the basis of a police officer's determination of probable cause, a judicial official must reconsider the officer's probable cause decision at a hearing, which may be nonadversarial. There is no right to counsel at a probable cause only hearing. Alternatively, when a judicial official has issued an arrest warrant prior to the arrest, the required determination of probable cause has been made and need not be done subsequent to the arrest, as a matter of routine procedure. See *Gerstein v. Pugh,* 420 U.S. 103 (1975).

CASE 12.2

Determining Bail: Individual Consideration of Factors Required

Stack v. Boyle
Supreme Court of the United States
342 U.S. 1 (1951)

FACTS

A federal grand jury returned an indictment against twelve defendants for violating the Smith Act, 18 U.S.C. sections 371 and 2385, that involved advocating the overthrow of the government of the United States and conspiracy with other conspirators to do the same. Subsequent to their arrest in New York, a federal district judge set bail at amounts ranging from $2,500 to $10,000.

One of the petitioners successfully moved for a reduction in bail prior to being moved to California to stand trial. When the defendants arrived in California, and pursuant to the prosecution's request that the amounts of bail be increased, the district court elevated bail to $50,000 for each defendant.

The petitioner filed a motion for a reduction in bail on the basis that the amount as determined violated the excessive bail prohibition of the Eighth Amendment. In support of the motion for bail reduction, the petitioners cited their varying financial situations, family relationships, health, prior criminal records, and other information. The prosecution did not focus on individual characteristics of each defendant during the bail reconsideration hearing. In opposition to the bail amount change, the prosecution argued that since other persons previously convicted of violating the Smith Act had jumped bail, a high bail was absolutely necessary for these defendants.

The federal district court denied the motion to reduce bail and refused to grant a motion for a writ of habeas corpus. The two decisions were affirmed by the Court of Appeals for the Ninth Circuit and the Supreme Court of the United States granted certiorari.

PROCEDURAL ISSUE

In a federal prosecution, is the amount of bail considered excessive where it is set without reference to individual circumstances in an amount greater than the minimum level necessary to assure the appearance of each defendant for all appropriate times?

HELD: YES

RATIONALE

Mr. Chief Justice Vinson delivered the opinion of the Court.

★ ★ ★

From the passage of the Judiciary Act of 1789, 1 Stat. 73, 91, the present Federal Rules of Criminal Procedure, Rule 46(a)(1), 18 U.S.C.A., federal law has unequivocally provided that a person arrested for a non-capital offense shall be admitted to bail. This traditional right to freedom before conviction permits the unhampered preparation of a defense, and serves to prevent the infliction of punishment prior to conviction. Unless this right to bail before trial is preserved, the presumption of innocence, secured only after centuries of struggle, would lose its meaning.

The right to release before trial is conditioned upon the accused's giving adequate assurance that he will stand trial and submit to sentence if found guilty. *Ex parte Milburn,* (1835) 9 Pet. 704, 710, 9 L.Ed. 280. Like the ancient practice of securing the oaths of responsible persons to stand as sureties for the accused, the modern practice of requiring a bail bond or the deposit of a sum of money subject to forfeiture serves as additional assurance of the presence of an accused. Bail set at a figure higher than an amount reasonably calculated to fulfill this purpose is "excessive" under the Eighth Amendment.

Since the function of bail is limited, the fixing of bail for any individual defendant must be based upon standards relevant to the purpose of assuring the presence of that defendant. The traditional standards as expressed in Federal Rules of Criminal Procedure are to be applied in each case to each defendant. In this case petitioners are charged with offenses under the Smith Act and, if found guilty, their convictions are subject to review with the scrupulous care demanded by our Constitution. Upon final judgment of conviction, petitioners face imprisonment of not more than five years and a fine of not more than $10,000. It is not denied that bail for each petitioner has been fixed in a sum much higher than usually imposed for offenses with like penalties and yet there has been no factual showing to justify such action in this case. The Government asks the courts to depart from the norm by assuming, without the introduction of evidence, that each petitioner is a pawn in a conspiracy and will, in obedience to a superior, flee the jurisdiction....

If bail in an amount greater than that usually fixed for serious charges of crimes is required in the case of any of the petitioners, that is a matter to which evidence should be directed in a hearing so that the constitutional rights of each petitioner may be preserved. In the absence of such a showing, we are of the opinion that the fixing of bail before trial in these cases cannot be squared with the statutory and constitutional standards for admission to bail.

★ ★ ★

The Court concludes that bail has not been fixed by proper methods in this case and that petitioners' remedy is by motion to reduce bail, with right of appeal to the Court of Appeals. Accordingly, the judgment of the Court of Appeals is vacated and the case is remanded to the District Court with directions to vacate its order denying petitioners' applications for writs of habeas corpus and to dismiss the applications without prejudice.

Petitioners may move for reduction of bail in the criminal proceeding so that a hearing may be held for the purpose of fixing reasonable bail for each petitioner.

It is so ordered.

COMMENTS, NOTES, AND QUESTIONS

1. Consistent with the federal bail statute provisions in force at the time, pretrial bail for the defendants in *Stack* was a possibility, and the first court to consider bail fixed it at different amounts for each defendant. As a consequence, the original court determined that the appropriate level of bail for each man, who presumably was differently situated than each of the others, would vary with individual circumstances. When the defendants arrived in California, bail was reconsidered by the California federal court. Should the bail for each defendant have been the same? Why or why not? Hypothetically, what factors could you suggest that would vary the amounts of bail for each of the defendants? What factor or factors would cause you as a judge to deny bail to one of the defendants?

2. In arriving at a bail determination, judges must decide whether to grant it, specify the amount, and consider any additional conditions that should be included. Judges have looked to the defendant's relationship with the local community, including business, family, and religious ties. Consideration is given to the seriousness of the crime; the penalty, if convicted; the strength of the prosecution's case; whether the defendant would intimidate potential witnesses; prior bail history, if any; relative wealth of the defendant; and the chance that the defendant would commit new crimes while on bail. At best, the decision concerning whether or not to grant bail and determining the amount is a calculated attempt to foretell the defendant's future conduct.

3. Would there be any reasons to alter the amount or conditions of bail once they have been determined by a court? What could the defendant do that would make the original bail determination no longer appropriate? Should it make any difference if the prosecution discovers other crimes that were not known at the time the original bail amount had been determined? Once pretrial bail has been set, as a general rule, either side may move for an addition or reduction of bail or for a change in bail conditions. Release on bail can be revoked for the commission of alleged new crimes, or the monetary amount may be lowered for good cause shown by the defendant.

4. In 1984, Congress amended the federal bail statutes to change the basic philosophy in many respects. Under the former law (the one in *Stack v. Boyle*), there was a basic presumption that most people arrested would be entitled to pretrial bail. In the time before the bail law was revisited by Congress in 1984, many persons who were accused of various drug violations, including trafficking, would pay their bail and then disappear to parts of the world beyond the jurisdiction of the United States. The new law provided that some individuals would not be admitted to bail regardless of the arguments of their counsel during the pretrial stage. A refusal to set bail could be argued by the government if a particular case involved crimes of violence, offenses for which the sentence could be life imprisonment or death, serious drug offenses, or certain repeat offenders. The philosophy appeared to reverse the theory that most people would have some level of bail set by the trial court during the pretrial stage.

CASE 12.3

Constitutionality of Pretrial Detention Statutes and Denial of Bail

United States v. Salerno
Supreme Court of the United States
481 U.S. 739 (1987)

FACTS

Agents of the United States government arrested Anthony Salerno and Vincent Cafaro after a federal grand jury returned a twenty-nine-count indictment which alleged several Racketeer Influenced and Corrupt Organizations (RICO) Act violations, mail and wire fraud, extortion, and various other crimes. The prosecution moved to have the men detained in custody, without bail, prior to trial under Section 3142(e) of the Bail Reform Act of 1984. According to arguments offered by federal prosecutors, bail should be denied because there existed no conditions of pretrial release which could assure the safety of the community or any person and which would ensure that Salerno would be present for trial.

At the bail hearing, the prosecutor offered evidence that Salerno was the leader of the Genovese Family of La Cosa Nostra and that Cafaro served as a "captain" in the same criminal organization. The government produced evidence the defendants had participated in several violent conspiracies, including two which involved murder.

Salerno questioned the credibility of the prosecutor's witnesses while he offered several character witnesses on his behalf. The District Court granted the prosecutor's motion to deny bail and to hold the defendants in custody since the judge concluded that the men, if on bail, would continue their organized crime activities and would expose the community to threats and future harm. Above all, the court concluded that they would continue their ongoing criminal enterprises. The District Court noted:

> The activities of a criminal organization such as the Genovese Family do not cease with the arrest of its principals and their release on even the most stringent of bail conditions. The illegal businesses, in place for many years, require constant attention and protection, or they will fail. Under these circumstances, this court recognizes a strong incentive on the part of its leadership to continue business as usual. When business as usual involves threats, beatings, and murder, the present danger such people pose in the community is self-evident. 631 F.Supp. 1364, 1375 (SDNY 1986).

Salerno and Cafaro successfully appealed the denial of bail and the pretrial detention order to the Court of Appeals. In construing the Bail Reform Act of 1984, the Court of Appeals concluded that due process would be violated if the courts permitted the government to detain persons who had been accused of crime merely because of a thought that the men might present a present danger to the community. The Supreme Court granted certiorari.

PROCEDURAL QUESTION

Consistent with the Eighth Amendment's provision on bail, may the federal government enforce a bail statute which permits pretrial, preconviction denial of bail upon proof of present or potential future danger to any person or danger to the community?

HELD: YES

RATIONALE

Chief Justice Rehnquist delivered the opinion of the Court.

The Bail Reform Act of 1984 allows a federal court to detain an arrestee pending trial if the Government demonstrates by clear and convincing evidence after an adversary hearing that no release conditions "will reasonably assure…the safety of any other person and the community." The United States Court of Appeals for the Second Circuit struck down this provision of the Act as facially unconstitutional, because, in the court's words, this type of pretrial detention violates "substantive due process." We granted certiorari because of a conflict among the Courts of Appeal regarding the validity of the Act. 479 U.S. 929 (1986). We hold that, as against the facial attack mounted by these respondents, the Act fully comports with constitutional requirements. We therefore reverse.

★ ★ ★

The Court of Appeals…found our decision in *Schall v. Martin,* 467 U.S. 253 (1984), upholding postarrest pretrial detention of juveniles, inapposite because juveniles have a lesser interest in liberty than do adults.

★ ★ ★

II

★ ★ ★

Respondents present two grounds for invalidating the Bail Reform Act's provisions permitting pretrial detention on the basis of future dangerousness. First, they rely upon the Court of Appeals' conclusion that the Act exceeds the limitations placed upon the Federal Government by the Due Process Clause of the Fifth Amendment. Second, they contend that the Act contravenes the Eighth Amendment's proscription against excessive bail. We treat these contentions in turn.

A

★ ★ ★

Respondents first argue that the Act violates substantive due process because the pretrial detention it authorizes constitutes impermissible punishment before trial. See *Bell v. Wolfish,* 441 U.S. 520, 535 (1979). The Government, however, has never argued that pretrial detention could be upheld if it were "punishment." The Court of Appeals assumed that pretrial detention under the Bail Reform Act is regulatory, not penal, and we agree that it is.

★ ★ ★

The legislative history of the Bail Reform Act clearly indicates that Congress did not formulate the pretrial detention provisions as punishment for dangerous individuals. Congress instead perceived pretrial detention as a potential solution to a pressing societal problem. There is no doubt that preventing danger to the community is a legitimate regulatory goal.

Nor are the incidents of pretrial detention excessive in relation to the regulatory goal Congress sought to achieve. The Bail Reform Act carefully limits the circumstances under which detention may be sought to the most serious of crimes. See 18 U.S.C. 3142(f) (detention hearings available if case involves crimes of violence, offenses for which the sentence is life imprisonment or death, serious drug offenses, or certain repeat offenders). The arrestee is entitled to a prompt detention hearing, *Ibid.,* and the maximum length of pretrial detention is limited by the stringent time limitations of the Speedy Trial Act. See 18 U.S.C. 3161 et seq. (1982 ed and Supp III). Moreover, as in *Schall v. Martin,* the conditions of confinement envisioned by the Act "appear to reflect the regulatory purposes relied upon by the" Government. 467 U.S. at 270. As in *Schall,* the statute at issue here requires that detainees be housed in a "facility separate, to the extent practicable, from persons awaiting or serving sentences or being held in custody pending appeal." 18 U.S.C. § 3142(i)(2). We conclude, therefore, that the pretrial detention contemplated by the Bail Reform Act is regulatory in nature, and does not constitute punishment before trial in violation of the Due Process Clause.

The Court of Appeals nevertheless concluded that

> the Due Process Clause prohibits pretrial detention on the ground of danger to the community as a regulatory measure, without regard to the duration of the detention. 794 F.2d 71.

Respondents characterize the Due Process Clause as erecting an impenetrable "wall" in this area that "no governmental interest—rational, important, compelling or otherwise—may surmount." Brief for Respondents 16.

★ ★ ★

The government's interest in preventing crime by arrestees is both legitimate and compelling. [Citation omitted]....The Bail Reform Act, in contrast, narrowly focuses on a particularly acute problem in which the Government interests are overwhelming. The Act operates only on individuals who have been arrested for a specific category of extremely serious offenses. 18 U.S.C. 3142(f). Congress specifically found that these individuals are far more likely to be responsible for dangerous acts in the community after arrest. Nor is the Act by any means a scattershot attempt to incapacitate those who are merely suspected of these serious crimes. The Government must first of all demonstrate probable cause to believe that the charged crime has been committed by the arrestee, but that is not enough. In a full-blown adversary hearing, the Government must convince a neutral decision maker by clear and convincing evidence that no conditions of release can reasonably assure the safety of the community or any person. 18 U.S.C. 3142(f). . . . While the Government's general interest in preventing crime is compelling, even this interest is heightened when the Government musters convincing proof that the arrestee, already indicted or held to answer for a serious crime, presents a demonstrable danger to the community. Under these narrow circumstances, society's interest in crime prevention is at its greatest.

★ ★ ★

Finally, we may dispose briefly of respondents' facial challenge to the procedures of the Bail Reform Act. To sustain them against such a challenge, we need only find them "adequate to authorize the pretrial detention of at least some [persons] charged with crimes." *Schall, supra,* at 264, whether or not they might be insufficient in some particular circumstances. We think they pass that test. As we stated in *Schall,* "there is nothing inherently unattainable about a prediction of future criminal conduct." 467 U.S. at 278. [Other citations omitted.]

★ ★ ★

Given the legitimate and compelling regulatory purpose of the Act and the procedural protections it offers, we conclude that the Act is not facially invalid under the Due Process Clause of the Fifth Amendment.

B

Respondents also contend that the Bail Reform Act violates the Excessive Bail Clause of the Eighth Amendment. The Court of Appeals did not address this issue because it found that the Act violates the Due Process Clause. We think that the Act survives a challenge founded upon the Eighth Amendment.

The Eighth Amendment addresses pretrial release by providing merely that "[e]xcessive bail shall not be required."

This Clause, of course, says nothing about whether bail shall be available at all. Respondents nevertheless contend that this Clause grants them a right to bail calculated solely upon considerations of flight. They rely on *Stack v. Boyle,* 342 U.S. 1, 5 (1951), in which the Court stated that "[b]ail set at a figure higher than an amount reasonably calculated [to ensure the defendant's presence at trial] is 'excessive' under the Eighth Amendment." In respondents' view, since the Bail Reform Act allows a court essentially to set bail at an infinite amount for reasons not related to the risk of flight, it violates the Excessive Bail Clause. Respondents concede that the right to bail they have discovered in the Eighth Amendment is not absolute. A court may, for example, refuse bail in capital cases. And, as the Court of Appeals noted and respondents admit, a court may refuse bail when the defendant presents a threat to the judicial process by intimidating witnesses.

★ ★ ★

The holding of *Stack* is illuminated by the Court's holding just four months later in *Carlson v. Landon,* 342 U.S. 524 (1952). In that case, remarkably similar to the present action, the detainees had been arrested and held without bail pending a determination of deportability. The Attorney General refused to release the individuals, "on the ground that there was reasonable cause to believe that [their] release would be prejudicial to the public interest and *would endanger the welfare and safety of the United States.*" *Id.,* at 529 (emphasis added). The detainees brought the same challenge that respondents bring to us today: the Eighth Amendment required them to be admitted to bail. The Court squarely rejected this proposition:

> The bail clause was lifted with slight changes from the English Bill of Rights Act. In England that clause has never been thought to accord a right to bail in all cases, but merely to provide that bail shall not be excessive in those cases where it is proper to grant bail. When this clause was carried over into our Bill of Rights, nothing was said that indicated any different concept. The Eighth Amendment has not prevented Congress from defining the classes of cases in which bail shall be allowed in this country. Thus, in criminal cases bail is not compulsory where the punishment may be death. Indeed, the very language of the Amendment fails to say all arrests must be bailable. *Id.,* at 545–546.

★ ★ ★

We believe that when Congress has mandated detention on the basis of a compelling interest other than prevention of flight, as it has here, the Eighth Amendment does require release on bail.

III

★ ★ ★

The judgment of the Court of Appeals is therefore reversed.

Justice Marshall, with whom Justice Brennan joins, dissenting.

This case brings before the Court for the first time a statute in which Congress declares that a person innocent of any crime may be jailed indefinitely, pending the trial of allegations which are legally presumed to be untrue, if the Government shows to the satisfaction of a judge that the accused is likely to commit crimes, unrelated to the pending charges, at any time in the future. Such statutes, consistent with the usages of tyranny and the excesses of what bitter experience teaches us to call the police state, have long been thought incompatible with the fundamental human rights protected by our Constitution. Today a majority of this Court holds otherwise. Its decision disregards basic principles of justice established centuries ago and enshrined beyond the reach of governmental interference in the Bill of Rights.

COMMENTS, NOTES, AND QUESTIONS

1. Is the Court's acceptance, that a denial of bail under the Bail Reform Act of 1984 constitutes mere regulation of the process and regulation of the individual and is not punitive in nature, dispositive of the Eight Amendment issue? Should it be? One could make the argument that since an accused person has not been convicted, any pretrial detention really constitutes punishment, no matter what label is attached to the practice. Because an individual under custody has not been to trial and has not been convicted, pretrial detention cannot be used as punishment. The bail statutes must clearly indicate that the intent is not punishment or the law will be subject to arguments of unconstitutionality.

2. Consider Justice Marshall's dissent and his assertion that the government could jail a defendant indefinitely. Would there be no outer limit to the time a defendant could be held without trial? Consider the effect of the Sixth Amendment right to a speedy trial and

the federal Speedy Trial Act. The combination of the Sixth Amendment and that act would appear to negate Justice Marshall's conclusion, at least for federal prosecutions. Most assuredly, a defendant could not be held longer than the statute of limitations that applied to a particular crime. However, not all crimes in all jurisdictions carry statutes of limitations, so theoretically, there may be a valid point to his argument.

3. Does the legislature set the basic law governing bailable offenses? In a given case, who potentially determines whether bail shall be available? The judge? The prosecutor? How much weight should be given to the seriousness and type of crimes with which the person has been accused of committing? The granting of bail is, at best, an educated guess concerning how the defendant will act and how he or she will behave during the pretrial and trial stage of the criminal justice process. As is the case with most forecasting of future human conduct, our predictions are often incorrect.

CASE 12.4

Effects of Failure to Hold Timely Pretrial Detention Hearing

United States v. Montalvo-Murillo
Supreme Court of the United States
495 U.S. 711 (1990)

FACTS

United States Customs Service agents stopped respondent at a New Mexico checkpoint near the Mexican border on February 8, 1989. Federal agents lawfully discovered approximately 72 pounds of cocaine hidden in respondent's truck. Montalvo-Murillo readily admitted to federal agents that he had plans to deliver the cocaine to purchasers in Chicago. Drug Enforcement Administration (DEA) officers persuaded Montalvo-Murillo to help them make a controlled delivery to the purchaser in Illinois.

When the buyers failed to appear, making the controlled delivery a failure, federal agents took respondent before a United States magistrate for an initial appearance. The defendant's day in court occurred two days after his initial arrest and resulted in an agreement between the government and Montalvo-Murillo that any bail or detention hearing would be held upon his transfer to New Mexico. Following his removal back to the juris-

diction of his arrest, the DEA requested a detention hearing on February 13, pursuant to the Bail Reform Act of 1984. At the first New Mexico detention hearing, and since the government did not have all of its paperwork completed, the magistrate's decision was delayed. As a result of the actual detention hearing on February 21, respondent was ordered released on $50,000 bond by the United States magistrate.

Pursuant to a *de novo* hearing on February 23, 1989, the District Court found that no condition of release would assure respondent's appearance or secure the safety of the community. However, the Court upheld the magistrate's decision to grant pretrial bail since the detention hearing had not been held upon respondent's first appearance as required by Section 3142(f) of the Bail Reform Act. The remedy for the violation of defendant Montalvo-Murillo's statutory rights under the Bail Reform Act, according to the District Court, under such circumstances was to release him under appropriate conditions.

As might have been predicted, once the Court released Montalvo-Murillo on bail, he skipped bail, becoming a federal fugitive, and he was not seen again.

The United States Supreme Court granted certiorari since federal circuit courts of appeal had rendered conflicting opinions concerning the remedy for a defendant where the government had not held detention hearings according to the statutory timetable.

PROCEDURAL ISSUE

Must a defendant be granted bail under the Bail Reform Act of 1984, where the government fails to comply with the legal requirements of a prompt detention hearing?

HELD: NO

RATIONALE

Justice Kennedy delivered the opinion of the Court.

★ ★ ★

Two provisions of the Bail Reform Act are relevant. The substantive provisions that allow detention are contained in subsection (e):

DETENTION—If, after a hearing pursuant to the provisions of subsection (f) of this section, the judicial officer finds that no condition or combination of conditions will reasonably assure the appearance of the person as required and the safety of any other person and the community, [he] shall order the detention of the person before trial.... Section 3142(e).

The controversy in this case centers around the procedures for a hearing, found in subsection (f):

DETENTION HEARING—The judicial officer shall hold a hearing to determine whether any condition or combination of conditions...will reasonably assure the appearance of such person as required and the safety of any other person and the community....

The hearing shall be held immediately upon the person's first appearance before the judicial officer unless that person, or the attorney for the Government, seeks a continuance. Except for good cause, a continuance on motion of the person may not exceed five days, and a continuance on motion of the attorney for the Government may not exceed three days. During a continuance, such person shall be detained....The person may be detained pending completion of the hearing.... Section 1342(f).

★ ★ ★

The sole question presented on certiorari is whether the Court of Appeals was correct in holding that respondent must be released as a remedy for the failure to hold a hearing at his first appearance.

II

In *United States v. Salerno,* 481 U.S. 739 (1987), we upheld the Bail Reform Act of 1984 against constitutional challenge. Though we did not refer in *Salerno* to the time limits for hearings as a feature which sustained the constitutionality of the Act, we recognize that a vital liberty interest is at stake. A prompt hearing is necessary, and the time limitations of the Act must be followed with care and precision. But the act is silent on the issue of a remedy for violations of its time limits. Neither the timing requirements nor any other part of the Act can be read to require, or even suggest, that a timing error must result in release of a person who should otherwise be detained.

The Act...requires pretrial detention of certain persons charged with federal crimes, and directs a judicial officer to detain a person charged, pending trial, if the Government has made the necessary showing of dangerousness or risk of flight. 18 U.S.C. Sections 3142(e), (f). The Act authorizes detention "after a hearing [held] pursuant to the provisions of subsection (f) of

this section." Section 3142(e). Subsection (f) provides that "[t]he judicial officer shall hold a hearing" and sets forth the applicable procedures. Nothing in Section 3142(f) indicates that compliance with the first appearance requirement is a precondition to holding the hearing or that failure to comply with the requirement renders such a hearing a nullity. It is conceivable that some combination of procedural irregularities could render a detention hearing so flawed that it would not constitute "a hearing pursuant to the provisions of subsection (f)" for purposes of Section 3142(e). A failure to comply with the first appearance requirement, however, does not so subvert the procedural scheme of Section 3142(f) as to invalidate the hearing. The contrary interpretation—that noncompliance with the time provisions in Section 3142(f) requires the release even of a person who presumptively should be detained under Section 3142(e)—would defeat the purpose of the Act.

We hold that a failure to comply with the first appearance requirement does not defeat the Government's authority to seek detention of the person charged. We reject the contention that if there had been a deviation from the time limits of the statute, the hearing necessarily is not one conducted "pursuant to the provisions of subsection (f)." There is no presumption or general rule that for every duty imposed upon the court or the government and its prosecutors there must exist some corollary punitive sanction for departures or omissions, even if negligent. See *French v. Edwards,* 13 Wall. 506, 511 (1872) ("[M]any statutory requisitions intended for the guide of officers in the conduct of business devolved upon them...do not limit their power or render its exercise in disregard of the requisitions ineffectual"). In our view, construction of the Act must conform to the "'great principle of public policy, applicable to all governments alike, which forbids that the public interests should be prejudiced by the negligence of the officers or agents to whose care they are confided.'" *Brock v. Pierce County,* 476 U.S. 253, 260 (1986) (quoting *United States v. Nashville, C & St. L. R. Co.,* 118 U.S. 120, 125 (1886)).

In *Brock v. Pierce County, supra,* the Court addressed a statute that stated that the Secretary of Labor "shall" act within a certain time on information concerning misuse of federal funds. The respondents there argued that a failure to act within the specified time divested the Secretary of authority to act to investigate a claim. We read the statute to mean that the Secretary did not lose the power to recover misused funds after the expiration of the time period. Congress' mere use of the word "shall" was not enough to remove the Secretary's power to act. ("We would be most reluctant to conclude that every failure of an agency to observe a procedural requirement voids subsequent agency action, especially when important public rights are at stake. When, as here, there are less drastic remedies available for failure to meet a statutory deadline, courts should not assume that Congress intended the agency to lose its power to act").

★ ★ ★

Our conclusion is consistent with the design and function of the statute. We have sustained the Bail Reform Act of 1984 as an appropriate regulatory device to assure the safety of persons in the community and to protect against the risk of flight. We have upheld the substantive right to detain based upon the Government's meeting the burden required by the statute. *United States v. Salerno,* 481 U.S. 739 (1987). Automatic release contravenes the object of the statute, to provide fair bail procedures while protecting the safety of the public and assuring the appearance at trial of defendants found likely to flee. The end of exacting compliance with the letter of Section 3142(f) cannot justify the means of exposing the public to an increased likelihood of violent crime by persons on bail, an evil the statute aims to prevent....The safety of society does not become forfeit to the accident of non-compliance with statutory time limits where the Government is ready and able to come forward with the requisite showing to meet the burden of proof required by the statute.

★ ★ ★

We find nothing in the statute to justify denying the Government an opportunity to prove that the person is dangerous or a risk of flight once the statutory time for hearing has passed. We do not agree that we should, or can, invent a remedy to satisfy some perceived need to coerce the courts and the Government into complying with the statutory time limits. Magistrates and district judges can be presumed to insist upon compliance with the law without the threat that we must embarrass the system by releasing a suspect certain to flee from justice, as this one did in such a deft and prompt manner. The district court, the court of appeals, and this Court remain open to order immediate release of anyone detained in violation of the statute. Whatever other remedies may exist for detention without a timely hearing or for conduct that is aggravated or intentional, a matter not before

us here, we hold that once the Government discovers that the time limits have expired, it may ask for a prompt detention hearing and make its case to detain based upon the requirements set forth in the statute.

★ ★ ★

We hold that respondent was not, and is not, entitled to release as a sanction for the delay in the case before us.

The judgment of the Court of Appeals is

Reversed.

Justice Stevens, with whom Justice Brennan and Justice Marshall join, dissenting.

This case involves two lawbreakers. Respondent, as the Court repeatedly argues,... failed to appear after his release on bail, an apparent violation of 18 U.S.C. Section 3146. Even before that, however, the Government imprisoned respondent without a timely hearing, a conceded violation of 18 U.S.C. Section 3142. In its haste to ensure the detention of respondent, the Court readily excuses the Government's prior and proven violation of the law. I cannot agree.

I

★ ★ ★

Our historical approach eschewing detention prior to trial reflects these concerns:

> From the passage of the Judiciary Act of 1789, 1 Stat. 73, 91, to the present Federal Rules of Criminal Procedure, Rule 46(a)(1), federal law has unequivocally provided that a person arrested for a non-capital offense *shall* be admitted to bail. This traditional right to freedom before conviction permits the unhampered preparation of a defense, and serves to prevent the infliction of punishment prior to conviction. See *Hudson v. Parker,* 156 U.S. 277, 285 (1895). Unless this right to bail before trial is preserved, the presumption of innocence, secured only after centuries of struggle, would lose its meaning. *Stack v. Boyle,* 342 U.S. 1, 4 (1951).

Sections 3142(e) and (f), allowing limited detention of arrestees, were enacted against this historical backdrop. Bail Reform Act of 1984, Publ. L. 98-473, 98 Stat. 1976, 18 U.S.C. Sections 3142(e), (f).

★ ★ ★

Section 3142(e) permits pretrial detention only

> [i]f, after a hearing pursuant to the provisions of subsection (f) of this section, the judicial officer finds that no condition or combination of conditions will reasonably assure the appearance of the person as required and the safety of any other person and the community. 18 U.S.C. Section 3142(e).

Subsection (f) in turn sets forth specific deadlines, chosen "in light of the fact that the defendant will be detained during such a continuance." S. Rep. No. 98–225, at 22, within which a detention hearing must be held:

> The hearing shall be held immediately upon the person's first appearance before the judicial officer unless that person, or the attorney for the Government, seeks a continuance. Except for good cause, a continuance on motion of such person may not exceed five days, and a continuance on motion of the attorney for the Government may not exceed three days. 18 U.S.C. Section 3142(f)(2).

There was no such hearing—or finding of good cause for continuance—when respondent was arrested on February 8, 1989, when he first appeared before a Northern District of Illinois Magistrate on February 10, or when the New Mexico Magistrate convened the parties on February 16. No court considered the basis of detention until February 21, after respondent had been incarcerated for 13 days.

★ ★ ★

A federal prosecutor should have no difficulty comprehending the unequivocal terms of Section 3142(f)(2) and complying with its deadlines by proceeding or obtaining a proper continuance at the arrestee's first appearance. The rare failure to meet the requirements of subsection (f) will mean only that the Government forfeits the opportunity to seek pretrial detention in that case. Because the provisions of Section 3142(f)(2) are a prerequisite only for hearings to consider this particular form of pretrial action, the prosecutor still may seek any conditions of release that are "reasonably necessary to assure the appearance of the person as required and to assure the safety of any other person and the community." 18 U.S.C. Section 3142 (c)(1)(B)(xiv). The range of options—the sole safeguards that were available in cases prior to the creation of the special detention provisions in 1984—remain viable.

II

The Court, however, concludes that no adverse consequences should flow from the prosecutor's violation of this plain statutory command. Treating the case as comparable to an agency's failure to audit promptly a grant recipient's use of federal funds, see *Brock v. Pierce County*, 476 U.S. 253 (1986), the Court concludes that there is no reason to penalize the public for a prosecutor's mistake. If a belated hearing eventually results in a determination that detention was justified, the error has been proved harmless. The Court apparently discards the possibility that the hearing might result in a determination that the arrestee is eligible for release—as the Magistrate so determined in this case—or that detention of any arrestee before establishing the legality of that intrusion on liberty could "affect substantial rights." 876 F.2d 826, 829 (CA10 1989); Fed. Rule Crim. Proc. 52(a). A harmless-error analysis fails to appreciate the gravity of the deprivation of liberty that physical detention imposes and the reality that "[r]elief in this type of case must be speedy if it is to be effective." *Stack*, 342 U.S., at 4.

★ ★ ★

I respectfully dissent.

COMMENTS, NOTES, AND QUESTIONS

1. If a defendant violates a criminal law of the United States government, people generally agree that there should be some penalty for the wrong act. When the federal government is the wrongdoer and fails to follow the clear dictates of a law which requires that a defendant receive various procedural benefits, should the government be penalized for breaking its own law? Why or why not? When a government agent violates the Fourth Amendment during a search, the government gets penalized by virtue of the exclusion of evidence from the criminal trial. Should the law provide for some benefit to a defendant when the government fails to follow its own laws? Or would such a penalty be a penalty against the whole population when a probable lawbreaker gains freedom to prey upon innocent people?

2. The Court held in *Montalvo-Murillo* that the person who has been detained in violation of the Bail Reform Act of 1984 has no remedy of release if a detention hearing is not held in accordance with law. Should there be a financial remedy for a detainee where the government breaks one of its laws? Do the dissenters have a valid point?

3. The Bail Reform Act of 1984 uses the word *shall* in its usually understood sense. According to the majority, we should not allow an accused person freedom as a remedy for a prosecutor's mistake, but should some action against a prosecutor be considered? Should the prosecutor suffer some sort of personal penalty for not following or trying to follow the clear dictate of the law? Personal loss of money? Internal discipline? Would discipline for the prosecutor help the individual defendant? Should it make a difference if a prosecutor deliberately delayed seeking a detention hearing for the explicit reason of keeping an arrestee in close custody?

CASE 12.5

Denial of the Right to a Speedy Trial: Four-Factors Test

Barker v. Wingo
Supreme Court of the United States
407 U.S. 514 (1972)

FACTS

Following the brutal killings of an elderly couple, Silas Manning and Willie Barker, the petitioner, were indicted for the murders. The trial court appointed attorneys for the pair on September 17 and set a tentative trial date of October 21, 1958. Since the Commonwealth of Kentucky had a stronger case against Manning and the prosecutor felt that Barker could only be convicted if Manning testified against Barker, the trial court granted the first of what eventually became sixteen continuances. Barker's trial finally began on October 9, 1963, some five years following his murder indictment. Barker spent ten months in custody prior to being released on pretrial bail.

The primary reason for the lengthy delay prior to Barker's trial was the difficulty of obtaining a valid conviction of Manning, so that Manning could be forced to testify against Barker. Subsequent delays involved the prosecutor and the health of his witnesses. Following Manning's conviction, the prosecutor requested a continuance of Barker's case for the twelfth time and Barker objected. The court granted the twelfth continuance in February 1962, and two subsequent continuances in June and September of 1962. Barker did not object to the latter two continuances. In February 1963, Barker's trial was set for March 19. On the March trial date, the prosecutor requested another continuance to which Barker objected and requested a dismissal of the case. The judge set the

case for a June trial in 1963. The June trial date came and went due to the continued illness of the former sheriff. The trial court announced that if the case were not tried in the October term of court for 1963, that the case would be dismissed with prejudice.

At the October trial, Manning testified against Barker with the result that Barker was convicted of murdering the elderly couple and sentenced to life in prison. Barker argued that his trial should never have occurred because his rights under the the speedy trial provision of the Sixth Amendment had been violated and the case should have been dismissed. The Supreme Court of the United States granted certiorari to consider whether the Sixth Amendment right to a speedy trial had been violated.

PROCEDURAL ISSUE

Where the prosecution delays a trial for valid reasons for longer than five years following an indictment for legitimate reasons, does the length of the delay by itself violate the Sixth Amendment right to a speedy trial?

HELD: NO

RATIONALE

Mr. Justice Powell delivered the opinion of the Court.

Although a speedy trial is guaranteed the accused by the Sixth Amendment to the Constitution, this Court has dealt with that right on infrequent occasions.

★ ★ ★

II

The right to a speedy trial is generically different from any of the other rights enshrined in the Constitution for the protection of the accused. In addition to the general concern that all accused persons be treated according to decent and fair procedures, there is a societal interest in providing a speedy trial which exists separate from, and at times in opposition to, the interests of the accused.

★ ★ ★

A second difference between the right to speedy trial and the accused's other constitutional rights is that deprivation of the right may work to the accused's advantage. Delay is not an uncommon defense tactic. As the time between the commission of the crime and trial lengthens, witnesses may become unavailable or their memories may fade. If the witnesses support the prosecution, its case will be weakened, sometimes seriously so....

Finally, and perhaps most importantly, the right to speedy trial is a more vague concept than other procedural rights. It is, for example, impossible to determine with precision when the right has been denied. We cannot definitely say how long is too long in a system where justice is supposed to be swift but deliberate. As a consequence, there is no fixed point in the criminal process when the State can put the defendant to the choice of either exercising or waiving the right to a speedy trial.

★ ★ ★

The amorphous quality of the right also leads to the unsatisfactorily severe remedy of dismissal of the indictment when the right has been deprived. This is indeed a serious consequence because it means that a defendant who may be guilty of a serious crime will go free, without having been tried. Such a remedy is more serious than an exclusionary rule or a reversal for a new trial, but it is the only possible remedy.

III

Perhaps because the speedy trial right is so slippery, two rigid approaches are urged upon us as ways of eliminating some of the uncertainty which courts experience in protecting the right. The first suggestion is that we hold that the Constitution requires a criminal defendant to be offered a trial within a specified time period. The result of such a ruling would have the virtue of clarifying when the right is infringed and of simplifying courts' application of it.

★ ★ ★

We find no constitutional basis for holding that the speedy trial right can be quantified into a specified number of days or months. The States, of course, are free to prescribe a reasonable period consistent with constitutional standards, but our approach must be less precise.

The second suggested alternative would restrict consideration of the right to those cases in which the accused has demanded a speedy trial. Most States have recognized what is loosely referred to as the "demand rule," although eight States reject it.... Under this rigid approach, a prior demand is a necessary condition to the consideration of the speedy trial right....

Such an approach, by presuming waiver of a fundamental right from inaction, is inconsistent with this Court's pronouncements on waiver of constitutional rights. The Court has defined waiver as "an intentional relinquishment or abandonment of a known right or privilege." *Johnson v. Zerbst,* 304 U.S. 458, 464 (1938). [Other citations omitted.] In *Carnley v. Cochran,* 369 U.S. 506 (1962), we held:

> Presuming waiver from a silent record is impermissible. The record must show, or there must be an allegation and evidence which show, that an accused was offered counsel but intelligently and understandably rejected the offer. Anything less is not waiver. *Id.* at 516.

★ ★ ★

We reject, therefore, the rule that a defendant who fails to demand a speedy trial forever waives his right. This does not mean, however, that the defendant has no responsibility to assert his right. We think the better rule is that the defendant's assertion of or failure to assert his right to a speedy trial is one of the factors to be considered in an inquiry into the deprivation of the right.

★ ★ ★

We, therefore, reject both of the inflexible approaches—the fixed-time period because it goes further than the Constitution requires; the demand-waiver rule because it is insensitive to a right which we have deemed fundamental. The approach we accept is a balancing test, in which the conduct of both the prosecution and the defendant are weighed.

IV

A balancing test necessarily compels courts to approach speedy trial cases on an *ad hoc* basis. We can do little more than identify some of the factors which courts should assess in determining whether a particular defendant has been deprived of his right. Though some might express them in different ways, we identify four such factors: Length of delay, the reason for the delay, the defendant's assertion of his right, and prejudice to the defendant.

The length of the delay is to some extent a triggering mechanism. Until there is some delay which is presumptively prejudicial, there is no necessity for inquiry into the other factors that go into the balance. Nevertheless, because of the imprecision of the right to speedy trial, the length of delay that will provoke such an inquiry is necessarily dependent upon the peculiar circumstances of the case. To take but one example, the delay that can be tolerated for an ordinary street crime is considerably less than for a serious, complex conspiracy charge.

Closely related to length of delay is the reason the government assigns to justify the delay. Here, too, different weights should be assigned to different reasons. A deliberate attempt to delay the trial in order to hamper the defense should be weighted heavily against the government. A more neutral reason such as negligence or overcrowded courts should be weighted less heavily but nevertheless should be considered since the ultimate responsibility for such circumstances must rest with the government rather than with the defendant. Finally, a valid reason, such as a missing witness, should serve to justify appropriate delay.

We have already discussed the third factor, the defendant's responsibility to assert his right. Whether and how a defendant asserts his right is closely related to the other factors we have mentioned. The strength of his efforts will be affected by the length of the delay, to some extent by the reason for the delay, and most particularly by the personal prejudice, which is not always readily identifiable, that he experiences. The more serious the deprivation, the more likely a defendant is to complain. The defendant's assertion of his speedy trial right, then, is entitled to strong evidentiary weight in determining whether the defendant is being deprived of the right. We emphasize that failure to assert the right will make it difficult for a defendant to prove that he was denied a speedy trial.

A fourth factor is prejudice to the defendant. Prejudice, of course, should be assessed in the light of the interests of defendants which the speedy trial right was designed to protect. This Court has identified three such interests: (i) to prevent oppressive pretrial incarceration; (ii) to minimize anxiety and concern of the accused; and (iii) to limit the possibility that the defense will be impaired. Of these, the most serious is the last, because the inability of a defendant adequately to prepare his case skews the fairness of the entire system. If witnesses die or disappear during a delay, the prejudice is obvious. There is also prejudice if defense witnesses are unable to recall accurately events of the distant past. Loss of memory, however, is not always reflected in the record because what has been forgotten can rarely be shown.

★ ★ ★

We regard none of the four factors identified above as either a necessary or sufficient condition to the finding of a deprivation of the right of speedy trial. Rather, they are related factors and must be considered together with such other circumstances as may be relevant. In sum, these factors have no talismanic qualities; the courts must still engage in a difficult and sensitive balancing process. But, because we are dealing with a fundamental right of the accused, this process must be carried out with full recognition that the accused's interest in a speedy trial is specifically affirmed in the Constitution.

V

The difficulty of the task of balancing these factors is illustrated by this case, which we consider to be close. It is clear that the length of delay between arrest and trial—well over five years—was extraordinary. Only seven months of that period can be attributed to a strong excuse, the illness of the ex-sheriff who was in charge of the investigation....

Two counterbalancing factors, however, outweigh these deficiencies. The first is that prejudice was minimal. Of course, Barker was prejudiced to some extent by living for over four years under a cloud of suspicion and anxiety. Moreover, although he was released on bond for most of the period, he did spend 10 months in jail before trial. But there is no claim that any of Barker's witnesses died or otherwise became unavailable owing to the delay. The trial transcript indicates only two very minor lapses of memory—one on the part of a prosecution witness—which were in no way significant to the outcome.

More important than the absence of serious prejudice, is the fact that Barker did not want a speedy trial. Counsel was appointed for Barker immediately after his indictment and represented him throughout the period. No question is raised as to the competency of such counsel. Despite the fact that counsel had notice of the motion for continuances, the record shows no action whatever taken between October 21, 1958, and February 12, 1962, that could be construed as the assertion of the speedy trial right. On the latter date, in response to another motion for continuance, Barker moved to dismiss the indictment. The record does not show on what ground this motion was based, although it is clear that no alternative motion was made for an immediate trial. Instead the record strongly suggests that while he hoped to take advantage of the delay in which he had acquiesced, and thereby obtain a dismissal of the charges, he definitely did not want to be tried.

★ ★ ★

That Barker was gambling on Manning's acquittal is also suggested by his failure, following the *pro forma* motion to dismiss filed in February 1962, to object to the Commonwealth's next two motions for continuances. Indeed, it was not until March 1963, after Manning's convictions were final, that Barker, having lost his gamble, began to object to further continuances. At that time, the Commonwealth's excuse was the illness of the ex-sheriff, which Barker has conceded justified the further delay.

We do not hold that there may never be a situation in which an indictment may be dismissed on speedy trial grounds where the defendant has failed to object to continuances. There may be a situation in which the defendant was represented by incompetent counsel, was severely prejudiced, or even cases in which the continuances were granted *ex parte*. But barring extraordinary circumstances, we would be reluctant indeed to rule that a defendant was denied this constitutional right on a record that strongly indicates, as does this one, that the defendant did not want a speedy trial. We hold, therefore, that Barker was not deprived of his due process to a speedy trial.

The judgment of the Court of Appeals is affirmed.

COMMENTS, NOTES, AND QUESTIONS

1. As clearly illuminated by the instant case, *Barker*, following an arrest, indictment, or other official accusation, an analysis of the four factors must be undertaken to determine whether a federal constitutional violation of the right to a speedy trial has occurred in a particular case. The length of the delay, the reason for the delay, the defendant's assertion or nonassertion of the right, and prejudice to the defendant all constitute factors that assist a court in making a decision.

2. Although usually no single factor is determinative, the prejudice to the defendant probably weighs the heaviest. If Barker could not win a speedy trial argument under the Constitution, what type of fact pattern, if added to Barker's case, would win such an argument? Could you alter or add to the facts of *Barker* to produce a situation in which the Supreme Court would find a violation of the right to a speedy trial? What could you suggest? Or consider a case where a prosecutor deliberately delayed bringing a case to trial because two defense witnesses were elderly and might soon pass away. If the prosecutor waits until the witnesses' deaths, would such a delay constitute a violation of the right to a speedy trail? Why or why not? Should it make much difference if the

defendant consistently desired a speedy trial and the prosecution "dragged its feet" until the witnesses died?

3. Before *Barker* and prior to *Klopfer v. North Carolina,* 386 U.S. 213 (1967), a state litigant had to argue that the protections of the individual state's constitution covered the speedy trial situation or that the defendant's case could be affected by the state's statutory speedy trial statute. The federal constitutional right to a speedy trial was not incorporated into the Due Process Clause of the Fourteenth Amendment until *Klopfer v. North Carolina,* 386 U.S. 213 (1967), so defendants after that date can contend that their Fourteenth Amendment rights under the Due Process Clause have been violated when delay lasts too long.

CASE 12.6

Pretrial Negligence in Bringing Indicted Defendant to Trial Violates Speedy Trial Right

Doggett v. United States
Supreme Court of the United States
505 U.S. 647 (1992)

FACTS

In February 1980 a federal grand jury indicted Marc Doggett and a few of his associates for conspiracy to import and distribute cocaine to the United States. Pursuant to a request by the Drug Enforcement Administration (DEA), police attempted to arrest Doggett at the home of his parents only to find that he was not present and had traveled to Colombia, South America, four days earlier.

Determined to apprehend Doggett on his return to the United States, the DEA sent word to all United States Customs stations and other law enforcement agencies that Doggett was to be arrested upon finding him. Doggett's name was entered in a United States Customs' computer and other law enforcement computer systems where it remained. The computer for the Treasury Enforcement Communication System entered his name but purged it after its expiration date.

The next year, in September 1981, the DEA discovered that Doggett had been arrested in Panama on drug charges and requested the Panamanian government to expel him to the United States once they were finished with his criminal charges. Panama officials did not deport Doggett to the United States but permitted him to travel to Colombia. Panama notified the State Department of Doggett's departure for Colombia. Apparently, the State

Department kept this information to itself and did not share it with federal law enforcement agencies. As a result, the DEA was unaware of Doggett's location until it discovered his 1982 travel to Colombia in 1985. The DEA assumed that Doggett had settled in Colombia and would not be returning to the United States.

Doggett returned to the United States in 1982 and passed unchallenged through United States Customs in New York and settled in Virginia, where he married, earned a college degree, and found employment. He made no effort to hide his whereabouts and Doggett lived openly under his own name.

In 1988, the United States Marshall's Service ran a credit check on several persons that turned up Doggett's address and place of employment. Almost nine years after his indictment, officials arrested Doggett pursuant to the original indictment. He raised an unsuccessful pretrial speedy trial argument and entered a conditional plea of guilt, reserving his right to appeal his Sixth Amendment speedy trial issue. The Court of Appeals rejected his constitutional claims and affirmed the conviction. The Supreme Court granted certiorari.

PROCEDURAL ISSUE

Where the government has obtained an indictment against a particular person, but the individual remained ignorant of the charges, and where the indicted individual lived openly under his own name and through government negligence has not been brought to trial for nearly nine years following the indictment, has the Sixth Amendment right to a speedy trial been violated?

HELD: YES

RATIONALE

Justice Souter delivered the opinion of the Court.

★ ★ ★

II

The Sixth Amendment guarantees that, "[i]n all criminal prosecutions, the accused shall enjoy the right to a speedy…trial…." On its face, the Speedy Trial Clause is written with such breadth that, taken literally, it would forbid the government to delay the trial of an "accused" for any reason at all. Our cases, however, have qualified the literal sweep of the provision by specifically recognizing the relevance of four separate enquiries: whether delay

before trial was uncommonly long, whether the government or the criminal defendant is more to blame for that delay, whether, in due course, the defendant asserted his right to a speedy trial, and whether he suffered prejudice as the delay's result. See *Barker* [*v. Wingo*, 407 U.S. 514], at 530.

The first of these is actually a double enquiry. Simply to trigger a speedy trial analysis, an accused must allege that the interval between accusation and trial has crossed the threshold dividing ordinary from "presumptively prejudicial" delay, since by definition, he cannot complain that the government had denied him a "speedy" trial if it has, in fact, prosecuted his case with customary promptness. If the accused makes this showing, the court must then consider, as one factor among several, the extent to which the delay stretches beyond the bare minimum needed to trigger judicial examination of the claim. This latter enquiry is significant to the speedy trial analysis because, as we discuss below, the presumption that pretrial delay has prejudiced the accused intensifies over time. In this case, the extraordinary $8^1/_2$ year lag between Doggett's indictment and arrest clearly suffices to trigger the speedy trial enquiry; its further significance within that enquiry will be dealt with later.

As for *Barker*'s second criterion, the Government claims to have sought Doggett with diligence. The findings of the courts below are to the contrary, however, and we review trial court determinations of negligence with considerable deference. [Citations omitted.] The Government gives us nothing to gainsay the findings that have come up to us, and we see nothing fatal to them in the record. For six years, Government's investigators made no serious effort to test their progressively more questionable assumption that Doggett was living abroad, and, had they done so, they could have found him within minutes.…

The Government goes against the record again in suggesting that Doggett knew of his indictment years before he was arrested. Were this true, Barker's third factor, concerning invocation of the right to a speedy trial, would be weighed heavily against him. But here again, the Government is trying to revisit the facts. At the hearing on Doggett's speedy trial motion, it introduced no evidence challenging the testimony of Doggett's wife, who said that she did not know of the charges until his arrest, and of his mother, who claimed not to have told him or anyone else that the police had come looking for him.

★ ★ ★

III

The Government is left, then, with its principal contention: that Doggett fails to make out a successful speedy trial claim because he has not shown precisely how he was prejudiced by the delay between his indictment and trial.

A

We have observed in prior cases that unreasonable delay between formal accusation and trial threatens to produce more than one sort of harm, including "oppressive pretrial incarceration," "anxiety and concern of the accused," and "the possibility that the [accused's] defense will be impaired" by dimming memories and loss of exculpatory evidence. *Barker,* 407 U.S., at 532; see also *Smith v. Hooey,* 393 U.S. 347, 377–379 (1969); *United States v. Ewell,* 383 U.S. 116, 120 (1966). Of these forms of prejudice, "the most serious is the last, because the inability of a defendant adequately to prepare his case skews the fairness of the entire system." 407 U.S., at 532. Doggett claims this kind of prejudice, and there is probably no other kind that he can claim, since he was subjected neither to pretrial detention nor, he has successfully contended, to awareness of unresolved charges against him.

The Government answers Doggett's claim by citing language in three cases, *United States v. Marion,* 404 U.S. 307, 320–323 (1971), *United States v. MacDonald,* 456 U.S. 1, 8 (1982), and *United States v. Loud Hawk,* 474 U.S. 302, 312 (1986), for the proposition that the Speedy Trial Clause does not significantly protect a criminal defendant's interest in fair adjudication. In so arguing, the Government asks us, in effect, to read part of *Barker* right out of the law, and that we will not do. In context, the cited passages support nothing beyond the principle, which we have independently based on textual and historical grounds that the Sixth Amendment right of the accused to a speedy trial has no application beyond the confines of a formal criminal prosecution. Once triggered by arrest, indictment, or other official accusation, however, the speedy trial enquiry must weigh the effect of delay on the accused's defense just as it has to weigh any other form of prejudice that *Barker* recognized.

As an alternative to limiting *Barker,* the Government claims Doggett has failed to make any affirmative showing that the delay weakened his ability to raise specific defenses, elicit specific testimony, or produce specific items of evidence. Though Doggett did indeed come up short in this respect, the Government's argument takes it only so far: consideration of prejudice is not limited to the specifically demonstrable, and, as it concedes, affirmative proof of particularized prejudice is not essential to every speedy trial claim. *Barker* explicitly recognized that impairment of one's defense is the most difficult form of speedy trial prejudice to prove because time's erosion of exculpatory evidence and testimony "can rarely be shown." 407 U.S., at 532.

★ ★ ★

B

This brings us to an enquiry into the role that presumptive prejudice should play in the disposition of Doggett's speedy trial claim. We begin with hypothetical and somewhat easier cases and work our way to this one.

Our speedy trial standards recognize that pretrial delay is often both inevitable and wholly justifiable. The government may need time to collect witnesses against the accused, oppose his pretrial motions, or if he goes into hiding, track him down. We attach great weight to such considerations when balancing them against the costs of going forward with a trial whose probative accuracy the passage of time has begun by degrees to throw into question. Thus, in this case, if the Government had pursued Doggett with reasonable diligence from his indictment to his arrest, his speedy trial claim would fail. Indeed, that conclusion would generally follow as a matter of course however great the delay, so long as Doggett could not show specific prejudice to his defense.

The Government concedes, on the other hand, that Doggett would prevail if he could show that the Government had intentionally held back in its prosecution of him to gain some impermissible advantage at trial. That we cannot doubt. *Barker* stressed that official bad faith in causing delay will be weighed heavily against the government, 407 U.S., at 531, and a bad-faith delay the length of this negligent one would present an overwhelming case for dismissal.

Between diligent prosecution and bad-faith delay, official negligence in bringing an accused to trial occupies the middle ground. While not compelling relief in every case where bad-faith delay would make relief virtually automatic, neither is negligence automatically tolerable simply because the accused cannot demonstrate exactly how it has prejudiced him. It was on this point that the Court of Appeals erred, and on the facts before us, it was reversible error.

Barker made it clear that "different weights [are to be] assigned to different reasons" for delay. Although negligence is obviously to be weighed more lightly than a deliberate intent to harm the accused's defense, it still falls on the wrong side of the divide between acceptable and unacceptable reasons for delaying a criminal prosecution once it has begun. And such is the nature of the prejudice presumed that the weight we assign to official negligence compounds over time as the presumption of evidentiary prejudice grows.

★ ★ ★

To be sure, to warrant granting relief, negligence unaccompanied by particularized trial prejudice must have lasted longer than negligence demonstrably causing such prejudice. But even so, the Government's egregious persistence in failing to prosecute Doggett is clearly sufficient. The lag between Doggett's indictment and arrest was 8 $^1/_2$ years, and he would have faced trial 6 years earlier than he did but for the Government's inexcusable oversights. The portion of the delay attributable to the Government's negligence far exceeds the threshold needed to state a speedy trial claim; indeed, we have called shorter delays "extraordinary." When the Government's negligence thus causes delay six times as long as that generally sufficient to trigger judicial review, and when the presumption of prejudice, albeit unspecified, is neither extenuated, as by the defendant's acquiescence, nor persuasively rebutted, the defendant is entitled to relief.

IV

We reverse the judgment of the Court of Appeals and remand the case for proceedings consistent with this opinion.

So ordered.

Justice O'Connor, dissenting.

I believe the Court of Appeals properly balanced the considerations set forth in *Barker v. Wingo,* 407 U.S. 514 (1972). Although the delay between indictment and trial was lengthy, petitioner did not suffer any anxiety or restriction on his liberty. The only harm to petitioner from the lapse of time was potential prejudice to his ability to defend his case. We have not allowed such speculative harm to tip the scales. Instead, we have required a showing of actual prejudice to the defense before weighing it in the balance. As we stated in *United States v. Loud Hawk,* 474 U.S. 302, 315 (1986), the

possibility of prejudice is not sufficient to support respondents' position that their speedy trial rights were violated. In this case, moreover, delay is a two-edged sword. It is the Government that bears the burden of providing its case beyond a reasonable doubt. The passage of time may make it difficult or impossible for the Government to carry this burden.

The Court of Appeals followed this holding, and I believe we should as well. For this reason,

I respectfully dissent.

COMMENTS, NOTES, AND QUESTIONS

1. Under the four-factors test of *Barker v. Wingo,* one of the factors that was necessary to prove a violation of the Sixth Amendment right to a speedy trial involved prejudice to the defendant. Did Doggett prove any prejudice to the merits of his defense? Did he have to prove prejudice? Is the Court presuming prejudice based on the length of the delay? If delay is all that is necessary, *Barker v. Wingo* should have had a different result! Since Doggett pled guilty, reserving his right of appeal, do you believe that his defense was impaired by the length of the delay?

2. The constitutional right to a speedy trial under the Sixth Amendment begins to run from the moment of arrest, indictment, or the filing of an information, whichever occurs first. Could the federal prosecutor have moved to have Doggett's indictment dismissed when he could not be located? Such a procedure would have stopped the running of the right to a speedy trial, and Doggett could have been indicted in the future if his location became known. Would the procedure have been fair to the prosecution and to the defense? Why or why not?

3. Should governmental negligence in bringing a strong case to trial allow a defendant to go free? In a somewhat similar situation, involving a timely federal bail hearing, when the hearing is delayed contrary to law, the defendant does not receive freedom as the remedy for the government's failure to follow the law. See *United States v. Montalvo-Murillo,* 495 U.S. 711 (1990). Dismissing a case with no clear prejudice to a defendant could be argued to be a rather drastic remedy. Is it? If the courts required defendants similarly situated to demonstrate prejudice to their defenses, would this serve as a better solution? Will a defendant who truly has a case that had been prejudiced by the delay be able to prove harm to his or her case? Would the lack of evidence help prove prejudice?

CASE 12.7

Pretrial Motion: Double Jeopardy Procedure in State Cases

Benton v. Maryland
Supreme Court of the United States
395 U.S. 784 (1969)

FACTS

The state of Maryland indicted and tried Benton for both burglary and larceny. The jury convicted him of the burglary charge and found Benton innocent of the larceny count. The court sentenced him to ten years in prison. Prior to the time his appeal would have been heard, the Maryland Court of Appeals decided a case which invalidated a portion of the Maryland constitution which had required jurors to swear their belief in the existence of God.

Benton was given an option for reindictment and retrial since both the grand jury which indicted Benton and the petit jury which convicted him had been selected under the invalid constitutional provision. He selected the option and received a new trial which resulted in a conviction for *both* burglary and robbery.

During the pretrial stage of the second prosecution, Benton alleged that the Fifth Amendment provision against double jeopardy precluded his being retried on the larceny charge since he had already been acquitted of the charge at the first trial. By making the double jeopardy argument prior to the second trial, the issue was properly preserved to be raised on appeal. The trial court denied Benton's contentions and the Maryland Court of Special Appeals considered the double jeopardy claim, but denied relief. Maryland's highest court refused discretionary review. The Supreme Court granted certiorari.

PROCEDURAL ISSUE

Does the Fifth Amendment prohibition against double jeopardy apply to the States through the Due Process Clause of the Fourteenth Amendment to prevent a second state trial of a previously tried criminal case?

HELD: YES

RATIONALE

Mr. Justice Marshall delivered the opinion of the Court.

★ ★ ★

III

In 1937, this Court decided the landmark case of *Palko v. Connecticut,* 302 U.S. 319. Palko, although indicted for first-degree murder, had been convicted of murder in the second degree after a jury trial in Connecticut state court. The State appealed and won a new trial. Palko argued that the Fourteenth Amendment incorporated, as against the States, the Fifth Amendment requirement that no person "be subject for the same offense to be twice put in jeopardy of life or limb." The Court disagreed. Federal double jeopardy standards [at that time in history] were not applicable against the States. Only when a kind of jeopardy subjected a defendant to "a hardship so acute and shocking that our polity will not endure it," *id.,* at 328, did the Fourteenth Amendment apply. The order for a new trial was affirmed. In subsequent appeals from state courts, the Court continued to apply this lesser *Palko* standard. *See, e.g., Brock v. North Carolina,* 344 U.S. 424 (1953).

Recently, however, this Court has "increasingly looked to the specific guarantees of the [Bill of Rights] to determine whether a state criminal trial was conducted with due process of law." *Washington v. Texas,* 388 U.S. 14, 18 (1967). In an increasing number of cases, the Court "has rejected the notion that the Fourteenth Amendment applies to the States only a 'watered-down, subjective version of the individual guarantees of the Bill of Rights....'" *Malloy v. Hogan,* 378 U.S. 1, 10–11 (1964). Only last Term we found that the right to trial by jury in criminal cases was "fundamental to the American scheme of justice," *Duncan v. Louisiana,* 391 U.S. 145 (1968), and held that the Sixth Amendment right to a trial by jury was applicable to the States through the Fourteenth Amendment. For the same reasons, we today find that the double jeopardy prohibition of the Fourteenth Amendment represents a fundamental ideal in our constitutional heritage, and that it should apply to the States through the Fourteenth Amendment. Insofar as it is inconsistent with this holding, *Palko v. Connecticut* is overruled.

Palko represented an approach to basic constitutional rights which this Court's recent decisions have rejected. It was out of the same cloth as *Betts v. Brady,* 316 U.S. 455 (1942), the case which held that a criminal defendant's right to counsel was to be determined by deciding in each case whether the denial of that right was "shocking to the universal sense of justice." *Id.* at 462. It relied upon *Twining v. New Jersey,* 211 U.S. 78 (1908), which held that the right against compulsory self-incrimination was not an element of Fourteenth Amendment due process. *Betts* was overruled by *Gideon v. Wainwright,* 372 U.S. 335 (1963); *Twining* by *Malloy v. Hogan,* 378 U.S. 1 (1964). Our recent cases have thoroughly rejected the *Palko* notion that basic constitutional rights can be denied by the States as long as the totality of the circumstances does not disclose a denial of "fundamental fairness." Once it is decided that a particular Bill of Rights guarantee is "fundamental to the American scheme of justice," *Duncan v. Louisiana, supra,* at 149, the same constitutional standards apply against both the State and Federal Governments. *Palko's* roots had thus been cut away years ago. We today only recognize the inevitable.

The fundamental nature of the guarantee against double jeopardy can hardly be doubted. Its origins can be traced to Greek and Roman times, and it became established in the common law of England long before this Nation's independence. As with many other elements of the common law, it was carried into the jurisprudence of this Country through the medium of Blackstone, who codified the doctrine in his Commentaries. "[T]he plea of *autrefois acquit,* or a former acquittal," he wrote, "is grounded on this universal maxim of the common law of England, that no man is to be brought into jeopardy of his life more than once for the same offence." Today, every State incorporates some form of the prohibition in its constitutional or common law. As this Court put it in *Green v. United States,* 355 U.S. 184 (1957), "[t]he underlying idea, one that is deeply ingrained in at least the Anglo-American system of jurisprudence, is that the State with all its resources and power should not be allowed to make repeated attempts to convict an individual for an alleged offense, thereby subjecting him to embarrassment, expense and ordeal and compelling him to live in a continuing state of anxiety and insecurity, as well as enhancing the possibility that even though innocent he may be found guilty." This underlying notion has from the very beginning been part of our constitutional tradition. Like the right to trial by jury, it is clearly "fundamental to the American scheme of justice." The validity of petitioner's larceny conviction must be judged, not by the watered-down standard enunciated in *Palko,* but under this Court's interpretations of the Fifth Amendment double jeopardy provision.

IV

It is clear that petitioner's larceny conviction cannot stand once federal double jeopardy standards are applied. Petitioner was acquitted of larceny in his first trial. Because he decided to appeal his burglary conviction, he is forced to suffer retrial on the larceny count as well. As this Court held in *Green v. United States, supra,* at 193–194,

> [c]onditioning an appeal of one offense on a coerced surrender of a valid plea of former jeopardy on another offense exacts a forfeiture in plain conflict with the constitutional bar against double jeopardy.

★ ★ ★

V

Petitioner argued that his burglary conviction should be set aside as well. He contends that some evidence, inadmissible under state law in a trial for burglary alone, was introduced in the joint trial for both burglary and larceny, and that the jury was prejudiced by this evidence. The question was not decided by the Maryland Court of Special Appeals because it found no double jeopardy violation at all....We do not think that this is the kind of determination we should make unaided by prior consideration by the state courts. Accordingly, we think it "just under the circumstances," 28 U.S.C. Section 2196, to vacate the judgment below and remand for consideration of this question. The judgment is vacated and the case is remanded for further proceedings not inconsistent with this opinion.

It so ordered.

COMMENTS, NOTES, AND QUESTIONS

1. Concerning an early attempt to have the Supreme Court recognize a federal requirement of double jeopardy in state prosecutions, consider the case of *Palko v. Connecticut,* 302 U.S. 319 (1937), mentioned in the first paragraph of the Court's opinion here. *Palko* involved a case where the Connecticut prosecutor tried Palko twice for the identical crime of first-degree murder. The first jury trial resulted in a conviction of second-degree murder and a life sentence. Pursuant to a state statute, the presiding trial judge granted permission for the *prosecution* to appeal the verdict. Upon proper consideration, the Supreme Court of Errors reversed Palko's conviction on the grounds that the trial judge improperly excluded defendant Palko's confession and evidence relating to his credibility. The court held that a jury instruction had been given to the prejudice of the state. Subsequently, Palko stood trial for a second time concerning the same activities for which he had originally been convicted. During this trial, he contended that the

retrial subjected him to jeopardy a second time for the same crime in violation of the Fifth Amendment's prohibition against double jeopardy. At the second trial, the jury found him guilty of first-degree murder, and the trial judge imposed the sentence of death.

In his appeal from the second conviction, Palko argued that the due process guarantees inherent in the Fourteenth Amendment included a prohibition against double jeopardy. The Supreme Court of the United States disagreed and refused to hold that the essence of the double jeopardy provision should have application against the states through the Due Process Clause of the Fourteenth Amendment. As the Court framed the issue:

> Is that kind of double jeopardy to which the statute has subject[ed] him a hardship so acute and shocking that our polity will not endure it? Does it violate those "fundamental principles of liberty and justice which lie at the base of all our civil and political institutions?" The answer surely must be "no." What the answer would have to be if the state were permitted after a trial free from error to try the accused over again or to bring another case against him, we have no occasion to consider. "We deal with the statute before us and no other. The state is not attempting to wear the accused out by a multitude of cases with accumulated trials. It asks no more than this, that the case against him shall go on until there shall be a trial free from the corrosion of substantial legal error." This is not cruelty at all, nor even vexation in any immoderate degree.

Connecticut executed Palko for his conviction of first-degree murder, his second conviction for the same crime. How would Palko's case be different today? Could the same result occur if Palko appealed his original conviction and won a new trial? Could Connecticut try him for the higher crime of first-degree murder? Or would it have to settle for a trial on second-degree murder?

2. Jeopardy is said to attach to a prosecution when the jury is empaneled and sworn,[500] and in a trial to a judge when the judge begins hearing evidence from the first witness.[501] At these times, the defendant has been in jeopardy once. The second prosecution for the same offense where jeopardy is about to attach or has attached constitutes the second jeopardy for which constitutional protection exists. A pretrial motion asking for a dismissal is required. The provision against double jeopardy is designed to prevent a defendant from having to undergo all the troubles and expense of a second trial; thus, to raise it after the second trial would be rather late.

3. Can jeopardy attach prior to the beginning of a trial? In *Serfass v. United States,* 420 U.S. 377 (1975), petitioner lost his pretrial motion that double jeopardy prevented his first trial. Serfass had refused armed forces induction, but the initial indictment had been dismissed prior to the holding of a trial. The dismissal was for procedural reasons that did not reach the merits of the case. The Supreme Court held that the double jeopardy protection did not bar a first trial following a prosecutor's successful appeal from a pretrial order dismissing the indictment. The erroneous dismissal was based on the records of the case and an affidavit. According to the Serfass Court, "Jeopardy had not attached...when the District Court dismissed the indictment, because petitioner had not then been put to trial." *Serfass* at 389. Since Serfass had never once been in jeopardy, there was no merit to his contention that he was being subjected to jeopardy a second time.

4. Once a first episode of jeopardy has attached, where or when does it terminate so that there is a possibility of a second jeopardy attachment? In a Michigan case that went to the Supreme Court, *Price v. Vincent,* 538 U.S. 634 (2003), the prosecution had levied an open charge of murder against a defendant who had been involved in a group brawl where one of those involved was killed. At the close of the prosecution's case, the defense attorney requested that the judge direct a verdict of acquittal on the first-degree murder charge, to which the judge replied that he agreed that premeditation had not been proven, but the judge granted the prosecutor's request to be heard on the matter the next morning.

When trial resumed, the defense counsel objected that to continue on first-degree murder, if the prosecutor convinced the judge, would constitute double jeopardy, since the judge had agreed that premeditation had not been proven and had, in effect, acquitted the defendant of the higher level of murder. The judged noted, "Oh, I granted a motion but I have not yet directed a verdict." However, rather cryptically, on the docket sheet, the court clerk had noted, "Motions by all atts for directed verdict. Court amended ct: 1 open murder to 2nd degree murder." The judge rejected the double jeopardy argument; the jury convicted the defendant of first-degree murder. The defendant pursued both appellate and collateral attack

---

[500]See *Downum v. United States,* 372 U.S. 734 (1963).
[501]See *Illinois v. Somerville,* 410 U.S. 458 (1973).

remedies. The Sixth Circuit Court of Appeals concluded that the state trial judge's actions constituted a ground of acquittal on the first-degree murder charge to which jeopardy then attached. For the trial judge to allow the jury to consider first-degree murder after the judge's ruling constituted double jeopardy, which then barred jury consideration of the higher charge.

The case arrived at the Supreme Court of the United States "clothed" in habeas corpus status, since a federal district court had issued a writ of habeas corpus and the court of appeals had affirmed. The Supreme Court reversed the court of appeals, since the Michigan Supreme Court decision against a finding of double jeopardy was not an objectively unreasonable application of clearly established law as defined by the Supreme Court of the United States. Thus, the trial judge's oral statement indicating that he did not believe first-degree murder had been proven but that he would entertain the prosecutor's rebuttal the next day did not operate as the termination of jeopardy that would make sending the case to the jury, as a first-degree murder case, a case of double jeopardy.

Had the trial judge made a clear statement on the record dismissing the higher charge, or signed an order indicating a directed verdict of first-degree murder, or given an instruction to the jury that the first-degree murder charge had been dismissed, or made a docket entry to that effect, a good argument that jeopardy had terminated could logically have been made.

5. While the Fifth Amendment provision against double jeopardy protects a defendant from having to stand trial twice for the same offense, the determination of which offense qualifies as the same offense as another has troubled courts for years. Could a person be tried on substantive criminal charges when the defendant had previously been convicted of criminal contempt of court based on the same criminal conduct? Would the proof in the substantive criminal case be different from the exact elements of a contempt of court case? Would each prosecution contain an element that was not in common to the other prosecution? The Court held that separate prosecutions would not be prohibited by the double jeopardy clause, since each case requires proof that the other does not, and they are separate crimes for double jeopardy purposes. *United States v. Dixon,* 509 U.S. 688 (1993).

6. In *Blockburger v. United States,* 284 U.S. 299 (1932), the Court fashioned a test designed to determine when two offenses are different for double jeopardy purposes. Two offenses are separate for double jeopardy purposes if "each provision requires proof of a fact which the other does not." *Blockburger* at 173. For example, in *Brown v. Ohio,* 432 U.S. 161 (1977), the Court held that motor vehicle theft and joyriding were part of the same offense, since automobile theft was simply joyriding coupled with an intent to permanently deprive. A second prosecution for automobile theft following a prosecution for joyriding violated the Fifth Amendment provision against double jeopardy.

7. In reality, a defendant need not actually have stood trial the first time for the double jeopardy clause to have impact on the government's prosecution. The defendant must merely have been in a position in which jeopardy attached. In *United States v. Jorn,* 400 U.S. 470 (1971), the trial judge dismissed the jury after it had been sworn because the judge believed that some of the prosecution witnesses did not properly understand their legal rights. On the judge's own motion and without the defendant's consent, the trial was aborted. When the retrial was scheduled, Jorn made a motion for dismissal, citing former jeopardy, which the judge granted. On the government's appeal, the Supreme Court refused to allow a second trial.

The Trial: Constitutional Rights and Trial Practice: Jury Trial, Right to Counsel, Due Process, and Equal Protection

Chapter Outline

1. Trial by Jury: A Constitutional Right
2. Application of the Basic Jury Trial Right
3. Selective Incorporation of the Sixth Amendment into the Due Process Clause
4. The Right to a Jury Trial: Petty Offenses Compared with Serious Offenses
5. Jury Selection: The Requirement of a Fair Cross Section of the Jurisdiction
6. Proving Violation of Fair Cross Section Requirement
7. Jury Size: Variety in State and Federal Juries
8. Experiments with Reducing Jury Size
9. Jury Unanimity: Variety in State Juries
10. Combination of Smaller Juries with Nonunanimous Verdicts
11. Trial by Jury: Racial and Gender Issues
12. Removal of Prospective Jurors: Rationales
13. Improper Rationales for Removal of Prospective Jurors
14. Waiver of the Right to a Trial by Jury
15. Development of the Sixth Amendment Right to Trial Counsel
16. Right to Appointed Counsel for Felonies
17. Right to Counsel: Where Possibility of Incarceration Exists
18. Major Cases
    - Case 13.1: The Sixth Amendment Right to a Jury Trial Applies in State Cases
    - Case 13.2: The Sixth Amendment Does Not Mandate Twelve-Person Jury in All State Cases
    - Case 13.3: Racial Animus May Not Be Basis of Peremptory Challenge for Juror Removal by Prosecutor

Key Terms

Challenge for cause
Fair cross section requirement
Federal jury size
Nonunanimous jury verdicts
Peremptory challenge
Petit jury
Petty offense compared with serious offense

Requirement of unanimity
Right to appointed counsel
Selective incorporation
Six-person jury
Trial by jury
Voire dire of jury
Waiver of trial by jury

1. TRIAL BY JURY: A CONSTITUTIONAL RIGHT

The concept that a group of individuals selected from the community should sit in judgment as a jury where one of their number had been accused of a crime was well known to the American colonists prior to the Revolutionary War. This practice continued in the colonies after the Revolution to the time when the United States Constitution replaced the Articles of Confederation. The Framers of the Constitution guaranteed the right to a trial by jury for defendants accused of federal crimes in Article 3, Section 2, where they wrote:

> The trial of all crimes, except in cases of impeachment, shall be by jury; and such trial shall be held in the State where the said crimes shall have been committed; but when not committed within any State, the trial shall be at such place or places as the Congress may by law have directed.

Although this section of Article 3 indicates that all crimes shall be tried by jury, in reality only persons accused of federal crimes received this guarantee, and the right to a trial by jury in the several states remained a creature of state law or of the constitution of an individual state. The federal guarantee was reiterated in Amendment Six as part of the Bill of Rights when the Framers wrote:

> In all criminal prosecutions, the accused shall enjoy the right to a speedy and public trial, by an impartial jury of the State and district wherein the crime shall have been committed, which district shall have been previously ascertained by law, and to be informed of the nature and cause of the accusation; to be confronted with the witnesses against him; to have compulsory process for obtaining witnesses in his favor, and to have the assistance of counsel for his defence.

This restated and reinforced right to a trial by jury required only the federal government to grant a trial by jury; the original intent of the amendment was not to give any guarantee to individual defendants in state criminal cases. The legal theory, often repeated in a variety of ways, was that there existed a fear of a strong national government, in relation to which the local states would have little power. For this reason, limitations on power and authority should be placed on the national government because the people in the states could control the way their respective state governments dealt with people with respect to criminal law and procedure.

2. APPLICATION OF THE BASIC JURY TRIAL RIGHT

The Sixth Amendment guarantee that "in all criminal prosecutions" the accused person shall have the right to have the case heard "by an impartial jury of the State and district" where the crime was committed could be interpreted as a guarantee to state criminal defendants. However, the reference to "the State" in the Sixth Amendment referred to the place of the trial, not the violation of state law. As originally conceived, this guarantee required the federal government to grant jury trials in federal criminal cases but left the states free to determine whether, when, and under what circumstances to offer a jury trial. Under the original legal theory, a state could amend its constitution and eliminate the particular state's jury requirement without running afoul of the federal Constitution. In a slightly different vein, a state could determine that the traditional jury of twelve should be reduced in number or could alter the jury system to allow for nonunanimous verdicts. In fact, both of these reforms have been tried by some of the states without transgressing any jury guarantee in the federal Constitution.

During the 1960s, the Supreme Court of the United States, under Chief Justice Earl Warren, began to decide cases involving the right of due process emanating from the Fourteenth Amendment. As various cases came to the United States Supreme Court, the justices took the position that some of the rights mentioned in the Bill of Rights were so crucial to fundamental fairness that they should be incorporated into the Due Process Clause of the Fourteenth Amendment. This gradual application of the Due Process Clause, based on case-by-case analysis, was known as the selective incorporation doctrine. As part of this doctrine, the Warren Court decided that the right to a trial by jury was so fundamental that it must be considered part of due process and enforced in state courts.

3. SELECTIVE INCORPORATION OF THE SIXTH AMENDMENT INTO THE DUE PROCESS CLAUSE

The Sixth Amendment jury trial provision was selectively incorporated into the Due Process Clause of the Fourteenth Amendment and made applicable to the states in *Duncan v. Louisiana* (see Case 13.1).[502] According to *Duncan,* since a jury trial was considered to be among the fundamental principles of liberty and justice that were part of the foundation of all our civil and political institutions, the federal Constitution required the states to offer jury trials. It is somewhat surprising, perhaps, that the Supreme Court concluded that the right to a trial by jury is fundamental to justice when many defendants decide to reject jury trials and instead opt for a trial by a judge. Once *Duncan* made the jury trial mandatory on the states, regardless of what the state constitutions had to say about the matter, the states were required to grant jury trials in much the same manner as did the federal government.

Even though the Sixth Amendment speaks of allowing a jury trial in all criminal cases, the drafters of the amendment did not contemplate that each minor offense charge should culminate in a jury trial. Once the right of trial by jury was required of the states, the Supreme Court had to determine exactly what the right meant in state courts and whether it might mean something different than in federal courts. In support of allowing petty offenses to be tried without juries, *Baldwin v. New York*[503] held that a jury trial is constitutionally required in a state case only where the potential sentence is greater than six months' incarceration. Thus, a reading of *Duncan v. Louisiana* and *Baldwin* requires a state to offer jury trials in serious cases punishable by incarceration longer than six months and permits a state to require bench trials for petty offenses for which six months or less is the maximum penalty.

---

[502]391 U.S. 145 (1968).
[503]399 U.S. 117 (1970).

4. THE RIGHT TO A JURY TRIAL: PETTY OFFENSES COMPARED WITH SERIOUS OFFENSES

Precisely what crime should be considered a "petty" offense has been the subject of litigation by individuals who have contended that some crimes, because of the fact of incarceration, significant fine, or collateral consequences, should be considered as serious crimes. If defendants had been successful in convincing the Supreme Court that other factors besides length of incarceration should classify other offenses as serious for Sixth Amendment purposes, such a decision would have had the effect of extending the right to a jury trial to additional situations. In *Banton v. City of North Las Vegas*,[504] the litigants contended that the offense of driving under the influence of alcohol should be construed as a serious offense for which the Sixth Amendment would mandate a jury trial. While the Court admitted that a crime's seriousness was to be judged by the maximum allowable custodial penalty,[505] and the Court was willing to consider the other penalties attached to such crime, it was not persuaded that the Nevada legislature considered the offense a serious crime. Thus, driving while intoxicated in Nevada did not require a trial by jury, but in some other contexts in other states, an allegation of driving while intoxicated may give rise to the right to a jury trial.[506]

5. JURY SELECTION: THE REQUIREMENT OF A FAIR CROSS SECTION OF THE JURISDICTION

To meet constitutional requirements and as a general rule, the actual jury empanelled must have been selected from a fair cross section of the community. The exclusion of identifiable groups or segments of the community prevents the excluded groups from sharing the civic responsibility of the administration of justice.[507] Congress has expressed the view that the requirement that a jury should be chosen from a fair cross section of the community is fundamental to the American system of justice.[508] To generate a pool of potential jurors, the jurisdiction must devise a method whereby all distinctive groups are represented and included as members of the pool from which actual jurors will be selected. For example, to call for jury service all citizens whose names appear on a list of income tax payers would fail to generate a representative pool, since the poorest citizens may not be included within the class of people who pay income taxes. A defendant does not possess the right to have an actual jury chosen that reflects the precise demographic composition of identifiable groups within the community, but the actual array of prospective jurors must generally be representative of a fair cross section of the community.

6. PROVING VIOLATION OF FAIR CROSS SECTION REQUIREMENT

Where a defendant believes that the jury was not chosen appropriately, the defendant usually must meet the burden of proof by presenting evidence that establishes

---

[504] 489 U.S. 538 (1989).
[505] For the offense and under the circumstances, the *Blanton* litigants faced a maximum of six months' incarceration under Nevada law.
[506] See *Solem v. Helm,* 463 U.S. 277, 280, n. 4 (1983).
[507] *Taylor v. Louisiana,* 419 U.S. 522, 530 (1975).
[508] Ibid.

a prima facie violation. As a general rule, a defendant's evidence should be able to demonstrate that the identifiable group alleged to be excluded from service possesses distinctive group characteristics in the community; that the representation of this group in the pool of potential jurors from which actual juries are selected is not fair and reasonable considering the number of such persons in the community; and that the underrepresentation is due to recurring attempts to exclude the group during the jury selection process.[509] Where a trial jury has been chosen from a pool of citizens in an irregular manner that failed to follow the state statute exactly but still produced a randomly selected jury pool that was not based on race, the fair cross section requirement was properly met and the jury was not constitutionally defective.[510] Merely demonstrating that African American and Hispanic persons constituted distinctive groups within the community was insufficient to prove a violation of the fair cross section requirement in the absence of proof that the jury pool excluded members of the recognizable groups and that any underrepresentation was the result of a systematic effort at exclusion.[511]

7. JURY SIZE: VARIETY IN STATE AND FEDERAL JURIES

The trial jury in a criminal case generally consists of twelve persons who possess citizenship and are representative of the local community who are empanelled to hear or judge a case. Federal criminal trials require twelve-person juries who generally must reach a verdict by a unanimous vote,[512] but may, with the consent of both parties, constitutionally render a verdict with fewer than twelve jurors.[513] The rules of criminal procedure for federal courts permit the use of a jury smaller than twelve if the judge and the parties consent in a written stipulation.[514] A federal court judge may allow a jury of eleven persons to return a verdict, even where the parties refuse to stipulate to a smaller jury, if deliberations have begun and the court finds good cause to excuse one of the twelve jurors.[515] State practice varies, since the tradition of a jury of twelve is not a federal constitutional requirement imposed by the United States Constitution upon the states.[516] However, most serious state criminal trials involve twelve-person jurors, and where a trial verdict carries the possibility of the death penalty or life in prison, a jury of twelve will be used.

---

[509]See *Duren v. Missouri,* 439 U.S. 357, 364 (1979).

[510]See *Boston v. Bowersox,* 202 F.3d 1001; 1999 U.S. LEXIS 30660 (8th Cir. 1999).

[511]*United States v. Brown,* 1997 U.S. App. LEXIS 13812 (2nd Cir. 1997).

[512]*Hawaii v. Mankichi,* 190 U.S. 197, 245 (1903). Justice Harlan, in dissent, offered his view on federal juries: "Whatever may be the power of the states in respect of grand and petit juries, it is firmly settled that the Constitution absolutely forbids the trial and conviction, in a federal civil tribunal, of anyone charged with crime otherwise than upon the presentment or indictment of a grand jury and the unanimous verdict of a petit jury composed, as at common law, of twelve jurors."

[513]*Patton et al. v. United States,* 281 U.S. 276, 312; 50 S. Ct. 253, 263 (1930).

[514]Federal Rules of Criminal Procedure, Rule 23(b)(2) (G.P.O. 2002).

[515]Ibid., Rule 23(b)(3).

[516]*Jordan v. Massachusetts,* 225 U.S. 167 (1912). "In criminal cases, due process of law is not denied by a state law which dispenses with a grand jury indictment and permits prosecution upon information, nor by a law which dispenses with the necessity of a jury of twelve, or unanimity in the verdict." *Jordan* was cited with approval in *Johnson v. Louisiana,* 406 U.S. 356 (1972), a case that held that less than unanimous verdicts in state criminal cases do not offend the Sixth Amendment as applied to the states.

Where a defendant possesses a right to a jury trial in a state criminal case, generally he or she may agree to accept a jury composed of fewer jurors than the state statute dictates. The right of a defendant to consent to a smaller jury stems from the right to completely waive a jury trial, and the same procedural safeguards that are required when formally waiving a jury trial should be followed prior to permitting a defendant to accept a reduction in jury size.[517] Among the reasons a defendant might wish to waive a right to a statutorily required number of jurors might be illness among the sitting jurors, removal of a juror for cause during a trial, or juror misconduct when alternative jurors are not available. The consent might be in the defendant's best interests, since the particular jury might appear to be leaning favorably toward the defendant and there would be a desire to keep that jury rather than accept a mistrial.

The jury hears the evidence and renders a verdict based on the facts and evidence presented by each party. To produce a decision, juror balloting, in most criminal cases, must be unanimous for either a conviction or an acquittal. The general rule is that a less than unanimous vote requires that the case be retried before a different jury. The costs of a jury trial (or retrial) to a municipality, county, or state can be significant, especially if the trial is lengthy. To be required to retry a case that has been terminated without a verdict because of a hung jury creates additional expense to the jurisdiction and has caused states to experiment with methods of reducing costs without reducing the quality of justice.

8. EXPERIMENTS WITH REDUCING JURY SIZE

With a view to reducing expenditures for jury trials, some states have experimented with different approaches designed to minimize the size of the jury while maximizing the chances that it will come to a verdict. The government costs required for selecting and managing the jury system of the several states are significant, so measures that make their respective systems less expensive and more decisive have proven attractive. The goal is to balance cost reduction with the maintenance of an appropriate level of justice, consistent with fairness and due process.

In *Williams v. Florida*,[518] the Court approved the use of unanimous six-person juries in a serious, noncapital case (see Case 13.2). The Court noted that the selection of the number twelve was probably a historical accident, even though that number appears in the Bible in connection with the twelve tribes and the Twelve Apostles. Since the required number of jurors may have been pure happenstance, and since the original intent of the Framers of the Sixth Amendment concerning jury size remains unknown, the *Williams* Court approved Florida's use of a six-person jury as consistent with the Constitution.

In utilizing the theory of *Williams,* Florida and other states that adopted the six-person jury could enjoy the financial benefits of lower costs, as well as the probability

[517]See *Kansas v. Roland,* 15 Kan. App.2d 296; 807 P.2d 705; 1991 Kan. App. LEXIS 149 (1991).
[518]399 U.S. 78 (1970).

that there would be fewer hung juries and thus fewer retrials. Of course, if a six-person jury offered monetary savings and other benefits, an even smaller jury would further enhance these advantages. Moving in the direction of a smaller jury system, Georgia attempted to reduce the six-person jury to a five-person jury for noncapital cases. In *Ballew v. Georgia,*[519] the Court refused to approve the five-person jury trial for serious, noncapital cases[520] on the theory that it would prove too small to allow for effective group deliberation and might produce a greater number of inaccurate verdicts. The *Ballew* Court noted:

> [R]ecent empirical data suggest that progressively smaller juries are less likely to foster effective group deliberation. At some point, this decline leads to inaccurate factfinding and incorrect application of the common sense of the community to the facts. Generally, a positive correlation exists between group size and the quality of both group performance and group productivity. *Ballew v. Georgia,* 435 U.S. 223, 232–233, n. 11 (1978).

The *Ballew* Court also noted that the smaller the group, the less likely it would be to overcome any biases held by its members and obtain an accurate result. Neither the financial nor the time-savings benefit of smaller juries influenced the Court; the benefit to Georgia would not offset the substantial threat to the constitutional guarantees that the Court believed would occur if it permitted Georgia to reduce the jury from six to five. Six-person juries are permissible, but the verdicts they render must be unanimous. In a Florida case, however, a defendant was permitted to waive his right to a six-person jury and have his case decided by the remaining five members. Since the right to a trial by jury has been deemed a waivable right, and although the federal Constitution has been construed as requiring at least a unanimous six-person jury in a state criminal case, a defendant may waive the right to a six-person jury and choose to accept the verdict from a five-member jury.[521]

9. JURY UNANIMITY: VARIETY IN STATE JURIES

In another area of jury reform, Louisiana and Oregon eliminated the unanimity requirement for serious, noncapital cases, permitting a 9-to-3 jury vote to be sufficient for either a conviction or an acquittal. Allowing nonunanimous jury verdicts lessened the number of hung juries, consequently lowering the number of retrials required and creating a savings to the adopting jurisdictions. The Supreme Court approved the procedure despite allegations that a nonunanimous verdict called into question whether proof beyond a reasonable doubt was possible where three persons believed in innocence. In *Johnson v. Louisiana,*[522] the Court upheld the nonunanimous verdict of 9 to 3 and rejected the contention that three dissenters would tend to impeach the vote of the other nine. In a companion case, the Court rejected an argument that the Sixth Amendment requires jury unanimity in order to

---

[519]435 U.S. 223 (1978).
[520]Ballew was initially sentenced to concurrent terms of one year in prison and a $1,000 fine for showing an obscene film, *Behind the Green Door.*
[521]See *Blair v. Florida,* 698 So. 2d 1210; 1997 Fla. LEXIS 1338 (1997).
[522]406 U.S. 356 (1972). Accord, *Apodaca v. Oregon,* 406 U.S. 404 (1972).

give effect to the burden of proof in criminal cases. The Court held that the reasonable doubt standard, while perhaps mandated by due process requirements, had no merit, since, in any event, the Sixth Amendment did not require proof beyond a reasonable doubt.[523]

10. COMBINATION OF SMALLER JURIES WITH NONUNANIMOUS VERDICTS

With costs savings available through the use of less than unanimous verdicts and reduced expenditures with smaller juries, it was not surprising that some state jurisdictions would try to achieve greater savings by combining the two concepts. However, efforts to unite reduction in juror numbers with nonunanimous jury verdicts ran aground in *Burch v. Louisiana*,[524] where the Court ruled that a nonunanimous six-person jury (a 5-to-1 vote) was not constitutionally permissible in serious, noncapital cases. According to the *Burch* Court, even though the state of Louisiana possessed a substantial interest in reducing the time and expense associated with administering its system of criminal justice, the state's interest proved to be an insufficient justification for its use of nonunanimous six-person juries. Where the state had reduced its jury size to the minimum permitted by the Court, any attempt to introduce nonunanimity in the legal equation began to threaten constitutional principles. The line had to be drawn somewhere concerning voting practice. The Court found the line in *Burch* and refused to move further away from the traditional unanimous vote of twelve persons of the community.

11. TRIAL BY JURY: RACIAL AND GENDER ISSUES

The federal Constitution, state constitutions, and case law require that fair and unbiased juries be empanelled as part of a guarantee of a fair trial. Although both the prosecution and the defense desire a fair jury trial, most often each side would prefer a jury more "fair" to that side than the other. In the not-so-distant past, various strategies have been employed by states and by various individuals, for a variety of reasons, to keep persons of color and other minorities from serving on juries altogether or from serving on some juries in particular. The use of the poll tax[525] prevented many minorities from registering to vote,[526] which kept persons from being selected when prospective jurors were summoned from voting lists. Literacy tests[527] as a prerequisite for voting registration had an effect similar to the poll tax, which indirectly prevented minority members of society from serving as jurors. In the past,

---

[523]See *Apodaca v. Oregon*, 406 U.S. 404, 411–412 (1972). Although the Court notes that the Sixth Amendment does not require proof beyond a reasonable doubt, the Due Process Clause of the Fourteenth Amendment was construed in *In re Winship*, 397 U.S. 358 (1970), as requiring proof beyond a reasonable doubt for proof of guilt in criminal cases.
[524]441 U.S. 130 (1979).
[525]A poll tax was a levy imposed on those citizens who wished to vote. The Supreme Court held that the tax constituted a violation of the Equal Protection Clause of the Fourteenth Amendment in *Harper v. Virginia*, 383 U.S. 663 (1966). Prior to this decision, if a citizen had not paid the poll tax, he or she could not vote. If a person were not on the voting rolls, there was a virtual certainty that a call to jury service would not be forthcoming, since jury service was often based on being listed as a voter.
[526]*South Carolina v. Katzenbach*, 383 U.S. 301 (1966).
[527]*Oregon v. Mitchell*, 400 U.S. 112 (1970).

some jurisdictions used what has been called a "key man" system, which resulted in members of identifiable minority groups from being underrepresented on trial and grand juries. Where courts appointed "key men" to select potential jurors, the tendency was to pick persons who were known to the "key men" and not to select other members of society who were members of minority groups.[528] "Key man" jury selection schemes have been known to keep minorities from jury service when white men were the "key men" doing the selecting.[529] Where jury service was permitted, other methods and intimidation had been devised to prevent particular individuals from seeing jury duty.

For more than 120 years, the Supreme Court has considered state-sponsored racial discrimination a transgression of the guarantees of the Fourteenth Amendment's Equal Protection Clause. In *Strauder v. West Virginia,* the Court held that a state violated the Fourteenth Amendment guarantee of equal protection of the laws when it put a black defendant before a jury "from which [all] members of his own race have been purposefully excluded."[530] The Court invalidated a state statute which provided that only white men could serve as jurors. This case seems to have been the genesis of efforts by the Supreme Court to remove factors involving racial discrimination from the courts in general and from jury selection in particular.

12. REMOVAL OF PROSPECTIVE JURORS: RATIONALES

During the jury selection process, both the prosecution and the defense are permitted to remove from a prospective jury any juror who can be shown to have a bias, prejudice, or interest involving the case. Since bias, prejudice, or interest may affect the juror's view of the merits of the case and could result in a decision on an improper basis, both parties are permitted unlimited removals of prospective jurors for cause. Alternatively, prospective jurors can be removed for any reason or for no stated reason if one side to a criminal case wishes to exclude a particular person using one of a limited number of peremptory challenges to a juror. A limitation on the use of peremptory challenges exists where a party uses a constitutionally prohibited, though unstated, reason to remove a potential juror. A defendant may not exercise a challenge to remove a prospective juror solely on the basis of the juror's gender, ethnic origin, or race. If a defendant could prove that a prosecutor both had used peremptory challenges to remove prospective black jurors and had historically followed a pattern of doing so, a violation of equal protection would be proven.[531] In *Swain v. Alabama,* the defendant was unable to demonstrate that the prosecutor in his case had practiced discrimination based on race because he could not prove that

---

[528]One "key man" system in Tennessee involved three jury commissioners who compiled a list of qualified potential jurors from which the actual grand jurors were selected at random. The Tennessee judge having criminal jurisdiction made all appointments of forepersons for the county grand juries. See *Rose v. Mitchell,* 443 U.S. 545 n.2 (1979). A "key man" system formerly followed in Texas allowed a state judge to appoint three to five jury commissioners who selected persons for jury duty who were believed to have a sound mind and who were of good moral character. But these "key man" systems did not always select from a fair cross section of the community. See *Castaneda v. Partida,* 430 U.S. 482, 484 (1977).
[529]*Hernandez v. Texas,* 347 U.S. 475, 479 (1954), and *Castaneda v. Partida,* 430 U.S. 482, 484 (1977).
[530]100 U.S. 303 (1880).
[531]*Swain v. Alabama,* 380 U.S. 202 (1965).

the prosecutor demonstrated a pattern of discrimination. Under the *Swain* test, a prosecutor who discriminatorily removed jurors in only one case was not likely to have a verdict disturbed on appeal based on equal protection grounds. The virtually insurmountable burden that a defendant had to meet required proof of a pattern of discrimination, data that would be expensive and difficult to obtain from the prosecutor's office and probably not available anywhere else.

13. IMPROPER RATIONALES FOR REMOVAL OF PROSPECTIVE JURORS

Swain remained good law until the Court faced a similar claim in an updated setting. In *Batson v. Kentucky*,[532] the judge conducted voir dire examination of the jury venire[533] and excused certain jurors for cause (see Case 13.3). Subsequently, the prosecutor used peremptory juror challenges to remove all four blacks from the jury, which left an all-white jury to hear the case of an African American defendant. The defendant could not meet the *Swain* test by showing that the prosecutor, in trial after trial, whatever the crime and whoever the defendant, had systematically removed blacks from serving as jurors. The Court announced that the *Swain* test had been slowly eroded by later decisions and that, henceforth, a defendant could establish a prima facie case of purposeful discrimination solely on evidence concerning the prosecutor's use of peremptory challenges in the very case at bar. According to *Batson,* the defendant would have to show that he or she is a member of a cognizable racial group and that the prosecutor exercised peremptory challenges to remove members of defendant's race from the jury. The defendant must show that the facts raise an inference that the prosecutor excluded the jurors due to race, implicating the Equal Protection Clause of the Fourteenth Amendment. The burden then shifts to the prosecutor to come forward with a race-neutral explanation for challenging African American jurors, and a court must determine whether the defendant has carried its burden of proving intentional discrimination. *Batson* effectively overturned the *Swain* test and substituted a more rational and workable approach that makes the allegation and proof of racial discrimination an easier path to follow. In *Batson,* the Court recognized that when a defendant makes an allegation of intentional racial discrimination on the part of the government in jury selection, such claim raises issues concerning the basic fairness of the trial at hand, as well as the fairness of other trials within that particular judicial system.

Following an allegation and offer of prima facie proof of discrimination in the use of peremptory challenges, a trial court must sort through the evidence offered by both the defense and the prosecution and render an initial decision on the allegation.

---

[532] 476 U.S. 79 (1986).

[533] *Voir dire* of the jury occurs when the judge asks questions of the prospective jurors concerning bias, interest, or prejudice in their beliefs. In some jurisdictions, the court asks the questions posed by the attorneys, and some jurisdictions allow the attorneys to do the questioning of the potential jurors. The word *venire* refers to the whole body of citizens summoned by the sheriff under an old writ called *venire facias* that directed the sheriff to summon qualified citizens of the jurisdiction to serve as jurors. The modern term *jury venire* refers similarly to the body composed of citizens qualified to serve as petit (trial) or grand jurors.

One Connecticut court identified numerous factors that should be considered in determining whether a prosecutor has used peremptory challenges in an unacceptable and discriminatory manner. The court noted that the issues include but are not limited to the following:

> (1) [T]he reasons given for the challenge were not related to the trial of the case…(2) the [party exercising the peremptory strike] failed to question the challenged juror or only questioned him or her in a perfunctory manner…(3) prospective jurors of one race [or gender] were asked a question to elicit a particular response that was not asked of the other jurors…(4) persons with the same or similar characteristics but not the same race [or gender] as the challenged juror were not struck…(5) the [party exercising the peremptory strike] advanced an explanation based on a group bias where the group trait is not shown to apply to the challenged juror specifically…and (6) the [party exercising the peremptory strike] used a disproportionate number of peremptory challenges to exclude members of one race [or gender].[534]

While the ultimate racial composition of the seated jury may not be determinative of the allegation of discrimination, it remains a factor that many courts consider in evaluating the prosecutor's explanation.[535]

Under the dictates of equal protection, defense attorneys may not exercise peremptory challenges in a racially discriminatory manner, and a trial judge does not cure the evil by permitting the prosecution to practice an equal degree of racial discrimination in an effort to level the field. In *Louisiana v. Lewis,*[536] when the defense began to exercise peremptory challenges with a view to removing white citizens from the jury, the prosecution objected, citing the *Batson* case. The ultimate court response involved allowing the prosecution the same latitude in striking prospective black jurors. When the defendant appealed his conviction, he contended that the prosecution practiced jury discrimination outlawed in *Batson.* The defendant proved successful in obtaining a reversal of his conviction because he demonstrated purposeful racial discrimination by the prosecution during the jury selection process, even though, arguably, he had engaged in similar discriminatory jury selection.

Although a member of a racial minority can use the *Batson* test for judging discrimination in jury selection, the same theory may be employed by a member of a racial majority. In *Powers v. Ohio,*[537] a white man objected to the prosecutor's use of peremptory challenges that removed seven black prospective jurors from the jury array. In deciding that a member of the majority racial group could use the *Batson*

---

[534]*Connecticut v. Morales,* 71 Conn. App. 790; 804 A.2d 902; 2002 Conn. App. LEXIS 453, n.17 (2002).

[535]In many cases, the defendant may face significant hurdles in proving that the prospective jurors removed actually possessed a particular racial identity or racial-ethnic identity. In *Collado v. Miller,* 157 F. Supp. 2d 227, 233; 2001 U.S. LEXIS 11788 (2001), the court noted that the defendant failed to show that challenged prospective jurors with Hispanic-sounding surnames were, in fact, Hispanic at all, or whether they simply carried Hispanic-sounding surnames with some different ethnic identity.

[536]795 So.2d 468; 2001 La. App. LEXIS 1938 (2001).

[537]499 U.S. 400 (1991).

test, the Court focused on the rights of jurors rather than on those belonging to a defendant. As the *Powers* Court noted:

> [T]he Equal Protection Clause prohibits a prosecutor from using the State's peremptory challenges to exclude otherwise qualified and unbiased persons from the petit jury solely by reason of their race, a practice that forecloses a significant opportunity to participate in civic life. An individual juror does not have a right to sit on any particular petit jury, but he or she does possess the right not to be excluded from one on account of race. 499 U.S. 400, 409.

In a further decision involving jury selection that involved racial discrimination, a white man had used peremptory challenges in a manner similar to what the prosecutor did in *Powers*. The defendant used his challenges to remove African Americans from the jury, partly because the victim in the case was a person of color. In *Georgia v. McCollum,*[538] the Court held that criminal defendants cannot use peremptory challenges based on race because the practice offends the Equal Protection Clause of the Fourteenth Amendment, and it harms the individual juror by subjecting him or her to open and public racial discrimination. In addition, such a racially discriminatory practice creates harm to the community by undermining public confidence in the jury system. Just as the prosecutor in *Batson* had been prohibited from using racial criteria, the Court applied a similar reasoning to prevent a defendant from doing the same thing.[539]

In selecting a jury, neither the prosecution nor the defense should pursue legal strategies designed to remove representatives of identifiable groups from jury service. Although the use of a racial animus in jury selection clearly transgresses the Constitution, the pursuit of gender goals resulting in discrimination was not always considered illegal. In *J.E.B. v. Alabama ex rel. T.B.,*[540] the government of Alabama used nine of its ten peremptory challenges allowed under state law to remove all males from a trial jury in a paternity case. The rationale of the state of Alabama was based on its perception that men who would otherwise be legally qualified to serve as jurors might be more sympathetic and receptive to the arguments of a man charged in a paternity action. The opposite view held by the defendant, that women equally qualified might be more sympathetic and receptive to the arguments of the child's mother, caused the defense to use peremptory challenges to remove female jurors. According to the Supreme Court, using gender as the factor in exercising peremptory challenges cannot be constitutionally supported since it is based on the very stereotypes the law condemns. The *J.E.B.* Court cited *Strauder v. West Virginia* in noting that the "defendant does have the right to be tried by a jury whose members are selected pursuant to nondiscriminatory criteria."[541] The *J.E.B.* Court went on to

---

[538]505 U.S. 42 (1992).

[539]In the interests of ensuring a fair trial, consistent with due process and equal protection, a white criminal defendant has the right to challenge state discrimination against African Americans in the selection of a grand jury foreman. In *Campbell v. Louisiana,* 523 U.S. 392 (1998), the court concluded that any accused suffers an "injury in fact" when a grand jury's composition has been tainted by racial discrimination. This theory applies equally to trial jury composition.

[540]511 U.S. 127 (1994).

[541]100 U.S. 303, 305 (1880). While *Strauder v. West Virginia* was a criminal case and *J.E.B. v. Alabama ex rel. T.B.* was a civil matter with criminal enforcement overtones, the prohibition against gender discrimination was not limited by the Court to civil cases; the decision was all-encompassing.

conclude that the Equal Protection Clause of the Fourteenth Amendment prohibits gender discrimination where it is based on the belief that jurors will possess stereotypical gender-based prejudices and decide cases based on that bias.

The purpose of selecting a proper jury for a trial is to insulate the defendant from an unfair or overzealous prosecutor or judge. This role cannot be successfully implemented where a jury is too small in number, where it has been selected based on racial characteristics, where an agreement of a significant number of the majority is not required for a decision, or where gender discrimination taints the selection of the jury. The goal of equal justice requires that a jury be selected appropriately and consistently with constitutional dictates.

14. WAIVER OF THE RIGHT TO A TRIAL BY JURY

Most constitutional rights, whether state or federal, may be waived by criminal defendants who desire to forgo the protections that the constitutional rights normally provide. Waiver of a right to a jury trial often occurs within the context of a negotiated plea bargain, and so long as the defendant understands the significance and substance of the rights being released, waiver is appropriate. Some defendants may waive the federal or state right to a trial by jury in order to obtain a bench trial where some of the evidence may be particularly gruesome or other facts might inflame the jury. Under the theory that most judges have seen and heard almost anything and everything, rough evidence may have less effect on a "case-hardened" judge. Where a defendant desires to waive the right to a jury trial, most states, through court decision or law, require that the trial judge make a concerted inquiry into this preference. For example, in Alabama, a defendant cannot waive a jury trial unless the waiver gains the consent of both the prosecutor and the trial judge. Additionally, the defendant may waive personally in writing or in open court or through the trial counsel if the waiver is made in open court and the defendant is present.[542] Similarly, Ohio courts allow a defendant to waive the right to a jury trial, but the waiver must be made in open court after arraignment and after the defendant has consulted with an attorney. The waiver must be contained in writing, signed by the defendant, and filed in the case as part of the record.[543] A failure to follow the strict Ohio requirements will be ineffective to waive a trial by jury and has the effect of removing jurisdiction of the court to hear the case.

15. DEVELOPMENT OF THE SIXTH AMENDMENT RIGHT TO TRIAL COUNSEL

As originally contemplated, the Sixth Amendment right to a jury trial existed for the most serious federal offenses and for some of the less serious offenses, but precisely where lines should be drawn was not always clear. In addition, the Sixth

---

[542]*Davis v. State,* 2003 Ark. App. LEXIS 112 (2003), citing Rule 31.1 and Rule 31.2 of the Arkansas Rules of Criminal Procedure.
[543]*Ohio v. Baer,* 1998 Ohio App. LEXIS 4152 (10th App. Dist. 1998).

Amendment appeared to permit the assistance of counsel to prepare one's criminal defense but did not advise a defendant how to find legal representation. The original intent of this right was that if a defendant could afford to pay for an attorney, he or she could have legal assistance in the preparation and presentation of a defense. The right to have the assistance of counsel meant very little to the person who could not afford to pay a lawyer. If the government, be it state, local, or federal, viewed a criminal matter as sufficiently important that it hired a lawyer to act as a prosecutor, it would seem that a defendant should be able to fairly meet the government by using a lawyer for the presentation of a defense. The inability to afford a proper defense created a legal mismatch for many indigent defendants. This handicapping of impoverished defendants who faced professionally trained prosecutors with no defense counsel existed from the founding of the nation until 1966. In a now famous case, Florida had charged Gideon with a serious felony but had not offered to furnish him with legal assistance. As a result, an impoverished Gideon proceeded to trial without counsel for having allegedly broken and entered a poolroom with intent to commit a misdemeanor, a felony. At his trial, where he was convicted, Gideon requested the assistance of counsel, but the judge followed state law and refused to appoint an attorney.

16. RIGHT TO APPOINTED COUNSEL FOR FELONIES

When Gideon's case reached the nation's top court in *Gideon v. Wainwright,*[544] the Court held that an indigent defendant charged with a serious, noncapital offense has the right to have appointed legal counsel to assist in his defense. The *Gideon* Court concluded that having the assistance of counsel was a fundamental right essential to a fair trial and that to force someone to trial without an attorney created a violation of the Sixth Amendment as applied to the states through the Due Process Clause of the Fourteenth Amendment. As Justice Black noted:

> From the very beginning, our state and national constitutions and laws have laid great emphasis on procedural and substantive safeguards designed to assure fair trials before impartial tribunals in which every defendant stands equal before the law. This noble ideal cannot be realized if the poor man charged with crime has to face his accusers without a lawyer to assist him. *Gideon v. Wainright,* 372 U.S. 335, 344 (1963).

For the very first time, the Court recognized the existence of the right to free legal counsel for any defendant charged in a state case when the accused could not afford to hire an attorney. The generally accepted view was that this decision significantly leveled the inherent advantages of the prosecution and helped move the states toward a fair criminal justice system. Yet to come was the extension of the right to counsel to other offenses of a less serious nature.

[544]372 U.S. 335 (1963).

17. RIGHT TO COUNSEL: WHERE POSSIBILITY OF INCARCERATION EXISTS

Following *Gideon,* in a series of cases culminating in *Argersinger v. Hamlin*[545] and *Scott v. Illinois,*[546] the Court extended the right to free assistance of counsel to any crime for which incarceration might be imposed. In *Argersinger,* the defendant was an indigent who was tried for an offense punishable by incarceration and for which he could have been imprisoned for up to six months, received a $1,000 fine, or both. He was actually given a ninety-day jail sentence after his court trial, at which he was given no right to court-appointed counsel. The state of Florida refused to grant free counsel on the ground that such a right extended only to trials involving serious offenses punishable by more than six months in prison. The Supreme Court rejected Florida's holding and determined that in the absence of counsel, no jail time may be given upon a conviction to an indigent who cannot afford legal representation and who has not been offered free assistance of counsel. In effect, if a judge determines not to appoint counsel for an indigent, the judge cannot later impose a jail or prison sentence. Incarceration cannot be imposed either at the end of a trial or later for a probation violation. As a further limitation, a conviction may not be used under a multiple offense statute or as a "strike offense" in a three-strikes law context to convert a subsequent misdemeanor into a felony with a prison term.[547]

MAJOR CASES

CASE 13.1

The Sixth Amendment Right to a Jury Trial Applies in State Cases

Duncan v. Louisiana
Supreme Court of the United States
391 U.S. 145 (1968)

FACTS

Appellant Duncan observed two of his cousins in a conversation with four white boys. Since racial incidents had occurred in the recent past, he stopped to see if anything was amiss. Duncan urged his cousins to come with him and was about to enter his automobile when a small altercation developed.

According to the white youths, appellant Duncan slapped one of them on the arm while Duncan and his partisans offered a story that indicated Duncan had only lightly touched the elbow of one of the white boys. As a result of the encounter and following a criminal complaint by the white boys, Duncan was charged with simple battery for which the maximum penalty was two years imprisonment and a $300 fine. The trial court rejected Duncan's request for a jury trial, citing Louisiana law which granted jury trials only where imprisonment at hard labor or the death penalty were potential sentences.

The trial court, sitting without a jury, rendered a conviction for simple battery and imposed a sentence that required Duncan to serve sixty days in the parish prison and pay a $150 fine. Having made an objection at trial to properly preserve the jury trial issue, Duncan requested that the Supreme Court of Louisiana hear the case. After the state supreme court denied to consider the case, Duncan applied to the Supreme Court of the United States for a grant of certiorari. Subsequently, the Court granted the writ.

---

[545]407 U.S. 25 (1972).
[546]440 U.S. 367 (1979).
[547]See *Baldasar v. Illinois,* 446 U.S. 222 (1980).

PROCEDURAL ISSUE

Should a crime be considered a serious criminal offense for which a jury trial must be offered where the potential punishment for that crime consists of up to two years' imprisonment and a $300 fine?

HELD: YES

RATIONALE

Mr. Justice White delivered the opinion of the Court.

★ ★ ★

I

★ ★ ★

The test for determining whether a right extended by the Fifth and Sixth Amendments with respect to federal criminal proceedings is also protected against state action by the Fourteenth Amendment has been phrased in a variety of ways in the opinions of this Court. The question has been asked whether a right is among those "fundamental principles of liberty and justice which lie at the base of all our civil and political institutions," *Powell v. State of Alabama,* 287 U.S. 45, 67 (1932); whether it is "basic in our system of jurisprudence," *In re Oliver,* 333 U.S. 257, 273 (1948); and whether it is "a fundamental right, essential to a fair trial," *Gidedon v. Wainright,* 372 U.S. 335, 343–344 (1963). The claim before us is that the right to trial by jury guaranteed by the Sixth Amendment meets these tests. The position of Louisiana, on the other hand, is that the Constitution imposes upon the States no duty to give a jury trial in any criminal case, regardless of the seriousness of the crime or the size of the punishment which may be imposed. Because we believe that trial by jury in criminal cases is fundamental to the American scheme of justice, we hold that the Fourteenth Amendment guarantees a right of jury trial in all criminal cases which—were they to be tried in a federal court—would come within the Sixth Amendment's guarantee. Since we consider the appeal before us to be such a case, we hold that the [federal] Constitution was violated when appellant's demand for jury trial was refused.

The history of trial by jury in criminal cases has been frequently told. It is sufficient for present purposes to say that by the time our Constitution was written, jury trial in criminal cases had been in existence in England for several centuries and carried impressive credentials traced by many to the Magna Carta. Its preservation and proper operation

as a protection against arbitrary rule were among the major objectives of the revolutionary settlement which was expressed in the Declaration and Bill of Rights of 1689.

★ ★ ★

The constitutions adopted by the original States guaranteed jury trials. Also, the constitution of every State entering the Union thereafter in one form or another protected the right to jury trial in criminal cases.

Even such skeletal history is impressive support for considering the right to jury trial in criminal cases to be fundamental to our system of justice, an importance frequently recognized in the opinions of this Court.

★ ★ ★

We are aware of prior cases in this Court in which the prevailing opinion contains statements contrary to our holding today that the right to jury trial in serious criminal cases is a fundamental right and hence must be recognized by the States as part of their obligation to extend due process of law to all persons within their jurisdiction. Louisiana relies especially on *Maxwell v. Dow,* 176 U.S. 581 (1900) [other citations omitted]. None of these cases, however, dealt with a State which had purported to dispense entirely with a jury trial in serious criminal cases. *Maxwell* held that no provision of the Bill of Rights applied to the States—a position long since repudiated—and that the Due Process Clause of the Fourteenth Amendment did not prevent a State from trying a defendant for a noncapital offense with fewer than 12 men on the jury.

★ ★ ★

The guarantees of jury trial in the Federal and State Constitutions reflect a profound judgment about the way in which law should be enforced and justice administered. A right to jury trial is granted to criminal defendants in order to prevent oppression by the Government. Those who wrote our constitutions knew from history and experience that it was necessary to protect against unfounded criminal charges brought to eliminate enemies and against judges too responsive to the voice of higher authority. The framers of the constitutions strove to create an independent judiciary but insisted upon further protection against arbitrary action. Providing an accused with the right to be tried by a jury of his peers gave him an inestimable safeguard against the corrupt or overzealous prosecutor and against the complaisant, biased, or eccentric judge. If the defendant preferred the common-sense judgment of a jury to the more tutored but perhaps less sympathetic reaction of the single judge, he was to have it. Beyond this, the jury trial provisions in the Federal and State Constitutions reflect a fundamental decision about the exercise of official power—a reluctance to entrust plenary powers over the life and liberty of the citizen to one judge or to a group of judges. Fear of unchecked power, so typical of our State and Federal governments in other respects, found expression in the criminal law in this insistence upon community participation in the determination of guilt or innocence. The deep commitment of the Nation to the right of jury trial in serious criminal cases as a defense against arbitrary law enforcement qualifies for protection under the Due Process Clause of the Fourteenth Amendment, and must therefore be respected by the States.

★ ★ ★

The State of Louisiana urges that holding that the Fourteenth Amendment assures a right to jury trial will cast doubt on the integrity of every trial conducted without a jury. Plainly this is not the import of our holding. Our conclusion is that in the American States, as in the federal judicial system, a general grant of jury trial for serious offenses is a fundamental right, essential for preventing miscarriages of justice and for assuring that fair trials are provided for all defendants. We would not assert, however, that every criminal trial—or any particular trial—held before a judge alone is unfair or that a defendant may never be as fairly treated by a judge as he would be by a jury. Thus we hold no constitutional doubts about the practices, common in both federal and state courts, of accepting waivers of jury trial and prosecuting petty crime without extending a right to jury trial. However, the fact is that in most places more trials for serious crimes are to juries than to a court alone; a great many defendants prefer the judgment of a jury to that of a court. Even where defendants are satisfied with bench trials, the right to a jury trial very likely serves its intended purpose of making judicial or prosecutorial unfairness less likely.

II

Louisiana's final contention is that even if it must grant jury trials in serious criminal cases, the conviction before us is valid and constitutional because here the petitioner was tried for simple battery and was sentenced to only 60 days in the parish prison. We are not persuaded. It is doubtless true that there is a category of petty crimes or offenses which is not subject to the Sixth Amendment jury trial provision and should not be subject to the Fourteenth Amendment jury trial requirement here applied to the States. Crimes carrying possible penalties of up to six months do not require a jury trial if they otherwise qualify as petty offenses, *Cheff v. Schnackenberg,* 384 U.S. 373 (1966). But the penalty authorized for a particular crime is of major relevance in determining whether it is serious or not and may in itself, if severe enough, subject the trial to the mandates of the Sixth Amendment. *District of Columbia v. Clawans,* 300 U.S. 617 (1937)....The question, then, is whether a crime carrying such a penalty is an offense which Louisiana may insist on trying without a jury.

We think not. So-called petty offenses were tried without juries both in England and in the Colonies and have always been held to be exempt from the otherwise comprehensive language of the Sixth Amendment's jury trial provisions. There is no substantial evidence that the framers intended to depart from this established common-law practice, and the possible consequences to defendants from convictions for petty offenses have been thought insufficient to outweigh the benefits to efficient law enforcement and simplified judicial administration resulting from the availability of speedy and inexpensive nonjury adjudications. These same considerations compel the same result under the Fourteenth Amendment. Of course the boundaries of the petty offense category have always been ill-defined, if not ambulatory. In the absence of an explicit constitutional provision, the definitional task necessarily falls on the courts, which must either pass upon the validity of legislative attempts to identify those petty offenses which are exempt from jury trial or, where the legislature has not addressed itself to the problem, themselves face the question in the first instance. In either case it is necessary to draw a line in the spectrum of crime, separating petty from serious infractions. This process, although essential, cannot be wholly satisfactory, for it requires attaching different consequences to events which, when they lie near the line, actually differ very little.

In determining whether the length of the authorized prison term or the seriousness of other punishment is enough in itself to require a jury trial, we are counseled by *District of Columbia v. Clawans, supra,* to refer to objective criteria, chiefly the existing laws and practices in the Nation. In the federal system, petty offenses are defined as those punishable by no more than six months in prison and a $500 fine. In 49 of the 50 States crimes subject to trial without a jury, which occasionally include simple battery, are punishable by no more than one year in jail. Moreover, in the late 18th century in America crimes triable without a jury were for the most part punishable by no more than a six-month prison term, although there appear to have been exceptions to this rule. We need not, however, settle in this case the exact location of the line between petty offenses and serious crimes. It is sufficient for our purposes to hold that a crime punishable by two years in prison is, based on past and contemporary standards in this country, a serious crime and not a petty offense. Consequently, appellant was entitled to a jury trial and it was error to deny it.

The judgment below is reversed and the case is remanded for proceedings not inconsistent with this opinion.

Reversed and remanded.

COMMENTS, NOTES, AND QUESTIONS

1. The Sixth Amendment appears to indicate that everyone gets a jury trial regardless of the seriousness of the charge, but limitations have been construed by the courts. *Duncan* did not determine the issue of when the length of potential incarceration allows the defendant to be granted a trial by jury. According to *Baldwin v. New York,* 399 U.S. 117 (1970), the right to a trial by jury begins for offenses for which the maximum penalty is greater than six months' incarceration. According to the *Baldwin* Court, a potential sentence of greater than six months' duration crossed the line between "petty" offenses and serious crimes. Would a defendant consider the possibility of six months a "non-serious" loss of freedom? Where would you have drawn the line if you had been a justice on the Supreme Court? The *Baldwin* decision would appear to reflect the collective personal opinions of the justices who decided the case, since the Sixth Amendment provides no assistance in limiting its coverage.

2. According to the *Duncan* Court, what motivated the Framers of the Constitution and the Bill of Rights to provide that citizens rather than judges should determine guilt or innocence? Is it possible for a judge to fairly render a decision concerning the outcome of a criminal trial? Why should our system use a jury? Is it because a trial to a judge casts doubt on the fairness of a nonjury trial? Does the option of a jury trial operate as a check on the power of judges?

3. While the right to a jury trial in a serious state criminal case constitutes a constitutional right after *Duncan,* what about a defendant who does not want to face a jury?

Is the right to a jury trial a waivable right? As a general rule, a trial by jury may be waived by a defendant provided proper procedures are followed. As a general rule, the defendant must be addressed by the judge concerning other collateral rights being relinquished. When the judge is satisfied that the defendant understands the effects of a guilty plea, the judge may accept the plea where the defendant clearly and unequivocally asks not to have a jury trial. Should a defendant have the right to waive a jury trial? Why or why not?

4. The manner in which the seriousness of a crime is evaluated could be addressed by determining whether it was classified as a felony or misdemeanor. Would that distinction be sufficient for determining when a jury trial existed? Could some crimes that carry sentences of six months or less be considered "serious" crimes for which a trial by jury should be allowed? Should a jury trial be a right for a person who has been charged with possession of recreational pharmaceuticals and who could lose a job? What about driving while under the influence of alcohol or drugs? Are these serious offenses? Why or why not? Consider *Blanton v. City of North Las Vegas,* 489 U.S. 538 (1989), where the court held that drunken driving was not a serious offense sufficient to require a jury trial under the circumstances. The *Blanton* Court felt that the most objective barometer of seriousness was the length of sentence attached to a particular crime. However, the Court suggested that if a defendant could demonstrate that additional statutory penalties, viewed in conjunction with the maximum potential sentence, could be deemed to be so harsh that they evidenced a legislative determination that the offense was a serious crime, an argument could be successfully made that a jury trial would be required. The Supreme Court has yet to find such a case.

CASE 13.2

The Sixth Amendment Does Not Mandate Twelve-Person Jury in All State Cases

Williams v. Florida
Supreme Court of the United States
399 U.S. 78 (1970)

FACTS

Prior to his trial for robbery, defendant Williams filed a pretrial motion to request a twelve-person jury to serve as the finder of fact for his trial. Williams was entitled to a six-person jury but not a twelve-person jury since

Florida criminal procedure permitted the larger jury for capital cases. In contending that he should have been entitled to a traditional jury of twelve, Williams noted that a twelve-person jury was the size commonly used at the time of the adoption of the Constitution and the Sixth Amendment. The trial court denied Williams' pretrial motion to have a twelve person jury empanelled and rejected some other pretrial motions concerning notice of alibi as defenses. The smaller jury convicted Williams as charged and he was sentenced to life in prison.

The Florida District Court of Appeal affirmed Williams' conviction and rejected, among other claims, Williams' Sixth Amendment claim that he possessed the constitutional right to have a twelve-person jury consider his case. In acting on Williams' petition, the Supreme Court granted a writ of certiorari to consider whether the Sixth Amendment requires a twelve-person jury in a serious, noncapital state prosecution.

PROCEDURAL ISSUE

When the nation ratified the Sixth Amendment, did the approval forever dictate that state criminal juries must be composed of twelve persons in serious, noncapital criminal prosecutions?

HELD: NO

RATIONALE

Mr. Justice White delivered the opinion of the Court.

★ ★ ★

In *Duncan v. Louisiana,* 391 U.S. 145 (1968), we held that the Fourteenth Amendment guarantees a right to trial by jury in all criminal cases that—were they to be tried in a federal court—would come within the Sixth Amendment's guarantee. Petitioner's trial for robbery on July 3, 1968, clearly falls within the scope of that holding. See *Baldwin v. New York, DeStefano v. Woods,* 392 U.S. 631 (1968). The question in this case then is whether the constitutional guarantee of a trial by "jury" necessarily requires trial by exactly 12 persons, rather than some lesser number—in this case six. We hold that the 12-man panel is not a necessary ingredient of "trial by jury," and that respondent's refusal to impanel more than the six members provided for by Florida law did not violate petitioner's Sixth Amendment rights as applied to the States through the Fourteenth.

We had occasion in *Duncan v. Louisiana, supra,* to review briefly the oft-told history of the development of trial by jury in criminal cases. That history revealed a long tradition attaching great importance to the concept of relying on a body of one's peers to determine guilt or innocence as a safeguard against arbitrary law enforcement. That same history, however, affords little insight into the considerations that gradually led the size of that body to be generally fixed at 12. Some have suggested that the number 12 was fixed upon simply because that was the number of the presentment jury from the hundred, from which the petit jury developed. Other, less circular but more fanciful reasons for the number 12 have been given, "but they were all brought forward after the number was fixed," and rest on little more than mystical or superstitious insights into the significance of "12." Lord Coke's explanation that the "*number of twelve* is much respected *in holy writ,* as 12 *apostles,* 12 *stones,* 12 *tribes,* etc.," is typical. In short, while sometime in the 14th century the size of the jury at common law came to be fixed generally at 12, that particular feature of the jury system appears to have been a historical accident, unrelated to the great purposes which gave rise to the jury in the first place. The question before us is whether this accidental feature of the jury has been immutably codified into our Constitution.

This Court's earlier decisions have assumed an affirmative answer to this question. The leading case so construing the Sixth Amendment is *Thompson v. Utah,* 170 U.S. 343 (1898). There the defendant had been tried and convicted by a 12-man jury for a crime committed in the Territory of Utah. A new trial was granted, but by that time Utah had been admitted as a State. The defendant's new trial proceeded under Utah's Constitution, providing for a jury of only eight members. This Court reversed the resulting conviction, holding that Utah's constitutional provision was an *ex post facto* law as applied to the defendant. In reaching its conclusion, the Court announced that the Sixth Amendment was applicable to the defendant's trial when Utah was a Territory, and that the jury referred to in the Amendment was a jury "constituted, as it was at common law, of twelve persons, neither more nor less." 170 U.S., at 349. Arguably unnecessary for the result, this announcement was supported simply by referring to the Magna Carta, and by quoting passages from treatises which noted—what has already been seen—that at common law the jury did indeed consist of 12. Noticeably absent was any discussion of the essential step in the argument: namely, that every feature of the jury as it existed at common law—whether incidental or essential to that institution—was necessarily included in the Constitution wherever that document referred to a "jury."...

While "the intent of the Framers" is often an elusive quarry, the relevant constitutional history casts considerable doubt on the easy assumption in our past decisions that if a given feature existed in a jury at common law in 1789, then it was necessarily preserved in the Constitution. Provisions for jury trial were first placed in the Constitution in Article III's provision that "[t]he Trial of all Crimes...shall be by Jury; and such Trial shall be held in the State where the said Crimes shall have been committed." The "very scanty history [of this provision] in the records of the Constitutional Convention" sheds little light either way on the intended correlation between Article III's "jury" and the features of the jury at common law.

★ ★ ★

We do not pretend to be able to divine precisely what the word "jury" imported to the Framers, the First Congress, or the States in 1789. It may well be that the usual expectation was that the jury would consist of 12, and that hence, the most likely conclusion to be drawn is simply that little thought was actually given to the specific question we face today. But there is absolutely no indication in "the intent of the Framers" of an explicit decision to equate the constitutional and common-law characteristics of the jury. Nothing in this history suggests, then, that we do violence to the letter of the Constitution by turning to other than purely historical considerations to determine which features of the jury system, as it existed at common law, were preserved in the Constitution. The relevant inquiry, as we see it, must be the function that the particular feature performs and its relation to the purposes of the jury trial. Measured by this standard, the 12-man requirement cannot be regarded as an indispensable component of the Sixth Amendment.

The purpose of the jury trial, as we noted in *Duncan,* is to prevent oppression by the Government.

> "Providing an accused with the right to be tried by a jury of his peers gave him an inestimable safeguard against the corrupt or overzealous prosecutor and against the compliant, biased, or eccentric judge." *Duncan v. Louisiana, supra,* at 156.

Given this purpose, the essential feature of a jury obviously lies in the interposition between the accused and his accuser of the commonsense judgment of a group of laymen, and in the community participation and shared responsibility that results from that group's determination of guilt or innocence. The performance of this role is not a function of the particular number of the body that makes up the jury. To be sure, the number should probably be large enough to promote group deliberation, free from outside attempts at intimidation, and to provide a fair possibility for obtaining a representative cross-section of the community. But we find little reason to think that these goals are in any meaningful sense less likely to be achieved when the jury numbers six, than when it numbers 12—particularly if the requirement of unanimity is retained. And, certainly the reliability of the jury as a factfinder hardly seems likely to be a function of its size.

It might be suggested that the 12-man jury gives a defendant a greater advantage since he has more "chances" of finding a juror who will insist on acquittal and thus prevent conviction. But the advantage might just as easily belong to the State, which also needs only one juror out of twelve insisting on guilt to prevent acquittal. What few experiments have occurred—usually in the civil area—indicate that there is no discernible difference between the results reached by the two different-sized juries. In short, neither currently available evidence nor theory suggests that the 12-man jury is necessarily more advantageous to the defendant than a jury composed of fewer members.

Similarly, while in theory the number of viewpoints represented on a randomly selected jury ought to increase as the size of the jury increases, in practice the difference between the 12-man and the six-man jury in terms of the cross-section of the community represented seems likely to be negligible. Even the 12-man jury cannot insure representation of every distinct voice in the community, particularly given the use of the peremptory challenge. As long as arbitrary exclusions of a particular class from the jury rolls are forbidden, see, e.g., *Carter v. Jury Commission,* 396 U.S. 320, 329–330 (1970), the concern that the cross-section will be significantly diminished if the jury is decreased in size from 12 to six seems an unrealistic one.

We conclude, in short, as we began: the fact that the jury at common law was composed of precisely 12 is a historical accident, unnecessary to effect the purposes of the jury system and wholly without significance "except to mystics." *Duncan v. Louisiana, supra,* at 182 (Harlan, J., dissenting). To read the Sixth Amendment as forever codifying a feature so incidental to the real purpose of the Amendment is to ascribe a blind formalism to the Framers which would require considerably more evidence than we have been able to discover in the history and language of the Constitution or in the reasoning of our past decisions. We do not mean to intimate that legislatures can never have good reasons for concluding that the 12-man jury is preferable to the smaller jury, or that such conclusions—reflected in the provisions of most States and in our federal system—are in any sense unwise. Legislatures may well have their own views about the relative value of the larger and smaller juries, and may conclude that, wholly apart from the jury's primary function, it is desirable to spread the collective responsibility for the determination of guilt among the larger group. In capital cases, for example, it appears that no State provides for less than 12 jurors—a fact that suggests implicit recognition of the value of the larger body as a means of legitimating society's decision to impose the death penalty. Our holding does no more than leave these considerations to Congress and the States, unrestrained by an interpretation of the Sixth Amendment that would forever dictate the precise number that can constitute a jury. Consistent with this holding, we conclude that petitioner's Sixth Amendment rights, as applied to the States through the Fourteenth Amendment, were not violated by Florida's decision to provide a six-man rather than a 12-man jury.

The judgment of the Florida District Court of Appeal is Affirmed.

COMMENTS, NOTES, AND QUESTIONS

1. Although the *Williams* Court approved using a six-person jury, instead of a twelve-person jury, for serious, noncapital cases, the number of jurors apparently reached the low-water mark with *Ballew v. Georgia,* 435 U.S. 223 (1978). In *Ballew,* a misdemeanor case, the Court held that a jury composed of five members was constitutionally too small to permit effective group deliberation and could produce inaccurate results in a greater number of cases. The Court expressed some concern that progressively smaller juries could reduce the chances of minority participation in the jury system. Would you rather be tried by a twelve-person jury or a five-person jury? Why? If you were the prosecutor, why would you like a five-person jury instead of a six- or twelve-person jury? What are your reasons? From the defendant's perspective, it would be easier to be acquitted, since the defendant would have to convince only five members rather than six or twelve. Should a defendant want a five-person jury? Why or why not?

2. When jury verdicts must be unanimous, one member can hang the jury and prevent a decision. A judge will have to declare a mistrial, which will require that the case be retried. With a view to enhancing the odds of reaching a verdict, the state of Louisiana enacted legislation

that permitted a nonunanimous twelve-person jury to reach a verdict where nine jurors voted either to acquit or to convict. In *Johnson v. Louisiana,* 406 U.S. 356 (1972), the Court sustained the 9-to-3 jury vote despite defense allegations that such a conviction creates a chance that the verdict might not have been based on proof beyond a reasonable doubt. Similarly, the Court rejected a defense contention that the dissent of three jurors had the effect of impeaching the verdict of the other nine jurors and would cast doubt concerning whether proof beyond a reasonable doubt could be based on nine of twelve votes. Do you think a vote of 9 to 3 for guilt calls into question whether the case has been proven beyond a reasonable doubt? Why or why not?

3. If a vote of three-fourths of a jury could produce a valid decision, it seemed logical that a 5-to-1 nonunanimous jury vote should pass constitutional muster because the vote constitutes a higher percentage of jurors than a 9-to-3 vote in a twelve-person jury. Louisiana lowered the number of jurors to six in noncapital cases and allowed a jury vote of 5 to 1 to produce a decision for criminal cases in which the punishment could be confinement for a period greater than six months. The practice would save the criminal justice system money; fewer jurors would have to be paid and fewer hung juries would occur. In *Burch v. Louisiana,* 441 U.S. 130 (1979), the Supreme Court ruled that the nonunanimous six-person jury failed to meet the Sixth Amendment guarantee of trial by jury in state cases. It rejected the theory that if 75 percent juror concurrence in *Johnson v. Louisiana* was permissible, juror concurrence of 83 percent in *Burch* should be sufficient. Is a nonunanimous six-person jury that much different than a unanimous six-person jury? Except for the *Burch* decision, the nonunanimous six-person jury might have been heading toward one of those constitutional "slippery slopes" where the right to a jury trial might otherwise have devolved to a one-person jury and effectively have ended the trial by jury. Thus, a six-person nonunanimous jury verdict in a state criminal case ran afoul of the Sixth Amendment right to trial by jury.

4. What practice should a court follow when a six-person jury cannot agree unanimously, but a defendant agrees (without knowing which way the vote swings) to accept a majority jury vote of 4 to 2 as a verdict? Since a person can waive a jury trial completely, should a defendant be permitted to accept a nonunanimous six-person jury vote? In *Nobles v. Florida,* 786 So.2d 56; 2001 Fla. App. LEXIS 6939 (2001); cert. denied, 535 U.S. 1022; 122 S. Ct. 1618 (2002), the Fourth District Court of Appeal held that a defendant may constitutionally waive his right

to a unanimous six-person jury verdict where he was fully informed of his options, had sufficient time to consider the merits, and made his decision after he and his counsel had observed the witnesses and jury during the trial. Additionally, the trial judge made a special inquiry to be sure that the defendant made a knowing and intelligent waiver of his constitutional and statutory rights. Would a defendant feel some pressure to accept a verdict of this type? Would a judge want a defendant to accept to prevent a mistrial and subsequent retrial? Since the defendant would not know the outcome of the jury vote, does this place justice in the same vein as gambling or "rolling the dice"? Why or why not?

5. Assume that you have attained the position of a court administrator. Would you support the use of nonunanimous juries composed of fewer than twelve members? Would financial considerations enter into your answer? Should they? Would your reasons be valid when less-than-unanimous-verdict juries are considered? Why or why not? Why would your answers probably be different if you were the defendant?

CASE 13.3

Racial Animus May Not Be Basis of Peremptory Challenge for Juror Removal by Prosecutor

Batson v. Kentucky
Supreme Court of the United States
476 U.S. 79 (1986)

FACTS

A Kentucky grand jury indicted petitioner Batson, an African American, on charges of second degree burglary and receipt of stolen goods. At the start of his trial, as was the local custom, the judge conducted *voir dire* examination of the venire, excused certain jurors for cause, and permitted the parties to exercise peremptory challenges as they wished. Skillfully, the prosecutor used the allotted peremptory challenges to strike all four black persons from sitting on the trial jury. The final selections resulted in a jury composed only of white persons. Defense counsel requested the trial judge to discharge the jury before jeopardy attached so that a jury differently composed could be selected. Defendant contended that the prosecutor's use of peremptory challenges to exclude members of defendant's race from the jury panel violated petitioner's rights under the Sixth and Fourteenth Amendments to

have a jury selected from a fair cross section of the community, and under the Fourteenth Amendment to equal protection of the laws. The trial judge observed that the parties were entitled to use their peremptory challenges to "strike anybody they want to." The judge denied petitioner's motion, reasoning that the cross-section requirement applies only to selection of the venire and not to selection of the trial jury itself.

Following his conviction on both charges, ultimately, Batson appealed to the Supreme Court of Kentucky. He continued his argument that the prosecutor's use of peremptory challenges based on the race of specific jurors deprived him of his right to a proper jury trial under the Sixth Amendment. Petitioner urged the court to follow persuasive decisions of other states and to hold that such conduct violated his rights to a jury drawn from a cross section of the community in violation of the Sixth Amendment and Section 11 of the Kentucky Constitution. Petitioner also contended that the facts showed that the prosecutor had engaged in a "pattern" of discriminatory challenges in this case and established an equal protection violation under *Swain v. Alabama,* 380 U.S. 202 (1965). In rejecting Batson's claims, the Kentucky Supreme Court noted that, in another case, it had relied on the rule of *Swain v. Alabama,* 380 U.S. 202 (1965), and had held that a defendant alleging lack of a fair cross section, in order to prevail, must demonstrate a systematic exclusion of a group of jurors from the venire. Batson had failed to make this demonstration so the Supreme Court of Kentucky affirmed Batson's convictions. The Supreme Court of the United States granted certiorari to decide the case.

PROCEDURAL ISSUE

Where a prosecutor, clothed with state authority, used peremptory challenges to remove all members of the defendant's race from the trial jury where it appeared that the goal was to remove all individuals of defendant's race, did such use of peremptory challenges violate a defendant's rights under the Sixth Amendment and under the Equal Protection Clause under the Fourteenth Amendment?

HELD: YES

RATIONALE

Justice Powell delivered the opinion of the Court.

This case requires us to reexamine that portion of *Swain v. Alabama,* 380 U.S. 202 (1965), concerning the evidentiary burden placed on a criminal defendant who claims that he has been denied equal protection through the State's use of peremptory challenges to exclude members of his race from [serving on] the petit jury.

I

In *Swain v. Alabama,* this Court recognized that a "State's purposeful or deliberate denial to [African Americans] on account of race of participation as jurors in the administration of justice violates the Equal Protection Clause." [*Swain*] 380 U.S., at 203–204. This principle has been "consistently and repeatedly" reaffirmed, in numerous decisions of this Court both preceding and following *Swain.* We reaffirm the principle today.

A

More than a century ago, the Court decided that the State denies a black defendant equal protection of the laws when it puts him on trial before a jury from which members of his own race have been purposefully excluded. *Strauder v. West Virginia,* 100 U.S. 303 (1880). The decision laid the foundation for the Court's unceasing efforts to eradicate racial discrimination in the procedures used to select the venire [i.e., the group] from which individual jurors are drawn.

★ ★ ★

…[T]he component of the jury selection process at issue here, the State's privilege to strike individual jurors through peremptory challenges, is subject to the commands of the Equal Protection Clause. Although a prosecutor ordinarily is entitled to exercise permitted peremptory challenges "for any reason at all, as long as that reason is related to his view concerning the outcome" of the case to be tried, the Equal Protection Clause forbids the prosecutor to challenge potential jurors solely on account of their race or on the assumption that black jurors as a group will be unable impartially to consider the State's case against a black defendant.

III

The principles announced in *Strauder* never have been questioned in any subsequent decision of this Court. Rather, the Court has been called upon repeatedly to review the application of those principles to particular facts. A recurring question in these cases, as in any case alleging a violation of the Equal Protection Clause, was whether the defendant has met his burden of proving purposeful discrimination on the part of the State.

A

Swain required the Court to decide, among other issues, whether a black defendant was denied equal protection by the State's exercise of peremptory challenges to exclude members of his race from the petit jury. The record in *Swain* showed that the prosecutor had used the State's peremptory challenges to strike the six black persons included on the petit jury venire. While rejecting the defendant's claim for failure to prove purposeful discrimination, the Court nonetheless indicated that the Equal Protection Clause placed some limits on the State's exercise of peremptory challenges.

The Court sought to accommodate the prosecutor's historical privilege of peremptory challenge free of judicial control, and the constitutional prohibition on exclusion of persons from jury service on account of race. While the Constitution does not confer a right to peremptory challenges, those challenges traditionally have been viewed as one means of assuring the selection of a qualified and unbiased jury. To preserve the peremptory nature of the prosecutor's challenge, the Court in *Swain* declined to scrutinize his actions in a particular case by relying on a presumption that he properly exercised the State's challenges.

★ ★ ★

Accordingly, a black defendant could make out a prima facie case of purposeful discrimination on proof that the peremptory challenge system was "being perverted" in that manner. For example, an inference of purposeful discrimination would be raised on evidence that a prosecutor, "in case after case, whatever the circumstances, whatever the crime and whoever the defendant or the victim may be, is responsible for the removal of Negroes who have been selected as qualified jurors by the jury commissioners and who have survived challenges for cause, with the result that no Negroes ever serve on petit juries." Evidence offered by the defendant in *Swain* did not meet that standard. While the defendant showed that prosecutors in the jurisdiction had exercised their strikes to exclude blacks from the jury, he offered no proof of the circumstances under which prosecutors were responsible for striking black jurors beyond the facts of his own case. [*Swain*], at 224–228.

A number of lower courts following the teaching of *Swain* reasoned that proof of repeated striking of blacks over a number of cases was necessary to establish a violation of the Equal Protection Clause. Since this interpretation of *Swain* has placed on defendants a crippling burden of proof, prosecutors' peremptory challenges are now largely immune from constitutional scrutiny. For reasons that follow, we reject this evidentiary formulation as inconsistent with standards that have been developed since *Swain* for assessing a prima facie case under the Equal Protection Clause.

B

Since the decision in *Swain,* we have explained that our cases concerning selection of the venire reflect the general equal protection principle that the "invidious quality" of governmental action claimed to be racially discriminatory "must ultimately be traced to a racially discriminatory purpose." As in any equal protection case, the "burden is, of course," on the defendant who alleges discriminatory selection of the venire "to prove the existence of purposeful discrimination."

★ ★ ★

Thus, since the decision in *Swain,* this Court has recognized that a defendant may make a prima facie showing of purposeful racial discrimination in selection of the venire by relying solely on the facts concerning its selection *in his case.* These decisions are in accordance with the proposition articulated in *Arlington Heights v. Metropolitan Housing Development Corp.,* that "a consistent pattern of official racial discrimination" is not "a necessary predicate to a violation of the Equal Protection Clause. A single invidiously discriminatory governmental act" is not "immunized by the absence of such discrimination in the making of other comparable decisions." 429 U.S., at 266, n.14. For evidentiary requirements to dictate that "several must suffer discrimination" before one could object, *McCray v. New York,* 461 U.S., at 965 (Marshall dissenting from denial of certiorari.), would be inconsistent with the promise of equal protection to all.

C

The standards for assessing a prima facie case in the context of discriminatory selection of the venire have been fully articulated since *Swain.* These principles support our conclusion that a defendant may establish a prima facie case of purposeful discrimination in selection of the petit jury solely on evidence concerning the prosecutor's exercise of peremptory challenges at the defendant's trial. To establish such a case, the defendant first must show that he is a member of a cognizable racial group, and that the prosecutor has exercised peremptory challenges to remove from the venire members of the defendant's race. Second, the defendant is entitled to rely on the fact, as to which there can be no dispute, that peremptory challenges constitute a jury selection practice that permits "those to discriminate who are of a mind to discriminate." *Avery v. Georgia,* 345 U.S., at 562. Finally, the defendant must show that these facts and any other relevant circumstances raise an inference that the prosecutor used that practice to exclude the veniremen from the petit jury on account of their race. This combination of factors in the empaneling of the petit jury, as in the selection of the venire, raises the necessary inference of purposeful discrimination.

In deciding whether the defendant has made the requisite showing, the trial court should consider all relevant circumstances. For example, a "pattern" of strikes against black jurors included in the particular venire might give rise to an inference of discrimination. Similarly, the prosecutor's questions and statements during *voir dire* examination and in exercising his challenges may support or refute an inference of discriminatory purpose. These examples are merely illustrative. We have confidence that trial judges, experienced in supervising *voir dire,* will be able to decide if the circumstances concerning the prosecutor's use of peremptory challenges creates a prima facie case of discrimination against black jurors.

Once the defendant makes a prima facie showing, the burden shifts to the State to come forward with a neutral explanation for challenging black jurors. Though this requirement imposes a limitation in some cases on the full peremptory character of the historic challenge, we emphasize that the prosecutor's explanation need not rise to the level justifying exercise of a challenge for cause. See *McCray v. Abrams,* 750 F.2d, at 1132; *Booker v. Jabe,* 775 F.2d 762, 773 (CA6 1985), cert. pending, No. 85-1028. But the prosecutor may not rebut the defendant's prima facie case of discrimination by stating merely that he challenged jurors of the defendant's race on the assumption—or his intuitive judgment—that they would be partial to the defendant because of their shared race. Just as the Equal Protection Clause forbids the States to exclude black persons from the venire on the assumption that blacks as a group are unqualified to serve as jurors, so it forbids the States to strike black veniremen on the assumption that they will be biased in a particular case simply because the defendant is black. The core guarantee of equal protection, ensuring citizens that their State will not discriminate on account of race, would be meaningless were we to approve the exclusion of jurors on the basis of such assumptions, which arise solely from the jurors' race. Nor may the prosecutor rebut the defendant's case merely by denying that he had a discriminatory motive or "affirm[ing] [his] good faith in individual selections."…The prosecutor therefore must articulate a neutral explanation related to the particular case to be tried. The trial court then will have the duty to determine if the defendant has established purposeful discrimination.

★ ★ ★

V

In this case, petitioner made a timely objection to the prosecutor's removal of all black persons on the venire. Because the trial court flatly rejected the objection without requiring the prosecutor to give an explanation for his action, we remand this case for further proceedings. If the trial court decides that the facts establish, prima facie, purposeful discrimination and the prosecutor does not come forward with a neutral explanation for his action, our precedents require that petitioner's conviction be

Reversed.

COMMENTS, NOTES, AND QUESTIONS

1. Discrimination in the justice system has long been illegal, but proving racial discrimination or other discrimination has been a tall order. In *Swain v. Alabama,* 380 U.S. 202 (1965), mentioned in the principal case, the facts indicated that no African American had served on a trial jury in that county from 1950 to 1964, although 26 percent of the African Americans in Talladega County were theoretically eligible. The *Swain* Court held that where a defendant could prove that a state purposefully or intentionally denied black citizens the right to participate as jurors in the administration of justice, a violation of the Equal Protection Clause of the Fourteenth Amendment would provably exist. In condemning racial discrimination, the *Swain* Court placed a difficult burden of proof on a litigant making such an allegation. The Court held that the person alleging a violation of equal protection had the burden to prove a pattern of discrimination, not merely what might appear to be discrimination in the defendant's particular case because of underrepresentation on the

jury as selected. The *Swain* burden proved to be virtually insurmountable. *Batson* altered the manner of proof so that an aggrieved defendant now has an opportunity to establish a prima facie case of discrimination solely on evidence concerning a prosecutor's conduct in exercising peremptory challenges at the defendant's trial. Following *Batson,* proof of long-standing discriminatory past practice will no longer be required.

2. Should a defendant have a constitutional right to have adult female citizens included within a fair cross section of the community? Would it make a difference in the interests of justice to exclude women from jury service? In contrast to *Batson,* where persons were being removed from jury service, in Louisiana if a woman wanted to serve on a jury, she had to affirmatively take steps to be considered. In the early 1970s, a woman in Louisiana was not eligible for jury service unless she filed a written declaration stating her desire to be available for jury duty. In some cases, no women were on the venire from which trial juries were drawn. In *Taylor v. Louisiana,* 419 U.S. 522 (1975), the defendant male challenged the Louisiana system of selecting jurors as being inconsistent with the Sixth Amendment. Taylor contended that the venire from which juries are selected should contain a fair cross section of community members, including adult female citizens. After surveying past jury trial cases, the *Taylor* Court noted that the unmistakable import of its jury selection opinions required that a jury be selected from a fair cross section of the community. According to that court:

> We accept the fair cross section requirement as fundamental to the jury trial guaranteed by the Sixth Amendment and are convinced that the requirement has solid foundation. The purpose of a jury is to guard against the exercise of arbitrary power—to make available the commonsense judgment of the community as the hedge against the overzealous prosecutor.…

The Court held that Louisiana's process of placing impediments to female jury service violated the Sixth Amendment concept of selecting jurors from a pool of persons representing a fair cross section of the community.

3. Subsequent to deciding *Batson,* the Court declined to hold that a defendant has the right to a fair possibility to a jury *actually* composed of a representative sample of the community. In *Holland v. Illinois,* 493 U.S. 474 (1990), the defendant unsuccessfully contended that the prosecutor should be prevented under the Sixth Amendment from exercising peremptory challenges in such a manner as to exclude all blacks from his jury. So

long as a prosecutor has a valid nonracial basis to exclude a juror by exercising a peremptory challenge, the removal of the prospective juror will stand. "In *Holland,* the Court held that a defendant could not rely on the Sixth Amendment to object to the exclusion of members of any distinctive group at the peremptory challenge stage."[548] The Court's decision made clear that there was no way that the fair-cross-section requirement could be interpreted to prohibit peremptory challenges. However, *Holland* did explicitly hold that the exclusion of jurors based on race violates the Fourteenth Amendment's Equal Protection Clause. Should a defendant be able to contest a case where the prosecutor seeks to eliminate a class of jurors from the jury? However, consider the *Holland* decision in light of the next note case, *Powers v. Ohio.*

4. In a case that appeared to be a mirror image of *Batson,* a Caucasian defendant objected to the prosecutor's repeated use of peremptory challenges that appeared to be designed to remove most or all prospective black jurors from sitting on his trial jury. In *Powers v. Ohio,* 499 U.S. 400 (1991), the Court rejected the state's argument that because Powers was white, he could not complain if black jurors were removed because of race. The *Powers* Court held that

> [T]he Equal Protection Clause prohibits a prosecutor from using the State's peremptory challenges to exclude otherwise qualified and unbiased persons from the petit jury solely by reason of their race, a practice that forecloses a significant opportunity to participate in civic life. An individual juror does not have a right to sit on any particular petit jury, but he or she does possess the right not to be excluded from one on account of race.

The *Powers* Court concluded that a person's race cannot be used as a barometer for determining the bias or competence of a juror and noted that the *Batson* Court held that the race of a person has no relationship to fitness as a juror. See *Batson v. Kentucky,* 476 U.S. 79, 87 (1986).

5. Should a Hispanic defendant be permitted to make a *Batson* argument that the exclusion of a particular ethnic group from the jury violates the Equal Protection Clause of the Fourteenth Amendment? For example, what action should a trial court take if a Hispanic defendant contests the systematic use of peremptory challenges designed to remove any juror of Portuguese ancestry? Should this make any difference? Should a trial court require that the prosecution offer a nondiscriminatory reason for exercising a peremptory challenge when the defendant claims the challenge is based on a prospective juror's ancestry or ethnic origin? In *Connecticut v. Rigual,* 256 Conn. 1; 771 A.2d 939; 2001 Conn. LEXIS 124 (2001), the Connecticut Supreme Court held that whenever a party alleges that illegal discrimination has occurred during the exercise of a peremptory challenge to a juror's selection, the trial court must determine whether the prosecution possessed a neutral, nondiscriminatory explanation for the removal of the juror. The equal protection clause of Connecticut's constitution prohibits discrimination based on ancestry or national origin, but other states do not all use this approach, and the federal Constitution does not contain such a prohibition. Are states going too far in efforts to ensure that no bias enters the judicial system? Or is this approach merely another step in assuring fair trials to all defendants? How far should this concept be driven? Should religion enter into the equation? Fraternal affiliation? Where do we end the inquiry concerning bias and prejudice in jury selection?

---

[548]See *Powers v. Ohio,* 499 U.S. 400, 409 (1991).

Appellate Practice and Other Posttrial Remedies

Chapter Outline

Key Terms

1. THE RIGHT TO APPEAL

[T]he right of review in an appellate court is purely a matter of state concern.
McKane v. Durston, 153 U.S. 684, 688 (1894).

While the right to appeal from a verdict rendered in a criminal trial would seem to be one of those constitutional rights found deeply embedded in the Due Process Clause of the Fifth or the Fourteenth Amendments, the opposite is true. The federal constitution does not guarantee any right to an appeal from a state criminal conviction. Justice Scalia, concurring in a recent case,[549] stated, "Since a State could, as far as the federal Constitution is concerned, subject its trial court determinations to no

---

[549]*Martinez v. Court of Appeal of California,* 528 U.S. 152, 165 (2000).

review whatever, it could *a fortiori* subject them to review which consists of a non-adversarial reexamination of convictions by a panel of government experts." The source for Justice Scalia's view on appellate rights comes from the language in an old case, which noted, "[T]he right of review in an appellate court is purely a matter of state concern."[550] From the perspective of the United States Supreme Court, states would not have to give any review to criminal case determinations but have chosen to do so as a matter of state law.

Although no state must give any criminal defendant the right of appeal from a trial court, all states permit at least one appeal from an initial court judgment. However, states do not and are not required to automatically allow appeals from an intermediate court of appeal to the top state court.[551] The ability to appeal is not based on a federal constitutional right but is either a creation of state law or required by an individual state constitution. While allowing at least one appeal, states may not condition this appeal in such a manner that the possibility or opportunity of an appeal depends upon the wealth of the appellant. As the Supreme Court of the United States once noted, "There is no meaningful distinction between a rule which would deny the poor the right to defend themselves in a trial court and one which effectively denies the poor an adequate appellate review accorded to all who have money enough to pay the costs in advance."[552]

The primary rationale for allowing appeals following a conviction involves the desire to correct errors or unfairness that may have improperly influenced the court verdict. Although both the prosecution and defense attorneys are obligated by their oaths taken upon the bar admission to support the United States Constitution and laws and to support and defend their respective state constitutions and state laws, it is unlikely that every law and rule has been properly applied and enforced in every criminal trial. Errors in procedure and practice, in admission and exclusion of evidence, in impeachment and cross-examination, in jury selection and exclusion, in the opening and closing statements, and in a variety of other areas create a virtual certainty that no criminal trial will be error-free. Some errors are so inconsequential that their effect on a verdict is minimal, but others may affect the outcome of a trial. Where a defendant can demonstrate a significant error to an appellate court, a reversal of the conviction may be the proper judicial remedy.

The zealous urge to prevail in a criminal case may prompt a defense counsel or a prosecutor to pursue a course of action that is, in the legal sense, erroneous. Some of these problems will be of a minor order of magnitude, and, when considering the whole body of evidence in a criminal case, the error will not be of great concern to either party. Such small errors will not be deemed to have created any lasting effect on the trial or any substantial influence on the overall outcome. In contrast, some errors have such a tremendous effect on the direction and outcome of a trial that it becomes impossible to say what the outcome of the case would have been without the error. The prosecutor and the defense counselor will most likely have different opinions concerning which errors have affected the outcome of a criminal case.

---

[550]*McKane v. Durston,* 153 U.S. 684, 688 (1894).
[551]See *Ross v. Moffit,* 417 U.S. 600, 610 (1974).
[552]*Griffin v. Illinois,* 351 U.S. 12, 18 (1965).

One way to test the effect of a legal or constitutional mistake on a trial involves taking the case to an appellate court and allowing a panel of judges to review it. Upon careful consideration of the appellant's briefs and oral argument by the parties, an appellate court will render an opinion concerning whether the alleged errors require reversal of the conviction.

2. THE APPEAL PROCESS: GENERALLY

The courts in most states have a process for appeal that takes the case from the trial court to an intermediate court of appeal as a matter of statutory right, with the possibility of having the top court in the state hear the case eventually. The move from the trial court to the court of appeal occurs as a matter of legal right because a court of appeal generally has no discretion concerning whether to hear a case. If the outcome is not favorable to the defendant in the court of appeal, additional litigation is possible within that state court system. Though theoretically it is possible to get a case to a state supreme court, in most instances these courts have the right to choose the cases they wish to hear. Where two separate courts of appeal within the same state have decided similar issues that have resulted in divergent and incompatible legal theories, a state supreme court may decide to take such a case to resolve the conflict between the lower courts of appeal. If a case contains a legal theory that has been decided in a way that is inconsistent with an earlier state supreme court decision, the state's high court may take the case and use it as a vehicle to revisit the issue or to adopt the new view offered by the lower court.

3. THE FIRST APPEAL: THE COURT OF APPEALS

The appellate procedure usually requires that the aggrieved defendant file a notice of appeal within a set period of time following the entry of the verdict. A failure to file the notice of appeal may preclude a higher court from considering the case. Subsequent to the notice of appeal, the defense attorney will consult the transcript of the trial and will conduct legal research covering the disputed areas of law, which will be incorporated within a legal brief presented to the appellate court and served on the prosecutor. In a similar manner, legal research and writing will result in a brief in which the prosecutor's office will present its view of the legal merits of the case. In some cases, the attorneys for both sides will simply submit the legal briefs and allow the appellate court to render its decision based on the briefs in the absence of oral argument. More typically, each side may determine that the best chance to prevail involves personally addressing the judges and putting the best face possible on the case.

Once the appellate judges have read the briefs and listened to and participated in oral arguments, they will take the case under advisement and, in due course, render a decision. Appellate decisions may take several directions. Perhaps the most common resolution in criminal cases is that the trial court decision is upheld and the conviction stands. The conviction also could be reversed, with directions to the trial court to dismiss the case and allow the defendant to walk free. The defendant's conviction could be reversed and the appellate court could order a retrial of the case. In many jurisdictions, an appellate court has the power to reduce the level of offense and to enter a conviction for a lesser included offense that the court considers appropriate under the circumstances.

4. THE APPELLATE ROLE OF A STATE SUPREME COURT

When the appellate court has rendered its decision, the prosecution and the defense are faced with some hard decisions. If the appellate court has rendered a verdict in the defendant's favor and has ordered a retrial or some other disposition, the attorneys for the government may request that the supreme court of the state consider hearing the case. As a general rule, state supreme courts have almost total discretion over which cases they will take. While there may be some cases under state law that state supreme courts must hear, criminal appeals do not normally fit into this category. Upon careful analysis of the appellate court decision, a prosecutor's office may conclude that its best efforts should be directed toward a retrial because the legal conclusions may predict a lack of success at the state supreme court level. If the appellate court has upheld the conviction of the defendant, few options realistically remain. The defense attorney may suggest that the case be appealed to the state supreme court, realizing that there is only a small possibility that the top court will take the case. The appeal to the supreme court may be a necessary prerequisite prior to filing a habeas corpus petition in the state or federal court system. For this reason, even though success in the supreme court may be only a distant hope, the attempt to obtain a hearing in a state supreme court may pave the way for other litigation.

If either party has proven successful in getting a review by the state's supreme court, each side will prepare a revised brief that will target the latest legal theories on the issues and will prepare for oral arguments in front of the high court. A process similar to that followed in the intermediate court of appeal will be repeated at the supreme court level. Each attorney tries to convince the court that his or her position is the most logical, reasonable, and intelligent resolution of the legal issues. While the decision rendered by a state supreme court will probably constitute the final resolution of the criminal case, either party may request a rehearing by the top court, but actually obtaining a rehearing will remain a remote possibility.

5. SUPREME COURT OF THE UNITED STATES: ONLY A POTENTIAL FOR REVIEW

A relatively small number of state supreme court decisions are successfully appealed to the Supreme Court of the United States, which, like state supreme courts, generally has control concerning whether to hear a particular case. Consistent with the Supreme Court's discretion in accepting cases, Rule 10 of the Rules of the Supreme Court states, "Review on a writ of certiorari is not a matter of right, but of judicial discretion. A petition for a writ of certiorari will be granted only for compelling reasons."[553] If the United States Supreme Court deems a case sufficiently important

---

[553]Rules of the Supreme Court of the United States, Rule 10, Considerations Governing Review on Certiorari. Adopted July 26, 1995.

where the case involves a federal question and where four justices vote to hear it, the Court will grant a writ of certiorari. The Court will be more likely to hear a case in which a state supreme court has decided a federal question in a manner that is in conflict with another top state court or where a state court has decided an important federal issue that should be settled by the Supreme Court of the United States.[554] Because the Supreme Court has no power to interpret state law or to reconsider the conclusions of fact based on what was presented at a state trial court, the Court must restrict its selection of cases and its decisions to cases involving federal questions. For that reason, in order to invoke the jurisdiction of the Court, litigants often contend that some federal right belonging to a defendant has been violated by the state government in bringing the case to trial and pursuing the criminal suit.

6. APPELLATE ASSISTANCE TO THE DEFENDANT: THE RIGHT TO COUNSEL

The Sixth Amendment guarantees that a person accused of a crime has the right to the assistance of counsel. Although this right is often thought to be primarily a right to counsel at trial, it has been extended to a variety of other situations. Assistance of counsel is available to the person undergoing custodial interrogation,[555] to a person in a postindictment or postinformation lineup,[556] and to a defendant involved in a preliminary hearing,[557] among other times. However, it is at the trial when assistance of counsel proves the most meaningful and where its absence is so devastating.[558] The value of appeal counsel to a defendant is almost the same as the importance of trial counsel because the pursuit of an appeal requires careful legal maneuvering and contending with arcane procedural paths to obtain meaningful appellate review.

In *Douglas v. California,*[559] a California trial court convicted the petitioners of thirteen felonies, including robbery and attempted murder (see Case 14.1). Douglas and his friend, both indigents, had rejected the assistance of counsel at their trial because they believed that the attorney was not properly prepared for trial. However, their preparation and performance in court as their own attorneys also proved to be inadequate, since they were convicted on all charges. At the time, California law allowed appeals by indigents but first required an appellate court to look over the trial record to preliminarily consider the merits of the appeal. If the appellate court determined that it would be of advantage to a defendant to have appellate counsel appointed, it would appoint such counsel but would otherwise deny the assistance of counsel for appellate purposes. In Douglas' case, the appellate court conducted the review and concluded that an appointed counsel for the

---

[554]Ibid.
[555]See *Miranda v. Arizona,* 384 U.S. 436 (1966).
[556]See *Gilbert v. California,* 388 U.S. 263 (1967).
[557]See *Coleman v. Alabama,* 399 U.S. 1 (1970).
[558]See *Gideon v. Wainwright,* 372 U.S. 335 (1963).
[559]372 U.S. 353 (1963).

appeal would not benefit the defendant or the court. A person in Mr. Douglas' position would be able to pursue an appeal so long as such a defendant possessed sufficient financial resources to afford an attorney. Because Douglas possessed no money, and the appellate court screened his case away, he had no avenue by which to make his one statutory appeal effective.

The Supreme Court considered the *Douglas* case with reference to an earlier one in which the kind of an appeal depended on the amount of money a person had. In *Griffin v. Illinois,* the Court observed that there could be no justice where justice depended on the amount of money a person possessed and held that a state may not grant appellate review in such a way as to discriminate against convicted defendants on account of their poverty.[560] In Douglas' case, the type of appeal he would have received would have been based on his ability to pay for private legal counsel, in the absence of a court determination on preliminary merits of the case. If he could have afforded legal counsel for appeal, he could have obtained the same appellate scrutiny as any other person. The Supreme Court found in favor of Douglas' argument that he should have a right to free counsel for his first appeal granted as a matter of right. Thus, an indigent defendant must be granted free assistance of counsel for the initial appeal. For Douglas and for future defendants, this decision assured a modicum of equality among the class of individuals who pursue criminal appeals.

Despite the precedent of *Douglas,* the strength of an appeal may still have some relationship to the financial well-being of a defendant. In *Smith v. Robbins,* 528 U.S. 259 (2000), the Supreme Court approved a California process in which the appellate attorney for the defendant evaluates the merits and grounds for an indigent's appeal (see Case 14.2). If the attorney finds strong grounds for the appeal, the appellate process continues along the typical path. However, if the facts of the case are less promising from an appellate perspective, California permits a reduced level of appellate advocacy. Where the attorney determines that the appeal possesses no meritorious legal basis, he or she files a brief with the appellate court attesting that no appealable issues exist. In contrast, a person who could afford a privately retained attorney would be able to have the case briefed and heard by the court of appeals on its merits, rather than having an attorney merely look over the record and potentially determine that no real meritorious appealable issues exist. According to the *Robbins* Court, the indigent appellate procedure does not have to be followed exactly as prior cases had proposed it should. The Court noted that proper appellate procedure was a "prophylactic framework" that it had established in *Douglas v. California* and later cases and was not to be viewed as a constitutional straitjacket. The states were permitted wide latitude in administering appellate procedures for indigents, subject to minimum standards of due process under the Fourteenth Amendment.

Assistance of counsel for indigents terminates following the one appeal granted as a matter of right by state laws or constitutions. In *Ross v. Moffitt,* 417 U.S. 600 (1974), an indigent wanted court-appointed appellate counsel to assist him in his

[560]351 U.S. 12 (1956).

discretionary appeals beyond the first level (see Case 14.3). In rejecting the argument favoring court-appointed counsel for discretionary appeals, Justice Rehnquist noted that the appellate level is significantly different from the trial level because the defendant has actually been convicted of a crime, stripped of the presumption of innocence, and had one appeal as a matter of right. Under either the Due Process Clause or Equal Protection Clause of the Fourteenth Amendment, the fact that a defendant wants to pursue additional litigation at the appellate level does not require a state to provide counsel for every legal maneuver a defendant might wish to pursue.

7. APPELLATE ASSISTANCE TO THE DEFENDANT: THE INDIGENT'S RIGHT TO A TRANSCRIPT

Essential to prosecuting a criminal appeal, besides the assistance of counsel, is the ability to get an appellate court to hear a defendant's case. The process of getting a criminal appeal in front of an appellate court involves more than just giving the notice of appeal. Appellate briefs that clearly state the legal reasons the defendant thinks the case should be reversed need to be prepared and served on the opposing counsel and transmitted to the court of appeals. The cost of an appeal will vary with the complexity of the criminal case, the legal issues involved, the length of the original criminal trial, and, to some extent, the jurisdiction.

In *Griffin v. Illinois*,[561] state law gave defendants a right to an appeal, but a full, direct appellate review could be obtained only by furnishing the appellate court with a report of the trial proceedings, certified by the trial judge. These documents were considered difficult to prepare without an expensive stenographic transcript of the trial proceedings. Because Griffin had no funds with which to purchase a transcript, he filed a motion in the trial court that a certified copy of the entire record, including a stenographic transcript of the proceedings, be furnished to him without cost. When the State of Illinois refused to furnish the trial transcripts, Griffin initiated a suit to force the state to pay for the transcript. When the case reached the United States Supreme Court, the Court expressed some concern that the only reason full appellate review was not available to Griffin was because he was too impoverished and that a person in better financial shape would have available a different legal remedy. The *Griffin* Court did not hold that a trial transcript had to be furnished in every case, but it did state that if a transcript was central to pursuing a meaningful appeal, the state was bound to furnish a free transcript.

The philosophy of *Douglas v. California* and of *Griffin v. Illinois* tends to indicate that the first appeal must be provided in a meaningful manner to all defendants, including those who are poor or of modest means, so that the type of justice one receives is not the type of justice that one can afford. These two cases and others involving related but similar issues are not recent decisions, but the Supreme Court of the United States has remained constitutionally sensitive to issues involving wealth that have the effect of denying substantially equal justice.

---

[561]Ibid.

8. LAYING THE GROUNDWORK FOR AN APPEAL: PRESERVING THE RECORD

During the trial, the defense counsel initiates the groundwork that will allow for an appeal if one is needed in the event of a conviction. Whenever the opposing side commits an error during the trial that is believed to be significant, the defense counsel will raise an objection. If the judge does not resolve the objection in favor of the defendant, this objection may become one of the grounds for a subsequent appeal. As potential appealable errors multiply throughout the course of a criminal trial, the trial attorney builds a significant record for appellate purposes. The defense generally is required to raise an objection at the time the alleged error occurs so that the trial judge is made aware of the problem and has a chance to correct it instead of waiting for an appeal with the hope of a reversal. Everyone's time would be more beneficially spent correcting the errors as they occur, rather than waiting to address the errors during the appellate process and potentially creating the need for a complete new trial.

9. THE PLAIN ERROR RULE: ABILITY TO APPEAL WITHOUT PRESERVING THE RECORD

Even where the defense attorney fails to notice errors committed by the judge, errors by the prosecution, or jury misconduct, some errors may be so egregious and outrageous that an appellate court would consider reversing a case even though they were observed by no one involved in the trial. This theory, known as the plain error rule,[562] constitutes an exception to the general rule that an objection must be made at the trial to preserve the issue for appeal. The plain error rule may have its best chance for appellate application where breaches of constitutional rights have occurred and where no functionary of the court system took notice during the trial. For example, plain error could be demonstrated where the prosecutor used evidence that clearly had been taken in violation of that defendant's Fourth Amendment rights against illegal searches, and through inadvertence, negligence, or ignorance, the defense counsel made no objection during the trial. Plain error has occurred where a trial court neglected to instruct the jury concerning one of the elements of the crime.[563] The plain error rule could be applied by an appellate court where a prosecutor used a coerced confession, known to the defense trial attorney, without objection. Such a fundamental breach of a constitutional right should trigger the ability for an appellate attorney successfully to argue the plain error rule upon appeal. As Justice Brennan, speaking of the plain error rule, stated in dissent in *United States v. Frady:*

> The Rule has been relied upon to correct errors that may have seriously prejudiced a possibly innocent defendant, *see, e.g., United States v. Mann,* 557 F.2d 1211, 1215–1216 (CA5 1977), and errors that severely undermine the integrity of the judicial proceeding, *see, e.g., United States v. Vaughan,* 443 F.2d 92, 94–95 (CA2 1971). The plain error Rule mitigates the harsh impact of the adversarial system, under

---

[562] Federal Rules of Criminal Procedure, Rule 52(b) (G.P.O. 2002).
[563] See *Penson v. Ohio,* 488 U.S. 75, 79 n. 1 (1988).

which the defendant is generally bound by the conduct of his lawyer, by providing relief in exceptional cases despite the lawyer's failure to object at trial. 456 U.S. 152, 180 (1982).

By following the principles that support the plain error rule, justice may be done by appellate courts when an attorney for a defendant has allowed an important legal point to pass unnoticed that, but for this theory, could result in substantial injustice.

10. SUBJECT MATTER JURISDICTION: ALWAYS AN APPEALABLE ISSUE

An issue that is always assertable upon appeal concerns the jurisdiction of the court to hear the case. Even when no objection was made at a trial, if later developments indicated that the crime occurred in a different state than the one in which the trial was held, it would become obvious that the trial court had no jurisdiction over the offense or the offender. The issue of jurisdiction over the crime is generally not a waivable defect and can be properly raised upon appeal even though no one raised the issue at, before, or during the trial.

11. THE APPELLATE PROCESS: MAKING IT WORK

Where a criminal appeal from a trial court decision has been briefed and argued before the appellate court, a variety of outcomes are possible when the court arrives at a decision. For the defendant, the best possible resolution would be for the appellate court to reverse the trial court decision and remand with instructions to dismiss the case with prejudice.[564]

In most cases, a court of appeals will affirm a trial court verdict, a decision that will most likely withstand additional litigation. A court's decision to affirm may be based on a clear view that the prosecution made its case beyond a reasonable doubt and that no substantial error affected the defendant's rights. Even an error that may appear to have a significant influence derogatory to a defendant's case may not cause an appellate court to reverse a conviction where the court deems the error to be "harmless error" beyond a reasonable doubt. In *Chapman v. California,* 366 U.S. 18 (1967), where the defendant's Fifth Amendment privilege against self-incrimination had been violated by the prosecution, the Supreme Court reversed the conviction since it could not say beyond a reasonable doubt that the constitutional violation had no effect on the outcome of the case (see Case 14.4). However, if there had been little chance that the error affected the outcome of the case and that the result would have been the same even in the absence of the error, the *Chapman* Court would have affirmed the convictions.[565]

---

[564]See *Burks v. United States,* 437 U.S. 1 (1978). The *Burks* Court held that the double jeopardy provision of the Fifth Amendment precluded a second trial once the appellate court determined the evidence insufficient to sustain the jury's verdict of guilty, and the only proper remedy available is to enter a verdict of acquittal. A retrial would not be barred if the reversal were based on trial error rather than on a failure of the prosecution to prove its case.

[565]The harmless error analysis has been applied, inter alia, where a jury instruction omitted an element of the crime, *Neder v. United States,* 527 U.S. 1 (1999); where an error in jury instructions proved not to be harmless error, *O'Neal v. McAninch,* 513 U.S. 432 (1995); in cases where the prosecution failed to disclose exculpatory evidence to the defense, *Kyles v. Whitley,* 514 U.S. 419 (1995); and where a jury instruction inadequately covered the concept of reasonable doubt, *Sullivan v. Louisiana,* 508 U.S. 275 (1993).

In a small number of cases, the court of appeals will reverse the case and order a new trial based on errors that occurred at the trial that substantially affected the original decision. Such errors that could be considered of sufficient magnitude to require a reversal include erroneous admission or exclusion of evidence, constitutional violations prior to or during the trial, prosecutorial misconduct, insufficiency of evidence, or jury misconduct, among other possibilities. If the appellate court has ordered a retrial, the prosecution must rethink its overall strategy and make a determination concerning whether to retry the individual as originally charged, offer a reduction in the charge in exchange for a plea bargain, or decide not to try the case again.

Alternatively, either the prosecution or the defense, depending on which side prevailed at the court of appeals, may elect to pursue the appeal to the next level. In most states that will be to the highest court of the state, often known as the supreme court. Since a court at this level generally possesses discretion considering which cases it will hear, the defendant may have a difficult time interesting the court in a single criminal case, but a prosecutor who has lost a case in the court of appeals may have a slightly easier time in getting the court to take the case. Where the top court of a state accepts a case from a state appellate court, the case resolution has much the same possible outcome as when the court of appeals first considered it.

12. ADVERSE APPELLATE RESULTS: THE NEXT STEP

The prosecution possesses some options where the state's highest court remands a case for retrial if the high court's decision was based on the United States Constitution; similarly, the defendant has some options if the case involves a federal question.[566] In either situation, when the case concerned an error involving a federal question, the losing appellate party may choose to petition the Supreme Court of the United States to consider the case. Such option may be effectively removed where a top state court decided a particular case based on adequate and independent state law grounds.[567] In most situations, the Supreme Court will decline review and will not issue a writ of certiorari.

Where the court of appeals or the supreme court of the state has returned a case to the lower court for a retrial, the prosecutor must start the prosecution from the beginning. Upon retrial, some rules and limitations govern what crime the prosecutor may charge the individual with having committed. On the assumption that a defendant has been tried for first-degree murder, has been convicted, and has had

---

[566]A federal question may be considered part of the case where the federal Constitution, federal law, or a federal treaty has been implicated in the case in some fashion. For example, a federal question exists where a defendant has alleged that her apartment was illegally searched and evidence seized in violation of the Fourth Amendment as applied to the states. If a federal question exists, an appeal to the Supreme Court of the United States is possible.

[567]For information concerning the doctrine that federal courts will not reverse state court decisions where they rest upon adequate and independent state grounds where no federal question is involved, see, e.g., *Murdock v. City of Memphis,* 87 U.S. 590 (1875); also see *Michigan v. Long,* 463 U.S. 1032, 1040 (1983), where Justice O'Connor noted, "Respect for the independence of state courts, as well as avoidance of rendering advisory opinions, have been the cornerstones of this Court's refusal to decide cases where there is an adequate and independent state ground." See also Westling, *Advisory Opinions and the "Constitutionally Required" Adequate and Independent State Grounds Doctrine,* 63 Tulane L.Rev. 379, 389, and n. 47 (1988).

the case reversed, the prosecutor may try the individual a second time for first-degree murder. Alternatively, if a defendant has been charged with first-degree murder but has been convicted only of second-degree murder, which was later reversed on appeal, the prosecution may not prosecute the defendant for first-degree murder. The legal theory in this case centers around the fact that the original trial court acquitted the defendant of first-degree murder and convicted of second-degree murder. A violation of the Fifth Amendment provision against double jeopardy would occur if the state were permitted to retry the defendant for the top level of murder. This limitation would also apply if the defendant had been originally charged only with second-degree murder, had been convicted of second-degree murder, and became subject to a retrial. The prosecution could not elevate the charge to first-degree murder on the retrial. These principles apply in any situation where the government wishes to levy a higher charge than was the subject crime at the first trial; in general, where there has been a conviction for a lesser offense, the government may not recharge at a higher level.

While double jeopardy provisions prevent a prosecutor from trying a defendant for a second time for a higher offense following a reversal, that type of limitation does not apply when a defendant has successfully procured a new trial and has been charged a second time for the same level of offense.[568] Following a second trial, case precedent allows a judge to give an enhanced sentence upon reconviction based on events that have come to light concerning the defendant's conduct since the first trial. The information may have come to the judge's attention from evidence presented at the second trial, from a subsequent presentence report, from the conduct record of the defendant while incarcerated on the original charge, and/or from general information available at the time of sentencing that was not presented at the earlier sentencing proceeding. A jury can impose an enhanced sentence following the second trial without offending due process so long as it remains unaware of the prior sentence so that the sentence enhancement could not have been given vindictively.[569] Sentence enhancement coexists with and is complementary to an extended sentence whether imposed under a habitual offender statute or under three-strikes legislation.

13. COLLATERAL ATTACK: THE WRIT OF HABEAS CORPUS

If a defendant has pursued a direct criminal appeal through the state appellate system and has not received satisfaction, the convicted defendant may consider pursuing a collateral attack that can be mounted in a state or federal court. In mounting a collateral attack on the conviction by filing a petition for a writ of habeas corpus, the defendant may initiate an action in the state criminal court that rendered the conviction or may file the petition in a federal district court. The general rule dictates that the defendant must have raised and fully litigated all potential legal issues at the proper times, whether at trial or upon appeal, so that the relevant courts have

---

[568]See *North Carolina v. Pearce,* 395 U.S. 711 (1969).
[569]See *Chaffin v. Stynchcombe,* 412 U.S. 17 (1973).

had an opportunity to correct any errors. An exception exists where the defendant is able to demonstrate that good cause existed for a failure to object or otherwise raise the issue at the proper time and that prejudice to the defendant's case has resulted. If the defendant succeeds in demonstrating good cause as the basis for the procedural default as well as "actual prejudice" to the case, there is the slight possibility of federal habeas corpus relief.[570]

In a collateral attack requesting a federal writ of habeas corpus, the defendant must make an allegation that he or she is being held in violation of the United States Constitution, federal law, or treaty. Whether the defendant seeks federal or state habeas corpus there must be a demonstration that all other possible avenues of relief have been pursued,[571] that relief has not been forthcoming, or that the pursuit would be futile.[572] Federal requirements decree that a litigant will not be deemed to have exhausted all state remedies if the defendant has the right under the law of the state that rendered the conviction to raise, by any available procedure, any federal question that is the center of the habeas corpus petition.[573] Where a federal district court determines that a defendant has remaining and unresolved state law claims, as a general rule, the district court must dismiss the petition. However, the defendant may return to federal court once the requisite exhaustion of remedies has occurred.[574] If a defendant meets the exhaustion test, the federal court will entertain the petition for the writ, but the burden of proof is on the applicant, who has the duty to rebut the presumption of state court correctness by clear and convincing evidence.[575]

When filing for a writ of habeas corpus, the defendant must allege the factual underpinnings of all of the constitutional errors in the case and is not permitted to save any errors to assert during later litigation in a subsequent habeas petition. A failure to bring all the claims at one time generally constitutes a waiver, and those claims will be forever barred as a basis for requesting a writ of habeas corpus. Part of the legal necessity of having some finality to a habeas petition surrounds the concept that there is no formal res judicata effect to a habeas corpus petition, whether granted or denied. Without a concept like abuse of the writ, a petitioning defendant could offer requests for relief without limit or merit, and courts would have to entertain them. Under modern court practice, the ready availability of appellate review dictated the need for some modification of the common-law rule that allowed endless habeas corpus petitions. Thus, under the legal theory of abuse of the writ, where a defendant brings a second or successive habeas corpus petition, a court will

---

[570]See *Engle v. Isaac,* 456 U.S. 107 (1982). See also *Reed v. Ross,* 468 U.S. 1 (1984), where the Supreme Court believed that there was good cause shown for not raising the issue during the trial and appellate stages, and that the issue properly could be first raised in a habeas corpus request.

[571]*Ex parte Hawk,* 321 U.S. 114, 116–117 (1944). In a per curiam opinion, the Court stated, "Ordinarily an application for *habeas corpus* by one detained under a state court judgment of conviction for crime will be entertained by a federal court only after all state remedies available, including all appellate remedies in the state courts and in this Court by appeal or writ of certiorari, have been exhausted."

[572]28 U.S.C. § 2254(b)(1) (Mathew Bender 2003).

[573]28 U.S.C. § 2254 (c) (Mathew Bender 2003).

[574]See *Rose v. Lundy,* 455 U.S. 509 (1982). The *Rose* Court held that a federal district court must dismiss habeas corpus petitions containing both exhausted and unexhausted claims.

[575]28 U.S.C. § 2254 (e) (Mathew Bender 2003).

generally dismiss the petition.[576] The government has the burden of pleading "abuse of the writ with particularity."[577] If the prosecution produces evidence that writ abuse has occurred, the burden of going forward with the evidence shifts to the other party. The defendant must demonstrate that there has been no abuse of the writ in seeking successive habeas corpus relief[578] involving an old claim or one that should have been included in the earlier habeas petition.

Where a federal district court grants the writ, the defendant will not normally gain immediate freedom but will remain in custody pending further litigation by the prosecution. The attorney for the state might decide to appeal the district court decision to the appropriate federal circuit court of appeal. Alternatively, if the federal district court denies the writ of habeas corpus, the defendant has a right of appeal similar to that of the prosecution. Once a court of appeal renders a judgment, either side is free to request a review by the Supreme Court of the United States.

A federal defendant who claims the right to be released upon the ground that the sentence was imposed in violation of the Constitution or laws of the United States is permitted to file an application for a writ of habeas corpus in the court that rendered the conviction with a request to vacate, set aside, or correct the conviction or sentence.[579] The federal prisoner must make a similar demonstration of exhaustion of remedies to be entitled to consideration for relief. Upon a favorable ruling in favor of the defendant, the federal prosecutor may appeal the decision; if the court fails to grant the writ of habeas corpus, the defendant may choose to appeal to the relevant federal circuit court of appeal and pursue the path of a state defendant seeking the same remedy.

MAJOR CASES

CASE 14.1

The Right to Counsel on Appeal

Douglas v. California
Supreme Court of the United States
372 U.S. 353 (1963)

FACTS

Following the filing of a thirteen-count information, which included robbery, assault with a deadly weapon, and assault with intent to commit murder, against defendants Douglas and Meyes, the defendant-petitioners were tried together and convicted. Prior to the trial, the single public defender appointed as counsel to represent both defendants requested a continuance so that separate counsel could be appointed. The trial court denied the motion and petitioners dismissed the defender, claiming he was unprepared, and again renewed motions for separate counsel and for a continuance. Subsequent to the conviction, petitioners requested, and were denied, the assistance of counsel on appeal, even though they were indigents. Under the California procedure at that time, the District Court of Appeal reviewed the record of the trial and came to the conclusion that the appeal was not meritorious and therefore refused to appoint appellate counsel. Although they pursued their appeal in the absence of an attorney, the appeal was heard without assistance of counsel, and their convictions were affirmed. The Supreme Court of California denied a discretionary review and the Supreme Court of the United States granted a writ of certiorari.

---

[576]See, generally, *McCleskey v. Zant,* 499 U.S. 467, 477–503 (1991).
[577]Ibid., 482.
[578]Ibid.
[579]28 U.S.C. § 2255 (Mathew Bender 2003).

PROCEDURAL ISSUE

Where the merits of the one appeal that an indigent legally possesses have been decided without the benefit of legal counsel, where fact of indigency was the only reason for lack of counsel, has there been a violation of the Sixth Amendment as applied to the states through the Due Process Clause of the Fourteenth Amendment?

HELD: YES

RATIONALE

Mr. Justice Douglas delivered the opinion of the Court.

★ ★ ★

[T]he type of an appeal a person is afforded in the District Court of Appeal hinges upon whether or not he can pay for the assistance of counsel. If he can, the appellate court passes on the merits of his case only after having the full benefit of written briefs and oral argument by counsel. If he cannot, the appellate court is forced to prejudge the merits before it can even determine whether counsel should be provided. At this stage in the proceedings, only the barren record speaks for the indigent, and, unless the printed pages show that an injustice has been committed, he is forced to go without a champion on appeal. Any real chance he may have had of showing that his appeal has hidden merit is deprived him when the court decides on an ex parte examination of the record that the assistance of counsel is not required.

★ ★ ★

[W]here the merits of the one and only appeal an indigent has as of right are decided without benefit of counsel, we think an unconstitutional line has been drawn between rich and poor.

When an indigent is forced to run this gauntlet of a preliminary showing of merit, the right to appeal does not comport with fair procedure. In the federal courts, on the other hand, an indigent must be afforded counsel on appeal whenever he challenges a certification that the appeal is not taken in good faith. *Johnson v. United States,* 352 U.S. 565. The federal courts must honor his request for counsel regardless of what they think the merits of the case may be; and "representation in the role of an advocate is required." *Ellis v. United States,* 356 U.S. 674. In California, however, once the court has "gone through"

the record and denied counsel, the indigent has no recourse but to prosecute his appeal on his own, as best he can, no matter how meritorious his case may turn out to be. The present case, where counsel was denied petitioners on appeal, shows that the discrimination is not between "possibly good and obviously bad cases," but between cases where the rich man can require the court to listen to argument of counsel before deciding on the merits, but a poor man cannot. There is lacking that equality demanded by the Fourteenth Amendment where the rich man, who appeals as of right, enjoys the benefit of counsel's examination into the record, research of the law, and marshalling of arguments on his behalf, while the indigent, already burdened by a preliminary determination that his case is without merit, is forced to shift for himself. The indigent, where the record is unclear or the errors are hidden, has only the right to a meaningless ritual, while the rich man has a meaningful appeal.

We vacate the judgment of the District Court of Appeal and remand the case to that court for further proceedings not inconsistent with this opinion.

It is so ordered.

NOTES, COMMENTS, AND QUESTIONS

1. With resources for appellate purposes in short supply, did California's provision for having the appellate court conduct a preliminary appellate merit review of the trial court record seem to make sense? Do you believe that an appellate court conducting an overview of a trial transcript would find most errors that might have been made during the trial? Would the merits of an appeal be best presented by an attorney-advocate for the defendant? Which procedure would you rather have if you happened to be in the position of the defendant? Would you prefer the decision be made by a trial judge who would have to second-guess personal mistakes to determine the merits of an appeal? Or would an aggressive attorney hoping to win the appellate case be more likely to properly and effectively represent an indigent defendant?

2. The *Douglas* Court was not extremely clear in offering its justification concerning the constitutional basis of its decision. In *Ross v. Moffitt,* 417 U.S. 600 (1974), Justice Rehnquist offered an explanation concerning the basis for the *Douglas* decision:

> The precise rationale for the *Griffin* and *Douglas* lines of cases has never been explicitly stated, some support being derived from the Equal Protection Clause of the Fourteenth Amendment, and some from the

Due Process Clause of that Amendment. Neither Clause, by itself, provides an entirely satisfactory basis for the result reached, each depending on a different inquiry which emphasizes different factors. "Due process" emphasizes fairness between the State and the individual dealing with the State, regardless of how other individuals in the same situation may be treated. "Equal protection," on the other hand, emphasizes disparity in treatment by a State between classes of individuals whose situations are arguably indistinguishable. *Moffit* at 608–609.

3. *Douglas* extended the Sixth Amendment right to counsel, free if a person cannot afford a lawyer, to the first appeal that all jurisdictions grant as a matter of state law or pursuant to the state constitution. Since the state does not have to give any right of appeal, why should it matter if the state provides a way for correcting errors without the use of a lawyer? Should the type of justice a person receives be dictated by the amount of wealth that person possesses? Despite this Court decision, does wealth (or lack of it) still have a role to play in the criminal justice system? Does it play a crucial role?

4. In *Douglas,* in a portion not printed here, the Court cited with approval the following passage dealing with differences in constitutional procedure: "But it is appropriate to observe that a State can, consistently with the Fourteenth Amendment, provide for differences so long as the result does not amount to a denial of due process or an 'invidious discrimination.'" *Williamson v. Lee Optical of Oklahoma,* 348 U.S. 483 (1955). The import seems to be that if California could devise a method of reviewing a trial for errors to determine the merits of a full appeal short of going through all the appellate procedure, the Court might approve. Could you think of a system that might meet constitutional muster? Would having the public defender's office take a close look over a defendant's criminal case be sufficient? The public defender would certainly have no vested interest in the status quo and could look aggressively to determine if appealable errors exist in a particular case. If you were an indigent person, would such a system be appropriate to defend your legal rights?

5. In an effort to meet the requirements of *Douglas v. California,* the California procedure adapted to the revised requirements for granting a meaningful appeal to those of indigent status. In *Anders v. California,* 386 U.S. 738 (1967), the court-appointed appellate counsel had a copy of the trial transcript but refused to write a formal brief or otherwise pursue the appeal. After looking over

the transcript, the appellate attorney concluded that there was no merit to the case. The attorney filed a "no merit" notice with the court of appeal. The court examined the record and affirmed the judgment of conviction. On a petition for a writ of habeas corpus, which Anders filed six years later, the court found the appeal lacked any merit. Upon appeal of the rejection of the writ, the California Supreme Court dismissed the habeas corpus application. Anders appealed to the Supreme Court of the United States, which reversed the California court result. The *Anders* Court suggested the following procedure, which, if followed, would meet the requirements of due process:

> The constitutional requirement of substantial equality and fair process can only be attained where counsel acts in the role of an active advocate in behalf of his client, as opposed to that of *amicus curiae.* The "no merit" letter and the procedure it triggers do not reach that dignity. Counsel should, and can with honor and without conflict, be of more assistance to his client and to the court. His role as advocate requires that he support his client's appeal to the best of his ability. Of course, if counsel finds his case to be wholly frivolous after a conscientious examination of it, he should so advise the court and request permission to withdraw. That request must, however, be accompanied by a brief referring to anything in the record that might arguably support the appeal. A copy of counsel's brief should be furnished the indigent, and time allowed him to raise any points that he chooses; the court—not counsel—then proceeds, after a full examination of all the proceedings, to decide whether the case is wholly frivolous. If it so finds, it may grant counsel's request to withdraw and dismiss the appeal insofar as federal requirements are concerned, or proceed to a decision on the merits, if state law so requires. On the other hand, if it finds any of the legal points arguable on their merits (and therefore not frivolous), it must, prior to decision, afford the indigent the assistance of counsel to argue the appeal. *Anders* at 744.

According to the Supreme Court, California did not meet the standards required under *Douglas v. California* as suggested in the preceding quotation. Could California revise its indigent appellate practice to comply with the suggestions? Since the practice outlined above was suggested by the Supreme Court, would strict compliance with the procedure satisfy the Supreme Court in the future? One could argue that California was looking after the interests of indigent defendants while at the same time not wasting limited state resources on cases that appeared to lack any real merit.

CASE 14.2

Denial of Indigent Appellate Assistance for Frivolous Appeals

Smith v. Robbins
Supreme Court of the United States
528 U.S. 259 (2000)

FACTS

A state court jury in California convicted Lee Robbins of second-degree murder. Upon appeal, the appointed counsel, after looking at all the material, concluded that appeal would be frivolous and of no merit. The attorney filed a brief with the state court of appeal which complied with the appellate procedure developed to meet constitutional dictates emanating from *Anders v. California,* 386 U.S. 738 (1967). The new procedure, established in *People v. Wende,* 25 Cal.3d 436 (1979), allowed an appellate attorney, if the attorney concluded that a case had no merit, to file

> a brief with the appellate court that summarizes the procedural and factual history of the case, with citations of the record. He also attests that he has reviewed the record, explained his evaluation of the case to his client, provided the client with a copy of the brief, and informed the client of his right to file a pro se supplemental brief. He further requests that the court independently examine the record for arguable issues. Unlike under the *Anders* procedure, counsel following *Wende* neither explicitly states that his review has led him to conclude that an appeal would be frivolous (although that is considered implicit, see *Wende,* 25 Cal.3d at 441–442, 600 P.2d at 1075) nor requests leave to withdraw. Instead, he is silent on the merits of the case and expresses his availability to brief any issues on which the court might desire briefing.

The procedure was followed in Robbins' case and the court of appeal agreed with the attorney's evaluation of the case that no arguable issues remained in the case. The court of appeal even considered two issues Robbins personally raised in a supplementary filing and denied Robbins' petition.

After Robbins exhausted his direct postconviction remedies, he filed a petition for a writ of habeas corpus in the appropriate federal district court. Robbins alleged that he had been denied the effective assistance of appellate counsel because his lawyer's brief to the court of appeal failed to comply with the suggestions in *Anders v. California* for cases where the attorney found no merit in the appeal. According to the district court, if an issue might arguably have supported an appeal it should have been included in the brief and since it was not, the district court concluded that a writ of habeas corpus should have been issued because the deviation in delivery of legal services amounted to deficient performance by counsel. The Ninth Circuit Court of Appeal agreed with the district and concluded that the brief filed by the appellate attorney was deficient because it did not, as the *Anders* procedure required, identify any legal issues that arguably could have supported the appeal. The Supreme Court of the United States granted certiorari.

PROCEDURAL ISSUE

Must states, while ensuring due process and adequate appellate equality between indigent litigants and more wealthy persons, follow exactly the suggestion of *Anders v. California*?

HELD: NO

RATIONALE

Justice Thomas delivered the opinion of the Court.

II

A

In *Anders,* we reviewed an earlier California procedure for handling appeals by convicted indigents. Pursuant to that procedure, Anders' appointed appellate counsel had filed a letter stating that he had concluded that there was "no merit to the appeal," *Anders,* 386 U.S. at 739–740. Anders, in response, sought new counsel; the State Court of Appeal denied the request, and Anders filed a *pro se* appellate brief. That court then issued an opinion that reviewed the four claims in his pro se brief and affirmed, finding no error (or no prejudicial error). *People v. Anders,* 167 Cal.App.2d 65, 333 P.2d 854 (1959). Anders thereafter sought a writ of *habeas corpus* from the State Court of Appeal, which denied relief, explaining that it had again reviewed the record and had found the appeal to be "'without merit.'" *Anders,* 386 U.S. at 740 (quoting unreported memorandum opinion).

We held that "California's action does not comport with fair procedure and lacks that equality that is required by the Fourteenth Amendment." *Id.* at 741. We placed the case within a line of precedent beginning with *Griffin v. Illinois,* 351 U.S. 12 (1956), and continuing with Douglas, *supra,* that imposed constitutional constraints on States when they choose to create appellate review. In finding the California procedure to have breached these constraints, we compared it to other procedures we had found invalid and to statutory requirements in the federal courts governing appeals by indigents with appointed counsel. We relied in particular on *Ellis v. United States,* 356 U.S. 674 (1958) *(per curiam),* a case involving federal statutory requirements, and quoted the following passage from it:

> "If counsel is convinced, after conscientious investigation, that the appeal is frivolous, of course, he may ask to withdraw on that account. If the court is satisfied that counsel has diligently investigated the possible grounds of appeal, and agrees with counsel's evaluation of the case, then leave to withdraw may be allowed and leave to appeal may be denied." *Anders, supra,* at 741–742 (quoting *Ellis, supra,* at 675).

In *Anders,* neither counsel, the state appellate court on direct appeal, nor the state *habeas* courts had made any finding of frivolity. We concluded that a finding that the appeal had "no merit" was not adequate, because it did not mean that the appeal was so lacking in prospects as to be "frivolous":

> We cannot say that there was a finding of frivolity by either of the California courts or that counsel acted in any greater capacity than merely as amicus curiae which was condemned in *Ellis.* 386 U.S. at 743.

★ ★ ★

In *Pennsylvania v. Finley,* 481 U.S. 551 (1987), we explained that the *Anders* procedure is not "an independent constitutional command," but rather is just "a prophylactic framework" that we established to vindicate the constitutional right to appellate counsel announced in *Douglas.* 481 U.S. at 555. We did not say that our *Anders* procedure was the only prophylactic framework that

could adequately vindicate this right; instead, by making clear that the Constitution itself does not compel the *Anders* procedure, we suggested otherwise. Similarly, in *Penson v. Ohio,* 488 U.S. 75 (1988), we described *Anders* as simply erecting "safeguards." 488 U.S. at 80.

★ ★ ★

Finally, any view of the procedure we described in the last section of *Anders* that converted it from a suggestion into a straitjacket would contravene our established practice, rooted in federalism, of allowing the States wide discretion, subject to the minimum requirements of the Fourteenth Amendment, to experiment with solutions to difficult problems of policy. In *Griffin v. Illinois,* 351 U.S. 12 (1956), which we invoked as the foundational case for our holding in *Anders,* see *Anders,* 386 U.S. at 741, we expressly disclaimed any pretensions to rulemaking authority for the States in the area of indigent criminal appeals. We imposed no broad rule or procedure, but merely held unconstitutional Illinois' requirement that indigents pay a fee to receive a trial transcript that was essential for bringing an appeal.

★ ★ ★

III

Having determined that California's *Wende* procedure is not unconstitutional merely because it diverges from the *Anders* procedure, we turn to consider the *Wende* procedure on its own merits. We think it clear that California's system does not violate the Fourteenth Amendment, for it provides "a criminal appellant pursuing a first appeal as of right [the] minimum safeguards necessary to make that appeal 'adequate and effective,'" *Evitts v. Lucey,* 469 U.S. 387, 392 (1985) (quoting *Griffin,* 351 U.S. at 20 (plurality opinion)).

A

As we have admitted on numerous occasions,

> "[t]he precise rationale for the *Griffin* and *Douglas* lines of cases has never been explicitly stated, some support being derived from the Equal Protection Clause of the Fourteenth Amendment and some from the Due Process Clause of that Amendment." *Evitts, supra,* at 403 (quoting *Ross v. Moffitt,* 417 U.S. 600, 608–609 (1974) (footnote omitted)).

But our case law reveals that, as a practical matter, the two clauses largely converge to require that a State's procedure "afford adequate and effective appellate review to indigent defendants," *Griffin,* 351 U.S. at 20 (plurality opinion). A State's procedure provides such review so long as it reasonably ensures that an indigent's appeal will be resolved in a way that is related to the merit of that appeal.

★ ★ ★

In determining whether a particular state procedure satisfies this standard, it is important to focus on the underlying goals that the procedure should serve—to ensure that those indigents whose appeals are not frivolous receive the counsel and merits brief required by *Douglas,* and also to enable the State to "protect itself so that frivolous appeals are not subsidized and public moneys not needlessly spent," *Griffin, supra,* at 24 (Frankfurter, J., concurring in judgment). For, although, under *Douglas,* indigents generally have a right to counsel on a first appeal as of right, it is equally true that this right does not include the right to bring a frivolous appeal and, concomitantly, does not include the right to counsel for bringing a frivolous appeal.

★ ★ ★

Since Robbins' counsel complied with a valid procedure for determining when an indigent's direct appeal is frivolous, we reverse the Ninth Circuit's judgment that the *Wende* procedure fails adequately to serve the constitutional principles we identified in *Anders.* But our reversal does not necessarily mean that Robbins' claim that his appellate counsel rendered constitutionally ineffective assistance fails. For it may be, as Robbins argues, that his appeal was not frivolous and that he was thus entitled to a merits brief rather than to a *Wende* brief.

★ ★ ★

The judgment of the Court of Appeals is reversed, and the case is remanded for further proceedings consistent with this opinion.

It is so ordered.

NOTES, COMMENTS, AND QUESTIONS

1. Under California's plan, an attorney who finds only frivolous legal grounds files a brief with the appellate court summarizing the procedural and factual history of the case and attests to having reviewed the case and having determined that it lacks substantive appellate merit. The attorney also informs the court that he or she has notified the client of the client's right to file a pro se supplemental brief with the court. The attorney requests that the appellate court independently examine the record for arguable issues, but he or she does not explicitly state why the review has led to the conclusion that an appeal would be frivolous. The attorney does not request permission to withdraw as defendant's counsel, but implicit in the procedure of giving notice to the court is the opinion by appellate counsel that a formal appeal would be frivolous. In filing the report with the court, the appellate attorney remains silent on the case's merits and indicates his or her availability to brief any arguable issues that an appellate court might determine to contain merit. Upon receipt of the report, the appellate court conducts a review of the entire record; if it finds that the appeal contains only frivolous grounds, that court will affirm the lower court decision. This seems to satisfy the Supreme Court so long as the essentials are followed. Has the Supreme Court of the United States backtracked on its original concern for the rights of indigent defendants and the concern that justice might be dependent upon one's wealth? What seemed like an original concern for equal justice may have eroded somewhat. Has it? Explain.

2. Do you think that appellant in *Smith v. Robbins* received roughly the same representation that a person who could afford an appellate attorney would have received? Why or why not? Does it seem close to providing the expected level of representation contemplated in *Douglas v. California*? Why or why not? If not, what would you improve with a view to making sure that the type of appeal a defendant receives is not driven by the amount of money he or she possesses?

3. If a convicted defendant privately retains an attorney, he or she will have the full benefit of a briefed and argued case before the appellate court in California. A poor person only has the benefit of having an attorney appointed to "scan" the record and send a report to the appellate court. Can you justify the difference in available justice? Does this procedure appear fair? Could it be considered substantively fair? Would our society be better served if we simply decided to give every defendant one real and substantial appeal rather than trying to serve legally needy persons with a reduced level of appellate representation in order to save public resources? Why or why not? Explain.

CASE 14.3

Sixth Amendment Right to Counsel Does Not Extend to Indigent's Discretionary Court Review

Ross v. Moffitt
Supreme Court of the United States
417 U.S. 600 (1974)

FACTS

A North Carolina trial court convicted an indigent, Claude Frank Moffitt, under a bill of indictment that charged him with forgery and with uttering and, in a separate case, with forgery. Moffitt was represented by a court-appointed attorney and had the benefit of legal counsel for his first appeal in each of the cases. In one of the cases that he wanted to take to the North Carolina Supreme Court, he was denied appointment of counsel for discretionary review by the North Carolina Supreme Court. In the other case, the North Carolina courts appointed counsel to prepare for an appeal to the Supreme Court of North Carolina. When Moffitt desired that counsel be appointed for an appeal to the Supreme Court of the United States, the North Carolina courts refused. Mr. Moffitt contended that the due process clause of the Fourteenth Amendment required that the state of North Carolina provide him with legal counsel for his appellate litigation. No North Carolina Court was receptive to his argument and he perfected his appeal to the Supreme Court of United States. When he pursued litigation in the federal court system, he had some initial success in the district courts, but the Fourth Circuit, 483 F.2d at 654, reversed portions of the federal district decision and remanded the case back to the lower courts. Moffitt appealed to the Supreme Court of the United States.

PROCEDURAL ISSUE

If state defendants wish to pursue discretionary appeals beyond the first appeal granted as a matter of right, does the due process clause of the Fourteenth Amendment require that indigent defendants be furnished with free legal counsel?

HELD: NO

RATIONALE

Mr. Justice Rehnquist delivered the opinion of the Court.

★ ★ ★

II

This Court, in the past 20 years, has given extensive consideration to the rights of indigent persons on appeal. In *Griffin v. Illinois,* 351 U.S. 12 (1956), the first of the pertinent cases, the Court had before it an Illinois rule allowing a convicted criminal defendant to present claims of trial error to the Supreme Court of Illinois only if he procured a transcript of the testimony adduced at his trial. No exception was made for the indigent defendant, and thus one who was unable to pay the cost of obtaining such a transcript was precluded from obtaining appellate review of asserted trial error. Mr. Justice Frankfurter, who cast the deciding vote, said in his concurring opinion:

> …Illinois has decreed that only defendants who can afford to pay for the stenographic minutes of a trial may have trial errors reviewed on appeal by the Illinois Supreme Court. *Id.* at 22.

The Court in *Griffin* held that this discrimination violated the Fourteenth Amendment.

Succeeding cases invalidated similar financial barriers to the appellate process, at the same time reaffirming the traditional principle that a State is not obliged to provide any appeal at all for criminal defendants. *McKane v. Durston,* 153 U.S. 684 (1894). The cases encompassed a variety of circumstances, but all had a common theme. For example, *Lane v. Brown,* 372 U.S. 477 (1963), involved an Indiana provision declaring that only a public defender could obtain a free transcript of a hearing on a *coram nobis* application. If the public defender declined to request one, the indigent prisoner seeking to appeal had no recourse. In *Draper v. Washington,* 372 U.S. 487 (1963), the State permitted an indigent to obtain a free transcript of the trial at which he was convicted only if he satisfied the trial judge that his contentions on appeal would not be frivolous. The appealing defendant was in effect bound by the trial court's conclusions in seeking to review the determination of frivolousness, since no transcript or its equivalent was made available to him. In *Smith v. Bennett,* 365 U.S. 708 (1961), Iowa had required a filing fee in order to process a state habeas corpus application by a convicted defendant, and in *Burns v. Ohio,* 360 U.S. 252 (1959), the State of Ohio required a $20 filing fee in order to move the Supreme Court of Ohio for leave to appeal from a judgment of the Ohio Court of Appeals affirming a criminal conviction. Each of these state-imposed financial barriers to the adjudication of a criminal defendant's appeal was held to violate the Fourteenth Amendment.

The decisions discussed above stand for the proposition that a State cannot arbitrarily cut off appeal rights for indigents while leaving open avenues of appeal for more affluent persons. In *Douglas v. California,* 372 U.S. 353 (1963), however, a case decided the same day as *Lane, supra,* and *Draper, supra,* the Court departed somewhat from the limited doctrine of the transcript and fee cases and undertook an examination of whether an indigent's access to the appellate system was adequate. The Court in *Douglas* concluded that a State does not fulfill its responsibility toward indigent defendants merely by waiving its own requirements that a convicted defendant procure a transcript or pay a fee in order to appeal, and held that the State must go further and provide counsel for the indigent on his first appeal as of right. It is this decision we are asked to extend today.

This Court held unconstitutional California's requirement that counsel on appeal would be appointed for an indigent only if the appellate court determined that such appointment would be helpful to the defendant or to the court itself. The Court noted that, under this system, an indigent's case was initially reviewed on the merits, without the benefit of any organization or argument by counsel. By contrast, persons of greater means were not faced with the preliminary "ex parte examination of the record," *id.* at 356, but had their arguments presented to the court in fully briefed form. The Court noted, however, that its decision extended only to initial appeals as of right....

★ ★ ★

We do not believe that the Due Process Clause requires North Carolina to provide respondent with counsel on his discretionary appeal to the State Supreme Court. At the trial stage of a criminal proceeding, the right of an indigent defendant to counsel is fundamental and binding upon the States by virtue of the Sixth and Fourteenth Amendments. *Gideon v. Wainwright,* 372 U.S. 335 (1963). But there are significant differences between the trial and appellate stages of a criminal proceeding. The purpose of the trial stage from the State's point of view is to convert a criminal defendant from a person presumed innocent to one found guilty beyond a reasonable doubt. To accomplish this purpose, the State employs a prosecuting attorney who presents evidence to the court, challenges any witnesses offered by the defendant, argues rulings of the court, and makes direct arguments to the court and jury seeking to persuade

them of the defendant's guilt. Under these circumstances, reason and reflection require us to recognize that, in our adversary system of criminal justice, any person haled into court, who is too poor to hire a lawyer, cannot be assured a fair trial unless counsel is provided for him.

By contrast, it is ordinarily the defendant, rather than the State, who initiates the appellate process, seeking not to fend off the efforts of the State's prosecutor, but rather to overturn a finding of guilt made by a judge or jury below. The defendant needs an attorney on appeal not as a shield to protect him against being "haled into court" by the State and stripped of his presumption of innocence, but rather as a sword to upset the prior determination of guilt. This difference is significant for, while no one would agree that the State may simply dispense with the trial stage of proceedings without a criminal defendant's consent, it is clear that the State need not provide any appeal at all. *McKane v. Durston,* 153 U.S. 684 (1894). The fact that an appeal has been provided does not automatically mean that a State then acts unfairly by refusing to provide counsel to indigent defendants at every stage of the way. *Douglas v. California, supra.* Unfairness results only if indigents are singled out by the State and denied meaningful access to the appellate system because of their poverty. That question is more profitably considered under an equal protection analysis.

★ ★ ★

This is not to say, of course, that a skilled lawyer, particularly one trained in the somewhat arcane art of preparing petitions for discretionary review, would not prove helpful to any litigant able to employ him. An indigent defendant seeking review in the Supreme Court of North Carolina is therefore somewhat handicapped in comparison with a wealthy defendant who has counsel assisting him in every conceivable manner at every stage in the proceeding. But both the opportunity to have counsel prepare an initial brief in the Court of Appeals and the nature of discretionary review in the Supreme Court of North Carolina make this relative handicap far less than the handicap borne by the indigent defendant denied counsel on his initial appeal as of right in *Douglas.* And the fact that a particular service might be of benefit to an indigent defendant does not mean that the service is constitutionally required. The duty of the State under our cases is not to duplicate the legal arsenal that may be privately retained by a criminal defendant in a continuing effort to reverse his conviction, but only to assure the indigent defendant an adequate opportunity to present his claims fairly in the context of the State's appellate process. We think respondent was given that opportunity under the existing North Carolina system.

★ ★ ★

VI

We do not mean by this opinion to in any way discourage those States which have, as a matter of legislative choice, made counsel available to convicted defendants at all stages of judicial review. Some States which might well choose to do so as a matter of legislative policy may conceivably find that other claims for public funds within or without the criminal justice system preclude the implementation of such a policy at the present time. North Carolina, for example, while it does not provide counsel to indigent defendants seeking discretionary review on appeal, does provide counsel for indigent prisoners in several situations where such appointments are not required by any constitutional decision of this Court. Our reading of the Fourteenth Amendment leaves these choices to the State, and respondent was denied no right secured by the Federal Constitution when North Carolina refused to provide counsel to aid him in obtaining discretionary appellate review.

The judgment of the Court of Appeals' holding to the contrary is

Reversed.

NOTES, COMMENTS, AND QUESTIONS

1. The *Moffitt* Court noted, "The fact that an appeal has been provided does not automatically mean that a state then acts unfairly by refusing to provide counsel to indigent defendants at every stage of the way." What is the logical difference between requiring that free counsel be given to an indigent defendant for the first appeal from the trial court decision and not mandating a similar level of legal assistance for a discretionary second or subsequent appeal? Does the *Moffitt* Court effectively make this distinction? Why or why not?

2. In *Griffin v. Illinois,* 351 U.S. 12 (1956), the Court determined that a state could not constitutionally place economic roadblocks that had the effect of allowing a wealthier defendant to have a meaningful and complete appeal, where a convicted defendant with no money or a defendant of very modest means might be precluded from prosecuting the first criminal appeal that is granted

as a matter of right. In *Griffin,* a complete appellate review could be obtained only by furnishing the appellate court with a bill of exceptions or report of the trial proceedings that had been certified by the trial judge. Frequently it was determined to be impossible to prepare such documents without a stenographic transcript of the trial proceedings, which were not furnished free of charge. Accordingly, in *Griffin* the Court determined, consistent with due process, that a transcript or whatever documentation was required must be supplied free to indigent defendants who want to prosecute the first appeal. As the Court stated, "There can be no equal justice where the kind of trial a man gets depends on the amount of money he has. Destitute defendants must be afforded as adequate appellate review as defendants who have money enough to buy transcripts." *Griffin* at 19. Does relative wealth play a strong role in the legal talent that one can afford to hire? Is this especially true where a defendant must rely upon appointed legal counsel? Why or why not?

CASE 14.4

Reversal Is Not Mandated under the Harmless Error Rule

Chapman v. California
Supreme Court of the United States
386 U.S. 18 (1967)

FACTS

A California trial jury convicted Ruth Chapman and Thomas Teale of a robbery, kidnapping, and murder of a bartender, after a trial where the defendants did not take the witness stand in their own defense. The legal theory and constitutional interpretation at the time of the trial permitted the prosecutor to comment upon their failure to testify and allowed the jury to be told that it could draw adverse inferences from their failure to testify. Subsequent to the trial, but before Chapman's case had been considered on appeal by the California Supreme Court, the Supreme Court decided *Griffin v. California,* 380 U.S. 609 (1965), which held as invalid California's constitutional provision and practice of commenting on a defendant's failure to testify, on the ground that it put a penalty on the exercise of a person's right not to be compelled to be a witness against himself, guaranteed by the Fifth Amendment to the United States Constitution and made applicable to the states by the Fourteenth Amendment.

The California Supreme Court agreed that the defendants had been subjected to an unconstitutional violation of rights by the lower court and the prosecutor who tried the case, but the Court refused to reverse Chapman's decision because it invoked the "harmless error rule." The harmless error rule holds that where a constitutional or other error has occurred, the verdict will stand despite the error if the reviewing court can determine that beyond a reasonable doubt, the error was not determinative of the outcome. The Supreme Court of the United States granted certiorari.

PROCEDURAL ISSUE

May a state court use the harmless error rule in order to refuse to reverse a decision in a criminal case where a defendant's constitutional rights have been violated?

HELD: YES

RATIONALE

Mr. Justice Black delivered the opinion of the Court.

★ ★ ★

I

Before deciding the two questions here—whether there can ever be harmless constitutional error and whether the error here was harmless—we must first decide whether state or federal law governs. The application of a state harmless error rule is, of course, a state question where it involves only errors of state procedure or state law. But the error from which these petitioners suffered was a denial of rights guaranteed against invasion by the Fifth and Fourteenth Amendments, rights rooted in the Bill of Rights, offered and championed in the Congress by James Madison, who told the Congress that the "independent" federal courts would be the "guardians of those rights." Whether a conviction for crime should stand when a State has failed to accord federal constitutionally guaranteed rights is every bit as much of a federal question as what particular federal constitutional provisions themselves mean, what they guarantee, and whether they have been denied. With faithfulness to the constitutional union of the States, we cannot leave to the States the formulation of the authoritative laws, rules, and remedies designed to protect people from infractions by the States of federally guaranteed rights. We have no hesitation in saying that the right of these petitioners not to be punished for exercising their Fifth and Fourteenth Amendment right to be silent—expressly created by the Federal Constitution itself—is a federal right which, in the absence of appropriate congressional action, it is our responsibility to protect by fashioning the necessary rule.

II

We are urged by petitioners to hold that all federal constitutional errors, regardless of the facts and circumstances, must always be deemed harmful. Such a holding, as petitioners correctly point out, would require an automatic reversal of their convictions and make further discussion unnecessary. We decline to adopt any such rule. All 50 States have harmless error statutes or rules, and the United States long ago, through its Congress, established for its courts the rule that judgments shall not be reversed for "errors or defects which do not affect the substantial rights of the parties." 28 U.S.C. § 2111. None of these rules, on its face, distinguishes between federal constitutional errors and errors of state law or federal statutes and rules. All of these rules, state or federal, serve a very useful purpose insofar as they block setting aside convictions for small errors or defects that have little, if any, likelihood of having changed the result of the trial. We conclude that there may be some constitutional errors which, in the setting of a particular case, are so unimportant and insignificant that they may, consistent with the Federal Constitution, be deemed harmless, not requiring the automatic reversal of the conviction.

III

In fashioning a harmless constitutional error rule, we must recognize that harmless error rules can work very unfair and mischievous results when, for example, highly important and persuasive evidence, or argument, though legally forbidden, finds its way into a trial in which the question of guilt or innocence is a close one. What harmless error rules all aim at is a rule that will save the good in harmless error practices while avoiding the bad, so far as possible.

★ ★ ★

We prefer the approach of this Court in deciding what was harmless error in our recent case of *Fahy v. Connecticut,* 375 U.S. 85. There we said: "The question is whether there is a reasonable possibility that the evidence complained of might have contributed to the conviction." *Id.* at 86–87. Although our prior cases have indicated that there are some constitutional rights so basic to a fair trial that their infraction can never be treated as harmless error, this statement in *Fahy* itself belies any belief that all trial errors which violate the Constitution automatically call for reversal. At the same time, however, like the federal harmless error statute, it emphasizes an intention not to treat as harmless those constitutional errors that "affect substantial rights" of a party. An error in admitting plainly relevant evidence which possibly influenced the jury adversely to a litigant cannot, under *Fahy,* be conceived of as harmless. Certainly error, constitutional error, in illegally admitting highly prejudicial evidence or comments, casts on someone other than the person prejudiced by it a burden to show that it was harmless. It is for that reason that the original common law harmless error rule put the burden on the beneficiary of the error either to prove that there was no injury or to suffer a reversal of his erroneously obtained judgment. There is little, if any, difference between our statement in *Fahy v. Connecticut* about "whether there is a reasonable possibility that the evidence complained of might have contributed to the conviction" and requiring the beneficiary of a constitutional error to prove beyond a reasonable doubt that the error complained of did not contribute to the verdict obtained. We therefore do no more than adhere to the meaning of our *Fahy* case when we hold, as we now do, that, before a federal constitutional error can be held harmless, the court must be able to declare a belief that it was harmless beyond a reasonable doubt. While appellate courts do not ordinarily have the original task of applying such a test, it is a familiar standard to all courts, and we believe its adoption will provide a more workable standard, although achieving the same result as that aimed at in our *Fahy* case.

IV

Applying the foregoing standard, we have no doubt that the error in these cases was not harmless to petitioners. To reach this conclusion, one need only glance at the prosecutorial comments compiled from the record by petitioners' counsel....[T]he state prosecutor's argument and the trial judge's instruction to the jury continuously and repeatedly impressed the jury that from the failure of petitioners to testify, to all intents and purposes, the inferences from the facts in evidence had to be drawn in favor of the State—in short, that, by their silence, petitioners had served as irrefutable witnesses against themselves. And though the case in which this occurred presented a reasonably strong "circumstantial

web of evidence" against petitioners, 63 Cal.2d at 197, 404 P.2d at 220, it was also a case in which, absent the constitutionally forbidden comments, honest, fair-minded jurors might very well have brought in not-guilty verdicts. Under these circumstances, it is completely impossible for us to say that the State has demonstrated, beyond a reasonable doubt, that the prosecutor's comments and the trial judge's instruction did not contribute to petitioners' convictions. Such a machine-gun repetition of a denial of constitutional rights, designed and calculated to make petitioners' version of the evidence worthless, can no more be considered harmless than the introduction against a defendant of a coerced confession. See, *e.g., Payne v. Arkansas,* 356 U.S. 560. Petitioners are entitled to a trial free from the pressure of unconstitutional inferences.

Reversed and remanded.

NOTES, COMMENTS, AND QUESTIONS

1. As a practical matter, using the harmless error rule makes a significant amount of sense; to follow another path and require a retrial when the result is already known would be a waste of scarce judicial resources. Alternatively, one might argue that when a federal constitutional right has been violated in a criminal trial, in order to give recognition to the Constitution, the error should require a new trial in every case. Which way do you believe produces the most logical outcome? Why? In the *Chapman* case itself, although the Court approved of the use of the harmless error rule, it reversed Chapman's conviction because the error was not harmless beyond a reasonable doubt. The conviction in *Chapman* could have been upheld if a reasonable person could have been convinced that the result (conviction) would have been the same with or without the error. The prosecutor's comments covered motive and procurement of firearms, the shooting of the deceased in an automobile, who did the shooting, and who possessed a loaded firearm upon arrest. Since the defendants had the right under the Fifth Amendment, as applied to the states through the Fourteenth Amendment, not to testify, the fact that the prosecutor mentioned evidence that was never explained by the defendants made the use of the Fifth Amendment legally costly to the defendants. Such conduct violated the Fifth Amendment.

2. According to Rule 52 of the Federal Rules of Criminal Procedure, a harmless error consists of any error, defect, irregularity, or variance that does not affect substantial rights of a defendant. The harmless error rule

has been used to preserve criminal convictions in a variety of contexts and involving a variety of errors. In *Neder v. United States,* 527 U.S. 1 (1999), the harmless error rule was applied to a jury instruction that omitted an element of the offense. In *Arizona v. Fulminante,* 499 U.S. 279 (1991), the erroneous admission of evidence of a coerced confession in violation of the Fifth Amendment's guarantee against self-incrimination was deemed to be subject to the harmless error standard. But where other types of constitutional issues have arisen, the harmless error rule may not be applied. In *Vasquez v. Hillery,* 474 U.S. 254 (1986), in a case involving admitted racial discrimination in the context of a grand jury, the Court rejected the use of the harmless error rule and overturned a murder verdict. Essentially, the Court held that racial discrimination can never be harmless error and must have affected substantial rights of the defendant when practiced by the government. In a recent Louisiana case decided by the Fifth Circuit court of Appeals, *Pickney v. Cain,* 2003 U.S. App. LEXIS 14566 (2003), the defendant had alleged a violation of equal protection due to racial discrimination in the selection of the grand jury foreperson, but the claim had been procedurally defaulted so the court declined to reach the racial discrimination claim. This decision calls into question the theory of automatic reversal for any case where racial discrimination exists, since the *Pickney* court felt that the outcome would not have changed even if the defendant had prevailed on his discrimination claim.

The Constitution of the United States

THE PREAMBLE

We the people of the United States, in order to form a more perfect union, establish justice, insure domestic tranquility, provide for the common defense, promote the general welfare, and secure the blessings of liberty to ourselves and our posterity, do ordain and establish this Constitution for the United States of America.

ARTICLE I

Section 1. All legislative powers herein granted shall be vested in a Congress of the United States, which shall consist of a Senate and House of Representatives.

Section 2. The House of Representatives shall be composed of members chosen every second year by the people of the several states, and the electors in each state shall have the qualifications requisite for electors of the most numerous branch of the state legislature.

No person shall be a Representative who shall not have attained to the age of twenty five years, and been seven years a citizen of the United States, and who shall not, when elected, be an inhabitant of that state in which he shall be chosen.

Representatives and direct taxes shall be apportioned among the several states which may be included within this union, according to their respective numbers, which shall be determined by adding to the whole number of free persons, including those bound to service for a term of years, and excluding Indians not taxed, three fifths of all other Persons. The actual Enumeration shall be made within three years after the first meeting of the Congress of the United States, and within every subsequent term of ten years, in such manner as they shall by law direct. The number of Representatives shall not exceed one for every thirty thousand, but each state shall have at least one Representative; and until such enumeration shall be made, the state of New Hampshire shall be entitled to choose three, Massachusetts eight, Rhode Island and Providence Plantations one, Connecticut five, New York six, New Jersey four, Pennsylvania eight, Delaware one, Maryland six, Virginia ten, North Carolina five, South Carolina five, and Georgia three.

When vacancies happen in the Representation from any state, the executive authority thereof shall issue writs of election to fill such vacancies.

The House of Representatives shall choose their speaker and other officers; and shall have the sole power of impeachment.

Section 3. The Senate of the United States shall be composed of two Senators from each state, chosen by the legislature thereof, for six years; and each Senator shall have one vote.

Immediately after they shall be assembled in consequence of the first election, they shall be divided as equally as may be into three classes. The seats of the Senators of the first class shall be vacated at the expiration of the second year, of the second class at the expiration of the fourth year, and the third class at the expiration of the sixth year, so that one third may be chosen every second year; and if vacancies happen by resignation, or otherwise, during the recess of the legislature of any state, the executive thereof may make temporary appointments until the next meeting of the legislature, which shall then fill such vacancies.

No person shall be a Senator who shall not have attained to the age of thirty years, and been nine years a citizen of the United States and who shall not, when elected, be an inhabitant of that state for which he shall be chosen.

The Vice President of the United States shall be President of the Senate, but shall have no vote, unless they be equally divided.

The Senate shall choose their other officers, and also a President pro tempore, in the absence of the Vice President, or when he shall exercise the office of President of the United States.

The Senate shall have the sole power to try all impeachments. When sitting for that purpose, they shall be on oath or affirmation. When the President of the United States is tried, the Chief Justice shall preside: And no person shall be convicted without the concurrence of two thirds of the members present.

Judgment in cases of impeachment shall not extend further than to removal from office, and disqualification to hold and enjoy any office of honor, trust or profit under the United States: but the party convicted shall nevertheless be liable and subject to indictment, trial, judgment and punishment, according to law.

Section 4. The times, places and manner of holding elections for Senators and Representatives, shall be prescribed in each state by the legislature thereof; but the Congress may at any time by law make or alter such regulations, except as to the places of choosing Senators.

The Congress shall assemble at least once in every year, and such meeting shall be on the first Monday in December, unless they shall by law appoint a different day.

Section 5. Each House shall be the judge of the elections, returns and qualifications of its own members, and a majority of each shall constitute a quorum to do business; but a smaller number may adjourn from day to day, and may be authorized to compel the attendance of absent members, in such manner, and under such penalties as each House may provide.

Each House may determine the rules of its proceedings, punish its members for disorderly behavior, and, with the concurrence of two thirds, expel a member.

Each House shall keep a journal of its proceedings, and from time to time publish the same, excepting such parts as may in their judgment require secrecy; and the yeas and nays of the members of either House on any question shall, at the desire of one fifth of those present, be entered on the journal.

Neither House, during the session of Congress, shall, without the consent of the other, adjourn for more than three days, nor to any other place than that in which the two Houses shall be sitting.

Section 6. The Senators and Representatives shall receive a compensation for their services, to be ascertained by law, and paid out of the treasury of the United States. They shall in all cases, except treason, felony and breach of the peace, be privileged from arrest during their attendance at the session of their respective Houses, and in going to and returning from the same; and for any speech or debate in either House, they shall not be questioned in any other place.

No Senator or Representative shall, during the time for which he was elected, be appointed to any civil office under the authority of the United States, which shall have been created, or the emoluments whereof shall have been increased during such time: and no person holding any office under the United States, shall be a member of either House during his continuance in office.

Section 7. All bills for raising revenue shall originate in the House of Representatives; but the Senate may propose or concur with amendments as on other Bills.

Every bill which shall have passed the House of Representatives and the Senate, shall, before it become a law, be presented to the President of the United States; if he approve he shall sign it, but if not he shall return it, with his objections to that House in which it shall have originated, who shall enter the objections at large on their journal, and proceed to reconsider it. If after such reconsideration two thirds of that House shall agree to pass the bill, it shall be sent, together with the objections, to the other House, by which it shall likewise be reconsidered, and if approved by two thirds of that House, it shall become a law. But in all such cases the votes of both Houses shall be determined by yeas and nays, and the names of the persons voting for and against the bill shall be entered on the journal of each House respectively. If any bill shall not be returned by the President within ten days (Sundays excepted) after it shall have been presented to him, the same shall be a law, in like manner as if he had signed it, unless the Congress by their adjournment prevent its return, in which case it shall not be a law.

Every order, resolution, or vote to which the concurrence of the Senate and House of Representatives may be necessary (except on a question of adjournment) shall be presented to the President of the United States; and before the same shall take effect, shall be approved by him, or being disapproved by him, shall be repassed by two thirds of the Senate and House of Representatives, according to the rules and limitations prescribed in the case of a bill.

Section 8. The Congress shall have power to lay and collect taxes, duties, imposts and excises, to pay the debts and provide for the common defense and general welfare of the United States; but all duties, imposts and excises shall be uniform throughout the United States;

To borrow money on the credit of the United States;
To regulate commerce with foreign nations, and among the several states, and with the Indian tribes;

To establish a uniform rule of naturalization, and uniform laws on the subject of bankruptcies throughout the United States;

To coin money, regulate the value thereof, and of foreign coin, and fix the standard of weights and measures;

To provide for the punishment of counterfeiting the securities and current coin of the United States;

To establish post offices and post roads;

To promote the progress of science and useful arts, by securing for limited times to authors and inventors the exclusive right to their respective writings and discoveries;

To constitute tribunals inferior to the Supreme Court;

To define and punish piracies and felonies committed on the high seas, and offenses against the law of nations;

To declare war, grant letters of marque and reprisal, and make rules concerning captures on land and water;

To raise and support armies, but no appropriation of money to that use shall be for a longer term than two years;

To provide and maintain a navy;

To make rules for the government and regulation of the land and naval forces;

To provide for calling forth the militia to execute the laws of the union, suppress insurrections and repel invasions;

To provide for organizing, arming, and disciplining, the militia, and for governing such part of them as may be employed in the service of the United States, reserving to the states respectively, the appointment of the officers, and the authority of training the militia according to the discipline prescribed by Congress;

To exercise exclusive legislation in all cases whatsoever, over such District (not exceeding ten miles square) as may, by cession of particular states, and the acceptance of Congress, become the seat of the government of the United States, and to exercise like authority over all places purchased by the consent of the legislature of the state in which the same shall be, for the erection of forts, magazines, arsenals, dockyards, and other needful buildings;—And

To make all laws which shall be necessary and proper for carrying into execution the foregoing powers, and all other powers vested by this Constitution in the government of the United States, or in any department or officer thereof.

Section 9. The migration or importation of such persons as any of the states now existing shall think proper to admit, shall not be prohibited by the Congress prior to the year one thousand eight hundred and eight, but a tax or duty may be imposed on such importation, not exceeding ten dollars for each person.

The privilege of the writ of habeas corpus shall not be suspended, unless when in cases of rebellion or invasion the public safety may require it.

No bill of attainder or ex post facto Law shall be passed.

No capitation, or other direct, tax shall be laid, unless in proportion to the census or enumeration herein before directed to be taken.

No tax or duty shall be laid on articles exported from any state.

No preference shall be given by any regulation of commerce or revenue to the ports of one state over those of another: nor shall vessels bound to, or from, one state, be obliged to enter, clear or pay duties in another.

No money shall be drawn from the treasury, but in consequence of appropriations made by law; and a regular statement and account of receipts and expenditures of all public money shall be published from time to time.

No title of nobility shall be granted by the United States: and no person holding any office of profit or trust under them, shall, without the consent of the Congress, accept of any present, emolument, office, or title, of any kind whatever, from any king, prince, or foreign state.

Section 10. No state shall enter into any treaty, alliance, or confederation; grant letters of marque and reprisal; coin money; emit bills of credit; make anything but gold and silver coin a tender in payment of debts; pass any bill of attainder, ex post facto law, or law impairing the obligation of contracts, or grant any title of nobility.

No state shall, without the consent of the Congress, lay any imposts or duties on imports or exports, except what may be absolutely necessary for executing its inspection laws: and the net produce of all duties and imposts, laid by any state on imports or exports, shall be for the use of the treasury of the United States; and all such laws shall be subject to the revision and control of the Congress.

No state shall, without the consent of Congress, lay any duty of tonnage, keep troops, or ships of war in time of peace, enter into any agreement or compact with another state, or with a foreign power, or engage in war, unless actually invaded, or in such imminent danger as will not admit of delay.

ARTICLE II

Section 1. The executive power shall be vested in a President of the United States of America. He shall hold his office during the term of four years, and, together with the Vice President, chosen for the same term, be elected, as follows:

Each state shall appoint, in such manner as the Legislature thereof may direct, a number of electors, equal to the whole number of Senators and Representatives to which the State may be entitled in the Congress: but no Senator or Representative, or person holding an office of trust or profit under the United States, shall be appointed an elector.

The electors shall meet in their respective states, and vote by ballot for two persons, of whom one at least shall not be an inhabitant of the same state with themselves. And they shall make a list of all the persons voted for, and of the number of votes for each; which list they shall sign and certify, and transmit sealed to the seat of the government of the United States, directed to the President of the Senate. The President of the Senate shall, in the presence of the Senate and House of Representatives, open all the certificates, and the votes shall then be counted. The person having the greatest number of votes shall be the President, if such number be a majority of the whole number of electors appointed; and if there be more than one who have such majority, and have an equal number of votes, then the House of Representatives shall immediately choose by ballot one of them for President; and if no person have a majority, then from the five highest on the list the said House shall in like manner choose the President. But in choosing the President, the votes shall be taken by States, the representation from each state having one vote; a quorum for this purpose shall consist of a member or members from two thirds of the states, and a majority of all the states shall be necessary to a choice. In every case, after the choice of the President, the person having the greatest number of votes of the electors shall be the Vice President. But if there should remain two or more who have equal votes, the Senate shall choose from them by ballot the Vice President.

The Congress may determine the time of choosing the electors, and the day on which they shall give their votes; which day shall be the same throughout the United States.

No person except a natural born citizen, or a citizen of the United States, at the time of the adoption of this Constitution, shall be eligible to the office of President; neither shall any person be eligible to that office who shall not have attained to the age of thirty five years, and been fourteen Years a resident within the United States.

In case of the removal of the President from office, or of his death, resignation, or inability to discharge the powers and duties of the said office, the same shall devolve on the Vice President, and the Congress may by law provide for the case of removal, death, resignation or inability, both of the President and Vice President, declaring what officer shall then act as President, and such officer shall act accordingly, until the disability be removed, or a President shall be elected.

The President shall, at stated times, receive for his services, a compensation, which shall neither be increased nor diminished during the period for which he shall have been elected, and he shall not receive within that period any other emolument from the United States, or any of them.

Before he enter on the execution of his office, he shall take the following oath or affirmation:—"I do solemnly swear (or affirm) that I will faithfully execute the office of President of the United States, and will to the best of my ability, preserve, protect and defend the Constitution of the United States."

Section 2. The President shall be commander in chief of the Army and Navy of the United States, and of the militia of the several states, when called into the actual service of the United States; he may require the opinion, in writing, of the principal officer in each of the executive departments, upon any subject relating to the duties of their respective offices, and he shall have power to grant reprieves and pardons for offenses against the United States, except in cases of impeachment.

He shall have power, by and with the advice and consent of the Senate, to make treaties, provided two thirds of the Senators present concur; and he shall nominate, and by and with the advice and consent of the Senate, shall appoint ambassadors, other public ministers and consuls, judges of the Supreme Court, and all other officers of the United States, whose appointments are not herein otherwise provided for, and which shall be established by law: but the Congress may by law vest the appointment of such inferior officers, as they think proper, in the President alone, in the courts of law, or in the heads of departments.

The President shall have power to fill up all vacancies that may happen during the recess of the Senate, by granting commissions which shall expire at the end of their next session.

Section 3. He shall from time to time give to the Congress information of the state of the union, and recommend to their consideration such measures as he shall judge necessary and expedient; he may, on extraordinary occasions, convene both Houses, or either of them, and in case of disagreement between them, with respect to the time of adjournment, he may adjourn them to such time as he shall think proper; he shall receive ambassadors and other public ministers; he shall take care that the laws be faithfully executed, and shall commission all the officers of the United States.

Section 4. The President, Vice President and all civil officers of the United States, shall be removed from office on impeachment for, and conviction of, treason, bribery, or other high crimes and misdemeanors.

ARTICLE III

Section 1. The judicial power of the United States, shall be vested in one Supreme Court, and in such inferior courts as the Congress may from time to time ordain and establish. The judges, both of the supreme and inferior courts, shall hold their offices during good behavior, and shall, at stated times, receive for their services, a compensation, which shall not be diminished during their continuance in office.

Section 2. The judicial power shall extend to all cases, in law and equity, arising under this Constitution, the laws of the United States, and treaties made, or which shall be made, under their authority;—to all cases affecting ambassadors, other public ministers and consuls;—to all cases of admiralty and maritime jurisdiction;—to controversies to which the United States shall be a party;—to controversies between two or more states;—between a state and citizens of another state;—between citizens of different states;—between citizens of the same state claiming lands under grants of different states, and between a state, or the citizens thereof, and foreign states, citizens or subjects.

In all cases affecting ambassadors, other public ministers and consuls, and those in which a state shall be party, the Supreme Court shall have original jurisdiction. In all the other cases before mentioned, the Supreme Court shall have appellate jurisdiction, both as to law and fact, with such exceptions, and under such regulations as the Congress shall make.

The trial of all crimes, except in cases of impeachment, shall be by jury; and such trial shall be held in the state where the said crimes shall have been committed; but when not committed within any state, the trial shall be at such place or places as the Congress may by law have directed.

Section 3. Treason against the United States, shall consist only in levying war against them, or in adhering to their enemies, giving them aid and comfort. No person shall be convicted of treason unless on the testimony of two witnesses to the same overt act, or on confession in open court.

The Congress shall have power to declare the punishment of treason, but no attainder of treason shall work corruption of blood, or forfeiture except during the life of the person attainted.

ARTICLE IV

Section 1. Full faith and credit shall be given in each state to the public acts, records, and judicial proceedings of every other state. And the Congress may by general laws prescribe the manner in which such acts, records, and proceedings shall be proved, and the effect thereof.

Section 2. The citizens of each state shall be entitled to all privileges and immunities of citizens in the several states.

A person charged in any state with treason, felony, or other crime, who shall flee from justice, and be found in another state, shall on demand of the executive authority of the state from which he fled, be delivered up, to be removed to the state having jurisdiction of the crime.

No person held to service or labor in one state, under the laws thereof, escaping into another, shall, in consequence of any law or regulation therein, be discharged from such service or labor, but shall be delivered up on claim of the party to whom such service or labor may be due.

Section 3. New states may be admitted by the Congress into this union; but no new states shall be formed or erected within the jurisdiction of any other state; nor any state be formed by the junction of two or more states, or parts of states, without the consent of the legislatures of the states concerned as well as of the Congress.

The Congress shall have power to dispose of and make all needful rules and regulations respecting the territory or other property belonging to the United States; and nothing in this Constitution shall be so construed as to prejudice any claims of the United States, or of any particular state.

Section 4. The United States shall guarantee to every state in this union a republican form of government, and shall protect each of them against invasion; and on application of the legislature, or of the executive (when the legislature cannot be convened) against domestic violence.

ARTICLE V

The Congress, whenever two thirds of both Houses shall deem it necessary, shall propose Amendments to this Constitution, or, on the application of the legislatures of two thirds of the several states, shall call a convention for proposing amendments, which, in either case, shall be valid to all intents and purposes, as part of this Constitution, when ratified by the legislatures of three fourths of the several states, or by conventions in three fourths thereof, as the one or the other mode of ratification may be proposed by the Congress; provided that no amendment which may be made prior to the year one thousand eight hundred and eight shall in any manner affect the first and fourth clauses in the ninth section of the first article; and that no state, without its consent, shall be deprived of its equal suffrage in the Senate.

ARTICLE VI

All debts contracted and engagements entered into, before the adoption of this Constitution, shall be as valid against the United States under this Constitution, as under the Confederation.

This Constitution, and the laws of the United States which shall be made in pursuance thereof; and all treaties made, or which shall be made, under the authority of the United States, shall be the supreme law of the land; and the judges in every state shall be bound thereby, anything in the Constitution or laws of any State to the contrary notwithstanding.

The Senators and Representatives before mentioned, and the members of the several state legislatures, and all executive and judicial officers, both of the United States and of the several states, shall be bound by oath or affirmation, to support this Constitution; but no religious test shall ever be required as a qualification to any office or public trust under the United States.

ARTICLE VII

The ratification of the conventions of nine states, shall be sufficient for the establishment of this Constitution between the states so ratifying the same.

Done in convention by the unanimous consent of the states present the seventeenth day of September in the year of our Lord one thousand seven hundred and eighty seven and of the independence of the United States of America the twelfth. In witness whereof We have hereunto subscribed our Names,

G. Washington—President and deputy from Virginia

New Hampshire: John Langdon, Nicholas Gilman
Massachusetts: Nathaniel Gorham, Rufus King
Connecticut: Wm. Saml. Johnson, Roger Sherman
New York: Alexander Hamilton
New Jersey: Wil. Livingston, David Brearly,
*   Wm. Paterson, Jona. Dayton*
Pennsylvania: B. Franklin, Thomas Mifflin,
*   Robt. Morris, Geo. Clymer, Thos. Fitzsimons,*
*   Jared Ingersoll, James Wilson, Gouv Morris*

Delaware: Geo. Read, Gunning Bedford Jun., John
*   Dickinson, Richard Bassett, Jaco. Broom*
Maryland: James McHenry, Dan of St Thos. Jenifer, Danl
*   Carroll*
Virginia: John Blair, James Madison Jr.
North Carolina: Wm. Blount, Richd. Dobbs Spaight,
*   Hu Williamson*
South Carolina: J. Rutledge, Charles Cotesworth
*   Pinckney, Charles Pinckney, Pierce Butler*
Georgia: William Few, Abr Baldwin

Attest: William Jackson

The Bill of Rights and Other Amendments to the Constitution

[The First Ten Amendments to the Constitution are known as the Bill of Rights.]

AMENDMENT I

(1791)

Congress shall make no law respecting an establishment of religion, or prohibiting the free exercise thereof; or abridging the freedom of speech, or of the press; or the right of the people peaceably to assemble, and to petition the Government for a redress of grievances.

AMENDMENT II

(1791)

A well regulated Militia, being necessary to the security of a free State, the right of the people to keep and bear Arms, shall not be infringed.

AMENDMENT III

(1791)

No Soldier shall, in time of peace be quartered in any house, without the consent of the Owner, nor in time of war, but in a manner to be prescribed by law.

AMENDMENT IV

(1791)

The right of the people to be secure in their persons, houses, papers, and effects, against unreasonable searches and seizures, shall not be violated, and no Warrants shall issue, but upon probable cause, supported by Oath or affirmation, and particularly describing the place to be searched, and the persons or things to be seized.

AMENDMENT V

(1791)

No person shall be held to answer for a capital, or otherwise infamous crime, unless on a presentment or indictment of a Grand Jury, except in cases arising in the land or naval forces, or in the Militia, when in actual service in time of war or public danger; nor shall any person be subject for the same offence to be twice put in jeopardy of life or limb; nor shall be compelled in any criminal case to be a witness against himself, nor be deprived of life, liberty, or property, without due process of law; nor shall private property be taken for public use, without just compensation.

AMENDMENT VI

(1791)

In all criminal prosecutions, the accused shall enjoy the right to a speedy and public trial, by an impartial jury of the State and district wherein the crime shall have been committed, which district shall have been previously ascertained by law, and to be informed of the nature and cause of the accusation; to be confronted with the witnesses against him; to have compulsory process for obtaining witnesses in his favor, and to have the Assistance of Counsel for his defence.

AMENDMENT VII

(1791)

In suits at common law, where the value in controversy shall exceed twenty dollars, the right of trial by jury shall be preserved, and no fact tried by a jury, shall be otherwise reexamined in any Court of the United States, than according to the rules of the common law.

AMENDMENT VIII

(1791)

Excessive bail shall not be required, nor excessive fines imposed, nor cruel and unusual punishments inflicted.

AMENDMENT IX

(1791)

The enumeration in the Constitution, of certain rights, shall not be construed to deny or disparage others retained by the people.

AMENDMENT X

(1791)

The powers not delegated to the United States by the Constitution, nor prohibited by it to the States, are reserved to the States respectively, or to the people.

[The Amendments that follow the Bill of Rights.]

AMENDMENT XI

(1798)

The judicial power of the United States shall not be construed to extend to any suit in law or equity, commenced or prosecuted against one of the United States by Citizens of another State, or by Citizens or Subjects of any Foreign State.

AMENDMENT XII

(1804)

The electors shall meet in their respective States, and vote by ballot for President and Vice-President, one of whom, at least, shall not be an inhabitant of the same state with themselves; they shall name in their ballots the person voted for as President, and in distinct ballots the person voted for as Vice-President, and they shall make distinct lists of all persons voted for as President, and of all persons voted for as Vice-President and of the number of votes for each, which lists they shall sign and certify, and transmit sealed to the seat of the Government of the United States, directed to the President of the Senate; The President of the Senate shall, in the presence of the Senate and House of Representatives, open all the certificates and the votes shall then be counted; the person having the greatest number of votes for President, shall be the President, if such number be a majority of the whole number of Electors appointed; and if no person have such majority, then from the persons having the highest numbers not exceeding three on the list of those voted for as President, the House of Representatives shall choose immediately, by ballot, the President. But in choosing the President, the votes shall be taken by states, the representation from each State having one vote; a quorum for this purpose shall consist of a member or members from two-thirds of the States, and a majority of all the States shall be necessary to a choice. And if the House of Representatives shall not choose a President whenever the right of choice shall devolve upon them, before the fourth day of March next following, then the Vice-President shall act as President, as in the case of the death or other constitutional disability of the President. The person having the greatest number of votes as Vice-President, shall be the Vice-President, if such number be a majority of the whole number of Electors appointed, and if no person have a majority, then from the two highest numbers on the list, the Senate shall choose the Vice-President; a quorum for the purpose shall consist of two-thirds of the whole number of Senators, and a majority of the whole number shall be necessary to a choice. But no person constitutionally ineligible to the office of President shall be eligible to that of Vice-President of the United States.

AMENDMENT XIII

(1865)

Section 1. Neither slavery nor involuntary servitude, except as a punishment for crime whereof the party shall have been duly convicted, shall exist within the United States, or any place subject to their jurisdiction.

Section 2. Congress shall have power to enforce this article by appropriate legislation.

AMENDMENT XIV

(1868)

Section 1. All persons born or naturalized in the United States, and subject to the jurisdiction thereof, are citizens of the United States and of the State wherein they reside. No State shall make or enforce any law which shall abridge the privileges or immunities of citizens of the United States; nor shall any State deprive any person of life, liberty, or property, without due process of law; nor deny to any person within its jurisdiction the equal protection of the laws.

Section 2. Representatives shall be apportioned among the several States according to their respective numbers, counting the whole number of persons in each State, excluding Indians not taxed. But when the right to vote at any election for the choice of Electors for President and Vice-President of the United States, Representatives in Congress, the executive and judicial officers of a State, or the members of the Legislature thereof, is denied to any of the male inhabitants of such State, being twenty-one years of age, and citizens of the United States, or in any way abridged, except for participation in rebellion, or other crime, the basis of representation therein shall be reduced in the proportion which the number of such male citizens shall bear to the whole number of male citizens twenty-one years of age in such State.

Section 3. No person shall be a Senator or Representative in Congress, or elector of President and Vice-President, or hold any office, civil or military, under the United States, or under any State, who, having previously taken an oath, as a member of Congress, or as an officer of the United States, or as a member of any State legislature, or as an executive or judicial officer of any State, to support the Constitution of the United States, shall have engaged in insurrection or rebellion against the same, or given aid or comfort to the enemies thereof. But Congress may by a vote of two-thirds of each House, remove such disability.

Section 4. The validity of the public debt of the United States, authorized by law, including debts incurred for payment of pensions and bounties for services in suppressing insurrection or rebellion, shall not be questioned. But neither the United States nor any State shall assume or pay any debt or obligation incurred in aid of insurrection or rebellion against the United States, or any claim for the loss or emancipation of any slave; but all such debts, obligations and claims shall be held illegal and void.

Section 5. The Congress shall have power to enforce, by appropriate legislation, the provisions of this article.

AMENDMENT XV

(1870)

Section 1. The right of citizens of the United States to vote shall not be denied or abridged by the United States or by any State on account of race, color, or previous condition of servitude.

Section 2. The Congress shall have power to enforce this article by appropriate legislation.

AMENDMENT XVI

(1913)

The Congress shall have power to lay and collect taxes on incomes, from whatever source derived, without apportionment among the several States and without regard to any census or enumeration.

AMENDMENT XVII

(1913)

The Senate of the United States shall be composed of two Senators from each State, elected by the people thereof, for six years; and each Senator shall have one vote. The electors in each State shall have the qualifications requisite for electors of the most numerous branch of the State legislatures.

When vacancies happen in the representation of any State in the Senate, the executive authority of such State shall issue writs of election to fill such vacancies: *Provided,* That the legislature of any State may empower the executive thereof to make temporary appointments until the people fill the vacancies by election as the legislature may direct. This amendment shall not be so construed as to affect the election or term of any Senator chosen before it becomes valid as part of the Constitution.

AMENDMENT XVIII

(1919)

Section 1. After one year from the ratification of this article, the manufacture, sale, or transportation of intoxicating liquors within, the importation thereof into, or the exportation thereof from the United States and all territory subject to the jurisdiction thereof for beverage purposes is hereby prohibited.

Section 2. The Congress and the several States shall have concurrent power to enforce this article by appropriate legislation.

Section 3. This article shall be inoperative unless it shall have been ratified as an amendment to the Constitution by the legislatures of the several States, as provided in the Constitution, within seven years from the date of the submission hereof to the States by Congress.

AMENDMENT XIX

(1920)

The right of citizens of the United States to vote shall not be denied or abridged by the United States or by any State on account of sex.

Congress shall have power to enforce this article by appropriate legislation.

AMENDMENT XX

(1933)

Section 1. The terms of the President and Vice-President shall end at noon on the twentieth day of January, and the terms of Senators and Representatives at noon on the third day of January, of the years in which such terms would have ended if this article had not been ratified; and the terms of their successors shall then begin.

Section 2. The Congress shall assemble at least once in every year, and such meeting shall begin at noon on the third day of January, unless they shall by law appoint a different day.

Section 3. If, at the time fixed for the beginning of the term of the President, the President-elect shall have died, the Vice-President-elect shall become President. If a President shall not have been chosen before the time fixed for the beginning of his term, or if the President-elect shall have failed to qualify, then the Vice-President-elect shall act as President until a President shall have qualified; and the Congress may by law provide for the case wherein neither a President-elect nor a Vice-President-elect shall have qualified, declaring who shall then act as President, or the manner in which one who is to act shall be selected, and such person shall act accordingly until a President or Vice-President shall have qualified.

Section 4. The Congress may by law provide for the case of the death of any of the persons from whom the House of Representatives may choose a President whenever the right of choice shall have devolved upon them, and for the case of the death of any of the persons from whom the Senate may choose a Vice-President whenever the right of choice shall have devolved upon them.

Section 5. Sections 1 and 2 shall take effect on the 15th day of October following the ratification of this article.

Section 6. This article shall be inoperative unless it shall have been ratified as an amendment to the Constitution by the legislatures of three-fourths of the several States within seven years from the date of its submission.

AMENDMENT XXI

(1933)

Section 1. The eighteenth article of amendment to the Constitution of the United States is hereby repealed.

Section 2. The transportation or importation into any State, Territory, or possession of the United States for delivery or use therein of intoxicating liquors, in violation of the laws thereof, is hereby prohibited.

Section 3. This article shall be inoperative unless it shall have been ratified as an amendment to the Constitution by conventions in the several States, as provided in the Constitution, within seven years from the date of the submission hereof to the States by the Congress.

AMENDMENT XXII

(1951)

Section 1. No person shall be elected to the office of the President more than twice, and no person who has held the office of President, or acted as President for more than two years of a term to which some other person was elected President shall be elected to the office of the President more than once. But this Article shall not apply to any person holding the office of President when this Article was proposed by the Congress, and shall not prevent any person who may be holding the office of President, or acting as President, during the term within which this Article becomes operative from holding the office of President or acting as President during the remainder of such term.

Section 2. This article shall be inoperative unless it shall have been ratified as an amendment to the Constitution by the legislatures of three-fourths of the several States within seven years from the date of its submission to the States by the Congress.

AMENDMENT XXIII

(1960)

Section 1. The District constituting the seat of government of the United States shall appoint in such manner as the Congress may direct:

A number of electors of President and Vice-President equal to the whole number of Senators and Representatives in Congress to which the District would be entitled if it were a State, but in no event more than the least populous State; they shall be in addition to those appointed by the States, but they shall be considered, for the purposes of the election of President and Vice-President, to be electors appointed by a State; and they shall meet in the District and perform such duties as provided by the twelfth article of amendment.

Section 2. The Congress shall have power to enforce this article by appropriate legislation.

AMENDMENT XXIV

(1964)

Section 1. The right of citizens of the United States to vote in any primary or other election for President or Vice-President, for electors for President or Vice-President, or for Senator or Representative in Congress, shall not be denied or abridged by the United States or any State by reason of failure to pay any poll tax or other tax.

Section 2. The Congress shall have power to enforce this article by appropriate legislation.

AMENDMENT XXV

(1967)

Section 1. In case of the removal of the President from office or of his death or resignation, the Vice-President shall become President.

Section 2. Whenever there is a vacancy in the office of the Vice-President, the President shall nominate a Vice-President who shall take office upon confirmation by a majority vote of both Houses of Congress.

Section 3. Whenever the President transmits to the President pro tempore of the Senate and the Speaker of the House of Representatives his written declaration that he is unable to discharge the powers and duties of his office, and until he transmits to them a written declaration to the contrary, such powers and duties shall be discharged by the Vice-President as Acting President.

Section 4. Whenever the Vice-President and a majority of either the principal officers of the executive departments or of such other body as Congress may by law provide, transmit to the President pro tempore of the Senate and the Speaker of the House of Representatives their written declaration that the President is unable to discharge the powers and duties of his office, the Vice-President shall immediately assume the powers and duties of the office as Acting President.

Thereafter, when the President transmits to the President pro tempore of the Senate and the Speaker of the House of Representatives his written declaration that no inability exists, he shall resume the powers and duties of his office unless the Vice-President and a majority of either the principal officers of the executive department or of such other body as Congress may by law provide, transmit within four days to the President pro tempore of the Senate and the Speaker of the House of Representatives their written declaration that the President is unable to discharge the powers and duties of his office. Thereupon Congress shall decide the issue, assembling within forty-eight hours for that purpose if not in session. If the Congress, within twenty-one days after receipt of the latter written declaration, or, if Congress is not in session, within twenty-one days after Congress is required to assemble, determines by two-thirds vote of both Houses that the President is unable to discharge the powers and duties of his office, the Vice-President shall continue to discharge the same as Acting President; otherwise, the President shall resume the powers and duties of his office.

AMENDMENT XXVI

(1971)

Section 1. The right of citizens of the United States, who are eighteen years of age or older, to vote shall not be denied or abridged by the United States or by any State on account of age.

Section 2. The Congress shall have power to enforce this article Amendment by appropriate legislation.

AMENDMENT XXVII

(1992)

No law, varying the compensation for the services of the Senators and Representatives, shall take effect, until an election of Representatives shall have intervened.

Glossary

Administrative probable cause: The level of suspicion, knowledge, or belief necessary to obtain a warrant for a noncriminal search of a home, business, or other location where the occupier of the premises will not consent to a search; a level of probable cause that requires a much lower level of suspicion or reason to justify a search directed toward enforcing administrative, zoning, or safety regulations. See *Camara v. Municipal Court,* 387 U.S. 523 (1967) (Case 5.1), and chapter 5.

Administrative search: A governmental search designed to enforce a civil (as opposed to criminal) law or regulation; a search conducted under a lower standard of probable cause than criminal probable cause that may or may not require a warrant depending on the circumstances. Administrative probable cause may be based on the passage of time, the nature of a building, or the condition of an area of a city, and does not have to be specific to the location being subjected to an administrative search. See *Camara v. Municipal Court,* 387 U.S. 523 (1967) (Case 5.1), and chapter 5.

Administrative search: business: A search of a commercial establishment to enforce zoning and regulatory and safety programs that can be conducted on a reduced level of probable cause that is lower than required for criminal probable cause. Absent consent or other theory permitting entry, an administrative search usually requires a warrant. See *Camara v. Municipal Court,* 387 U.S. 523 (1967) (Case 5.1), and chapter 5.

Administrative search: home: A search of a private dwelling, not directed at a finding of criminal wrongdoing but focused on assuring compliance with zoning, safety, architectural, and other regulatory programs, that does not require traditional probable cause but does require a warrant or some recognized exception to a warrant. See *Camara v. Municipal Court,* 387 U.S. 523 (1967) (Case 5.1), and chapter 5.

Adverse prosecutorial comment: A violation of the Fifth Amendment privilege against self-incrimination occurs whenever a prosecutor calls attention to the fact that a defendant has not testified in his or her criminal case. A prosecutor's comment may or may not be a reversible error depending on the circumstances. See *Chapman v. California,* 386 U.S. 18 (1967) (Case 14.4), and chapter 8.

Affidavit: A written and sworn statement of fact or of belief given under oath and signed in front of a person legally qualified to execute oaths. See chapter 1.

Affidavit for a warrant: The written and sworn statement offered by a law enforcement official to a judicial official that describes the facts and circumstances that the official believes constitute probable cause sufficient for the judicial official to issue a search or an arrest warrant. See chapter 1.

Airport passenger search: A consent-based search of airline passengers and luggage designed to detect the presence of objects that could be used to hijack the aircraft or to cause harm to the passengers or crew. The search must be reasonable and no more extensive or intrusive than necessary to meet the goal of airline safety. See chapter 5.

***Alford* plea:** A plea of guilt to the charges, admitting to the truthfulness of the accusation while at the same time alleging that the defendant is not guilty of the charges. See *Alford v. North Carolina,* 400 U.S. 25 (1970), and chapter 11.

Amicus curiae: An organization or a person not a party to a lawsuit who receives court permission to file a brief supporting the position of one party in an existing lawsuit with a view toward influencing the outcome; literally, "friend of the court."

Arraignment: An early postarrest hearing of the criminal justice process in which the charges are read to the arrestee, where counsel is often appointed, where bail may be set, and where the court typically asks the arrestee to enter a plea to the charges.

Arrest: The seizure of the body of a person, under the authority of a government, for whom probable cause exists to warrant a person of reasonable caution to hold the belief that the seized person has committed a crime or crimes.

Arrest in the home: A warrant is required for police to make a lawful seizure of a person who is inside that person's home. Several exceptions to the general rule allow a warrantless arrest under exigent circumstances (an emergency), hot pursuit into the home, or consent to enter the home. See *Payton v. New York,* 445 U.S. 573 (1980) (Case 4.1), *New York v. Harris,* 495 U.S. 14 (1990), *Kirk v. Louisiana,* 536 U.S. 635 (2002), and chapter 3.

Arrest of third party in home: A warrantless seizure of a person while he or she is a guest at another person's home violates the Fourth Amendment. See *Steagald v. United States,* 451 U.S. 204 (1981), *Minnesota v. Carter,* 525 U.S. 83 (1998) (Case 6.7), and chapter 3.

Attachment of jeopardy: A defendant is deemed to have been once at risk of a criminal conviction when a judge at a bench trial begins hearing evidence from the first witness and when the jury has been empanelled and sworn in a trial to a jury. See *Downum v. United States,* 372 U.S. 734 (1963), *Crist v. Bretz,* 437 U.S. 28 (1978), and chapter 12.

Attenuation: See **Doctrine of Attenuation.**

Automatic standing: The principle that anyone "legitimately on the premises" who becomes the subject of a police search has legal grounds to contest the illegality of the search under the Fourth Amendment. This doctrine has no application in federal trials and has been rejected in most state criminal proceedings. See *Jones v. United States,* 362 U.S. 257 (1960), *Rakas v. Illinois,* 439 U.S. 128 (1978) (Case 6.5), and *United States v. Salvucci,* 488 U.S. 83 (1980).

Bail: The method of procuring the release of a person accused of a crime by payment of money; an amount of money or approved property that a judge or magistrate

believes will cause an arrested person to comply with all conditions of release and to appear at court at all appropriate times; pretrial release on conditions set by the court. See *United States v. Salerno,* 481 U.S. 739 (1987) (Case 12.3), and chapter 12.

Bailable offense: Any offense that a legislature has determined would be appropriate for pretrial release on conditions; any offense other than those that a state or the federal legislature has determined do not merit consideration of pretrial release. See chapter 12.

Bail provision of Eighth Amendment: The part of the Eighth Amendment that prohibits excessive federal bail and regulates the manner in which federal bail statutes may be structured by Congress; the section of the Eighth Amendment that has never been incorporated into the Due Process Clause of the Fourteenth Amendment and therefore does not apply to the states and does not regulate state bail practice.

Bench trial: Where the defendant elects to have the judge or a three-judge panel hear and decide the case in which the defendant has waived various legal rights, especially the Sixth Amendment right to a trial by jury. See chapter 13.

***Bivens* remedy:** The court-created remedy for an egregious violation of the Fourth Amendment by federal law enforcement officials in which the wronged individual may file a federal civil suit for money damages against the agents.

***Blockburger* test for double jeopardy:** Offenses are separate offenses for double jeopardy purposes if each crime requires proof of an element that the other does not. See *Blockburger v. United States,* 284 U.S. 299 (1932), and chapter 12.

Blood alcohol tests: Scientific examinations that are conducted to determine the alcoholic content of individuals' blood following arrests for driving while intoxicated and that do not violate the Fifth Amendment privilege against self-incrimination. See *Schmerber v. California,* 384 U.S. 757 (1966) (Case 8.1).

Bond: An amount of money or the value of assets placed with a court to obtain pretrial release of an accused; in misdemeanor cases, the amount of money set by a court, police agency, or statute to ensure the subject's appearance in court at all appropriate times.

Breach of plea agreement: Following the execution of a negotiated plea, if either party fails to perform its respective obligations, the plea may be withdrawn and the parties will be left where they were prior to the plea agreement. In some cases, specific performance of a plea agreement may be possible. See *Santobello v. New York,* 404 U.S. 257 (1971) (Case 11.4), *Ricketts v. Adamson,* 483 U.S. 1 (1987), and chapter 11.

Burden of proof: The quantum of evidence required to be produced by the prosecution to win a criminal case; a level of proof required to be demonstrated in affirmative defenses for criminal cases; the prosecution must introduce evidence to prove the case beyond a reasonable doubt.

***Carroll* doctrine:** Judicial principle that permits a warrantless search of a moving or readily movable motor vehicle for which probable cause exists; an exception to the Fourth Amendment warrant requirement that permits searches of readily movable or moving vehicles, boats, and aircraft. See *Carroll v. United States,* 267 U.S. 132 (1925) (Case 1.1), *Chambers v. Maroney,* 399 U.S. 42 (1970) (Case 4.4), *California v. Carney,* 471 U.S. 386 (1985), and chapter 4.

Challenge for cause: The concept that a prospective juror can be removed for bias, interest, or prejudice in a criminal case where the attorney for a party can demonstrate lack of impartiality. Challenges for cause are theoretically unlimited in number.

Closely (heavily) regulated industry: A business or industry that has traditionally been subject to intensive or pervasive governmental regulation such that persons engaging in such a business or industry may expect a diminished expectation of privacy and may expect searches of their premises without prior notice, probable cause, or warrant. Firearms and explosives manufacturing, the production of distilled spirits, and automobile dismantling are examples of businesses and industries that have traditionally been closely regulated by different levels of government. See *Colonnade Catering Corporation v. United States,* 397 U.S. 72 (1970), and chapter 5.

Collateral attack: When a defendant has exhausted all direct state and federal appellate reviews and appeals without success and files court papers requesting that a court issue a writ of habeas corpus if it finds that the defendant is currently being held under a judgment in violation of, respectively, the state or federal constitution or laws.

Collateral estoppel: Where a fact necessary to the prosecution of a second but different case against the defendant has been clearly found in the defendant's favor at the first trial, the defendant cannot be forced to relitigate the same fact a second time at a second trial involving the same sovereign. See *Ashe v. Swenson,* 397 U.S. 436 (1970), *Dowling v. United States,* 493 U.S. 342 (1990), and chapter 12.

Compelled testimony: No witness has the right to refuse to testify in front of a grand jury where the witness has been given use or transactional immunity that is coextensive with the protections of the Fifth Amendment. See *United States v. Hubbell,* 530 U.S. 27 (2000), and chapter 10.

Competency: The mental ability of a defendant to comprehend the nature and importance of court proceedings and to have sufficient mental comprehension to properly assist counsel in preparing a defense; the requirement that a witness in a court case take an oath to tell the truth, to have possessed original perception of the events, to have a recollection of what happened, and to have the ability to communicate the facts to the judge or jury.

Composition of grand jury: Members of a grand jury must be selected from a pool of citizens who represent a fair cross section of the jurisdiction. See *Vazquez v. Hillery,* 474 U.S. 254 (1986) (Case 10.3), and chapter 10.

Concept of standing: The requirement under the Fourth Amendment that an aggrieved party must demonstrate that a personal right of his or hers has been violated in order to be permitted to argue for suppression of evidence illegally seized in violation the rule of *Mapp v. Ohio,* 367 U.S. 643 (1961), and the Fourth Amendment. See *Rakas v. Illinois,* 439 U.S. 128 (1978) (Case 6.5), and chapter 6.

Confession: The free and voluntary act by an accused of admitting to the material elements of a crime that are generally sufficient to generate proof beyond a reasonable doubt if believed by a trier of fact. See chapter 8.

Consent search: A search conducted by a governmental agent following the granting of permission by the individual holding dominion and control over the object or premises; a search justified where the occupier of the premises freely and voluntarily relinquished his or her Fourth

Amendment rights and permitted a search. Voluntariness of consent is measured by the "totality of the circumstances" test. See *Schneckloth v. Bustamonte,* 412 U.S. 218 (1973) (Case 4.8), and chapter 4.

Counsel: Every accused possesses the right to an attorney under the Sixth Amendment, and where the accused has insufficient funds to afford legal representation, the government must furnish reasonably competent legal representation. See chapter 13.

Custody: For *Miranda* purposes, exists when a governmental agent deprives an individual of his or her freedom of movement in any significant manner; one of the two triggering factors under *Miranda* that require police officers to offer *Miranda* warnings. See chapter 7.

Derivative evidence: Evidence discovered or disclosed by reference to exploiting other evidence already known; evidence that may be excluded if the original evidence was "tainted" or illegally seized under the Fourth Amendment. See *Wong Sun v. United States,* 371 U.S. 471 (1963) (Case 6.2), and chapter 6.

Determination of bail amount: The factors that courts use to evaluate the amount of money or approved property required to assure that a bailed defendant will appear at all appropriate times. Courts consider, among other factors, the strength of the prosecution's case, the alleged offender's prior history while on bail, the severity of the charged offense, the alleged offender's ties to the community, the wealth of the individual, and whether the alleged offender will harm members of the community or witnesses in the case.

Doctrine of attenuation: The theory that an illegally seized item of evidence, normally excluded under the Fourth Amendment's exclusionary rule, may be admissible where that evidence and the act of illegal seizure have significant separation by time and distance sufficiently to break the chain of causation between the evidence and the illegal seizure. See *Wong Sun v. United States,* 371 U.S. 471 (1963) (Case 6.2).

Double jeopardy: A provision of the Fifth Amendment of the United States Constitution that has been construed to prohibit an individual from being tried twice for the same crime prosecuted by the same sovereign jurisdiction unless the defendant waives the constitutional protection by appealing a conviction or otherwise.

See *Bartkus v. Illinois,* 359 U.S. 121 (1959), *Benton v. Maryland,* 395 U.S. 784 (1969) (Case 12.7), *Heath v. Alabama,* 474 U.S. 82 (1985), and chapter 11.

Drug courier profile: A set of characteristics developed from past encounters with drug dealers and traffickers that may be used to identify persons who are not known to be involved in the drug trade but who may be drug carriers based on their possession of the stereotypical characteristics. The profile may include demeanor, age, travel origin or destination, time of arrival at a transportation facility, lack of luggage or use of expensive luggage, and other factors. When properly applied, law enforcement agents may use the profile to briefly stop and inquire about a person's travel plans and ask other routine questions. See *Florida v. Royer,* 460 U.S. 491 (1983) (Case 2.4), and chapter 2.

Dual sovereignty: The concept that each of the several states is sovereign for the purposes of determining its criminal law and that the federal government is sovereign for the purposes of determining its criminal law. A state that prosecutes a person following a prosecution by a different state for the same act does not constitute a violation of double jeopardy, and both the federal government and one of the states may successively prosecute an individual for one act that consists of two separate crimes.

Dual sovereignty doctrine: A person may be prosecuted successively by one state and then another or by the state and then by the federal government for the same acts, which constitute different crimes under two or more separate jurisdictions. See *Heath v. Alabama,* 474 U.S. 82 (1985).

Due process: A constitutional guarantee found in the Fifth and Fourteenth Amendments to the United States Constitution which mandates that the state and central governments treat individuals with "fundamental fairness" when interacting with them, whether the situation involves lawmaking or law enforcement.

Due Process Clause of the Fourteenth Amendment: The constitutional guarantee that the governments of the states will treat all persons found within their borders with "fundamental fairness" in all interactions between a state government and an individual.

Effect of discrimination: Where racial discrimination has been proved to have tainted a criminal case, the case will be reversed and will not generally be decided using the harmless error doctrine. See *Vasquez v. Hillery,* 474 U.S. 254 (1986) (Case 10.3).

Emergency administrative search: A search directed toward discovering items or conditions that pose actual or potential harms to the general public or to a specific group of persons. It does not require a warrant and may not require administrative probable cause. Examples of emergency administrative searches include entry to a farm to destroy tubercular cattle, seizure of botulism-tainted tuna, and confiscation of misbranded prescription drugs. See *Camara v. Municipal Court,* 387 U.S. 523 (1967) (Case 5.1), and chapter 5.

Emergency exception: The doctrine that permits governmental action under the Fourth Amendment where life or property may be in danger, and when compliance with usual procedural requirements would not be reasonable. See *Warden v. Hayden,* 387 U.S. 294 (1967), and chapter 7.

Emergency exception to *Miranda*: An excuse for conducting limited custodial interrogation of an arrestee where an immediate danger exists to the safety of the arresting officer or other persons; permissible custodial interrogation generally characterized by the presence of an unlocated firearm or explosive device. See *New York v. Quarles,* 467 U.S. 649 (1984).

Exceptions to warrant: Arrest warrants will not be required to arrest within the home where exigent circumstances exist, where the arrest follows a hot pursuit, or under circumstances of consent. Search warrants generally will not be required for motor vehicle searches and are not necessary for consent searches, inventory searches, exigent circumstances, and searches incident to lawful arrests. See chapter 3.

Excessive bail: For federal bail purposes and under many state interpretations, bail has been deemed excessive when it has been set at an amount higher than the amount minimally necessary to assure a defendant's appearance at all appropriate times. See *Stack v. Boyle,* 342 U.S. 1 (1951) (Case 12.2), and chapter 12.

Exclusionary rule: A court-made rule that prevents the use of evidence illegally seized in violation of the Fourth Amendment during the prosecution's case in chief; a court-made rule designed to ensure respect for the Fourth

Amendment by law enforcement officials by removing the incentive to conduct illegal searches and seizures. See *Mapp v. Ohio,* 367 U.S. 643 (1961) (Case 6.1), and chapter 6.

Executory plea: A negotiated plea that had received mutual assent by the parties but which has not been performed by both sides. Either party may withdraw at any time from an executory plea agreement since no constitutional rights are enforceable in an executory plea bargain due to lack of performance. See *Mabry v. Johnson,* 467 U.S. 504 (1984) (Case 11.6), and chapter 11.

Exigent circumstances: An emergency situation characterized by a law enforcement official lawfully entering private premises or property without a warrant; situations where life may hang in the balance, which justifies an extraordinary law enforcement response involving a warrantless search and/or seizure.

Expectation of privacy: A judicially recognized constitutional right based on the Fourth Amendment that limits governmental intrusion on areas of a person's life, property, papers, and effects. An expectation of privacy is not absolute and may be breached by a demonstration of an important and sufficient governmental interest. See *Mapp v. Ohio,* 367 U.S. 643 (1961) (Case 6.1), *Kyllo v. United States,* 533 U.S. 27 (2001) (Case 4.2), and chapter 3.

Eyewitness identification: A process in which a witness to a crime identifies the proper person, following procedures that must meet due process requirements to prevent misidentification; a process involving a lineup, photographic array, or one-on-one show-up where the law enforcement agents do not attempt to steer or otherwise assist in making an identification and during which the defendant may have a right of counsel. See *United States v. Wade,* 388 U.S. 218 (1967) (Case 9.1), *Neil v. Biggers,* 409 U.S. 188 (1972) (Case 9.3), and chapter 8.

Factors used in determining bail: In making a bail decision, courts typically consider the strength of the prosecution's case, prior history while on bail, severity of the charged offense, the alleged offender's ties to the community, the wealth of the individual, and whether the alleged offender will harm members of the community or witnesses in the case.

Fair cross section requirement: The concept that the pool of citizens from which a grand jury or a trial jury is to be selected must represent identifiable groups within the judicial community. Where identifiable groups have been intentionally excluded, there is the possibility of reversible error. See chapter 12.

Federal jury size: The Sixth Amendment right to a trial by jury has been judicially determined to require a jury of twelve unless a defendant consents to a lower number. See chapter 12.

Federal question: Denotes that a particular cause of action may be tried in a federal court as federal cause of action; in the appellate or habeas corpus context, where a legal issue involves a federal law, the federal constitution, or a federal treaty, it may be litigated in a federal court. See chapter 14.

Felony: A serious offense for which the punishment may include a heavy fine and/or significant imprisonment (often greater than one year) up to life imprisonment or the death penalty; an offense of a serious nature that is greater than a misdemeanor but lower than treason.

Fifth Amendment privilege: The constitutional right granted to every person to not serve as a witness against him- or herself. A defendant has no duty to assist the prosecution in obtaining a conviction of the defendant. See *Malloy v. Hogan,* 378 U.S. 1 (1964), and chapter 8.

Fifth Amendment privilege at lineup: A defendant has no constitutional right to refuse to participate in a lineup, even though it may prove to be a link in a chain of evidence that results in a conviction. See *United States v. Wade,* 388 U.S. 218 (1967) (Case 9.1), *Gilbert v. California,* 388 U.S. 263 (1967), and chapter 8.

First hearing: The initial appearance of an arrestee before a judicial official where probable cause to hold may be judicially evaluated, where a not guilty plea or no plea may be entered, where the charges are read to the arrestee, and where the judge may set a bail amount. See chapter 12.

Fourth Amendment: The portion of the Bill of Rights that generally requires warrants for searches and seizures but has been construed to permit warrantless arrests in most situations.

Frisk: A limited search of the outer garments of a detainee to discern whether the individual possesses a

weapon or weapons that could be used to harm the officer or surrounding persons. See *Terry v. Ohio,* 392 U.S. 1 (1968) (Case 2.1), and chapter 2.

Fruit of the poisonous tree doctrine: A corollary to the exclusionary rule whereby evidence may be excluded from an individual's criminal trial where the individual would have normally possessed no standing to suppress evidence; the theory that excludes evidence from a defendant's trial when the evidence was derivatively obtained in violation of the defendant's Fourth Amendment rights and would not have been discovered but for the violation of defendant's rights. See *Wong Sun v. United States,* 371 U.S. 471 (1963) (Case 6.2), and chapter 6.

Functional equivalent of international border: Any location similar to an airport or seaport where products and people enter or leave a nation, and where customs and immigration services may be required. Searches and seizures conducted at these locations have minimal Fourth Amendment limitations concerning probable cause or scope of search. See chapter 5.

Functional equivalent of interrogation: Where police speak in front of a suspect in their custody in a manner that is clearly designed to elicit an incriminating response from a suspect who has decided not to talk following receipt of *Miranda* warnings; any words or actions on the part of the police (other than those normally incident to arrest and taking a person into custody) that the police should know are reasonably likely to elicit an incriminating response from the suspect. See *Rhode Island v. Innis,* 446 U.S. 291 (1980) (Case 7.2), and chapter 7.

Fundamental fairness: Description often given to explain the essential dictates of the Fifth and/or Fourteenth Amendment requirement of due process; the proposition that the government must offer each accused person sufficient notice and opportunity to be heard and to have a meaningful opportunity to defend against criminal charges.

Good-faith exception: A judicially recognized exception to the *Mapp* exclusionary rule that permits prosecution use of evidence illegally obtained where the searching officers were reasonably unaware of the defect in the search warrant; permits use of illegally seized evidence where the judge or magistrate has made an error in issuing a search warrant where the law enforcement officials acted in an "objectively reasonable" manner and were ignorant of the error. See *United States v. Leon,* 468 U.S. 897 (1984), *Massachusetts v. Sheppard,* 468 U.S. 981 (1984), and chapter 6.

Grand jury: A group of qualified persons, theoretically eligible to be voters (often numbering from nine to twenty-four) selected from a fair cross section of the community whose function is to determine whether probable cause exists to believe that a person has committed a specific offense or offenses; a body of persons who make the determination of whether or not to indict a person. See chapter 10.

Grand jury secrecy: limitations: The secrecy surrounding a grand jury proceeding cannot be violated except to prevent an injustice in a separate case (and therefore the need for disclosure is greater than the need for continued secrecy). However, individual grand jury witnesses may reveal the substance of offered testimony, and grand jurors may speak after the grand jury's term has expired. See chapter 10.

Grand jury standard: probable cause: To render an indictment, the grand jury, by a majority vote, must be convinced that a person of reasonable caution, when presented with the facts and circumstances, would conclude that a particular person had committed a particular crime or crimes. See chapter 10.

Grand jury target: Refers to the individual who the prosecutor believes committed the crime or crimes and who is the subject of the grand jury's particular investigation. See chapter 10.

Guilty plea: Admission by a criminal defendant that he or she is guilty of the crime or crimes for which charges have been alleged; a confession of guilt that allows the trial court to impose a sentence; a plea that waives the right to a jury trial, the right to confront and cross-examine adverse witnesses, the Fifth Amendment privilege against self-incrimination, the right to force witnesses to testify on one's behalf, the right to complain of violations of protections against illegal search and seizure, and generally, the right to appeal the conviction. See chapter 11.

Guilty plea effect: Upon the acceptance of a guilty plea, the defendant has given up the right to a trial by jury, the right to contest most grand jury issues, the right to be represented by counsel at trial, the privilege against self-incrimination, the right to compel witnesses to testify, the

right to confront and cross-examine adverse witnesses, the right to contest Fourth Amendment issues, the right to a public trial, the right to a speedy trial, and the right to an appeal. See chapter 11.

Habeas corpus: a common-law writ that survives to the present that permits a criminal defendant or convict to request that a court issue the writ where the individual can prove that he or she is being held in violation of the particular state constitution or the national constitution; a writ that will permit the person who is illegally held to be freed from present custody or obtain a new trial where the defendant demonstrates that he or she has been held illegally in absence of due process of law. See chapter 14.

Hearsay: A statement offered in court substantially repeating a statement made by someone outside of that court and offered for its substantive truth; in-court statements made by a witness who is quoting someone else who was not under oath and made a statement while outside of the court.

Hot pursuit: An exception to the usual requirement of a warrant where an arrest is effectuated within the arrestee's home or other place by directly following the suspect inside the structure; the doctrine that permits a warrantless arrest within a suspect's home where probable cause to arrest exists and the officer closely followed the suspect inside after a chase. See *Warden v. Hayden,* 387 U.S. 294 (1967).

Identification of defendant: An eyewitness must make a fairly positive determination that the defendant is the one responsible for the crime and must make this determination in a manner that comports with due process for the accused. See *Neil v. Biggers,* 409 U.S. 188 (1972) (Case 9.3), and chapter 9.

Identification: the *Neil* five-factors test: In order to determine whether an eyewitness had made a proper identification of a suspect, the court must evaluate the opportunity of the witness to view the criminal at the time of the crime, the witness's degree of attention, the accuracy of the witness's original description of the criminal, the level of certainty demonstrated by the witness at the time of the confrontation, and the length of time between the crime scene identification and the confrontation. See *Neil v. Biggers,* 409 U.S. 188 (1972) (Case 9.3), and chapter 8.

Impeachment: The art of placing a courtroom witness in a position where the truthfulness of the witness's testimony is called into question; a showing that the witness may intentionally not be telling the truth or a demonstration that the witness may have been mistaken for any of several reasons concerning what the witness thought he or she observed.

Impeachment use of confession: The principle that a confession taken in violation of the *Miranda* warnings, but not in violation of the Fifth Amendment privilege against self-incrimination, may be used to cast doubt on a defendant's testimony when a defendant takes the witness stand and offers evidence that is contradictory to the *Miranda*-barred statement or confession. See *Harris v. New York*, 401 U.S. 222 (1971), and chapter 8.

Impeachment use of *Miranda*: Evidence that has been received in violation of the principles of *Miranda* may be used to impeach a defendant where the defendant takes the witness stand and offers a contradictory story from the one given subsequent to a defective *Miranda* warning. See chapter 7.

Improper steering: The making of subtle or overt suggestions to witnesses by government law enforcement agents during identification procedures. A violation of due process may render the eyewitness's testimony excluded from admission to evidence. See chapter 8.

Independent source rule: An exception to the exclusionary rule that permits the use of evidence that has been discovered through an illegal means where the evidence also has a lawful means of discovery; introduction of evidence discovered during an illegal search and seizure so long as the evidence was later obtained independently by legal law enforcement activity unrelated to the initial illegality. See *Murray v. United States*, 487 U.S. 533 (1988) (Case 6.3), *Segura v. United States*, 468 U.S. 796 (1984), and chapter 6.

Indictment: The written product of a grand jury issued when a simple majority of the members conclude that probable cause exists to believe that a particular person has committed a specific crime or crimes; a true bill returned by a grand jury that charges a person with a crime. See chapter 10.

Indigent right to appellate counsel: Where a state or the federal government allows one appeal as a matter of

statutory right, a person too poor to afford to hire an attorney to pursue the appeal must be furnished with free counsel to prosecute the first appeal. See *Douglas v. California*, 372 U.S. 353 (1963) (Case 14.1), and chapter 14.

Indigent right to transcript: Where an appeal requires a trial transcript to obtain meaningful appellate review, a person who is too poor to afford the price of a transcript is entitled under due process to have the proper number of transcripts prepared at governmental expense. See *Griffin v. Illinois*, 351 U.S. 12 (1956).

Individual show-up: The identification procedure conducted prior to indictment or the filing of an information where the police exhibit a single suspect to an eyewitness for possible identification. See *Stovall v. Denno*, 388 U.S. 293 (1967) (Case 9.2), and chapter 8.

Infamous crime: Under the Fifth Amendment, the crime required to initiate a federal criminal prosecution must be an offense punishable by hard labor or death or otherwise labeled an infamous crime. See *United States v. Moreland*, 258 U.S. 433 (1922) (Case 10.2), and chapter 10.

Informants: Individuals, whether paid or unpaid, who deliver information to law enforcement officials in an effort to assist in the apprehension of criminals or to frustrate criminal plans; individuals who must have a sufficient level of believability to help establish probable cause for arrest or for search. See *Illinois v. Gates*, 462 U.S. 213 (1983) (Case 1.2).

Information: One method of initiating a serious criminal case whereby the prosecutor, in a writing filed with the proper court, accuses, in plain language and with sufficient particularity, a person with having committed a specific crime or crimes; a method of initiating a criminal lawsuit that often requires that the potential defendant waive his or her right to a grand jury indictment and consent to the entering of criminal charges against him or her. See chapter 10.

Infrared scan: A process that uses a thermal imaging device, which detects heat escaping from homes or other structures, to produce a picture that assists law enforcement agents in determining whether a building is being used to grow marijuana. The use of this technology to uncover details of the interiors of private homes implicates the Fourth Amendment and generally constitutes an illegal search when conducted without a warrant. See *Kyllo v. United States,* 533 U.S. 27 (2001) (Case 4.2), and chapter 4.

Initial appearance: Often called an arraignment; the first instance where an accused meets a magistrate or judge to hear a reading of the charge(s) against him or her and where the accused may make an initial plea or response.

International border search: Persons crossing a United States international border may be searched for any reason and without a showing of probable cause, since the Fourth Amendment has a diminished effect on international travelers at the point of entry or exit of the nation. See chapter 5.

Interrogation: The process of acquiring information from a suspect or eyewitness; under *Miranda,* questioning a suspect by speaking in a declarative voice with a view toward eliciting incriminating statements from the arrestee; the functional equivalent of questioning a suspect while in custody. See *Miranda v. Arizona,* 384 U.S. 436 (1966) (Case 7.1), and chapter 7.

Inventory search: An exception to the usual requirement of probable cause to search that permits a warrantless inventory or cataloging of items found on an arrestee or items in the immediate dominion and control of the arrestee. See *Illinois v. Lafayette,* 462 U.S. 640 (1983) (Case 5.2), *Colorado v. Bertine,* 479 U.S. 367 (1987) (Case 5.3), *Florida v. Wells,* 495 U.S. 1 (1990), chapter 4, and chapter 5.

Inventory search: motor vehicle: A lawful search not requiring probable cause that police may conduct following receipt of a vehicle as evidence or for safekeeping. The purpose is to protect police from false claims of loss of personal items and to protect the owner from theft of personal property while the property remains in police custody. If a police agency has and follows a written policy regulating these searches, criminal evidence produced by the search will be admissible in court. See *Illinois v. Lafayette,* 462 U.S. 640 (1983) (Case 5.2), *Colorado v. Bertine,* 479 U.S. 367 (1987) (Case 5.3), *Florida v. Wells,* 495 U.S. 1 (1990), and chapter 4.

Inventory search: personal property: Police may without a warrant and without probable cause conduct a search of personal property that comes into police custody or possession following an arrest. The purpose is to

protect police from false claims of loss of personal items and to protect the owner from theft of personal property while it is in police custody. If a police agency has and follows a written policy regulating these searches, criminal evidence produced by the search will be admissible in court. See *Illinois v. Lafayette,* 462 U.S. 640 (1983) (Case 5.2), and chapter 5.

Inventory search policy: Every jurisdiction that wishes to conduct searches based on an inventory search theory must have and routinely follow a departmental policy that regulates inventory searches. In the absence of policy regulation, the parameters of an inventory search will have no limits, and the search will be deemed unreasonable under the Fourth Amendment. See *Florida v. Wells,* 495 U.S. 1 (1990), and chapter 5.

Involuntary confession: Where the mind and will of an accused are overcome by governmental tactics, and he or she offers evidence sufficient to meet the standard of proof beyond a reasonable doubt. See *Arizona v. Fulminante,* 499 U.S. 279 (1991) (Case 8.3), and chapter 8.

Jeopardy: When a defendant has been placed in danger of losing money, freedom, or life; it attaches to a defendant in a bench trial when the judge begins hearing the first witness and attaches in a jury trial when the jury has been empaneled and sworn. See chapter 12.

Judgment: The decision rendered by a judge or jury following a trial, or the entry made by a judge following the acceptance of a negotiated plea. See chapter 11.

Knock and announce: Fourth Amendment requirement that law enforcement officials notify occupants of real property that police are outside and have the legal authority of a warrant to enter. The necessity of notice is not absolute, and notice need not be given where the announcement would clearly expose police officers to unreasonable levels of risk or where officers reasonably believe that evidence might be destroyed. See *Atwater v. City of Lago Vista,* 532 U.S. 318 (2001) (Case 3.3), *Wilson v. Arkansas,* 514 U.S. 927 (1995) (Case 1.4), and chapter 1.

Lesser included offense: An offense below the initially charged offense that lacks one or more elements necessary to prove the more serious offense. For example, second-degree murder would be a lesser included offense of first-degree murder, since second-degree murder would not require proof of premeditation. See chapter 11.

Limitations on scope: Refers to the extent that a police officer may lawfully search for a specifically defined object. An officer may only search where an object or material might reasonably be found and may not search in places where the object could not be hidden. For example, in an automobile an officer could lawfully search for drugs almost anywhere, but if a stolen desktop computer were the object of the search the officer could not lawfully look for it in the automobile console. See chapter 2.

Lineup: An identification process whereby a witness observes several individuals, one of whom may be the police suspect, and is requested to indicate whether the person the witness observed at the crime scene is a member of the array; an identification procedure that requires the presence of counsel for the defendant if the process occurs following an indictment or the filing of an information.

Material witness: An observer of the essential elements of the crime whose presence in court may be essential to the prosecution or the defense; an essential witness who may be placed under bail or kept in official custody to ensure his or her presence at a criminal trial.

***Miranda* warnings:** Legal advisement that must be made by a governmental official to an arrestee concerning constitutional rights that must be explained prior to any interrogation; a warning to a person who is in custody that the individual has the right to remain silent and to consult with counsel prior to speaking, that anything that is said may be used against the individual in a court of law, and that a free lawyer is available for the arrestee. See *Miranda v. Arizona,* 384 U.S. 436 (1966), and chapter 7.

Misdemeanor: A criminal violation that is less severe than a felony; an offense often punished by custody of less than a year (time varies by jurisdiction) and/or a fine; a criminal violation that is punishable by local incarceration rather than custody in a state prison.

Misdemeanor bail: An amount of bail or bond that normally does not involve individual consideration of a defendant and is set by a fee schedule based on the type of crime that has been charged. See chapter 12.

Motion to suppress: A request, normally filed with the court prior to trial, that seeks to have evidence excluded from consideration by the judge or jury; a pretrial request that the judge order evidence illegally seized in violation of the Fourth or Fifth Amendment excluded from trial consideration.

Necessary conditions for warning: To be required to offer the *Miranda* warnings, custody of a subject must exist and police must desire to conduct interrogation of the subject. See *Miranda v. Arizona,* 384 U.S. 436 (1966), and chapter 7.

Neutral and detached judicial official: A person who serves in a judicial capacity who has authority to issue arrest and search warrants and who has no preconceived reason either to grant or refuse to grant a warrant but makes his or her decision based only on the merits of the evidence. See *Coolidge v. New Hampshire,* 403 U.S. 443 (1971), *California v. Acevedo,* 500 U.S. 565 (1991) (Case 4.6), *Arizona v. Evans,* 514 U.S. 1 (1995), and chapter 3.

Nolo contendere: The Latin phrase denoting that a defendant has decided not to put on a defense and to allow the judge to determine guilt or innocence, most frequently resulting in a guilty adjudication. See chapter 11.

Nontestimonial evidence: Evidence that does not come from the mouth of a witness and may include conduct; physical evidence that may have the operative effect of proving guilt but has not been deemed to have the same effect as speech. See *Schmerber v. California,* 384 U.S. 757 (1966) (Case 8.1), and chapter 8.

Nonunanimous jury verdicts: In state cases the right to a jury trial does not dictate that a jury of twelve must be used to comply with the Sixth Amendment requirement of unanimity, which is required in federal criminal prosecutions. See *Apodaca v. Oregon,* 406 U.S. 404 (1972), *Johnson v. Louisiana,* 406 U.S. 356 (1972), and chapter 13.

Notice of appeal: The procedural requirement that alerts the trial court that a convicted defendant plans to appeal the conviction. As a general rule, if the defendant fails to notify the trial court within 30 days, the right of appeal extinguishes by operation of law. See chapter 14.

Open field doctrine: The principle that an uncovered field, which the occupier has not taken steps to prevent individuals from observing, is not a house or an effect and does not merit Fourth Amendment protection. Erection of a farm or cattle fence has been held to be insufficient to create an expectation of privacy in an open field. See *United States v. Dunn,* 480 U.S. 294 (1987) (Case 1.5), and chapter 1.

Parole: Discharge from traditional confinement prior to the time originally scheduled for release; early discharge from custody under conditions that may include staying away from specific individuals, not consuming alcohol, not gambling, not committing additional crimes, maintaining employment, and/or other conditions believed relevant to rehabilitation.

Particularity of description: A requirement under the Fourth Amendment that items that are the subject of a search must be clearly and carefully described, so that any law enforcement official may know what items can be seized what items are not subject to seizure. In the context of a search warrant the items must be carefully described in language placed on an affidavit for a search warrant, and this description is carried over to the language used in a subsequent search warrant. See the Fourth Amendment and chapter 1.

Peremptory challenge: The practice of removing a prospective petit juror from trial service for any reason or no particular reason by requesting that the prospective juror be excused from further jury consideration; a method of eliminating a trial juror without offering a reason for so doing, limited by the fact that removal cannot be based on the race or gender of the prospective juror. See *Georgia v. McCollum,* 505 U.S. 42 (1992).

Petit jury: The jury of citizens that determines the guilt or innocence of the accused. See chapter 12.

Petty offense compared with serious offense: A trial by jury must be accorded to any defendant who faces greater than six months in custody. See *Baldwin v. New York,* 399 U.S. 117 (1970), and chapter 12.

Photographic array: The functional equivalent of an identification lineup conducted by law enforcement officials by the use of still photographs of persons who are similar in appearance to the suspect; a method of identifying suspects that does not require the presence of an attorney for the accused regardless of whether an indictment been issued or information has been filed. See *United States v. Ash,* 413 U.S. 300 (1973), and chapter 9.

Plain error rule: The principle that, in the interests of justice, an appellate court may reverse a criminal conviction based on an extreme error that was not preserved for appeal by an objection at trial and would not normally be considered by an appellate court. See chapter 14.

Plain feel doctrine: A corollary of the plain view doctrine that permits instantaneous seizure of the object whose criminal nature becomes immediately apparent to a law enforcement officer who senses the seizable material during a lawful pat-down or frisk of a person. See *Minnesota v. Dickerson,* 508 U.S. 366 (1993), and chapter 4.

Plain feel search: See **Plain feel doctrine.**

Plain view doctrine: An exception to the usual requirement that an officer possess probable cause prior to conducting a search; permits the warrantless seizure and introduction of evidence taken by an officer who was lawfully in a position to observe the seizable property. See *Coolidge v. New Hampshire,* 403 U.S. 443 (1971), *Horton v. California,* 496 U.S. 128 (1990) (Case 4.9), and chapter 4.

Plea: The response a defendant offers to a judge during an arraignment, preliminary hearing, or other early judicial hearing that takes the form of a plea of guilty, a plea of not guilty, or a plea of nolo contendere. See chapter 11.

Plea bargain: Where a defendant agrees to plead guilty to a specific charge or charges in exchange for the government's agreement to dismiss other charges and/or for an agreed sentence or recommendation of sentence; an agreement by the government to lower the level of the criminal charge in exchange for the defendant's agreement to admit guilt to the lesser crime. See chapter 11.

Preliminary hearing: An early hearing in the criminal justice process where a court determines probable cause to detain, where the bail amount may be set, where early psychiatric examinations may be requested, and where the prosecution may be required to put on a prima facie case. See *Coleman v. Alabama,* 399 U.S. 1 (1970) (Case 12.1).

Pretrial detention: When a judge or magistrate denies bail to an arrestee and the accused must remain in full custody awaiting trial; under the federal Bail Reform Act of 1984, a person deemed to be dangerous to others or who has been accused of particular federal crimes may be denied bail completely and kept in custody until and during trial. See *United States v. Montalvo-Murillo,* 495 U.S. 711 (1990) (Case 12.4), and chapter 12.

Prima facie case: The level of evidence sufficient to convict if no adverse evidence were introduced; the level of evidence necessary to survive a motion to dismiss for lack of proof beyond a reasonable doubt. See chapter 11.

Private employer search: Where workers employed by private corporations are subject to Fourth Amendment searches of personal property and searches of the person under the order of a government where the search may be based on less than probable cause. For example, federal railroad regulations specify testing employees for drugs or alcohol upon the occurrence of specified events like train wrecks or the personal injury of a worker. See chapter 5.

Privilege against self-incrimination: The right of an accused under the Fifth Amendment to refuse to testify or otherwise give evidence against himself or herself. See *Malloy v. Hogan,* 378 U.S. 1 (1964), and *Schmerber v. California,* 384 U.S. 757 (1966); one of the constitutional rights that law enforcement officers must explain to a person who is in official custody prior to initiating interrogation. See *Miranda v. Arizona,* 384 U.S. 436 (1966) (Case 7.1), and chapter 8.

Probable cause: Where the facts and circumstances known to a person of reasonable caution would permit him or her to conclude that seizable property would be found in a particular place or that a particular person has committed a particular crime. See *Beck v. Ohio,* 379 U.S. 89 (1964) (Case 3.1), *Draper v. United States,* 358 U.S. 307 (1959) (Case 3.2), chapter 1, and chapter 3.

Probable cause only hearing: A judicial procedure required when a person has been arrested without a warrant and without an indictment where the hearing determines only probable cause to hold the individual and must be held within forty-eight hours after arrest. See *County of Riverside v. McLaughlin,* 500 U.S. 44 (1991).

Probable cause to arrest: The level of proof that a police officer must have to take a subject into custody lawfully; the level of proof that would permit a person of reasonable caution to form the belief that a particular person had committed or was committing an offense for which an arrest was permitted. See *Beck v. Ohio,* 379 U.S. 89 (1964) (Case 3.1).

Probation: Release of a convicted person by the judicial system without that person serving the sentence of incarceration; release prior to execution of sentence on condition that the convict obey the law, maintain employment, not drink alcohol, not consume recreational pharmaceuticals, or not gamble, among other possible conditions.

Protective sweep: A cursory inspection of premises beyond the area permitted under a search warrant (or arrest warrant) for the purposes of discerning whether other persons might be present who might harm the officers or frustrate the search or arrest; a quick and limited search of the premises, incident to an arrest, conducted to protect the safety of police officers and others, which is narrowly confined to a cursory visual inspection of places in which a person might be hiding. See *Maryland v. Buie,* 494 U.S. 325 (1990).

Public safety exception to *Miranda*: Where an arrestee presents or appears to present an immediate danger to the safety of the arresting officer or other persons, the officer is permitted to interrogate the subject concerning the danger prior to offering the warnings required by *Miranda;* permissible custodial interrogation generally permitted when unresolved dangers to the public exist. See *New York v. Quarles,* 467 U.S. 649 (1984).

Rationale for bail: The purposes for granting bail: It assists the defendant in planning a defense with his or her attorney, it allows the defendant to freely search for and interview witnesses, and it prevents preconviction punishment and preserves the presumption of innocence while assuring the defendant's appearance before a court as appropriate. See chapter 12.

Rationale for double jeopardy: The purposes for forbidding double jeopardy: This prevents the prosecution with all the resources of the state from continuing to retry a defendant until, through successive prosecutions, it wears down the defendant's will to oppose the government; a government should have one and only one chance to make its case or refrain from additional efforts toward one defendant. See chapter 12.

Reasonable basis to suspect: The standard of proof necessary for a police officer to initiate a brief stop of a person where there exists some question as to whether the individual is involved in criminal activity. If the suspicion extends to a fear that the subject may be armed and dangerous, a pat-down of the subject's outer garments is permissible. This standard will allow a brief motor vehicle stop where there is articulable reason to suspect that criminality may be present. See *Terry v. Ohio,* 392 U.S. 1 (1968) (Case 2.1), *Alabama v. White,* 496 U.S. 325 (1990) (Case 2.3), and chapter 2.

Reasonable suspicion: Virtually the same as probable cause in some contexts; may be used in the context of a *Terry v. Ohio*-type search in which the terminology may be phrased as "reasonable basis to suspect criminal activity," which would permit a police officer to initiate a brief detention, discussion, and perhaps a pat-down of a suspect. See *Terry v. Ohio,* 392 U.S. 1 (1968) (Case 2.1).

Reduced expectation of privacy: juveniles: Children do not have the same Fourth Amendment rights as adults and can be searched by school officials on a showing of less than probable cause. Public school children, with parental consent, can be forced to submit to drug screens as a condition of engaging in after-school activities like football or the Latin club. See *New Jersey v. T.L.O.,* 469 U.S. 325 (1985) (Case 5.4), *Vernonia School District 47J v. Acton,* 515 U.S. 646 (1995) (Case 5.5), *Board of Education v. Earls,* 536 U.S. 822 (2002) (Case 5.6), and chapter 5.

Requirement of unanimity: Federal criminal cases must be decided by unanimous jury verdicts. See *Johnson v. Louisiana,* 406 U.S. 356 (1972), and chapter 13.

Requirement to claim double jeopardy: Defendant must allege and prove that the same sovereign is attempting to try him or her a second time for a crime that has already been adjudicated to a conclusion; defendant must show that the crime or crimes the prosecution wants to try for a second time do not have a separate element different from the first crime charged.

Reservation of right to appeal: Where a defendant enters a plea of guilty but specifically does not give up all rights of appeal, such that he or she reserves the right to appeal one or more narrow legal issues as part of a plea bargain. See chapter 11.

Right assertable against government: Constitutional rights possessed by defendants that they may use to prevent evidence seized against their rights from being used by a government to prove guilt. Examples include alleged *Miranda* and self-incrimination violations, as well as the right to demand a jury trial.

Right to a grand jury indictment: Absent waiver, all serious federal criminal prosecutions must be initiated by the use of a grand jury, but states are free to develop individual alternatives because the right to a grand jury indictment has never been applied to the states through the Due Process Clause of the Fourteenth Amendment. See *Hurtado v. California,* 110 U.S. 516 (1884) (Case 10.1), and chapter 10.

Right to counsel: A benefit given to all accused persons under the Sixth Amendment to the federal constitution as well as a right granted by state constitutions. The right includes the furnishing by the government of free legal counsel to those accused individuals who cannot afford to hire attorneys. See *Gideon v. Wainwright,* 372 U.S. 335 (1963), *Argersinger v. Hamlin,* 407 U.S. 25 (1972), *Scott v. Illinois,* 440 U.S. 367 (1979), and chapter 13.

Right to counsel: postarrest limitations: No general right to counsel exists following an arrest unless other procedures, like interrogation, a postindictment lineup, or a postinformation lineup, occur. See *United States v. Ash,* 413 U.S. 300 (1973), and chapter 9.

Right to counsel: postindictment: A defendant has the right to counsel at all critical stages of the criminal justice process. See *Coleman v. Alabama,* 399 U.S. 1 (1970) (Case 12.1).

Right to counsel: postinformation: A defendant has the right to counsel following the filing of an information against the defendant, since proceedings following the filing of an information are considered critical stages of the criminal process. See chapter 8.

Right to remain silent: A constitutional right guaranteed to persons under the Fifth Amendment that permits a person to refuse to assist the government in prosecuting a criminal case against that individual; a right guaranteed by the Fifth Amendment and reinforced by the case of *Miranda v. Arizona,* 384 U.S. 436 (1966), allowing a person in custody to refuse to speak with police about any substantive matter.

Rule of inevitable discovery: The exception to the exclusionary rule that allows the admission of evidence that has been illegally discovered where the evidence clearly would have been discovered by lawful means at a later time. See *Nix v. Williams,* 467 U.S. 431 (1984) (Case 6.4), and chapter 6.

Scope of frisk: The area on the person or in a place that may be searched under the rationale of *Terry v. Ohio* and its progeny. A frisk following a lawful stop allows an officer to pat down the outer garments of a subject with whom the officer is dealing in an effort to ascertain whether the subject is armed and may extend to any area of outer clothing under which weapons may reasonably be hidden. See *Terry v. Ohio,* 392 U.S. 1 (1968) (Case 2.1), and chapter 2.

Scope of search: The places where law enforcement officials may lawfully look where an object of the search could reasonably have been hidden. Example: cocaine could be hidden almost anywhere, but a stolen television could not be found in a medicine chest above a sink in a bathroom.

Scope of search of a home: The type and extent of a search of a home that can be considered reasonable based on the size and type of property that is the object of a home search. Searching officers may search for an object in any home location where the object of the search could reasonably be hidden. See *Wilson v. Layne,* 526 U.S. 603 (1999).

Scope of search of a motor vehicle: The type and extent of a search that may be conducted of a motor vehicle when due consideration has been given to the object of the search. Officers may search anywhere inside a motor vehicle, including any containers, that could reasonably be the location of seizable property. See *Wyoming v. Houghton,* 526 U.S. 295 (1999), *United States v. Ross,* 456 U.S. 798 (1982) (Case 4.5), and chapter 4.

Search: A governmental inspection, survey, or examination of the premises of a person's home, automobile, papers, person, or other area where private material may be stored.

Search incident to arrest: A specialized type of search that requires only a lawful arrest of a person as its justification; a search that permits inquiry into areas under the immediate "dominion and control" of the arrestee, such as a purse or backpack and personal effects, but does not generally include a search of an entire house or automobile. See *Chimel v. California,* 395 U.S. 752 (1969), *United States v. Robinson,* 414 U.S. 218 (1973), and chapter 4.

Secrecy of grand jury: purpose: A grand jury is not open for public scrutiny because there is no such constitutional requirement, and secrecy prevents targeted individuals from escaping or influencing witnesses or jurors while it protects those individuals who are never indicted. See *Butterworth v. Smith,* 494 U.S. 624 (1990), and chapter 10.

Seizure: The act by law enforcement officials of acquiring dominion and control over a person, property, or contraband.

Selective incorporation: The process whereby the Supreme Court of the United States, on a case-by-case basis, determined that various rights in the Bill of Rights should be incorporated into the Due Process Clause of the Fourteenth Amendment. See chapter 13.

Separate offense interrogation: Where an arrestee has requested counsel following receipt of *Miranda* warnings, the law prohibits any additional police interrogation on any separate offense unrelated to the offense for which the person is in custody. See *Arizona v. Roberson,* 486 U.S. 675 (1988), and chapter 7.

Serious criminal case: For purposes of the Sixth Amendment, any offense that carries a maximum penalty of greater than six months in prison creates the right to jury trial for a defendant. See *Duncan v. Louisiana,* 391 U.S. 145 (1968) (Case 13.1), and chapter 10.

Silver platter doctrine: Legal theory, no longer used, whereby a federal officer, who had illegally seized evidence in violation of the Fourth Amendment, could offer the evidence for use by a state official in a state prosecution.

Six-person jury: The smaller trial jury that has been approved by the Supreme Court of the United States for state cases as not violating the Sixth Amendment right to a trial by jury so long as unanimity is maintained. See *Williams v. Florida,* 399 U.S. 78 (1970) (Case 13.2), and chapter 13.

Sixth Amendment right to a speedy trial: While not specifying any particular time frame, the Sixth Amendment, as interpreted, requires that an accused be tried within a reasonable time following arrest, indictment, or the filing of an information. See *Barker v. Wingo,* 407 U.S 514 (1972) (Case 12.5), and chapter 12.

Specific performance: In cases of plea bargains breached by the prosecution, the trial court has discretion to allow the defendant to completely withdraw the original plea and start the prosecution anew, or to order that the prosecution exactly perform the duties under the plea bargain to which it had originally agreed. See *Santobello v. New York,* 404 U.S. 257 (1971) (Case 11.4), and chapter 11.

Speedy trial: The requirement under the Sixth Amendment, federal law, state law, and/or state constitution that a person accused of a crime be brought to trial within a specific time or within a reasonable time following the filing of an information, apprehension, or indictment. The remedy for a violation of the Sixth Amendment speedy trial right is prejudicial dismissal against the prosecution. See *Barker v. Wingo,* 407 U.S. 514 (1972) (Case 12.5), *Doggett v. United States,* 505 U.S. 647 (1992) (Case 12.6), and chapter 12.

Speedy trial: factors to consider: The four-factors test evaluates the length of time, the reason for the delay, the defendant's assertion or nonassertion of the right, and prejudice to the defendant and the case. See *Barker v. Wingo,* 407 U.S. 514 (1972) (Case 12.5), *Doggett v. United States,* 505 U.S. 647 (1992) (Case 12.6), and chapter 12.

Stale probable cause: The rationale sufficient to search for an object may exist only for a short time, since some illegal activity depends upon movement of the object. When the probable cause becomes stale, the search for the object becomes unreasonable under the Fourth Amendment. Example: Drug dealers must move their product and sell it as part of the normal course of business, so that probable cause for a search at a particular time for a particular place may not exist several days later. Probable cause for arrest does not typically become stale, since the information pointing to a particular perpetrator does not often change with the passage of time.

Standing: The legal position that an accused must hold in order to be able to successfully litigate a motion to suppress evidence under the exclusionary rule of *Mapp v. Ohio* and the Fourth Amendment; the position of possessing a reasonable expectation of privacy under the Fourth Amendment. See *Rakas v. Illinois,* 439 U.S. 128 (1978) (Case 6.5).

Statutory right to a speedy trial: Many states and the federal government have laws that help enforce both the Sixth Amendment and state constitutional rights to speedy trials by specifying the time requirements necessary to

meet the goal of having swift trials. These laws have the effect of moving criminal cases in danger of not meeting time requirements to the top of the docket.

Stop and frisk: The reasonable limited restriction on freedom of movement and the potential limited search of the outer garments permitted under the doctrine announced in *Terry v. Ohio,* 392 U.S. 1 (1968); limited detention or search permitted whenever an officer observes unusual conduct that leads the officer to suspect criminal activity, and the officer reasonably believes that the person with whom he or she is presently dealing may be armed and dangerous. See chapter 2.

Stop and identify: A rejected theory, related to the stop and frisk doctrine, that would allow police officers to stop anyone who seemed out of place or who seemed remotely suspicious, and that would allow a police officer to force a subject to give a positive identification. No person who is merely abroad in the night or day can be required to carry identification. See *Kolender v. Lawson,* 461 U.S. 352 (1983), and chapter 2.

Straight plea: When a defendant pleads guilty to exactly the charges that the prosecutor has levied without any promises or consideration made by the prosecution. See chapter 11.

Subpoena: A lawful order issued by a court of competent jurisdiction commanding an individual to appear in court or another place under penalty of law for failure to comply; an order requiring a person to personally appear and bring particularly described items to court at a specified time is called a *subpoena duces tecum.*

Suggestiveness at lineup: Where improper steering or undue influencing of eyewitnesses occurrs during an in-person lineup, an in-person show-up, or a photographic lineup (array), a violation of due process has occurred that generally will require exclusion of the evidence.

Suspicionless public school search: Schools may require that children, with parental consent, submit to drug screens and testing as a condition of playing sports or engaging in extracurricular activities. See *Board of Education v. Earls,* 536 U.S. 822 (2002) (Case 5.6), and chapter 5.

Suspicionless workplace search: A privately or publicly employed worker, holding a position where the safety of the public could be injured, may be required to submit to a warrantless drug test or screen as a condition of continued employment. Probable cause or reasonable suspicion is not required to make this search reasonable for some occupations. See *Treasury Employees v. Von Raab,* 489 U.S. 656 (1989), and chapter 5.

Testimonial evidence: Oral evidence offered from the witness stand or by deposition by a witness who has taken an oath to tell the truth and who is generally subject to cross-examination. See chapter 8.

Thermal imaging: The picture produced when police subject a building to a scan with an infrared detector to measure the differences in the heat signature offered by particular parts of the building. The imaging machine converts infrared radiation into an image based on the relative warmth or coolness of the surface of the building. For example, on the screen of an infrared scanner, white indicates a relatively hot surface, gray colors demonstrate cooler temperatures, and black indicates a relatively cold surface. See *Kyllo v. United States,* 533 U.S. 27 (2001) (Case 4.2), and chapter 4.

Time limitations on detention: A person cannot be held in custody in the absence of a judicial or grand jury determination of probable cause longer than forty-eight hours, but the remedy for a person who has been held longer without judicial intervention is not automatic release. See *Riverside v. McLaughlin,* 500 U.S. 44 (1991), and chapter 2. Also, under the stop and frisk rationale, a subject may be detained only for a brief time without the detention maturing into an illegal arrest. See *Terry v. Ohio,* 392 U.S. 1 (1968) (Case 2.1).

Totality of the circumstances test: A test used to determine whether an informant has met the requirements necessary for a judge or police officer to be able to find probable cause for an arrest or search. See *Illinois v. Gates,* 462 U.S. 213 (1983) (Case 1.2). Also, a test used to determine whether a person has given a valid consent to search the person or an area controlled by the person that involves an analysis of the person's age and education, coerciveness of the circumstances, knowledge of the right to refuse consent, and other factors. See *Schneckloth v. Bustamonte,* 412 U.S. 218 (1973) (Case 4.8).

Transactional immunity: The type of immunity given to a witness and potential defendant in which the government gives up its right to pursue criminal sanctions against the individual in exchange for testimony against other defendants; a type of immunity under which the defendant or target can never be prosecuted for crimes for which the immunity extends. See chapter 8.

Trial by jury: A federal and state constitutional right where members of the community are called to sit in judgment of the defendant to determine guilt or lack of guilt; a process of determining whether the prosecution has proven its case by having a body of community members numbering twelve or fewer evaluate the evidence to determine whether guilt beyond a reasonable doubt exists. See *Ballew v. Georgia,* 435 U.S. 223 (1978), *Burch v. Louisiana,* 441 U.S. 130 (1979), and chapter 13.

Trial by the court: Where the defendant elects to have the judge or a three-judge panel hear and decide the case in which the defendant has waived various legal rights, especially the Sixth Amendment right to a trial by jury. See chapter 13.

Two-pronged test: The test to determine whether an informant has sufficient standing to permit the facts offered by the informant to equal probable cause for a search or arrest; under *Aguilar v. Texas,* 378 U.S. 108 (1964), the informant's story must contain sufficient facts that would equal probable cause, and there had to be sufficient reason to believe that the informant was telling the truth. The requirements of the two-pronged test were overruled by the Supreme Court in *Illinois v. Gates,* 462 U.S. 213 (1983). See chapter 1.

Unexplained flight: Where an individual takes immediate steps to place distance between the individual and a police officer upon observing the officer's presence where some additional factor is present. Nervous, evasive behavior in a high-crime area coupled with flight upon sight of a police officer may be sufficient to meet the reasonable-basis-to-suspect standard for a stop and frisk under *Terry v. Ohio.* See *Illinois v. Wardlow,* 528 U.S. 119 (2000) (Case 2.5), and chapter 2.

Unlawful arrest: An arrest for which probable cause does not exist; a warrantless arrest conducted within the home of the arrestee in the absence of exigent circumstances.

Unlawfully seized evidence: admissible: A grand jury may consider illegally seized evidence because the Fourth Amendment and the exclusionary rule possess very little application at a grand jury proceeding. See chapter 10.

Use immunity: A guarantee offered by the prosecution to a prospective witness, typically at a grand jury proceeding, that the prosecution will not affirmatively use the information offered by the witness against the same witness; a type of immunity that is coextensive with the protections of the Fifth Amendment privilege against self-incrimination that still permits the government to use independently sourced evidence to prosecute the immunized person. See chapter 8.

Vehicle forfeiture search: A warrantless search having no limitations on its scope that does not require probable cause and that is conducted by law enforcement agents following the acquiring of custody of a vehicle that is subject to forfeiture under the laws of the jurisdiction. No person possesses an expectation of privacy under the Fourth Amendment in a motor vehicle that is owned by a government or that is subject to forfeiture. See *Florida v. White,* 526 U.S. 559 (1999), and chapter 4.

Vicarious standing: A generally unsuccessful legal theory whereby an individual who has not personally been the victim of a Fourth Amendment violation attempts to suppress evidence where the evidence is sought to be offered against that person or a third party. See *United States v. Salvucci,* 448 U.S. 83 (1980), and chapter 6.

Voire dire of jury: An inquiry under the direction of the trial judge or the trial attorneys in which jurors are questioned concerning possible bias or interest in the case in which they are about to be seated; an interrogation of a prospective witness concerning the witness's qualifications.

Voluntary confession: Evidence offered without governmental duress or compulsion by a suspect or defendant that includes admissions containing all the elements necessary to prove guilt of the crime in question.

Waivable rights: Legal entitlements belonging to a defendant that an accused may knowingly and intelligently determine to relinquish as part of a plea bargain or a straight plea of guilt. See chapter 11.

Waiver: The decision by an accused to forgo some statutory or constitutional protections, which requires that the decision be based on knowledge and understanding of the right being relinquished. A decision not to obtain the benefits of the *Miranda* warnings and subsequent submission to interrogation constitutes a waiver of the right against self-incrimination. A waiver is the

intentional abandonment of a known right or privilege. See *Miranda v. Arizona,* 384 U.S. 436 (1966) (Case 7.1), and chapter 7.

Waiver of privilege: The decision of an accused not to assert a Fifth Amendment privilege against self-incrimination and to offer a free and voluntary confession to the crime alleged. See chapter 8.

Waiver of right to indictment: A federal defendant may decline to force the government to procure an indictment and, usually as part of a plea bargain, allow the government to file an information against the defendant. See chapter 10.

Waiver of trial by jury: Under the Sixth Amendment, the process under which a defendant may choose to have a criminal case decided by a judge rather than by a jury; the waiver must be done knowingly, intelligently, and with understanding of the rights being relinquished.

Warrant: A legal order of a court directed to a law enforcement official to seize a particular person or property and return the individual or property to the court.

Warrant exception for vehicles: Where probable cause to search a motor vehicle exists, the general rule allows an immediate warrantless search of the vehicle whose scope is regulated by the nature of the objects of the search. See *Carroll v. United States,* 267 U.S. 132 (1925) (Case 1.1), *Chambers v. Maroney,* 399 U.S. 42 (1970) (Case 4.4), *California v. Carney,* 471 U.S. 386 (1985), and chapter 4.

Warrant requirement for house: Police may neither warrantlessly search a place of residence nor warrantlessly arrest a resident inside a home. The home possesses the highest expectation of privacy under the Fourth Amendment and generally requires a warrant or some exception for law enforcement officials to breach its privacy. See *Payton v. New York,* 445 U.S. 573 (1979) (Case 4.1), and *Kaupp v. Texas,* 538 U.S. ___ (2003) (page number not available at time of publication).

Warrant to arrest: A court order based on probable cause issued by a neutral and detached judicial official directed to law enforcement agents ordering them to obtain official custody of a particularly described individual. See chapter 3.

Weapons frisk of automobile: A cursory and limited search of the interior of a motor vehicle, permitted when a person is stopped under a stop and frisk standard, that permits the officer to ascertain whether weapons are in close proximity that could be used to frustrate the purpose of the brief stop. The officer must possess a reasonable belief based on specific and articulable facts that warrant an officer in believing that the subject may be dangerous and that the subject could gain immediate control of weapons. See *Michigan v. Long,* 463 U.S. 1032 (1983), and chapter 2.

Writ of assistance: Blanket warrant used by British officials that permitted searches of homes and effects of colonists in the absence of any individual suspicion; a blank search warrant that allowed British Crown officials to search private houses for personal items, personal documents and effects, and other evidence that could be used in court to convict the possessor. See chapter 6.

Writ of certiorari: The court order that indicates the Supreme Court of the United States will hear a case from a state appellate or state supreme court; the court order granted when four justices of the Supreme Court of the United States vote to hear a case. See chapter 14.

Writ of habeas corpus: A common-law writ that survives to the present that allows a criminal defendant or convict to petition a court when the individual believes that he or she is being held in violation of the particular state constitution or the national constitution; a writ that will permit the person who is illegally held to be freed from custody or obtain a new trial, if the applicant for the writ demonstrates that he or she has been held illegally in absence of due process of law. See chapter 14.

Table of Cases

Boldface case name indicates principal case treatment, and boldface page number indicates location of principal case.

Index